Major Problems
in American Constitutional History

MAJOR PROBLEMS IN AMERICAN HISTORY SERIES

GENERAL EDITOR
THOMAS G. PATERSON

Major Problems
in American Constitutional
History

DOCUMENTS AND ESSAYS

SECOND EDITION

EDITED BY

KERMIT L. HALL, Late

UNIVERSITY AT ALBANY,
STATE UNIVERSITY OF NEW YORK

TIMOTHY S. HUEBNER

RHODES COLLEGE

Australia • Brazil • Japan • Korea • Mexico • Singapore • Spain • United Kingdom • United States

WADSWORTH
CENGAGE Learning™

Major Problems in American Constitutional History: Documents and Essays, Second Edition
Kermit L. Hall, Late
Timothy S. Huebner

Senior Publisher: Suzanne Jeans

Sponsoring Editor: Jeffrey Greene

Development Editor: Terri Wise

Assistant Editor: Megan Curry

Editorial Assistant: Megan Chrisman

Senior Marketing Manager: Katherine Bates

Marketing Coordinator: Lorreen Pelletier

Marketing Communications Manager: Christine Dobberpuhl

Associate Content Project Manager: Sara Abbott

Senior Art Director: Cate Barr

Print Buyer: Paula Vang

Senior Rights Acquisition Account Manager: Katie Huha

Production Service/Compositor: Integra

Cover Designer: Gary Regaglia, Metro Design

Cover Image: Lamb, A. A., *Emancipation Proclamation*, Gift of Edgar William and Bernice Chrysler Garbisch, Image courtesy of the board of Trustees, National Gallery of Art, Washington, 1864 or after, oil on canvas, .825 × 1,372 (32 3/8 × 54); framed: .965 × 1.510 × .053 (38 × 59 7/16 × 2 1/8)

For product information and technology assistance, contact us at **Cengage Learning Academic Resource Center, 1-800-423-0563**
For permission to use material from this text or product, submit all requests online at **www.cengage.com/permissions**
Further permissions questions can be e-mailed to **permissionrequest@cengage.com**

Library of Congress Control Number: 2009920385

ISBN-13: 978-0-618-54333-5

ISBN-10: 0-618-54333-3

Wadsworth
20 Channel Center Street
Boston, MA 02210
USA

Cengage Learning is a leading provider of customized learning solutions with office locations around the globe, including Singapore, the United Kingdom, Australia, Mexico, Brazil, and Japan. Locate your local office at **www.cengage.com/international.**

Cengage Learning products are represented in Canada by Nelson Education, Ltd.

For your course and learning solutions, visit **www.cengage.com/ wadsworth**

Purchase any of our products at your local college store or at our preferred online store **www.ichapters.com.**

Printed in Canada
1 2 3 4 5 6 7 13 12 11 10 09

Dedicated to the memory of Kermit L. Hall—scholar, teacher, mentor

Contents

C H A P T E R   3

Rights in the New Republic

Page 76

C H A P T E R   4

The Departmental Theory and the Establishment of Judicial Review

Page 110

CHAPTER 5
Andrew Jackson, Nullification, and Indian Removal
Page 157

CHAPTER 6
Abraham Lincoln, Slavery, and the Civil War
Page 192

CHAPTER 11
Race and Civil Rights in the Cold War Era
Page 383

CHAPTER 12
Abortion Rights: The United States and South Africa Compared
Page 417

C H A P T E R   1 3
Freedom of and Freedom from Religion
Page 451

C H A P T E R   1 4
Federalism and Judicial Review
Page 484

C H A P T E R   1 5
Presidential Power from the Cold War to the War on Terror
Page 518

A P P E N D I X   I
Page 557

A P P E N D I X   I I
Page 575

Preface

By any measure, the U.S. Constitution is a remarkable document. Viewed in historical context, the principles it enunciates were revolutionary in nature. The opening words of its preamble—"We the People"—boldly proclaimed to a world of monarchs and aristocrats that in America the people were sovereign. In 1787, never had any nation made such a claim. During the next two centuries, the words of the American founders echoed across the oceans and helped usher in a modern era of democratic constitutionalism and human rights. Whatever debt the founders owed to their ancient forbears or to their immediate English ancestors, the American experiment in constitutional government had a profound effect on the world. In our time, when the efficacy of such principles as the separation of powers and the freedom of speech, for example, seems self-evident, it is easy to lose sight of the founders' achievement.

More than a charter of ideals, though, for 220 years the Constitution has served as a workable and adaptable blueprint for governing a nation. Through a bitter battle over its ratification, a bloody civil war over slavery, a wrenching transition to an industrial economy, and popular movements for the civil rights of African Americans and women, the Constitution has evolved yet endured. In its long history, the document has been amended 27 times. Ten of those amendments, the Bill of Rights, came in the immediate aftermath of ratification. Another three resulted from the Civil War, while other flourishes of constitutional revision occurred during the Progressive Era and the post–World War II period. The ability of the Constitution to absorb the social and political shocks of American life certainly stands out as one of its most striking attributes.

The judiciary has played a particularly significant role in adapting the Constitution to changing social realities. The founders' drafting of a brief constitutional text—it contains approximately 4,500 words—had the effect, perhaps unintended, of placing extraordinary power in the hands of judges. Although famously described as the "least dangerous branch" by Alexander Hamilton, beginning in the early nineteenth century the American judiciary assumed a significant role in constitutional interpretation. This fact has prompted some critics to charge that the Supreme Court acts as a sort of sitting constitutional convention, in which un-elected judges exercise the power to say what the Constitution means at any given time. Such an imprecise term as "due process of law," for example, has undergone considerable judicial interpretation over the past century, thus spawning fierce debates over the meaning of the constitutional text and the nature of the judicial role.

The study of the Constitution's history is important on a number of levels. In the most basic sense, in our precedent-based common law system, in order for present law to be legitimate, it must have some historical connection. In other words, we achieve stability in our constitutional polity by linking the past to the present. For this reason, constitutional history has figured prominently in our public life and has continually emerged as a source of political and scholarly controversy. Time and again public officials, whether in Congress, the White House, or the Supreme Court, have turned to the history of the Constitution to support their positions. Just as often, given the ambiguity of the past, historians and legal scholars have clashed with one another over what lessons previous constitutional struggles actually teach us. Whether inside or outside of the academy, conservatives, liberals, and radicals alike invoke the Constitution in support of their respective political agendas, and in order to assess the validity of their claims, informed citizens need to know what the Constitution says. During the past decade alone, Americans have witnessed the impeachment of a president, the settling of a disputed election by the Supreme Court, and the emergence of contentious debate over the scope of executive power and the meaning of civil liberties in wartime. Because the Constitution is the one text the interpretation of which truly affects the lives of all Americans, the study of its historical development remains as important and as relevant as ever.

This book attempts to capture some of the controversies that have marked America's constitutional history. Like other volumes in the *Major Problems in American History* series, the chapters that follow contain both primary documents and scholarly essays. Primary sources give instructors and students a chance to read firsthand accounts from the past, while the essays provide the perspective and context that only scholars can provide. Although the first edition was divided into two separate volumes, the second edition is condensed into one, in order to accommodate the large number of instructors who teach constitutional history in a single-semester format. The content of the second edition, moreover, includes significant changes from the first, which reflect recent scholarship on such topics as race, gender, popular constitutionalism, and comparative constitutionalism. Thus, the book contains a number of new selections, such as Paul Finkelman's piece on the slavery issue at the Constitutional Convention and Julie Novkov's essay on women's protective legislation during the Progressive Era. Among the new documents, moreover, are several landmark Supreme Court decisions of the past decade on such issues as religion, federalism, and executive power. Still, many of the classic cases and documents in American constitutional history are included here.

Numerous individuals have contributed in important ways to this volume. I thank Thomas Paterson for inviting me to undertake this project and Robert McMahon for initially suggesting that I complete the work that Kermit Hall had begun. Robert Wagner in Albany, as well as Ashley Cundiff and Joseph Doyle in Memphis, ably assisted in locating materials at various stages along the way. Meredith "Murfy" Nix, in the Department of History at Rhodes College, provided expert assistance with a variety of tasks, including editing, sorting, and paginating multiple versions of the manuscript. I could not have completed this book without her Herculean labors. Rhodes colleagues Michael Drompp, Dee Garceau-Hagen, David McCarthy, Gail Murray, Michael Nelson, James Vest, and Lynn Zastoupil all offered moral support at several points along the way, while Dean Robert Llewellyn and Provost Charlotte Borst provided institutional support that allowed me to complete the book in a timely fashion. I am especially grateful for the encouragement given to me by Phyllis Hall.

In addition, I thank the following colleagues whose valuable comments helped guide this revision: Steven R. Boyd, University of Texas at San Antonio; Christopher Capozzola, Massachusetts Institute of Technology; Paul G.E. Clemens, Rutgers University; Gregory Schmidt, Winona State University; and Christopher Waldrep, San Francisco State University.

The editors at Wadsworth/Cengage—Jean Woy, Jeff Greene, Terri Wise, Sara Abbott, and Anita Iyer—were models of professionalism from start to finish, and I express my deep appreciation to all of them for helping to make this a better book. Finally, my wife Kristin, as always, encouraged and supported me in every way. She remains my "biggest fan."

When Kermit L. Hall published the first edition of this book in 1992, I was one of his doctoral students at the University of Florida. Although best known for his accomplishments as a scholar and his talents as an academic administrator, Kermit was above all an exceptional teacher and mentor. Remarkably, not only did he remain an active scholar while he served as a university president, Kermit also continued to teach. In fact, at the time of his tragic death of a heart attack in August 2006, he was preparing to offer a course on the history of the Supreme Court at the State University of New York at Albany. With his extraordinary ability to analyze and synthesize the past, Kermit stands out as the most effective, engaging, and demanding instructor whom I have ever encountered. It has been an honor to complete this project, and it is with deep admiration that I dedicate this volume to his memory.

T.S.H.

CHAPTER

1

Interpreting American Constitutional History

Scholars approach the history of the U.S. Constitution from a variety of perspectives. Law professors, political scientists, and historians study the past in different ways and for different reasons. In general, law professors approach the past as present-minded advocates who <u>seek historical</u> support for a specific side in a current <u>public policy debate</u> or to illustrate a particular legal theory. They may also seek to find the historical origins of a particular doctrine in order to understand current law. Political scientists who study American constitutional history usually focus on the relationship among governmental institutions, the allocation of power, and the development of doctrine. For political scientists, history serves as a methodological tool or approach used to <u>understand</u> a particular theory of politics or constitutionalism. For their part, <u>historians generally approach the nation's constitutional history for the sake of studying the past, perhaps in hopes that it may help us to gain insight into ourselves and our</u> society. Because of their emphasis on studying change over time, historians pay <u>stricter</u> attention to the chronology of events than lawyers and political scientists generally do. Moreover, because they are situated in departments of history, which usually pay a great deal of attention to social and cultural forces, historians tend to exhibit a greater sensitivity to extra-legal factors in studying the nation's constitutional past. Despite these different purposes and approaches, legal scholars, political scientists, and historians have all made significant contributions to scholarship in the field of American constitutional history. Lawyers and political scientists have provided sophisticated interpretations of constitutions, laws, institutions, and doctrines, while historians have ensured that the study of constitutional and legal development remains firmly rooted in the context of the times.

To be sure, all of these approaches reflect a <u>range of ideological</u> perspectives that inform their interpretations. The radical tradition in American constitutional scholarship originated in the progressive era of the early twentieth century, when leading historians emphasized the role of private property ownership in the writing and ratification of the Constitution. This strain of thought continues to manifest itself through the work of those who focus on how the judicial interpretation of the Constitution has supported the existing structures of power and benefited economic elites. Conservative constitutional thought, in contrast, has taken a drastically different approach. Conservative scholars have emphasized the important role that ideological principles played at the time of the founding. Because of their high opinion of the Constitution's framers, many conservative scholars and judges have emphasized the need for the American judiciary to adhere to a jurisprudence of original intent—the belief that judges should interpret the Constitution by strictly upholding the principles articulated at the founding. Suspicious of activist judges and national regulatory power, conservative scholars tend to celebrate the vision of limited government and the strict protection of private property rights that prevailed from the time of the founding up through the early twentieth century. Finally, liberal scholars have stressed the evolution of American constitutional principles, particularly the advancement of the rights of free expression and the government's regulation of the excesses of capitalism. Generally speaking, during the past 50 years, liberals have been more sympathetic than either radicals or conservatives to the exercise of judicial power, for judges acted as the prime movers in the rights revolution of the late twentieth century. The liberal vision of American constitutionalism thus encompasses faith in the power of law to protect individual liberty and bring about a more just society. Liberals and conservatives generally share an optimistic belief that American constitutionalism embodies core values—despite their emphasis on different values— while radicals hold a more critical view of the constitutional order as defined by power and property.

Such widely divergent approaches and perspectives raise a host of questions for students of U.S. constitutional history. How should we engage in the study of the history of American constitutionalism? By taking constitutional ideals at face value or by attempting to uncover the economic interests that might lie behind them? Should our study of constitutional interpretation focus on the opinions of the U.S. Supreme Court, or should we look to "the people" as the source of the Constitution's meaning? If we emphasize the decisions of the Supreme Court, do we view those rulings as a unifying feature of our constitutional tradition or as expressions of political power? If we view the people as most important, do we celebrate their work or stress their cultural prejudices? Does the legitimacy of constitutional values endure because succeeding generations maintain fidelity to the assumptions of those who have come before them? Or does the maintenance of an effective constitutional order depend on each generation's creatively adapting the Constitution to ever-changing social and economic circumstances? Scholars of American constitutional history continue to disagree vigorously about such matters.

✣ E S S A Y S

The following four essays reflect these spirited debates over American constitutionalism and present some of the major themes of this book. Jennifer Nedelsky, a law professor at the University of Toronto, offers a critique from within the progressive tradition. She emphasizes the role of the Constitution's framers and, subsequently, the nation's courts in attempting to protect private property from democratic majorities. The essay by John Semonche, a historian at the University of North Carolina, represents a very different perspective. Semonche applies the concept of "civil religion" to the work of the Supreme Court. Rather than viewing the judiciary as protective of elite interests, Semonche describes the Court as a unifying and legitimizing force in American culture. The third essay, by Stanford law professor Larry D. Kramer, stresses "the people themselves" as the primary movers in the nation's constitutional past. Rejecting altogether an emphasis on the judiciary, Kramer provides a provocative alternative to more conventional court-centered accounts. Because of his emphasis on the work of popular majorities, Kramer's approach has won respect from an interesting combination of radical and conservative scholars. Finally, historian Linda K. Kerber of the University of Iowa urges us to think about how the concept of gender has informed our nation's constitutional discourse. Despite the apparently generic language of citizenship, she shows how a 2001 decision of the U.S. Supreme Court in fact treated men and women quite differently.

The Constitution and the Protection of Private Property

JENNIFER NEDELSKY

Private property has shaped the structure of the American political system. The framework of our political institutions and the categories through which we understand politics developed around the problems of making popular government compatible with the security of property. This focus on property has been the source of the greatest strengths of the American Constitution, of its greatest weaknesses, and of the distorted quality even of its strengths.

Our Constitution maintains a working tension between democratic values and the privileged status of private rights. This impressive achievement has its roots in the Framers' concern with protecting property from democratic incursion. Their sense of the vulnerability of property in a republic became the focus for the broader task of securing individual rights against the tyranny of the majority. This focus, in turn, led to the greatest weakness of our system: its failure to realize its democratic potential. The Framers' preoccupation with property generated a shallow conception of democracy and a system of institutions that allocates political power unequally and fails to foster political participation. Finally, the focus on property distorted the very strength it provided: the conception and institutionalization of rights as limits to the legitimate scope of the state. With property as the paradigmatic instance of the vulnerability of rights in a democracy, inequality became both a presumption and an object of protection which skewed the conception of limited government that underlies our Constitution. Both the skewed conception and the stunted forms of democracy have outlasted the primacy of property itself as a constitutional barrier to democratic action.

To understand the enduring significance of property in our system, we must understand the original formation of the United States Constitution: the Federalist victory at the Constitutional Convention in 1787, ratified in 1788 and consolidated with the rise of judicial review in the first decades of the nineteenth century. The struggles over the formation involved fundamental choices about the allocation of power, the hierarchy of values the system would foster and protect, and the relation between citizens and their government. And the terms in which the choices were framed were as important as the choices themselves. The choices shaped our institutions; the categories and priorities still shape our perception of alternatives and the grounds on which we choose among them.

The core of my argument is that those who won the formative contests over the nature of the new republic were preoccupied with the protection of private property. This is not a repetition of the Progressives' claim that "the new government was a republic rigged up with contrivances to protect the interests of the propertied minority." That claim is crudely true, but it misses what is most important about property in the formation of the Constitution: the distortion of the problems and potential of republican government. My emphasis is not on economic interest, but on the structure of ideas and institutions.

In the 1780s, the urgent sense that property rights had to be protected from democratic legislatures became the focus for formulating the principle that individual rights set limits to the legitimate power of government. That property-centered formulation shaped the Constitution in 1787 and then hardened into a notion of rights as judicially enforced boundaries dividing the legitimate scope of government from the protected sphere of individual liberty. This formative focus on property resulted in the neglect of two crucial issues: the means of fostering popular participation in government and the relationship between economic and political power. Both our institutions and our tradition of political thought still betray this original neglect.

These neglected issues are part of the basic problem: the original focus on property placed inequality at the center of American constitutionalism. For the Framers, the protection of property meant the protection of *unequal* property and thus the insulation of both property and inequality from democratic transformation. Effective insulation, in their view, required wealth-based inequality of access to political power. It also meant that the illegitimacy of redistribution defined the legitimate scope of the state. The inherent vulnerability of all individual rights became transformed into a fear of "the people" as a threatening propertyless mass whose power must be contained. The lesson of the formation is that when inequality is built into the conception of rights as limits to legitimacy, both our institutions and our understanding of constitutionalism must be distorted. Those distortions remain to be grappled with in the post-New Deal era of contested egalitarianism.

The modern welfare state does not fit easily within the Federalists' conceptual framework. Property once provided the conceptual boundary to the legitimate scope of government. That boundary is now threatened by the changing meaning of property and the demands of equality which simultaneously challenge traditional rights of property and the traditional scope of the state. In many crucial respects, we have accepted the New Deal but rejected its conceptual underpinnings. As a country, we routinely engage in redistribution to ameliorate social ills, but we have not simply accepted property as a mere social construct to be redefined or redistributed without constraint. The status of property as boundary lingers despite its disintegration as a constitutional concept. We countenance redistribution as a means, but we have no consensus on a vision of the state that clearly defines redistribution as a legitimate goal. And we tacitly rely upon, but have no clear means of justifying, this distinction between means and goal. In short, because the original structure of constitutionalism rested on an effort to prevent democratic control of property, our post-New Deal state requires a rethinking not just of the meaning of property, but also of the scope and purpose of the state. As such, it requires new foundations for constitutionalism.

I should clarify my claims about property: I do not claim that any particular property regime has inevitable consequences for democracy and constitutionalism. The links I do claim are the following: the Federalists' focus on protecting property from redistribution and, more broadly, from democratic redefinition, led to a misunderstanding of both the problems and the potential of democracy; and treating the protection of unequal property as the paradigm case of the problem of protecting individual rights in a democracy led to a misconception of the complex relation between democracy and individual autonomy, which is the true problem of constitutionalism. It was thus not property as such, but the effort to protect property and inequality from democratic revision, that has had distorting consequences.…

[T]he emergence of the American conception of limited government is a story of contests, not of monolithic forces. No one strain of thought, no single set of ideas or interests entirely shaped the American Constitution. But despite ongoing conflict and even accommodation, one strain of thought, that of the Federalists, won out. And in that dominant mode of thought, property was the focus around which the basic issues of limited government were worked out. The story of limited government in America is thus, in part, the story of the triumph of the Federalist perspective and of the priority it accorded to property.

. . . The principle of consent was the core of political discourse in the debates over independence and the early discussions of the new forms of government for the former colonies. There was a consensus that men had the right to be bound only by laws to which they had consented, and that consent was essential to republican government. The agreement on this general principle was deep and broad enough to obscure the uncertainties and disagreements about just what consent should mean in practice.

By the 1780s, the confidence of the revolutionary era had waned, and the emphasis on consent had shifted. Almost all the new state governments had issued paper money and passed debtor relief laws which were widely perceived as attacks on property rights. These events appeared to many as dramatic evidence of the limits of the principle of consent as the foundation for good and just government. The revolutionary claim that a man is a slave if his property can be taken without his consent gave way to the grim realization that consent alone was not adequate protection; property was now threatened by duly elected republican legislatures. The first stage in the development of limited government was characterized by a focus on this threat.

For many of the leading figures in American politics, the events of the 1780s signaled the need to replace the Articles of Confederation with a central government strong enough to take a respected place among the nations of the world and capable of avoiding and controlling the unjust propensities of the state governments. The Federalists were the chief proponents of such views in the debates over the Constitution. To say that they treated republican principles primarily as a problem, rather than a goal, would be a slight overstatement. It would, however, capture an important matter of emphasis: they took the principle of consent as a given and turned their attention to the dangers inherent in governments based on such principles. The result was a subtle but important shift in focus from the promise of republican government to the containment of its threats.

James Madison provided the most thoughtful formulation of the basic problem which republican government posed for the Federalists. Good government must be able to protect both the "rights of persons" and the "rights of property." In republican government, those two objectives were in tension with one another because of a third category of rights, the right of all men to be governed only by those laws to which they consent. The problem was that if political rights were granted equally to all, the rights of persons and the rights of property would not be equally protected. The propertied could be relied upon to respect the rights of persons, in which they also had an interest. But the propertyless had no corresponding interest in property. The rights of property would thus be at risk whenever the sheer numerical advantage of the poor was translated into political power through equal political rights. The threat to property in America was particularly insidious because it took indirect forms such as depreciation of currency rather than direct expropriation. No one denied that property was a basic right, but the propertyless majority would nevertheless demand measures that destroyed the security of property. The problem of providing equal protection for the rights of persons and the rights of property in a manner consistent with republican principles was, Madison said, the most difficult of all political problems.

Part of the American solution to this problem was the formulation of important categories and hierarchies of rights. Civil rights, which included both the rights of persons and of property, were to be distinguished from political rights. Political rights, moreover, were conceived of as mere means to the true end of government, the protection of civil rights. In this view, political rights had no intrinsic value. By designating political rights as means, it was possible to treat them as purely instrumental and entirely contingent, and thus to make compromises of these rights appear not to involve compromise of principle.

In 1787, however, the choice implicit in these categories was still preliminary, its precise formulation and implementation unclear. The Constitutional Convention of that year can be seen as an effort to create a government which could protect all the competing rights of citizens: political rights as well as the rights of persons and property. Madison and his fellow Federalists were certain in their conviction that civil rights provided independent standards by which to measure the outcome of democratic processes. They felt acutely that when property rights were infringed by legislatures—that is, were infringed with the consent of the governed—such consent did not make the infringements legitimate. There was, however, no comparable certainty among the Framers about the way to give effect to those independent standards. In a republic where the people are, in principle, their own governors, the question of limited government becomes a question of *self*-limiting government—which, as we shall see, poses the irreducible problem of a government setting and enforcing its own limits.

The solution that emerged from the 1787 convention was one which did not rely heavily on limits as such. State governments were limited by specific prohibitions, but the Federal government would rely primarily on a structure of institutions designed to check each other and to minimize the likelihood of effective majoritarian tyranny. This solution had several advantages. It sustained the tensions between the competing categories of civil and political rights, as well as the particular tensions among the rights of persons, property, and participation. The Constitution of 1787 could encompass all of the competing values by avoiding a clear subordination of one to the other. It provided a fluid kind of solution which left somewhat vague whether the conceptual primacy of civil over political rights was to be translated into an institutionalized hierarchy of enforceable limits. It was important to the development of limited government in America that the Constitution of 1787 left the tensions between competing values open and alive. It was equally important that the balance struck between them was skewed by the Framers' preoccupation with property.

For those whose views prevailed at the Convention, property was the central instance of rights at risk in a republic. It was property that alerted them to the inherent vulnerability of minority rights in popular government, and thus property that became the focal point for the broader problem. And property was not just an abstract symbol. It was a right whose security was essential to the economic and political success of the new republic. If property could not be protected, not only prosperity, but liberty, justice, and the international strength of the nation would ultimately be destroyed. The focus on property bred a general suspicion of the people. Influential Framers, such as Madison, foresaw a permanent propertyless majority which would be fluid in its composition, but fixed in its inevitability. "The people" thus posed a permanent threat to the rights of property, rights whose protection was demanded not only by "the rules of justice," but by the requirements of political and economic stability.

Under the Constitution of 1787, the people were to be the base of the government, but their participation and efficacy was to be controlled, channeled, and contained by the structure of government. Both Federalists and Anti-Federalists agreed that the structure of the institutions outlined in the Constitution would draw the elite into the government. The people would have the role of periodically selecting among those elite and trying to evaluate their performance, but the ongoing control of public affairs would be left in the hands of the suitable (and propertied) few. The Anti-Federalists raised what we would today call democratic objections. But the potential value of active self-governance never engaged the attention of the Federalists.

They were committed to republican government, which they thought allowed for the highest degree of popular participation possible without disintegration into anarchy or oligarchy. But theirs was not a literal vision of self-governance. They wanted the elite to rule. They treated the ability to govern as essentially fixed (rather than as a capacity that could be developed) and as class-based. Thus they were not concerned with expanding or enhancing the people's competence and involvement in public affairs. For the Federalists, the challenge was to make republican government compatible with the security of rights, not to design institutions that would foster men's ability to govern themselves. The democratic values that prevailed in 1787 were shallow values, and, in the subsequent tradition of American political thought, they have remained so.

The preoccupation with property had another important consequence for the structure of American government and the dominant tradition of political thought: the neglect of the problems arising from the relationship between economic and political power. For those preoccupied with containing the popular threat to property, the dangers posed by wealth commanded little attention; the problem of economic power remained submerged.

In sum, the Constitution of 1787 institutionalized the principle of consent in ways that left open important questions about what to do in a conflict between the rights of the people to implement their will through their representatives and the independent rights of property. The Constitution did not simply give precedence to property (or other private rights) over the republican principles of government by consent. However, the primacy of the Federalist concern with protecting property so shaped the structure of the Constitution that it was characterized as much by this implicit priority as by the absence of its formal institutionalization. The tensions remained, but the balance was tipped.

The remaining step in the formation of the Constitution, the rise of judicial review, tipped the balance further. The establishment of judicial review may be seen as the culmination and consolidation of the Federalist conception of politics. The Marshall Court took the Federalist hierarchy of rights to its logical, institutional conclusion (a conclusion which Madison resisted, preferring balanced tensions to logical consistency). By the end of the 1820s, the American approach to limited government had come to be characterized by its focus on clear limits, by its vision of hard boundaries as giving meaning and efficacy to the idea of limited government.

Judicial review was established in the context of the rise of early party divisions, the battles between the Hamiltonian Federalists and the Jeffersonian Republicans. With the victory of the Jeffersonians in 1800, it seemed clear to the Federalists that winning in 1787 had not been enough. The carefully crafted federal structure alone was not sufficient protection for certain basic rules and rights—property and contract in particular. Property was thus one of the crucial issues around which judicial review and the law-politics distinction was built. The courts could make a strong claim that property belonged in a distinctly legal realm, which had the sanction of the long and honorable tradition of common law. The need for the judiciary to protect this venerable realm from legislative encroachment could then be seen to rest on a neutral legal tradition rather than on the fear and suspicion of the people. Once the crucial boundaries were defined as a matter of law, the judiciary's claim to draw them was virtually unassailable.

Limited government thus took the form of judicially enforced boundaries. The dilemma of self-limiting government—of the political entity requiring limits being the one to set those limits—was "solved" by placing those limits in an arena declared to be outside of politics. The bifurcation of law and politics separated the limits from their object while giving the judicial source of limits a status exalted enough to stand against the claims of democracy. The neutrality of law stood above the petty squabbles of politics. The particular American dilemma of circumscribing the democratic power of a sovereign could thus also be evaded by recourse to a distinct legal arena which provided an ostensibly apolitical basis for defining and enforcing limits. Law, according to the model, did not thwart the will of the people; law gave effect to it in a loftier, truer way than politics.

The idea of boundaries and of a sharp distinction between law and politics has been central to the American conception of limited government. Property was for 150 years the quintessential instance of rights as boundaries. It has been the symbol and source of a protected sphere into which the state cannot enter. Property has also carried with it the paradox of self-limiting government: it is the limit to the state; it is also the creature of the state. In property, the state sets its own limits.

Despite all the ways in which the state has changed those limits when it has suited some "public purpose," the paradox has been kept obscured by the distinction between law and politics. This distinction has sustained a mythic quality of property as not merely a social construct, but a basic right, linked in powerful ways to cherished values of freedom and autonomy. The myth of property and the image of the law-politics distinction have sustained each other and have together provided the foundation for the American conception of limited-government.

Property remains central to our conception of government. The basic issues of the legitimate scope of government, indeed the desirable nature of government, continue to be fought over the issue of property. From the early challenges to workmen's compensation, to the continuing regulation-vs-market debate, to new claims for equal protection on the grounds of wealth, property has stood at the center of conflicts that shape the kind of political system we have. The context for these contests continues to be the property-centered ideas and institutions shaped during the formation of the Constitution. . . .

The Supreme Court as a Unifying Force in American Culture

JOHN E. SEMONCHE

At a time in American history when group seems to be pitted against group, when irradicable differences are stressed to the detriment of commonalities, when there seems to be no end to claims of victimization, and when social critics worry about the society falling apart, we need to take a fresh look at the ties that have bound a diverse people together.

Americans are united within a civic culture that is much stronger and more durable than current worries suggest. These ties that bind are primarily legal, political, and spiritual; they nurture and promote the interests of the individual within a national community; and they are institutionalized within the American constitutional system. The Supreme Court of the United States, which is at the apex of the country's legal system, plays a central role in explicating, reinforcing, and expanding the range of these ties. . . .

From the beginning, Americans, lacking any traditional basis for nationhood, defined themselves in terms of ideas—liberty, equality, and republican government founded upon the people's consent—and embarked upon an experiment to determine whether a people so defined could constitute an enduring nation. Although many generations have passed since the founding of the United States, the experiment continues, and the unfinished nature of American society remains one of its most distinguishing characteristics. So it must be, for this joining together on the basis of shared principles leaves much in a person's identity to be determined outside the parameters of this limited community. Those who seek to tighten the embrace of this community by attempting to read into it their cultural preferences as further tests of one's Americanism contradict the community's core principles. On the other hand, those who stress their diversity and attack the cultural grafts that their opponents would attach to being American too often fail to distinguish these vulnerable grafts from the core principles themselves. No

From Semonche, John E., *Keeping the Faith: A Cultural History of the U.S. Supreme Court.* Copyright 1998 Rowman and Littlefield. Reproduced with permission of the publisher.

matter how strident and seemingly total is the identification with a particular group, the American remains a member of the national community and both implicitly and explicitly works within its understood parameters. For instance, "claims for tolerance, equality and justice must be based on the democratic principles of the national ideology," for by itself membership in any group "creates no claim on others for tolerance, respect, equality, or anything else."

From the time of the Declaration of Independence, Americans were challenged to fulfill a founding myth that viewed the country "as a divinely inspired asylum for those who sought liberty and opportunity." Blessings, therefore, were to be shared with new arrivals. The idealistic core of American identity was only strengthened as immigrants eagerly accepted "the universal norms of a moral and social order which gave them equality of status, liberty of expression, and the right to consider themselves citizens." Throughout its history, the country staked its identity "on the peculiar faith that the One and the Many are not only mutually compatible but essential to freedom."

As successive waves of immigrants peopled the new land, they quickly absorbed a legal tradition that responded to them as individuals. "It is this easily transferred and easily absorbed idea of a constitutional system that protects the individual ... that harmonizes great social, economic and even ethnic differences in American society." In the long run, this legal emphasis on the individual works against the stigmatization or subordination of any group of individuals.

When Thomas Paine exhorted Americans to shed their loyalty to King George III in 1776, he suggested that they crown law as their king. And this is precisely what Americans proceeded to do. What eighteenth-century Americans had in mind when they spoke of the rule of law was the common law tradition, as they had interpreted it, with its emphasis on the protection of individual rights and its restraint on arbitrary authority. The rule of law sought to embrace all official conduct under standards of fairness, impartiality, and equality. Its legitimacy stemmed from a faith in procedures and reasoned justification. ...

[L]aw, itself, should be taken seriously. Those who see it as a tool of powerful interests or those who search for hidden motivations behind its text are refusing to come to terms with its significance in American culture, a significance it had at the time of national creation and a significance that it retains today. ...

American unity, however, is not based upon overwhelming agreement upon substantive matters but rather on procedural and relational ones; that is, how are differences among persons to be resolved and how can opposing parties be accorded the equal respect due them. The American legal system provides the arena for resolving such disputes. In submitting the dispute to the resolution of courts, opposing parties are subscribing to a substantial consensus. They believe that the process will justly resolve their differences, that it respects them as individuals, and that it gives them the opportunity to be heard.

Such access to the judicial system provides an important means to present and argue new claims and eventually to bring about changes in the law. In this adversarial process lawyers play an important role. By transforming individual grievances into legal issues, lawyers contribute indispensably to making judges both understand and respond to the claims presented. In undertaking this responsibility, courts define and also educate a national community. The vocabulary of this conversation provides "a rhetorical coherence to public life by compelling those who disagree about one thing to speak a language which expresses their actual or pretended agreement about everything else." By forcing litigants to speak the language of the law, something new is created—"a place and mode of discourse, a set of relations, that form a central part of our civilization." The language and operation of the law thus define the political community in which contesting parties find their home.

Such a community cannot be created or maintained by force; this is why governmental repression, which seeks to replace difference with sameness, is so counterproductive. In fact, such diversity among individuals is the best testament to unity. Within this national community "the most fundamental notion of legality" requires that the government "justify, by reference to its legitimate interests and concerns, any intrusions on the liberty and bodily integrity of its citizens." The legal system provides a structure in which the search for liberty and justice can continue while managing conflict within the parameters of a prevailing consensus—precisely what the rule of law was designed to do. Conflict could not be eliminated, but its disrupting potential could be reduced. The continued success of the American experiment rests upon the maintenance of this consensus.

The law provides so many roles that virtually all people in society have parts in the continuing drama, and over a lifetime the roles they play can and do change. First, we have the initial lawmakers—legislators and those administrators charged with formulating rules. Then, we have the initial law enforcers—the police and other governmental officials armed with the authority of the law. In the position of mediators between those who enforce and those who are the subject of enforcement are lawyers and arbitrators. And, finally, we have ordinary citizens, who are grand and trial jurors and who may be summoned as either civil or criminal defendants or who themselves, as plaintiffs, may summon others to the bar to redress some grievance.

Overseeing this drama and both directing and playing a complex major role, both as lawmaker and law enforcer, is the judiciary. The term "director" may be too limited, for it implies a script much more finished than the drama of the law provides. Perhaps the judiciary can be most usefully viewed as a dramaturge, that is, as a specialist in the art or technique of dramatic composition and theatrical presentation. This dramaturge's work is ongoing and can never be completed, but continually it must explain, justify, and develop the drama in the direction of the essential goals of a rule of law.

This is what makes the judicial opinion such a rich source for viewing law as a culture-shaping force. Judges are not necessarily wiser than the other legal players, but the task imposed upon them is appreciably different. Legal texts are not self-interpretive, and eventually the authority of the law must rest upon "the process of writing opinions by which the decisions reached by the courts are given their meaning." Judges must indeed respect the texts of the past, but they must also take responsibility for an interpretation that can only be their own. Regularly the meaning of the opinions is broader than first perceived, for underpinning the resolution are conclusions about who we are and what we do or should desire. In dipping into the past and establishing continuity with the present, the judge "establishes or modifies a discursive and political community with his readers." In the process, generations are connected and so are different individuals and groups in the present.

The tradition of a rule of law is strong in the popular mind. All polls and surveys reveal a strong American commitment to obey the law that is not explained in terms of rational calculations of self-interest—the so-called instrumental approach. The normative approach, which suggests that people voluntarily obey the law because it is the right or moral or the just thing to do, continues to be a much more accurate description. There is a prevailing faith in the law, its relationship to common morality, and the essential fairness of its procedures.

In fact, the law's protections are so ingrained in the popular mind that they become generalized standards of judgment. "Life in modern America," one legal historian has said, "is a vast, diffuse school of law." Back in Jacksonian America the French traveler Alexis de Tocqueville had noted both the incorporation of legal language into everyday speech and a legalistic spirit pervading the whole society. In the century and a half since that time, public language has become even more legalistic in a continuing search for common values; it creeps "into the languages that Americans employ around the kitchen table, in the neighborhood, and in their diverse communities of memory and mutual aid." Legal standards become minimum moral standards, and an American commitment to the rule of law becomes no less than a matter of fundamental faith, a subject to which we now turn.

Much of what we have been considering is part of an American faith structure, a creed, even a civil or public religion. This creed commands belief, operates as a vehicle for public discourse, becomes a spur to reduce gaps between belief and practice, and serves as a code that can be legally implemented. In 1967, Robert Bellah introduced the term "American civil religion" into the arena of contemporary scholarly debate, drawing his evidence from presidential addresses with their references to God, the nation's mission, and the transcendent standards to which the American people are held accountable.

That a search for evidence of an American civil religion should seek out and find this God-talk in formal presidential addresses is understandable. The nation has no other single spokesman, and the words of reference to divine providence are regularly found in such speeches. But such references get us only so far in an attempt to explore the viability of the concept of an American civil religion. Talk is cheap, and although such references seem to strike a popular chord, they provide limited evidence of an operative faith structure. Too often, such references seem to be a matter of political gloss, all surface and little substance. In fact, this search for God-talk may well lead us astray.

In the sociological search for a spiritual tie that bound the diverse people called Americans together, Bellah did fasten on a concept that has led to substantial debate and criticism. The debate demonstrated that civil religion can be defined in diverse and contradictory ways, a result that called into question its serviceability as an analytical tool. However, if Americans are defined in terms of their beliefs and if their actions are to be judged in terms of standards established by those beliefs, then the term civil religion may advance an understanding of what unites Americans.

Instead of beginning with an example of what we would agree was a religion and then measuring a claimant against the standards the example established, sociologists, cultural anthropologists, and even theologians have defined religion in terms of its functions. These definitions have stressed symbolism, meaning, transcendence, and wholeness as characteristics by which to grasp religion's place in the modern world. Although much in this world can be explained, "lingering contingencies" or the human being's need for holistic explanations that lie beyond the competence of empirical science remain. Arguing that "any durable society seems to possess important collective religious aspects instrumental in its achievement of coherence and in its continuing viability," these writers have focused our attention on the many aspects of the culture that have religious characteristics. "A society acquires and maintains its legitimacy over time and through space on the basis of a meaning system which has been, empirically or historically speaking, most frequently religious," and "the possession of a common set of ideas, rituals, and symbols can supply an overarching sense of unity even in a society riddled with conflict." One theologian has defined religion as a comprehensive interpretive scheme that structures "human experience and understanding of self and world," or alternatively "as a kind of cultural and/or linguistic framework or medium that shapes the entirety of life and thought." A civil religion seeks to embrace the totality of public life and thought. To be more specific, the term "civil religion," as it is applied to the United States and used in this work, means "a public perception of our national experience, in the light of universal and transcendent claims upon human beings, but especially upon Americans; a set of values, symbols, and rituals institutionalized as the cohesive force and center of meaning uniting our many peoples."

None of the critics of the concept of an American civil religion have denied that the adjective "religious" can and should be attached to various aspects of American culture. Look at the way Americans have glorified the origin of their nation and insisted upon their destiny. George Washington was deified before he died, and the practical politicians of the late eighteenth century who wrestled with the details of establishing governments are hallowed as "Founding Fathers."

One of the problems with the civil religion concept, however, is that it has been the preserve of academicians, who have paid too little attention to the everyday world that the faithful inhabit. We need to look at the essentials of the American creed and see how they have become transcendent standards, not only for criticizing official action but also for promoting communication in the diverse society. To give more substance to the concept of an American civil religion, we eventually have to find some evidence of its social institutionalization.

American nationhood rests upon a common faith in a civil theology, largely composed of the principles of the Declaration of Independence, the Preamble to the Constitution, and the elaborated rights of the individual as found in the Constitution with its Bill of Rights. All of this is housed within the concept of a rule of law, which promises fair, equal, and just treatment to all. Americans become, then, a "'covenanting community' in which the commitment to freedom under law, having transcended the 'natural' bonds of race, religion, and class, itself takes on transcendent importance." From the beginning, then, law for Americans was necessarily concerned with what can best be described as "religio-moral issues" and courts provided "a major arena for airing transcendental issues." Sidney Mead, a historian of religion, has argued that Americans were adherents of a religion that "is essentially prophetic, which is to say that its ideals and aspirations stand in constant judgment over the passing shenanigans of the people, reminding them of the standards by which their current practices and those of their nation are ever being judged and found wanting."

As Joseph Vining, a thoughtful legal scholar, has suggested, law within American culture can be most usefully perceived not in terms of science, economics, or even history, but rather of theology. First of all, lawyers and theologians tend to rely on "texts produced by hierarchical authorities." Second, for both professions, faith is a prerequisite; only then can understanding follow. This faith involves belief that human life has meaning and that it can be ordered to help individuals fulfill their destiny. Third, both studies encompass all of human life in the "effort to make sense of our experience and make statements that are consistent and understandable in light of it all." Finally, the parallels between the courtroom and the church are obvious, including the solemnity of both temples and the formality of the discourse between the supplicant "praying for relief" and the robed figures of priestly authority.

To expand on Vining's first common characteristic—the existence of authoritative texts—the writing at the pinnacle of the civil religion's theological hierarchy is the Constitution. This document of fundamental law is unlike any other in that "it represents the lifeblood of the American nation, its supreme symbol and manifestation. It is so intimately welded to national existence that the two have become inseparable." The Constitution is the official embodiment of the nation's values, which, when articulated, "provide an important part of the 'moral cohesion' that is the cement for our national community." Supreme Court Justice Hugo L. Black went even further when he called the Constitution "my legal bible; its plan of our government is my plan and its destiny my destiny." It binds the American people because they regard it as supreme and as having a capacity to answer the "most troubling national questions."

This secular codification of fundamental law gains its predominant position because it flows from the mythical will of the whole people, the same way that the Bible represents the voice of God captured by His agents. Both texts contain most of the essentials of the theology and delineate the culture of believers. Priestly interpreters in both spheres rest their authority on their ability to extract meaning from the words and to draw conclusions in the form of judgments based upon the texts themselves. This task is far from a mechanical enterprise, for it involves the attempt to give moral structure to the world in which both the text and its interpreters live. As a rule of law seeks to define a culture, a society, and a world or cosmic view, it takes on a religious character. In drawing an analogy between a religious community and the American political community, one observer has said that the American constitutional text bears a close relationship to a sacred text in that the interpreter is charged with the responsibility of mediating "the past of the tradition with its present" for the purpose of infusing new life in the tradition. He adds that "for the American political community, the constitutional text is not (simply) a book of answers to particular questions. . . . It is, rather, a principal symbol, perhaps *the* principal symbol of fundamental aspirations of the tradition. . . ."

The basic theological principles are not so general that they lack any meaning or fail to provide a text that can be translated with some faithfulness to the original. For instance, take Thomas Jefferson's words in the Declaration, "All men are created equal." We know from human experience that not all persons are equally endowed with intelligence and material benefits. Were we God would we so create them? Or, less pretentiously, with our ability to allocate material benefits and our increasing ability to manipulate human matter, should we strive to achieve this goal? These are legitimate questions arising from the Declaration's text, and future generations may well take them quite seriously. Our history illustrates the way in which such fanciful questions of an earlier time can become real and demanding ones later.

To remain more faithful to Jefferson's text, clearly he was saying that all human beings are created with equal rights that their fellow creatures should respect and that government should protect. In Jefferson's time blacks were not considered the equal of whites, nor were women considered the equal of men. The problem, however, is not with the text but rather with the limitations of the times and of the translators of the text. Not all translators were equally circumscribed by such limitations. Abigail Adams warned her husband, John, of the rebellious potential of women who were denied the rights commanded by principles to which American males said they subscribed. Many blacks as well wondered how their profound inequality could be supported by a text acknowledging that God had ordained a basic equality among all human beings. Such disparities lead us to a recognition that in the practice of any faith gaps exist between belief and action. Before any progress can be made in bridging the distance between the two, the faithful must perceive the gap. Inevitably, we more easily perceive our ancestors' failings than our own.

What we are dealing with, then, is not a changing American faith over time, but a remarkably consistent faith in which its practitioners contend with the task, first, of recognizing that gaps between faith and practice do exist, and, second, of attempting to close them. A nation founded by conscious political action that rests its continuing existence upon a set of principles incorporated in a constitutional order may seem fragile indeed, for survival depends upon its people keeping their faith. One might well expect that such a people could easily become cynical, hypocritical, complacent, or apathetic. When Americans could be so characterized, however, such attitudes have been exposed and condemned by fellow Americans in every imaginable literary and pictorial form. These critics ask no more than that their compatriots live up to the demands of their shared faith. In fact, most, if not all, internal criticism of American society is premised upon the critic calling attention to a discrepancy between belief and action. Challenges to the core beliefs themselves are indeed rare.

At times, these ever-present critics are successful in stirring the people to action. As an illustration, the modern civil rights movement's success is in part explained by an identification of its aspirations with the civil theology. When Gunnar Myrdal, a Swedish social scientist, surveyed the condition of blacks in American society in the late 1930s and early 1940s, he found hope in what he called a spiritual consensus built around the ideas of dignity, equality, freedom, justice, and opportunity subscribed to by both "the rich and secure, out of pride and conservatism, and the poor and insecure, out of dire need." He concluded that the blacks and other disadvantaged groups "could not possibly have invented a system of political ideals which better corresponded to their interests." For Myrdal, these ideals constituted a creed that was "the cement in the structure of this great and disparate nation." The ensuing civil rights movement was solidly anchored in the American creed. When Presidents John F. Kennedy and Lyndon B. Johnson sought to get the monumental Civil Rights Act of 1964 through Congress, their speeches were filled with references to the need for Americans to live up to the demands of their civil theology by making its benefits available to all.

These eras when creedal politics supplant interest-group politics are relatively rare, but the system does contain an ongoing institution that is at the heart of the civil religion—the United States Supreme Court. In recognizing and helping to close gaps between common belief and common practice, the Supreme Court has played a major role. The Court is the priestly interpreter of the holy writ, the one agency in government that has the assigned duty to respond to the claims of individuals that the rights they have been promised have not been realized. Those cases involving a claim of individual right interposed against governmental action are real-life dramas, in which seemingly trivial events are transformed "into narratives with meanings that touch our largest concerns as a people engaged in self-government under the law." The Court's decisions reinforce a culture and speak to all about the integrity of the individual, the limits placed upon government, and how people should act.

In the process of writing opinions, the Court does far more than justify its decisions: it describes and defines American culture, it promotes unity, and it educates the people as to their responsibilities under the civil faith. All in all, the Court seeks to make the rule of law worthy of the faith a diverse people repose in it. This is as much a moral task as it is a legal one, and the Court has repeatedly insisted that it is the only agency that is both equipped and entitled to play the role of supreme priestly interpreter of the Constitution. In interpreting the holy writ, the Court not only describes, integrates, and preserves the law, it prioritizes, explicates, and then reinforces "the basic values...that make us a nation." In its opinions the Court articulates and perpetuates "the ideals and aspirations that define the national character." It explains both who we are and who we can be. As such, it maintains both the basic theology of the civil religion and the community it serves. As one longtime student of the Court has said, "it has remained true to its assumed role as our national conscience and our institutional common sense." Another critic of the Court has defended judicial review as "one important way the American political community struggles to remain faithful to its" basic principles. That community, he continues, is one "of political-moral judgment" involving how people are to be treated and how their rights and liberties are to be secured.

As any interpreter of the written word, the Supreme Court has considerable discretion; and in the task of interpreting, it is itself a creator. Precedent can, and at times should, be overruled, for the High Bench must enter into a dialogue with the past, not to accept its authority blindly but to inquire substantially into what has changed and what effect that change should have on the present ruling. In this dialogue with the past and with the advocates of the present, the Court explores "an enormous reservoir of intellectual and practical experience" and tends to make the law "a mode of communal self-education and self-constitution." In their opinions, the justices constantly synthesize the old with the new, respecting tradition but reevaluating and reconstituting it in response to new problems. By summoning up the past and then reshaping it as they rationalize their decisions, they continually reconstruct the culture itself. . . .

This is not to say that all justices at all times were protective of individual rights and of a national unity that would overcome local particularism. Nor is it contended that the approach taken here embraces all the important decisions that constitute the respective canons of constitutional law and constitutional history. What is being argued is that, first, the Supreme Court viewed union as a precondition for the protection of individual rights; second, that from the very beginning the justices saw their role in terms of safeguarding these rights; third, that the current protection of individual rights builds upon a long, evolutionary process; and finally, that this emphasis throughout its history has made the Court an increasingly significant unifying force within the pluralistic society. To say that "the Supreme Court has established itself as a central institution for the self-conscious and authoritative reconstitution of our language, culture, and community" may not be an exaggeration. Some of this work has been done quite consciously by the justices, and generally in both their decisions and their rhetoric they have lent credibility to their role as high priests of the American civil religion.

Popular Constitutionalism

LARRY D. KRAMER

By the early 1840s, popular constitutionalism and judicial supremacy were sharing space in American political culture, coexisting in an uncertain and sometimes tense relationship. The very diffuseness and decentralization of popular constitutionalism, combined with uncertainty over the means through which it was expressed, helped make this possible by leaving room for advocates of judicial supremacy to continue nursing their claim. The resulting dialectical tug of war continues even today. Struggle has not been constant. It has consisted of periodic confrontations or blowups occurring after years or sometimes decades during which active backers of the two perspectives jostled for position while ordinary citizens remained largely indifferent or unconcerned. Though we cannot know for sure, it is possible, and maybe even probable, that popular constitutionalism was the dominant public understanding during most of these latent periods, even as judicial supremacy was favored by and within the legal profession. What is certain is that popular constitutionalism was the clear victor each time matters came to a head. Yet the end of one cycle simply began another in which the Court and its supporters eventually renewed their efforts to establish judicial supremacy. Resurgent claims of judicial authority, in turn, gave rise to a new wave of criticism as opponents of the judiciary pushed back by advocating a revived or restored commitment to popular constitutionalism.

This claim runs counter to today's prevailing wisdom, which holds that "[f]or most of our history, most Americans have seen the Supreme Court as the ultimate interpreter of the Constitution, entitled (this side of an amendment) to impose its understanding of the Constitution on the states, the other branches of the federal government, and the people." It seems quite likely, however, that this conventional wisdom is wrong. The Constitution was written against a background of popular constitutionalism, and while an argument for judicial supremacy had emerged by the end of the 1790s, it was decisively repudiated both then and later. The idea did not disappear: there were always those who favored giving courts final say over the Constitution "this side of an amendment." But they were a minority. Not surprisingly, this minority included prominent judges and members of the legal profession—men like Marshall, Webster, and Story—and we have tended (understandably perhaps, but

From Kramer, Larry D., *The People Themselves: Popular Constitutionalism and Judicial Review.* Reproduced with permission of Oxford University Press.

without any real basis) to treat their views as authoritative, as reflecting an established practice and position. Yet the reality is that we have been privileging the views of men who suffered overwhelming political defeats each time they tried to establish their position. It was the views of Jefferson, Jackson, and Van Buren that carried the day and that reflected how most Americans apparently understood their Constitution.

Perhaps the point should not be stated so baldly, for we really have no way of knowing for sure who "most Americans" thought should have final authority to interpret the Constitution. A better inference to draw from the historical record might be that departmentalism and popular constitutionalism—which clearly were the rule in the beginning—probably continued to embody most people's intuitive sense of the matter. This conclusion rests partly on an assumption that prior beliefs normally persist unless and until something causes them to change. Change may occur either gradually or convulsively, but once realized it tends to be visible and easily spotted. Viewed in this light, it seems significant, as this chapter briefly recounts, that each time a controversy did arise—each time, that is, an event occurred affording us some opportunity to measure public sentiment—it resulted in a clear rejection of judicial supremacy and a reaffirmation of preexisting commitments to popular constitutionalism.

Bear in mind that popular constitutionalism never denied courts the power of judicial review: it denied only that judges had final say. During periods when no major controversies arose, most citizens (and most political leaders) were content to leave the Court's rulings unchallenged and to respect its status as, in Madison's words, "the surest expositor of the Constitution." Even during these periods, there were groups and movements that called upon the tradition of popular constitutionalism to press their own visions of the Constitution. Some of these movements sought and gained control of the political branches or the judiciary. Others had little immediate success but still helped to reshape American consciousness. Many simply petered out while a few suffered cataclysmic defeats. Yet what is most noteworthy is that whenever an issue or a leader managed to capture the general public's attention—whenever, in other words, circumstances impelled Americans to crystallize their latent beliefs and choose sides—they consistently chose popular constitutionalism over the view that the Constitution was subject to authoritative control by the judiciary.

That popular constitutionalism remained ascendant in the antebellum era seems uncontroversial. One sees this reflected, for example, in the judiciary's general quiescence on constitutional matters for most of the period, which stood in sharp contrast to the openly instrumental jurisprudence courts employed when it came to private law. . . .

Because little happened to force the issue for a generation after John Marshall's death in 1835, the distinction between judicial review and judicial supremacy received little attention. Certainly this was true for ordinary citizens, but even politicians and party leaders had little reason to worry about the distinction in these years. Popular constitutionalism embodied their prior beliefs, and its preeminence could be taken for granted because it was reflected in everyday practice. The Justices did address some important questions, but not in ways that threatened prevailing Jacksonian orthodoxies or caused serious political friction. The Supreme Court remained a presence on the constitutional scene, with a potential question respecting the nature of its authority lurking in the background.

The tensions implicit in this state of affairs were ultimately exposed by the problem of slavery in the territories—which brought the period of latency to an abrupt ending and produced yet another strong reaffirmation of popular constitutionalism with a matching repudiation of judicial supremacy. Whether and where to permit slavery in the territories dominated national politics for a decade and a half, from the moment in 1846 when David Wilmot introduced his famous proviso to prevent the introduction of slavery outside the old South, until the question was finally overtaken by secession in 1861. Framed on both sides as a constitutional problem, the issue was dealt with by the parties in politics as a matter for popular constitutionalism. The unhappy efforts of party leaders to find a solution were reflected in such brittle legislation as the Kansas–Nebraska Act and the Compromise of 1850. A small group lobbied to turn the dispute over to the Supreme Court, but their efforts to obtain legislation to this effect went nowhere as Whigs and Democrats alike questioned whether the Court was "a fit tribunal for the determination of a great political question like this." And then the Justices rendered the issue of legislation moot by reaching out to address the slavery problem without it in *Dred Scott v. Sandford*, perhaps the single most reviled decision in the canon of American constitutional law.

Dred Scott was, by almost any measure, a mistake. Mark Graber has recently produced some interesting data suggesting that Chief Justice Taney's opinion was initially received by many as a useful and moderate compromise, enabling Northern Democrats to make modest gains in state elections held soon after the decision. If so, this acceptance was short lived, as opponents immediately set about discrediting the Court in the press. Their efforts soon bore fruit—unintentionally aided by Southern extremists, whose actions in Kansas destroyed any hopes for moderation or compromise. The wounds inflicted on the Supreme Court's reputation as a result of this assault took nearly a generation to heal. Recoiling from what was perceived as Taney's high-handed assertion of judicial supremacy, Republicans and Northerners savagely denounced the Court for its "atrocious," "wicked," "abominable" decision and declared their support for the departmental theory. The *New York Evening Post* charged the majority with "judicial impertinence" for presuming to "act as the interpreter of the Constitution for the other branches of the government", while its competitor, the *New York Tribune*, commented that "[i]t has come to a pretty pass, indeed, if this Court, created by the people, is to be considered ... as utterly irresponsible. If this were so, we might as well give up the executive and legislative branches of the Government at once."

Southerners and some Northern Democrats continued to defend the Court and to insist on obeisance to its opinion, though the leading study of *Dred Scott* concluded that "the literature of defense was less impressive in both volume and quality." Outside the South, the prevailing attitude became one of outrage at the majority, and especially at Chief Justice Taney. Old Democrats like Martin Van Buren and Thomas Hart Benton stirred themselves from retirement to write elaborate attacks, the first of a raft of books and articles critically examining the decision. Van Buren, who was willing to support the jurisdictional holding in *Dred Scott*, wrote his *Inquiry into the Origin and Course of Political Parties in the United States* largely to criticize the Court's assertion of supremacy respecting the Missouri Compromise and to urge Democrats not to enter "upon a path ... which would in time substitute for the present healthful and beneficial action of public opinion the selfish and contracted rule of a judicial oligarchy." Benton, in the meantime, rushed out a 130-page book in which he likewise attacked the Justices. The chief effect of *Dred Scott* was thus to raise political consciousness in the North, rousing a considerable segment of the public to adopt views that were openly anti-Court and anti-judicial supremacy as well as anti-slave power.

Abraham Lincoln, who had criticized *Dred Scott* on departmental grounds when he campaigned for the Senate against Stephen Douglas in 1858, returned to the decision in his First Inaugural Address. Lincoln agreed that the Court's judgments should be enforced as to the parties immediately involved. "At the same time," he continued:

> [T]he candid citizen must confess that if the policy of the government upon vital questions, affecting the whole people, is to be irrevocably fixed by decisions of the Supreme Court, the instant they are made, in ordinary litigation between parties, in personal actions, the people will have ceased to be their own rulers, having to that extent practically resigned their government into the hands of that eminent tribunal.

Lincoln's Administration acted consistently with these views, too, by ignoring the Court's opinion and recognizing black citizenship in a range of contexts, such as the regulation of coastal shipping and the issuance of passports and patents (not to mention by abolishing slavery in the territories and the District of Columbia).

At the same time, Lincoln's critique of judicial supremacy was carefully phrased to reflect changes in the departmental position since Jefferson's and Jackson's time. In particular, Lincoln questioned only the finality of Supreme Court decisions dealing with "vital questions, affecting the whole people," and even with respect to these, he asked only whether they become binding "the instant they are made" when they had been rendered "in ordinary litigation" and "personal actions." Apparently, Lincoln was prepared to concede the Court something more than were its opponents of fifty or even thirty years earlier.

We should be careful to read Lincoln in context, however. He spoke against a background in which the Court's actual role was still confined almost exclusively to enforcing constitutional limits against states, a role the new President seemed willing to accept. This was, of course, the easiest setting in which to justify aggressive judicial intervention, as it was expressly intended, arguably authorized by the text of the Constitution, well established as a matter of practice, and theoretically justified on the ground that the Court spoke as a national institution against a sub-national unit. That the contrary position was now closely associated with nullification and secession did not hurt either.

When it came to general federal legislation, in contrast, the judicial practice had been one of invariable and virtually complete deference. *Dred Scott* stuck out like a sore thumb partly because it was so unprecedented for the Supreme Court to assert its will over and against Congress. Having denounced the Court's pretensions in this respect, Lincoln had no particular interest in upsetting the preexisting balance or rejecting judicial authority across the board.

Modern commentators have tended mistakenly to view Lincoln's endorsement of departmentalism as something unusual and extraordinary, a departure from what they assume was a normal background rule of judicial supremacy. If anything, the opposite was true: rather than evoking a departure from "normal" practice, *Dred*

Scott produced but the latest reaffirmation of what had always been the prevailing, if not always spoken, understanding. There were in the 1850s, as there had been in the 1790s and in the 1830s, people eager to promote judicial supremacy. So far, however, these advocates had failed to establish their position and had, in fact, been decisively repudiated each time they tried.

The effects of *Dred Scott* were slow to expire. What Robert Jackson would later call "the struggle for judicial supremacy" thus did not resume until the final decades of the nineteenth century, at which point the Justices tried once again to assert their authority in an aggressive manner. Though it took a good decade for the new jurisprudence to gather steam, a marked change overtook the Court between 1865 and 1905, the year of *Lochner v. New York*. Having found only two federal laws unconstitutional during the entire antebellum period (in *Marbury* and *Dred Scott*), the Court struck down four federal statutes in the 1860s alone, followed by seven in the 1870s, four more in the 1880s, and five in the 1890s. While these numbers seem small by comparison to today (the Court struck down thirty federal laws between 1990 and 2000, for example, the most in its history), the change was striking enough to convince some commentators that it was only in this period that judicial review "really" became established.

A variety of factors contributed to the turnabout. The weight of *Dred Scott* gradually lifted as time passed and the Court's personnel changed. The political scene shifted as the nation grew weary of Reconstruction politics. The Republican party's ascendancy gave way after 1874 to several decades of divided government, which naturally gave the Justices more freedom to act. Their desire to do so was very much influenced by politics, as the equal rights rhetoric of the Civil War era evolved among conservatives into a new anti-democratic, anti-redistributive orthodoxy. Morally committed to a particular notion of property rights and fearful of the labor movement and other seemingly ominous signs of social unrest, the Court set about deliberately enlarging its role—seeking, as Robert Burt has convincingly demonstrated, "to transform all popular partisan disputes into questions for final determination by courts." In a talk delivered in 1893, Justice Brewer spoke about "magnifying, like the apostle of old, my office" because "the salvation of the nation … rests upon the independence and vigor of the judiciary." It was at this time, too, that we begin to hear again the old discredited Federalist arguments about how "what is now to be feared and guarded against is the depotism of the many—of the majority" and how through judicial review the "people had effectually protected themselves against themselves."

Like most such developments, the Court's new activism was overdetermined, for change was facilitated as well by a significant jurisprudential shift when the pragmatic functionalism of the mid-nineteenth century gave way to formalism and what Duncan Kennedy has called "Classical Legal Thought." Morton Horwitz succinctly described the central characteristics of this mode of legal reasoning as consisting of a sharp distinction between public and private spheres—and so between legitimate and illegitimate objects of government regulation—together with a pronounced tendency to emphasize broad, abstract legal categories, and a greater emphasis on deductive reasoning and bright-line classifications.

Gradually, these developments altered the Court's constitutional jurisprudence. Because the change occurred slowly and (at least, initially) affected mainly laws that no longer had strong political support, it took a few years before the Court began to draw fire. By the early 1880s, however, legal commentators and political leaders had begun to take notice. A prolonged struggle began, eventually culminating in the New Deal crisis of the 1930s.

There is no need to review that struggle here, for it has been extensively documented and analyzed by others. Suffice it to say that the Justice continued and even accelerated their aggressive ways in the early decades of the twentieth century, subjecting more and more legislation to one test or another of judicial approval. Yet every step in this judicial campaign was contested, both on and off the Court. Indeed, if the years between Reconstruction and the New Deal were a period of judicial expansion, they were also a kind of golden age for popular constitutionalism: a time rife with popular movements mobilizing support for change by invoking constitutional arguments and traditions that neither depended upon nor recognized—and often denied—imperial judicial authority. It was partly for this reason that politics in these years were so turbulent. . . .

While many of the Progressives' democratic reforms were adopted, recall of judges or judicial decisions failed to attract broad public support. Apart from abolition of the short-lived and ill-conceived Commerce Court, the judiciary survived the Progressive onslaught largely undamaged. Yet the battle hardly ceased. Support for "the people" as the court of last resort in clashes between the judiciary and the legislature remained strong among liberal lawyers and intellectuals, and opposition to the judiciary continued to fester. For a variety of reasons, matters did not explode publicly until the 1930s, at which point the Supreme Court collided head-on with FDR's New Deal. The Court's role became a contested political issue for the general public, and the triumphant New Dealers reasserted the right of the people to decide the meaning of their Constitution. As William Forbath has shown, Roosevelt made his case by appealing to "the legacy of popular constitutionalism, with its emphasis on the people's and popular leaders' interpretive authority." "The Constitution of the United States," Roosevelt insisted, was "a layman's document, not a lawyer's contract". . . .

The basic terms of this New Deal settlement are familiar, having been a centerpiece of constitutional law for more than three generations. Without getting sidetracked by the many doctrinal intricacies that emerged over the course of sixty years, the heart of the arrangement consisted of a sharp division between constitutional questions regarding the definition or scope of affirmative powers delegated by the Constitution to Congress and the Executive, and constitutional questions pertaining to a broad category of individual rights that limit the form or circumstances in which those powers can be exercised.

With respect to the former category—claims that a law is unconstitutional because not encompassed within an enumerated power—the determination of constitutionality was left for Congress and the Executive to make, subject only to a highly deferential "rational basis scrutiny" in the courts. The limits on judicial oversight built into this form of scrutiny consisted of two ingredients. First, Congress possessed nearly unreviewable discretion in its choice of whether and how to implement the Constitution's grants of power. In practice, this meant that courts would not second-guess congressional motives or means so long as a law could rationally be said to further a constitutional purpose. Second, courts were extremely respectful of legislative findings that some such purpose was served, which in practice meant

Originally

deferring to Congress unless the legislature's factual conclusions were patently illogical or wholly unsupportable.

The critical thing to understand about rational basis scrutiny is that it was a rule of judicial restraint, not substantive constitutional law. It did not mean that laws were constitutional if they were rational. Rather, the decision whether a particular law was constitutional was made by the legislature, with the Court's power of review limited to questioning the legislature's determination only in the rare case where Congress could not be said to have had a "rational basis" for what it did. By using this device, the Court ceded a quite substantial area of constitutional authority to political officials.

In sharp contrast, the New Deal settlement preserved a more active role for courts in the second category of cases, which encompassed claims based on a range of individual rights, including those specified in or inferred from the Bill of Rights and Reconstruction Amendments; those pertaining to voting and the political process; and those necessary to protect racial, religious, or other "discrete and insular minorities." Even within this category of rights, the Court reserved substantial room for the political branches to make constitutional judgments. It did so by limiting heightened judicial scrutiny over the most potentially capacious provisions—the Due Process and Equal Protection Clauses—to a subset of issues where judicial intervention was deemed most necessary, mainly those involving race and, later, privacy and gender. As to other issues, especially economic ones, the democratic pedigree and superior evaluative capacities of the political branches, and particularly of the legislature, were thought to warrant the use of minimal (i.e., rational basis) scrutiny.

On the surface of things, the New Deal settlement proved surprisingly durable. For nearly six decades, from the late 1930s to the mid-1990s, this basic allocation of constitutional responsibilities endured. The Warren and Burger Courts were definitely "activist," but their activism remained for the most part within the terms of the New Deal accommodation. While making their presence felt on questions of individual right, these Courts carefully respected the space carved out for popular constitutionalism at the time of the New Deal and left questions respecting the scope of national powers to the political process.

The Justices of the Warren and Burger Courts nevertheless planted seeds, perhaps unwittingly, that set in motion a process of unraveling the constitutional settlement of 1937. For while these Courts may have confined their activism to the limited sphere marked out in the New Deal, within that sphere they effectuated tremendous change. When New Dealers advocated a two-tiered system of judicial review, they probably envisioned the courts' role protecting individual rights as a relatively small thing. This would have been a reasonable expectation given prior experience, and it was an accurate prediction, too—at first. But beginning with *Brown v. Board of Education*, the Supreme Court showed what a really ambitious judiciary was capable of accomplishing even within the previously limited domain of individual rights. To name only a few of the most well-known cases in addition to *Brown*, consider *Baker v. Carr* and reapportionment, *Roe v. Wade* and abortion, *Engle v. Vitale* and school prayer, *Craig v. Boren* and sex discrimination, *Brandenburg v. Ohio* and political speech, *Miranda v. Arizona* and police interrogation, and *Furman v. Georgia* and the death penalty. Constitutional settlement or not, decisions like these were not likely to pass unnoticed, and the Supreme Court was still frequently embroiled in controversy as different segments of society bridled at particular rulings.

Ultimately, to be sure, these challenges had only limited success. For while they may have played a role in getting the Court to pull back in some areas, they also induced it forcefully to reassert its supremacy: most famously in 1958, when all nine Justices signed an extraordinary opinion in *Cooper v. Aaron* insisting that *Marbury* had "declared the basic principle that the federal judiciary is supreme in the exposition of the law of the Constitution" and that this idea "has ever since been respected by this Court and the Country as a permanent and indispensable feature of our constitutional system."

This was, of course, just bluster and puff. As we have seen, *Marbury* said no such thing, and judicial supremacy was not cheerfully embraced in the years after *Marbury* was decided. The Justices in *Cooper* were not reporting a fact so much as trying to manufacture one, and notwithstanding the Eisenhower Administration's reluctant decision to send troops to Little Rock to enforce the Court's judgment, the declaration of judicial interpretive supremacy evoked considerable skepticism at the time.

But here is the striking thing: after *Cooper v. Aaron*, the idea of judicial supremacy seemed gradually, at long last, to find wide public acceptance. The Court's decisions were still often controversial. State legislatures sometimes enacted laws they knew the Court would strike down, and compliance with the Justices' most contentious rulings, like those on abortion and school prayer, was willfully slack in many places. But sometime in the 1960s, these incidents of noncompliance evolved into forms of protest rather than claims of interpretive superiority. Outright defiance, in the guise of denying that Supreme Court decisions define constitutional law, seemed largely to disappear.

Popular constitutionalism remained very much alive at first, as evidenced by the period's many protest movements, for example, or by Richard Nixon's law-and-order campaign in 1968. But by the 1980s, most protests that touched on constitutional matters were being directed *at* rather than against the Court, and acceptance of judicial supremacy seemed to become the norm. Witness the conniptions evoked in 1986 when former Attorney General Edwin Meese dared to invoke the departmental theory and suggest that Supreme Court decisions might be binding only on the parties to a case. Meese was accused of inviting anarchy and of "making a calculated assault on the idea of law in this country: on the role of judges as the balance wheel in the American system." He quickly backed down, softening his criticism to concede that judicial decisions "are the law of the land" and "do indeed have general applicability."

Explaining this rather extraordinary development is not easy. One factor in the background, certainly, was the general skepticism about popular government that came to characterize western intellectual thought after World War II. The seeming eagerness with which mass publics in Europe had embraced fascism and communism eroded intellectual faith in what political scientist Robert Dahl derisively referred to in the 1950s as "populist democracy." The new thinking, associated most closely with Dahl and with Joseph Schumpeter, denigrated democratic politics as a site for developing substantive values and replaced it instead with a self-interested competition among interest groups. Viewing electoral politics in this unflattering light, in turn, made it easier to defend courts as a comparatively better setting in which to preserve constitutional commitments and carry on the moral deliberation that everyone agreed was a crucial aspect of democratic government. Thus was born the curious notion of the judiciary as a "forum of principle." ...

Gender and American Citizenship

LINDA K. KERBER

The Constitution's language of equality is wholesomely generic. The Fourteenth Amendment declares, "All persons, born or naturalized in the United States, are citizens." But the practices of equality have been problematic. *Nguyen v. INS*, decided by the U.S. Supreme Court in June 2001, captures the state of judicial thought about one important dimension of the contested meaning of citizenship.

American legal tradition and practice has long been shaped by the assumption that married women's domestic obligations to their husbands trump their civic obligations to the state. The corollary, of course, is that married men and married women are not equal. In theory, the civic infirmities of married women should not affect single women—the never married, divorced, or widowed who at any moment make up a substantial proportion of the population. In practice, however, all women were generally treated as if they were married.

As a result the rights and obligations of citizenship have been invoked differently for men and for women. The differences in rights are easier to see. We know that the right to vote has varied greatly by gender and race, across time and place. Despite the nation's founding principle of "no taxation without representation," most of the vast numbers of people excluded from the suffrage (most African Americans for most of American history, most white women until 1920, and until deep into the twentieth century, Asian immigrants ineligible for citizenship) paid taxes.

Inequality can be traced not only in the well-known history of unequal rights but quite as deeply in the history of unequal obligations to the state. Women have not been excused from civic obligation, but rather civic obligation has burdened them in different forms than it has burdened men. These asymmetries have occurred in the various categories of specific rights and obligations, including not only voting and taxation, but inclusion in the pool of jurors, the obligation to avoid vagrancy, and entitlement to birthright citizenship.

Which babies born outside the U.S. count as Americans from birth? And which men and women can bestow U.S. citizenship, automatically, upon their children? For centuries, with minor variations, the practices that define which children born abroad are to be considered American citizens and which must be naturalized have treated the status of the mother and the status of the father asymmetrically. And in June 2001, just in time for Father's Day, the U.S. Supreme Court handed down its decision in *Tuan Anh Nguyen et al. v. Immigration and Naturalization Service*, a case that sustains traditional ideas about fathers and the meaning of their citizenship.

As is often true of significant cases, *Nguyen* was full of ironies: a challenge to sex discrimination brought by a man jailed for sexual assault; a claim to the rights of citizenship brought by a convicted felon. Tanh Anh Nguyen was born in 1969. His father, Joseph Boulais, was an American veteran who, after his discharge from service

Originally published by Common-Place. Reproduced with permission of the publisher.

in Germany, went to Vietnam as a civilian employee of a construction company. He had a son with a Vietnamese woman who abandoned them both after Nguyen's birth. Boulais remained in Vietnam, cared for his son and developed a new relationship with a Vietnamese woman—not Nguyen's mother—whom he would later marry. When Saigon fell in April 1975, Boulais was out of Vietnam; the child was being cared for by his wife's mother. She managed to flee the city, taking the boy with her. They reached the United States as refugees and the family was reunited. Nguyen grew up in Houston in his father's home.

Had his birth parents been married to each other, U.S. law would have embraced Nguyen as a citizen from birth. Children of American citizens are automatically citizens, so long as one parent had lived in the United States for ten years, at least five of which were after age fourteen. (The number of years has since been reduced to five and two.) Joseph Boulais clearly met this requirement, which seeks to ensure that we do not develop a class of citizens who from one generation to the next have never lived in the United States. But he had not married Nguyen's mother.

If Nguyen's *mother*, although unmarried, had been a citizen, U.S. law would also have defined Nguyen as a citizen from birth so long as she had lived in the United States for twelve months before her baby was born. But it was Joseph Boulais who was the citizen, and in order to secure Nguyen's status as a citizen, Boulais was legally required to do three things on his son's behalf: to establish by "clear and convincing evidence" the blood relationship between them; to provide financial support until his son reached age eighteen; and to acknowledge his paternity formally before the child reached legal adulthood.

So long as life moved along quietly, so long as Boulais supported his son, what did formal paperwork matter? But in 1992 Nguyen, then age twenty-three and still, in legal terms, a resident alien, was convicted of sexually assaulting a minor, and sentenced to an eight-year prison term. Four years into Nguyen's sentence, Congress, responding to a rising tide of anti-immigrant sentiment, tightened the rules controlling legal aliens like Nguyen: conviction of a felony now meant deportation. And so, as Nguyen's prison time neared its end, the INS moved to deport him. Released from prison, Nguyen remained in confinement at the INS detention center in Houston.

Had his parents been married, Nguyen would have been counted a citizen at birth. Flip the coin: had his unmarried citizen-parent been his mother, he would also have been a citizen at birth and invulnerable to deportation. Not illogical, Justice John Paul Stevens had declared in the last similar case to reach the Supreme Court, *Miller v. Albright*, decided in the spring of 1998. Parenthood, the Court effectively found, *was* asymmetrical. Motherhood counted for more. Everyone knows who the mother is; there are witnesses to the birth. (Such reasoning has a long history; a member of the medieval Guild of Fishwives had the right to be in the birthing room of Marie Antoinette, charged with the responsibility to witness that the heir to the French throne had actually emerged from the body of his mother.) Not illogical, wrote Justice Stevens, but rather "entirely reasonable for Congress to require special evidence of [ties to this country] ... between an illegitimate child and its father. A mother is far less likely to ignore the child she has carried in her womb than is the natural father, who may not even be aware of its existence ... [T]he time limitation ... deters fraud."

Justice Ruth Bader Ginsburg disagreed. In a vigorous dissent joined by Justices Souter and Breyer, she assailed the law as "one of the few provisions remaining in the United States Code that uses sex as a criterion in delineating citizens' rights." Ginsburg's dissent argued that opposing arguments were soaked with stereotypes about the parental roles of men and women. The three dissenting justices waited impatiently for another chance to consider this principle in a case without some of the technicalities raised by *Miller*.

Nguyen gave them one. His suit challenged the threat to deport him on the grounds that he should have been a citizen from the moment of his birth. Boulais argued that he, an American man, should have the same right American women have to transmit citizenship to nonmarital children. He arranged for DNA testing that demonstrated his paternity. He might well have imagined he would prevail. Indeed, court decisions in Canada underline how fluid stereotypes can be. Until very recently, it was the child born abroad to a Canadian woman, fathered by a U.S. man, who required a security check in order to take up Canadian citizenship; the child born abroad to a Canadian citizen-father was automatically a citizen.

In *Miller* four years ago, and then again, in *Nguyen*, much of the discussion focused on stereotypes. The treatment is unequal because fathers are burdened; they have to go through more hoops to establish paternity than women do to establish maternity. But there is another, ugly history lurking in the subtext to these arguments. In the Anglo-American legal tradition—the body of law that Americans received as colonists and retained despite the Revolution—the father was the head of the household, and his wife's citizenship largely depended on his. In American family law, husbands traditionally controlled children as well as wives. Fathers made the final decision, for example, on where a child should be apprenticed. In the event of divorce fathers usually got custody. A father had responsibility for financial support of the children born during his marriage.

But a long tradition also held that a man became accountable for the children he fathered *outside* of marriage only if he wished to claim them. If legitimate heirs were the responsibility of their fathers, illegitimate children were the responsibilities of their mothers. To make doubly sure, American colonists passed laws that specified that children of free fathers and enslaved mothers "followed the condition of the mother." (That is why Thomas Jefferson's father-in-law, John Wayles, could use his own daughter as a slave; that is how Sally Hemings—Jefferson's own sister-in-law—ended up a slave in Jefferson's household.) In 2001, Nguyen's "condition"—as citizen or noncitizen—was governed by the status of his mother.

Last June, barely thirty years after the Court in *Reed v. Reed* ruled for the first time that discrimination on the basis of sex may be a denial of equal protection of the law, the Supreme Court ruled against Nguyen. The decision was five to four. The majority opinion, written by Justice Anthony Kennedy, emphasized—as the Justice Department had done in oral argument—the reasonableness, even generosity of the rules. Citizen-fathers have an extended period of time—eighteen years—to satisfy the requirements of the statute. "Fathers and mothers are not similarly situated with regard to the proof of biological parenthood," and gender-neutral language—language like that of the Fourteenth Amendment, say—would have been "a hollow neutrality." Kennedy observed, "Given the nine-month interval between conception and birth, it is not always certain that a father will know that a child was conceived, nor is it always clear that even the mother will be sure of the father's identity ... One concern in this context has always been with young people, men for the most part, who are on duty with the Armed Forces in foreign countries ... "

During oral argument, when this point was made, Justice Ruth Bader Ginsburg remarked that it implied that the Court approved of military men fathering children out of wedlock and abandoning them. "I expect very few of these are the children of female service personnel," Ginsburg observed to the amusement of the audience. "There are these men out there who are being Johnny Appleseed."

But the majority of justices remained unpersuaded. To the contrary, Kennedy's opinion continued, "[Considering] the conditions which prevail today ... the ease of travel and the willingness of Americans to visit foreign countries have resulted in numbers of trips abroad that must be of real concern when we contemplate the prospect of accepting petitioners' argument, which would mandate ... citizenship by male parentage subject to no condition save the father's previous length of residence in this country ... " To insist that citizenship must be consciously claimed, rather than "unwitting," was not, Kennedy insisted, a stereotype. As the Court had previously established, "Physical differences between men and women ... are enduring."

Kennedy's opinion came as a disappointment to observers who had trusted that, given facts different from those in *Miller*, he could be persuaded to focus on the similar situation of the newborn rather than the different situation of the mother and father. Still, as Gerald Neuman of Columbia University School of Law pointed out, the opinion could also count as strengthening another important American tradition of citizenship: that descent alone should not be enough, that citizenship should be claimed. "U.S. citizenship isn't racial," Neuman observed. "We are not a descent group. We are tied together by something else. I think it may be useful not to lose sight of this positive aspect of the decision."

The other vote that Nguyen's supporters had hoped to swing swung. Justice Sandra Day O'Connor, who had voted with the majority in *Miller*, wrote an extensive dissent joined by Justices Ginsburg, Souter, and Breyer. She rejected the idea that the case was about immigration and naturalization; it actually concerned birthright citizenship. Quoting an observation made in *J.E.B. v. Alabama ex rel. T.B.*, a 1994 case that had addressed gender-based peremptory challenges in jury selection, she situated *Nguyen* squarely "in the context of our Nation's long and unfortunate history of sex discrimination," a history that required "the application of heightened scrutiny" and the showing of "an exceedingly persuasive justification of the sex-based classification substantially related[d] to the achievement of important governmental objectives." In *Ngyuen*, she maintained, "The different statutory treatment is solely on account of the sex of the similarly situated individuals. This type of treatment is patently inconsistent with the promise of equal protection of the laws." She challenged the arguments made by the Department of Justice: if the Court were truly interested in establishing that the citizen-parent had a substantial relationship to the child, she thought, it would logically have placed burdens of proof of parenthood on mothers as well as fathers. Were it interested primarily in biological connection, it would not have shrugged off DNA testing so cavalierly. And so the decision fell back on stereotypes: "the generalization that mothers are significantly more likely than fathers ... to develop caring relationships with their children." The facts in this case contradicted the stereotype: Boulais, not the child's birth mother, had raised Nguyen.

Nguyen, the dissent continued, belonged in the "historic regime that left women with responsibility, and freed men from responsibility, for non-marital children." O'Connor ended by castigating the majority for deviating from "a line of cases in which we have vigilantly applied heightened scrutiny"; she ended with the hope "that today's error remains an aberration."

And so Tuan Anh Nguyen and Joseph Boulais—and the lawyers who threw their hearts into helping them make their arguments—lost their battle. At this writing, Nguyen is no longer in confinement but he continues to face deportation. But in the long run the law is also shaped by valiant dissents. The dissenters here make clear that the deep-rooted belief that women are likely to be tricksters, and that men should be able to pick and choose for which of their children they will be responsible, still infects the integrity of American law.

✤ F U R T H E R   R E A D I N G

Amar, Akhil Reed. *America's Constitution: A Biography* (2005).

Beard, Charles A. *An Economic Interpretation of the Constitution of the United States* (1913).

Belz, Herman. "New Left Reverberations in the Academy: The Antipluralist Critique of Constitutionalism," *Review of Politics*, 36 (1974): 265–283.

Benedict, Michael Les. *The Blessings of Liberty: A Concise History of the Constitution of the United States*, 2nd ed. (2005).

Dahl, Robert. *How Democratic is the American Constitution?* (2003).

Friedman, Lawrence M. *A History of American Law*, 3rd ed. (2005).

Hall, Kermit L. and Peter Karsten. *The Magic Mirror: Law in American History*, 2nd ed. (2008).

Hartog, Hendrik. "The Constitution of Aspiration and 'The Rights that Belong to Us All,'" *Journal of American History*, 74 (1987): 1013–1034.

Irons, Peter. *A People's History of the Supreme Court* (2006).

Kammen, Michael. *A Machine That Would Go of Itself: The Constitution in American Culture* (1986).

Kelly, Alfred H., Winfred A. Harbison, and Herman J. Belz. *The American Constitution: Its Origins and Development*, 7th ed. (1991).

Kerber, Linda K. *No Constitutional Right to be Ladies: Women and the Obligations of Citizenship* (1998).

Murphy, Paul. "Time to Reclaim: The Current Challenge of American Constitutional History," *American Historical Review*, 69 (1963): 64–79.

Rowe, Gary D. "Constitutionalism in the Streets," *Southern California Law Review*, 78 (2005): 401–456.

Schwartz, Bernard. *A History of the Supreme Court* (1993).

Urofsky, Melvin I. and Paul Finkelman. *A March of Liberty: A Constitutional History of the United States*, 2nd ed. (2001).

VanBurkleo, Sandra. *"Belonging to the World": Women's Rights and American Constitutional Culture* (2001).

Wiecek, William M. *Liberty under Law: The Supreme Court in American Life* (1988).

_____ "Clio as Hostage: The United States Supreme Court and the Uses of History," *California Western Law Review*, 24 (1988): 227–276.

CHAPTER

2

Creating the American
Republic

*The origins of the American republic lay in the history of English political and
constitutional thought. Because colonial Americans identified their political fortunes
with events back home, they closely followed England's political struggles. They took
particular note of the opposition faction in Parliament that developed in the aftermath of the Glorious Revolution of 1688–1689, which had established Parliament's
primacy over the crown. The so-called "country" faction criticized the King, his ministers, and the majority in Parliament for their corruption. This struggle between
the country party and the court party in England became especially significant
for the American colonists after the conclusion of the French and Indian War in
1763. At that point, the British government adopted an aggressive imperial policy
designed to make the colonists pay the cost of their own defense. This new program
thrust British officials into the day-to-day affairs of the colonists, many of whom
reacted strongly against new taxes and trade regulations. These measures, moreover,
raised questions about the meaning of representation and government by consent,
ideas which were central to colonists' understanding of their rights and their place
within the empire.*

*Deeply committed to the idea that they possessed certain rights as Englishmen,
Americans by the end of the eighteenth century came to believe that only by separating themselves from England could those rights be preserved. In making the
argument for independence, Americans drew from two major lines of thinking in
English political history. First, they took from the country party tradition, which
had criticized the corruption associated with concentrated power. Second, they owed
a debt to political theorist John Locke, whose liberal ideology stressed private rights,
government by consent, and the right of revolution. In order to justify and proclaim
their independence to England and the rest of the world, American leaders signed a
formal Declaration of Independence on July 4, 1776.*

*Once they declared their independence, the colonists faced a more daunt-
ing task—that of forming a new government. If, as the Declaration claimed,
the British monarch no longer held sway over Americans, who was sovereign
in the new United States of America? When the Declaration proclaimed the
colonies to be "free and independent states," it was clear that it meant free*

from English rule. But were they also "free and independent" of each other? Colonial leaders initially seemed to think so. In 1777, while Americans fought the War of Independence, they united under their first constitution, the Articles of Confederation, which established a weak central government and affirmed the sovereignty of the 13 states. (Each state, under the Articles, possessed an equal vote in the Confederation Congress, regardless of its population.) Eventually, the inability of this government to handle matters of national significance—for example, the regulation of interstate commerce—proved to be a driving force in the movement to revise the Articles. In 1787, delegates from all of the 13 states except Rhode Island assembled in Philadelphia. Although they met initially only to alter the Articles, after 3 months they ended up drafting an entirely new constitution. The new document, subsequently ratified in 1788, seemed to estab- lish (as least in its preamble) "the people" of the United States as sovereign, for it nowhere described the states in this way and conferred significant new pow- ers upon the central government. At the same time, the Convention settled on a bicameral legislature as the best compromise between those who wanted represen- tation to be based on population and those who favored maintaining the equal power of states. The Articles of Confederation had stated that its provisions could be changed only by the unanimous consent of the states, but in order to increase the likelihood of the new Constitution's ratification, the delegates provided that the assent of only nine states would be necessary. Within 10 months, ratifying conventions in the requisite nine states approved the Constitution.

Historians have spilled a tremendous amount of ink describing the events of the founding era, particularly the motives of the nation's founders. For decades, progressive historian Charles Beard's economic interpretation set the terms of the debate. Beard argued that the framers undermined the democratic impulses of the Revolution and placed property interests above human liberty, by establishing a strong central government to promote commerce and manufacturing at the expense of agriculture. Scholars writing during the second half of the twentieth century, while stressing ideology rather than the founders' status as property holders, gener- ally accepted Beard's claim that the Constitution was more socially and economically conservative than the Revolution. Still, subsequent historians noted the unique and revolutionary nature of the founders' achievement. The delegates in Philadelphia succeeded in giving an entirely new meaning to ideas such as separation of powers, representation, and popular sovereignty. In this respect, the American Constitution was distinctive worldwide.

Judging from the vast outpouring of works on the founding, Americans continue to possess an extraordinary interest in the Revolution and the writing of the Constitution. And the debates among historians remain as high-pitched as ever. Were the founders motivated more by interests or ideas? If ideas were more important, which ideas? Were the founders forward-looking visionaries who created a democratic government and a Lockean liberal social order based on the pursuit of self-interest? Or were they backward-looking "classical republicans," acting in the country party tradition, who believed that civic virtue—devotion to the public good—outweighed individual interests? How important was the notion of popular sovereignty during the founding? Were the founders really concerned about "the people," or did the Constitution represent a betrayal of revolution- ary notions of political equality, particularly with regard to African Americans and women? What are we in the twenty-first century to make of the framers' handiwork?

John Locke published *Two Treatises on Civil Government*, excerpted here as Document 1, in an attempt to rationalize the Glorious Revolution. Locke contributed significantly to the development of Western constitutional thought by synthesizing existing ideas into a coherent liberal ideology. Locke's influence was especially clear in the Declaration of Independence, Document 2, written by Thomas Jefferson. By affirming the Lockean notions of inalienable rights and the right to revolution, in the Declaration, Jefferson succeeded in providing a legal justification for the American revolutionaries' apparently "illegal" actions. The king's abuses had left Americans, as a matter of fundamental law, no choice but to rebel. Significantly, Jefferson directed his ire not at Parliament—which had enacted every one of the measures against which the colonists complained—but at the monarchy. Excerpts from the Articles of Confederation, Document 3, show the colonists' first plan of government. Although the Articles did not prove workable, they demonstrate the founders' initial attempt to establish a union that preserved the sovereignty of states.

The next several documents provide glimpses of the debates at the Constitutional Convention, particularly over representation and the structure of the new government. Edmund Randolph submitted the large-state plan, known as the Virginia plan, Document 4, and William Paterson urged the small-state or New Jersey plan, Document 5. The former would have based representation on population, while the latter would have preserved the principle of state equality. The discussion of the establishment of a national legislature, Document 6, taken from James Madison's *Debates in the Federal Convention of 1787*, illustrates how delegates grappled with popular sovereignty, the relationship between the national government and the states, and the structure of the new republic. The issue of representation also figured in the debates over slavery. Document 7, also from Madison's *Debates*, shows how the delegates arrived at the Three-Fifths Compromise—the provision that three-fifths of the slave population would be counted for purposes of representation in the House of Representatives.

Document 8, Madison's famous *Federalist X*—one of the many essays he authored in support of the ratification of the Constitution—illustrates how the "Father of the Constitution" attempted to explode contemporary political theory, which held that a republic could only exist in a small geographic area with a homogenous population.

✠ D O C U M E N T   1

Political Theorist John Locke Describes the Ends of Political Society and Government, 1690

. . . 95. Men being by nature all free, equal, and independent, no one can be put out of this state and subjected to the political power of another without his own consent. The only way one divests himself of his natural liberty and puts on the bonds of civil society is by agreeing with other men to join and unite into a community for their comfortable, safe, and peaceable living. This any number of men may do, because it injures not the freedom of the rest; they are left in the state of nature. When any number of men have so consented to make one community or government, they constitute one body politic wherein the majority have a right to act and include the rest. . . .

123. If man in the state of nature be so free, as has been said; if he be absolute lord of his own person and possessions, equal to the greatest, and subject to nobody, why will he part with his freedom and subject himself to the control of any other power? To which it is obvious to answer that though in the state of nature he had such right, yet the enjoyment of it is very uncertain and constantly exposed to the invasion of others. For all being kings as much as he, every man his equal, and the greater part of mankind no strict observers of equity and justice, the enjoyment of the property he has in this state is very unsafe, very insecure. This makes him willing to surrender this condition, which, however free, is full of fears and continual dangers. And it is not without reason that he seeks out and is willing to join in society with others who are already united, or have a mind to unite, for the mutual preservation of their lives, liberties, and estates, which I call by the general name "property."

124. The great and chief end, therefore, of men's uniting into commonwealths and putting themselves under government is the preservation of their property, to which in the state of nature there are many things lacking:

First, there is no established, settled, known law, received and agreed by common consent to be the standard of right and wrong, and the common measure to decide all controversies. For though the law of nature be plain and intelligible to all rational creatures, yet men, being biased by their interest as well as ignorant for lack of studying of it, are not apt to allow of it as a law binding to them in the application of it to their particular cases.

125. *Second*, in the state of nature there is no known and impartial judge with authority to determine all differences according to the established law. For everyone in that state being both judge and executioner of the law of nature, passion and revenge are apt to carry men too far and with too much heat in their own cases, as well as negligence and unconcernedness to make them too remiss in other men's.

126. *Thirdly*, in the state of nature, there often is no power to back and support the sentence when right, and to give it due execution. They who commit injustice will seldom lack the force to make good their injustice. Such resistance many times makes the punishment dangerous and frequently destructive to those who attempt it.

127. Thus mankind, notwithstanding all the privileges of the state of nature, being but in an ill condition while they remain in it, are quickly driven into society. Hence it comes to pass that we seldom find any number of men live any time together in this state. It is this makes them so willingly give up everyone his single power of punishing, to be exercised by such alone as shall be appointed to it among them, and by such rules as the community shall agree on. And here we have the original right of both the legislative and the executive power, as well as of governments and societies themselves.

128. In the state of nature a man has two powers: The first is to do whatsoever he thinks fit for the preservation of himself and others within the permission of the law of nature. And, were it not for the corruption and viciousness of degenerate men, there would be no need of any other, no necessity that men should separate from this great and natural community and by positive agreements combine into smaller and divided associations.

The other power a man has in the state of nature is the power to punish the crimes committed against that law. Both these he gives up when he joins a private, if I may so call it, or particular political society and incorporates into any commonwealth separate from the rest of mankind.

129. The first power he gives up to be regulated by laws made by the society, which laws in many things confine the liberty he had by the law of nature.

130. Secondly, the power of punishing he wholly gives up, and engages his natural force to assist the executive power of the society, as the law thereof shall require.

131. But though men when they enter into society give up the equality, liberty, and executive power they had in the state of nature into the hands of the society, to be so far disposed of by the legislative as the good of the society shall require, yet it remains the intention of everyone the better to preserve himself, his liberty, and his property by entering society. Therefore, the power of that society can never be supposed to extend farther than the common good. For a government is obliged to secure everyone's property by providing against those three defects above-mentioned that made the state of nature so unsafe and uneasy. And so whoever has the legislative or supreme power of any commonwealth is bound to govern by established standing laws, promulgated and known to the people, and not by extemporary decrees; and these laws are to be administered by impartial and upright judges who are to decide controversies by these laws. The force of the community is to be employed at home only in the execution of such laws, or abroad to prevent or redress foreign injuries, and secure the community from inroads and invasion. And all this to be directed to no other end but the peace, safety, and public good of the people.

132. The majority, having the whole power of the community naturally in them, may employ all the power of the community in making laws from time to time, and executing those laws by officers of their own appointing. Then the form of government is a perfect democracy. Or else they may put the power of making laws into the hands of a few select men, and their heirs or successors, and then it is an oligarchy; or else into the hands of one man, and then it is a monarchy; if to him and his heirs, it is a hereditary monarchy; if to him only for life, but upon his death the power only of nominating a successor to return to the majority, then an elective monarchy. And so accordingly of these the community may make compounded and mixed forms of government, as they think good. For since the form of government depends on the placing of supreme power, which is the legislative—it being impossible to conceive that an inferior power should prescribe to a superior, or any but the supreme make laws—according as the power of making laws is placed, such is the form of the commonwealth. . . .

✤ D O C U M E N T   2

American Colonists Declare Their Independence, 1776

In Congress, July 4, 1776

The Unanimous Declaration of the Thirteen United States of America

When in the Course of human events, it becomes necessary for one people to dissolve the political bands which have connected them with another, and to assume among the Powers of the earth, the separate and equal station to which the Laws of

Nature and of Nature's God entitle them, a decent respect to the opinions of mankind requires that they should declare the causes which impel them to the separation.

We hold these truths to be self-evident, that all men are created equal, that they are endowed by their Creator with certain unalienable Rights, that among these are Life, Liberty and the pursuit of Happiness. That to secure these rights, Governments are instituted among Men, deriving their just powers from the consent of the governed, That whenever any Form of Government becomes destructive of these ends, it is the Right of the People to alter or to abolish it, and to institute new Government, laying its foundation on such principles and organizing its powers in such form, as to them shall seem most likely to effect their Safety and Happiness. Prudence, indeed, will dictate that Governments long established should not be changed for light and transient causes; and accordingly all experience hath shown, that mankind are more disposed to suffer, while evils are sufferable, than to right themselves by abolishing the forms to which they are accustomed. But when a long train of abuses and usurpations, pursuing invariably the same Object evinces a design to reduce them under absolute Despotism, it is their right, it is their duty, to throw off such Government, and to provide new Guards for their future security.—Such has been the patient sufferance of these Colonies; and such is now the necessity which constrains them to alter their former Systems of Government. The history of the present King of Great Britain is a history of repeated injuries and usurpations, all having in direct object the establishment of an absolute Tyranny over these States. To prove this, let Facts be submitted to a candid world.

He has refused his Assent to Laws, the most wholesome and necessary for the public good.

He has forbidden his Governors to pass Laws of immediate and pressing importance, unless suspended in their operation till his Assent should be obtained; and when so suspended, he has utterly neglected to attend to them.

He has refused to pass other Laws for the accommodation of large districts of people, unless those people would relinquish the right of Representation in the Legislature, a right inestimable to them and formidable to tyrants only.

He has called together legislative bodies at places unusual, uncomfortable, and distant from the depository of their Public Records, for the sole purpose of fatiguing them into compliance with his measures.

He has dissolved Representative Houses repeatedly, for opposing with manly firmness his invasions on the rights of the people.

He has refused for a long time, after such dissolutions, to cause others to be elected; whereby the Legislative Powers, incapable of Annihilation, have returned to the People at large for their exercise; the State remaining in the mean time exposed to all the dangers of invasion from without, and convulsions within.

He has endeavoured to prevent the population of these States; for that purpose obstructing the Laws of Naturalization of Foreigners; refusing to pass others to encourage their migration hither, and raising the conditions of new Appropriations of Lands.

He has obstructed the Administration of Justice, by refusing his Assent to Laws for establishing Judiciary Powers.

He has made Judges dependent on his Will alone, for the tenure of their offices, and the amount and payment of their salaries.

He has erected a multitude of New Offices, and sent hither swarms of Officers to harass our People, and eat out their substance.

He has kept among us, in times of peace, Standing Armies without the Consent of our legislature.

He has affected to render the Military independent of and superior to the Civil Power.

He has combined with others to subject us to a jurisdiction foreign to our constitution, and unacknowledged by our laws; giving his Assent to their acts of pretended legislation:

For quartering large bodies of armed troops among us;

For protecting them, by a mock Trial, from Punishment for any Murders which they should commit on the Inhabitants of these States;

For cutting off our Trade with all parts of the world;

For imposing taxes on us without our Consent;

For depriving us in many cases, of the benefits of Trial by Jury;

For transporting us beyond Seas to be tried for pretended offences;

For abolishing the free System of English Laws in a neighbouring Province, establishing therein an Arbitrary government, and enlarging its Boundaries so as to render it at once an example and fit instrument for introducing the same absolute rule into these Colonies;

For taking away our Charters, abolishing our most valuable Laws, and altering fundamentally the Forms of our Governments;

For suspending our own Legislature, and declaring themselves invested with Power to legislate for us in all cases whatsoever.

He has abdicated Government here, by declaring us out of his Protection and waging War against us.

He has plundered our seas, ravaged our Coasts, burnt our towns, and destroyed the lives of our people.

He is at this time transporting large armies of foreign mercenaries to compleat the works of death, desolation and tyranny, already begun with circumstances of Cruelty & perfidy scarcely paralleled in the most barbarous ages, and totally unworthy the Head of a civilized nation.

He has constrained our fellow Citizens taken Captive on the high Seas to bear Arms against their Country, to become the executioners of their friends and Brethren, or to fall themselves by their Hands.

He has excited domestic insurrections amongst us, and has endeavoured to bring on the inhabitants of our frontiers, the merciless Indian Savages, whose known rule of warfare, is an undistinguished destruction of all ages, sexes and conditions.

In every stage of these Oppressions We have Petitioned for Redress in the most humble terms: Our repeated Petitions have been answered only by repeated injury. A Prince, whose character is thus marked by every act which may define a Tyrant, is unfit to be the ruler of a free People.

Nor have We been wanting in attention to our British brethren. We have warned them from time to time of attempts by their legislature to extend an unwarrantable jurisdiction over us. We have reminded them of the circumstances of our emigration and settlement here. We have appealed to their native justice and magnanimity, and we have conjured them by the ties of our common kindred to disavow these usurpations, which, would inevitably interrupt our connections and correspondence. They too have been deaf to the voice of justice and of consanguinity. We must, therefore, acquiesce in the necessity, which denounces our Separation, and hold them, as we hold the rest of mankind, Enemies in War, in Peace Friends.

We, therefore, the Representatives of the United States of America, in General Congress, Assembled, appealing to the Supreme Judge of the world for the rectitude of our intentions, do, in the Name, and by Authority of the good People of these Colonies, solemnly publish and declare, That these United Colonies are, and of Right ought to be Free and Independent States; that they are Absolved from all Allegiance to the British Crown, and that all political connection between them and the State of Great Britain, is and ought to be totally dissolved; and that as Free and Independent States, they have full Power to levy War, conclude Peace, contract Alliances, establish Commerce, and to do all other Acts and Things which Independent States may of right do. And for the support of this Declaration, with a firm reliance on the Protection of Divine Providence, we mutually pledge to each other our Lives, our Fortunes and our sacred Honor.

✛ *D O C U M E N T   3*

The American Colonies Form a Confederation, 1777

Articles of Confederation

To all to whom these Presents shall come, we the undersigned Delegates of the States affixed to our Names send greeting.

Articles of Confederation and perpetual Union between the states of New Hampshire, Massachusetts-bay, Rhode Island and Providence Plantations, Connecticut, New York, New Jersey, Pennsylvania, Delaware, Maryland, Virginia, North Carolina, South Carolina and Georgia.

I.

The Stile of this Confederacy shall be
"The United States of America".

II.

Each state retains its sovereignty, freedom, and independence, and every power, jurisdiction, and right, which is not by this Confederation expressly delegated to the United States, in Congress assembled.

III.

The said States hereby severally enter into a firm league of friendship with each other, for their common defense, the security of their liberties, and their mutual and general welfare, binding themselves to assist each other, against all force offered to, or attacks made upon them, or any of them, on account of religion, sovereignty, trade, or any other pretense whatever.

IV.

The better to secure and perpetuate mutual friendship and intercourse among the people of the different States in this Union, the free inhabitants of each of these States, paupers, vagabonds, and fugitives from justice excepted, shall be entitled to all privileges and immunities of free citizens in the several States; and the people of each State shall free ingress and regress to and from any other State, and shall enjoy therein all the privileges of trade and commerce, subject to the same duties, impositions, and restrictions as the inhabitants thereof respectively, provided that such restrictions shall not extend so far as to prevent the removal of property imported into any State, to any other State, of which the owner is an inhabitant; provided also that no imposition, duties or restriction shall be laid by any State, on the property of the United States, or either of them....

V.

For the most convenient management of the general interests of the United States, delegates shall be annually appointed in such manner as the legislatures of each State shall direct, to meet in Congress on the first Monday in November, in every year, with a powerreserved to each State to recall its delegates, or any of them, at any time within the year, and to send others in their stead for the remainder of the year.

No State shall be represented in Congress by less than two, nor more than seven members; and no person shall be capable of being a delegate for more than three years in any term of six years; nor shall any person, being a delegate, be capable of holding any office under the United States, for which he, or another for his benefit, receives any salary, fees or emolument of any kind.

Each State shall maintain its own delegates in a meeting of the States, and while they act as members of the committee of the States.

In determining questions in the United States in Congress assembled, each State shall have one vote....

VI.

No State, without the consent of the United States in Congress assembled, shall send any embassy to, or receive any embassy from, or enter into any conference, agreement, alliance or treaty with any King, Prince or State; nor shall any person holding any office of profit or trust under the United States, or any of them, accept any present, emolument, office or title of any kind whatever from any King, Prince or foreign State; nor shall the United States in Congress assembled, or any of them, grant any title of nobility.

No two or more States shall enter into any treaty, confederation or alliance whatever between them, without the consent of the United States in Congress assembled, specifying accurately the purposes for which the same is to be entered into, and how long it shall continue.

No State shall lay any imposts or duties, which may interfere with any stipulations in treaties, entered into by the United States in Congress assembled, with any King, Prince or State, in pursuance of any treaties already proposed by Congress, to the courts of France and Spain.

No vessel of war shall be kept up in time of peace by any State, except such number only, as shall be deemed necessary by the United States in Congress assembled, for the defense of such State, or its trade; nor shall any body of forces be kept up by any State in time of peace, except such number only, as in the judgement of the United States in Congress assembled, shall be deemed requisite to garrison the forts necessary for the defense of such State; but every State shall always keep up a well-regulated and disciplined militia, sufficiently armed and accoutered, and shall provide and constantly have ready for use, in public stores, a due number of filed pieces and tents, and a proper quantity of arms, ammunition and camp equipage.

No State shall engage in any war without the consent of the United States in Congress assembled, unless such State be actually invaded by enemies, or shall have received certain advice of a resolution being formed by some nation of Indians to invade such State, and the danger is so imminent as not to admit of a delay till the United States in Congress assembled can be consulted; nor shall any State grant commissions to any ships or vessels of war, nor letters of marque or reprisal, except it be after a declaration of war by the United States in Congress assembled, and then only against the Kingdom or State and the subjects thereof, against which war has been so declared, and under such regulations as shall be established by the United States in Congress assembled, unless such State be infested by pirates, in which case vessels of war may be fitted out for that occasion, and kept so long as the danger shall continue, or until the United States in Congress assembled shall determine otherwise. ...

VIII.

All charges of war, and all other expenses that shall be incurred for the common defense or general welfare, and allowed by the United States in Congress assembled, shall be defrayed out of a common treasury, which shall be supplied by the several States in proportion to the value of all land within each State, granted or surveyed for any person, as such land and the buildings and improvements thereon shall be estimated according to such mode as the United States in Congress assembled, shall from time to time direct and appoint.

The taxes for paying that proportion shall be laid and levied by the authority and direction of the legislatures of the several States within the time agreed upon by the United States in Congress assembled.

IX.

The United States in Congress assembled, shall have the sole and exclusive right and power of determining on peace and war, except in the cases mentioned in the sixth article—of sending and receiving ambassadors—entering into treaties and alliances, provided that no treaty of commerce shall be made whereby the legislative power of the respective States shall be restrained from imposing such imposts and duties on foreigners, as their own people are subjected to, or from prohibiting the exportation or importation of any species of goods or commodities whatsoever—of establishing rules for deciding in all cases, what captures on land or water shall be legal, and in what manner prizes taken by land or naval forces in the service of the United States shall be divided or appropriated—of granting letters of marque and reprisal in times of peace—appointing courts for the trial of piracies and felonies commited on the high seas and establishing courts for receiving and determining finally appeals in all cases of captures, provided that no member of Congress shall be appointed a judge of any of the said courts. ...

The United States in Congress assembled shall never engage in a war, nor grant letters of marque or reprisal in time of peace, nor enter into any treaties or alliances, nor coin money, nor regulate the value thereof, nor ascertain the sums and expenses necessary for the defense and welfare of the United States, or any of them, nor emit bills, nor borrow money on the credit of the United States, nor appropriate money, nor agree upon the number of vessels of war, to be built or purchased, or the number of land or sea forces to be raised, nor appoint a commander in chief of the army or navy, unless nine States assent to the same: nor shall a question on any other point, except for adjourning from day to day be determined, unless by the votes of the majority of the United States in Congress assembled. ...

XIII.

Every State shall abide by the determination of the United States in Congress assembled, on all questions which by this confederation are submitted to them. And the Articles of this Confederation shall be inviolably observed by every State, and the Union shall be perpetual; nor shall any alteration at any time hereafter be made in any of them; unless such alteration be agreed to in a Congress of the United States, and be afterwards confirmed by the legislatures of every State. ...

✛ *D O C U M E N T   4*

Convention Delegate Edmund Randolph Proposes the Virginia Plan, May 29, 1787

1. Resolved that the Articles of Confederation ought to be so corrected and enlarged as to accomplish the objects proposed by their institution; namely "common defence, security of liberty and general welfare."

2. Resolved therefore that the rights of suffrage in the National Legislature ought to be proportioned to the Quotas of contribution, or to the number of free inhabitants, as the one or the other rule may seem best in different cases.

3. Resolved that the National Legislature ought to consist of two branches.

4. Resolved that the members of the first branch of the National Legislature ought to be elected by the people of the several States every   for the terms of   ; to be of the age of   years at least, to receive liberal stipends by which they may be compensated for the devotion of their time to public service, to be ineligible to any office established by a particular State, or under the authority of the United States, except those peculiarly belonging to the functions of the first branch, during the term of service, and for the space of   after its expiration; to be incapable of reelection for the space of   after the expiration of their term of service, and to be subject to recall.

5. Resolved that the members of the second branch of the National Legislature ought to be elected by those of the first, out of a proper number of persons nominated

by the individual Legislatures, to be of the age of   years at least; to hold their offices for a term sufficient to ensure their independency; to receive liberal stipends, by which they may be compensated for the devotion of their time to public service; and to be ineligible to any office established by a particular State, or under the authority of the United States, except those peculiarly belonging to the functions of the second branch, during the term of service, and for the space of   after the expiration thereof.

6. Resolved that each branch ought to possess the right of originating Acts; that the National Legislature ought to be impowered to enjoy the Legislative Rights vested in Congress by the Confederation and moreover to legislate in all cases to which the separate States are incompetent, or in which the harmony of the United States may be interrupted by the exercise of individual Legislation; to negative all laws passed by the several States, contravening in the opinion of the National Legislature the articles of Union; and to call forth the force of the Union against any member of the Union failing in its duty under the articles thereof.

7. Resolved that a National Executive be instituted; to be chosen by the National Legislature for the term of   years; to receive punctually, at stated times, a fixed compensation for the services rendered, in which no increase or diminution shall be made so as to affect the Magistracy, existing at the time of the increase or diminution, and to be ineligible a second time; and that besides a general authority to execute the National laws, it ought to enjoy the Executive rights vested in Congress by the Confederation.

8. Resolved that the Executive and a convenient number of the National Judiciary, ought to compose a Council or revision with authority to examine every act of the National Legislature before it shall operate, and every act of a particular Legislature before a Negative thereon shall be final; and that the dissent of the said Council shall amount to a rejection, unless the Act of the National Legislature be passed again, or that of a particular Legislature be again negatived by   of the members of each branch.

9. Resolved that a National Judiciary be established to consist of one or more supreme tribunals, and of inferior tribunals to be chosen by the National Legislature, to hold their offices during good behaviour; and to receive punctually at stated times fixed compensation for their services, in which no increase or diminution shall be made so as to affect the persons actually in office at the time of such increase or diminution. That the jurisdiction of the inferior tribunals shall be to hear and determine in the first instance, and of the supreme tribunal to hear and determine in the dernier resort, all piracies and felonies on the high seas, captures from an enemy; cases in which foreigners or citizens of other States applying to such jurisdictions may be interested, or which respect the collection of the National revenue; impeachments of any National officers, and questions which may involve the national peace and harmony.…

14. Resolved that the Legislative, Executive, and Judiciary powers within the several States ought to be bound by oath to support the articles of Union.

15. Resolved that the amendments which shall be offered to the Confederation, by the Convention ought at a proper time, or times, after the approbation of Congress to be submitted to an assembly or assemblies of Representatives, recommended by the several Legislatures to be expressly chosen by the people, to consider and decide thereon.

✣ D O C U M E N T   5

William Paterson Proposes the New Jersey Plan,
June 15, 1787

1. Resolved that the Articles of Confederation ought to be so revised, corrected, and enlarged as to render the federal Constitution adequate to the exigencies of Government, and the preservation of the Union.

2. Resolved that in addition to the powers vested in the United States in Congress, by the present existing articles of Confederation, they be authorized to pass acts for raising a revenue, by levying a duty or duties on all goods or merchandizes of foreign growth or manufacture, imported into any part of the United States, by Stamps on paper, vellum or parchment, and by a postage on all letters or packages passing through the general post-office, to be applied to such federal purposes as they shall deem proper and expedient; to make rules and regulations for the collection thereof; and the same from time to time, to alter and amend in such manner as they shall think proper: to pass Acts for the regulation of trade and commerce as well with foreign nations as with each other; provided that all punishments, fines, forfeitures and penalties to be incurred for contravening such acts rules and regulations shall be adjudged by the Common law Judiciaries of the State in which any offence contrary to the true intent and meaning of such Acts rules and regulations shall have been committed or perpetrated, with liberty of commencing in the first instance all suits and prosecutions for that purpose, in the superior common law Judiciary in such state, subject nevertheless, for the correction of errors, both in law and fact in rendering Judgement, to an appeal to the Judiciary of the United States.

3. Resolved that whenever requisitions shall be necessary, instead of the rule for making requisitions mentioned in the articles of Confederation, the United States in Congress be authorized to make such requisitions in proportion to the whole number of white and other free citizens and inhabitants of every age sex and condition including those bound to servitude for a term of years and three fifths of all other persons not comprehended in the foregoing description, except Indians not paying taxes; that if such requisitions be not complied with, in the time specified therein, to direct the collection thereof in the non-complying States and for that purpose to devise and pass acts directing and authorizing the same; provided that none of the powers hereby vested in the United States in Congress shall be exercised without the consent of at least   States, and in that proportion if the number of Confederated States should hereafter be increased or diminished.

4. Resolved that the United States in Congress be authorized to elect a federal Executive to consist of   persons, to continue in office for the term of   years, to receive punctually at stated times a fixed compensation for their services, in which no increase or diminution shall be made so as to affect the persons composing the Executive at the time of such increase or diminution, to be paid out of the federal treasury; to be incapable of holding any other office or appointment during their time of service and for   years thereafter; to be ineligible a second time, and removeable by Congress on application by a majority of the Executive of the several States;

that the Executives besides their general authority to execute the federal acts ought to appoint all federal officers not otherwise provided for, and to direct all military operations; provided that none of the persons composing the federal Executive shall on any occasion take command of any troops so as personally to conduct any enterprise as General or in other capacity.

5. Resolved that a federal Judiciary be established to consist of a supreme tribunal the Judges of which to be appointed by the Executive, and to hold their offices during good behaviour, to receive punctually at stated times a fixed compensation for their services in which no increase or diminution shall be made so as to affect persons actually in office at the time of such increase or diminution; that the Judiciary so established shall have authority to hear and determine in the first instance on all impeachments of federal officers, and by way of appeal in the dernier resort in all cases touching the rights of Ambassadors, in all cases of captures from an enemy, in all cases of piracies and felonies on the high Seas, in all cases in which foreigners may be interested, in the construction of any treaty or treaties, or which may arise on any of the Acts for regulation of trade, or the collection of the federal Revenue: that none of the Judiciary shall during the time they remain in office be capable of receiving or holding any other office or appointment during the time of service, or for thereafter.

6. Resolved that all Acts of the United States in Congress made by virtue and in pursuance of the powers hereby and by the articles of Confederation vested in them, and all Treaties made and ratified under the authority of the United States, shall be the supreme law of the respective States so far forth as those Acts or Treaties shall relate to the said States or their Citizens, and that the Judiciary of the several States shall be bound thereby in their decisions, any thing in the respective laws of the Individual States to the contrary notwithstanding; and that if any State, or any body of men in any State shall oppose or prevent carrying into execution such acts or treaties, the federal Executive shall be authorized to call forth the power of the Confederated States, or so much thereof as may be necessary to enforce and compel an obedience to such Acts or an observance of such Treaties....

✠ *D O C U M E N T   6*

Delegates Debate the Creation of a National Legislature, May–June, 1787

Thursday, May 31

Resol: 4. first clause "that the members of the first branch of the National Legislature ought to be elected by the people of the several States" being taken up,

Mr. Sherman opposed the election by the people, insisting that it ought to be by the State Legislatures. The people he said, immediately should have as little to do as may be about the Government. They want information and are constantly liable to be misled.

Mr. Gerry. The evils we experience flow from the excess of democracy. The people do not want virtue, but are the dupes of pretended patriots. In Massts. it had been fully confirmed by experience that they are daily misled into the most baneful measures and opinions by the false reports circulated by designing men, and which no one on the spot can refute. One principal evil arises from the want of due provision for those employed in the administration of Governmt. It would seem to be a maxim of democracy to starve the public servants. He [Mr. Gerry] mentioned the popular clamour in Massts. for the reduction of salaries and the attack made on that of the Govt. though secured by the spirit of the Constitution itself. He had he said been too republican heretofore: he was still however republican, but had been taught by experience the danger of the levelling spirit.

Mr. Mason, argued strongly for an election of the larger branch by the people. It was to be the grand depository of the democratic principle of the Govts. It was, so to speak, to be our House of Commons—It ought to know & sympathise with every part of the community; and ought therefore to be taken not only from different parts of the whole republic, but also from different districts of the larger members of it, which had in several instances particularly in Virga., different interests and views arising from difference of produce, of habits &c &c. He admitted that we had been too democratic but was afraid we sd. incautiously run into the opposite extreme. We ought to attend to the rights of every class of people. He had often wondered at the indifference of the superior classes of society to this dictate of humanity & policy; considering that however affluent their circumstances, or elevated their situations, might be, the course of a few years, not only might but certainly would, distribute their posterity throughout the lowest classes of Society. Every selfish motive therefore, every family attachment, ought to recommend such a system of policy as would provide no less carefully for the rights and happiness of the lowest than of the highest orders of Citizens.

Mr. Wilson contended strenuously for drawing the most numerous branch of the Legislature immediately from the people. He was for raising the federal pyramid to a considerable altitude, and for that reason wished to give it as broad a basis as possible. No government could long subsist without the confidence of the people. In a republican Government, this confidence was peculiarly essential. ...

Mr. Madison considered the popular election of one branch of the National Legislature as essential to every plan of free Government. He observed that in some of the States one branch of the Legislature was composed of men already removed from the people by an intervening body of electors. That if the first branch of the general legislature should be elected by the State Legislatures, the second branch elected by the first—the Executive by the second together with the first; and other appointments again made for subordinate purposes by the Executive, the people would be lost sight of altogether; and the necessary sympathy between them and their rulers and officers, too little felt. He was an advocate for the policy of refining the popular appointments by successive filtrations, but thought it might be pushed too far. He wished the expedient to be resorted to only in the appointment of the second branch of the Legislature, and in the Executive & judiciary branches of the Government. He thought too that the great fabric to be raised woult be more stable and durable, if it should rest on the solid foundation of the people themselves, than if it should stand merely on the pillars of the Legislatures.

Mr. Gerry did not like the election by the people. The maxims taken from the British constitution were often fallacious when applied to our situation which was extremely different. Experience he said had shewn that the State legislatures drawn immediately from the people did not always possess their confidence. He had no objection however to an election by the people if it were so qualified that men of honor & character might not be unwilling to be joined in the appointments. ...

On the question for an election of the first branch of the national Legislature by the people.

Massts. ay. Connect. divd. N. York ay. N. Jersey no. Pena. ay. Delawe. divd. Va. ay. N. C. ay. S. C. no. Georga. ay.

The Committee proceeded to Resolution 5. "that the second, [or senatorial] branch of the National Legislature ought to be chosen by the first branch out of persons nominated by the State Legislatures."

Mr. Spaight contended that the 2d. branch ought to be chosen by the State Legislatures and moved an amendment to that effect.

Mr. Wilson opposed both a nomination by the State Legislatures, and an election by the first branch of the national Legislature, because the second branch of the latter, ought to be independent of both. He thought both branches of the National Legislature ought to be chosen by the people, but was not prepared with a specific proposition. He suggested the mode of chusing the Senate of N. York to wit of uniting several election districts, for one branch, in chusing members for the other branch, as a good model.

Mr. Madison observed that such a mode would destroy the influence of the smaller States associated with larger ones in the same district; as the latter would chuse from within themselves, altho' better men might be found in the former. The election of Senators in Virga. where large & small counties were often formed into one district for the purpose, had illustrated this consequence Local partiality, would often prefer a resident within the County or State, to a candidate of superior merit residing out of it. Less merit also in a resident would be more known throughout his own State. ...

Wednesday, June 6

Mr. Pinkney according to previous notice & rule obtained, moved "that the first branch of the national Legislature be elected by the State Legislatures, and not by the people," contending that the people were less fit Judges in such a case, and that the Legislature would be less likely to promote the adoption of the new Government, if they were to be excluded from all share in it.

Mr. Rutlidge 2ded. the motion.

Mr. Gerry. Much depends on the mode of election. In England, the people will probably lose their liberty from the smallness of the proportion having a right of suffrage. Our danger arises from the opposite extreme: hence in Massts. the worst men get into the Legislature. Several members of that Body had lately been convicted of infamous crimes. Men of indigence, ignorance & baseness, spare no pains, however dirty to carry their point agst. men who are superior to the artifices practised. He was not disposed to run into extremes. He was as much principled as ever agst. aristocracy and monarchy. It was necessary on the one hand that the people should appoint one branch of the Govt. in order to inspire them with the necessary confidence. But he wished the election on the other to be so modified as to secure more effectually a just preference of merit. His idea was that the people should nominate certain persons in certain districts, out of whom the State Legislature shd. make the appointment. ...

Mr. Sherman. If it were in view to abolish the State Govt. the elections ought to be by the people. If the State Govts. are to be continued, it is necessary in order to preserve harmony between the National & State Govts. that the elections to the former shd. be made by the latter. The right of participating in the National Govt. would be sufficiently secured to the people by their election of the State Legislatures. The objects of the Union, he thought were few. 1. defence agst. foreign danger. 2 agst. internal disputes & a resort to force. 3. Treaties with foreign nations. 4 regulating foreign commerce, & drawing revenue from it. These & perhaps a few lesser objects alone rendered a Confederation of the States necessary. All other matters civil & criminal would be much better in the hands of the States. The people are more happy in small than large States. States may indeed be too small as Rhode Island, & thereby be too subject to faction. Some others were perhaps too large, the powers of Govt. not being able to pervade them. He was for giving the General Govt. power to legislate and execute within a defined province.

Col. Mason. Under the existing Confederacy, Congs. represent the *States* not the *people* of the States: their acts operate on the *States*, not the individuals. The case will be changed in the new plan of Govt. The people will be represented; they ought therefore to choose the Representatives. The requisites in actual representation are that the Reps. should sympathize with their constituents; shd. think as they think, & feel as they feel; and that for these purposes shd. even be residents among them. ...

Mr. Madison considered an election of one branch at least of the Legislature by the people immediately, as a clear principle of free Govt. and that this mode under proper regulations had the additional advantage of securing better representatives, as well as of avoiding too great an agency of the State Governments in the General one.—He differed from the member from Connecticut [Mr. Sherman] in thinking the objects mentioned to be all the principal ones that required a National Govt. Those were certainly important and necessary objects; but he combined with them the necessity of providing more effectually for the security of private rights, and the steady dispensation of Justice. Interferences with these were evils which had more perhaps than any thing else, produced this convention. ...

Mr. Read. Too much attachment is betrayed to the State Governts. We must look beyond their continuance. A national Govt. must soon of necessity swallow all of them up. They will soon be reduced to the mere office of electing the National Senate. He was agst. patching up the old federal System: he hoped the idea wd. be dismissed. It would be like putting new cloth on an old garment. The confederation was founded on temporary principles. It cannot last: it cannot be amended. If we do not establish a good Govt. on new principles, we must either go to ruin, or have the work to do over again. The people at large are wrongly suspected of being averse to a Genl. Govt. The aversion lies among interested men who possess their confidence. ...

Mr. Wilson, would not have spoken again, but for what had fallen from Mr. Read; namely, that the idea of preserving the State Govts. ought to be abandoned. He saw no incompatibility between the National & State Govts. provided the latter were restrained to certain local purposes; nor any probability of their being devoured by the former. In all confederated Systems antient & modern the reverse had happened; the Generality being destroyed gradually by the usurpations of the parts composing it.

On the question for electing the 1st. branch by the State Legislatures as moved by Mr. Pinkney: it was negatived:

Mass. no. Ct. ay. N. Y. no. N. J. ay. Pa. no. Del. no. Md. no. Va. no. N. C. no. S. C. ay. Geo. no.

Thursday, June 7

The Clause providing for ye. appointment of the 2d. branch of the national Legislature, having lain blank since the last vote on the mode of electing it, to wit, by the 1st. branch, Mr. Dickenson now moved "that the members of the 2d. branch ought to be chosen by the individual Legislatures."

Mr. Sherman seconded the motion; observing that the particular States would thus become interested in supporting the national Governt. and that a due harmony between the two Governments would be maintained....

Mr. Dickenson had two reasons for his motion. 1. because the sense of the States would be better collected through their Governments; than immediately from the people at large; 2. because he wished the Senate to consist of the most distinguished characters, distinguished for their rank in life and their weight of property, and bearing as strong a likeness to the British House of Lords as possible; and he thought such characters more likely to be selected by the State Legislatures, than in any other mode. The greatness of the number has no objection with him. He hoped there would be 80 and twice 80. of them. If their number should be small, the popular branch could not be balanced by them. The legislature of a numerous people ought to be a numerous body.

Mr. Wilson. If we are to establish a national Government, that Government ought to flow from the people at large. If one branch of it should be chosen by the Legislatures, and the other by the people, the two branches will rest on different foundations, and dissensions will naturally arise between them. He wished the Senate to be elected by the people as well as the other branch, and the people might be divided into proper districts for the purpose & moved to postpone the motion of Mr. Dickenson, in order to take up one of that import.

Mr. Morris 2ded. him.

Mr. Madison, if the motion [of Mr. Dickenson] should be agreed to, we must either depart from the doctrine of proportional representation; or admit into the Senate a very large number of members. The first is inadmissible, being evidently unjust. The second is inexpedient.

On Mr. Dickinson's motion for an appointment of the Senate by the State Legislatures.

Mass. ay. Ct. ay. N. Y. ay. Pa. ay. Del. ay. Md. ay. Va. ay. N. C. ay. S. C. ay. Geo. ay.

✠ *D O C U M E N T   7*

Delegates Debate Slavery and Representation, June–July, 1787

Saturday, June 30

Mr. Madison. But he contended that the States were divided into different interests not by their difference of size, but by other circumstances; the most material of which resulted partly from climate, but principally from the effects of their having or not having slaves. These two causes concurred in forming the great division of interests in the U. States. It did not lie between the large & small States: It lay between the

Northern & Southern, and if any defensive power were necessary, it ought to be mutually given to these two interests. He was so strongly impressed with this important truth that he had been casting about in his mind for some expedient that would answer the purpose. The one which had occurred was that instead of proportioning the votes of the States in both branches, to their respective numbers of inhabitants computing the slaves in the ratio of 5 to 3, they should be represented in one branch according to the number of free inhabitants only; and in the other according to the whole no. counting the slaves as if free. By this arrangement the Southern Scale would have the advantage in one House, and the Northern in the other. ...

Wednesday, July 11

Mr. Randolph's motion requiring the Legislre. to take a periodical census for the purpose of redressing inequalities in the Representation, was resumed.

Mr. Sherman was agst. shackling the Legislature too much. We ought to choose wise & good men, and then confide in them.

Mr. Mason. The greater the difficulty we find in fixing a proper rule of Representation, the more unwilling ought we to be, to throw the task from ourselves, on the Genl. Legislre. He did not object to the conjectural ratio which was to prevail in the outset; but considered a Revision from time to time according to some permanent & precise standard as essential to ye. fair representation required in the 1st. branch. ...

Mr. Butler & Genl. Pinkney insisted that blacks be included in the rule of Representation, *equally* with the Whites: and for that purpose moved that the words "three fifths" be struck out.

Mr. Gerry thought that $\frac{3}{5}$ of them was to say the least the full proportion that could be admitted.

Mr. Ghorum. This ratio was fixed by Congs. as a rule of taxation. Then it was urged by the Delegates representing the States having slaves that the blacks were still more inferior to freemen. At present when the ratio of representation is to be established, we are assured that they are equal to freemen. The arguments on ye. former occasion had convinced him that $\frac{3}{5}$ was pretty near the just proportion and he should vote according to the same opinion now.

Mr. Butler insisted that the labour of a slave in S. Carola. was as productive & valuable as that of a freeman in Massts., that as wealth was the great means of defence and utility to the Nation they were equally valuable to it with freemen; and that consequently an equal representation ought to be allowed for them in a Government which was instituted principally for the protection of property, and was itself to be supported by property.

Mr. Mason, could not agree to the motion, notwithstand it was favorable to Virga. because he thought it unjust. It was certain that the slaves were valuable, as they raised the value of land, increased the exports & imports, and of course the revenue, would supply the means of feeding & supporting an army, and might in case of emergency become themselves soldiers. As in these important respects they were useful to the community at large, they ought not to be excluded from the estimate of Representation. He could not however regard them as equal to freemen and could not vote for them as such. He added as worthy of remark, that the Southern States have this peculiar species of property, over & above the other species of property common to all the States.

Mr. Williamson reminded Mr. Ghorum that if the Southn. States contended for the inferiority of blacks to whites when taxation was in view, the Eastern States on the same occasion contended for their equality. He did not however, either then or now, concur in either extreme, but approved of the ratio of $\frac{3}{5}$.

On Mr. Butler's motion for considering blacks as equal to Whites in the apportionmt. of Representation.

Massts. no. Cont. no. [N. Y. not on floor.] N. J. no. Pa. no. Del. ay. Md. no. Va. no. N. C. no. S. C. ay. Geo. ay.

Mr. Govr. Morris said he had several objections to the proposition of Mr. Williamson. 1. It fettered the Legislature too much. 2. it would exclude some States altogether who would not have a sufficient number to entitle them to a single Representative. 3. it will not consist with the Resolution passed on Saturday last authorising the Legislature to adjust the Representation from time to time on the principles of population & wealth or with the principles of equity. If slaves were to be considered as inhabitants, not as wealth, then the sd. Resolution would not be pursued: If as wealth, then why is no other wealth but slaves included? These objections may perhaps be removed by amendments. His great objection was that the number of inhabitants was not a proper standard of wealth. The amazing difference between the comparative numbers & wealth of different Countries, rendered all reasoning superfluous on the subject. Numbers might with greater propriety be deemed a measure of strength, than of wealth, yet the late defence made by G. Britain, agst. her numerous enemies proved in the clearest manner, that it is entirely fallacious even in this respect.

Mr. King thought there was great force in the objections of Mr. Govr. Morris: he would however accede to the proposition for the sake of doing something.

Mr. Rutlidge contended for the admission of wealth in the estimate by which Representation should be regulated. The Western States will not be able to contribute in proportion to their numbers; they shd. not therefore be represented in that proportion. The Atlantic States will not concur in such a plan. He moved that "at the end of   years after the 1st. meeting of the Legislature, and of every   years thereafter, the Legislature shall proportion the Representation according to the principles of wealth & population."

Mr. Sherman thought the number of people alone the best rule for measuring wealth as well as representation; and that if the Legislature were to be governed by wealth, they would be obliged to estimate it by numbers. He was at first for leaving the matter wholly to the discretion of the Legislature; but he had been convinced by the observations of [Mr. Randolph & Mr. Mason,] that the *periods* & the *rule*, of revising the Representation ought to be fixt by the Constitution.

Mr. Reid thought the Legislature ought not to be too much shackled. It would make the Constitution like Religious Creeds, embarrassing to those bound to conform to them & more likely to produce dissatisfaction and scism, than harmony and union.

Mr. Mason objected to Mr. Rutlidge's motion, as requiring of the Legislature something too indefinite & impracticable, and leaving them a pretext for doing nothing.

Mr. Wilson had himself no objection to leaving the Legislature entirely at liberty. But considered wealth as an impracticable rule.

Mr. Ghorum. If the Convention who are comparatively so little biassed by local views are so much perplexed, How can it be expected that the Legislature hereafter under the full biass of those views, will be able to settle a standard. He was convinced by the arguments of others & his own reflections, that the Convention ought to fix some standard or other. . . .

On the question on the first clause of Mr. Williamson's motion as to taking a census of the *free* inhabitants; it passed in the affirmative Masts. ay. Cont. ay. N. J. ay. Pa. ay. Del. no. Md. no. Va. ay. N. C. ay. S. C. no. Geo. no.

The next clause as to $\frac{3}{5}$ of the negroes considered.

Mr. King being much opposed to fixing numbers as the rule of representation, was particularly so on account of the blacks. He thought the admission of them along with Whites at all, would excite great discontents among the States having no slaves. . . .

Mr. Sherman. S. Carola. had not more beyond her proportion than N. York & N. Hampshire, nor either of them more than was necessary in order to avoid fractions or reducing them below their proportion. Georgia had more; but the rapid growth of that State seemed to justify it. In general the allotment might not be just, but considering all circumstances, he was satisfied with it.

Mr. Ghorum supported the propriety of establishing numbers as the rule. He said that in Massts. estimates had been taken in the different towns, and that persons had been curious enough to compare these estimates with the respective numbers of people; and it had been found even including Boston, that the most exact proportion prevailed between numbers & property. He was aware that there might be some weight in what had fallen from his colleague, as to the umbrage which might be taken by the people of the Eastern States. But he recollected that when the proposition of Congs. for changing the 8th. art: of Confedn. was before the Legislature of Massts. the only difficulty then was to satisfy them that the negroes ought not to have been counted equally with whites instead of being counted in the ratio of three fifths only.*

Mr. Wilson did not well see on what principle the admission of blacks in the proportion of three fifths could be explained. Are they admitted as Citizens? then why are they not admitted on an equality with White Citizens? are they admitted as property? then why is not other property admitted into the computation? These were difficulties however which he thought must be overruled by the necessity of compromise. He had some apprehensions also from the tendency of the blending of the blacks with the whites, to give disgust to the people of Pena. as had been intimated by his Colleague [Mr. Govr. Morris]. But he differed from him in thinking numbers of inhabts. so incorrect a measure of wealth. . . .

Mr. Govr. Morris was compelled to declare himself reduced to the dilemma of doing injustice to the Southern States or to human nature, and he must therefore do it to the former. For he could never agree to give such encouragement to the slave trade as would be given by allowing them a representation for their negroes, and he did not believe those States would ever confederate on terms that would deprive them of that trade.

---

*They were then to have been a rule of taxation only. [Footnote by Madison.]

On Question for agreeing to include $\frac{3}{5}$ of the blacks.

Masts. no. Cont. ay. N. J. no. Pa. no. Del. no. Mard. no. Va. ay. N. C. ay. S. C. no. Geo. ay. . . .

Thursday, July 12

Mr. Govr. Morris moved to add to the clause empowering the Legislature to vary the Representation according to the principles of wealth & number of inhabts. a "proviso that taxation shall be in proportion to Representation."

Mr. Butler contended again that Representation sd. be according to the full number of inhabts. including all the blacks; admitting the justice of Mr. Govr. Morris's motion.

Mr. Mason also admitted the justice of the principle, but was afraid embarrassments might be occasioned to the Legislature by it. It might drive the Legislature to the plan of Requisitions.

Mr. Govr. Morris, admitted that some objections lay agst. his motion, but supposed they would be removed by restraining the rule to *direct* taxation. With regard to indirect taxes on *exports* & imports & on consumption, the rule would be inapplicable. Notwithstanding what had been said to the contrary he was persuaded that the imports & consumption were pretty nearly equal throughout the Union.

General Pinkney liked the idea. He thought it so just that it could not be objected to. But foresaw that if the revision of the census was left to the discretion of the legislature, it would never be carried into execution. The rule must be fixed, and the execution of it enforced by the Constitution. He was alarmed at what was said yesterday, concerning the negroes. He was now again alarmed at what had been thrown out concerning the taxing of exports. S. Carola. has in one year exported to the amount of £600,000 Sterling all which was the fruit of the labor of her blacks. Will she be represented in proportion to this amount? She will not. Neither ought she then to be subject to a tax on it. He hoped a clause would be inserted in the system, restraining the Legislature from a taxing Exports.

Mr. Wilson approved the principle, but could not see how it could be carried into execution; unless restrained to direct taxation.

Mr. Govr. Morris having so varied his Motion by inserting the word "direct." It passd. nem. con. as follows—"provided the always that direct taxation ought to be proportioned to representation."

Mr. Davie, said it was high time now to speak out. He saw that it was meant by some gentlemen to deprive the Southern States of any share of Representation for their blacks. He was sure that N. Carola. would never confederate on any terms that did not rate them at least as $\frac{3}{5}$. If the Eastern States meant therefore to exclude them altogether the business was at an end.

Dr. Johnson, thought that wealth and population were the true, equitable rule of representation; but he conceived that these two principles resolved themselves into one; population being the best measure of wealth. He concluded therefore that ye. number of people ought to be established as the rule, and that all descriptions including blacks *equally* with the whites; ought to fall within the computation. As various opinions had been expressed on the subject, he would move that a Committee might be appointed to take them into consideration and report thereon.

Mr. Govr. Morris. It has been said that it is high time to speak out, as one member, he would candidly do so. He came here to form a compact for the good of America. He was ready to do so with all the States. He hoped & believed that all would enter into such a Compact. If they would not he was ready to join with any States that would. But as the Compact was to be voluntary, it is in vain for the Eastern States to insist on what the Southn. States will never agree to. It is equally vain for the latter to require what the other States can never admit; and he verily believed the people of Pena. will never agree to a representation of Negroes. What can be desired by these States more than has been already proposed; that the Legislature shall from time to time regulate Representation according to population & wealth.

Genl. Pinkney desired that the rule of wealth should be ascertained and not left to the pleasure of the Legislature; and that property in slaves should not be exposed to danger under a Govt. instituted for the protection of property.

The first clause in the Report of the first Grand Committee was postponed.

Mr. Elseworth. In order to carry into effect the principle established, moved to add to the last clause adopted by the House the words following "and that the rule of contribution by direct taxation for the support of the Government of the U. States shall be the number of white inhabitants, and three fifths of every other description in the several States, until some other rule that shall more accurately ascertain the wealth of the several States can be devised and adopted by the Legislature."

Mr. Butler seconded the motion in order that it might be committed.

Mr. Randolph was not satisfied with the motion. The danger will be revived that the ingenuity of the Legislature may evade or pervert the rule so as to perpetuate the power where it shall be lodged in the first instance. He proposed in lieu of Mr. Elseworth's motion, "that in order to ascertain the alterations in Representation that may be required from time to time by changes in the relative circumstances of the States, a census shall be taken within two years from the 1st. meeting of the Genl Legislature of the U. S., and once within the term of every year afterwards, of all the inhabitants in the manner & according to the ratio recommended by Congress in their resolution of the 18th day of Apl. 1783; [rating the blacks at $\frac{3}{5}$ of their number] and, that the Legislature of the U. S. shall arrange the Representation accordingly."—He urged strenuously that express security ought to be provided for including slaves in the ratio of Representation. He lamented that such a species of property existed. But as it did exist the holders of it would require this security. It was perceived that the design was entertained by some of excluding slaves altogether; the Legislature therefore ought not to be left at liberty.

Mr. Elseworth withdraws his motion & seconds that of Mr. Randolph. . . .

Mr. Pinkney moved to amend Mr. Randolph's motion so as to make "blacks equal to the whites in the ratio of representation." This he urged was nothing more than justice. The blacks are the labourers, the peasants of the Southern States: they are as productive of pecuniary resources as those of the Northern States. They add equally to the wealth, and considering money as the sinew of war, to the strength of the nation. It will also be politic with regard to the Northern States, as taxation is to keep pace with Representation. . . .

On Mr. Pinkney's motion for rating blacks as equal to Whites instead of as $\frac{3}{5}$—

Mas. no. Cont. no. [Dr. Johnson ay] N. J. no. Pa. no. [3 agst. 2.] Del. no. Md. no. Va. no. N. C. no. S. C. ay. Geo.—ay.

Mr. Randolph's proposition as varied by Mr. Wilson being read for question on the whole.

Mr. Gerry, urged that the principle of it could not be carried into execution as the States were not to be taxed as States. With regard to taxes in imports, he conceived they would be more productive. Where there were no slaves than where there were; the consumption being greater—

Mr. Elseworth. In case of a poll tax there wd. be no difficulty. But there wd. probably be none. The sum allotted to a State may be levied without difficulty according to the plan used by the State in raising its own supplies. On the question on ye. whole proposition; as proportioning representation to direct taxation & both to the white & $\frac{2}{3}$ of black inhabitants, & requiring a Census within six years—& within every ten years afterwards.

Mas. divd. Cont. ay. N. J. no. Pa. ay. Del. no. Md. ay. Va. ay. N. C. ay. S. C. divd. Geo. ay.

✠ *D O C U M E N T   8*

Delegate James Madison Advocates an Extended Republic, 1788

Among the numerous advantages promised by a well-constructed Union, none deserves to be more accurately developed than its tendency to break and control the violence of faction. ....

By a faction I understand a number of citizens, whether amounting to a majority or minority of the whole, who are united and actuated by some common impulse of passion, or of interest, adverse to the rights of other citizens, or to the permanent and aggregate interests of the community.

There are two methods of curing the mischiefs of faction: the one, by removing its causes; the other, by controlling its effects.

There are again two methods of removing the causes of faction: the one, by destroying the liberty which is essential to its existence; the other, by giving to every citizen the same opinions, the same passions, and the same interests.

It could never be more truly said than of the first remedy that it was worse than the disease. Liberty is to faction what air is to fire, an aliment without which it instantly expires. But it could not be a less folly to abolish liberty, which is essential to political life, because it nourishes faction than it would be to wish the annihilation of air, which is essential to animal life, because it imparts to fire its destructive agency.

The second expedient is as impracticable as the first would be unwise. As long as the reason of man continues fallible, and he is at liberty to exercise it, different opinions will be formed. As long as the connection subsists between his reason and his self-love, his opinions and his passions will have a reciprocal influence on each other; and the former will be objects to which the latter will attach themselves. The diversity in the faculties of men, from which the rights of property originate, is not less an insuperable obstacle to a uniformity of interests. The protection of these faculties is the first object of government. From the protection of different and unequal faculties of acquiring property, the possession of different degrees and kinds of property immediately results; and from the influence of these on the sentiments and views of the respective proprietors ensues a division of the society into different interests and parties.

The latent causes of faction are thus sown in the nature of man; and we see them everywhere brought into different degrees of activity, according to the different circumstances of civil society. A zeal for different opinions concerning religion, concerning government, and many other points, as well of speculation as of practice; an attachment to different leaders ambitiously contending for pre-eminence and power; or to persons of other descriptions whose fortunes have been interesting to the human passions, have, in turn, divided mankind into parties, inflamed them with mutual animosity, and rendered them much more disposed to vex and oppress each other than to co-operate for their common good. So strong is this propensity of mankind to fall into mutual animosities that where no substantial occasion presents itself the most frivolous and fanciful distinctions have been sufficient to kindle their unfriendly passions and excite their most violent conflicts. But the most common and durable source of factions has been the verious and unequal distribution of property. Those who hold and those who are without property have ever formed distinct interests in society. Those who are creditors, and those who are debtors, fall under a like discrimination. A landed interest, a manufacturing interest, a mercantile interest, a moneyed interest, with many lesser interests, grow up of necessity in civilized nations, and divide them into different classes, actuated by different sentiments and views. The regulation of these various and interfering interests forms the principal task of modern legislation and involves the spirit of party and faction in the necessary and ordinary operations of government....

It is in vain to say that enlightened statesmen will be able to adjust these clashing interests and render them all subservient to the public good. Enlightened statesmen will not always be at the helm. Nor, in many cases, can such an adjustment be made at all without taking into view indirect and remote considerations, which will rarely prevail over the immediate interest which one party may find in disregarding the rights of another or the good of the whole.

The inference to which we are brought is that the *causes* of faction cannot be removed and that relief is only to be sought in the means of controlling its *effects*.

If a faction consists of less than a majority, relief is supplied by the republican principle, which enables the majority to defeat its sinister views by regular vote. It may clog the administration, it may convulse the society; but it will be unable to execute and mask its violence under the forms of the Constitution. When a majority is included in a faction, the form of popular government, on the other hand, enables it to sacrifice to its ruling passion or interest both the public good and the rights of other citizens. To secure the public good and private rights against the danger of such a faction, and at the same time to preserve the spirit and the form of popular government, is then the great object to which our inquiries are directed. Let me add that it is the great desideratum by which alone this from of government can be rescued from the opprobrium under which it has so long labored and be recommended to the esteem and adoption of mankind.

By what means is this object attainable? Evidently by one of two only. Either the existence of the same passion or interest in a majority at the same time must be prevented, or the majority, having such coexistent passion or interest, must be rendered, by their number and local situation, unable to concert and carry into effect schemes of oppression. If the impulse and the opportunity be suffered to coincide, we well know that neither moral nor religious motives can be relied on as an adequate control. They are not found to be such on the injustice and violence of individuals, and lose their efficacy in proportion to the number combined together, that is, in proportion as their efficacy becomes needful.

From this view of the subject it may be concluded that a pure democracy, by which I mean a society consisting of a small number of citizens, who assemble and administer the government in person, can admit of no cure for the mischiefs of faction. A common passion or interest will, in almost every case, be felt by a majority of the whole; a communication and concert results from the form of government itself; and there is nothing to check the inducements to sacrifice the weaker party or an obnoxious individual. Hence it is that such democracies have ever been spectacles of turbulence and contention; have ever been found incompatible with personal security or the rights of property; and have in general been as short in their lives as they have been violent in their deaths. ...

A republic, by which I mean a government in which the scheme of representation takes place, opens a different prospect and promises the cure for which we are seeking. Let us examine the points in which it varies from pure democracy, and we shall comprehend both the nature of the cure and the efficacy which it must derive from the Union.

The two great points of difference between a democracy and a republic are: first, the delegation of the government, in the latter, to a small number of citizens elected by the rest; secondly, the greater number of citizens and greater sphere of country over which the latter may be extended.

The effect of the first difference is, on the one hand, to refine and enlarge the public views by passing them through the medium of a chosen body of citizens, whose wisdom may best discern the true interest of their country and whose patriotism and love of justice will be least likely to sacrifice it to temporary or partial considerations. ... On the other hand, the effect may be inverted. Men of factious tempers, of local prejudices, or of sinister designs, may, by intrigue, by corruption, or by other means, first obtain the suffrages, and then betray the interests of the people. The question resulting is, whether small or extensive republics are most favorable to the election of proper guardians of the public weal; and it is clearly decided in favor of the latter by two obvious considerations.

In the first place it is to be remarked that however small the republic may be the representatives must be raised to a certain number in order to guard against the cabals of a few; and that however large it may be they must be limited to a certain number in order to guard against the confusion of a multitude. Hence, the number of representatives in the two cases not being in proportion to that of the constituents, and being proportionally greatest in the small republic, it follows that if the proportion of fit characters be not less in the large than in the small republic, the former will present a greater option, and consequently a greater probability of a fit choice.

In the next place, as each representative will be chosen by a greater number of citizens in the large than in the small republic, it will be more difficult for unworthy candidates to practise with success the vicious arts by which elections are too often carried; and the suffrages of the people being more free, will be more likely to center on men who possess the most attractive merit and the most diffusive and established characters.

It must be confessed that in this, as in most other cases, there is a mean, on both sides of which inconveniencies will be found to lie. By enlarging too much the number of electors, you render the representative too little acquainted with all their local circumstances and lesser interests; as by reducing it too much, you render him unduly attached to these, and too little fit to comprehend and pursue great and national objects. The federal Constitution forms a happy combination in this respect; the great and aggregate interests being referred to the national, the local and particular to the State legislatures.

The other point of difference is the greater number of citizens and extent of territory which may be brought within the compass of republican than of democratic government; and it is this circumstance principally which renders factious combinations less to be dreaded in the former than in the latter. The smaller the society, the fewer probably will be the distinct parties and interests composing it; the fewer the distinct parties and interests, the more frequently will a majority be found of the same party; and the smaller the number of individuals composing a majority, and the smaller the compass within which they are placed, the more easily will they concert and execute their plans of oppression. Extend the sphere and you take in a greater variety of parties and interests; you make it less probable that a majority of the whole will have a common motive to invade the rights of other citizens; or if such a common motive exists, it will be more difficult for all who feel it to discover their own strength and to act in unison with each other. Besides other impediments, it may be remarked that, where there is a consciousness of unjust or dishonorable purposes, communication is always checked by distrust in proportion to the number whose concurrence is necessary.

Hence, it clearly appears that the same advantage which a republic has over a democracy in controlling the effects of faction is enjoyed by a large over a small republic—is enjoyed by the Union over the States composing it. Does this advantage consist in the substitution of representatives whose enlightened views and virtuous sentiments render them superior to local prejudices and to schemes of injustice? It will not be denied that the representation of the Union will be most likely to possess these requisite endowments. Does it consist in the greater security afforded by a greater variety of parties, against the event of any one party being able to outnumber and oppress the rest? In an equal degree does the increased variety of parties comprised within the Union increase this security. Does it, in fine, consist in the greater obstacles opposed to the concert and accomplishment of the secret wishes of an unjust and interested majority? Here again the extent of the Union gives it the most palpable advantage.

The influence of factious leaders may kindle a flame within their particular States but will be unable to spread a general conflagration through the other States. A religious sect may degenerate into a political faction in a part of the Confederacy; but the variety of sects dispersed over the entire face of it must secure the national councils against any danger from that source. A rage for paper money, for an abolition of debts, for an equal division of property, or for any other improper or wicked project, will be less apt to pervade the whole body of the Union than a particular member of it, in the same proportion as such a malady is more likely to taint a particular county or district than an entire State.

In the extent and proper structure of the Union, therefore, we behold a republican remedy for the diseases most incident to republican government....

✥ E S S A Y S

The essays included here provide a sampling of how historians have approached the work of the founders. Paul Finkelman, a historian at the Albany Law School, is the foremost scholar of the relationship between the Constitution and slavery. In this selection, he argues that slavery pervaded the founders' Constitution (although the word "slavery" never appeared in the text) and that white southerners won a key victory with the inclusion of the Three-Fifths Clause. Sectional loyalties and economic interests loom large in his account. The second essay is by Forrest McDonald, who taught history for many years at the University of Alabama. In this selection, McDonald sees a very different and more complicated set of factions operating at the Convention, which he claims had a great deal to do with the variety of political ideologies at work among the delegates. In the final essay, Jan Lewis, a professor of history at Rutgers University, argues for the essential radicalism of the founders' view of representation with regard to women. The weight of English tradition to the contrary, the founders viewed women as members of the body politic.

Slavery and the Debate Over Representation

PAUL FINKELMAN

The word "slavery" appears in only one place in the Constitution—in the Thirteenth Amendment, where the institution is abolished. Throughout the main body of the Constitution, slaves are referred to as "other persons," "such persons," or in the singular as a "person held to Service or Labour." Why is this the case?

Throughout the debates, the delegates talked about "blacks," "Negroes," and "slaves." But the final document avoided these terms. The change in language was clearly designed to make the Constitution more palatable to the North. In a debate over representation, William Paterson of New Jersey pointed out that under the Articles of Confederation Congress "had been ashamed to use the term 'Slaves' & had substituted a description." This shame over the word "slave" came up at the Convention during the debate over the African slave trade. The delegates from the Carolinas and Georgia vigorously demanded that the African trade remain open under the new Constitution. Gouverneur Morris of Pennsylvania, furious at this immoral compromise, suggested that the proposed clause read: the "Importation of slaves into N. Carolina, S—Carolina & Georgia" shall not be prohibited. Connecticut's Roger Sherman, who voted with the Deep South to allow the trade, objected, not only to the singling out of specific states, but also to the term "slave." He declared he "liked a description better than the terms proposed, which had been declined by the old Congs & were not pleasing to some people." George Clymer of Pennsylvania "concurred" with Sherman. In the North Carolina ratifying convention, James Iredell, who had been a delegate in Philadelphia, explained that "the word *slave* is not mentioned" because "the northern delegates, owing to their particular scruples on the subject of slavery, did not choose the word *slave* to be mentioned." Thus, southerners avoided the term because they did not want unnecessarily to antagonize their colleagues from the

North. As long as they were assured of protection for their institution, the southerners at the Convention were willing to do without the word "slave."

Despite the circumlocution, slavery was sanctioned throughout the Constitution. Five provisions dealt directly with slavery.

Article I, Section 2, Paragraph 3. The three-fifths clause provided for counting three-fifths of all slaves for purposes of representation in Congress. This clause also provided that, if any "direct tax" was levied on the states, it could be imposed only proportionately, according to population, and that only three-fifths of all slaves would be counted in assessing what each state's contribution would be.

Article I, Section 9, Paragraph 1. Popularly known as the "slave trade clause," this provision prohibited Congress from banning the "Migration or Importation of such Persons as any of the States now existing shall think proper to admit" before the year 1808. Awkwardly phrased and designed to confuse readers, this clause prevented Congress from ending the African slave trade before 1808, but did not require Congress to ban the trade after that date. The clause was a significant exception to the general power granted to Congress to regulate all commerce.

Article I, Section 9, Paragraph 4. This clause declared that any "capitation" or other "direct tax" had to take into account the three-fifths clause. It ensured that, if a head tax were ever levied, slaves would be taxed at three-fifths the rate of whites. The "direct tax" portion of this clause was redundant, because that was provided for in the three-fifths clause.

Article V, Section 2, Paragraph 3. The fugitive slave clause prohibited the states from emancipating fugitive slaves and required that runaways be returned to their owners "on demand."

Article V. This article prohibited any amendment of the slave importation or capitation clauses before 1808.

Taken together, these five provisions gave the South a strong claim to "special treatment" for its peculiar institution. The three-fifths clause also gave the South extra political muscle—in the House of Representatives and in the electoral college—to support that claim.

Numerous other clauses of the Constitution supplemented the five clauses that directly protected slavery. Some provisions that indirectly guarded slavery, such as the prohibition on taxing exports, were included primarily to protect the interests of slaveholders. Others, such as the guarantee of federal support to "suppress Insurrections" and the creation of the electoral college, were written with slavery in mind, although delegates also supported them for reasons having nothing to do with slavery....

When they arrived at the Convention, the delegates probably did not think slavery would be a pressing issue. Rivalries between large and small states appeared to pose the greatest obstacle to a stronger Union. The nature of representation in Congress; the power of the national government to levy taxes, regulate commerce, and pay off the nation's debts; the role of the states under a new constitution; and the power of the executive were on the agenda. Yet, as the delegates debated these issues, the importance of slavery—and the sectional differences it caused—became clear. Throughout the summer of 1787, slavery emerged to complicate almost every debate. Most important by far was the way slavery figured in the lengthy debate over representation....

Randolph's plan called for a radical restructuring of the American government by making population the basis for representation in the national Congress. Under the Articles of Confederation, each state had one vote in Congress. By changing the basis of representation to population, Randolph's plan immediately created tensions between the large and small states at the Convention. But the plan also raised the dilemma of whether slaves would be counted in allocating representation in the new Congress. This dilemma of how to count slaves, or whether to count them at all, would trouble the delegates throughout the Convention.

Virginia was the most populous state in the nation, and thus Randolph had a vested interest in basing Congressional representation on population. But how that population would be counted greatly affected the potential representation of Virginia and the rest of the South. Virginia's white population, as the 1790 census would reveal, was only slightly larger than Pennsylvania's. If representation were based solely on free persons, the North would over-whelm the South. But if slaves were counted equally with free persons, the Virginia delegation would be the largest, and the South would have more members of Congress than the North. The Virginians of course realized that the northern states were unlikely to support counting slaves for purposes of representation. Thus, Randolph's plan hedged the issue, declaring "that the rights of suffrage in the National Legislature ought to be proportioned to the Quotas of contribution, or to the number of free inhabitants, as the one or the other rule may seem best in different cases." Randolph's avoidance of the term "slaves" by referring to "quotas of contribution" indicates the sensitivity of the subject.

Squabbling over slavery began in earnest the next day, May 30. James Madison moved to delete the term "free inhabitants" from the Virginia Plan because he felt the phrase "might occasion debates which would divert" attention "from the general question whether the principle of representation should be changed" from states to population. Madison understood that an early debate on the role of slavery in the Union might destroy the Convention before it got started. But his proposal would have left representation based solely on "quotas of contribution," and this was also unacceptable to most of the northern delegates. Madison himself agreed "that some better rule ought to be found." Alexander Hamilton then proposed that representation be based solely on the number of "free inhabitants" in each state. This proposal was also too volatile and the delegates quickly tabled it. Other attempts at compromise failed. Finally, the Delaware delegates put a temporary end to this divisive discussion by telling the Convention that they "were restrained by their commission from assenting to any change on the rule of suffrage," and if the body endorsed any change in representation, they would be forced to leave the Convention. The Convention, having successfully postponed this acrimonious debate, adjourned for the day.

The Convention intermittently debated representation for the next two weeks, but on June 11 slavery reemerged to complicate the debate, when the Convention considered for the first time, and also approved provisionally, the three-fifths clause. Over the next three months the Convention would, on a number of occasions, redebate and reconsider the three-fifths clause before finally adopting it.

The evolution of the three-fifths clause during the Convention shows that the clause was not essentially a compromise over taxation and representation, as historians have traditionally claimed and as the structure of Article I, Section 2, Paragraph 3 implies. Rather, it began as a compromise between those who wanted to count slaves at all. On this crucial question, the slave states won a critical victory without making any important concessions.

On June 11, Roger Sherman of Connecticut proposed that representation be based on the "numbers of free inhabitants" in each state. John Rutledge and Pierce Butler of South Carolina objected, arguing for representation according to "quotas of contribution," which had become a euphemism for counting slaves for representation. James Wilson and Charles Pinckney, the younger cousin of General Charles Cotesworth Pinckney, skillfully headed off the Rutledge-Butler proposal.

Wilson proposed and Pinckney seconded a motion that ultimately became the three-fifths clause. Here for the first time was an example of cooperation between the North and the South over slavery. Significantly, Wilson was known to oppose slavery and came from a state, Pennsylvania, which had already adopted a gradual emancipation scheme. Nevertheless, harmony at the Convention was more important to Wilson than the place of slavery in the new nation. By teaming up, the nominally antislavery Pennsylvanian and the rabidly proslavery Carolinian may have hoped to undercut the anti-slavery sentiments of other northern delegates while also satisfying the demands of the proslavery delegates like Butler and Rutledge.

Most delegates seemed to accept this proposal. However, Elbridge Gerry of Massachusetts was unwilling to compromise. With some irony he protested, "Blacks are property, and are used to the southward as horses and cattle to the northward; and why should their representation be increased to the southward on account of the number of slaves, than horses or oxen to the north?" Gerry believed this would be an appropriate rule for taxation, but not for representation, because under it four southern voters would have more political power than ten northern voters. He also argued that this clause would degrade freemen in the North by equating them with slaves. He wondered "Are we to enter into a Compact with Slaves?" No other northerner opposed counting slaves for representation at this time.

Thus, with little debate, the Convention initially accepted the three-fifths clause as a basis for representation. The clause, giving the South enormous political leverage in the nation, was accepted without any quid pro quo from the North. Application of the clause to taxation would not come until later in the Convention. Indeed, there was no reason in mid-June to believe it would ever be applied to taxation. A brief history of the three-fifths ratio, prior to 1787, bears this out.

The ratio of three slaves to five free persons was first proposed in the Congress in 1783 as part of an overall program for the national government to raise revenue from the states. The ratio was controversial. Southerners thought it overvalued slaves, and northerners thought it undervalued them. Delegates from Virginia and South Carolina, the states with the most slaves, wanted taxation based on land values. Congress initially rejected and then later resurrected the entire package, which called for taxation based on population. Congress then sent the package to the states as an amendment to the Articles of Confederation. However, this amendment failed to achieve the necessary unanimous support of all the states and so was not added to the Articles of Confederation. . . .

The meaning of the three-fifths clause to the delegates in Philadelphia was clear in the report of the Committee of the Whole on June 13, which stated that representation would be "in proportion to the whole number of white and other free citizens and inhabitants, of every age, sex and condition, including those bound to servitude for a term of years and three fifths of all other persons not comprehended in the foregoing description, except Indians, not paying taxes in each State." The phrasing of the term "white and other free citizens and inhabitants" clearly implied that the "other persons" were neither white nor free. By mid-June a majority in the Convention had accepted the principle that representation in the national Congress would be based on population and that three-fifths of the slave population would be added to the free population in determining representation. However, a minority of the delegates, led by those from New Jersey, were still unhappy with this plan.

On June 15 William Paterson introduced what is commonly known as the New Jersey Plan. The plan rejected congressional representation based on population and, instead, retained the system of representation then in force under the Articles of Confederation: that the states would have an equal number of delegates in the Congress. . . .

By June 30 the Convention was at a standstill. The states in favor of population-based representation had enough votes to adopt their scheme. But if they were unable to persuade the delegates from the smaller states to acquiesce on this point, the Convention itself would fail. In the middle of this debate, Madison offered a new mode of analysis for the delegates. He argued

> that the States were divided into different interests not by their difference of size, but by other circumstances; the most material of which resulted partly from climate, but principally from their having or not having slaves. These two causes concurred in forming the great division of interests in the U. States. It did not lie between the large and small States: it lay between the Northern and Southern, and if any defensive power were necessary, it ought to be mutually given to these two interests.

So Madison proposed two branches of Congress, one in which slaves would be counted equally with free people to determine how many representatives each state would have, and one in which slaves would not be counted at all. Under this arrangement, "the Southern Scale would have the advantage in one House, and the Northern in the other." Madison made this proposal despite his reluctance to "urge any diversity of interests" among the delegates.

The Convention ignored Madison's proposal. He may have offered it simply to divert attention from the heated debate between the large and small states. If this was indeed his goal, he was not immediately successful. The small states, led by Delaware, continued to express fear that they would be swallowed up by larger states if representation in the Congress were based solely on population.

Subsequent debates, however, reveal the validity of Madison's analysis that sectionalism—caused by slavery—created a major division within the Convention and the nation. Indeed, slavery continued to complicate the Convention debates long after the conflict between large and small states had evaporated. On July 2, Charles Pinckney argued that there was "a solid distinction as to interest between the southern and northern states." He noted that the Carolinas and Georgia "in their Rice and Indigo had a peculiar interest which might be sacrificed" if they did not have sufficient power in any new Congress. Immediately after this speech the Convention accepted a proposal by General Charles Cotesworth Pinckney to send the entire question of representation to a committee of one delegate from each state. The Convention then adjourned until July 5.

On July 5 the committee proposed what historians have since called the Great Compromise. Under this plan, representation in the lower house of the legislature would be based on population, and in the upper house the states would have an equal vote. The three-fifths clause was a part of this proposal.

On July 6 the Convention once again approved the concept of representation based on population for the lower house of the Congress. The Convention then chose a five-man committee to redraft the clause. In the absence of a census, this committee would also have to recommend to the Convention the number of representatives that each state would get in the first congress. Before the Convention adjourned for the day, Charles Pinckney again raised sectional issues connected to slavery, arguing that "blacks ought to stand on an equality with whites," but he "w[oul]d.... agree to the ratio settled by Congs."

Pinckney's argument here was doubly significant. First, in a debate that had nothing to do with slavery per se, Pinckney raised the issue, as if to warn the Convention not to forget the special needs of the South. Second, Pinckney made it clear that he (and presumably other southerners) thought that the three-fifths rule for counting slaves was a great concession. . . .

After various unsuccessful attempts to reduce representation for some northern states or increase representation for some southern states, the Convention adopted an apportionment scheme for representation in the first congress by a vote of nine to two. The negative votes did not come from the smallest states, but from the most southern. The delegates from South Carolina and Georgia made their point: they must have protection for slavery or they would oppose the Constitution.

The next day, July 11, the Convention debated the provision for a census to determine future representation in Congress. Hugh Williamson of North Carolina amended the provision under consideration to explicitly include the three-fifths clause for counting slaves. Still dissatisfied with the three-fifths clause, Butler and Charles Cotesworth Pinckney of South Carolina "insisted that blacks be included in the rule of Representation, equally with the Whites," and moved to delete the three-fifths clause. Butler argued that "the labour of a slave in South Carolina was as productive and valuable as that of a freeman in Massachusetts," and since the national government "was instituted principally for the protection of property," slaves should be counted fully for representation. The Convention quickly rejected the Butler-Pinckney proposal.

The defeat of the Butler-Pinckney resolution did not end the debate over slavery and representation. A motion to require Congress to take a census of all "free inhabitants" passed on a slim six-to-four vote, with four slave states voting no. The Convention then began debating the motion to count three-fifths of all slaves. King and Gorham of Massachusetts expressed reservations, and Sherman of Connecticut urged conciliation.

James Wilson of Pennsylvania, who had initially proposed the three-fifths clause, supported it on pragmatic grounds. Admitting he "did not well see on what principle the admission of blacks in the proportion of three fifths could be explained," he asked, if slaves were citizens, "why are they not admitted on an equality with White Citizens?" But, if slaves were "admitted as property," it was reasonable to ask, "Then why is not other property admitted into the computation?" Wilson argued, however, that these logical inconsistencies "must be overruled by the necessity of compromise." Gouverneur Morris, also representing Pennsylvania, was not so willing to sacrifice principle. Having been "reduced to the dilemma of doing injustice to the Southern States or to human nature," Morris chose the former, asserting that he "could never agree to give such encouragement to the slave trade" by allowing the slave states "a representation for their negroes." The three-fifths clause then failed, by a vote of four to six. However, this defeat was not solely the result of Morris's arguments in favor of principle: two slave states that were still holding out for fully counting slaves for representation opposed the measure, while three northern states hoped not to count slaves at all.

The next day, July 12, the three-fifths clause was back on the floor, directly tied to taxation for the first time. The debate on slavery was the most divisive yet. Six southerners, representing Virginia, North Carolina, and South Carolina, addressed the issue. Their collective demand was clear: either give the South substantial representation for its slave population or the South would oppose the Constitution. Randolph, who had so far avoided the debates over slavery, "lamented that such a species of property existed," but nevertheless "urged strenuously that express security ought to be provided for including slaves in the ratio of Representation." Meanwhile, the South Carolinians, as might be expected, demanded full representation for slaves, declaring themselves willing, even eager, to be taxed fully for their slaves in return for full representation for their slaves. William R. Davie of North Carolina, who had been virtually silent throughout the Convention, declared "it was high time now to speak out." Davie warned that North Carolina would "never confederate" unless slaves were counted, at the very least, under a three-fifths ratio. Davie threatened that if some representation for slaves was not adopted, "the business [of the convention] was at an end."

Only Gouverneur Morris was prepared to call Davie's bluff, warning that Pennsylvania would "never agree to a representation of Negroes." But he also agreed that it was "vain for the Eastern states to insist on what the Southern States will never agree to." As much as Morris wished "to form a compact for the good of America," he seemed ready to risk failure on the issue of slave representation. No other northerner joined Morris on this issue. However, Oliver Ellsworth and William Samuel Johnson of Connecticut strongly supported southern interests, foreshadowing an emerging compromise between New England and the South over slavery and commerce. After a heated debate, the Convention finally adopted the three-fifths clause by a vote of six to two, with two states divided.

After more than a month and a half of anguished argument, the Convention had finally resolved the issue of representation for what would become the House of Representatives. Throughout, slavery had constantly confused the issue and thwarted compromise. Sectional interests caused by slavery had emerged as a major threat to the Union. At this juncture in the Convention, the smaller states still feared the larger ones; however, the northern and southern states had also come to openly distrust each other. ...

The Power of Ideas in the Convention

FORREST MCDONALD

Almost all the delegates who attended the Constitutional Convention were nationalists in the narrow sense that they believed it necessary to reorganize and strengthen the central authority. A vote on that question was taken at the outset of the deliberations, and only three individuals are known to have voted in the negative. Few delegates, however, thought of themselves as representing America or the American people. The others thought of themselves as representing the people of the several states severally—or to put it differently, they were there as representatives of separate political societies—and the rules of the debates, including the rule that each state's delegation had but one vote, no matter what the number of its delegates, reflected that distinction.

Most of the delegates also attached reservations or conditions to their willingness to strengthen the central authority. Some of the reservations were ideological, though doctrinaire ideologues by no means constituted a majority of those in attendance. (Fortunately for the nation, John Adams was in London and Jefferson was in Paris, and Sam Adams, Richard Henry Lee, Patrick Henry, and most of the other archrepublican Patriot leaders of Seventy-six were either not chosen as delegates by their legislatures or declined to attend.) Other reservations arose from personal or group prejudices or interests, such as those of public-security holders, land speculators, merchants, and slave owners. The strongest reservations arose from the perceived interests, political or economic, of the individual political societies that the delegates represented. Thus, one absolutely central issue—perhaps the absolutely central issue—before the convention was the role, if any, that the states would play in the reorganized and strengthened common authority.

To understand the motives and the actions of the Framers, it is necessary to ascertain, in regard to as many of them as possible, where they stood on this issue and also where they stood in respect to the various and conflicting interests and ideological and philosophical positions that we have been considering.

Possibly the most important group of delegates consisted of those whose nationalism was undiluted or nearly so. Heading the list was Washington, who was crucial to the successful outcome of the convention even though he contributed little to the debates. Two in this group were from Massachusetts, Nathaniel Gorham and Rufus King; King had overcome the fear of an "aristocratical conspiracy" that he had so shrilly expressed in 1785, his perspective having been shifted by Shays's Rebellion, by his marriage to the daughter of a wealthy New York merchant, and by more than a year of intimate association with Alexander Hamilton. Seven were from the Middle States: Hamilton, Gouverneur Morris, Robert Morris, James Wilson, George Clymer, Thomas Fitzsimons, and George Read. Franklin should probably be added to the list, along with William R. Davie of North Carolina and perhaps William Pierce of Georgia. In several respects, Madison and Charles Pinckney can also be counted as being in this group, for they were in agreement with the nationalists on many points;

From *Novus Ordo Seclorum: The Intellectual Origins of the Constitution*, by Forrest McDonald, pp. 185–191, 199–209, University of Kansas Press, 1985. Reprinted with permission of the publisher.

but the two differed from them in certain fundamental ways, and therefore must properly be considered as being in categories by themselves.

All of these men, who might loosely be described as "court-party" national-ists, shared a complex of experiences and attitudes. In the backgrounds of all except the convert King were one or more of the following elements: they had been born or educated abroad or had traveled extensively abroad; they had served for a considerable time as officers in the Continental Line; or they had held important civilian positions in the Confederation during the climactic years 1781 to 1783. All or nearly all of them admired the British system, were somewhat elitist in their lean-ings (or at least wanted to create a national government that would be high-toned as well as powerful), and were concerned with national honor and glory in addition to the protection of liberty and property. They were hard-nosed and tough-minded, but they were also idealistic, some to the point of romanticism. They were practical men of experience and talent who were scornful of ideology and abstract speculation, but some of them were extremely learned in history and political thought. The intel-lectual influences upon them were varied. For example, Gouverneur Morris, Wilson, and Hamilton were thoroughly versed in ancient history and in English legal and constitutional history, and all three expressed ideas derived from Hume and Smith; but in other respects, Morris seems to have been most influenced by Blackstone, Wilson by Burlamaqui and Francis Hutcheson, and Hamilton by Steuart, Vattel, and Necker.

The court-party nationalists were in agreement that in framing a constitution, it was prudent to act on the assumption that most men in government would put their own interests ahead of the public interest much of the time. This way of thinking, together with the key to the problem that it posed to republican constitution makers, was familiar to them from, among other sources, Hume's essay "On the Independency of Parliament." It was a maxim, Hume wrote, "that, in contriving any system of government, and fixing the several checks and controuls of the constitution, every man ought to be supposed a *knave*, and to have no other end, in all his actions, than private interest. By this interest we must govern him, and, by means of it, make him, notwithstanding his insatiable avarice and ambition, co-operate to public good." Hume was proposing a modified Mandevillean scheme: modified in the sense that the "vice-ridden" hive was to be deliberately constructed by men who were themselves dedicated to the public good.

Several of the court-party men spoke in the convention as if they had committed Hume's essay to memory. Franklin declared that men were governed by ambition and avarice, as if he had coined the thought. Hamilton paraphrased Hume at length: "Take mankind as they are, and what are they governed by? Their passions. There may be in every government a few choice spirits, who may act from more worthy motives. One great error [however] is that we suppose mankind more honest than they are. Our prevailing passions are ambition and interest; and it will ever be the duty of a wise government to avail itself of those passions, in order to make them subservient to the public good."

It is a grave mistake, however, to assume from this that the Framers (or even the court-party nationalists or even Hamilton) cynically abandoned the whole notion of virtue in the republic and opted to substitute crass self-interest in its stead. Several historians have made that assumption, and at least one has gone so far as to pronounce the judgement that the very tradition of civic humanism, of men finding their highest fulfillment in service to the public, thereby was brought to an end. To commit that mistake is to fail to understand two subtle but crucial aspects of the concept that men are driven by their passions.

The first is the simpler of the two. Men are driven by their passions, and in devising governments, it is wise to assume that ambition and avarice are the ruling passions of all. Hume himself, however, in the very passage just cited, indicated that the assumption was "false in *fact*." To prepare for the worst was to err on the side of prudence, but the court-party nationalists actually expected something better, for men are driven by a variety of passions, and many of these—love of fame, of glory, of country, for example—are noble. When any such passion becomes a man's ruling passion, he must necessarily live his life in virtuous service to the public; and it was such men whom the nationalists counted on to govern others through their baser passions. Sir James Steuart put the matter succinctly. Self-interest, he wrote, is the "only motive which a statesman should make use of, to engage a free people to concur in the plans which he lays down for their government." But he adds, immediately: "I beg I may not here be understood to mean, that self-interest should conduct the statesman: by no means. Self-interest, when considered with regard to him, is public spirit."

It was generally agreed that the love of fame—the desire for secular immortality in the grateful remembrance of posterity—is the noblest of the passions. Fame is bestowed upon men for a variety of achievements which writers from Plutarch to Machiavelli to Sir Francis Bacon to Hume had ranked on hierarchical scales. On Bacon's scale (from the bottom upwards), those who won fame were fathers of their country, who "reign justly, and make the times good wherein they live"; champions of empire, who in honorable wars "enlarge their territories or make noble defence against invaders"; saviors of empire, who deliver their country from civil war or from tyrants; lawgivers, who provide constitutions by which they govern wisely and well after they are gone; and at the pinnacle, "FOUNDERS OF STATES AND COMMONWEALTHS." Clearly, quite a number of delegates to the convention were driven, to lesser and greater degrees, by a passion for fame, and so were many others of the founding generation. Moreover, they were convinced that—during their generation, at least—enough men were driven by the love of fame and other noble passions to permit the establishment of government on solid foundations. . . .

Court-party nationalists in the convention were considerably more influential, but only slightly more numerous, than republican ideologues. In attempting to determine which delegates were of the latter description, one key issue is especially useful. Whereas the first group sought to establish a government on Humean-Mandevillean lines, moderated by Addisonian-Smithian "honor," the ideologues, taught by Bolingbroke, Montesquieu, or classical republicanism, shrank with horror at the prospect of admitting the baser passions as operating principles of government. On four occasions during the convention the delegates confronted a question that turned upon beliefs as to whether virtue or the baser passions should be depended upon as the operating principle of government. The issue was the extent to which congressmen should be excluded from holding other offices. Permeating the debates was the question of "corruption," in the British sense of the term. Bolingbroke had raged repeatedly in denunciation of "placemen," and Montesquieu had more moderately warned against entrusting people with power if it was to their personal advantage to abuse it. Both views had been accepted by the Patriots of 1776. Hume, by contrast, had contended that corruption in the form of the power to manage Parliament by passing out lucrative offices was necessary to the balance of the British constitution. Those delegates to the convention who insisted upon the absolute exclusion of congressmen from other offices during and for a time after their service in Congress can be regarded as being in the Bolingbroke-Montesquieu camp; they still hoped to found the republic upon classical principles, which is to say upon public virtue. Those who were willing to forbid dual officeholding, but who would allow congressmen to resign their seats to accept appointive offices, can be regarded as being in the Hume-Mandeville camp; they rejected as chimerical the idea that virtue alone could activate the republic, choosing instead to erect it on new principles, which is to say upon the channeling of self-interested motives. The first group might be roughly described as corresponding to the country party in England. Judging by their positions on the issue of congressional exclusion, the "country party" in the convention included Abraham Baldwin of Georgia; Pierce Butler, John Rutledge, and Charles Cotesworth Pinckney of South Carolina; Hugh Williamson of North Carolina; George Mason and Edmund Randolph of Virginia; Luther Martin and Daniel Jenifer of Maryland; John Lansing and Robert Yates of New York; Roger Sherman of Connecticut; and Elbridge Gerry of Massachusetts. The court party, by that criterion, included John Langdon and Nicholas Gilman of New Hampshire; Nathaniel Gorham, Rufus King, and Caleb Strong of Massachusetts; Oliver Ellsworth of Connecticut; Hamilton of New York; Wilson, Thomas Mifflin, and Gouverneur Morris of Pennsylvania; John Francis Mercer of Maryland; Charles Pinckney of South Carolina; and William Few, William Pierce, and William Houstoun of Georgia. Madison, along with Alexander Martin of North Carolina, favored a modified Humean position which turned out to be close to what was finally adopted. It is to be observed that the personnel of the court party on this issue is similar to but not identical with the group described earlier as court-party nationalists. Moreover, as will be seen, Sherman and the South Carolinians, identified on this issue as being country party, can more properly be described as advocates of a "foederal," as opposed to a national, system.

The court-party nationalists had a number of advantages. They were, for the most part, young, energetic, bold, articulate, and extremely gifted. They knew one another, knew what they wanted to accomplish, had taken the initiative in bringing the convention about, and were able to seize the initiative once the convention had begun. The republican ideologues, or country party, by contrast, were generally older, less imaginative, and on the defensive. They recognized that something must be done to establish order and to strengthen the Union, and they were willing to make a number of concessions toward that end. Only gradually would they become aware of the nature and extent of the designs to create a national government far more high-toned, far more powerful, and far less compatible with traditional dogmas than anything that a Bolingbrokean or Montesquieuan republican could stomach.

The ablest of the ideologues were Gerry, Mason, Luther Martin, and Randolph. Gerry was a disciple of Sam Adams and may almost be considered to have been Adams's surrogate at the convention. Mason, the author of Virginia's bill of rights, was ideologically and politically pretty much at one with Richard Henry Lee, though he was both more principled and more intelligent than Lee. Luther Martin, the attorney general of Maryland, was a tiresome dipsomaniac, but he was also a man of learning and had great skills as a lawyer. In actuality, he was in the camp of the ideologues more as a matter of opportunism than of temperament or conviction. The same is at least partly true of Randolph, the governor of Virginia, who was the kind of politician known in the eighteenth century as a trimmer.

Though these men were archrepublicans, they were among the most outspoken enemies of democracy in the convention. Randolph declared: "Our chief danger arises from the democratic parts of our constitutions. It is a maxim which I hold incontrovertible, that the powers of government exercised by the people swallows up the other branches. None of the constitutions have provided sufficient checks against the democracy." Gerry echoed, "The evils we experience flow from the excess of democracy." Curiously, he added that the people were not lacking in virtue, but were "the dupes of pretended patriots." Mason agreed "that we had been too democratic," though he was afraid that the convention might "incautiously run into the opposite extreme."

The republican ideologues (except for Martin) were anxious to check the excess of democracy in the state governments by strengthening the central authority, but only on condition that the strengthening be accompanied by attention to several basic principles. Among these were the complete separation of the three departments of government, both in function and in personnel; either a plural executive or a single executive whose power was shared and checked by an executive council; a bicameral legislature, the two houses being chosen by some means that would ensure that they checked one another; explicit enumeration of the powers of each branch of government and a declaration that all other powers were reserved to the states; explicit separation of the "power of the purse" from the "power of the sword," an explicit repudiation of standing armies, and an explicit denial of the power of the national government to charter corporations or to create monopolies; and a bill of rights. They were ill disposed to compromise on these points.

Occupying positions somewhere between those of the court-party nationalists and the republican ideologues were James Madison and Charles Pinckney. Madison was an ideologue in search of an ideology: he was a man of doctrinaire temperament, marked by what Jean-Paul Sartre called "a nostalgia for the absolute"; but he had not yet found or formulated a body of doctrine that he could reconcile with his immense range of reading and his ongoing public experience. It is true that in 1787 and 1788 he pronounced with great certainty his theory of refining public servants by means of complex electoral processes and his theory of checking factions by "extending the sphere." But his certainty was predicated partly on temperament—a preference for the untried but theoretically appealing, as opposed to the imperfections of reality—and partly on the reality that the unchecked legislature of his beloved Virginia (in whose virtue he had once believed with equal confidence) was currently under the sway of his hated political rival Patrick Henry. In a short time the inefficaciousness of his theories would, in his own eyes, be abundantly demonstrated by the triumph of Hamiltonianism, and Henry would lose his power; and then Madison would find it necessary to begin theorizing anew.

The Madison of the 1780s, however, is generally regarded as having been as solidly entrenched in the nationalist camp as Hamilton was. This view of Madison as ardent nationalist must be tempered by at least two major sets of qualifications. One was that throughout his career on the national stage, at least until Jefferson became president, Madison was always mindful of the interests of his state and was rarely if ever willing to do anything in the national interest which he believed to be inconsonant with the interests of Virginia. That alone repeatedly set him apart from such nationalists as Gouverneur Morris, Hamilton, and Washington.

The other qualification to Madison's nationalism was that it was a matter of vital concern with him that the national government be appropriately balanced and checked and refined, lest it become an engine of tyranny. The difference between him and Hamilton in this respect was evident even during the convention and even as they were cooperating in the writing of *The Federalist*. Hamilton was concerned that the national government be given stability, strength, and energy; and though he had ideas about how this might best be done, it was almost a matter of indifference to him as to how the government's powers should be organized or what forms they should take. Madison's attitude is clear from an often-quoted passage: "If men were angels, no government would be necessary. If angels were to govern men, neither external nor internal controls on government would be necessary. In framing a government which is to be administered by men over men, the great difficulty lies in this: you must first enable the government to control the governed; and in the next place oblige it to control itself." Hamilton thought that such precautions were unnecessary: he believed that the states were and ever would be an adequate, and probably an excessive, restraint upon the national authority. At bottom, Hamilton and other court-party nationalists trusted themselves and therefore trusted power if it was in their own hands. Madison and other men of his temperament did not trust themselves and therefore did not trust power in anyone's hands. ...

Representation of Women in the Constitution

JAN LEWIS

It is axiomatic among scholars of the Constitution that women are nowhere mentioned in that document. What to make of that omission, however, has been a matter of debate. Some have read the Constitution's silence as implied inclusiveness. Just think of the contortions through which we put ourselves when we try to write in gender-neutral language. Surely, the Constitution's avoidance of "he" and "him," "male" and "man" must have been intentional. Just look at the Fourteenth Amendment, which for the first time introduced the word "male" into the Constitution: It was easy enough to make the Constitution an explicitly gendered document when that was the intention.

At the same time, others have argued that the Constitution's failure to mention women was no mistake. At best, the framers of the Constitution were not thinking of women. At worst, they intended to exclude them. After all, republican political thought was misogynist, and the compact theory of government imagined that compact as a deal cut among men. If the political theories upon which the Constitution was based did not designate a role for women in the state, then neither could the Constitution.

Some years ago, the historian Richard Morris bemoaned the Constitution's ambiguous silence on gender, saying "it would have been very helpful" if that document's authors "had given us a hint." In fact, the framers of the Constitution did leave us a hint, and a very helpful one at that. It is to be found in James Madison's notes on the Federal Convention, which, although they were not published until 1840, have been available to students of the Constitution ever since. I do not believe, however, that this passage has until now attracted the attention of scholars.

The place: Philadelphia. The date: Monday, June 11, 1787. The delegates are discussing the thorny topic of representation in the new national legislature that the delegates are proposing. James Wilson, delegate from Pennsylvania, suggests that representation in the lower house should be "in proportion to the whole number of white & other free Citizens & inhabitants of every age sex & condition including those bound to servitude for a term of years and three fifths of all other persons not comprehended in the foregoing description, except Indians not paying taxes, in each state." Edited down into a more concise form, this formulation became the infamous Three Fifths Clause.

Significantly, the words that are of interest to us here—"of every age sex & condition"—attracted no attention whatsoever. It's not that the general issue, representation, was uncontroversial. After all, it was this very issue that would hold the delegates up most of that long summer. Nor was it that the states explicitly included women when they were apportioning representatives. In fact, none of the state constitutions then in effect explicitly included women (or children), and two states that wrote their constitutions in the 1790s allocated representatives on the basis of the number of free adult white males (Kentucky) and taxpayers (Tennessee). Including women, then, was an innovation and, in terms of the state constitutions, not to mention the Northwest Ordinance, an anomaly as well. Yet in the four volumes of the Records of the Federal Convention there is not a single comment upon the inclusion of women.

The delegates accepted Wilson's language and sent it off for editing to the Committee of Style (the Convention's copy editors, who were charged with improving the document's rhetoric without changing its substance). What came back became, after one subsequent minor amendment, the language that we recognize from Article I, Section 2 of the Constitution: "whole number of free persons, including those bound to service for a terms of years and excluding Indians not taxed, three fifths of all other persons." All free men, women, and children were now comprised in the more succinct term free "persons." The term "women" ended up on the cutting room floor, but we can, and should, understand that women were indeed included in the term "free persons," and, hence, that every place that the Constitution uses the term "person" or "persons" and probably every other place that it uses gender-neutral language as well, women were implicitly included....

[T]he canonical texts of American politics and political thought are not, as is sometimes thought, irrelevant to women and their history. Instead, they are deeply relevant, not only because, as we historians of gender are always insisting, gender is every-where but because those texts did, in fact, concern themselves with women. My larger project is to ask where women fit into the doctrines of American liberalism. Was the American republic constructed, as Joan Landes has argued for the French one, "against women, not just without them"? Are women permanently and necessarily outside the state? Or are women inside it, and if they are, on what terms? ...

We might begin by examining the context in which Wilson offered his language about "every age sex & condition." The practical issue was apportionment of representatives in Congress. Should representation be based upon some measure of population? Some states gave representatives, after all, to counties or districts of unequal sizes. And if representation were to be based upon population, what about the slaves? Counting them obviously enhanced the power of the slave states. Counting women and children, on the other hand, had virtually no practical effect. With sex and age ratios almost the same, including women in the basis for apportionment neither gave some states more representation nor others less.

The theoretical issue, particularly as it applied to women, was more complex. The critical issue here, and it is one that the delegates discussed at some length, albeit without mentioning women, was who was to be represented in the new nation. The preamble to the Constitution, of course, begins "We the People," yet, as Edmund S. Morgan has noted, "the people" was a fiction. The compact theory of government held that, as Massachusetts's James Sullivan put it in the spring of 1776, when Massachusetts was writing its first state constitution, "Laws and Government are founded on the Consent of the people, and that consent should by each member of Society be given in proportion to his Right. Every member of Society has a Right to give his Consent to the Laws of the Community or he owes no Obedience to them." But who were the people? As Sullivan acknowledged—indeed, this was his point— "a very great number of the people of this Colony have at all times been bound by Laws to which" they had never consented, not meeting the property requirement for voting. "[Y]et by Fiction of Law"—sometimes the documents that we historians work with are so good that it almost seems as if we made them up—"every Man is supposed to consent."

Sullivan did not mention women, but it seems pretty clear that he had women in mind and wondered by what logic—or illogic—they were excluded from the imaginary social compact that created the state. Several years later, while serving as Massachusetts attorney general, he defended the state from James Martin's suit to reclaim the property that the state had seized from his Loyalist mother, who had fled the state with her Loyalist husband. Part of the case turned on whether women were among the "every *inhabitant* and *member*" covered by the Massachusetts confiscation statute. Martin's attorney asserted that as a *feme covert*, a married woman whose legal capacity was absorbed by her husband, Anna Martin was "not a member" and had "no *political relation* to the *state* any more than an alien." She had no choice but to abandon her property and to follow her Loyalist husband when he left the country. In response, Sullivan insisted that "surely a *feme covert* can be an inhabitant in every sense of the word. Who are the members of the body-politic? are not all the *citizens*, members: infants, idiots, insane, or whatever may be their *relative* situations in society?" Women, then, were inhabitants, members, and citizens; the state constitution secured them their rights and privileges, and entailed upon them responsibilities. They were part of the social compact.

Martin won his case, and Sullivan lost his argument. The justices adhered to an older, more patriarchal notion of the family and the state both: A woman's first obligation was to her husband; she related to the state only through him, and consequently, as far as the state was concerned, she was not a member of it.

It is in the context of this case, and the majority opinion upholding coverture as a political principle, that the Constitution's doctrine of representation appears so radical. With nothing practical to be gained by it, James Wilson proposed and his fellow delegates accepted the principle that women—and children, and every inhabitant of the nation except for 2/5 of the slaves and all the untaxed Indians—were part of the body politic, to be represented by the elected officials of the new nation.

From our perspective, two centuries later, knowing how arduous the struggle for women's rights has been and still is, it is easy for us to overlook the radicalism of this doctrine of representation. Yet it is only by recovering this moment that we can understand the subsequent history of the women's rights struggle. James Wilson, James Sullivan, and other liberals developed a radical doctrine of representation, one that said that women were part of the body politic, among those whom the new nation was supposed to serve, but its promise—of inclusion and protection for women—has still not yet been realized. Why not?

If we want to discover what became of the liberal doctrine of representation, we might begin by considering—and acknowledging—what it was able to accomplish. When men such as Wilson and Sullivan asserted that women were members of the body politic and entitled to representation, they thought of women as rights-bearing individuals. In their simplest terms, the rights guaranteed by the Bill of Rights were guaranteed to women, as well as to men, whether they were married or single, propertied or not. Moreover, these rights—of speech, of religion, of assembly, of trial by jury—are by no means trivial. Coverture—and republican theories of dependency—have had their limits.

To say that women did not, at the time of the writing and ratification of the Constitution, enjoy all the rights, let alone exercise all the obligations, of citizenship is to state the obvious. But the compact theory of government, which made women rights-bearing members of the body politic, necessarily presented a challenge to those exclusions and denials. It meant, at the very least, that the bases for exclusion and the denial of rights would have to be crafted anew, in a new language compatible with the compact theory. That is what John Adams realized when he and James Sullivan discussed the state constitution that Massachusetts was writing in 1776. Sullivan's letter to Adams has been lost, but a letter he wrote Elbridge Gerry that Gerry forwarded to Adams makes it clear that Sullivan accepted the Lockean premises of the compact theory. Adams accepted them too. "It is certain in Theory, that the only moral Foundation of Government is the Consent of the People." What Adams gave with one hand, however, he took away with the other: "But to what an Extent Shall We carry this Principle?" This was the problem that compact theory—that is, liberalism—presented: Accept its premises, and where do you stop?

Adams saw the problem immediately. "Shall We Say, that every Individual of the Community, old and young, male and female, as well as rich and poor [and note that he's anticipating perfectly Wilson's formulation of age, sex, and condition], must consent, expressly to every Act of Legislation?" This horrible question was, for Adams, rhetorical. "This is impossible." But it was also a problem. "Whence arises the Right of the Men to govern the Women, without their Consent?" Adams's real fear was that men without property, who, according to republican theory were dependents, lacking in virtue, and too easily bent to the will of the powerful, would be allowed to vote. His big concern was the "condition" part of the phrase "age sex & condition." But he understood that to some extent, the elements were interchangeable: Recognize one group as citizens whose consent was required, and what was the logic of excluding others? As Adams asked rhetorically, "Why exclude women?" And he warned Sullivan: "Depend upon it, sir, it is dangerous to open So fruitfull a Source of Controversy and Altercation. ... There would be no End of it." Those like Adams who feared the destabilizing effects of making women full beneficiaries of democracy would have to craft new bases of exclusion, ones at least nominally consistent with liberal principles. In due course opponents of women's rights would come to assert that women were by nature different from men and hence disqualified for government by their very nature, but we should understand that this way of thinking was not intrinsic to liberalism; instead, it was an attempt to thwart its potential.

If the question of women's rights has remained controversial and called forth a powerful opposition, another facet of the representation of women has not. At its simplest, most literal level, the representation of women in the Constitution means that women are among those whom the new government—now an old government— was supposed to serve. Sometimes we lose sight of this aspect of political thought and structure. Most of our focus, as women's historians, has been on rights, and in particular, the right to vote. If we have not thought much about the meaning of representation, perhaps that is because American national government in the nine-teenth century, and especially before the Civil War, was so weak. What, substantively, would it mean to represent the interests of women in government?

And so we return, once again, to the compact theory of government. We begin with Locke, and his observation that the purpose of government was to protect "Life, Liberty, and Estate." Then we filter Locke through the philosophers of the Scottish Enlightenment, men such as Thomas Reid and Francis Hutcheson who developed the notion of *society*. Locke used the terms "community" and "government" almost inter-changeably. By the time that the Scots had elaborated the concept of society, Thomas Paine would be able to draw a sharp distinction between society and government. In the second paragraph of *Common Sense*, Paine proclaimed as if it were conventional wisdom that "society is in every state a blessing, but government even in its best state is but a necessary evil." It was this notion of society that James Wilson, himself a Scot by birth, had in mind when he said that women should be counted in apportion-ing representatives.

Lecturing on the law several years later to an audience of both men and women in Philadelphia, Wilson built upon Paine: "By some politicians, society has been considered as only the scaffolding of government; very improperly, in my judgment. In the just order of things, government is the scaffolding of society: and if society could be built and kept entire without government, the scaffolding might be thrown down." Or, to put it more succinctly, "Government was instituted for the happiness of society." And by society, he meant what Jürgen Habermas has called the "bourgeois public sphere"—all those places where men and women came together to create a public, for example, the hall at the University of Pennsylvania where Wilson was lecturing on the law.

Again borrowing from the Scots, Wilson explained that women made a particular contribution to society. Women trained men in the ways of affection, and affection was the glue that held society together. It was the basis for humanitarianism— "we feel delight in the agreeable conception of the improvement and happiness of mankind"—and patriotism—"we entertain for our country an animated and vigorous zeal"—both. This notion of affection made its way into the *Federalist Papers*, too. In No. 14, for example, in one of the most lyrical passages in the *Papers*, Madison urged ratification of the Constitution by telling the "people of America" that they were "knit together ... by so many chords of affection," living "together as members of the same family."

In liberal thought, the purpose of government was to protect society. It was to protect property as well, but liberals such as Madison, Sullivan, and Wilson did not see any conflict or contradiction here. For all of them, as for Paine, the family, society, and private enterprise were all on one—on the better—side of the sharp line that divided government from that which had to be protected from government. And if government was, almost by definition, suspect, then the family and private enterprise were imagined as unproblematic realms. The exclusion of women from government should be read in the context of early American liberals' profound suspiciousness of government—and their concomitant idealization of the private sphere.

Women were members of society, and government was supposed to protect society. The purpose of government, in Lockean terms, was to protect those who could not protect themselves. To some extent, the measure of any particular government was how well it protected those who could not protect themselves—the weak, the infirm, the aged, the young, the women. To make such a statement is not simply to make a logical inference from the liberalism of the Founding Fathers; it is to hit upon its bedrock.

But it is also to come up against its greatest obstacle, that is, the obstacle that is presented and continues to present to women—and to the weak, the poor, the infirm, the helpless. Yes, the Constitution included women. Yes, it represented them. Yes, it implicitly offered them protection. But it did not allow them to represent themselves. Instead, it entrusted their care to the men in their families, just as it entrusted the care of slaves to their owners. This comparison is not a mere figure of speech, an inflammatory analogy equating the position of women to the position of slaves. Rather, it is a precise description of the way in which women and slaves were represented in and by the Constitution. The Constitution made women rights-bearing citizens and represented them as members of the body politic, but it gave them no means of securing their rights. American feminists pointed out this discrepancy almost a century and a half ago, and like them, we are still working and waiting for the promise of liberalism to be fulfilled.

✣ F U R T H E R   R E A D I N G

Adams, Willi Paul. *The First American Constitutions: Republican Ideology and the Making of the State Constitutions in the Revolutionary Era* (1980).

Bailyn, Bernard. *The Ideological Origins of the American Revolution* (1967).

Beard, Charles A. *An Economic Interpretation of the Constitution of the United States* (1913).

acute during the late 1790s, as the new nation struggled to survive in a world beset by conflict between revolutionary France and Great Britain. The Federalist Party of President John Adams and former Treasury Secretary Alexander Hamilton wanted to cement America's trading relationship with the English and to keep the dangerous fires of social revolution from spreading to America. The Republican Party of Thomas Jefferson and James Madison, in contrast, saluted the ideas of liberty manifested in the French Revolution. When the Adams Administration embarked on a "quasi-war" with France, Federalists attempted to silence Republican critics by passing the Alien and Sedition Acts, which prohibited political criticism of the government. The Jeffersonians questioned the constitutionality of the acts, particularly in light of the First Amendment's wording that Congress could make no law "abridging the freedom of speech or of the press." The question of individual expression, moreover, was closely linked to the structure of the new government. The Anti-Federalists and then the Jeffersonian Republicans claimed that since the national government's powers were strictly limited, it could not enact laws like the Alien and Sedition Acts. They also asserted that the Sedition Act in particular provided evidence of the baneful centralizing tendencies of the national government.

Whom should we credit with advancing individual liberties in the new republic? Were the Anti-Federalists the first great American champions of liberty, particularly given their stubborn insistence on a bill of rights? Or should we credit the Jeffersonian Republicans of the 1790s, since they stood up to the Federalists in opposing the Alien and Sedition Acts? How significant were the debates over the structure of the new government in securing rights? Were the Anti-Federalists and the Jeffersonians defending individual rights, or did they really just want to preserve state sovereignty? How seriously should we take the rhetoric of rights during this time? Did the Jeffersonians conceive of the Bill of Rights as protecting the rights of unpopular minorities, or were they just as guilty as the Federalists in attempting to silence their political opponents?

✣ D O C U M E N T S

That liberty was a prime concern in the early republic is evident in the following selections. A few years before the Constitutional Convention, as a member of the Virginia legislature, James Madison wrote the *Memorial and Remonstrance Against Religious Assessments*, Document 1, in opposition to a proposed tax to aid Christian teachers. Madison's essay is a classic statement of religious freedom, one of the most significant liberties championed by the American founders.

Virginian George Mason, who had refused to sign the Constitution because he believed it posed a threat to liberty, composed a lengthy list of reasons for opposing ratification, published here as Document 2. The influence of Anti-Federalists such as Mason proved significant. Although Madison initially believed a bill of rights to be unnecessary, as a member of the House of Representatives in the first Congress he ended up leading the movement to amend the Constitution to protect rights. Madison's speech of June 8, 1789, Document 3, was the most important moment in the House debates over the amendments.

Documents 4–6 pertain to the crisis over rights that commenced with the passage of the Alien and Sedition Acts in 1798. Although the Federalist-dominated Congress actually passed four different repressive and restrictive measures aimed at Republican newspaper editors and pamphleteers, the Sedition Act posed the most problems from a constitutional standpoint. The Act (Document 4) seemed to violate the Constitution's First Amendment. In 1798, the Republican response to these measures came in the form of the Virginia and Kentucky Resolutions (Document 5), authored by Madison and Jefferson, respectively, and endorsed by the legislatures of those states. The refusal of most states to embrace the resolutions prompted a second and more strident round of resolutions in 1799, which supported the theory of nullification—the idea that a state could nullify acts of the federal government that it considered unconstitutional. Republicans took their protest to the state legislatures primarily because they viewed the states as the guarantors of individual rights. They also feared that the federal courts, staffed by Federalist judges, would prove unfriendly. *Lyon's Case* (Document 6), in which a Republican member of Congress was convicted of seditious libel in a federal circuit court, confirmed their fears. Eventually, 14 people were arrested under the Sedition Act, and 10 of them were convicted. The Sedition Act expired, by its own terms, on March 3, 1801, President Adams' last day in office.

✢ D O C U M E N T   1

Virginian James Madison Champions Religious Liberty, 1785

To the Honorable the General Assembly of the Commonwealth of Virginia

We, the subscribers, citizens of the said Commonwealth, having taken into serious tled "A Bill establishing a provision for Teachers of the Christian Religion," and conceiving that the same, if finally armed with the sanctions of a law, will be a dangerous abuse of power, are bound as faithful members of a free State, to remonstrate against it, and to declare the reasons by which we are determined. We remonstrate against the said Bill,

1. Because we hold it for a fundamental and undeniable truth, "that Religion or the duty which we owe to our Creator and the Manner of discharging it, can be directed only by reason and conviction, not by force or violence." The Religion then of every man must be left to the conviction and conscience of every man; and it is the right of every man to exercise it as these may dictate. This right is in its nature an unalienable right. It is unalienable; because the opinions of men, depending only on the evidence contemplated by their own minds, cannot follow the dictates of other men: It is unalienable also, because what is here a right towards men, is a duty towards the Creator. It is the duty of every man to render to the Creator such homage, and such only, as he believes to be acceptable to him. This duty is precedent both in order of time and degree of obligation, to the claims of Civil Society. Before any man can be considered as a member of Civil Society, he must be considered as a subject of the Governor of the Universe: And if a member of Civil Society, who enters into any subordinate Association, must always do it with a reservation of his duty to the general authority; much more must every man who becomes a member of any particular Civil Society, do it with a saving of his allegiance to the Universal Sovereign. We maintain therefore that in matters of Religion, no man's right is abridged by the institution of Civil Society, and that Religion is wholly exempt from

its cognizance. True it is, that no other rule exists, by which any question which may divide a Society, can be ultimately determined, but the will of the majority; but it is also true, that the majority may trespass on the rights of the minority.

2. Because if religion be exempt from the authority of the Society at large, still less can it be subject to that of the Legislative Body. The latter are but the creatures and vicegerents of the former. Their jurisdiction is both derivative and limited: it is limited with regard to the co-ordinate departments, more necessarily is it limited with regard to the constituents. The preservation of a free government requires not merely, that the metes and bounds which separate each department of power may be invariably maintained; but more especially, that neither of them be suffered to overleap the great Barrier which defends the rights of the people....

3. Because, it is proper to take alarm at the first experiment on our liberties. We hold this prudent jealousy to be the first duty of citizens, and one of [the] noblest characteristics of the late Revolution. The freemen of America did not wait till usurped power had strengthened itself by exercise, and entangled the question in precedents. They saw all the consequences in the principle, and they avoided the consequences by denying the principle. We revere this lesson too much, soon to forget it....

4. Because, the bill violates that equality which ought to be the basis of every law, and which is more indispensable, in proportion as the validity or expediency of any law is more liable to be impeached. If "all men are by nature equally free and independent," all men are to be considered as entering into Society on equal conditions; as relinquishing no more, and therefore retaining no less, one than another, of their natural rights. Above all are they to be considered as retaining an "*equal* title to the free exercise of Religion according to the dictates of conscience." ...

5. Because the bill implies either that the Civil Magistrate is a competent Judge of Religious truth; or that he may employ Religion as an engine of Civil policy. The first is an arrogant pretension falsified by the contradictory opinions of Rulers in all ages, and throughout the world: The second an unhallowed perversion of the means of salvation.

6. Because the establishment proposed by the Bill is not requisite for the support of the Christian Religion. To say that it is, is a contradiction to the Christian Religion itself; for every page of it disavows a dependence on the powers of this world: it is a contradiction to fact; for it is known that this Religion both existed and flourished, not only without the support of human laws, but in spite of every opposition from them; and not only during the period of miraculous aid, but long after it had been left to its own evidence, and the ordinary care of Providence ...

7. Because experience witnesseth that ecclesiastical establishments, instead of maintaining the purity and efficacy of Religion, have had a contrary operation....

8. Because the establishment in question is not necessary for the support of Civil Government. If it be urged as necessary for the support of Civil Government only as it is a means of supporting Religion, and it be not necessary for the latter purpose, it cannot be necessary for the former.... A just government, instituted to secure & perpetuate it, needs them not. Such a government will be best supported by protecting every citizen in the enjoyment of his Religion with the same equal hand which protects his person and his property; by neither invading the equal rights of any Sect, nor suffering any Sect to invade those of another.

9. Because the proposed establishment is a departure from that generous policy, which, offering an asylum to the persecuted and oppressed of every Nation and Religion, promised a lustre to our country, and an accession to the number of its citizens. What a melancholy mark is the Bill of sudden degeneracy? Instead of holding forth an asylum to the persecuted, it is itself a signal of persecution. It degrades from the equal rank of Citizens all those whose opinions in Religion do not bend to those of the Legislative authority. ...

10. Because, it will have a likely tendency to banish our Citizens. The allurements presented by other situations are every day thinning their number. To superadd a fresh motive to emigration, by revoking the liberty which they now enjoy, would be the same species of folly which has dishonoured and depopulated flourishing kingdoms.

11. Because, it will destroy that moderation and harmony which the forbearance of our laws to intermeddle with Religion, has produced amongst its several sects. Torrents of blood have been spilt in the old world, by vain attempts of the secular arm to extinguish Religious discord, by proscribing all difference in Religious opinions. Time has at length revealed the true remedy. Every relaxation of narrow and rigorous policy, wherever it has been tried, has been found to assuage the disease. ...

12. Because, the policy of the bill is adverse to the diffusion of the light of Christianity. The first wish of those who enjoy this precious gift, ought to be that it may be imparted to the whole race of mankind. Compare the number of those who have as yet received it with the number still remaining under the dominion of false Religions; and how small is the former! Does the policy of the Bill tend to lessen the disproportion? No; it at once discourages those who are strangers to the light of [revelation] from coming into the Region of it; and countenances, by example the nations who continue in darkness, in shutting out those who might convey it to them. Instead of levelling as far as possible, every obstacle to the victorious progress of truth, the Bill with an ignoble and unchristian timidity would circumscribe it, with a wall of defence, against the encroachments of error.

13. Because attempts to enforce by legal sanctions, acts obnoxious to so great a proportion of Citizens, tend to enervate the laws in general, and to slacken the bands of Society. ...

14. Because a measure of such singular magnitude and delicacy ought not to be imposed, without the clearest evidence that it is called for by a majority of citizens: and no satisfactory method is yet proposed by which the voice of the majority in this case may be determined, or its influence secured. ...

15. Because, finally, "the equal right of every citizen to the free exercise of his Religion according to the dictates of conscience" is held by the same tenure with all our other rights. If we recur to its origin, it is equally the gift of nature; if we weigh its importance, it cannot be less dear to us; if we consult the Declaration of those rights which pertain to the good people of Virginia, as the "basis and foundation of Government," it is enumerated with equal solemnity, or rather studied emphasis. ... We the subscribers say, that the General Assembly of this Commonwealth have no such authority: And that no effort may be omitted on our part against so dangerous an usurpation, we oppose to it, this remonstrance; earnestly praying, as we are in duty bound, that the Supreme Lawgiver of the Universe, by illuminating those to whom it

is addressed, may on the one hand, turn their councils from every act which would affront his holy prerogative, or violate the trust committed to them: and on the other, guide them into every measure which may be worthy of his [blessing, may re]dound to their own praise, and may establish more firmly the liberties, the prosperity, and the Happiness of the Commonwealth.

✠ D O C U M E N T   2

Anti-Federalist George Mason Outlines His Objections to the Proposed Constitution, 1787

There is no Declaration of Rights; and the Laws of the general Government being paramount to the Laws and Constitutions of the several States, the Declaration of Rights in the separate States are no Security. Nor are the people secured even in the Enjoyment of the Benefits of the common-Law: which stands here upon no other Foundation than its having been adopted by the respective Acts forming the Constitutions of the several States.

In the House of Representatives there is not the Substance, but the Shadow only of Representation; which can never produce proper Information in the Legislature, or inspire Confidence in the People: the Laws will therefore be generally made by Men little concern'd in, and unacquainted with their Effects and Consequences.

The Senate have the Power of altering all Money-Bills, and of originating Appropriations of Money and the Sallerys of the Officers of their own Appointment in Conjunction with the President of the United States; altho' they are not the Representatives of the People, or amenable to them.

These with their other great Powers (vizt. their Power in the Appointment of Ambassadors and all public Officers, in making Treaties, and in trying all Impeachments) their Influence upon and Connection with the supreme Executive from these Causes, their Duration of Office, and their being a constant existing Body almost continually sitting, joined with their being one compleat Branch of the Legislature, will destroy any Balance in the Government, and enable them to accomplish what Usurpations they please upon the Rights and Libertys of the People.

The Judiciary of the United States is so constructed and extended, as to absorb and destroy the Judiciarys of the several States; thereby rendering Law as tedious[,] intricate and expensive, and Justice as unattainable, by a great part of the Community, as in England, and enabling the Rich to oppress and ruin the Poor.

The President of the United States has no constitutional Council (a thing unknown in any safe and regular Government) he will therefore be unsupported by proper Information and Advice; and will generally be directed by Minions and Favourites—or He will become a Tool to the Senate—or a Council of State will grow out of the principal Officers of the great Departments; the worst and most dangerous of all Ingredients for such a Council, in a free Country; for they may be induced to join in any dangerous or oppressive Measures, to shelter themselves, and prevent an Inquiry into their own Misconduct in Office; whereas had a constitutional Council been formed (as was proposed) of six Members; vizt. two from the Eastern, two from the Middle, and two from the Southern States, to be appointed by Vote of the States in the House of Representatives, with the same Duration and Rotation of Office as the Senate, the Executive wou'd always have had safe and proper Information and Advice, the President of such a Council might have acted as Vice President of the United States, pro tempore, upon any Vacancy or Disability of the chief Magistrate; and long continued Sessions of the Senate wou'd in a great Measure have been prevented.

From this fatal Defect of a constitutional Council has arisen the improper Power of the Senate, in the Appointment of public Officers, and the alarming Dependence and Connection between that Branch of the Legislature, and the supreme Executive.

Hence also sprung that unnecessary and dangerous Officer, the Vice President; who for want of other Employment, is made President of the Senate; thereby dangerously blending the executive and legislative Powers; besides always giving to some one of the States an unnecessary and unjust Preeminence over the others.

The President of the United States has the unrestrained Power of granting Pardon for Treason; which may be sometimes exercised to screen from Punishment those whom he had secretly instigated to commit the Crime, and thereby prevent a Discovery of his own Guilt.

By declaring all Treaties supreme Laws of the Land, the Executive and the Senate have in many Cases, an exclusive Power of Legislation; which might have been avoided by proper Distinctions with Respect to Treaties, and requiring the Assent of the House of Representatives, where it cou'd be done with Safety.

By requiring only a Majority to make all commercial and navigation Laws, the five Southern States (whose Produce and Circumstances are totally different from that of the eight Northern and Eastern States) will be ruined; for such rigid and premature Regulations may be made, as will enable the Merchants of the Northern and Eastern States not only to demand an exorbitant Freight, but to monopolize the Purchase of the Commodities at their own Price, for many years: to the great Injury of the landed Interest, and Impoverishment of the People: and the Danger is the greater, as the Gain on one Side will be in Proportion to the Loss on the other. Whereas requiring two thirds of the members present in both Houses wou'd have produced mutual moderation, promoted the general Interest, and removed an insuperable Objection to the Adoption of the Government.

Under their own Construction of the general Clause at the End of the enumerated powers the Congress may grant Monopolies in Trade and Commerce, constitute new Crimes, inflict unusual and severe Punishments, and extend their Power as far as they shall think proper; so that the State Legislatures have no Security for the Powers now presumed to remain to them; or the People for their Rights.

There is no Declaration of any kind for preserving the Liberty of the Press, the Tryal by Jury in civil Causes; nor against the Danger of standing Armys in time of Peace.

The State Legislatures are restrained from laying Export Duties on their own Produce.

The general Legislature is restrained from prohibiting the further Importation of Slaves for twenty odd Years; tho' such Importations render the United States weaker, more vulnerable, and less capable of Defence.

Both the general Legislature and the State Legislature are expressly prohibited [from] making ex post facto Laws; tho' there never was, or can be a Legislature but must and will make such Laws, when necessity and the public Safety require them; which will hereafter be a Breach of all the Constitutions in the Union, and afford precedents for other Innovations.

This Government will commence in a moderate Aristocracy; it is at present impossible to foresee whether it will, in its Operation, produce a Monarchy, or a corrupt oppressive Aristocracy; it will most probably vibrate some Years between the two, and then terminate in the one or the other.

✠ D O C U M E N T   3

Madison Advocates a Bill of Rights, 1789

…It cannot be a secret to the gentlemen in this House, that, notwithstanding the ratification of this system of Government by eleven of the thirteen United States, in some cases unanimously, in others by large majorities; yet still there is a great number of our constituents who are dissatisfied with it; among whom are many respectable for their talents and patriotism, and respectable for the jealousy they have for their liberty, which, though mistaken in its object, is laudable in its motive. There is a great body of the people falling under this description, who at present feel much inclined to join their support to the cause of Federalism, if they were satisfied on this one point. We ought not to disregard their inclination, but, on principles of amity and moderation, conform to their wishes, and expressly declare the great rights of mankind secured under this Constitution.

But I will candidly acknowledge, that, over and above all these considerations, I do conceive that the Constitution may be amended; that is to say, if all power is subject to abuse, that then it is possible the abuse of the powers of the General Government may be guarded against in a more secure manner than is now done, while no one advantage arising from the exercise of that power shall be damaged or endangered by it. We have in this way something to gain, and, if we proceed with caution, nothing to lose.

I believe that the great mass of the people who opposed it, disliked it because it did not contain effectual provisions against the encroachments on particular rights, and those safeguards which they have been long accustomed to have interposed between them and the magistrate who exercises the sovereign power; nor ought we to consider them safe, while a great number of our fellow-citizens think these securities necessary.

It is a fortunate thing that the objection to the Government has been made on the ground I stated; because it will be practicable, on that ground, to obviate the objection, so far as to satisfy the public mind that their liberties will be perpetual, and this without endangering any part of the Constitution, which is considered as essential to the existence of the Government by those who promoted its adoption.

The amendments which have occurred to me, proper to be recommended by Congress to the State Legislatures, are these:

First. That there be prefixed to the Constitution a declaration, that all power is originally vested in, and consequently derived from, the people.

That Government is instituted and ought to be exercised for the benefit of the people; which consists in the enjoyment of life and liberty, with the right of acquiring and using property, and generally of pursuing and obtaining happiness and safety.

That the people have an indubitable, unalienable, and indefeasible right to reform or change their Government, whenever it be found adverse or inadequate to the purposes of its institution.

Secondly. That in article 1st, section 2, clause 3, these words be struck out, to wit: "The number of Representatives shall not exceed one for every thirty thousand, but each State shall have at least one Representative, and until such enumeration shall be made," and that in place thereof be inserted these words, to wit: "After the first actual enumeration, there shall be one Representative for every thirty thousand, until the number amounts to——, after which the proportion shall be so regulated by Congress, that the number shall never be less than, nor more than——, but each State shall, after the first enumeration, have at least two Representatives; and prior thereto."

Thirdly. That in article 1st, section 6, clause 1, there be added to the end of the first sentence, these words, to wit: "But no law varying the compensation last ascertained shall operate before the next ensuing election of Representatives."

Fourthly. That in article 1st, section 9, between clauses 3 and 4, be inserted these clauses, to wit: The civil rights of none shall be abridged on account of religious belief or worship, nor shall any national religion be established, nor shall the full and equal rights of conscience be in any manner, or on any pretext, infringed.

The people shall not be deprived or abridged of their right to speak, to write, or to publish their sentiments; and the freedom of the press, as one of the great bulwarks of liberty, shall be inviolable.

The people shall not be restrained from peaceably assembling and consulting for their common good; nor from applying to the Legislature by petitions, or remonstrances, for redress of their grievances.

The right of the people to keep and bear arms shall not be infringed; a well armed and well regulated militia being the best security of a free country: but no person religiously scrupulous of bearing arms shall be compelled to render military service in person.

No soldier shall in time of peace be quartered in any house without the consent of the owner; nor at any time, but in a manner warranted by law.

No person shall be subject, except in cases of impeachment, to more than one punishment or one trial for the same offence; nor shall be compelled to be a witness against himself; nor be deprived of life, liberty, or property without due process of law; nor be obliged to relinquish his property, where it may be necessary for public use, without a just compensation.

Excessive bail shall not be required, nor excessive fines imposed, nor cruel and unusual punishments inflicted.

The rights of the people to be secured in their persons, their houses, their papers, and their other property, from all unreasonable searches and seizures, shall not be violated by warrants issued without probable cause, supported by oath or affirmation, or not particularly describing the places to be searched, or the persons or things to be seized.

In all criminal prosecutions, the accused shall enjoy the right to a speedy and public trial, to be informed of the cause and nature of the accusation, to be confronted with his accusers, and the witnesses against him; to have a compulsory process for obtaining witnesses in his favor; and to have the assistance of counsel for his defence.

The exceptions here or elsewhere in the Constitution, made in favor of particular rights, shall not be so construed as to diminish the just importance of other rights retained by the people, or as to enlarge the powers delegated by the Constitution; but either as actual limitations of such powers, or as inserted merely for greater caution.

Fifthly. That in article 1st, section 10, between clauses 1 and 2, be inserted this clause, to wit:

No State shall violate the equal rights of conscience, or the freedom of the press, or the trial by jury in criminal cases.

Sixthly. That, in article 3d, section 2, be annexed to the end of clause 2d, these words, to wit:

But no appeal to such court shall be allowed where the value in controversy shall not amount to——dollars: nor shall any fact triable by jury, according to the course of common law, be otherwise re-examinable than may consist with the principles of common law.

Seventhly. That in article 3d, section 2, the third clause be struck out, and in its place be inserted the clauses following, to wit:

The trial of all crimes (except in cases of impeachments, and cases arising in the land or naval forces, or the militia when on actual service, in time of war or public danger) shall be by an impartial jury of freeholders of the vicinage, with the requisite of unanimity for conviction, of the right of challenge, and other accustomed requisites; and in all crimes punishable with loss of life or member, presentment or indictment by a grand jury shall be an essential preliminary, provided that in cases of crimes committed within any county which may be in possession of an enemy, or in which a general insurrection may prevail, the trial may by law be authorized in some other county of the same State, as near as may be to the seat of the offence.

In cases of crimes committed not within any county, the trial may by law be in such county as the laws shall have prescribed. In suits at common law, between man and man, the trial by jury, as one of the best securities to the rights of the people, ought to remain inviolate.

Eighthly. That immediately after article 6th, be inserted, as article 7th, the clauses following, to wit:

The powers delegated by this Constitution are appropriated to the departments to which they are respectively distributed: so that the Legislative Department shall never exercise powers vested in the Executive or Judicial, nor the Executive exercise the powers vested in the Legislative or Judicial, nor the Judicial exercise the powers vested in the Legislative or Executive Departments.

The powers not delegated by this Constitution, nor prohibited by it to the States, are reserved to the States respectively.

Ninthly. That article 7th be numbered as article 8th. ...

But I confess that I do conceive, that in a Government modified like this of the United States, the great danger lies rather in the abuse of the community than in the Legislative body. The prescriptions in favor of liberty ought to be levelled against that quarter where the greatest danger lies, namely, that which possesses the highest prerogative of power. But this is not found in either the Executive or Legislative departments of Government, but in the body of the people, operating by the majority against the minority. ...

It may be said, indeed it has been said, that a bill of rights is not necessary, because the establishment of this Government has not repealed those declarations of rights which are added to the several State constitutions; that those rights of the people which had been established by the most solemn act, could not be annihilated by a subsequent act of that people, who meant and declared at the head of the instrument, that they ordained and established a new system, for the express purpose of securing to themselves and posterity the liberties they had gained by an arduous conflict.

I admit the force of this observation, but I do not look upon it to be conclusive. In the first place, it is too uncertain ground to leave this provision upon, if a provision is at all necessary to secure rights so important as many of those I have mentioned are conceived to be, by the public in general, as well as those in particular who opposed the adoption of this Constitution. Besides, some States have no bills of rights, there are others provided with very defective ones, and there are others whose bills of rights are not only defective, but absolutely improper; instead of securing some in the full extent which republican principles would require, they limit them too much to agree with the common ideas of liberty.

It has been objected also against a bill of rights, that, by enumerating particular exceptions to the grant of power, it would disparage those rights which were not placed in that enumeration; and it might follow by implication, that those rights which were not singled out, were intended to be assigned into the hands of the General Government, and were consequently insecure. This is one of the most plausible arguments I have ever heard urged against the admission of a bill of rights into this system; but, I conceive, that it may be guarded against. I have attempted it, as gentlemen may see by turning to the last clause of the fourth resolution.

It has been said that it is unnecessary to load the Constitution with this provision, because it was not found effectual in the constitution of the particular States. It is true, there are a few particular States in which some of the most valuable articles have not, at one time or other, been violated; but it does not follow but they may have to a certain degree, a salutary effect against the abuse of power. If they are incorporated into the Constitution, independent tribunals of justice will consider themselves in a peculiar manner the guardians of those rights; they will be an impenetrable bulwark against every assumption of power in the Legislative or Executive; they will be naturally led to resist every encroachment upon rights expressly stipulated for in the Constitution by the declaration of rights. Besides this security, there is a great probability that such a declaration in the federal system would be enforced; because the State Legislatures will jealously and closely watch the operations of this Government, and be able to resist with more effect every assumption of power, than any other power on earth can do; and the greatest opponents to a Federal Government admit the State Legislatures to be sure guardians of the people's liberty. I conclude, from this view of the subject, that it will be proper in itself, and highly politic, for the tranquility of the public mind, and the stability of the Government, that we should offer something, in the form I have proposed, to be incorporated in the system of Government, as a declaration of the rights of the people.

I wish, also, in revising the Constitution, we may throw into that section, which interdicts the abuse of certain powers in the State Legislatures, some other provisions of equal, if not greater importance than those already made. The words, "No State shall pass any bill of attainder, *ex post facto* law," &c., were wise and proper restrictions in the Constitution. I think there is more danger of those powers being abused by the State Governments than by the Government of the United States. The same may be said of other powers which they possess, if not controlled by the general principle, that laws are unconstitutional which infringe the rights of the community. I should, therefore, wish to extend this interdiction, and add, as I have stated in the 5th resolution, that no State shall violate the equal right of conscience, freedom of the press, or trial by jury in criminal cases; because it is proper that every Government should be disarmed of powers which trench upon those particular rights.

[T]he State Governments are as liable to attack these invaluable privileges as the General Government is, and therefore ought to be as cautiously guarded against.

I think it will be proper, with respect to the judiciary powers, to satisfy the public mind on those points which I have mentioned. Great inconvenience has been apprehended to suitors from the distance they would be dragged to obtain justice in the Supreme Court of the United States, upon an appeal on an action for a small debt. To remedy this, declare that no appeal shall be made unless the matter in controversy amounts to a particular sum; this, with the regulations respecting jury trials in criminal cases, and suits at common law, it is to be hoped, will quiet and reconcile the minds of the people to that part of the Constitution.

I find, from looking into the amendments proposed by the State conventions, that several are particularly anxious that it should be declared in the Constitution, that the powers not therein delegated should be reserved to the several States. Perhaps other words may define this more precisely than the whole of the instrument now does. I admit they may be deemed unnecessary; but there can be no harm in making such a declaration, if gentlemen will allow that the fact is as stated. I am sure I understand it so, and do therefore propose it.

✚ *D O C U M E N T   4*

The Sedition Act Limits Criticism of the National Government, 1798

An Act in Addition to the Act, Entitled "An Act for the Punishment of Certain Crimes Against the United States."

Sec. 1. *Be it enacted* …, That if any persons shall unlawfully combine or conspire together, with intent to oppose any measure or measures of the government of the United States, which are or shall be directed by proper authority, or to impede the operation of any law of the United States, or to intimidate or prevent any person holding a place or office in or under the government of the United States, from undertaking, performing or executing his trust or duty; and if any person or persons, with intent as aforesaid, shall counsel, advise or attempt to procure any insurrection, riot, unlawful assembly, or combination, whether such conspiracy, threatening, counsel, advice, or attempt shall have the proposed effect or not, he or they shall be deemed guilty of a high misdemeanor, and on conviction, before any court of the United States having jurisdiction thereof, shall be punished by a fine not exceeding five thousand dollars, and by imprisonment during a term not less than six months nor exceeding five years; and further, at the discretion of the court may be holden to find sureties for his good behaviour in such sum, and for such time, as the said court may direct.

Sec. 2. That if any person shall write, print, utter, or publish, or shall cause or procure to be written, printed, uttered or published, or shall knowingly and willingly assist or aid in writing, printing, uttering or publishing any false, scandalous and malicious writing or writings against the government of the United States, or either house of the Congress of the United States, or the President of the United States, with intent to defame the said government, or either house of the said Congress, or the said President, or to bring them, or either of them, into contempt or disrepute; or to excite against them, or either or any of them, the hatred of the good people of the United States, or to stir up sedition within the United States, or to excite any unlawful combinations therein, for opposing or resisting any law of the United States, or any act of the President of the United States, done in pursuance of any such law, or of the powers in him vested by the constitution of the United States, or to resist, oppose, or defeat any such law or act, or to aid, encourage or abet any hostile designs of any foreign nation against the United States, their people or government, then such person, being thereof convicted before any court of the United States having jurisdiction thereof, shall be punished by a fine not exceeding two thousand dollars, and by imprisonment not exceeding two years.

Sec. 3. That if any person shall be prosecuted under this act, for the writing or publishing any libel aforesaid, it shall be lawful for the defendant, upon the trial of the cause, to give in evidence in his defence, the truth of the matter contained in the publication charged as a libel. And the jury who shall try the cause, shall have a right to determine the law and the fact, under the direction of the court, as in other cases.

Sec. 4. That this act shall continue to be in force until March 3, 1801, and no longer. ...

✠ D O C U M E N T   5

The Virginia and Kentucky Resolutions Decry the Abuse of National Power, 1798–1799

The Virginia Resolutions, December 24, 1798

Resolved, That the General Assembly of Virginia doth unequivocally express a firm resolution to maintain and defend the Constitution of the United States, and the Constitution of this state, against every aggression either foreign or domestic; and that they will support the Government of the United States in all measures warranted by the former.

That this Assembly most solemnly declares a warm attachment to the union of the states, to maintain which it pledges all its powers; and that, for this end, it is their duty to watch over and oppose every infraction of those principles which constitute the only basis of that Union, because a faithful observance of them can alone secure its existence and the public happiness.

That this Assembly doth explicitly and peremptorily declare that it views the powers of the Federal Government as resulting from the compact to which the states are parties, as limited by the plain sense and intention of the instrument constituting that compact; as no further valid than they are authorized by the grants enumerated in that compact; and that, in case of a deliberate, palpable, and dangerous exercise of other powers not granted by the said compact, the states, who are parties thereto, have the right and are in duty bound to interpose for arresting the progress of the evil, and for maintaining within their respective limits the authorities, rights, and liberties appertaining to them.

That the General Assembly doth also express its deep regret, that a spirit has in sundry instances been manifested by the Federal Government to enlarge its powers by forced constructions of the constitutional charter which defines them; and that indications have appeared of a design to expound certain general phrases (which, having been copied from the very limited grant of powers in the former Articles of Confederation, were the less liable to be misconstrued) so as to destroy the meaning and effect of the particular enumeration which necessarily explains and limits the general phrases; and so as to consolidate the states, by degrees, into one sovereignty, the obvious tendency and inevitable consequence of which would be to transform the present republican system of the United States into an absolute, or, at best, a mixed monarchy.

That the General Assembly doth particularly PROTEST against the palpable and alarming infractions of the Constitution in the two late cases of the "Alien and Sedition Acts," passed at the last session of Congress; the first of which exercises a power nowhere delegated to the Federal Government, and which, by uniting legislative and judicial powers to those of [the] executive, subverts the general principles of free government, as well as the particular organization and positive provisions of the Federal Constitution: and the other of which acts exercises, in like manner, a power not delegated by the Constitution, but, on the contrary, expressly and positively forbidden by one of the amendments thereto,—a power which, more than any other, ought to produce universal alarm, because it is levelled against the right of freely examining public characters and measures, and of free communication among the people thereon, which has ever been justly deemed the only effectual guardian of every other right.

That this state having, by its Convention which ratified the Federal Constitution, expressly declared that, among other essential rights, "the liberty of conscience and of the press cannot be cancelled, abridged, restrained or modified by any authority of the United States," and from its extreme anxiety to guard these rights from every possible attack of sophistry or ambition, having, with other states, recommended an amendment for that purpose, which amendment was in due time annexed to the Constitution,—it would mark a reproachful inconsistency and criminal degeneracy, if an indifference were now shown to the palpable violation of one of the rights thus declared and secured, and to the establishment of a precedent which may be fatal to the other.

That the good people of this commonwealth, having ever felt and continuing to feel the most sincere affection for their brethren of the other states, the truest anxiety for establishing and perpetuating the union of all and the most scrupulous fidelity to that Constitution, which is the pledge of mutual friendship, and the instrument of mutual happiness, the General Assembly doth solemnly appeal to the like dispositions of the other states, in confidence that they will concur with this Commonwealth in declaring, as it does hereby declare, that the acts aforesaid are unconstitutional; and that the necessary and proper measures will be taken by each for co-operating with this state, in maintaining unimpaired the authorities, rights, and liberties reserved to the states respectively, or to the people. ...

The Kentucky Resolutions, February 22, 1799

... Our opinions of these alarming measures of the general government, together with our reasons for those opinions, were detailed with decency, and with temper, and submitted to the discussion and judgment of our fellow-citizens throughout the Union. Whether the like decency and temper have been observed in the answers of most of those States, who have denied or attempted to obviate the great truths contained in those resolutions, we have now only to submit to a candid world. Faithful to the true principles of the federal Union, unconscious of any designs to disturb the harmony of that Union, and anxious only to escape the fangs of despotism, the good people of this commonwealth are regardless of censure or calumniation. Lest, however, the silence of this commonwealth should be construed into an acquiescence in the doctrines and principles advanced and attempted to be maintained by the said answers, or at least those of our fellow-citizens throughout the Union who so widely differ from us on those important subjects, should be deluded by the expectation, that we shall be deterred from what we conceive our duty, or shrink from the principles contained in those resolutions—therefore,

Resolved, That this commonwealth considers the federal Union, upon the terms and for the purposes specified in the late compact, conducive to the liberty and happiness of the several states: That it does now unequivocally declare its attachment to the Union, and to that compact, agreeably to its obvious and real intention, and will be among the last to seek its dissolution: That if those who administer the general government be permitted to transgress the limits fixed by that compact, by a total disregard to the special delegations of power therein contained, an annihilation of the state governments, and the creation upon their ruins of a general consolidated government, will be the inevitable consequence: That the principle and construction contended for by sundry of the state legislatures, that the general government is the exclusive judge of the extent of the powers delegated to it, stop not short of *despotism*—since the discretion of those who administer the government, and not the *Constitution*, would be the measure of their powers: That the several states who formed that instrument being sovereign and independent, have the unquestionable right to judge of the infraction; and, *That a nullification of those sovereignties, of all unauthorized acts done under color of that instrument is the rightful remedy*: That this commonwealth does, under the most deliberate reconsideration, declare, that the said Alien and Sedition Laws are, in their opinion, palpable violations of the said Constitution; and, however cheerfully it may be disposed to surrender its opinion to a majority of its sister states, in matters of ordinary or doubtful policy, yet, in momentous regulations like the present, which so vitally wound the best rights of the citizen, it would consider a silent acquiescence as highly criminal: That although this commonwealth, as a party to the federal compact, will bow to the laws of the Union, yet, it does, at the same time declare, that it will not now, or ever hereafter, cease to oppose in a constitutional manner, every attempt at what quarter soever offered, to violate that compact. And, finally, in order that no pretext or arguments may be drawn from a supposed acquiescence, on the part of this commonwealth in the constitutionality of those laws, and be thereby used as precedents for similar future violations of the federal compact—this commonwealth does now enter against them its solemn PROTEST.

✠ *D O C U M E N T   6*

Lyon's Case, 1798

U.S. Circuit Court, District of Vermont

[This was an indictment, under the act of July 14, 1798, against Matthew Lyon, for the publication of a seditious libel.]

The indictment which was found on October 5, 1798, contained three counts, the first of which, after averring the intent to be "to stir up sedition, and to bring the president and government of the United States into contempt," laid the following libel-lous matter: "As to the executive, when I shall see the efforts of that power bent on the promotion of the comfort, the happiness, and accommodation of the people, that executive shall have my zealous and uniform support: but whenever I shall, on the part of the executive, see every consideration of the public welfare swallowed up in a con-tinual grasp for power, in an unbounded thirst for ridiculous pomp, foolish adulation, and selfish avarice; when I shall behold men of real merit daily turned out of office, for no other cause but independency of sentiment; when I shall see men of firmness, merit, years, abilities, and experience, discarded in their applications for office, for fear they possess that independence, and men of meanness preferred for the ease with which they take up and advocate opinions, the consequence of which they know but little of—when I shall see the sacred name of religion employed as a state engine to make mankind hate and persecute one another, I shall not be their humble advocate."

The second count consisted of having maliciously, &c., and with intent, &c., published a letter, said to be a letter from a diplomatic character in France, containing two paragraphs in the words following: "The misunderstanding between the two governments (France and the United States), has become extremely alarming; confidence is completely destroyed, mistrusts, jealousy, and a disposition to a wrong attribution of motives, are so apparent, as to require the utmost caution in every word and action that are to come from your executive. I mean, if your object is to avoid hostilities. Had this truth been understood with you before the recall of Monroe, before the coming and second coming of Pinckney; had it guided the pens that wrote the bullying speech of your president, and stupid answer of your senate, at the opening of congress in November last, I should probably had no occasion to address you this letter.—But when we found him borrowing the language of Edmund Burke, and telling the world that although he should succeed in treating with the French, there was no dependence to be placed on any of their engagements, that their religion and morality were at an end, that they would turn pirates and plunderers, and it would be necessary to be perpetually armed against them, though you were at peace: we wondered that the answer of both houses had not been an order to send him to a mad house. Instead of this the senate have echoed the speech with more servility than ever George III experienced from either house of parliament."

The third count was for assisting, counselling, aiding, and abetting the publication of the same.

Saturday, Oct. 7. The defendant, being still in custody, (having been arrested on a bench warrant immediately after the finding of the bill,) pleaded not guilty, and put in bail for his appearance on Monday, October 9.

Monday, Oct. 9. The panel being called, a juror named Board, was challenged for cause by the district attorney, (Mr. Charles Marsh.) Question. Have you formed or expressed an opinion as to the guilt or innocence of the accused? Answer. No.

The district attorney then produced one of the deputy sheriffs who had summoned the jury, who testified that he heard the juror say he thought Mr. Lyon would not, or should not, be condemned.

Paterson, Circuit Justice. Let the juror stand aside, and unless there is not enough to form a jury without him, you need inquire no further.

Two jurors were challenged by the defendant for cause. Against one no evidence was produced, and there appears to have been no examination of him on his venire dire. The other was shown to have been the author of an article in a newspaper, inveighing politically and personally against the defendant.

Paterson, Circuit Justice. The cause shown is sufficient, as a difference of this nature is a disqualification.

The box having been filled, and the jury sworn, the defendant interposed an additional plea, to the effect that the sedition law was unconstitutional, which plea was stricken off by the court.

The district attorney having opened the case, produced a letter from the defendant, dated Philadelphia, July 7, 1798, and postmarked on the same day, which was printed in Vermont on July 23. The authorship of the letter and the fact of publication were admitted by the defendant. It was further proved that the defendant had several times read at public meetings in Vermont the letter (known at the time as the "Barlow" letter) from which the libellous matter in the second count was taken. Several witnesses were called to show that the defendant, both in public and in private, had extensively used the letter for political purposes, and in doing so had frequently made use of language highly disrespectful to the administration. On cross examination it appeared that on one occasion he had endeavoured to prevent it from being printed.

The prosecution having closed its case, the defendant stated his defence to consist in three points: First, that the court had no jurisdiction of the offence, the act of congress being unconstitutional and void, if not so generally, at least, as to writings composed before its passage; second, that the publication was innocent; and third, that the contents were true.

On the first two points he offered no testimony, but on the third he proposed to call Judge Paterson, the presiding judge, and Judge Smith.

Judge Paterson being then on the bench, was then asked by the defendant, whether he had not frequently "dined with the president, and observed his ridiculous pomp and parade?" Judge Paterson replied that he had sometimes, though rarely, dined with the president, but that he had never seen any pomp or parade; he had seen, on the contrary, a great deal of plainness and simplicity. The defendant then asked whether he (the judge) had not seen at the president's more pomp and servants there, than at the tavern at Rutland? To this no answer was given. No other witness was called.

Mr. Marsh, district attorney, addressed the jury at length, urging, (1) the libellous nature of the offensive passages, which were clearly within the act of congress, and (2) the declared intentions with which they had been used by the defendant, which expressly came up to the innuendoes.

Judge Smith, (the then chief justice of Vermont,) who then appeared as counsel for the defendant, declining to reply, in consequence of the shortness of time allowed him for preparation, he having been called into the case at the bar, the defendant addressed the jury at great length, insisting on the unconstitutionality of the law, and the insufficiency of the evidence to show anything more than a legitimate opposition.

Before Paterson, Circuit Justice, and Hitchcock, District Judge.

Paterson, Circuit Justice (charging jury). "You have nothing whatever to do with the constitutionality or unconstitutionality of the sedition law. Congress has said that the author and publisher of seditious libels is to be punished; and until this law is declared null and void by a tribunal competent for the purpose, its validity cannot be disputed. Great would be the abuses were the constitutionality of every statute to be submitted to a jury, in each case where the statute is to be applied. The only question you are to determine is, that which the record submits to you. Did Mr. Lyon publish the writing given in the indictment? Did he do so seditiously? On the first point, the evidence is undisputed, and in fact, he himself concedes the fact of publication as to a large portion of libellous matter. As to the second point, you will have to consider whether language such as that here complained of could have been uttered with any other intent than that of making odious or contemptible the president and government, and bringing them both into disrepute. If you find such is the case, the offence is made out, and you must render a verdict of guilty. Nor should the political rank of the defendant, his past services, or the dependent condition of his family, deter you from this duty. Suchconsiderations are for the court alone in adjusting the penalty they will bestow. The fact of guilt is for you, for the court, the grade of punishment. As to yourselves, one point, in addition, in exercising the functions allotted to you, you must keep in mind; and that is, that in order to render a verdict of guilty, you must be satisfied beyond all reasonable substantial doubt that the hypothesis of innocence is unsustainable. Keeping these instructions in your mind, you will proceed to deliberate on your verdict."

At about eight o'clock in the evening of the same day, after about an hour's absence, the jury returned with a verdict of guilty.

The defendant being called up for sentence, a postponement was obtained till the next morning, when, after upon a representation of his circumstances, it appearing that he was almost insolvent, Judge Paterson addressed him as follows: "Matthew Lyon, as a member of the federal legislature, you must be well acquainted with the mischiefs which flow from an unlicensed abuse of government, and of the motives which led to the passage of the act under which this indictment is framed. No one, also, can be better acquainted than yourself with the existence and nature of the act. Your position, so far from making the case one which might slip with a nominal fine through the hands of the court, would make impunity conspicuous should such a fine alone be imposed. What, however, has tended to mitigate the sentence which would otherwise have been imposed, is, what I am sorry to hear of, the reduced condition of your estate. The judgment of the court is, that you stand imprisoned four months, pay the costs of prosecution, and a fine of one thousand dollars, and stand committed until this sentence be complied with."

In the first essay, Saul Cornell, a professor of history at Ohio State University, highlights the important contributions of the Anti-Federalists to Americans' conception of liberty. Contrary to generations of scholars who ignored the Anti-Federalists as the "losers" in the struggle over constitutional ratification, Cornell portrays them sympathetically as the founders of a dissenting tradition in the United States. In this selection, Cornell describes how Anti-Federalists in the first Congress believed that Madison's proposed bill of rights did not go far enough in ensuring the protection of liberty.

In contrast, in the second essay, the late Leonard Levy, a noted constitutional historian who for many years taught at Claremont Graduate School, emphasized the contributions of the Jeffersonian Republicans to American notions of freedom of speech and press during the late 1790s. The First Amendment's guarantee of free speech, he argued, had been based on the English common law definition of no prior restraint. That is, under the existing understanding of freedom of speech, laws could not be enacted to prohibit speech but prosecution for seditious libel after the fact could still occur. According to Levy, the Jeffersonian Republicans understood that, in a government based on popular sovereignty, the widest possible latitude had to be given to rights.

The Anti-Federalists and American Liberty

SAUL CORNELL

Elections to the First Congress were profoundly influenced by the politics of ratification. In many instances, a candidate's original stance on the Constitution was at least as important as any other issue put before the public. Despite the efforts of Federalists to discredit those who had been Anti-Federalists, the new Senate contained three vocal Anti-Federalists, and the new House contained a distinct Anti-Federalist minority of eleven representatives. Although not the only voting bloc to emerge in the House, the voting pattern of these individuals consistently reflected their Anti-Federalist commitments. On a number of issues ranging from the right of the president to declare days of thanksgiving to his power to remove heads of executive departments without congressional approval and administer the Post Office, former Anti-Federalists broadcast their objections in terms reminiscent of the recent debate over ratification....

The debate most self-consciously linked to the ratification contest concerned amendments to the Constitution. The job of framing amendments that would satisfy the Anti-Federalist objections fell to James Madison, who was eager to prevent Anti-Federalists from obtaining structural changes in the federal system that would weaken the new government.

The terms of the debate over the Bill of Rights in the First Congress were largely derivative of the arguments between Federalists and Anti-Federalists. Describing the politics there, one contemporary observed, "The Antis viz. Gerry Tucker etc. appear determined to obstruct and embarrass the Business as much as possible." Pennsylvania's Frederick A. Muhlenberg even believed that the Anti-Federalist sympathies of some members had become more pronounced as a result of the political conflicts of the First Congress. "Mr. Gerry and Tucker had each of them a long string of Amendts. which were not comprised in the Report of the Special Committee, and which they stiled amendments proposed by the several States. There was a curious medley of them, and such as even our Minority in Pennsylvania would rather have pronounced dangerous."

A distinctive Anti-Federalist agenda emerged. The goal of Anti-Federalists was to limit the powers of the new government and bolster the states so that they would continue to be in a position to protect the liberty of their citizens. William Grayson confided to Patrick Henry that amendments being considered in Congress "shall affect personal liberty alone, leaving the great points of the Jud[iciar]y and direct taxation etc. to stand as they are." This claim reiterated the central concern of Anti-Federalists: that the organization of federal authority was essential to the preservation of liberty. Grayson's observation that the proposed amendments "are good for nothing, and I believe as many others do, that they will do more harm than benefit" reflected his concern that issues of taxation and the structure of the new federal judiciary could render all other amendments protecting personal liberty nugatory. Grayson explicitly faulted Congress for failing to address Anti-Federalist concerns about those potential threats to liberty. Taxation and impartial administration of justice had been central in the Revolutionary struggle with Britain and were crucial to the Anti-Federalist critique of the Constitution. To Grayson, the threat that the new government would overstep its bounds and use the power of taxation arbitrarily and oppressively negated any paper check on governmental authority. This threat was compounded by the nature of federal judicial power. Where the only legal recourse to challenge federal authority would be through the federal courts, without structural change mere parchment barriers could not protect liberty. Anti-Federalists' view of liberty and rights was still closely akin to the one patriot leaders espoused in 1776. Grayson's concerns about the judiciary and taxation can be understood only within the context of this tradition. Written guarantees of individual liberty were meaningless if the new government contained large, unrestricted grants of authority, especially in the area of taxation.

No issue was more bitterly contested than the Anti-Federalist effort to limit the powers of the new government to those expressly delegated by the Constitution. Madison's response was an amendment: "The powers not delegated by this Constitution, nor prohibited by it to the states, are reserved to the states respectively." Anti-Federalist Thomas Tudor Tucker moved to insert the word "expressly" between "not" and "delegated." Madison responded, "This question was agitated in the Convention of Virginia; it was brought forward by those who were opposed to the Constitution, and was finally given up by them." Without the insertion of the word "expressly," many Anti-Federalists believed that amendments were of little consequence: the new government would eventually absorb all power within its orbit. Tucker's argument with Madison foreshadowed later arguments over the proper strategy for interpreting what would become the Tenth Amendment. More than any other issue, the notion of restricting the powers of the government to those expressly delegated by the Constitution would define the core around which a distinctively Anti-Federalist interpretation of federalism would evolve into a dissenting constitutional discourse. . . .

Throughout the debate over amendments, Anti-Federalist congressmen sought to secure structural changes that would augment the power of the states and to block any wording that might provide the new government with a pretext for expanding its authority. In every instance Madison and his allies effectively blunted the Anti-Federalist agenda.

Anti-Federalists were not satisfied with Madison's amendments. Elbridge Gerry reminded his fellow congressmen, "Those who were called anti-federalists at that time, complained that they had injustice done them by the title, because they were in favor of a Federal Government, and the others were in favor [o]f a national one." A number of prominent Anti-Federalists, including Gerry, believed that the amendments adopted by the First Congress failed to achieve the structural changes necessary to protect the rights of individuals and the power of the states. Still, few, if any, prominent Anti-Federalist politicians were willing to challenge the legitimacy of the Constitution, a move that would have undermined the new government.

It is easy to understand the dissatisfaction of many Anti-Federalists with the final form of the Bill of Rights presented by Congress. In the view of Aedanus Burke, those amendments "likely to be adopted by this house, are very far from giving satisfaction to our constituents." The amendments adopted were not "those solid and substantial amendments which the people expect; they are little better than whip-syllabub, and frothy and full of wind, formed only to please the palate, or they are like a tub thrown out to a whale, to secure the freight of the ship and its peaceable voyage."

Richard Henry Lee, like other Anti-Federalists, assessed the amendments approved by Congress even less optimistically. "The idea of subsequent Amendments was delusion altogether, and so intended by the greater part of those who arrogated to themselves the name of Federalists." He echoed the arguments of his fellow Virginians: "The great points of free election, Jury trial in criminal cases much loosened, the unlimited right of Taxation, and Standing Armies in peace, remain as they were. Some valuable Rights are indeed *declared*, but the powers that remain are very sufficient to render them nugatory at pleasure." Lee's judgment reflected the Anti-Federalist belief that, without serious structural change, a declaration of rights would remain a flimsy barrier against encroachments on popular liberty.

Some Anti-Federalists were more sanguine, and George Mason was more optimistic than many: "I received much Satisfaction from the Amendments to the federal Constitution, which have lately passed the House of Representatives." Yet, even Mason believed that such amendments were still woefully inadequate on a number of points:

> With two or three further Amendments such as confining the federal Judiciary to Admiralty and Maritime Jurisdiction, and to Subjects merely federal—fixing the Mode of Elections either in the Constitution itself (which I think would be preferable) or securing the Regulation of them to the respective States—Requiring more than a bare Majority to make Navigation and Commercial laws, and appointing a constitutional amenable Council to the President, and lodging with them most of the Executive Powers now rested in the Senate—I cou'd chearfully put my Hand and Heart to the new Government.

Mason reiterated the Anti-Federalists' concerns about the structural defects of the new government, particularly their fears that the judiciary represented a palpable threat and that the new Constitution failed to provide adequate representation.

It was not only Anti-Federalists who viewed the final amendments as little more than a political expediency. Federalist George Clymer wrote to Tench Coxe, describing "Madison's amendments" as a mere placebo: "Like a sensible physician," Madison "has given his malades imaginaires bread pills powder of paste and neutral mixtures to keep them in play." Thus, even some influential Federalists supported the view that Madison's amendments were designed to assuage Anti-Federalist fears without answering Anti-Federalist objections.

Anti-Federalists were united in seeking substantial amendments to the Constitution. Understanding the logic of their demand for a Bill of Rights is essential in order to appreciate their reaction to the draft proposed by James Madison. The final form adopted by Congress failed to remedy many of the most serious defects identified by Anti-Federalist critics. That Anti-Federalists were dissatisfied with the version of amendments did not mean that their earlier support for a Bill of Rights was hollow or a cynical maneuver. Their disappointment made perfect sense, given their beliefs that liberty could be protected only in a properly structured federal system.

With the controversy over amendments concluded, the stage was set for a new political debate. With the amended Constitution now firmly in place, the most pressing issue facing former Federalists and Anti-Federalists was how to interpret the new frame of government. The old divisions between Anti-Federalists and Federalists did not disappear, but were radically transformed by the conclusion of the debate over amendments. The last remaining issue directly inherited from ratification was now settled. Increasingly, the struggle turned on how the Constitution would be interpreted by citizens, Congress, and the courts.

One of the most interesting sources for charting the gradual transition from a distinctively Anti-Federalist style of opposition to a new Democratic-Republican constitutional opposition is the detailed diary kept by Senator William Maclay of Pennsylvania. A supporter of the Constitution in 1787–1788 and a Democratic-Republican during the 1790s, Maclay's observations about politics provide important clues to the evolution of political discourse in this period. Early in his diary, Maclay described Virginia's Richard Henry Lee as "a notorious Antifederalist" and Massachusetts's Elbridge Gerry as "highly Antifederal." Yet, as new issues came before Congress, Maclay's description of the terms of political debate changed. He noted the emergence of a new group, which he described as the "Court party." This group was committed to strengthening the executive branch and generally expanding the powers of the federal government. Maclay even found himself in agreement with the "notorious Antifederalist" from Virginia, Lee. Maclay was flattered that Lee had adopted his own argument against this new, emerging court party. Maclay's shifting response to Lee suggests an erosion of the older lines of political controversy. The emergence of new divisions and alliances did not completely obliterate old animosities. While Maclay showed considerable sympathy for Lee, he took exception to William Grayson's suggestion that the court party was merely carrying forward the designs of the original supporters of the Constitution. Having himself supported the Constitution, Maclay rejected this argument. He thought Grayson's reference to Patrick Henry's charge that "consolidation is the object of the New Government" was "remarkable." Certainly, not all former Anti-Federalists were of a single mind in interpreting new developments in Congress. Clearly, Lee's more conciliatory approach seemed more likely to win over those former Federalists who opposed the emerging "court interest." That Maclay sided with the former Anti-Federalists in opposing the court faction did not mean that he had adopted Anti-Federalist principles. Maclay clearly believed that new political divisions had emerged in Congress. For many Anti-Federalists, the actions of the court faction vindicated their earlier stance during ratification; the most politically astute realized that it was vital to forge a working alliance with those members of the old Federalist coalition who were alarmed by the rise of a court-style political faction. Doubtless, for some, such a move grew out of political expediency, but for others it arose out of a recognition that some who supported the Constitution might not have intended to create a court-style government.

Maclay was especially puzzled by the newfound affection for British government expressed by members of the court party. He was particularly confused by the "conduct of [William] Patterson," who had "been characterized to me as a Staunch Revolution man and Genuine Whig." Despite this reputation, Patterson "has in every republican Question deserted and in some instances betrayed Us." A clear pattern had emerged in the First Congress, and Maclay sincerely believed that "the desi[gns] of a certain party" were to use "the General Power to carry the Constitution into effect by a constructive interpretation." This strategy "wou[l]d extend to every Case That Congress may deem necessar[y] or expedient." In Maclay's view, the Supreme Court's interpretation of the Constitution proved to be an "open point," an "unguarded pass" that if unchecked would render "the General Government compleatly incontrolable." Maclay was astonished that politicians boasted that they had "cheated the People" and established "a form of Government over them which none of them expected." Ultimately, Maclay believed, the arrogance of this new faction would be its undoing: "I think they have made but a bungling hand of it." In their arrogance, the supporters of the court faction had confessed their true intentions. It would now be possible to alert the people and rally those who sought to preserve the spirit of the Constitution against those who would use it as an engine of aristocratic influence. The idea that the court interest had departed from traditional Whig republican ideals and now intended to transform the Constitution through "constructive interpretation" was a stance that former Anti-Federalists could readily accept. The rise of a court "faction" made possible a rapprochement between former Anti-Federalists and many who had originally supported the Constitution.

The development of the court party had profound consequences for both former Anti-Federalists and Federalists. At the same time that the court was energizing former Anti-Federalists, it was providing the basis for those original supporters of the Constitution who feared greater centralization to reassess their views of their former Anti-Federalist opponents. Once again, a common enemy effectively united what might otherwise have remained a loose and, in many respects, incompatible coalition of interests. The stage was set for the creation of a dissenting political and constitutional movement that would draw on a rich ideological legacy that included a generous dose of Anti-Federalism.

The death of Anti-Federalism as an active political movement provided the means for resurrecting the spirit of Anti-Federalism. While the decision to assume the role of a loyal constitutional opposition was crucial to this transformation, the rehabilitation also benefited from the efforts of Thomas Jefferson and James

Madison. Jefferson had conditionally supported the Constitution and was among the most outspoken proponents of incorporating a bill of rights. Madison had been one of the most outspoken supporters of the Constitution and critics of Anti-Federalism. Confronting the threat of the new court faction of Federalists, both men reassessed their views of Anti-Federalism.

By 1792, Jefferson reevaluated his initial assessment of Anti-Federalist arguments. Writing to Washington, he confided, "The Antifederal champions are now strengthened in argument by the fulfilment of their predictions." By contrast, "the republican federalists who espoused the same government for its intrinsic merits, are disarmed of their weapons." Jefferson had come to believe that Anti-Federalist "prophecy" had now "become true history."

A similar effort at reevaluating the legitimacy of Anti-Federalism was undertaken by James Madison in his 1792 essay "A Candid State of Parties." Madison laid out for the public his own analysis of the evolution of American political life since the Revolution. His explanation of the transition from the political situation of the 1780s to that of the 1790s was one of the most important contemporary discussions of how Anti-Federalism had been transformed into a loyal opposition.

Madison contrasted the local character of partisan politics during the Confederation period with the national scope of politics during the struggle over ratification. The debate over the Constitution, he maintained, had transformed the nature of American politics: "The Federal Constitution, proposed in the latter year, gave birth to a second and most interesting division of the people. Every one remembers it, because every one was involved in it." As for the Federalists of 1788, Madison wrote, "Among those who embraced the Constitution, the great body were unquestionably friends to republican liberty; tho' there were, no doubt, some who were openly or secretly attached to monarchy and aristocracy." While defending the supporters of the Constitution, Madison conceded an essential point that had been central to the Anti-Federalist critique: the desire of some Federalists to use the Constitution as the instrument of an aristocratic counterrevolution. At the same time that Madison revised his estimation of the Federalists, he conceded a new respect for the Anti-Federalists. Madison's assessment of the Anti-Federalists was unusually generous, given his frustration with them during ratification. "Among those who opposed the constitution, the great body were certainly well affected to the union and to good government, tho' there might be a few who had a leaning unfavourable to both." The adoption of the Constitution, Madison asserted, had effectively rendered these older labels obsolete.

Madison preferred to characterize the two sides as the "antirepublican party" and the "Republican party." The "antirepublican party," Madison observed, included those who "from natural temper, or from the habits of life are, more partial to the opulent than to the other classes of society." The leaders had "debauched themselves into a persuasion that mankind are incapable of governing themselves" and "that government can be carried on only by the pageantry of rank, the influence of money and emoluments, and the terror of military force."

The willingness of former Anti-Federalists to support the amended Constitution allowed Madison and Jefferson to recognize the legitimacy of Anti-Federalist fears. The creation of a Democratic-Republican opposition was an amalgam of ideas drawn from various parts of Anti-Federalism and those more closely associated with Jefferson and Madison.

While Jefferson and Madison worked to forge a new coalition that included former opponents of the Constitution, Federalists seized the opportunity that this new alliance created to attack the opposition. Federalists freely used the charge of Anti-Federalism to undermine their opposition. The term "Anti-Federalist" continued to be a political slur. In the controversial elections of 1792, the charge of Anti-Federalism once again circulated to discredit opposition to the Federalist agenda. The choice of the popular Anti-Federalist politician George Clinton to oppose John Adams for the vice-presidency served only to intensify the debate over the continuing status of Anti-Federalism in American politics. The list of evils paraded before the people by Clinton's enemies was lengthy. The New Yorker's Anti-Federalism was linked to a variety of other unsavory characters opposed to true republican principles including "demagogues, democrats, mobocrats, non-contents, dis-contents, mal-contents, enemies to the government, hostile to the constitution, friends of anarchy, haters of good order, promoters of confusion, exciters of mobs, sowers of sedition." In response, Clinton supporters strenuously insisted that no virtuous citizen in America would claim to be an Anti-Federalist if that meant opposing the amended Constitution.

Former Anti-Federalists worked hard to stress that the original opponents of the Constitution were now its greatest supporters. William Findley captured the attitudes of many former opponents when he rejected the present validity of the label "Anti-Federalist," sharing the view of most Anti-Federalists, who were never comfortable with the label in the first place. Anti-Federalists had always maintained that they were the true supporters of federalist ideas. Eager to rid themselves of the opprobrium attached to the epithet "Anti-Federalist," they still adhered to many of the same constitutional principles. Findley argued that the term "Anti-Federalism" had become an anachronism: it deserved an honorable place in history, but it no longer was useful in the political struggles of the post-Constitution period. "The artful cry of the danger of antifederalism is gradually ceasing to have its effect," he was happy to report. "The more the people examine, the more they are convinced, that no body of antifederalists exists in the United States, and that no design for overturning the government has been entertained since the commencement of its operation." No former Anti-Federalist wished to oppose the amended Constitution; the goal was to maintain a loyal opposition that would actually preserve the Constitution against its current enemies. The key was to limit the government to those powers that the people acting through their state conventions had intended to cede to the federal government.

Even as Findley acknowledged the merits of the amended Constitution, he reiterated his fear about the continuing danger of the Federalist agenda. If anything, that program appeared more sinister than in the predictions made in 1787.

> Those who opposed adopting the government without amendments, in their zealous criticism on the Constitution, said the time might come, when an insidious faction would get into the legislature, and expound these expressions in such a manner as to bottom a subversion of the governments on them; but those who advocated the Constitution in the State Convention, pronounced this apprehension to be absurd.

Findley not only felt that Anti-Federalist warnings had been prescient; he was somewhat astonished that this view was shared by many so others. Neither party expected "that what the one thought might possibly happen at some future period, and the other believed to be impossible, should be realized so soon."

Most Anti-Federalists followed Findley's explanation of the nature of Anti-Federalist opposition to the Constitution: "Those who were designated antifederalists when the Constitution was in a probationary state, were not opposed to a Federal government, but ... they objected to the proposed instrument as not being defined with that precision, nor guarded with those restraints that were necessary." He was quick to add that the majority of Americans shared this view, and the demands for amendments by the states demonstrated that this was "the general opinion in the majority of the states." Anti-Federalists sought "greater precision in the definition of the powers, and more explicit guards were recommended." Once those objections were "removed, those who had been called antifederalists are not only well satisfied, but zealously attached to the government." Although Findley was satisfied with the amended Constitution, he retained some concerns. The failure of the amendments to eliminate all Anti-Federalist concerns, to restrain those sections of the Constitution that sanctioned broad grants of authority to the federal government, worried Findley. With amendments adopted, "the monarchical party," Findley remarked, was forced to place its hopes in "the ambiguity of the Constitution." The adoption of the Constitution necessarily inaugurated a debate over the politics of constitutional interpretation, because amendments had not prevented the danger from constructive interpretations.

Despite the intensity of Anti-Federalist opposition to the Constitution, no Anti-Constitution party emerged after ratification. With the demise of the second-convention movement, Anti-Federalists turned their attention to seeking office under the new government. Federalist efforts to discredit Anti-Federalists only further diminished the likelihood of a distinctive Anti-Federalist party's emerging. Instead, Anti-Federalists set about becoming a loyal opposition. A number of other factors facilitated this transformation. The rapid adoption of the Bill of Rights, even if it failed to satisfy many Anti-Federalists, deprived them of an important rallying point. Reverence for the principles of constitutionalism and a belief that, when properly amended, the new frame of government would effectively protect liberty further weakened the chances of an Anti-Federal party's forming. The respect accorded George Washington, the new president, also worked against continued opposition. When coupled with renewed economic prosperity, all of those factors helped promote the formal demise of Anti-Federalism. Yet, though Anti-Federalism did not generate an Anti-Constitution party, the term "Anti-Federalist," the various texts produced by the Anti-Federalists during ratification, and the alternative constitutional discourses that shaped Anti-Federalism did not simply disappear. The emergence of a court faction among Federalists caused many former supporters of the Constitution to rethink the original Anti-Federalist critique. The efforts of former Federalists, most notably James Madison, and former Anti-Federalists, such as William Findley, were crucial to the creation of a Democratic-Republican opposition. That loyal opposition drew important ideas and rhetorical themes from Anti-Federalism and adapted them to the exigencies of political conflict in the 1790s.

The Republicans and the Transformation
of Libertarian Thought

LEONARD W. LEVY

In 1798 there was a sudden break-through in American libertarian thought on freedom of speech and press—sudden, radical, and transforming, like an underwater volcano erupting its lava upward from the ocean floor to form a new island. The Sedition Act, which was a thrust in the direction of a single-party press and a monolithic party system, triggered the Republican surge. The result was the emergence of a new promontory of libertarian thought jutting out of a stagnant Blackstonian sea.

To appreciate the Republican achievement requires an understanding of American libertarian thought on the meaning and scope of freedom of political discourse. Contrary to the accepted view, neither the Revolution nor the First Amendment superseded the common law by repudiating the Blackstonian concept that freedom of the press meant merely freedom from prior restraint. There had been no rejection of the concept that government may be criminally assaulted, that is, seditiously libeled, simply by the expression of critical opinions that tended to lower it in the public's esteem.

To be sure, the principle of a free press, like flag, home, and mother, had no enemies. Only seditious libels, licentious opinions, and malicious falsehoods were condemned. The question, therefore, is not whether freedom of the press was favored but what it meant and whether its advocates would extend it to a political opponent whose criticism cut to the bone on issues that counted. Jefferson once remarked that he did not care whether his neighbor said that there are twenty gods or no God, because "It neither picks my pocket nor breaks my leg." But in drafting a constitution for Virginia in 1776 he proposed that freedom of religion "shall not be held to justify any seditious preaching or conversation against the authority of the civil government." And in the same year he helped frame a statute on treasonable crimes, punishing anyone who "by any word" or deed defended the cause of Great Britain. Apparently political opinions could break his leg or pick his pocket, thus raising the question of what he meant by freedom of the press. We can say that he and his contemporaries supported an unrestricted public discussion of issues if we understand that "unrestricted" meant merely the absence of censorship in advance of publication: no one needed a government license to express himself, but he was accountable under the criminal law for abuse of his right to speak or publish freely.

Before 1798 the *avant-garde* among American libertarians staked everything on the principles of the Zenger case, which they thought beyond improvement. No greater liberty could be conceived than the right to publish without restriction if only the defendant might plead truth as a defense in a criminal prosecution for seditious, blasphemous, obscene, or personal libel, and if the criminality of his words might be determined by a jury of his peers rather than by a judge. The substantive law of criminal libels was unquestioned.

From *Constitutional Opinions: Aspects of the Bill of Rights* by Leonard W. Levy, pp. 163–170. Copyright © 1986 by Leonard W. Levy. Reprinted with permission of Oxford University Press, Inc.

Zengerian principles, however, were a frail prop for a broad freedom of the press. Granted, a defendant representing a popular cause against the administration in power might be acquitted, but if his views were unpopular, God help him—for a jury would not, nor would his plea of truth as a defense. A jury, then as today, was essentially a court of public opinion, often synonymous with public prejudice. Moreover, the opinions of men notoriously differ: one man's truth is another's falsehood. Indeed political opinions may be neither true nor false and are usually not capable of being proved by the rules of evidence, even if true. An indictment for seditious libel, based on a defendant's accusation of bribery or corruption by a public official, can be judged by a jury. But the history of sedition trials indicates that indictments are founded on accusations of a different order, namely, that the government, or one of its measures or officials, is unjust, tyrannical, or contrary to the public interest. Libertarians who accepted Zengerian principles painted themselves into a corner. If a jury returned a verdict of guilty despite a defense of truth, due process had been accorded, and protests were groundless, for the substance of the law that made the trial possible had not been challenged.

American acquiescence in the British or common-law definition of a free press was so widespread that even the frail Zengerian principles seemed daring, novel, and had few adherents. It was not until 1790, after the framing, but before the ratification, of the First Amendment, that the first state, Pennsylvania, took the then radical step of adopting the Zengerian principles which left the common law of seditious libel intact. The Pennsylvania provision was drafted by James Wilson, who (in the state convention that ratified the Constitution) declared, without challenge by any of the ardent proponents of a bill or rights: "what is meant by the liberty of the press is that there should be no antecedent restraint upon it; but that every author is responsible when he attacks the security or welfare of the government. ... " The mode of proceeding, Wilson added, should be by prosecution. The state constitutional provision of 1790 reflected this proposition, as did state trials before and after 1790.

Delaware and Kentucky followed Pennsylvania's lead in 1792, but elsewhere the *status quo* prevailed. In 1789 William Cushing and John Adams worried about whether the guarantee of a free press in Massachusetts ought to mean that truth was a good defense to a charge of criminal libel, but they agreed that false publications against the government were punishable. In 1791, when a Massachusetts editor was prosecuted for a criminal libel against a state official, the Supreme Judicial Court divided on the question of truth as a defense, but, like the Pennsylvania judges, agreed that the state constitutional guarantee of a free press was merely declaratory of the common law in simply prohibiting a licensing system.

The opinions of Jefferson, the acknowledged libertarian leader in America, and of Madison, the father of the Bill of Rights, are especially significant. Jefferson, in 1783, when proposing a new constitution for Virginia, exempted the press from prior restraints, but carefully provided for prosecution—a state criminal trial—in cases of false publication. In 1788, when urging Madison to support a bill of rights to the new federal Constitution, Jefferson made the same recommendation. Madison construed it in its most favorable light, observing: "The Exemption of the press from liability in every case for *true facts* is ... an innovation and as such ought to be well considered." On consideration, however, he did not add truth as a defense to the amendment that he offered on the press when proposing a bill of rights to Congress. Yet his phrasing appeared too broad for Jefferson who stated that he would be pleased if the press provision were altered to exclude freedom to publish "false facts ... affecting the peace of the confederacy with foreign nations," a clause whose suppressive possiblities can be imagined in the context of a foreign policy controversy such as the one on Jay's Treaty.

Madison fortunately ignored Jefferson's proposal but there is no evidence warranting the belief that he dissented from the universal American acceptance of the Blackstonian definition of a free press. At the Virginia ratifying convention in 1788 Madison remained silent when George Nicholas, one of his closest supporters, declared that the liberty of the press was secure because there was no power to license the press. Again Madison was silent when John Marshall rose to say that Congress would never make a law punishing men of different political opinions "unless it be such a case as much satisfy the people at large." In October 1788, when replying to Jefferson's argument that powers of the national government should be restricted by a bill of rights, Madison declared: "absolute restrictions in cases that are doubtful, or where emergencies may overrule them, ought to be avoided." When Madison proposed an amendment in Congress guaranteeing freedom of the press, he did not employ the emphatic language of the Virginia ratifying convention's recommendation that the press cannot be abridged "by any authority of the United States." The amendment, in the form in which Madison introduced it, omitted the important clause "by any authority of the United States," which would have covered the executive and the judiciary as well as Congress. The omitted clause would have prohibited the federal courts from exercising any common-law jurisdiction over criminal libels. As ratified, the First Amendment declared only that Congress should make no law abridging the freedom of speech or press.

What did the amendment mean at the time of its adoption? More complex than it appears, it meant several things, and it did not necessarily mean what it said or say what it was intended to mean. First, as is shown by an examination of the phrase "the freedom of the press," the amendment was merely an assurance that Congress was powerless to authorize restraints in advance of publication. On this point the evidence for the period from 1787 to 1797 is uniform and nonpartisan. For example, Hugh Williamson of North Carolina, a Federalist signatory of the Constitution, used freedom of the press in Blackstonian or common-law terms, as did Melancthon Smith of New York, an Antifederalist. Demanding a free press guarantee in the new federal Constitution, despite the fact that New York's constitution lacked that guarantee, Smith argued that freedom of the press was "fully defined and secured" in New York by "the common and statute law of England" and that a state constitutional provision was therefore unnecessary. No other definition of freedom of the press by anyone anywhere in America before 1798 has been discovered. Apparently there was, before that time, no dissent from the proposition that the punishment of a seditious libeler did not abridge the proper or lawful freedom of the press.

That freedom was so narrowly understood that its constitutional protection did not, per se, preclude the enactment of a sedition law. The security of the state against libelous attack was always and everywhere regarded as outweighing any social interest in completely unfettered discussion. The thought and experience of a lifetime, indeed the taught traditions of law and politics extending back many generations, supplied an unquestioned assumption that freedom of political discourse, however broadly conceived, stopped short of seditious libel.

The injunction of the First Amendment, nevertheless, was not intended to imply that a sedition act might be enacted without abridging "the freedom of the press." A sedition act would not be an abridgment, but that was not the point of the amendment. To understand its framers' intentions, the amendment should not be read with the focus on the meaning of "the freedom of the press." It should not, in other words, be read merely to mean that Congress could impose no prior restraints. It should be read, rather, with the stress on the opening clause: "Congress shall make no law. ... " The injunction was intended and understood to prohibit any congressional regulation of the press, whether by means of a licensing law, a tax, or a sedition act. The framers meant Congress to be totally without power to enact legislation respecting the press. They intended a federal system in which the central government could exercise only such powers as were specifically enumerated or were necessary and proper to carry out the enumerated ones. Thus James Wilson declared that, because the national government had "no power whatsoever" concerning the press, "no law ... can possibly be enacted" against it. Thus Hamilton, referring to the demand for a free press guarantee, asked, "why declare that things shall not be done which there is no power to do?" The illustrations may be multiplied fiftyfold. In other words, no matter what was meant or understood by freedom of speech and press, the national government, *even in the absence of the First Amendment*, could not make speech or press a legitimate subject of restrictive legislation. The amendment itself was superfluous. To quiet public apprehension, it offered an added assurance that Congress would be limited to the exercise of its delegated powers. The phrasing was intended to prohibit the possibility that those powers might be used to abridge speech and press. From this viewpoint, the Sedition Act of 1798 was unconstitutional.

That act was also unnecessary as a matter of law, however necessary as a matter of Federalist party policy. It was unnecessary because the federal courts exercised jurisdiction over nonstatutory or common-law crimes against the United States. At the Pennsylvania ratifying convention James Wilson declared that, while Congress could enact no law against the press, a libel against the United States might be prosecuted in the state where the offense was committed, under Article III, Section 2, of the Constitution which refers to the judicial power of the United States. A variety of common-law crimes against the United States were, in fact, tried in the federal courts during the first decade of their existence. There were, in the federal courts, even a couple of common-law indictments for the crime of seditious libel. All the early Supreme Court judges, including several who had been influential in the Philadelphia Convention, or in the state ratifying conventions, or in the Congress that passed the Judiciary Act of 1789, assumed the existence of a federal common law of crimes. Ironically, it was a case originating as a federal prosecution of Connecticut editors for seditious libels against President Jefferson that finally resulted in a ruling by a divided Supreme Court in 1812 that there was no federal common law of crimes.

There was unquestionably a federal common law of crimes at the time of the Sedition Act. Why then was the act passed if it was not legally needed? Even in England, where the criminal courts exercised an unquestioned jurisdiction over seditious libels, it was politically advisable in the 1790s to declare public policy in unmistakable terms by the enactment of sedition statutes. Legislation helped ensure effective enforcement of the law and stirred public opinion against its intended victims. The Federalists, hoping to control public opinion and elections, emulated the British model. A federal statute was expedient also because the Republicans insisted that libels against the United States might be tried only by the state courts.

This suggests another original purpose of the First Amendment. It has been said that a constitutional guarantee of a free press did not, in itself, preclude a sedition act, but that the prohibition on Congress did, though leaving the federal courts free to try cases of seditious libel. It now appears that the prohibition on Congress was motivated far less by a desire to give immunity to political expression than by a solicitude for states' rights and the federal principle. The primary purpose of the First Amendment was to reserve to the states an exclusive legislative authority in the field of speech and press.

This is clear enough from the countless states' rights arguments advanced by the Antifederalists during the ratification controversy, and it is explicit in the Republican arguments during the controversy over the Sedition Act. In the House debates on the bill, Albert Gallatin, Edward Livingston, John Nicholas, and Nathaniel Macon all agreed—to quote Macon on the subject of liberty of the press: "The States have complete power on the subject...." Jefferson's Kentucky Resolutions of 1798 expressed the same proposition, as did Madison's "Address of the General Assembly to the People of the Commonwealth of Virginia" in 1799.

It is possible that the opponents of the Sedition Act did not want or believe in state prosecutions, but argued for an exclusive state power over political libels because such an argument was tactically useful as a means of denying national jurisdiction, judicial or legislative. If so, how shall we explain the Republican prosecution in New York in 1803 against Harry Croswell, a Federalist editor, for a seditious libel against President Jefferson? How shall we explain the Blackstonian opinions of the Republican judges in that case? How shall we explain Jefferson's letter to the governor of Pennsylvania in the same year? The President, enclosing a newspaper piece that unmercifully attacked him, urged a "few prosecutions" because they "would have a wholesome effect in restoring the integrity of the presses." How shall we explain Jefferson's letter to Abigail Adams in 1804 in which he said: "While we deny that Congress have a right to controul the freedom of the press, we have ever asserted the right of the states, and their exclusive right to do so." And if exclusive state power was advanced not as a principle but as a tactic for denying federal jurisdiction, how shall we explain what Jefferson's opponents called his "reign of terror": the common-law indictments in 1806 in the United States Circuit Court in Connecticut against six men charged with seditious libel of the President? How shall we explain his letter of 1807 in which he said of the "prosecutions in the Court of the U.S." that they could "not lessen the useful freedom of the press," if truth were admitted as a defense?

Earlier, in 1798, the Federalists had also felt that the true freedom of the press would benefit if truth—their truth—were the measure of freedom. Their infamous Sedition Act, in the phrase of Gilbert and Sullivan, was the true embodiment of everything excellent. It was, that is, the very epitome of libertarian thought since the time of Zenger's case, proving that American libertarianism went from Zengerian principles to the Sedition Act in a single degeneration. Everything that the libertarians had ever demanded was, however, incorporated in the Sedition Act: a requirement that criminal intent be shown; the power of the jury to decide whether the accused's statement was libelous as a matter of law as well as of fact; and truth as a defense—an innovation not accepted in England until 1843. By every standard the Sedition Act was a great victory for libertarian principles of freedom of the press—except that libertarian standards abruptly changed because the Republicans immediately recognized a Pyrrhic victory.

The Sedition Act provoked them to develop a new libertarian theory. It began to emerge when Congressmen Albert Gallatin, John Nicholas, Nathaniel Macon, and Edward Livingston argued against the enactment of the sedition bill. It was further developed by defense counsel, most notably George Blake, in Sedition Act prosecutions. It reached its most reflective and systematic expression in tracts and books which are now unfortunately rare and little known even by historians. The main body of original Republican thought on the scope, meaning, and rationale of the First Amendment is to be found in George Hay's tract, *An Essay on the Liberty of the Press*; in Madison's *Report* on the Virginia Resolutions for the Virginia House of Delegates; in the book *A Treatise Concerning Political Enquiry, and the Liberty of the Press*, by Tunis Wortman of New York; in John Thomson's book *An Enquiry, Concerning the Liberty, and Licentiousness of the Press*; and in St. George Tucker's appendix to his edition of Blackstone's *Commentaries*, a most significant place for the repudiation of Blackstone on the liberty of the press. Of these works, Wortman's philosophical book is preeminent; it is an American masterpiece, the only equivalent on this side of the Atlantic to Milton and Mill.

The new libertarians abandoned the strait-jacketing doctrines of Blackstone and the common law, including the recent concept of a federal common law of crimes. They scornfully denounced the no prior restraints definition. Said Madison: "this idea of the freedom of the press can never be admitted to be the American idea of it" because a law inflicting penalties would have the same effect as a law authorizing a prior restraint. "It would seem a mockery to say that no laws shall be passed preventing publications from being made, but that laws might be passed for punishing them in case they should be made." As Hay put it, the "British definition" meant that a man might be jailed or even put to death for what he published provided that no notice was taken of him before he published. ...

Wholesale abandonment of the common law's limitations on the press was accompanied by a withering onslaught against the constrictions and subjectivity of Zengerian principles. The Sedition Act, Hay charged, "appears to be directed against falsehood and malice only; in fact ... there are many truths, important to society, which are not susceptible of that full, direct, and positive evidence, which alone can be exhibited before a court and a jury. If, argued Gallatin, the administration prosecuted a citizen for his opinion that the Sedition Act itself was unconstitutional, would not a jury, composed of the friends of that administration, find the opinion "ungrounded, or, in other words, false and scandalous, and its publication malicious? And by what kind of argument or evidence, in the present temper of parties, could the accused convince them that his opinions were true?" The truth of opinions, the new libertarians concluded, could not be proved. Allowing "truth" as a defense and thinking it to be a protection for freedom, Thomson declared, made as much sense as letting a jury decide which was "the most palatable food, agreeable drink, or beautiful color." A jury, he asserted, cannot give an impartial verdict in political trials. The result, agreed Madison, is that the "baleful tendency" of prosecutions for seditious libel "is little diminished by the privilege of giving in evidence the truth of the matter contained in political writings."

The renunciation of traditional concepts reached its climax in the assault on the very idea that there was a crime of seditious libel. That crime, Wortman concluded, could "never be reconciled to the genius and constitution of a Representative Commonwealth." He and the others constructed a new libertarianism that was genuinely radical because it broke sharply with the past and advocated an absolute freedom of political expression. One of their major tenets was that a free government cannot be criminally attacked by the opinions of its citizens. Hay, for example, insisted that freedom of the press, like chastity, was either "absolute" or did not exist. Abhorring the idea of verbal political crimes, he declared that a citizen should have a right to "say everything which his passions suggest; he may employ all his time, and all his talents, if he is wicked enough to do so, in speaking against the government matters that are false, scandalous and malicious." He should be "safe within the sanctuary of the press" even if he "condemns the principle of republican institutions.... If he censures the measures of our government, and every department and officer thereof, and ascribes the measures of the former, however salutary, and the conduct of the latter, however upright, to the basest motives; even if he ascribes to them measures and acts, which never had existence; thus violating at once, every principle of decency and truth."

In brief the new libertarians advocated that only "injurious conduct," as manifested by "overt acts" or deeds, rather than words, might be criminally redressable. They did not refine this proposition except to recognize that the law of libel should continue to protect private reputations against malicious falsehoods. They did not even recognize that under certain circumstances words may immediately and directly incite criminal acts.

This absolutist interpretation of the First Amendment was based on the now familiar but then novel and democratic theory that free government depends for its existence and security on freedom of political discourse. According to this theory, the scope of the amendment is determined by the nature of the government and its relationship to the people. Since the government is their servant, exists by their consent and for their benefit, and is constitutionally limited, responsible, and elective, it cannot, said Thomson, tell the citizen, "You shall not think this, or that upon certain subjects; or if you do, it is at your peril." The concept of seditiousness, it was argued, could exist only in a relationship based on inferiority, when people are subjects rather than sovereigns and their criticism implies contempt of their master. "In the United States," Madison declared, "the case is altogether different." Coercion or abridgment of unlimited political opinion, Wortman explained, would violate the very "principles of the social state," by which he meant a government of the people. Because such a government depended upon popular elections, all the new libertarians agreed that the widest possible latitude must be maintained to keep the electorate free, informed, and capable of making intelligent choices. The citizen's freedom of political expression had the same scope as the legislator's, and for the same reasons. That freedom might be dangerously abused, but the people would decide men and measures wisely if exposed to every opinion.

This brief summary of the new libertarianism scarcely does justice to its complexity, but suggests its boldness, originality, and democratic character. It developed, to be sure, as an expediency of self-defense on the part of a besieged political minority struggling to maintain its existence and right to function unfettered. But it established virtually all at once and in nearly perfect form a theory justifying the rights of individual expression and of opposition parties. That the Jeffersonians in power did not always adhere to their new principles does not diminish the enduring nobility and rightness of those principles. It proves only that the Jeffersonians set the highest standards of freedom for themselves and posterity to be measured against. Their legacy was the idea that there is an indispensable condition for the development of free men in a free society: the state must be bitted and bridled by a bill of rights which is to be construed in the most generous terms and whose protections are not to be the playthings of momentary majorities.

✣ *F U R T H E R   R E A D I N G*

Amar, Akhil Reed. *The Bill of Rights: Creation and Reconstruction* (1998).

Anderson, David A. "The Origins of the Press Clause," *UCLA Law Review*, 30 (1983): 455–540.

Bailyn, Bernard and John B. Hench, eds. *The Press and the American Revolution* (1980).

Berns, Walter. *The First Amendment and the Future of American Democracy* (1976).

Dry, Murray. "The Anti-Federalists and the Constitution," in Robert L. Utley Jr., ed., *Principles of the Constitutional Order: The Ratification Debates* (1989): 68–84.

Foner, Eric. *The Story of American Freedom* (1998).

Hoffman, Ronald and Peter J. Albert, eds. *The Bill of Rights: Government Proscribed* (1997).

Hunt, Lynn. *Inventing Human Rights: A History* (2007).

Hutson, James H. "Country, Court and Constitution: Antifederalism and the Historians," *William and Mary Quarterly*, 38 (1981): 337–368.

Kelly, Alfred H. "Constitutional Liberty and the Law of Libel," *American Historical Review*, 74 (1968): 429–452.

Levy, Leonard W. "Did the Zenger Case Really Matter?" *William and Mary Quarterly*, 3rd Ser., 17 (1960): 35–50.

——. *Emergence of a Free Press* (1985).

——. *Origins of the Bill of Rights* (1999).

Main, Jackson Turner. *The Antifederalists: Critics of the Constitution 1781–1788* (1961).

Miller, John C. *Crisis in Freedom: The Alien and Sedition Acts* (1952).

Rosenberg, Norman. *Protecting the Best Men: An Interpretive History of the Law of Libel* (1986).

Rutland, Robert A. *The Birth of the Bill of Rights, 1776–1791* (1983).

Schwartz, Bernard, ed. *The Roots of the Bill of Rights*, vol. 1 (1980).

Shapiro, Martin. *Freedom of Speech: The Supreme Court and Judicial Review* (1966).

Storing, Herbert J., ed. *The Complete Anti-Federalist*, 7 vols. (1981).

CHAPTER
4

The Departmental Theory and the Establishment of Judicial Review

Who decides what the Constitution means? That important question has bedeviled the republic from its earliest days, as the Constitution itself provides no clear answer. The first major constitutional controversy in the nation's history involved whether Congress had the power to charter a national bank, a private corporation that would assist the nation in developing a more robust economy. Because the Constitution nowhere specifically provided that Congress possessed such a power, the nation's leaders debated whether such a measure was constitutional. When Congress passed a bill chartering a bank in 1791, President George Washington sought advice about its constitutionality from two members of his Cabinet, Secretary of State Thomas Jefferson and Secretary of the Treasury Alexander Hamilton. Washington ended up accepting Hamilton's arguments that the implied powers of Congress permitted such legislation, and he signed the bill into law. Congress and the president agreed, there-fore, that the Constitution permitted Congress to charter a bank.

Although the Congress and the president implicitly claimed the power to define the scope of the national government's powers under the Constitution—the Congress by passing the bill and the president by signing it—the status of the judiciary as an interpreter of the Constitution remained more ambiguous. Precedent for the judicial review of legislative acts existed in England from the early seventeenth century, and many of the framers seemed to support the idea that federal courts could declare acts of Congress null and void if they were repugnant to the Constitution. State courts, moreover, began exercising such a power over state legislative acts during the 1780s, and the U.S. Supreme Court similarly reviewed a few congressional enactments during the following decade. Still, the Supreme Court during the 1790s was a weak institution that lacked effective leadership. Not until Chief Justice John Marshall in 1803 asserted the Supreme Court's power of judicial review, a practice nowhere specifically provided for in the Constitution, did the Court emerge as a major force in the American constitutional order.

110

As with the debates over American foreign policy and the rights of free expression in the early republic, Marshall's actions must be understood in the context of an intense partisan divide between Federalists and Jeffersonian Republicans. Led by Washington, Hamilton, and John Adams, Federalists held control over the new national government during the first decade of its existence. However, when Thomas Jefferson won the presidency and the Republicans took control of Congress in the election of 1800, the United States experienced the political equivalent of an earthquake. Between the time of the election in November and the swearing in of the new president and Congress the following March, the lame-duck Federalist Congress enacted the Judiciary Act of 1801. A combination of reform and partisanship, the act created a new tier of federal judges. At the time, justices of the Supreme Court "rode the circuit," meaning that they traveled hundreds of miles (under primitive conditions) to hear cases as members of federal circuit courts. By providing for a new group of federal circuit judges to assume this task, Congress in effect gave the outgoing President Adams a chance to appoint 16 new Federalist judges. Because all federal judges serve "during good behavior," meaning for life unless impeached, Federalists saw the act as a way to preserve their influence in the national government. Predictably, Republicans cried foul and labeled Adams' appointees "midnight judges," since many of them were literally appointed during Adams' last hours in office. In 1802, the Republican-dominated Congress responded by repealing the judiciary act that had been passed the previous year, and in 1804 the radical wing of the Republican Party led the charge to impeach Supreme Court Justice Samuel Chase, an ardent and outspoken Federalist. (He was acquitted and remained on the bench for several more years.)

Marshall, appointed by Adams in early 1801, vigorously championed judicial review during his tenure on the Supreme Court. One of the most famous cases in American history, Marbury v. Madison, involved a midnight appointee, Federalist William Marbury, who sued to receive his undelivered commission for his post as justice of the peace in the District of Columbia. Although he denied Marbury relief, Chief Justice Marshall claimed that it was "emphatically the province of the judicial department to say what the law is." Rarely did the nineteenth-century Supreme Court declare acts of Congress unconstitutional (Marbury was the only instance in which the Marshall Court did so), and the exercise of judicial review usually involved rendering a state legislative enactment unconstitutional. Whether involving an act of Congress or not, federal judicial review raised significant questions about the role of the courts. Should unelected judges have the authority to overturn popularly elected legislatures? The matter of federalism (the relationship between the national and state governments) complicated the issue further. Did federal judges have power to review state legislative enactments or state judicial decisions? Finally, did the power of judicial review imply judicial supremacy?

During the first several decades of the history of the republic, the departmental theory of review held sway. According to this theory, the political branches had responsibility for political-constitutional controversies within their spheres, and the judicial branch assumed the role of settling legal disputes. From this perspective, judicial review was a negative, defensive practice intended to protect the courts from legislative and executive encroachments. Marshall, most historians argue, did not claim that the Supreme Court held a superior position relative to the other departments of government when it came to constitutional interpretation. Instead, they contend, Marshall simply attempted to establish the rightful place of the judiciary among the other two co-equal branches of government. Still, the exercise of judicial *review by Marshall, as well as his successor, Roger B. Taney, played a significant role in resolving disputes relating to state–federal relations, economic development, and eventually slavery. In deciding cases with such large policy implications—often in grandiose constitutional language—the early-nineteenth-century Supreme Court contributed to the gradual waning of the departmental theory and the rise of the controversial notion of judicial supremacy.*

✣ *D O C U M E N T S*

The idea of judicial review had its American origins in the late eighteenth century. Alexander Hamilton in *Federalist 78* (Document 1) argued that the power of the judiciary flowed from its apolitical character and its independence of the political branches. Because it possessed neither the power of the sword nor the purse, he claimed, the judiciary was the "least dangerous branch." At around the time Hamilton was writing, a number of state courts put forth some version of judicial review. Spencer Roane, a leading Virginia jurist, championed the practice in *Kamper v. Hawkins* (Document 2). *Kamper* involved a Virginia law that transferred powers from constitutionally created courts to legislatively created tribunals, an act that Roane and his colleagues believed violated the state's constitution and the independence of the judiciary.

Republican John Breckinridge's speech on the repeal of the Judiciary Act of 1801 (Document 3) shows the deep partisan struggle over the federal courts in the early republic and provides the context for understanding *Marbury v. Madison* (Document 4). Chief Justice Marshall, like Roane, believed deeply in the independence of the judiciary. Still, Marshall realized that the political environment, as well as the Court's precarious position, would not allow him to push too far. When Federalists challenged the constitutionality of the Republicans' repeal of the Judiciary Act of 1801, the Court upheld the validity of the repeal act on narrow grounds. In *Marbury*, Marshall also treaded cautiously. Writing for a unanimous Court, the chief justice argued forcefully that the Federalist appointee Marbury had a right to his commission and to his office as justice of the peace. At the same time, realizing that President Jefferson would ignore such a ruling, Marshall denied Marbury relief, by claiming that the Judiciary Act of 1789 had unconstitutionally expanded the jurisdiction of the Court. By conferring upon the Court the power to issue writs of mandamus in the 1789 Act, Marshall ruled, the Congress had unconstitutionally expanded the Court's authority. Thus, by holding that Congress lacked the power to pass such a law, Marshall claimed the power to declare acts of Congress unconstitutional.

In the final two cases included here, *Martin v. Hunter's Lessee* (Document 5) and *McCulloch v. Maryland* (Document 6), the Marshall Court overruled a state judicial decision and overturned a state legislative enactment, respectively. In *Martin*, a unanimous Court held that Virginia had to adhere to a previous ruling of the Court invalidating a Virginia land confiscation act, notwithstanding a defiant ruling to the contrary by that state's highest court. At issue was Section 25 of the Judiciary Act of 1789, which had allowed for the removal of certain cases from state courts to federal courts. Because of a conflict of interest, Marshall recused himself from *Martin*, and Justice Joseph Story wrote the opinion. In *McCulloch*, Marshall's unanimous decision invalidated a state law that effectively prevented the branch of the Second Bank of the United States in Maryland from doing business. (The charter of the First Bank of the United States had expired in 1811, and in 1816 Congress had established a new bank.) Both *Martin* and

McCulloch directly challenged the theory of state sovereignty by emphasizing the idea that the people, rather than states, had ratified the Constitution.

Despite the success of the Marshall Court in advancing judicial review, the departmental theory persisted. Nearly four decades after Washington had signed the first bill chartering a bank and 13 years after *McCulloch*, in 1832 President Andrew Jackson vetoed a bill re-chartering the bank. In his veto message (Document 7), Jackson refuted the Court's arguments in *McCulloch* and asserted the president's authority to decide what the Constitution means. Jackson's veto remains a classic statement of the departmental theory.

✠ D O C U M E N T   1

Federalist Alexander Hamilton Defends Judicial Review, 1788

… In unfolding the defects of the existing Confederation, the utility and necessity of a federal judicature have been clearly pointed out. It is the less necessary to recapitulate the considerations there urged as the propriety of the institution in the abstract is not disputed; the only questions which have been raised being relative to the manner of constituting it, and to its extent. To these points, therefore, our observations shall be confined.

The manner of constituting it seems to embrace these several objects: 1st. The mode of appointing the judges. 2nd. The tenure by which they are to hold their places. 3rd. The partition of the judiciary authority between different courts and their relations to each other.

First. As to the mode of appointing the judges: this is the same with that of appointing the officers of the Union in general and has been so fully discussed in the two last numbers that nothing can be said here which would not be useless repetition.

Second. As to the tenure by which the judges are to hold their places: this chiefly concerns their duration in office, the provisions for their support, the precautions for their responsibility.

According to the plan of the convention, all judges who may be appointed by the United States are to hold their offices *during good behavior;* which is conformable to the most approved of the State constitutions, and among the rest, to that of this State. Its propriety having been drawn into question by the adversaries of that plan is no light symptom of the rage for objection which disorders their imaginations and judgments. The standard of good behavior for the continuance in office of the judicial magistracy is certainly one of the most valuable of the modern improvements in the practice of government. In a monarchy it is an excellent barrier to the despotism of the prince; in a republic it is a no less excellent barrier to the encroachments and oppressions of the representative body. And it is the best expedient which can be devised in any government to secure a steady, upright, and impartial administration of the laws.

Whoever attentively considers the different departments of power must perceive that, in a government in which they are separated from each other, the judiciary, from the nature of its functions, will always be the least dangerous to the political rights of the Constitution; because it will be least in a capacity to annoy or injure them. The executive not only dispenses the honors but holds the sword of the community. The legislature not only commands the purse but prescribes the rules by which the duties and rights of every citizen are to be regulated. The judiciary, on the contrary, has no influence over either the sword or the purse; no direction either of the strength or of the wealth of the society, and can take no active resolution whatever. It may truly be said to have neither FORCE nor WILL but merely judgment; and must ultimately depend upon the aid of the executive arm even for the efficacy of its judgments.

This simple view of the matter suggests several important consequences. It proves incontestably that the judiciary is beyond comparison the weakest of the three departments of power; that it can never attack with success either of the other two; and that all possible care is requisite to enable it to defend itself against their attacks. It equally proves that though individual oppression may now and then proceed from the courts of justice, the general liberty of the people can never be endangered from that quarter; I mean so long as the judiciary remains truly distinct from both the legislature and the executive. For I agree that "there is no liberty if the power of judging be not separated from the legislative and executive powers." And it proves, in the last place, that as liberty can have nothing to fear from the judiciary alone, but would have everything to fear from its union with either of the other departments; that as all the effects of such a union must ensue from a dependence of the former on the latter, not with standing a nominal and apparent separation; that as, from the natural feebleness of the judiciary, it is in continual jeopardy of being overpowered, awed, or influenced by its co-ordinate branches; and that as nothing can contribute so much to its firmness and independence as permanency in office, this quality may therefore be justly regarded as an indispensable ingredient in its constitution, and, in a great measure, as the citadel of the public justice and the public security.

The complete independence of the courts of justice is peculiarly essential in a limited Constitution. By a limited Constitution, I understand one which contains certain specified exceptions to the legislative authority; such, for instance, as that it shall pass no bills of attainder, no *ex post facto* laws, and the like. Limitations of this kind can be preserved in practice no other way than through the medium of courts of justice, whose duty it must be to declare all acts contrary to the manifest tenor of the Constitution void. Without this, all the reservations of particular rights or privileges would amount to nothing.

Some perplexity respecting the rights of the courts to pronounce legislative acts void, because contrary to the Constitution, has arisen from an imagination that the doctrine would imply a superiority of the judiciary to the legislative power. It is urged that the authority which can declare the acts of another void must necessarily be superior to the one whose acts may be declared void. As this doctrine is of great importance in all the American constitutions, a brief discussion of the grounds on which it rests cannot be unacceptable.

There is no position which depends on clearer principles than that every act of a delegated authority, contrary to the tenor of the commission under which it is exercised, is void. No legislative act, therefore, contrary to the Constitution, can be valid. To deny this would be to affirm that the deputy is greater than his principal; that the servant is above his master; that the representatives of the people are superior to the people themselves; that men acting by virtue of powers may do not only what their powers do not authorize, but what they forbid.

If it be said that the legislative body are themselves the constitutional judges of their own powers and that the construction they put upon them is conclusive upon the other departments it may be answered that this cannot be the natural presumption where it is not be collected from any particular provisions in the Constitution. It is not otherwise to be supposed that the Constitution could intend to enable the representatives of the people to substitute their *will* to that of their constituents. It is far more rational to suppose that the courts were designed to be an intermediate body between the people and the legislature in order, among other things, to keep the latter within the limits assigned to their authority. The interpretation of the laws is the proper and peculiar province of the courts. A constitution is, in fact, and must be regarded by the judges as, a fundamental law. It therefore belongs to them to ascertain its meaning as well as the meaning of any particular act proceeding from the legislative body. If there should happen to be an irreconcilable variance between the two, that which has the superior obligation and validity ought, of course, to be preferred; or, in other words, the Constitution ought to be preferred to the statute, the intention of the people to the intention of their agents.

Nor does this conclusion by any means suppose a superiority of the judicial to the legislative power. It only supposes that the power of the people is superior to both, and that where the will of the legislature, declared in its statutes, stands in opposition to that of the people, declared in the Constitution, the judges ought to be governed by the latter rather than the former. They ought to regulate their decisions by the fundamental laws rather than by those which are not fundamental. ...

If, then, the courts of justice are to be considered as the bulwarks of a limited Constitution against legislative encroachments, this consideration will afford a strong argument for the permanent tenure of judicial offices, since nothing will contribute so much as this to that independent spirit in the judges which must be essential to the faithful performance of so arduous a duty.

This independence of the judges is equally requisite to guard the Constitution and the rights of individuals from the effects of those ill humors which the arts of designing men, or the influence of particular conjunctures, sometimes disseminate among the people themselves, and which, though they speedily give place to better information, and more deliberate reflection, have a tendency, in the meantime, to occasion dangerous innovations in the government, and serious oppressions of the minor party in the community. Though I trust the friends of the proposed Constitution will never concur with its enemies in questioning that fundamental principle of republican government which admits the right of the people to alter or abolish the established Constitution whenever they find it inconsistent with their happiness; yet it is not to be inferred from this principle that the representatives of the people, whenever a momentary inclination happens to lay hold of a majority of their constituents incompatible with the provisions in the existing Constitution would, on that account, be justifiable in a violation of those provisions; or that the courts would be under a greater obligation to connive at infractions in this shape than when they had proceeded wholly from the cabals of the representative body. Until the people have, by some solemn and authoritative act, annulled or changed the established form, it is binding upon themselves collectively, as well as individually; and no presumption, or even knowledge of their sentiments, can warrant their representatives in a departure from it prior to such an act. But it is easy to see that it would require an uncommon portion of fortitude in the judges to do their duty as faithful guardians of the Constitution, where legislative invasions of it had been instigated by the major voice of the community. . . .

That inflexible and uniform adherence to the rights of the Constitution, and of individuals, which we perceive to be indispensable in the courts of justice, can certainly not be expected from judges who hold their offices by a temporary commission. Periodical appointments, however regulated, or by whomsoever made, would, in some way or other, be fatal to their necessary independence. If the power of making them was committed either to the executive or legislature there would be danger of an improper complaisance to the branch which possessed it; if to both, there would be an unwillingness to hazard the displeasure of either; if to the people, or to persons chosen by them for the special purpose, there would be too great a disposition to consult popularity to justify a reliance that nothing that nothing would be consulted but the Constitution and the laws. . . .

✣ *D O C U M E N T   2*

Kamper v. Hawkins, 1793
Virginia General Court

Judge Roane.

This great question was adjourned by me from the district court of Dumfries. I thought it necessary to obtain the opinion of this court, for the government of the several district courts, who might otherwise have differed in their construction of the clause in question, and the administration of the law in this instance been consequently partial.

My opinion then was, upon a short consideration, that the district courts ought to execute this law; for I doubted how far the judiciary were authorized to refuse to execute a law, on the ground of its being against the spirit of the Constitution.

My opinion, on more mature consideration, is changed in this respect, and I now think that the judiciary may and ought not only to refuse to execute a law expressly repugnant to the Constitution; but also one which is, by a plain and natural construction, in opposition to the fundamental principles thereof.

I consider the people of this country as the only sovereign power.—I consider the legislature as not sovereign but subordinate; they are subordinate to the great constitutional charter, which the people have established as a fundamental law, and which alone has given existence and authority to the legislature. I consider that at the time of the adoption of our present Constitution, the British government was at an end in Virginia: it was at an end, because among many other weighty reasons very emphatically expressed in the first section of our Constitution, "George the Third, heretofore entrusted with the exercise of the kingly office in this colony, had abandoned the helm of government, and declared us out of his allegiance and protection."

The people were therefore at that period, they were at the period of the election of the Convention, which formed the Constitution, absolved from the former kingly government, and free, as in a state of nature, to establish a government for themselves. But admitting for a moment that the old government was not then at an end, I assert that the people have a right by a convention, or otherwise, to change the existing government, whilst such existing government is in actual operation, for the ordinary purposes thereof. The example of all America in the adoption of the federal government, and that of several of the states in changing their state constitutions in this temperate and peaceable manner, undeniably proves my position. The people of Virginia, therefore, if the old government should not be considered as then atanend, permitted it to proceed, and by a convention chosen by themselves, with full powers, for they were not restrained, established then a Constitution.

This convention was not chosen under the sanction of the former government; it was not limited in its powers by it, if indeed it existed, but may be considered as a spontaneous assemblage of the people of Virginia, under a recommendation of a former convention, to consult for the good of themselves, and their posterity. They established a bill of rights, purporting to appertain to their posterity, and a constitution evidently designed to be permanent. This constitution is sanctioned by the consent and acquiescence of the people for seventeen years; and it is admitted by the almost universal opinion of the people, by the repeated adjudications of the courts of this commonwealth, and by very many declarations of the legislature itself, to be of superior authority to any opposing act of the legislature. ...

But if the legislature may infringe this Constitution, it is no longer fixed; it is not this year what it was the last; and the liberties of the people are wholly at the mercy of the legislature.

A very important question now occurs, viz. whose province it is to decide in such cases. It is the province of the judiciary to expound the laws, and to adjudge cases which may be brought before them—the judiciary may clearly say, that a subsequent statue has not changed a former for want of sufficient words, though it was perhaps intended it should do so. It may say too, that an act of assembly has not changed the Constitution, though its words are expressly to that effect; because a legislature must have both the power and the will (as evidenced by words) to change the law, and it is conceived, for the reasons above mentioned, that the legislature have not power to change the fundamental laws. In expounding laws, the judiciary considers *every* law which relates to the subject: would you have them to shut their eyes against that law which is of the highest authority of any, or against a part of that law, which either by its words or by its spirit, denies to any but the people the power to change it? ...

From the above premises I conclude that the judiciary may and ought to adjudge a law unconstitutional and void, if it be plainly repugnant to the letter of the Constitution, or the fundamental principles thereof. By fundamental principles I understand, those great principles growing out of the Constitution, by the aid of which, in dubious cases, the Constitution may be explained and preserved inviolate; those landmarks, which it may be necessary to resort to, on account of the impossibility to foresee or provide for cases within the spirit, but without the letter of the Constitution.

To come now more immediately to the question before the court; can those who are appointed judges in chancery, by an act of assembly, without ballot, and

without commission during good behaviour, constitutionally exercise that office?—
The fourteenth article of the Virginia Constitution recites "that the people have a right
to uniform government; and therefore, that no government separate from, or independent of, the government of VIRGINIA, ought to be erected or established within the
limits thereof." Here then is a general principle pervading all the courts mentioned
in the Constitution—from which, without an exception, we ought not to depart. If
those may be judges who are not appointed by joint ballot, but by an act of assembly, the senate have in that instance more power than the Constitution intended; for
they control the other branch, by their negative upon the law, whereas if they mixed
with that branch in a joint ballot, a plurality of votes of senators and delegates would
decide.

If there can be judges in chancery who have no commission during good behaviour, their tenure of office is absolutely at the will of the legislature, and they consequently are not independent. The people of Virginia intended that the judiciary should
be independent of the other departments: they are to judge where the legislature is
a party, and therefore should be independent of it, otherwise they might judge cor-
ruptly, in order to please the legislature, and be consequently continued in office.
It is an acknowledged principle in all countries, that no man shall be judge in his
own cause; but it is nearly the same thing, where the tribunal of justice is under the
influence of a party. If the legislature can transfer from constitutional to legislative
courts, all judicial powers, these dependent tribunals being the creatures of the legislature itself, will not dare to oppose an unconstitutional law, and the principle I set
out upon, viz. that such laws ought to be opposed, would become a dead letter, or in
other words, this would pave the way to an uncontrolled power in the legislature. The
constitution requires the concurrence of the legislature to appoint, and the executive
to commission a judge:—but an appointment by act of assembly, will invest with
this high power one who has not the sanction of the executive; and will throw a new
office upon a man, without the liberty of declining such appointment, if he thinks
proper. For these reasons, and others which it would be tedious to enumerate, I am
of opinion, that the clause in question, is repugnant to the fundamental principles of
the Constitution, in as much as the judges of the general court have not been balloted
for and commissioned as judges in chancery, pursuant to the fourteenth article of the
Constitution.

✢ *D O C U M E N T   3*

Republican John Breckenridge Advocates the Repeal of the Federalists' Judiciary Act, 1802

Friday, January 8.

Agreeably to the order of the day, the Senate proceeded to the consideration of
the motion made on the 6th instant, to wit:

"That the act of Congress passed on the 13th day of February, 1801, entitled
'An act to provide for the more convenient organization of the Courts of the United
States,' ought to be repealed."

Mr. BRECKENRIDGE then rose and addressed the President, as follows:

It will be expected of me, I presume, sir, as I introduced the resolution now under consideration, to assign my reasons for wishing a repeal of this law. This I shall do; and shall endeavor to show.

1. That the law is unnecessary and improper, and was so at its passage; and
2. That the courts and judges created by it, can and ought to be abolished.

1st. That the act under consideration was unnecessary and improper, is, to my mind, no difficult task to prove. No increase of courts or judges could be necessary or justifiable, unless the existing courts and judges were incompetent to the prompt and proper discharge of the duties consigned to them. To hold out a show of litigation, when in fact little exists, must be impolitic; and to multiply expensive systems, and create hosts of expensive officers, without having experienced an actual necessity for them, must be a wanton waste of the public treasure.

The document before us shows that, at the passage of this act, the existing courts, not only from their number, but from the suits depending before them, were fully competent to a speedy decision of those suits. It shows, that on the 15th day of June last, there were depending in all the circuit courts, (that of Maryland only excepted, whose docket we have not been furnished with,) one thousand five hundred and thirty-nine suits. It shows that eight thousand two hundred and seventy-six suits of every description have come before those courts, in ten years and upwards. From this it appears, that the annual average amount of suits has been about eight hundred.

But sundry contingent things have conspired to swell the circuit court dockets. In Maryland, Virginia, and in all the Southern and Southwestern States, a great number of suits have been brought by British creditors; this species of controversy is nearly at an end.

In Pennsylvania, the docket has been swelled by prosecutions in consequence of the Western insurrection, by the disturbances in Bucks and Northampton counties; and by the sedition act. These I find amount in that State to two hundred and forty suits.

In Kentucky, non-resident land claimants have gone into the federal court from a temporary convenience: because, until within a year or two past, there existed no court of general jurisdiction co-extensive with the whole State. I find, too, that of the six hundred and odd suits which have been commenced there, one hundred and ninety-six of them have been prosecutions under the laws of the United States.

In most of the States there have been prosecutions under the sedition act. This source of litigation is. I trust, forever dried up. And, lastly, in *all* the States a number of suits have arisen under the excise law; which source of controversy will, I hope, before this session terminates, be also dried up.

But this same document discloses another important fact; which is, that notwithstanding all these untoward and temporary sources of federal adjudication, the suits in those courts are *decreasing*; for, from the dockets exhibited (except Kentucky and Tennessee, whose suits are summed up in the aggregate) it appears, that in 1799 there were one thousand two hundred and seventy-four, and in 1800 there were six hundred and eighty-seven suits commenced; showing a decrease of five hundred and eighty-seven suits.

Could it be necessary then to *increase* courts when suits were *decreasing*? Could it be necessary to multiply judges, when their duties were diminishing? And will I not be justified, therefore, in affirming, that the law was unnecessary, and that Congress acted under a mistaken impression when they multiplied courts and judges at a time when litigation was actually decreasing?

But, sir, the decrease of business goes a small way in fixing my opinion on this subject. I am inclined to think, that so far from there having been a necessity at this time for an increase of courts and judges, that the time never will arrive when America will stand in need of thirty-eight federal judges. Look, sir, at your Constitution, and see the judicial power there consigned to federal courts, and seriously ask yourself, can there be fairly extracted from those powers subjects of litigation sufficient for six supreme and thirty-two inferior court judges? To me it appears impossible.

The judicial powers given to the federal courts were never intended by the Constitution to embrace, exclusively, subjects of litigation, which could, with propriety, be left with the State courts. Their jurisdiction was intended principally to extend to great national and foreign concerns. Except cases arising under the laws of the United States. I do not at present recollect but three or four kinds in which their power extends to subjects of litigation, in which private persons only are concerned. And can it be possible, that with a jurisdiction embracing so small a portion of private litigation, in a great part of which the State courts might, and ought to participate, that we can stand in need of thirty-eight judges, and expend in judiciary regulations the annual sum of $137,000? ...

I will now inquire into the power of Congress to put down these additional courts and judges.

First, as to the courts, Congress are empowered by the Constitution "from time to time, to ordain and establish inferior courts." The act now under consideration, is a legislative construction of this clause in the Constitution, that Congress may abolish as well as create these judicial officers; because it does expressly, in the twenty-seventh section of the act, abolish the then existing inferior courts, for the purpose of making way for the present. This construction, I contend, is correct; but it is equally pertinent to my object, whether it be or be not. If it be correct, then the present inferior courts may be abolished as constitutionally as the last; if it be not, then the law for abolishing the former courts, and establishing the present, was unconstitutional, and consequently repealable.

But independent of this legislative construction, on which I do not found my opinion, nor mean to rely my argument, there is little doubt indeed, in my mind, as to the power of Congress on this law. The first section of the third article vests the judicial power of the United States in one Supreme Court and such inferior courts as Congress may, from time to time, ordain and establish. By this clause Congress *may*, from time to time, establish inferior courts; but it is clearly a discretionary power, and they *may not* establish them. The language of the Constitution is very different when regulations are not left discretional. For example, "The trial," says the Constitution, "of all crimes (except in cases of impeachment) shall be by jury: representatives and direct taxes shall be apportioned according to numbers. All revenue bills shall originate in the House of Representatives," &c. It would, therefore, in my opinion, be a perversion, not only of language, but of intellect, to say, that although Congress may, from time to time, establish inferior courts, yet, when established, that they shall not be abolished by a subsequent Congress possessing equal powers. It would be a paradox in legislation.

2d. As to the judges. The Judiciary department is so constructed as to be sufficiently secured against the improper influence of either the Executive or Legislative departments. The courts are organized and established by the Legislature, and the Executive creates the judges. Being thus organized, the Constitution affords the proper checks to secure their honesty and independence in office. It declares they shall not be removed from office during good behaviour; nor their salaries diminished during their continuance in office. From this it results, that a judge, after his appointment, is totally out of the power of the President, and his salary secured against legislative diminution, during his continuance in office. The first of these checks, which protects a judge in his office during good behaviour, applies to the President only who would otherwise have possessed the power of removing him, like all other officers, at pleasure; and the other check, forbidding a diminution of their salaries, applies to the Legislature only. They are two separate and distinct checks, furnished by the Constitution against two distinct departments of the Government; and they are the only ones which are or ought to have been furnished on the subject.

But because the Constitution declares that a judge shall hold his office during good behaviour, can it be tortured to mean, that he shall hold his office after it is abolished? Can it mean, that his tenure should be limited by behaving well in an office which did not exist? Can it mean that an office may exist, although its duties are extinct? Can it mean, in short, that the shadow, to wit, the judge, can remain, when the substance, to wit, the office, is removed? It must have intended all these absurdities, or it must admit a construction which will avoid them.

The construction obviously is, that a judge should hold an existing office, so long as he did his duty in that office; and not that he should hold an office that did not exist, and perform duties not provided by law. ...

I conceive, sir, that the tenure by which a judge holds his office, is evidently bottomed on the idea of securing his honesty and independence, whilst exercising his office. The idea was introduced in England, to counteract the influence of the Crown over the judges; but if the construction now contended for shall prevail, we shall, in our mistaken imitation of this our favorite prototype, butstrip them, by establishing what they have not, a judicial bligarchy; for there their judges are removable by a joint vote of Lords and Commons. Here ours are not removable, except for malfeasance in office; which malfeasance could not be committed, as they would have no office.

Upon the whole, sir, as all courts under any free Government must be created with an eye to the administration of justice only; and not with any regard to the advancement or emolument of individual men; as we have undeniable evidence before us that the creation of the courts now under consideration was totally unnecessary; and as no Government can, I apprehend, seriously deny that this Legislature has a right to repeal a law enacted by a preceding one, we will, in any event, discharge our duty by repealing this law; and thereby doing all in our power to correct the evil. If the judges are entitled to their salaries under the Constitution, our repeal will not affect them; and they will, no doubt, resort to their proper remedy. For where there is a Constitutional right, there must be a Constitutional remedy.

✣ *D O C U M E N T   4*

Marbury v. Madison, 1803

... **Marshall, C. J.** ... The peculiar delicacy of this case, the novelty of some of its circumstances, and the real difficulty attending the points which occur in it, require a complete exposition of the principles on which the opinion to be given by the court is founded. ...

In the order in which the court has viewed this subject, the following questions have been considered and decided:

1st.   Has the applicant a right to the commission he demands?

2dly.   If he has a right, and that right has been violated, do the laws of his country afford him a remedy?

3rdly.   If they do afford him a remedy, is it a *mandamus* issuing from this court? ...

The first object of enquiry is,

Has the applicant a right to the commission he demands? ...

It is therefore decidedly the opinion of the court, that when a commission has been signed by the President, the appointment is made; and that the commission is complete, when the seal of the United States has been affixed to it by the secretary of state. ...

Mr. Marbury, then, since his commission was signed by the President, and sealed by the secretary of state, was appointed; and as the law creating the office, gave the officer a right to hold for five years, independent of the executive, the appointment was not revocable; but vested in the officer legal rights, which are protected by the laws of his country.

To withhold his commission, therefore, is an act deemed by the court not warranted by law, but violative of a vested legal right.

2. This brings us to the second enquiry: which is,

If he has a right, and that right has been violated, do the laws of his country afford him a remedy? ...

The government of the United States has been emphatically termed a government of laws, and not of men. It will certainly cease to deserve this high appellation, if the laws furnish no remedy for the violation of a vested legal right.

If this obloquy is to be cast on the jurisprudence of our country, it must arise from the peculiar character of the case. ...

By the constitution of the United States, the President is invested with certain important political powers, in the exercise of which he is to use his own discretion, and is accountable only to his country in his political character, and to his own conscience. To aid him in the performance of these duties, he is authorized to appoint certain officers, who act by his authority and in conformity with his orders.

In such cases, their acts are his acts; and whatever opinion may be entertained of the manner in which executive discretion may be used, still there exists, and can exist, no power to control that discretion. The subjects are political. ...

The conclusion from this reasoning is, that where the heads of departments are the political or confidential agents of the executive, merely to execute the will of the President, or rather to act in cases in which the executive possesses a constitutional or legal discretion, nothing can be more perfectly clear than that their acts are only politically examinable. But where a specific duty is assigned by law, and individual rights depend upon the performance of that duty, it seems equally clear that the individual who considers himself injured, has a right to resort to the laws of his country for a remedy....

It is, then, the opinion of the Court,

1st.   That by signing the commission of Mr. Marbury, the president of the United States appointed him a justice of peace for the county of Washington in the District of Columbia; and that the seal of the United States, affixed thereto by the secretary of state, is conclusive testimony of the verity of the signature, and of the completion of the appointment; and that the appointment conferred on him a legal right to the office for the space of five years.

2ndly.   That, having this legal title to the office, he has a consequent right to the commission; a refusal to deliver which, is a plain violation of that right, for which the laws of his country afford him a remedy.

It remains to be enquired whether,

3rdly.   He is entitled to the remedy for which he applies. This depends on

1st.   The nature of the writ applied for, and

2dly.   The power of this court....

This, then, is a plain case for a mandamus, either to deliver the commission, or a copy of it from the record; and it only remains to be enquired,

Whether it can issue from this court.

The act to establish the judicial courts of the United States authorizes the supreme court "to issue writs of mandamus, in cases warranted by the principles and usages of law, to any courts appointed, or persons holding office, under the authority of the United States."

The secretary of state, being a person holding an office under the authority of the United States is precisely within the letter of the description; and if this court is not authorized to issue a writ of mandamus to such an officer, it must be because the law is unconstitutional, and therefore absolutely incapable of conferring the authority and assigning the duties which its words purport to confer and assign.

The constitution vests the whole judicial power of the United States in one supreme court, and such inferior courts as congress shall, from time to time, ordain and establish. This power is expressly extended to all cases arising under the laws of the United States; and consequently, in some form, may be exercised over the present case; because the right claimed is given by a law of the United States.

In the distribution of this power it is declared, that "the supreme court shall have original jurisdiction in all cases affecting ambassadors, other public ministers and consuls, and those in which a state shall be a party. In all other cases, the supreme court shall have appellate jurisdiction." ...

If it had been intended to leave it in the discretion of the legislature to apportion the judicial power between the supreme and inferior courts according to the will of that body, it would certainly have been useless to have proceeded further than to have defined the judicial power, and the tribunals in which it should be vested. The subsequent part of the section is mere surplusage, is entirely without meaning, if such is to be the construction. If congress remains at liberty to give this court appellate jurisdiction, where the constitution has declared their jurisdiction shall be original; and original jurisdiction where the constitution has declared it shall be appellate; the distribution of jurisdiction, made in the constitution, is form without substance.

Affirmative words are often, in their operation, negative of other objects than those affirmed; and in this case, a negative or exclusive sense must be given to them or they have no operation at all.

It cannot be presumed, that any clause in the constitution is intended to be without effect; and therefore such a construction is inadmissible, is inadmissible, unless the words require it. . . .

The authority, therefore, given to the supreme court, by the act establishing the judicial courts of the United States, to issue writs of mandamus to public officers, appears not to be warranted by the constitution; and it becomes necessary to inquire whether a jurisdiction so conferred can be exercised.

The question whether an act repugnant to the constitution can become the law of the land, is a question deeply interesting to the United States; but, happily not of an intricacy porportioned to its interest. It seems only necessary to recognize certain principles supposed to have been long and well established, to decide it.

That the people have an original right to establish for their future government such principles as, in their opinion, shall most conduce to their own happiness, is the basis on which the whole American fabric has been erected. The exercise of this original right is a very great exertion, nor can it nor ought it to be frequently repeated. The principles therefore so established are deemed fundamental. And as the authority from which they proceed is supreme and can seldom act, they are designed to be permanent.

This original and supreme will organizes the government, and assigns to different departments their respective powers. It may either stop here or establish certain limits not to be transcended by those departments.

The government of the United States is of the latter description. The powers of the legislature are defined and limited; and that those limits may not be mistaken or forgotten, the constitution is written. To what purpose are powers limited, and to what purpose is that limitation committed to writing, if these limits may, at any time, be passed by those intended to be restrained? The distinction between a government with limited and unlimited powers is abolished if those limits do not confine the persons on whom they are imposed and if acts prohibited and acts allowed are of equal obligation. It is a proposition too plain to be contested, that the constitution controls any legislative act repugnant to it; or, that the legislature may alter the constitution by an ordinary act.

Between these alternatives there is no middle ground. The constitution is either a superior paramount law, unchangeable by ordinary means, or it is on a level with ordinary legislative acts, and, like other acts, is alterable when the legislature shall please to alter it.

If the former part of the alternative be true, then a legislative act contrary to the constitution is not law; if the latter part be true, then written constitutions are absurd attempts, on the part of the people, to limit a power in its own nature illimitable.

Certainly all those who have framed written constitutions contemplate them as forming the fundamental and paramount law of the nation, and consequently the theory of every such government must be that an act of the legislature repugnant to the Constitution is void.

This theory is essentially attached to a written constitution, and is consequently to be considered, by this court as one of the fundamental principles of our society. It is not, therefore, to be lost sight of in the further consideration of this subject.

If an act of the legislature repugnant to the constitution is void, does it, notwithstanding its invalidity, bind the courts and oblige them to give it effect? Or, in other words, though it be not law, does it constitute a rule as operative as if it was a law? This would be to overthrow in fact what was established in theory, and would seem, at first view, an absurdity too gross to be insisted on. It shall, however, receive a more attentive consideration.

It is emphatically the province and duty of the judicial department to say what the law is. Those who apply the rule to particular cases must of necessity expound and interpret that rule. If two laws conflict with each other, the courts must decide on the operation of each.

So if a law be in opposition to the constitution; if both the law and the constitution apply to a particular case, so that the court must either decide that case conformably to the law, disregarding the constitution, or conformably to the constitution, disregarding the law, the court must determine which of these conflicting rules governs the case. This is of the very essence of judicial duty.

If, then, the courts are to regard the constitution, and the constitution is superior to any ordinary act of the legislature, the constitution, and not such ordinary act, must govern the case to which they both apply.

Those, then, who controvert the principle that the constitution is to be considered in court as a paramount law, are reduced to the necessity of maintaining that courts must close their eyes on the constitution and see only the law.

This doctrine would subvert the very foundation of all written constitutions. It would declare that an act which, according to the principles and theory of our government, is entirely void, is yet, in practice, completely obligatory. It would declare that if the legislature shall do what is expressly forbidden, such act, notwithstanding the express prohibition, is in reality effectual. It would be giving to the legislature a practical and real omnipotence with the same breath which professes to restrict their powers within narrow limits. It is prescribing limits and declaring that those limits may be passed at pleasure.

That it thus reduces to nothing what we have deemed the greatest improvement on political institutions, a written constitution, would of itself be sufficient, in America, where written constitutions have been viewed with so much reverence, for rejecting the construction. But the peculiar expressions of the constitution of the United States furnish additional arguments in favor of its rejection.

The judicial power of the United States is extended to all cases arising under the constitution.

Could it be the intention of those who gave this power to say that in using it the constitution should not be looked into? That a case arising under the constitution should be decided without examining the instrument under which it arises?

This is too extravagant to be maintained.

In some cases, then, the constitution must be looked into by the judges. And if they can open it at all, what part of it are they forbidden to read or to obey?

There are many other parts of the constitution which serve to illustrate this subject.

It is declared that "no tax or duty shall be laid on articles exported from any state." Suppose a duty on the export of cotton, of tobacco, or of flour, and a suit instituted to recover it, ought judgment to be rendered in such a case? Ought the judges to close their eyes on the constitution, and only see the law?

The constitution declares "that no bill of attainder or *ex post facto* law shall be passed." If, however, such a bill should be passed, and a person should be prosecuted under it, must the court condemn to death those victims whom the constitution endeavors to preserve?

"No person," says the constitution, "shall be convicted of treason unless on the testimony of two witnesses to the same overt act, or on confession in open court."

Here the language of the constitution is addressed especially to the courts. It prescribes, directly for them, a rule of evidence not to be departed from. If the legislature should change that rule, and declare one witness, or a confession out of court, sufficient for conviction, must the constitutional principle yield to the legislative act?

From these, and many other selections which might be made, it is apparent that the framers of the constitution contemplated that instrument as a rule for the government of *courts*, as well as of the legislature. Why otherwise does it direct the judges to take an oath to support it? This oath certainly applies in an especial manner to their conduct in their official character. How immoral to impose it on them if they were to be used as the instruments, and the knowing instruments, for violating what they swear to support!

The oath of office, too, imposed by the legislature, is completely demonstrative of the legislative opinion on this subject. It is in these words: "I do solemnly swear that I will administer justice without respect to persons, and do equal right to the poor and to the rich; and that I will faithfully and impartially discharge all the duties incumbent on me as——, according to the best of my abilities and understanding, agreeably to *the constitution* and laws of the United States." Why does a judge swear to discharge his duties agreeably to the constitution of the United States, if that constitution forms no rule for his government?—if it is closed upon him, and cannot be inspected by him?

If such be the real state of things, this is worse than solemn mockery. To prescribe, or to take this oath, becomes equally a crime.

It is also not entirely unworthy of observation, that in declaring what shall be the *supreme* law of the land, the constitution itself is first mentioned, and not the laws of the United States generally, but those only which shall be made in *pursuance* of the constitution, have that rank.

Thus, the particular phraseology of the constitution of the United States confirms and strengthens the principle, supposed to be essential to all written constitutions, that a law repugnant to the constitution is void, and that courts, as well as other departments, are bound by that instrument.

[Mandamus denied.]

✤ *D O C U M E N T   5*

Martin v. Hunter's Lessee, 1816

Story, J. delivered the opinion of the Court.

... The questions involved in this judgment are of great importance and delicacy. Perhaps it is not too much to affirm, that, upon their right decision, rest some of the most solid principles which have hitherto been supposed to sustain and protect the constitution itself. The great respectability, too, of the court whose decisions we are called upon to review, and the entire deference which we entertain for the learning and ability of that court, add much to the difficulty of the task which has so unwelcomely fallen upon us. It is, however, a source of consolation, that we have had the assistance of most able and learned arguments to aid our inquiries; and that the opinion which is now to be pronounced has been weighed with every solicitude to come to a correct result, and matured after solemn deliberation.

Before proceeding to the principal questions, it may not be unfit to dispose of some preliminary considerations which have grown out of the arguments at the bar.

The constitution of the United States was ordained and established, not by the states in their sovereign capacities, but emphatically, as the preamble of the constitution declares, by "the people of the United States." There can be no doubt that it was competent to the people to invest the general government with all the powers which they might deem proper and necessary; to extend or restrain these powers according to their own good pleasure, and to give them a paramount and supreme authority. As little doubt can there be, that the people had a right to prohibit to the states the exercise of any powers which were, in their judgment, incompatible with the objects of the general compact; to make the powers of the state governments, in given cases, subordinate to those of the nation, or to reserve to themselves those sovereign authorities which they might not choose to delegate to either. The constitution was not, therefore, necessarily carved out of existing state sovereignties, nor a surrender of powers already existing in state institutions, for the powers of the states depend upon their own constitutions; and the people of every state had the right to modify and restrain them, according to their own views of policy or principle. On the other hand, it is perfectly clear that the sovereign powers vested in the state governments, by their respective constitutions, remained unaltered and unimpaired, except so far as they were granted to the government of the United States. . . .

The third article of the constitution is that which must principally attract our attention. The 1st. section declares, "the judicial power of the United States shall be vested in one supreme court, and in such other inferior courts as the congress may, from time to time, ordain and establish." The 2d section declares, that "the judicial power shall extend to all cases in law or equity, arising under this constitution, the laws of the United States, and the treaties made, or which shall be made, under their authority; to all cases affecting ambassadors, other public ministers and consuls; to all cases of admiralty and maritime jurisdiction; to controversies to which the United States shall be a party; to controversies between two or more states; between a state and citizens of another state; between citizens of different states; between citizens of the same state, claiming lands under the grants of different states; and between a state or the citizens thereof, and foreign states, citizens, or subjects." It then proceeds to declare, that "in all cases affecting ambassadors, other public ministers and consuls, and those in which a state shall be a party, the supreme court shall have original jurisdiction. In all the other cases before mentioned the supreme court shall have appellate jurisdiction, both as to law and fact, with such exceptions, and under such regulations, as the congress shall make."

Such is the language of the article creating and defining the judicial power of the United States. It is the voice of the whole American people solemnly declared, in establishing one great department of that government which was, in many respects, national, and in all, supreme. It is a part of the very same instrument which was to act not merely upon individuals, but upon states; and to deprive them altogether of the exercise of some powers of sovereignty, and to restrain and regulate them in the exercise of others. ...

This leads us to the consideration of the great question as to the nature and extent of the appellate jurisdiction of the United States. We have already seen that appellate jurisdiction is given by the constitution to the supreme court in all cases where it has not original jurisdiction; subject, however, to such exceptions and regulations as congress may prescribe. It is, therefore, capable of embracing every case enumerated in the constitution, which is not exclusively to be decided by way of original jurisdiction. But the exercise of appellate jurisdiction is far from being limited by the terms of the constitution to the supreme court. There can be no doubt that congress may create a succession of inferior tribunals, in each of which it may vest appellate as well as original jurisdiction. The judicial power is delegated by the constitution in the most general terms, and may, therefore, be exercised by congress under every variety of form, of appellate or original jurisdiction. And as there is nothing in the constitution which restrains or limits this power, it must, therefore, in all other cases, subsist in the utmost latitude of which, in its own nature, it is susceptible.

As, then, by the terms of the constitution, the appellate jurisdiction is not limited as to the supreme court, and as to this court it may be exercised in all other cases than those of which it has original cognizance, what is there to restrain its exercise over state tribunals in the enumerated cases? The appellate power is not limited by the terms of the third article to any particular courts. The words are, "the judicial power (which includes appellate power) shall extend to all cases," &c., and "in all other cases before mentioned the supreme court shall have appellate jurisdiction." It is the case, then, and not the court, that gives the jurisdiction. If the judicial power extends to the case, it will be in vain to search in the letter of the constitution for any qualification as to the tribunal where it depends. It is incumbent, then, upon those who assert such a qualification to show its existence by necessary implication. If the text be clear and distinct, no restriction upon its plain and obvious import ought to be admitted, unless the inference be irresistible.

If the constitution meant to limit the appellate jurisdiction to cases pending in the courts of the United States, it would necessarily follow that the jurisdiction of these courts would, in all the cases enumerated in the constitution, be exclusive of state tribunals. How otherwise could the jurisdiction extend to all cases arising under the constitution, laws, and treaties of the United States, or to all cases of admiralty and maritime jurisdiction? If some of these cases might be entertained by state tribunals, and no appellate jurisdiction as to them should exist, then the appellate power would not extend to all, but to some, cases. If state tribunals might exercise concurrent jurisdiction over all or some of the other classes of cases in the constitution without control, then the appellate jurisdiction of the United States might, as to such cases, have no real existence, contrary to the manifest intent of the constitution. ...

But it is plain that the framers of the constitution did contemplate that cases within the judicial cognizance of the United States not only might but would arise in the state courts, in the exercise of their ordinary jurisdiction. With this view the sixth article declares, that "this constitution, and the laws of the United States which shall be made in pursuance thereof, and all treaties made, or which shall be made, under the authority of the United States, shall be the supreme law of the land, and the judges in every state shall be bound thereby, any thing in the constitution or laws of any state to the contrary notwithstanding." It is obvious that this obligation is imperative upon the state judges in their official, and not merely in their private, capacities. From the very nature of their judicial duties they would be called upon to pronounce the law applicable to the case in judgment. They were not to decide merely according to the laws or constitution of the state, but according to the constitution, laws and treaties of the United States—"the supreme law of the land." ...

It must, therefore, be conceded that the constitution not only contemplated, but meant to provide for cases within the scope of the judicial power of the United States, which might yet depend before state tribunals. It was foreseen that in the exercise of their ordinary jurisdiction, state courts would incidentally take cognizance of cases arising under the constitution, the laws, and treaties of the United States. Yet to all these cases the judicial power, by the very terms of the constitution, is to extend. It cannot extend by original jurisdiction if that was already rightfully and exclusively attached in the state courts, which (as has been already shown) may occur; it must, therefore, extend by appellate jurisdiction, or not at all. It would seem to follow that the appellate power of the United States must, in such cases, extend to state tribunals; and if in such cases, there is no reason why it should not equally attach upon all others within the purview of the constitution. ...

This is not all. A motive of another kind, perfectly compatible with the most sincere respect for state tribunals, might induce the grant of appellate power over their decisions. That motive is the importance, and even necessity of uniformity of decisions throughout the whole United States, upon all subjects within the purview of the constitution. Judges of equal learning and integrity, in different states, might differently interpret a statute, or a treaty of the United States, or even the constitution itself: If there were no revising authority to control these jarring and discordant judgments, and harmonize them into uniformity, the laws, the treaties, and the constitution of the United States would be different in different states, and might, perhaps, never have precisely the same construction, obligation, or efficacy, in any two states. The public mischiefs that would attend such a state of things would be truly deplorable; and it cannot be believed that they could have escaped the enlightened convention which formed the constitution. What, indeed, might then have been only prophecy, has now become fact; and the appellate jurisdiction must continue to be the only adequate remedy for such evils.

There is an additional consideration, which is entitled to great weight. The constitution of the United States was designed for the common and equal benefit of all the people of the United States. The judicial power was granted for the same benign and salutary purposes. It was not to be exercised exclusively for the benefit of parties who might be plaintiffs, and would elect the national forum, but also for the protection of defendants who might be entitled to try their rights, or assert their privileges, before the same forum. Yet, if the construction contended for be correct, it will follow, that as the plaintiff may always elect the state court, the defendant may be deprived of all the security which the constitution intended in aid of his rights. Such a state of things can, in no respect, be considered as giving equal rights. ...

On the whole, the court are of opinion, that the appellate power of the United States does extend to cases pending in the state courts; and that the 25th section of the judiciary act, which authorizes the exercise of this jurisdiction in the specified cases, by a writ of error, is supported by the letter and spirit of the constitution. We find no clause in that instrument which limits this power; and we dare not interpose a limitation where the people have not been disposed to create one.

Strong as this conclusion stands upon the general language of the constitution, it may still derive support from other sources. It is an historical fact, that this exposition of the constitution, extending its appellate power to state courts, was, previous to its adoption, uniformly and publicly avowed by its friends, and admitted by its enemies, as the basis of their respective reasonings, both in and out of the state conventions. It is an historical fact, that at the time when the judiciary act was submitted to the deliberations of the first congress, composed, as it was, not only of men of great learning and ability, but of men who had acted a principal part in framing, supporting, or opposing that constitution, the same exposition was explicitly declared and admitted by the friends and by the opponents of that system. It is an historical fact, that the supreme court of the United States have, from time to time, sustained this appellate jurisdiction in a great variety of cases, brought from the tribunals of many of the most important states in the union, and that no state tribunal has ever breathed a judicial doubt on the subject, or declined to obey the mandate of the supreme court, until the present occasion. This weight of contemporaneous exposition by all parties, this acquiescence of enlightened state courts, and these judicial decisions of the supreme court through so long a period, do, as we think, place the doctrine upon a foundation of authority which cannot be shaken, without delivering over the subject to perpetual and irremediable doubts. . . .

✠ D O C U M E N T   6

McCulloch v. Maryland, 1819

Marshall, Chief Justice, delivered the opinion of the Court.

. . . The first question made in the cause is—has Congress power to incorporate a bank?

The power now contested was exercised by the first Congress elected under the present Constitution. The bill for incorporating the Bank of the United States did not steal upon an unsuspecting legislature and pass unobserved. Its principle was completely understood, and was opposed with equal zeal and ability. After being resisted first in the fair and open field of debate, and afterwards in the executive cabinet, with as much persevering talent as any measure has ever experienced, and being supported by arguments which convinced minds as pure and as intelligent as this country can boast, it became a law. The original act was permitted to expire, but a short experience of the embarrassments to which the refusal to revive it exposed the Government convinced those who were most prejudiced against the measure of its necessity, and induced the passage of the present law. It would require no ordinary share of intrepidity to assert that a measure adopted under these circumstances was a bold and plain usurpation to which the Constitution gave no countenance. These observations belong to the cause;

but they are not made under the impression that, were the question entirely new, the law would be found irreconcilable with the Constitution.

In discussing this question, the counsel for the State of Maryland have deemed it of some importance, in the Construction of the Constitution, to consider that instrument not as emanating from the people, but as the act of sovereign and independent States. The powers of the General Government, it has been said, are delegated by the States, who alone are truly sovereign, and must be exercised in subordination to the States, who alone possess supreme dominion.

It would be difficult to sustain this proposition. The convention which framed the Constitution was indeed elected by the State legislatures. But the instrument, when it came from their hands, was a mere proposal, without obligation or pretensions to it. It was reported to the then existing Congress of the United States with a request that it might

> be submitted to a convention of delegates, chosen in each State by the people thereof, under the recommendation of its legislature, for their assent and ratification.

This mode of proceeding was adopted, and by the convention, by Congress, and by the State legislatures, the instrument was submitted to the people. They acted upon it in the only manner in which they can act safely, effectively and wisely, on such a subject—by assembling in convention. It is true, they assembled in their several States—and where else should they have assembled? No political dreamer was ever wild enough to think of breaking down the lines which separate the States, and of compounding the American people into one common mass. Of consequence, when they act, they act in their States. But the measures they adopt do not, on that account, cease to be the measures of the people themselves, or become the measures of the State governments.

From these conventions the Constitution derives its whole authority. The government proceeds directly from the people; is "ordained and established" in the name of the people, and is declared to be ordained,

> in order to form a more perfect union, establish justice, insure domestic tranquillity, and secure the blessings of liberty to themselves and to their posterity.

The assent of the States in their sovereign capacity is implied in calling a convention, and thus submitting that instrument to the people. But the people were at perfect liberty to accept or reject it, and their act was final. It required not the affirmance, and could not be negatived, by the State Governments. The Constitution, when thus adopted, was of complete obligation, and bound the State sovereignties. ...

This Government is acknowledged by all to be one of enumerated powers. The principle that it can exercise only the powers granted to it would seem too apparent to have required to be enforced by all those arguments which its enlightened friends, while it was depending before the people, found it necessary to urge; that principle is now universally admitted. But the question respecting the extent of the powers actually granted is perpetually arising, and will probably continue to arise so long as our system shall exist. In discussing these questions, the conflicting powers of the

General and State Governments must be brought into view, and the supremacy of their respective laws, when they are in opposition, must be settled.

If any one proposition could command the universal assent of mankind, we might expect it would be this—that the Government of the Union, though limited in its powers, is supreme within its sphere of action. This would seem to result necessarily from its nature. It is the Government of all; its powers are delegated by all; it represents all, and acts for all. Though any one State may be willing to control its operations, no State is willing to allow others to control them. The nation, on those subjects on which it can act, must necessarily bind its components parts. But this question is not left to mere reason; the people have, in express terms, decided it by saying, "this Constitution, and the laws of the United States, which shall be made in pursuance thereof," "shall be the supreme law of the land," and by requiring that the members of the State legislatures and the officers of the executive and judicial departments of the States shall take the oath of fidelity to it. The Government of the United States, then, though limited in its powers, is supreme, and its laws, when made in pursuance of the Constitution, form the supreme law of the land, "anything in the Constitution or laws of any State to the contrary notwithstanding."

Among the enumerated powers, we do not find that of establishing a bank or creating a corporation. But there is no phrase in the instrument which, like the Articles of Confederation, excludes incidental or implied powers and which requires that everything granted shall be expressly and minutely described. Even the 10th Amendment, which was framed for the purpose of quieting the excessive jealousies which had been excited, omits the word "expressly," and declares only that the powers "not delegated to the United States, nor prohibited to the States, are reserved to the States or to the people," thus leaving the question whether the particular power which may become the subject of contest has been delegated to the one Government, or prohibited to the other, to depend on a fair construction of the whole instrument. The men who drew and adopted this amendment had experienced the embarrassments resulting from the insertion of this word in the Articles of Confederation, and probably omitted it to avoid those embarrassments. A Constitution, to contain an accurate detail of all the subdivisions of which its great powers will admit, and of all the means by which they may be carried into execution, would partake of the prolixity of a legal code, and could scarcely be embraced by the human mind. It would probably never be understood by the public. Its nature, therefore, requires that only its great outlines should be marked, its important objects designated, and the minor ingredients which compose those objects be deduced from the nature of the objects themselves. That this idea was entertained by the framers of the American Constitution is not only to be inferred from the nature of the instrument, but from the language. Why else were some of the limitations found in the 9th section of the 1st article introduced? It is also in some degree warranted by their having omitted to use any restrictive term which might prevent its receiving a fair and just interpretation. In considering this question, then, we must never forget that it is *a Constitution* we are expounding.

Although, among the enumerated powers of Government, we do not find the word "bank" or "incorporation," we find the great powers, to lay and collect taxes; to borrow money; to regulate commerce; to declare and conduct a war; and to raise and support armies and navies. The sword and the purse, all the external relations, and no inconsiderable portion of the industry of the nation are intrusted to its Government. It can never be pretended that these vast powers draw after them others of inferior importance merely because they are inferior. Such an idea can never be advanced. But it may with great reason be contended that a Government intrusted with such ample powers, on the due execution of which the happiness and prosperity of the Nation so vitally depends, must also be intrusted with ample means for their execution. The power being given, it is the interest of the Nation to facilitate its execution. It can never be their interest, and cannot be presumed to have been their intention, to clog and embarrass its execution by withholding the most appropriate means. ...

But the Constitution of the United States has not left the right of Congress to employ the necessary means for the execution of the powers conferred on the Government to general reasoning. To its enumeration of powers is added that of making.

> all laws which shall be necessary and proper for carrying into execution the foregoing powers, and all other powers vested by this Constitution in the Government of the United States or in any department thereof. ...

Is it true that this is the sense in which the word "necessary" is always used? Does it always import an absolute physical necessity so strong that one thing to which another may be termed necessary cannot exist without that other? We think it does not. If reference be had to its use in the common affairs of the world or in approved authors, we find that it frequently imports no more than that one thing is convenient, or useful, or essential to another. To employ the means necessary to an end is generally understood as employing any means calculated to produce the end, and not as being confined to those single means without which the end would be entirely unattainable. Such is the character of human language that no word conveys to the mind in all situations one single definite idea, and nothing is more common than to use words in a figurative sense. Almost all compositions contain words which, taken in a their rigorous sense, would convey a meaning different from that which is obviously intended. It is essential to just construction that many words which import something excessive should be understood in a more mitigated sense—in that sense which common usage justifies. The word "necessary" is of this description. It has not a fixed character peculiar to itself. It admits of all degrees of comparison, and is often connected with other words which increase or diminish the impression the mind receives of the urgency it imports. A thing may be necessary, very necessary, absolutely or indispensably necessary. To no mind would the same idea be conveyed by these several phrases. The comment on the word is well illustrated by the passage cited at the bar from the 10th section of the 1st article of the Constitution. It is, we think, impossible to compare the sentence which prohibits a State from laying "imposts, or duties on imports or exports, except what may be absolutely necessary for executing its inspection laws," with that which authorizes Congress "to make all laws which shall be necessary and proper for carrying into execution" the powers of the General Government without feeling a conviction that the convention understood itself to change materially the meaning of the word "necessary," by prefixing the word "absolutely." This word, then, like others, is used in various senses, and, in its construction, the subject, the context, the intention of the person using them are all to be taken into view. ...

In ascertaining the sense in which the word "necessary" is used in this clause of the Constitution, we may derive some aid from that with which it it is associated. Congress shall have power "to make all laws which shall be necessary and proper to carry into execution" the powers of the Government. If the word "necessary" was used in that strict and rigorous sense for which the counsel for the State of Maryland contend, it would be an extraordinary departure from the usual course of the human mind, as exhibited in composition, to add a word the only possible effect of which is to qualify that strict and rigorous meaning, to present to the mind the idea of some choice of means of legislation not strained and compressed within the narrow limits for which gentlemen contend.

But the argument which most conclusively demonstrates the error of the construction contended for by the counsel for the State of Maryland is founded on the intention of the convention as manifested in the whole clause. To waste time and argument in proving that, without it, Congress might carry its powers into execution would be not much less idle than to hold a lighted taper to the sun. As little can it be required to prove that, in the absence of this clause, Congress would have some choice of means. That it might employ those which, in its judgment, would most advantageously effect the object to be accomplished. That any means adapted to the end, any means which tended directly to the execution of the Constitutional powers of the Government, were in themselves Constitutional. This clause, as construed by the State of Maryland, would abridge, and almost annihilate, this useful and necessary right of the legislature to select its means. That this could not be intended is, we should think, had it not been already controverted, too apparent for controversy.

We think so for the following reasons:

1st. The clause is placed among the powers of Congress, not among the limitations on those powers.

2d. Its terms purport to enlarge, not to diminish, the powers vested in the Government. It purports to be an additional power, not a restriction on those already granted. No reason has been or can be assigned for thus concealing an intention to narrow the discretion of the National Legislature under words which purport to enlarge it. The framers of the constitution wished its adoption, and well knew that it would be endangered by its strength, not by its weakness. Had they been capable of using language which would convey to the eye one idea and, after deep reflection, impress on the mind another, they would rather have disguised the grant of power than its limitation. If, then, their intention had been, by this clause, to restrain the free use of means which might otherwise have been implied, that intention would have been inserted in another place, and would have been expressed in terms resembling these. "In carrying into execution the foregoing powers, and all others," etc., "no laws shall be passed but such as are necessary and proper." Had the intention been to make this clause restrictive, it would unquestionably have been so in form, as well as in effect.

The result of the most careful and attentive consideration bestowed upon this clause is that, if it does not enlarge, it cannot be construed to restrain, the powers of Congress, or to impair the right of the legislature to exercise its best judgment in the selection of measures to carry into execution the Constitutional powers of the Government. If no other motive for its insertion can be suggested, a sufficient one is found in the desire to remove all doubts respecting the right to legislate on that vast mass of incidental powers which must be involved in the Constitution if that instrument be not a splendid bauble.

We admit, as all must admit, that the powers of the Government are limited, and that its limits are not to be transcended. But we think the sound construction of the Constitution must allow to the national legislature that discretion with respect to the means by which the powers it confers are to be carried into execution which will enable that body to perform the high duties assigned to it in the manner most beneficial to the people. Let the end be legitimate, let it be within the scope of the Constitution, and all means which are appropriate, which are plainly adapted to that end, which are not prohibited, but consist with the letter and spirit of the Constitution, are Constitutional. ...

After the most deliberate consideration, it is the unanimous and decided opinion of this Court that the act to incorporate the Bank of the United States is a law made in pursuance of the Constitution, and is a part of the supreme law of the land. ...

It being the opinion of the Court that the act incorporating the bank is constitutional, and that the power of establishing a branch in the State of Maryland might be properly exercised by the bank itself, we proceed to inquire:

2. Whether the State of Maryland may, without violating the Constitution, tax that branch? ...

That the power of taxing it by the States may be exercised so as to destroy it is too obvious to be denied. But taxation is said to be an absolute power which acknowledges no other limits than those expressly prescribed in the Constitution, and, like sovereign power of every other description, is intrusted to the discretion of those who use it. But the very terms of this argument admit that the sovereignty of the State, in the article of taxation itself, is subordinate to, and may be controlled by, the Constitution of the United States. How far it has been controlled by that instrument must be a question of construction. In making this construction, no principle, not declared, can be admissible which would defeat the legitimate operations of a supreme Government. It is of the very essence of supremacy to remove all obstacles to its action within its own sphere, and so to modify every power vested in subordinate governments as to exempt its own operations from their own influence. This effect need not be stated in terms. It is so involved in the declaration of supremacy, so necessarily implied in it, that the expression of it could not make it more certain. We must, therefore, keep it in view while construing the Constitution.

The argument on the part of the State of Maryland is not that the States may directly resist a law of Congress, but that they may exercise their acknowledged powers upon it, and that the Constitution leaves them this right, in the confidence that they will not abuse it. ...

That the power to tax involves the power to destroy; that the power to destroy may defeat and render useless the power to create; that there is a plain repugnance in conferring on one Government a power to control the constitutional measures of another, which other, with respect to those very measures, is declared to be supreme over that which exerts the control, are propositions not to be denied. But all inconsistencies are to be reconciled by the magic of the word CONFIDENCE. Taxation, it is said, does not necessarily and unavoidably destroy. To carry it to the excess of destruction would be an abuse, to presume which would banish that confidence which is essential to all Government.

But is this a case of confidence? Would the people of any one State trust those of another with a power to control the most insignificant operations of their State Government? We know they would not. Why, then, should we suppose that the people of any one State should be willing to trust those of another with a power to control the operations of a Government to which they have confided their most important and most valuable interests? In the Legislature of the Union alone are all represented. The Legislature of the Union alone, therefore, can be trusted by the people with the power of controlling measures which concern all, in the confidence that it will not be abused. This, then, is not a case of confidence, and we must consider it is as it really is.

If we apply the principle for which the State of Maryland contends, to the Constitution generally, we shall find it capable of changing totally the character of that instrument. We shall find it capable of arresting all the measures of the Government, and of prostrating it at the foot of the States. The American people have declared their Constitution and the laws made in pursuance thereof to be supreme, but this principle would transfer the supremacy, in fact, to the States.

If the States may tax one instrument, employed by the Government in the execution of its powers, they may tax any and every other instrument. They may tax the mail; they may tax the mint; they may tax patent rights; they may tax the papers of the custom house; they may tax judicial process; they may tax all the means employed by the Government to an excess which would defeat all the ends of Government. This was not intended by the American people. They did not design to make their Government dependent on the States....

The Court has bestowed on this subject its most deliberate consideration. The result is a conviction that the States have no power, by taxation or otherwise, to retard, impede, burden, or in any manner control the operations of the constitutional laws enacted by Congress to carry into execution the powers vested in the General Government. This is, we think, the unavoidable consequence of that supremacy which the Constitution has declared.

We are unanimously of opinion that the law passed by the Legislature of Maryland, imposing a tax on the Bank of the United States is unconstitutional and void....

DOCUMENT 7

President Andrew Jackson Defies the Supreme Court and Vetoes the Bank Bill, 1832

To the Senate.

The bill "to modify and continue" the act entitled "An act to incorporate the subscribers to the Bank of the United States" was presented to me on the 4th July instant. Having considered it with that solemn regard to the principles of the Constitution which the day was calculated to inspire, and come to the conclusion that it ought not to become a law, I herewith return it to the Senate, in which it originated, with my objections.

A bank of the United States is in many respects convenient for the Government and useful to the people. Entertaining this opinion, and deeply impressed with the belief that some of the powers and privileges possessed by the existing bank are unauthorized by the Constitution, subversive of the rights of the States, and dangerous to the liberties of the people, I felt it my duty at an early period of my Administration to call the attention of Congress to the practicability of organizing an institution combining all its advantages and obviating these objections. I sincerely regret that in the act before me I can perceive none of those modifications of the bank charter which are necessary, in my opinion, to make it compatible with justice, with sound policy, or with the Constitution of our country. . . .

It is maintained by the advocates of the bank that its constitutionality in all its features ought to be considered as settled by precedent and by the decision of the Supreme Court. To this conclusion I can not assent. Mere precedent is a dangerous source of authority, and should not be regarded as deciding questions of constitutional power except where the acquiescence of the people and the States can be considered as well settled. So far from this being the case on this subject, an argument against the bank might be based on precedent. One Congress, in 1791, decided in favor of a bank; another, in 1811, decided against it. One Congress, in 1815, decided against a bank; another, in 1816, decided in its favor. Prior to the present Congress, therefore, the precedents drawn from that source were equal. If we resort to the States, the expressions of legislative, judicial, and executive opinions against the bank have been probably to those in its favor as 4 to 1. There is nothing in precedent, therefore, which, if its authority were admitted, ought to weigh in favor of the act before me.

If the opinion of the Supreme Court covered the whole ground of this act, it ought not to control the coordinate authorities of this Government. The Congress, the Executive, and the Court must each for itself be guided by its own opinion of the Constitution. Each public officer who takes an oath to support the Constitution swears that he will support it as he understands it, and not as it is understood by others. It is as much the duty of the House of Representatives, of the Senate, and of the President to decide upon the constitutionality of any bill or resolution which may be presented to them for passage or approval as it is of the supreme judges when it may be brought before them for judicial decision. The opinion of the judges has no more authority over Congress than the opinion of Congress has over the judges, and on that point the President is independent of both. The authority of the Supreme Court must not, therefore, be permitted to control the Congress or the Executive when acting in their legislative capacities, but to have only such influence as the force of their reasoning may deserve. . . .

✣ *E S S A Y S*

Scholars continue to debate the origins and significance of *Marbury* and the other decisions of the Marshall Court. In the first essay, Larry D. Kramer, a professor of law at Stanford, places *Marbury* in the context of the rivalry between Federalists and Jeffersonian Republicans, particularly with regard to their attitudes toward the judiciary.

In Kramer's view, the very weakness of the judiciary at the time of *Marbury* helps explain Marshall's attempt to establish a role for the Court. Viewing the decision as fully compatible with the departmental theory and the notion of popular constitutionalism, Kramer downplays the significance of *Marbury*.

Sylvia Snowiss, a political scientist at California State University at Northridge, takes the opposite view, arguing that the Marshall Court's employment of judicial review constituted a bold and innovative shift in the history of the American judiciary. Breaking the history of judicial review into three periods, Snowiss contends that the Marshall Court transformed the understanding of the Constitution into that of a supreme written law, thereby enlarging the scope of judicial control over the legislative branch. Both *Marbury* and *McCulloch*, in Snowiss' assessment, stand out as important cases in the expansion of judicial power.

Timothy S. Huebner, a historian at Rhodes College and the co-editor of this volume, examines judicial review at the state level. Huebner shows how Judge Spencer Roane's efforts to establish the power of the Virginia Court of Appeals paralleled—and collided with—Marshall's efforts to engage in judicial review of state legislation. The contest between the Marshall Court and Virginia over national supremacy versus state sovereignty, in other words, represented the clash of two judicial leaders who sought more power for their respective tribunals.

Marshall, *Marbury,* and the Defense of Judicial Review

LARRY D. KRAMER

...The case of *Marbury v. Madison* played a supporting role in a bigger drama about the place of the judiciary in American government, and while only a minor player, its part turned out to be important in unexpected ways. The stage was set by the election of 1800, in which Jefferson and the Republicans trounced the divided and demoralized Federalists. Jefferson's and Burr's margin over Adams in the Electoral College was only 73–65, but peculiarities in the way electors were chosen obscure from us (though not from contemporaries) the actual strength of the Republican showing. The elections for Congress more clearly evinced just how sweeping a victory Jefferson's party had won. Going into the election, Federalists held sixty-three seats in the House of Representatives to the Republicans' forty-three. The vote in 1800 more than reversed these numbers, leaving the Republicans with a 65–41 edge and a clear mandate to change the government's direction.

Faced with the loss of the executive and legislative branches, the lame duck Federalist Congress acted quickly to secure its adherents a sanctuary in the judiciary. Federalists had talked about court reform for years: Attorney General Edmund Randolph had recommended steps as early as 1790; the Supreme Court had repeatedly petitioned for relief; and President Adams had urged Congress to take some sort of action as recently as December 1799. But nothing came of these efforts until the embarrassment of Jefferson's election finally spurred the Federalists to act. Gouverneur Morris justified their doing so in a letter to Robert Livingston:

From Kramer, Larry D., *The People Themselves: Popular Constitutionalism and Judicial Review.* Reproduced with permission of Oxford University Press.

"[T]he leaders of the federal party ... are about to experience a heavy gale of adverse wind; can they be blamed for casting many anchors to hold their ship through the storm?"

These anchors were to consist chiefly of new judgeships in a substantially restructured third branch. The main feature of the Judiciary Act of 1801 was thus to relieve the Supreme Court Justices of circuit-riding duties by creating six new circuit courts staffed by sixteen new judges; the Supreme Court was at the same time reduced in size from six to five, said reduction to take effect when the next vacancy occurred. By this none-too-subtle means, the Federalists rewarded themselves with numerous appointments to the inferior courts—not just the judges, but also marshals, clerks, federal attorneys, and all the other supporting personnel attached to a court—while simultaneously requiring the incoming Republican Administration to wait for two vacancies on the Supreme Court before it could make its first appointment there.

But time was short. The Judiciary Act became law on February 13, 1801. The new Administration was scheduled to take over at 12:01 a.m. on March 4. This meant the outgoing Federalists had less than three weeks to select, nominate, and confirm all the new judges and support staff. Nor was the bonanza of last-minute appointments limited to circuit courts created in the Judiciary Act. For on February 27, just four days before Jefferson's inauguration, Congress rushed through yet another law creating yet another circuit court, this one for the District of Columbia; the President was authorized to nominate three more judges and also to appoint "such number of discreet persons to be justices of the peace, as the President of the United States shall from time to time think expedient, to continue in office five years." President Adams immediately nominated the allotted circuit judges, and the Senate hurriedly confirmed his choices. In addition, Adams selected forty-two justices of the peace, most stout Federalists. The outgoing President thus spent his last days in office signing commissions prepared for him by his overworked Secretary of State, John Marshall, who was also already serving as Chief Justice of the Supreme Court.

Once the commissions were signed, it was Marshall's responsibility to make them official by affixing the seal of the United States and arranging to have them delivered. Commissions for the circuit judges went out before Adams's term expired, but some justices of the peace were still waiting when time ran out—including one William Marbury. Legend has it that Marshall was frantically scribbling away in his office when Jefferson's Attorney General Levi Lincoln flung open the door and interrupted him carrying a watch whose hands showed midnight, March 3, 1801.

Republicans were plenty angry about the federal courts even before these last-minute shenanigans. They had not forgiven the exuberance with which Federalist judges tried to muzzle Republicans under the Sedition Act; nor had they forgotten the judges' frequently outrageous conduct of the trials and aggressive use of the bench to campaign for Federalist candidates and policies. There were other issues, too, like the claim that common law was available to federal courts, which Jefferson called an "audacious, barefaced, and sweeping pretension" in comparison to which other Federalist doctrines were "unconsequential, timid things."

Yet despite all this, Jefferson and most Republicans were prepared to live and let live. Jefferson was furious at Adams for his last-minute appointments—he later singled them out as the only "personally unkind" act Adams had ever committed against him—but Jefferson was also willing to forgo a purge if the newly appointed officeholders would act honorably and responsibly. The new President went out of his way to be conciliatory in his inaugural address, and he pursued (at some considerable political cost) a restrained policy with respect to patronage. For example, Jefferson reduced the number of justices of the peace in the District of Columbia from forty-two to thirty, but he included twenty-five of Adams's original appointees in this group.

Jefferson's correspondence in the months between March and December 1801, when the new Congress finally convened, indicates that he continued to brood about the judiciary. Yet Jefferson barely alluded to the matter in his December 8 opening address to Congress, and he recommended no specific action. "The Judiciary system of the United States, and especially that portion of it recently erected will, of course, present itself to the contemplation of Congress," was all that he said, adding a hint in the guise of some hastily compiled (and not very accurate) caseload statistics. While a number of historians interpret this as evidence that Jefferson was already intent on repealing the Judiciary Act of 1801, most now believe he had not yet committed to such a policy. Strong elements within Jefferson's party were pushing for action—infuriated by, among other things, continued diatribes in the Federalist press and the audacity of Federalist judges in the new D.C. circuit who, despite the election results, instituted a common law libel prosecution against the editor of the Republican *National Intelligencer*. But moderates in the party had doubts about the propriety of repeal and were not anxious to begin their turn at the helm by plunging into what promised to be a bitter partisan affair, and Jefferson probably felt the same way. So he equivocated, neither advocating nor ignoring the possibility of repeal.

Then, on December 16, Secretary of State James Madison was served with notice that a motion would be made in the Supreme Court the following day asking Madison to show cause why a writ of mandamus should not be issued directing him to deliver commissions as justices of the peace to William Marbury, Dennis Ramsay, Robert R. Hooe, and William Harper. Madison ignored the summons and Chief Justice Marshall granted the motion to show cause; argument about whether the petitioners were entitled to a writ was scheduled for the beginning of the next term. Richard Ellis hypothesizes that Federalists deliberately chose this moment to challenge Jefferson, believing "a show of determination would deter the Republicans on the court issue before they could unite themselves. If so, the strategy backfired, for filing *Marbury v. Madison* turned out to be the crucial act that united Republicans behind the repeal effort. Interpreting the Court's show cause order as confirmation of Federalist plans to use the judiciary to obstruct Jefferson's Administration, angry Republicans—including now, most importantly, the President himself—decided to strike first. "The conduct of the Judges on this occasion," Virginia Senator Stevens Thomas Mason told Madison, "has excited a very general indignation and will secure the repeal of the Judiciary Law of the last session, about the propriety of which some of our Republican friends were hesitating."

The repeal debate proved to be every bit as ugly and contentious as moderate Republicans had feared. Overwrought Federalists ranted about the demise of an independent judiciary and hysterically charged Republicans with bringing the nation to "the brink of that revolutionary torrent, which deluged in blood one of the fairest countries in Europe." Republicans shrieked back that repeal was justified to counter a Federalist abuse of power and preserve a proper constitutional balance as well as to protect the public fisc. The pending *Marbury* case was referred to by both sides—Republicans offering it as evidence of judicial overreaching, Federalists citing it as an example of why an independent judiciary was necessary. Numerous arguments both for and against judicial review were heard, including some Republican denunciations of the practice in any and all forms. In the end, which came on March 3, 1802, the Act was of course repealed. ...

But the most crushing blow came when the Federalists' various court actions challenging repeal were summarily rejected in the circuit courts. Anticipating the possibility of such challenges, the Republican Congress had already passed legislation designed to put off a ruling from the Supreme Court. This was accomplished by legislation adopted in early April that abolished the Supreme Court's June and December terms, thus delaying the Court's next sitting until February 1803, by which time Jefferson hoped that tempers in the capital would have cooled. An incidental effect of this legislation was to put off the hearing in *Marbury v. Madison*, which otherwise would have been heard in June.

Undeterred, some of the removed Federalist judges challenged the constitutionality of repeal in four lower court cases. They argued, first, that Congress had no power to order the transfer of actions already pending in courts established under the Judiciary Act of 1801. Second, they said it was unconstitutional for Supreme Court Justices also to sit as judges in the circuit courts. But mainly they argued that Congress had no power to remove judges who were guilty of no malfeasance or dereliction in office. In three of these challenges—presided over by Justices Washington and Cushing and by Chief Justice Marshall—their arguments were rejected on the spot. In the fourth, heard by Justice Paterson, the proceedings were adjourned overnight, leaving time for conversations that led a "very much mortified" Theophilus Parsons to withdraw his plea the next morning.

Incredibly, though four of six Supreme Court Justices had now indicated their unwillingness to rule against the Administration, the pigheaded Federalists pressed on by appealing Chief Justice Marshall's ruling to the full Court. The argument and decision in the case, captioned *Stuart v. Laird*, trailed those in *Marbury* by a few days each. Predictably, given what they had already said and done, the Justices affirmed the lower court. Justice Paterson's opinion for a unanimous Supreme Court was brief, though not fully to the point. It was clear that Congress could abolish the inferior courts set up in the Judiciary Act of 1801 and transfer their cases to a different tribunal, the Court said, there being "no words in the constitution to prohibit or restrain" Congress's authority to "establish from time to time such inferior tribunals as they think proper." As for the objection that Supreme Court Justices could not sit on circuit courts, "it is sufficient to observe, that practice and acquiescence under it for a period of several years, commencing with the organization of the judicial system, affords an irresistible answer, and has indeed fixed the construction. ... [T]he question is at rest, and ought not to be disturbed. Remarkably, Paterson and the Court ignored the appellant's most fundamental objection, which was that Congress could not remove Article III judges by any means other than impeachment or for any reasons other than misbehavior in office. But that argument was no longer essential to the case once the Court had concluded that Congress could transfer pending actions from one court to another, and the Justices chose in *Stuart* to say no more than was absolutely necessary to decide the case before them.

We are now, finally, in a position to understand the many-sided calculation that lay behind Chief Justice Marshall's enigmatic opinion in *Marbury*. Like every Federalist, Marshall worried about how far Republicans would go to vitiate the political order established under the leadership of Washington and Hamilton. Bear in mind that disagreements between the parties were not confined to questions of policy, but reflected profoundly different social philosophies. A major organizing principle of Federalism was fear of populism and demagoguery. In its most extreme manifestations, Federalism exhibited open contempt for ordinary citizens and a sure conviction that republicanism would fail unless those citizens left problems of governing to their social and intellectual betters. Gouverneur Morris perfectly expressed this tenet during the debate over repeal: "Look into the records of time, see what has been the ruin of every Republic. The vile love of popularity. Why are we here? To save the people from their most dangerous enemy; to save them from themselves." A week later, Morris took umbrage at the suggestion that he had sought popular approval by one of his arguments. "[S]ure I am that I uttered nothing in the style of an *appeal to the people*," he sneered. "I hope no member of this House has so poor a sense of its dignity as to make such an appeal." Marshall himself seldom spoke this bluntly, and he was generally moderate when it came to particular policies. But he shared with all Federalists these core convictions as well as the belief that Jefferson and the Republicans pandered too much to popular opinion.

Marshall was, at the same time, reasonably certain that any attempt by the Court to stand in Jefferson's way would be crushed. What doubts he may have harbored in this respect, moreover, were presumably laid to rest when, just before the Court reconvened in February, Jefferson asked the House of Representatives to look into whether New Hampshire District Judge John Pickering's erratic behavior warranted impeachment. There was, as a result, a new "overhanging threat" to unsettle the Justices as they sat down to decide *Stuart* and *Marbury*....

Effectively silenced in *Stuart*, *Marbury* became the Court's only outlet for making a statement. Yet the prospects for getting away with something here were scarcely more promising than in *Stuart*. Secretary of State Madison had simply ignored the initial motion to show cause, and he displayed equal disregard for the Court's proceedings on whether to grant the petitioners' request—not bothering to appear or even to offer an argument. It was abundantly clear that an order directing Madison to deliver the commissions would likewise be ignored. Unwilling to say that Jefferson was right, but also not wanting to have its impotence openly put on display, the Court decided instead to dismiss for lack of jurisdiction.

Yet Marshall could not bring himself simply to rule that Marbury and his co-petitioners were entitled to no relief. This would have meant letting Jefferson completely off the hook in both cases, and that was to concede too much to the Republicans. Marshall deemed it imperative to make some kind of statement: to send a message that the Court had views and might step in at some point. Marshall therefore prefaced his jurisdictional ruling with a lengthy dissertation explaining why the Administration had acted unlawfully by with holding the petitioners' commissions. By coupling this essay with a dismissal for want of jurisdiction, Marshall was, in effect, leaving open the question whether the Court would stand up to the Executive.

He was also, as one biographer has put it, "throwing a sop to the High Federalists," offering something to take the edge off their disappointment.

It was a risky strategy. Marshall's lecture infuriated Jefferson, who perceived it as a politically motivated attack on his presidency. And not just because, having already decided that the Court lacked jurisdiction, Marshall's discussion was gratuitous and wholly improper (which it was) but also because, in Jefferson's eyes, Marshall was so obviously wrong on the merits (which he was). Marshall nevertheless decided to gamble. Richard Ellis explains: "[T]he Chief Justice was an experienced politician, and he probably realized that Jefferson, preoccupied as he was with the diplomatic intricacies of the Louisiana Purchase and with the clashing interests within the Republican Party, was not likely to get into a fight over a lecture that had no practical meaning." Marshall's gamble paid off, and he succeeded in rebuking Jefferson without triggering a Republican backlash or even strong criticism in the press.

And what about judicial review? Marshall definitely went out of his way (quite a bit out of his way, in fact) to address the issue. It would have been perfectly easy to have reached the same result in the case—that the Supreme Court lacked original jurisdiction to entertain Marbury's petition—without striking anything down. Section 13 of the Judiciary Act of 1789 did not read like a grant of jurisdiction, and the better interpretation was that it authorized writs of mandamus only in cases where the Court otherwise had jurisdiction. Indeed, this would have been a stronger legal position than the one Marshall actually took, for (as countless scholars have argued) Marshall's conclusion that Article III prohibited Congress from enlarging the Supreme Court's original jurisdiction was anything but obvious. As it was, Marshall had to stretch very far to reach the result he did through an exercise of judicial review.

Why did he do it? Why force a potentially controversial question that no one had raised or even hinted at, particularly one wholly unnecessary to accomplish the Court's main objective? And why do so at this highly charged moment, when the Court's position was so precarious? The answer may be that the very precariousness of the Court's position is what led Marshall to conclude that he needed to do something about judicial review. The federal courts had been under attack for five years, beginning with Republican denunciations of their role in enforcing the Sedition Act. This assault had become a full-fledged siege after Republicans took office and assumed the offensive by repealing the Judiciary Act of 1801. In the course of debating repeal, the Supreme Court's authority had been questioned and condemned, and the concept of judicial review had come under challenges of a type and temper not heard since before the Constitution was adopted. Suddenly, a practice that had seemed so uncontroversial throughout the 1790s no longer seemed immune to attack.

At the same time, outright rejection of judicial review was not yet a position embraced officially by Republicans, most of whom shared Jefferson's more moderate departmental theory and were willing to live with review on his theory's limited terms. This was the moment to make a statement, Marshall apparently decided, before more extreme sentiments against judicial review spread or grew into something more threatening. Yet such a statement would be effective only if the Court could make it in a way that dampened rather than inflamed further hostility. Marshall's goal was, in effect, to get judicial review into the record—not to establish its existence, but to deflect an incipient movement to delegitimate it. ...

It is tempting, and perhaps too easy, to assume that since Marshall was daring in finding a way to introduce judicial review into the case, he must have been equally bold and imaginative in developing the doctrine. If anything, the opposite was true. The circumstances of *Marbury* led Marshall to write cautiously and to formulate the Court's authority to nullify legislation conservatively.

Many Federalists had, by the time of *Marbury*, begun to espouse a theory of judicial review broader and more ambitious than anything we have seen so far—a theory recognizable today as judicial supremacy, or the notion that judges have the last word when it comes to constitutional interpretation and that their decisions determine the meaning of the Constitution for everyone. A few had pushed this theory aggressively during the debates over the Repeal Act, in turn prompting the most forceful Republican denunciations of judicial review. But judges were generally more circumspect than politicians in declaring the scope of their authority, and Marshall was doubly inclined to be cautious in *Marbury*. His opinion thus carefully and self-consciously avoided the language and arguments of his Federalist allies. Instead, it offered a straightforward application of principles that were widely accepted by most Republicans (including, significantly, President Jefferson), and fully consistent with the premises of popular constitutionalism. Marshall himself acknowledged as much, for he was being neither ironic nor misleading when he introduced the topic by observing that it was "not of an intricacy proportioned to its interest" and could be decided by "certain principles, supposed to have been long and well established.

Like every other writer of the period, Marshall began with the principle that the Constitution is "a superior, paramount law," and that, therefore, "an act of the legislature, repugnant to the constitution, is void." He then asked, again like every other writer of the period, "does [such a law], notwithstanding its invalidity, bind the courts, and oblige them to give it effect?" Though this would seem, "at first view, an absurdity too gross to be insisted on," Marshall proposed nevertheless to say more and explain why. Then, the famous line: "It is emphatically the province and duty of the judicial department to say what the law is."

Read in context, this sentence did not say what, to modern eyes, it seems to say when read in isolation. That is, it did not say "it is the job of courts, alone, to say what the Constitution means." Nor did it say, "it is the job of courts, more so than others, to say what the Constitution means." What it said was "courts, too, can say what the Constitution means." Marshall thus followed his celebrated sentence with exactly the same point as that made by Tucker and Roane in *Kamper*. "Those who apply the rule to particular cases, must of necessity expound and interpret that rule. ... Those then who controvert the principle that the constitution is to be considered, in court, as a paramount law, are reduced to the necessity of maintaining that courts must close their eyes on the constitution, and see only the law." ...

To contemporary readers, Marshall was simply insisting—like practically every other judge and writer of the era—that courts had the same duty and the same obligation to enforce the Constitution as everyone else, both in and out of government. ...

Judicial Review and the Law of the Constitution

SYLVIA SNOWISS

Judicial authority to enforce the Constitution against unconstitutional acts is conventionally traced to Chief Justice John Marshall's opinion in *Marbury v. Madison* and its claim that the written Constitution is included within that law for which it is "the province and duty of the judicial department to say what the law is." The extent to which Marshall's assertion reflected a shared agreement has yet to be conclusively determined, while powerful criticism of the *Marbury* reasoning made over succeeding centuries stands unanswered. Nevertheless, the *Marbury* claim remains the basis for judicial authority to invalidate legislation and overrule executive action.

I shall argue here that this proposition was no part of the understanding of those who before *Marbury* supported a judicial check on legislation, and that the conventional reading of *Marbury* did not develop until some time in the middle of the nineteenth century. Judicial review as we know it developed over three distinct periods: from Independence to *Federalist 78; Federalist 78* to *Marbury*; and from *Marbury* to the end of Marshall's tenure on the Court. During the first period judicial authority over unconstitutional acts was often claimed, but its legitimacy was just as often denied. In this unresolved controversy, judicial invalidation of legislation remained an essentially controversial practice. Moreover, the judicial power then claimed, although resembling modern judicial review, was nevertheless decisively different from it. In its most important difference, it understood the Constitution, or fundamental law, to be a political instrument different in kind from ordinary law. As a restraint on sovereign power rather than individual behavior fundamental law was no part of that law subject to authoritative judicial application and interpretation. The judicial authority to enforce the Constitution asserted in period I was, accordingly, understood to be an extraordinary political act, a judicial substitute for revolution. Although it was to be exercised by the judiciary in the course of its enforcement of ordinary law, constitutional enforcement was not part of conventional legal responsibility. During period 1, however, there existed no coherent or uniform defense of this power. In refusing to execute particular laws, period 1 judges leaned on a variety of justifications, all of which were closer to outdated English precedent than subsequent American doctrine.

Period 2 provided the coherent defense of judicial authority over unconstitutional legislation that had been absent in period 1. It was presented first by James Iredell in a North Carolina newspaper in 1786 and reformulated and popularized by Alexander Hamilton in *Federalist 78* and James Wilson in *Lectures on the Law*. It quickly gained widespread support, putting opposition to judicial authority over unconstitutional legislation on the defensive—as it had not been before but has remained ever since—and articulating for the first time a single standard defense.

This period 2 argument was the forerunner of the *Marbury* doctrine, but it did not then carry the meaning since attributed to *Marbury*. Period 2 judicial review, first, was not derived from the written constitution per se, as *Marbury* suggests, but from the existence in the American states of real, explicit social contracts or fundamental law, which came into being in the aftermath of the revolutionary break from England. The distinctive characteristics of American as opposed to European fundamental law, which made the former enforceable in court, were the reality of American social contracts, in contrast to the fictional or imaginary status of European ones, and the explicitness of its content, in contrast to the traditional and customary content of European fundamental law. That American fundamental law was written was, before Marshall, only of incidental importance, serving merely as the vehicle for its explicitness. The most telling evidence of the relative unimportance of the American state and national Constitutions' commitment to writing is the absence of any mention of, or reliance on it in the three major period 2 defenses of judicial review: Iredell's "To the Public," Hamilton's *Federalist 78*, and Wilson's *Lectures on the Law*.

Next, period 2 judicial review maintained the period 1 understanding that judicial enforcement of the Constitution was an extraordinary political act, a judicial substitute for revolution. Its great achievement was the demonstration that this act was one which judges were nevertheless allowed and even required to perform. Period 2 judicial review, furthermore, derived its authority over legislation from an equality of the governmental branches under explicit fundamental law, not, as does the *Marbury* doctrine, from a uniquely judicial responsibility to a written constitution. Last, its exercise was accompanied by political restraints appropriate for judicial defense of fundamental law.

Period 3 began with Marshall's assumption of the chief justiceship and consisted of his reworking of the period 2 position. Marshall's key innovations did not come in *Marbury*, which was only a peculiarly worded restatement of the ground already won in period 2, but in the way he treated the Constitution in his opinions of the 1810s and 1820s. First, Marshall ended seriatim opinion writing and, with it, public airing of alternate approaches to fundamental law. Next, under this near monopoly of opinion writing, he introduced an unprecedented application to the Constitution of the rules for statutory interpretation, an application not to be found in period 2 cases or in the Court, concurring, or dissenting opinions of his Supreme Court colleagues. Last, he effected a seemingly slight but portentous shift in the significance to be attributed to the written constitution. In Marshall's hands the written constitution lost its period 2 meaning as vehicle of explicit fundamental law and became instead testimony to the Constitution's status as supreme ordinary law. Through this use of the written constitution, coupled with its subjection to the rules for statutory interpretation, Marshall transformed explicit fundamental law, different in kind from ordinary law, into supreme written law, different only in degree. In the process judicial enforcement of the Constitution lost its character as revolutionary defense of explicit fundamental law and became judicial application and interpretation of supreme written law. At the same time the restraints that had been part of period 2 judicial review lost their applicability. This changed the character and enlarged the scope of judicial control over legislation while introducing the judicial supremacy that had been absent from period 2 judicial review but that remains the controversial core of the modern practice.

Legalization of the Constitution took about half a century to complete. Although there was some recognition that Marshall's actions exceeded the terms of the period

2 agreement, there was no general awareness of the magnitude or import of his innovations. Marshall was able to achieve this silent unrecognized legalization and judicial enforcement of the Constitution through maintenance of period 2 language and form, by virtue of the seeming superficiality of the difference between explicit fundamental law and supreme written law, and by confining his results to those which could be accommodated under period 2 terms. At the same time, the rapid elimination of the circumstances that had given rise to the original practice, and Marshall's skillful manipulation and exploitation of the agreement underlying that practice, have blinded succeeding generations to the original understanding and to Marshall's transformation of it.

From the beginning the legalized form of judicial review was accorded deep public acceptance. There has also been a certain scholarly awareness that in the course of its development American constitutional law was, in some way, "legalized." But to the extent the issue is addressed, it is assumed that legalization was the product of an evolving consensus achieved before *Marbury*. There has been no recognition that it was the product of Marshall's deliberate actions and, more important, that it came to be accepted with no public awareness of its implications and commitments. This has resulted in a confesed inconclusiveness in our understanding of the pre-Marshall sources and, in place of understanding, attribution to them of internal contradiction and ambiguity. It has also thwarted our capacity to come to terms with the complex legal-political institution that is modern judicial review. This failure is reflected in the perpetual controversy and periodic crisis that accompanies constitutional law. ...

In *Marbury*, Marshall divided the issue of judicial review into its standard two parts. The first was "whether an act, repugnant to the constitution, can become the law of the land." This inquiry into the status of legislative omnipotence was the starting point for the period 1 rejection of Blackstone. By 1803 the argument against legislative omnipotence hardly had to be made, but Marshall made it nevertheless. The opening paragraphs of the defense of judicial review in *Marbury* repeated the period 1 agreement that explicit fundamental law ended legislative omnipotence and that "an act of the legislature, repugnant to the constitution, is void." Marshall's only innovation was to stress the written character of the "superior," "paramount," and "fundamental" law that bound the branches.

The period 1 and 2 rejection of legislative omnipotence had always been asserted in contemplation of a concededly unconstitutional act, as it was in *Marbury*. Marshall inquired whether an unconstitutional act could be valid law only after declaring void a section of the Judiciary Act of 1789. He did so, following the precedent established in *Kamper*, for a law dealing with organization of the judiciary. Marshall did reverse the order followed in *Kamper* and declared the act void before inquiring into judicial authority to do so. Nevertheless, in making the standard period 2 defense of judicial review, Marshall was under no more obligation to discuss who should determine the constitutionality of legislation than was any period 2 source.

The second inquiry, as stated in *Marbury*, was, "Does [an act which is void] notwithstanding its invalidity, bind the courts, and oblige them to give it effect?" This was the standard second question of period 1 and 2 debate. In answering, Marshall drew on the period 2 answers, particularly on Hamilton's and Tucker's formulations. The key paragraphs of *Marbury* read as follows:

It is emphatically the province and duty of the judicial department to say what the law is. Those who apply the rule to particular cases, must of necessity expound and interpret that rule. If two laws conflict with each other, the courts must decide on the operation of each.

So if a law be in opposition to the constitution: if both the law and the constitution apply to a particular case, so that the court must either decide that case conformably to the law, disregarding the constitution; or conformably to the constitution, disregarding the law; the court must determine which of these conflicting rules governs the case. This is of the very essence of judicial duty.

If then the courts are to regard the constitution; and the constitution is superior to any ordinary act of the legislature; the constitution, and not such ordinary act, must govern the case to which they both apply.

The first sentence in this formulation combined key phrases from *Federalist 78* and Tucker's *Kamper* opinion. In Tucker's opinion the word *law* referred to ordinary law, not the Constitution. For at least the last century the law mentioned in this first sentence, as in the third, has been read to include the Constitution. I am convinced that none of Marshall's contemporaries read the words that way. In context, following the assertion that an unconstitutional act was void, this paragraph introduced the conflict of laws analogy as used in period 2 to support the argument that the judicial responsibility to expound ordinary law precluded enforcement of an act that, in its invalidity, was not law.

The second sentence of this key paragraph used the word *rule* rather than *law* or *constitution*. In period 2 usage *rule* was widely used to refer to the Constitution, but Wilson also used it to refer to legislative acts. In this same second sentence Marshall described the judicial function as it applied to ordinary law. In the next paragraph Marshall included both the Constitution and ordinary legislation within the term *rule* and spoke of the Constitution and ordinary law as applying to the same case. This is as close as Marshall ever came to a direct assertion that applying, expounding, and interpreting the Constitution was part of the province and duty of the judicial department. There is only the barest support for such a reading of *Marbury*, and that only because of subsequent events. These key paragraphs, aside from the enigmatic second sentence, are pure period 2 judicial review. They linked the judiciary's authority over legislation to its responsibility to expound ordinary law, used the conflict of laws analogy to justify refusal to enforce a concededly unconstitutional act, and reaffirmed Court authority "to regard" the Constitution and thereby the key period 2 innovation, the rejection of Blackstone.

The rest of *Marbury* maintained the period 2 analysis and language. Marshall asserted the right of courts "to regard," "to look into," and "to examin[e]" the Constitution. In asserting that "the constitution is to be considered, in court, as a paramount law," Marshall was only denying that the Constitution was a rule to the legislature only. His examples of clear constitutional violations practically duplicated a section of Tucker's *Kamper* opinion. Reference to "the supreme law of the land" echoed James Wilson's usage, and the statement that the invalidity of an act repugnant to the Constitution is a principle not "to be lost sight of" was taken directly from Paterson in *VanHorne's Lessee*. Marshall's argument on the judicial oath was intended to demonstrate that "the framers of the constitution contemplated that instrument, as a rule for the government of *courts*, as well as of the legislature." The inability of the judicial oath to sustain the judicial supremacy of period 3 is a staple of the modern criticism of *Marbury*. But in context *Marbury* merely repeated the period 2 claim of the equality of the branches in rejection of the legislative supremacy of period 1. The concluding paragraph made the same point: "Thus, the particular phraseology of the constitution of the United States confirms and strengthens the principle, supposed to be essential to all written constitutions, that a law repugnant to the constitution is void; and that *courts, as well as other departments,* are bound by that instrument." ...

Marbury departed from the period 2 defense of judicial power over unconstitutional legislation in only two ways, neither of them recognizable at the time. The first was the hidden suggestion that the province and duty of the judicial department included saying what the law of the Constitution is, and the second was its liberal references to the written constitution. There were almost as many references to the written constitution in *Marbury* as in all the period 2 discussions combined. The references to the written constitution in *Marbury* were bland. They carried neither the period 2 meaning of explicit fundamental law not the period 3 meaning of supreme ordinary law. They served more than anything to associate the judicial refusal to execute an unconstitutional act with the written constitution, and to prepare the ground for judicial exposition of the constitutional text that was to begin at some opportune time in the future. ...

McCulloch reviewed the constitutionality of the national bank established by Congress and of a state tax on a bank branch. The central issue was whether Congress had authority under the necessary and proper clause to charter a bank. Marshall held that it did, but in reaching this conclusion he drew more on the objects or intent of the Constitution than on definitional and textual analysis. At the same time, opponents of the bank's constitutionality relied heavily on such analysis.

In *McCulloch*, Marshall also uncharacteristically called attention to the differences between a constitution and ordinary law. In one of the most quoted passages in American constitutional law he reminded his readers, "We must never forget that it is *a constitution* we are expounding." By so arguing against treating the Constitution in terms devised for ordinary law and by relying in *McCulloch* on the objects or intent of the Constitution to establish the constitutionality of the bank, Marshall seemed to contradict the thrust of the analysis presented here.

McCulloch clearly did depart from Marshall's rule that the Constitution's intent is to be gathered from its words. Perhaps he followed this course because he thought that the necessary and proper clause text, by itself, could not sustain the substantive analysis he wanted to make. That his opponents relied heavily on a textual and definitional analysis may also have turned him away from it. Nevertheless, despite this departure from his usual approach, *McCulloch* did not undermine Marshall's larger effort.

For one thing, although Marshall's *McCulloch* opinion emphasized constitutional objects more than his other opinions usually did, it established these objects from the nature of the Constitution and not, ... from external sources such as the "history of the times" or "contemporaneous construction." Nor did Marshall abandon definitions or textual analysis altogether. He gave his own definition of *necessary*, showed why the contending one was wrong, and reinforced his reading by comparing use of the word *necessary* in the clause under consideration with that in the provision barring state taxes on imports "except what may be *absolutely* necessary for executing [state] inspection laws."

Next, Marshall's insistence on expounding the Constitution differently from statutes, rather than contradicting his general approach to constitutional law, assumed the very point in contention between his own and period 2 judicial review, namely, judicial authority to expound the Constitution in the first place. It was precisely because a Constitution was not thought amenable to authoritative judicial exposition that period 2 judicial review sought its meaning in sources external to the text. To remind his readers that it is a constitution we are expounding was to assume judicial authority for such exposition and to reduce the differences between the Constitution and ordinary law to those of degree rather than kind. Such a difference in degree, as invoked by Marshall, remains to this day in the legalized modern judicial review with which we are familiar. The Constitution is universally acknowledged to be more general than statutes and to be open to adaptation to meet future unknowable needs. But it remains subject to authoritative *judicial* exposition, and that is the main difference between period 2 and 3 judicial review. ...

The differences between Marshall and his colleagues in determinations of constitutionality were not random ones, nor was modern judicial review the product of an undirected evolutionary process. Both followed from Marshall's deliberate design, one that transformed fundamental law into the supreme law of the land, subject on that ground to authoritative judicial rather than public or legislative exposition. This change, furthermore, was carried out with no public acknowledgment or discussion. The deliberateness of Marshall's design, as well as its public concealment, is visible, but only by hindsight, in *Marbury v. Madison*, in Marshall's portentous transformation of Tucker's argument made in *Kamper v. Hawkins*. What had been in *Kamper* a claim of judicial authority to "regard" the Constitution in order to make a just exposition of the ordinary law became, in *Marbury*, the suggestion of a judicial authority to say what the law of the Constitution is. This suggestion lay dormant and did not become the operative reading of *Marbury* until Marshall had applied and interpreted the Constitution and had gained public acceptance for such interpretation. Likewise, the period 3 willingness to invalidate legislation as contrary to general principles or the spirit of the Constitution and the absence of any textual exposition in opinions written by Marshall's colleagues indicate that, despite *Marbury*'s liberal references to the written constitution, the significance of that commitment to writing was not yet that attributed to it today. ...

Marshall transformed fundamental law by taking existing raw materials and, with consummate skill, redirecting them to other purposes. By the time he came to the Court judicial refusal to enforce an unconstitutional act was well established and beyond controversy. Nor was judicial exposition of the constitutional text Marshall's invention, foisted on a compliant Court. Precedents for both existed, but what was unprecedented was the simultaneous exposition of the constitutional text and the invalidation of legislation supported by a plausible legislative construction to the contrary. In linking the two, Marshall asserted a judicial claim to be authoritative expounder of the Constitution in the same way the judiciary functions with respect to ordinary law. ...

Spencer Roane, Judicial Power, and State Sovereignty

TIMOTHY S. HUEBNER

By the end of the eighteenth century, many southern appellate judges began to assert the power of judicial review, and through more than three decades of judicial service, Roane played a key role in this expansion of judicial power in his own state. During the decade before his first judicial appointment in 1789, the Virginia Court of Appeals first began to expand its role in the state's new government by asserting the power to review legislative acts. In *Commonwealth v. Caton* (1782), a case involving an extralegal attempt by the House of Delegates to pardon three prisoners condemned for treason, Wythe asserted what was at that time an unprecedented degree of judicial power. "If the whole legislature ... should attempt to overleap the bounds, prescribed to them by the people," he wrote, "I, in administering the public justice of the country, will meet the united powers at my seat in this tribunal; and, pointing to the constitution, will say to them, here is the limit of your authority; and hither shall you go, but no further." In at least two more cases, the Virginia Court of Appeals again asserted the power to review acts of the legislature. At about the same time, the supreme courts of North Carolina and South Carolina claimed this right, while northern state courts in New York, Rhode Island, Massachusetts, Pennsylvania, and New Hampshire did the same.

At a time of confusion over the exact relationship of the courts to the legislative branch, Roane vigorously championed judicial review. While a member of the General Court, Roane delivered an important opinion in *Kamper v. Hawkins* (1793), a case involving a 1792 law that eliminated some of the important distinctions between courts of law and equity. The act allowed district court judges to grant injunctions to stay proceedings on any judgment obtained in a district court and declared that district courts might proceed to the final hearing of all suits commenced by injunction—powers previously reserved to the state's High Court of Chancery. While Roane and Judge St. George Tucker were sitting at the Dumfries District Court, Peter Kamper petitioned under the new law for an injunction to stay the proceeding on a judgment Mary Hawkins had previously obtained against him. When Tucker declined to hear the motion on jurisdictional grounds, Roane, not wanting to decide this important matter by himself, adjourned the case to the General Court because of the subject's "novelty and difficulty."

When a five-member General Court convened to decide the case, Roane and Tucker took similarly strong stands in favor of judicial review. Born in Bermuda in 1752, Tucker had arrived in Virginia in 1770 and, like Roane, studied law under Wythe. Tucker later succeeded his mentor as professor of law at William and Mary, where he prepared and published a multivolume annotated edition of Blackstone's *Commentaries*. Already regarded among the leaders of the Virginia legal community, Tucker's learned and lengthy opinion in *Kamper* further contributed to his reputation. Drawing on the accumulated wisdom of William Blackstone, Thomas Paine, and Alexander Hamilton, among others, Tucker eloquently argued for constitutional

From Huebner, Timothy S., *The Southern Judicial Tradition: State Judges and Sectional Distinctiveness, 1790-1890.* Published by University of Georgia Press, 1999. Reproduced with permission of The University of Georgia Press.

supremacy and judicial review. The commonwealth's constitution, he believed, stood above acts of the legislature, and, because it was a written constitution, all branches of the government were clearly subject to its dictates. Moreover, Tucker contended, "the duty of expounding" the constitution "must be exclusively vested in the judiciary." "The judiciary are bound to take notice of the constitution, as the first law of the land," he summarized, "and that what soever is contradictory thereto, is not the law of the land."

Equal to Tucker's opinion in its substantive support for judicial review, the style of Roane's decision was less doctrinal and more practical. Roane reversed his position from when the case had first come before him in the district court; at that time he had doubted whether the judiciary possessed the power to prevent the execution of an act passed by the legislature. "My opinion, on more mature considerations," he wrote in *Kamper*, "is changed in this respect." Roane's turnaround was dramatic, for he supported judicial review in more explicit language than did any of his fellow judges, including Tucker. "I now think that the judiciary may and ought not only to refuse to execute a law expressly repugnant to the Constitution," he wrote, "but also one which is, by a plain and natural construction, in opposition to the fundamental principles thereof." While Tucker described the judiciary in defensive terms—as "a barrier against the possible usurpation or abuse of power in other departments"— Roane portrayed the courts as active agents of review, as the branch of government that "may and ought to adjudge a law unconstitutional and void."

Roane, like Tucker, argued that the constitution—not legislative action—was the expression of the people's sovereign will and that the judiciary alone could determine a law's constitutionality. In his view, by severing ties with England, the Revolution had created a unique set of circumstances for Virginians. The commonwealth's constitutional convention, because it neither served nor derived any power under the former government, constituted "a spontaneous assemblage of the people of Virginia." Moreover, according to Roane, the decisions of the courts and even the proclamations of the legislature had continually upheld the idea that the constitution, as the product of the people's work, was superior to any legislative act. Constitutional interpretation, Roane concluded, was the domain of the judiciary. Because the courts examined all laws dealing with a particular subject when deciding a case, Roane reasoned that it was also within the bounds of judicial responsibility to assess a law within the context of the constitution. "In expounding laws," he argued, "the judiciary considers every law which relates to the subject: would you have them to shut their eyes against that law which is of the highest authority of any, or against a part of that law, which either by its words of by its spirit, denies to any but the people the power to change it?" On the issue of judicial review, Roane's opinion in *Kamper v. Hawkins* was decisive.

Roane then declared the law unconstitutional. Because the legislation in question transferred important powers from the chancery courts to the district courts—from constitutionally created tribunals to legislatively created tribunals—Roane viewed the act as an unlawful expansion of legislative authority. The act not only violated the theory of separation of powers but also threatened the independence and power of the judiciary, especially the principle of judicial review. "If the legislature can transfer from constitutional to legislative courts all judicial powers," Roane argued, "these dependent tribunals being the creatures of the legislature itself, will not dare to oppose an unconstitutional law, and the principle I set out upon, viz. that such laws ought to be opposed, would become a dead letter, or in other words, this would pave the way to an uncontrolled power in the legislature." In Roane's view, judicial review and judicial independence were inseparable. Because the 1792 law seemed to violate both of these principles, Roane deemed the act unconstitutional....

The court's decision in *Kamper v. Hawkins*, as well as Roane's and his successors' continued assertions of judicial power, firmly established the practice of judicial review in Virginia. Drawing on the ideas of Wythe and Tucker, Roane explicitly described the judiciary as the agent of review when legislative acts violated either the letter or the "fundamental principles" of the constitution. Because of his directness on the issue, Roane earned a reputation as one of the progenitors of judicial review in Virginia....

...Roane worried that a consolidated national government, in the form of a powerful U.S. Supreme Court, threatened to undermine the power of both state legislatures and state courts. As Roane once wrote to James Monroe, "The only fear is, that carried away by the Vortex of Power—feeling power and forgetting right—the safeguard for our liberties by the virtue of our fathers, will be demolished." Rather than a precursor to mid-nineteenth-century secessionists, Roane was more the heir to late-eighteenth-century patriots in his defense of states....

Roane began his crusade against the Supreme Court with his opinion in *Hunter v. Martin* (1814), a case involving Virginia's postrevolutionary confiscation of Tory lands. After the U.S. Supreme Court voided the state's confiscation act in *Fairfax's Devisee v. Hunter's Lessee* (1813) on the grounds that the law violated the Treaty of 1794 with England, Roane led the way both in declaring Section 25 of the Judiciary Act of 1789 unconstitutional and in refusing to obey the mandate of the Supreme Court. Roane viewed the dispute as a judicial clash, involving the independence, power, and jurisdiction of two distinct court systems, one of which was trying to overrun the other. His lengthy opinion in *Hunter v. Martin*, reprinted in the *Richmond Enquirer*, earned the Virginia judge a national reputation as the Supreme Court's chief foe and initiated a crusade against the Court that ended only with Roane's death.

Roane attacked Section 25 of the 1789 act, which allowed for appeals from state courts to the federal judiciary, as inconsistent with the U.S. Constitution's provisions regarding judicial power and jurisdiction. Roane believed that unless stated otherwise, all of the Constitution's provisions regarding the jurisdiction of courts applied only to the federal judiciary. "Naturally the jurisdiction granted to a government is confined to the courts of that government," Roane claimed. "It does not, naturally, run into and affect the courts of another and distinct government." With the exception of Article 6, which specifically referred to state judges, Roane found no constitutional provisions regulating state courts. Section 2 of Article 3, for example, which provided for trial by jury in the state in which the crime was committed, applied only to federal courts. Such was also the case with the Seventh Amendment's establishment of the right of trial by jury in civil cases. "It will not be contended that it relates to the jurisdiction of the state courts," Roane wrote, "as most of the state constitutions had already provided for the inviolability of jury trial." And in Roane's view, when the Eighth Amendment afforded the right of speedy trial in the state in which the crime was committed, the reference again was undoubtedly to the federal courts. To Roane, in short, Section 25 of the Judiciary Act of 1789, by intruding into the jurisdiction of state courts, was inconsistent with the Constitution's exclusive concern with federal court jurisdiction. Because the Constitution did not subordinate the state judiciary to the federal, the two court systems stood on equal footing, with neither holding power over the other. Therefore, the Virginia Court of Appeals, as a coequal judicial body, had legitimate grounds on which to oppose the Supreme Court's decision. ...

In subsequent political writings, state sovereignty emerged as the centerpiece of Roane's challenge to Marshall. In advancing this argument, Roane drew upon the Antifederalist tradition of the 1780s as well as the Kentucky and Virginia Resolutions of 1798–99. Roane's attachment to Jefferson, the author of the Kentucky Resolution, accelerated Roane's devotion to the doctrine of state sovereignty. In 1815 Roane sought Jefferson's view of the decision in *Hunter v. Martin*, initiating an important political friendship that continued until Roane's death. When Jefferson said that he agreed with Roane's opinion in *Hunter v. Martin*, Roane expressed a renewed sense of confidence about the ruling. "The opinion here seem pretty general in favour of the decision," he wrote to James Barbour, one of Virginia's U.S. senators. "If we have erred, we have erred with Plato & Socrates—for Mr. Jefferson is with us." Roane's deep respect for Jefferson, coupled with the former president's long-standing commitment to state sovereignty, help to explain Roane's fervent adoption of the theory and his renewed sense of determination on the matter. With Jefferson on his side, Roane made it known that future Supreme Court decisions of a like nature would meet with similar defiance. "The 25th Section of the judicial act," he asserted to Barbour, "can never be enforced in Virginia."

Backed by Jefferson, Roane continued his campaign against the Supreme Court. Marshall's vigorous endorsement of national supremacy and implied powers in *McCulloch v. Maryland* (1819) provoked a series of essays by Roane in the *Richmond Enquirer. McCulloch* involved the constitutionality of the national bank and the ability of the state of Maryland to tax a branch of that institution. Roane supported the national bank. In at least two instances, he affirmed the necessity of the bank, once observing that "a great a general distress would pervade all classes" were the bank to disappear. He even purchased fifty shares of stock in the bank for his son, William. In response to the *McCulloch* decision, therefore, Roane did not write as an opponent of the national bank itself. Even though the Virginia Court of Appeals was not involved in *McCulloch*, Roane viewed Marshall's decision as a flagrant perversion of the Supreme Court's proper role and a threat to the sovereignty of the states.

As in *Hunter v. Martin*, Roane used state sovereignty to attack the Supreme Court's jurisdiction in particular and the national government's power in general. "It is not competent to the general government to usurp rights reserved to the states, nor for its courts to adjudicate them away. ... Our government is a federal and not a consolidated government." This distinction was important. If the nation were truly federal in character, the Supreme Court would have no jurisdiction over a state matter, as such issues would remain the domain of the states' legislators and judges. By augmenting the Supreme Court's jurisdiction to permit review of state laws, Roane believed, Marshall threatened to replace the federal system with a consolidated scheme in which the national government was superior. To combat this idea, Roane turned again to state sovereignty. "The Constitution of the United

States was not adopted by the people of the United States, as one people," he wrote, countering the Court's popular sovereignty and national supremacy argument. "It was adopted by the several states, in their highest sovereign character, that is, by the people of the said states, respectively; such people being competent, and they only competent, to alter the preexisting governments operating in the said states." Under this theory of sovereignty, the Supreme Court, as an agent of the national government, possessed no jurisdiction over state laws, whether judicial decisions or statutes.

While Roane employed state sovereignty to make the jurisdictional argument, he drew on the common-law tradition to undermine Marshall's notion of the implied powers of Congress. Roane contended that the Necessary and Proper Clause in no way extended the powers that the Constitution specifically granted to the legislative branch. Instead, the words of the clause, he wrote, were "tautologous and redundant, though harmless." In other words, the Necessary and Proper Clause, in Roane's view, was a mere truism that had no meaning in and of itself and certainly did not augment the enumerated powers of the national government. Citing the works of Littleton, Coke, and Blackstone, Roane contended that grants of power included only those accessory powers that were "fairly incident" to the enumerated powers. Roane thus disagreed with Marshall's liberal interpretation of the Necessary and Proper Clause as out of line with established principles of the common law. Again, Roane did not attack the specific act of Congress establishing the national bank. Rather, he condemned Marshall's broad grant of authority to Congress seemingly to assume whatever powers it wished at the expense of the states. "I principally make war against the declaratory decision of the Supreme Court," Roane wrote, "giving Congress power to 'bind us in all cases whatsoever.'"

Finally, Roane assailed Marshall for his expansive view of judicial power. Marshall's broad attempt to establish national supremacy and to expand the central government's implied powers struck Roane as a flagrant perversion of the Supreme Court's role. In a case that dealt with specific issues regarding the national bank, Marshall's sweeping pronouncements on the scope of congressional power and the nature of the Union appeared to Roane to be "entirely extrajudicial and without authority." Moreover, Roane saw the Court assuming the form of a legislative body. The Supreme Court "often puts its veto upon the acts of the immediate representatives of the people," he charged. "It in fact assumes legislative powers by repealing laws which the legislature have enacted."

When taken within the context of Roane's own spirited assertions of judicial review of legislation at the state level, these statements in support of legislative supremacy seem out of character or at least ironic. However, one of the key issues in this debate for Roane was that of defending his position as a state judge. If the Supreme Court under Marshall were allowed to continue unabated its dramatic expansion of national judicial power and jurisdiction, what would become of the Virginia Court of Appeals and other state courts? Prodded by Jefferson, Roane argued that Marshall's decision in *McCulloch* was another step in the creation of a consolidated national judiciary that presented a looming threat to state judicial power. "While I would consent to … support the federal judiciary within the states, in all its legitimate objects," Roane wrote in 1819, "I would not set up without necessity a batch of courts strong enough to withdraw from the state courts their proper powers." In Roane's view, the Supreme Court's continued attempts to further its power threatened to render state courts—including his own Court of Appeals—weak and ineffective.

✛ F U R T H E R   R E A D I N G

Bickel, Alexander. *The Least Dangerous Branch: The Supreme Court at the Bar of Politics* (1962).

Choper, Jesse H. *Judicial Review and the National Political Process: A Functional Reconsideration of the Role of the Supreme Court* (1980).

Clinton, Robert Lowry. *Marbury v. Madison and Judicial Review* (1989).

Ellis, Richard. *The Jeffersonian Crisis: Courts and Politics in the Young Republic* (1971).

Hall, Kermit L., ed., *Judicial Review in American History: Major Historical Interpretations* (1987).

———. *The Supreme Court and Judicial Review in American History* (1985).

Hall, Kermit T. and Kevin T. McGuire, eds., *Institutions of Democracy: The Judicial Branch* (2005).

Hamilton, Daniel W., ed., "A Symposium on *The People Themselves: Popular Constitutionalism and Judicial Review*," *Chicago-Kent Law Review*, 81 (2006): 809–1182.

Harrington, Matthew. *Jay and Ellsworth, The First Courts: Justices, Rulings, Legacy* (2008).

Haskins, George L. and Herbert A. Johnson, *Foundations of Power: John Marshall, 1801–1815*; vol. II of *The Oliver Wendell Holmes Devise History of the Supreme Court of the United States* (1981).

Hobson, Charles. *The Great Chief Justice: John Marshall and the Rule of Law* (1996).

Hobson, Charles, *et al.*, eds., *The Papers of John Marshall*, 12 vols. (1974–2006).

Johnson, Herbert A. *The Chief Justiceship of John Marshall* (1997).

Killenbeck, Mark Robert, *M'Culloch v. Maryland: Securing a Nation* (2006).

Klarman, Michael, "How Great were the 'Great' Marshall Court Decisions?" *Virginia Law Review*, 87 (2001): 1111–1184.

Levy, Leonard W. "Judicial Review, History, and Democracy," in L.W. Levy, ed., *Judgments: Essays on American Constitutional History* (1972).

McDowell, Gary L. *Curbing the Courts: The Constitution and the Limits of Judicial Power* (1988).

Nelson, William E. *Marbury v. Madison: The Origins and Legacy of Judicial Review* (2000).

Newmyer, R. Kent. *John Marshall and the Heroic Age of the Supreme Court* (2001).

———. *Supreme Court Justice Joseph Story: Statesman of the Old Republic* (1985).

———. *The Supreme Court under Marshall and Taney*, 2nd ed. (2006).

Simon, James. *What Kind of Nation: Thomas Jefferson, John Marshall, and the Epic Struggle to Create a United States* (2002).

Smith, Jean Edward. *John Marshall: Definer of a Nation* (1996).

White, G. Edward. *The American Judicial Tradition: Profiles of Leading American Judges* (1988).

———. *The Marshall Court and Cultural Change, 1815–1835* (1988).

Wolfe, Christopher. *The Rise of Modern Judicial Review: From Constitutional Interpretation to Judge-Made Law* (1986).

CHAPTER
5

Andrew Jackson, Nullification,
and Indian Removal

For decades, historians referred to most of the first half of the nineteenth century as "the Age of Jackson," and for good reason. The most powerful of all of nineteenth-century presidents save for Abraham Lincoln, Andrew Jackson served two terms in office and transformed the nation's political landscape. As Americans moved westward during the early nineteenth century, new states entered the Union, usually without the property qualifications for suffrage that had previously limited voting to propertied (mostly white) males. Older states gradually began eliminating these property qualifications as well, until near universal white male suffrage prevailed by the 1830s. The first president born west of the Appalachian Mountains, Jackson became a hero to many Americans because of his frontier origins, and he seemed to embody the democratic spirit of the age.

Jackson interpreted the Constitution as providing for a vigorous chief executive. Article II of the document stated that the president was to be elected indirectly by the people through an electoral college composed of members from each state, with the number of electors dependant on state population. The president was to share certain powers, such as the appointment of judges and the making of war, with the Congress. This hedging of presidential power reflected the ambivalence of late eighteenth-century Americans about leadership. They recognized that the new nation would benefit from continuous, effective, and unified administration of government, but they also worried that, as the nation grew in population and territory, these same qualities might create an opportunity for one person to accumulate power sufficient to re-create the monarchical forms of Great Britain's government. Nevertheless, Jackson exercised the veto power more than all of his predecessors combined (12 times), and he stubbornly staked out strong positions on all of the major policy disputes of the day. Two of these disputes—over South Carolina's attempt to nullify the federal tariff and over the removal of Native Americans from the southeastern United States—proved to be defining moments of Jackson's presidency.

The nullification crisis had its origins in the "Tariff of Abominations" of 1828, which increased import duties to record-high levels. Many southern political leaders, led by John C. Calhoun of South Carolina, believed that a high tariff benefited northern manufacturers at the expense of the southern economy, in that it kept imported manufactured goods from competing with northern industry. In 1832 Congress passed a new, somewhat milder tariff, but the measure retained the protective principle. To combat the tariff, Calhoun championed the doctrine of nullification—the idea that a state could invalidate an act of Congress. In essence, he argued, states were the final arbiters of the Constitution. As a constitutional principle, nullification built on the Virginia and Kentucky Resolutions of the late 1790s, written in opposition to the Alien and Sedition Acts. Calhoun argued that the national government was a mere trustee for the sovereign states, which had entered into a compact to create the national government. This "compact theory" mocked the twin concepts of nationalism and federal judicial review that Chief Justice Marshall had been pressing. Nullification also drew the ire of President Jackson. While a southerner sympathetic to states' rights, he was strongly nationalistic in his attitude toward the Union. The fact that Calhoun, his vice president, assumed leadership of the nullification movement only aggravated Jackson's raw political nerves.

The controversy surrounding Indian removal began when Jackson announced his clear intention to support such a policy. As a military leader, Jackson had fought Indians for years, and as a presidential candidate he indicated his support for relocating thousands of Native Americans from the southeastern states to present-day Oklahoma. Jackson, in fact, argued that removal would protect Indians from land-hungry whites. Once Jackson announced his support of this policy in his first annual message to Congress, states moved aggressively to enact laws invalidating claims of Indian sovereignty. Because these state laws seemingly violated treaties negotiated between Indian tribes and the U.S. government, some of these laws ended up being challenged in court. The most famous of these cases involved the Cherokee, the tribe that had gone the farthest in adopting European-American cultural norms. Demonstrating their faith in American legal institutions, the Cherokee hired one of the nation's top attorneys, William Wirt, to argue their case against Georgia, and three times the issue came before the Supreme Court. When the Marshall Court ruled in Worcester v. Georgia (1832), the last of these cases, that the Cherokee constituted a political nation over which Georgia had no control, Georgia and Jackson ignored the decision. Although Indians who resided on private rather than tribal lands stayed behind and a group of Seminoles in Florida fought against removal, eventually some 60,000 American Indians made the difficult journey to Oklahoma. Another 15,000 or so died along the way, most from disease.

Jackson's presidency raises a host of constitutional questions. What exactly was Jackson's view of the Constitution, the Union, and the states? Did he hold a unified constitutional vision that allowed for both his strong opposition to nullification and his advocacy of state sovereignty over Indians, or were his actions motivated more by politics and personal dislike of both nullifiers and Native Americans? What are we to make of Jackson's defiance of the Supreme Court in Worcester, particularly in light of his challenge to McCulloch v. Maryland in his veto of the bank's re-charter? Was Jackson blatantly anti-Court, or do his actions simply reflect the idea of the departmental theory of review? What was the relationship between nullification, Indian removal, and slavery? South Carolina, after all, was the only state in which slaves outnumbered whites. Was South Carolina—and perhaps Georgia—really motivated by underlying concerns over federal interference with their "peculiar institution"?

✢ D O C U M E N T S

The following documents demonstrate the tensions surrounding the issues of state sovereignty and Indian removal during the Jackson Administration. In 1828, the then Vice President John C. Calhoun put forth the "South Carolina Exposition and Protest," an anonymously written treatise on state sovereignty and nullification, excerpted here as Document 1. (Calhoun also served as vice president under John Quincy Adams, Jackson's predecessor.) When Calhoun's authorship of the "South Carolina Exposition" became apparent, a rift developed between him and Jackson that resulted in Jackson selecting a new vice presidential candidate in 1832. Calhoun eventually resigned from office in December of that year and went on to serve in the U.S. Senate from South Carolina.

In an address to Congress in December 1829, excerpted here as Document 2, Jackson announced his formal support for Indian removal. The following May, Congress passed the Indian Removal Act, which granted the authority to the president to negotiate the transfer of lands west of the Mississippi and outside of any state at the time to Indian tribes in exchange for their lands in the southeastern United States. With the support of both Congress and the president, states had a free hand to enact legislation terminating Indian rights within their borders. Georgia had already begun this process, and other southern states soon followed.

The Cherokee nation mounted a legal challenge to Georgia's law. In *Cherokee Nation v. Georgia*, Document 3, Chief Justice Marshall refused to issue a definitive ruling on the question of Cherokee sovereignty. Although sympathetic to the plight of the Cherokee, Marshall hesitated to hold outright, in opposition to the president and Congress, that the Cherokee were a sovereign nation. Describing the Cherokee as a "domestic dependent nation," Marshall and his colleagues (by a 4–2 vote) denied the request for an injunction against the Georgia law on the grounds that the Court lacked jurisdiction. Still, Marshall hinted that another case with a different set of facts might allow the Court to make a ruling on the status of Cherokee lands. Another case the following year, *Worcester v. Georgia*, Document 4, gave Marshall a chance to reconsider his decision. *Worcester* involved the arrest of two missionaries by the state of Georgia within the Cherokee nation. The missionaries' appeal directly challenged the Georgia law and asked the Court to rule that the Cherokee constituted a sovereign nation, over which Georgia had no control. This time (in a 5–1 vote) Marshall and his colleagues ruled against the state.

While supporting Georgia's claim to state sovereignty, Jackson forcefully opposed South Carolina's attempt to nullify the tariff. In October 1832, the South Carolina legislature called a nullification convention, which the following month issued an "Ordinance of Nullification," Document 5, declaring the federal tariff laws of 1828 and 1832 null and void. In December 1832, Jackson responded with a "Proclamation to the People of South Carolina," Document 6, which bluntly rejected nullification. The following year Congress ended the crisis. It passed a law giving Jackson the power to collect the tariff in South Carolina and keep the state in the Union, while at the same time adopting legislation that gradually lowered the tariff.

✢ D O C U M E N T   1

South Carolinian John C. Calhoun Proposes Nullification, 1828

… The General Government is one of specific powers, and it can rightfully exercise only the powers expressly granted, and those that may be "necessary and proper" to carry them into effect; all others being reserved expressly to the States, or to the people. It results necessarily, that those who claim to exercise a power under the Constitution, are bound to shew, that it is expressly granted, or that it is necessary and proper, as a means to some of the granted powers. The advocates of the Tariff have offered no such proof. It is true, that the third [*sic*] section of the first article of the Constitution of the United States authorizes Congress to lay and collect an impost duty, but it is granted as a tax power, for the sole purpose of revenue; a power in its nature essentially different from that of imposing protective or prohibitory duties. The two are incompatable [*sic*]; for the prohibitory system must end in destroying the revenue from impost. It has been said that the system is a violation of the spirit and not the letter of the Constitution. The distinction is not material. The Constitution may be as grossly violated by acting against its meaning as against its letter; but it may be proper to dwell a moment on the point, in order to understand more fully the real character of the acts, under which the interest of this, and other States similarly situated, has been sacrificed. The facts are few and simple. The Constitution grants to Congress the power of imposing a duty on imports for revenue; which power is abused by being converted into an instrument for rearing up the industry of one section of the country on the ruins of another. The violation then consists in using a power, granted for one object, to advance another, and that by the sacrifice of the original object. It is, in a word, *a violation of perversion*, the most dangerous of all, because the most insidious, and difficult to resist. Others cannot be perpetrated without the aid of the judiciary; this may be, by the executive and legislative alone. The courts by their own decisions cannot look into the motives of legislators—they are obliged to take acts by their titles and professed objects, and if *they* be constitutional they cannot interpose their power, however grossly the acts may violate the Constitution. The proceedings of the last session sufficiently prove, that the House of Representatives are aware of the distinction, and determined to avail themselves of the advantage. . . .

On the great and vital point, the industry of the country, which comprehends nearly all the other interests, two great sections of the Union are opposed. We want free trade; they, restrictions. We want moderate taxes, frugality in the government, economy, accountability, and a rigid application of the public money, to the payment of the public debt, and the objects authorized by the Constitution; in all these particulars, if we may judge by experience, their views of their interest are the opposite. They act and feel on all questions connected with the American System, as sovereigns; as those always do who impose burdens on others for their own benefit; and we, on the contrary, like those on whom such burdens are imposed. In a word, to the extent stated, the country is divided and organized into two great opposing parties, one sovereign and the other subject; marked by all the characteristics which must ever accompany that relation, under whatever from it may exist. That our industry is controlled by the many, instead of one, by a majority in Congress elected by a majority in the community having an opposing interest, instead of hereditary rulers, forms not the slightest mitigation of the evil. In fact, instead of mitigating, it aggravates. In our case one opposing branch of industry cannot prevail without associating others, and thus instead of a single act of oppression we must bear many. . . . Liberty comprehends the idea of *responsible power*, that those who make and execute the laws should be controlled by those on whom they operate; that the governed should govern. Thus to prevent rulers from abusing their trust, constituents must controul [*sic*] them through elections; and so to prevent the major from oppressing the minor interests of society, the constitution must provide . . . a check founded on the same principle, and equally efficacious. In fact the abuse of delegated power, and the tyranny of the greater over the less interests of society, are the two great dangers, and the only two, to be guarded against; and if *they* be effectually guarded liberty must be *eternal*. ... No government based on the naked principle, that the majority ought to govern, however true the maxim in its proper sense and under proper restrictions, ever preserved its liberty, even for a single generation. ... Those governments only, which provide checks, which limit and restrain within proper bounds the power of the majority, have had a prolonged existence, and been distinguished for virtue, power and happiness. Constitutional government, and the government of a majority, are utterly incompatible, it being the sole purpose of a constitution to impose limitations and checks upon the majority. An unchecked majority, is a despotism—and government is free, and will be permanent in proportion to the number, complexity and efficiency of the checks, by which its powers are controlled. ...

Our system, then consists of two distinct and independent sovereignties. The general powers conferred on the General Government, are subject to its sole and separate control, and the States cannot, without violating the Constitution, interpose their authority to check, or in any manner counteract its movements, so long, as they are confined to its proper sphere; so also the peculiar and local powers, reserved to the States, are subject to their exclusive control, nor can the General Government interfere with them, without on its part, also violating the Constitution. In order to have a full and clear conception of our institutions, it will be proper to remark, that there is in our system a striking distinction between the government and the sovereign power. Whatever may be the true doctrine in regard to the sovereignty of the States individually, it is unquestionably clear that while the government of the union is vested in its legislative, executive and political departments, the actual sovereign power, resides in the several States, who created it, in their separate and distinct political character. ...

... The constitutional power to protect their rights as members of the confederacy, results necessarily, by the most simple and demonstrable arguments, from the very nature of the relation subsisting between the States and General Government. If it be conceded, as it must by every one who is the least conversant with our institutions, that the sovereign power is divided between the States and General Government, and that the former holds its reserved rights, in the same high sovereign capacity, which the latter does its delegated rights; it will be impossible to deny to the States the right of deciding on the infraction of their rights, and the proper remedy to be applied for the correction. The right of judging, in such cases, is an essential attribute of sovereignty of which the States cannot be divested, without losing their sovereignty itself; and being reduced to a subordinate corporate condition. In fact, to divide power, and to give to one of the parties the exclusive right of judging of the portion allotted to each, is in reality not to divide at all; and to reserve such exclusive right to the General Government, (it matters not by what department it be exercised,) is in fact to constitute it one great consolidated government, with unlimited powers, and to reduce the States to mere corporations. It is impossible to understand the force of terms, and to deny these conclusions. The opposite opinion can be embraced only on hasty and imperfect views of the relation existing between the States and the General Government. But the existence of the right of judging of their powers, clearly established from the sovereignty of the States, as clearly implies a veto, or controul on the action of the General Government on contested points of authority; and this very controul is the remedy, which the Constitution has provided to prevent the enroachment of the General Government on the reserved right of the States; and by the exercise of which, the distribution of power between the General and State Governments, may be preserved forever inviolate, as is established by the Constitution; and thus afford effectual protection to the great minor interest of the community, against the oppression of the majority.

✤ D O C U M E N T   2

President Andrew Jackson Advocates Indian Removal, 1829

Fellow Citizens of the Senate and of the House of Representatives:

... The condition and ulterior destiny of the Indian tribes within the limits of some of our States have become objects of much interest and importance. It has long been the policy of Government to introduce among them the arts of civilization, in the hope of gradually reclaiming them from a wandering life. This policy has, however, been coupled with another wholly incompatible with its success. Professing a desire to civilize and settle them, we have at the same time lost no opportunity to purchase their lands and thrust them farther into the wilderness. By this means they have not only been kept in a wandering state, but been led to look upon us as unjust and indifferent to their fate. Thus, though lavish in its expenditures upon the subject, Government has constantly defeated its own policy, and the Indians in general, receding farther and farther to the west, have retained their savage habits. A portion, however, of the Southern tribes, having mingled much with the whites and made some progress in the arts of civilized life, have lately attempted to erect an independent government within the limits of Georgia and Alabama. These States, claiming to be the only sovereigns within their territories, extended their laws over the Indians, which induced the latter to call upon the United States for protection.

Under these circumstances the question presented was whether the General Government had a right to sustain those people in their pretensions. The Constitution declares that "no new State shall be formed or erected within the jurisdiction of any other State" without the consent of its legislature. If the General Government is not permitted to tolerate the erection of a confederate State within the territory of one of the members of this Union against her consent, much less could it allow a foreign and independent government to establish itself there.

Georgia became a member of the Confederacy which eventuated in our Federal Union as a sovereign State, always asserting her claim to certain limits, which, having been originally defined in her colonial charter and subsequently recognized in the treaty of peace, she has ever since continued to enjoy, except as they have been circumscribed by her own voluntary transfer of a portion of her territory to the United States in the articles of cession of 1802. Alabama was admitted into the Union on the same footing with the original States, with boundaries which were prescribed by Congress.

There is no constitutional, conventional, or legal provision which allows them less power over the Indians within their borders than is possessed by Maine or New York. Would the people of Maine permit the Penobscot tribe to erect an independent government within their State? And unless they did would it not be the duty of the General Government to support them in resisting such a measure? Would the people of New York permit each remnant of the six Nations within her borders to declare itself an independent people under the protection of the United States? Could the Indians establish a separate republic on each of their reservations in Ohio? And if they were so disposed would it be the duty of this Government to protect them in the attempt? If the principle involved in the obvious answer to these questions be abandoned, it will follow that the objects of this Government are reversed, and that it has become a part of its duty to aid in destroying the States which it was established to protect.

Actuated by this view of the subject, I informed the Indians inhabiting parts of Georgia and Alabama that their attempt to establish an independent government would not be countenanced by the Executive of the United States, and advised them to emigrate beyond the Mississippi or submit to the laws of those States.

Our conduct toward these people is deeply interesting to our national character. Their present condition, contrasted with what they once were, makes a most powerful appeal to our sympathies. Our ancestors found them the uncontrolled possessors of these vast regions. By persuasion and force they have been made to retire from river to river and from mountain to mountain, until some of the tribes have become extinct and others have left but remnants to preserve for a while their once terrible names. Surrounded by the whites with their arts of civilization, which by destroying the resources of the savage doom him to weakness and decay, the fate of the Mohegan, the Narragansett, and the Delaware is fast over-taking the Choctaw, the Cherokee, and the Creek. That this fate surely awaits them if they remain within the limits of the States does not admit of a doubt. Humanity and national honor demand that every effort should be made to avert so great a calamity. It is too late to inquire whether it was just in the United States to include them and their territory within the bounds of new States, whose limits they could control. That step can not be retraced. A State can not be dismembered by Congress or restricted in the exercise of her constitutional power. But the people of those States and of every State, actuated by feelings of justice and a regard for our national honor, submit to you the interesting question whether something can not be done, consistently with the rights of the States, to preserve this much-injured race.

As a means of effecting this end I suggest for your consideration the propriety of setting apart an ample district west of the Mississippi, and without the limits of any State or Territory now formed, to be guaranteed to the Indian tribes as long as they shall occupy it, each tribe having a distinct control over the portion designated for its use. There they may be secured in the enjoyment of governments of their own choice, subject to no other control from the United States than such as may be necessary to preserve peace on the frontier and between the several tribes. There the benevolent may endeavor to teach them the arts of civilization, and, by promoting union and harmony among them, to raise up an interesting commonwealth, destined to perpetuate the race and to attest the humanity and justice of this Government.

This emigration should be voluntary, for it would be as cruel as unjust to compel the aborigines to abandon the graves of their fathers and seek a home in a distant land. But they should be distinctly informed that if they remain within the limits of the States they must be subject to their laws. In return for their obedience as individuals they will without doubt be protected in the enjoyment of those possessions which they have improved by their industry. But it seems to me visionary to suppose that in this state of things claims can be allowed on tracts of country on which they have neither dwelt nor made improvements, merely because they have seen them from the mountain or passed them in the chase. Submitting to the laws of the States, and receiving, like other citizens, protection in their persons and property, they will ere long become merged in the mass of our population.

✠ D O C U M E N T   3

Cherokee Nation v. Georgia, 1831

Mr Chief Justice Marshall delivered the opinion of the Court.

This bill is brought by the Cherokee nation, praying an injunction to restrain the state of Georgia from the execution of certain laws of that state, which, as is alleged, go directly to annihilate the Cherokees as a political society, and to seize, for the use of Georgia, the lands of the nation which have been assured to them by the United States in solemn treaties repeatedly made and still in force.

If courts were permitted to indulge their sympathies, a case better calculated to excite them can scarcely be imagined. A people once numerous, powerful, and truly independent, found by our ancestors in the quiet and uncontrolled possession of an ample domain, gradually sinking beneath our superior policy, our arts and our arms, have yielded their lands by successive treaties, each of which contains a solemn guarantee of the residue, until they retain no more of their formerly extensive territory than is deemed necessary to their comfortable subsistence. To preserve this remnant, the present application in made.

Before we can look into the merits of the case, a preliminary inquiry presents itself. Has this court jurisdiction of the cause?

The third article of the constitution describes the extent of the judicial power. The second section closes an enumeration of the cases to which it is extended, with "controversies" "between a state or the citizens thereof, and foreign states, citizens, or subjects." A subsequent clause of the same section gives the supreme court original jurisdiction in all cases in which a state shall be a party. The party defendant may then unquestionably be sued in this court. May the plaintiff sue in it? Is the Cherokee nation a foreign state in the sense in which that term is used in the constitution?

The counsel for the plaintiffs have maintained the affirmative of this proposition with great earnestness and ability. So much of the argument as was intended to prove the character of the Cherokees as a state, as a distinct political society, separated from others, capable of managing its own affairs and governing itself, has, in the opinion of a majority of the judges, been completely successful. They have been uniformly treated as a state from the settlement of our country. The numerous treaties made with them by the United States recognize them as a people capable of maintaining the relations of peace and war, of being responsible in their political character for any violation of their engagements, or for any aggression committed on the citizens of the United States by any individual of their community. Laws have been enacted in the spirit of these treaties. The acts of our government plainly recognize the Cherokee nation as a state, and the courts are bound by those acts.

A question of much more difficulty remains. Do the Cherokees constitute a foreign state in the sense of the constitution?

The counsel have shown conclusively that they are not a state of the union, and have insisted that individually they are aliens, not owing allegiance to the United States. An aggregate of aliens composing a state must, they say, be a foreign state. Each individual being foreign, the whole must be foreign.

This argument is imposing, but we must examine it more closely before we yield to it. The condition of the Indians in relation to the United States is perhaps unlike that of any other two people in existence. In the general, nations not owing a common allegiance are foreign to each other. The term foreign nation is, with strict propriety, applicable by either to the other. But he relation of the Indians to the United States is marked by peculiar and cardinal distinctions which exist no where else.

The Indian territory is admitted to compose a part of the United States. In all our maps, geographical treatises, histories, and laws, it is so considered. In all our intercourse with foreign nations, in our commercial regulations, in any attempt at intercourse between Indians and foreign nations, they are considered as within the jurisdictional limits of the United States, subject to many of those restraints which are imposed upon our own citizens. They acknowledge themselves in their treaties to be under the protection of the United States; they admit that the United States shall have the sole and exclusive right of regulating the trade with them, and managing all their affairs as they think proper; and the Cherokees in particular were allowed by the treaty of Hopewell, which preceded the constitution, "to send a deputy of their choice, whenever they think fit, to congress." Treaties were made with some tribes by the state of New York, under a then unsettled construction of the confederation, by which they ceded all their lands to that state, taking back a limited grant to themselves, in which they admit their dependence.

Though the Indians are acknowledged to have an unquestionable, and, heretofore, unquestioned right to the lands they occupy, until that right shall be extinguished by a voluntary cession to our government; yet it may well be doubted whether those tribes which reside within the acknowledged boundaries of the United States can, with strict accuracy, be denominated foreign nations. They may, more correctly, perhaps, be denominated domestic dependent nations. They occupy a territory to which we assert a title independent of their will, which must take effect in point of possession when their right of possession ceases. Meanwhile they are in a state of pupilage. Their relation to the United States resembles that of a ward to his guardian.

They look to our government for protection; rely upon its kindness and its power; appeal to it for relief to their wants; and address the president as their great father. They and their country are considered by foreign nations, as well as by ourselves, as being so completely under the sovereignty and dominion of the United States, that any attempt to acquire their lands, or to form a political connexion with them, would be considered by all as an invasion of our territory, and an act of hostility.

These considerations go far to support the opinion, that the framers of our constitution had not the Indian tribes in view, when they opened the courts of the union to controversies between a state or the citizens thereof, and foreign states.

In considering this subject, the habits and usages of the Indians, in their intercourse with their white neighbours, ought not to be entirely disregarded. At the time the constitution was framed, the idea of appealing to an American court of justice for an assertion of right or a redress of wrong, had perhaps never entered the mind of an Indian or of his tribe. Their appeal was to the tomahawk, or to the government. This was well understood by the statesmen who framed the constitution of the United States, and might furnish some reason for omitting to enumerate them among the parties who might sue in the courts of the union. Be this as it may, the peculiar relations between the United States and the Indians occupying our territory are such, that we should feel much difficulty in considering them as designated by the term foreign state, were there no other part of the constitution which might shed light on the meaning of these words. But we think that in construing them, considerable aid is furnished by that clause in the eighth section of the third article; which empowers congress to "regulate commerce with foreign nations, and among the several states, and with the Indian tribes."

In this clause they are as clearly contradistinguished by a name appropriate to themselves, from foreign nations, as from the several states composing the union. They are designated by a distinct appellation; and as this appellation can be applied to neither of the others, neither can the appellation distinguishing either of the others be in fair construction applied to them. The objects, to which the power of regulating commerce might be directed, are divided into three distinct classes—foreign nations, the several states, and Indian tribes. When forming this article, the convention considered them as entirely distinct. We cannot assume that the distinction was lost in framing a subsequent article, unless there be something in its language to authorize the assumption.

The counsel for the plaintiffs contend that the words "Indian tribes" were introduced into the article, empowering congress to regulate commerce, for the purpose of removing those doubts in which the management of Indian affairs was involved by the language of the ninth article of the confederation. Intending to give the whole power of managing those affairs to the government about to be instituted, the convention conferred it explicitly; and omitted those qualifications which embarrassed the exercise of it as granted in the confederation. This may be admitted without weakening the construction which has been intimated: Had the Indian tribes been foreign nations, in the view of the convention; this exclusive power of regulating intercourse with them might have been, and most probably would have been, specifically given, in language indicating that idea, not in language contradistinguishing them from foreign nations. Congress might have been empowered "to regulate commerce with foreign nations, including the Indian tribes, and among the several states." This language would have suggested itself to statesmen who considered the Indian tribes as foreign nations, and were yet desirous of mentioning them particularly.

It has been also said, that the same words have not necessarily the same meaning attached to them when found in different parts of the same instrument: their meaning is controlled by the context. This is undoubtedly true. In common language the same word has various meanings, and the peculiar sense in which it is used in any sentence is to be determined by the context. This may not be equally true with respect to proper names. Foreign nations is a general term, the application of which to Indian tribes, when used in the American constitution, is at best extremely questionable. In one article in which a power is given to be exercised in regard to foreign nations generally, and to the Indian tribes particularly, they are mentioned as separate in terms clearly contradistinguishing them from each other. We perceive plainly that the constitution in this article does not comprehend Indian tribes in the general term "foreign nations;" not we presume because a tribe may not be a nation, but because it is not foreign to the United States. When, afterwards, the term "foreign state" is introduced, we cannot impute to the convention the intention to desert its former meaning, and to comprehend Indian tribes within it, unless the context force that construction on us. We find nothing in the context, and nothing in the subject of the article, which leads to it.

The court has bestowed its best attention on this question, and, after mature deliberation, the majority is of opinion that an Indian tribe or nation within the United States is not a foreign state in the sense of the constitution, and cannot maintain an action in the courts of the United States.

A serious additional objection exists to the jurisdiction of the court. Is the matter of the bill the proper subject for judicial inquiry and decision? It seeks to restrain a state from the forcible exercise of legislative power over a neighbouring people, asserting their independence; their right to which the state denies. On several of the matters alleged in the bill, for example on the laws making it criminal to exercise the usual powers of self government in their own country by the Cherokee nation, this court cannot interpose; at least in the form in which those matters are presented.

That part of the bill which respects the land occupied by the Indians, and prays the aid of the court to protect their possession, may be more doubtful. The mere question of right might perhaps be decided by this court in a proper case with proper parties. But the court is asked to do more than decide on the title. The bill requires us to control the legislature of Georgia, and to restrain the exertion of its physical force. The propriety of such an interposition by the court may be well questioned. It savours too mch of the exercise of political power to be within the proper province of the judicial department. But the opinion on the point respecting parties makes it unnecessary to decide this question.

If it be true that the Cherokee nation have rights, this is not the tribunal in which those rights are to be asserted. If it be true that wrongs have been inflicted, and that still greater are to be apprehended, this is not the tribunal which can redress the past or prevent the future.

The motion for an injunction is denied.

✠ *D O C U M E N T   4*

Worcester v. Georgia, 1832

Mr Chief Justice Marshall delivered the opinion of the Court.

...From the commencement of our government, congress has passed acts to regulate trade and intercourse with the Indians; which treat them as nations, respect their rights, and manifest a firm purpose to afford that protection which treaties stipulate. All these acts, and especially that of 1802, which is still in force, manifestly consider the several Indian nations as distinct political communities, having territorial boundaries, within which their authority is exclusive, and having a right to all the lands within those boundaries, which is not only acknowledged, but guarantied by the United States.

In 1819, congress passed an act for promoting those humane designs of civilizing the neighbouring Indians, which had long been cherished by the executive. It enacts, "that, for the purpose of providing against the further decline and final extinction of the Indian tribes adjoining to the frontier settlements of the United States, and for introducing among them the habits and arts of civilization, the president of the United States shall be, and he is hereby authorized, in every case where he shall judge improvement in the habits and condition of such Indians practicable, and that the means of instruction can be introduced with their own consent, to employ capable persons, of good moral character, to instruct them in the mode of agriculture suited to their situation; and for teaching their children in reading, writing and arithmetic; and for performing such other duties as may be enjoined, according to such instructions and rules as the president may give and prescribe for the regulation of their conduct in the discharge of their duties."

This act avowedly contemplates the preservation of the Indian nations as an object sought by the United States, and proposes to effect this object by civilizing and converting them from hunters into agriculturists. Though the Cherokees had already made considerable progress in this improvement, it cannot be doubted that the general words of the act comprehend them. Their advance in the "habits and arts of civilization," rather encouraged perseverance in the laudable exertions still farther to meliorate their condition. This act furnishes strong additional evidence of a settled purpose to fix the Indians in their country by giving them security at home.

The treaties and laws of the United States contemplate the Indian territory as completely separated from that of the states; and provide that all intercourse with them shall be carried on exclusively by the government of the union.

Is this the rightful exercise of power, or is it usurpation?

While these states were colonies, this power, in its utmost extent, was admitted to reside in the crown. When our revolutionary struggle commenced, congress was composed of an assemblage of deputies acting under specific powers granted by the legislatures, or conventions of the several colonies. It was a great popular movement, not perfectly organized; nor were the respective powers of those who were entrusted with the management of affairs accurately defined. The necessities of our situation produced a general conviction that those measures which concerned all, must be transacted by a body in which the representatives of all were assembled, and which could command the confidence of all: congress, therefore, was considered as invested with all the powers of war and peace, and congress dissolved our connexion with the mother country, and declared these United Colonies to be independent states. Without any written definition of powers, they employed diplomatic agents to represent the United States at the several courts of Europe; offered to negotiate treaties with them, and did actually negotiate treaties with France. From the same necessity, and on the same principles, congress assumed the management of Indian affairs; first in the name of these United Colonies; and, afterwards, in the name of the United States. Early attempts were made at negotiation, and to regulate trade with them. These not proving successful, war was carried on under the direction, and with the forces of the United States, and the efforts to make peace, by treaty, were earnest and incessant. The confederation found congress in the exercise of the same powers of peace and war, in our relations with Indian nations, as with those of Europe.

Such was the state of things when the confederation was adopted. That instrument surrendered the powers of peace and war to congress, and prohibited them to the states, respectively, unless a state be actually invaded, "or shall have received certain advice of a resolution being formed by some nation of Indians to invade such state, and the danger is so imminent as not to admit of delay till the United States in congress assembled can be consulted." This instrument also gave the United States in congress assembled the sole and exclusive right of "regulating the trade and managing all the affairs with the Indians, not members of any of the states: provided, that the legislative power of any state within its own limits be not infringed or violated."

The ambiguous phrases which follow the grant of power to the United States, were so construed by the states of North Carolina and Georgia as to annual the power itself. The discontents and confusion resulting from these conflicting claims, produced representations to congress, which were referred to a committee, who made their report in 1787. The report does not assent to the construction of the two states, but recommends an accommodation, by liberal cessions of territory, or by an admission, on their part, of the powers claimed by congress. The correct exposition of this article is rendered unnecessary by the adoption of our existing constitution. That instrument confers on congress the powers of war and peace; of making treaties, and of regulating commerce with foreign nations, and among the several states, and with the Indian tribes. These powers comprehend all that is required for the regulation of our intercourse with the Indians. They are not limited by any restrictions on their free actions. The shackles imposed on this power, in the confederation, are discarded.

The Indian nations had always been considered as distinct, independent political communities, retaining their original natural rights, as the undisputed possessors of the soil, from time immemorial, with the single exception of that imposed by irresistible power, which excluded them from intercourse with any other European potentate than the first discoverer of the coast of the particular region claimed: and this was a restriction which those European potentates imposed on themselves, as well as on the Indians. The very term "nation," so generally applied to them, means "a people distinct from others." The constitution, by declaring treaties already made, as well as those to be made, to be the supreme law of the land, has adopted and sanctioned the previous treaties with the Indian nations, and consequently admits their rank among those powers who are capable of making treaties. The words "treaty" and "nation" are words of our own language, selected in our diplomatic and legislative proceedings, by ourselves, having each a definite and well understood meaning. We have applied them to Indians, as we have applied them to the other nations of the earth. They are applied to all in the same sense.

Georgia, herself, has furnished conclusive evidence that her former opinions on this subject concurred with those entertained by her sister states, and by the government of the United States. Various acts of her legislature have been cited in the argument, including the contract of cession made in the year 1802, all tending to prove her acquiescence in the universal conviction that the Indian nations possessed a full right to the lands they occupied, until that right should be extinguished by the United States, with their consent: that their territory was separated from that of any state within whose chartered limits they might reside, by a boundary line, established by treaties: that, within their boundary, they possessed rights with which no state could interfere: and that the whole power of regulating the intercourse with them, was vested in the United States. A review of these acts, on the part of Georgia, would occupy too much time, and is the less necessary, because they have been accurately detailed in the argument at the bar. Her new series of laws, manifesting her abandonment of these opinions, appears to have commenced in December 1828.

In opposition to this original right, possessed by the undisputed occupants of every country; to this recognition of that right, which is evidenced by our history, in every change through which we have passed; is placed the charters granted by the monarch of a distant and distinct region, parcelling out a territory in possession of others whom he could not remove and did not attempt to remove, and the cession made of his claims by the treaty of peace.

The actual state of things at the time, and all history since, explain these charters; and the king of Great Britain, at the treaty of peace, could cede only what belonged to his crown. These newly asserted titles can derive no aid from the articles so often repeated in Indian treaties; extending to them, first, the protection of Great Britain, and afterwards that of the United States. These articles are associated with others, recognizing their title to self government. The very fact of repeated treaties with them recognizes it; and the settled doctrine of the law of nations is, that a weaker power does not surrender its independence—its right to self government, by associating with a stronger, and taking its protection. A weak state, in order to provide for its safety, may place itself under the protection of one more powerful, without stripping itself of the right of government, and ceasing to be a state. Examples of this kind are not wanting in Europe. "Tributary and feudatory states," says Vattel, "do not thereby cease to be sovereign and independent states, so long as self government and sovereign and independent authority are left in the administration of the state." At the present day, more than one state may be considered as holding its right of self government under the guarantee and protection of one or more allies.

The Cherokee nation, then, is a distinct community occupying its own territory, with boundaries accurately described, in which the laws of Georgia can have no force, and which the citizens of Georgia have no right to enter, but with the assent of the Cherokees themselves, or in conformity with treaties, and with the acts of congress. The whole intercourse between the United States and this nation, is, by our constitution and laws, vested in the government of the United States.

The act of the state of Georgia, under which the plaintiff in error was prosecuted, is consequently void, and the judgment a nullity. Can this court revise, and reverse it?

If the objection to the system of legislation, lately adopted by the legislature of Georgia, in relation to the Cherokee nation, was confined to its extra-territorial operation, the objection, though complete, so far as respected mere right, would give this court no power over the subject. But it goes much further. If the review which has been taken be correct, and we think it is, the acts of Georgia are repugnant to the constitution, laws, and treaties of the United States.

They interfere forcibly with the relations established between the United States and the Cherokee nation, the regulation of which, according to the settled principles of our constitution, are committed exclusively to the government of the union.

They are in direct hostility with treaties, repeated in a succession of years, which mark out the boundary that separates the Cherokee country from Georgia; guaranty to them all the land within their boundary; solemnly pledge the faith of the United States to restrain their citizens from trespassing on it; and recognize the pre-existing power of the nation to govern itself.

They are in equal hostility with the acts of congress for regulating this intercourse, and giving effect to the treaties.

The forcible seizure and abduction of the plaintiff in error, who was residing in the nation with its permission, and by authority of the president of the United States, is also a violation of the acts which authorise the chief magistrate to exercise this authority.

Will these powerful considerations avail the plaintiff in error? We think they will. He was seized, and forcibly carried away, while under guardianship of treaties guarantying the country in which he resided, and taking it under the protection of the United States. He was seized while performing, under the sanction of the chief magistrate of the union, those duties which the humane policy adopted by congress had recommended. He was apprehended, tried, and condemned, under colour of a law which has been shown to be repugnant to the constitution, laws, and treaties of the United States. Had a judgment, liable to the same objections, been rendered for property, none would question the jurisdiction of this court. It cannot be less clear when the judgment affects personal liberty, and inflicts disgraceful punishment, if punishment could disgrace when inflicted on innocence. The plaintiff in error is not less interested in the operation of this unconstitutional law than if it affected his property. He is not less entitled to the protection of the constitution, laws, and treaties of his country.

This point has been elaborately argued and, after deliberate consideration, decided, in the case of Cohens v. The Commonwealth of Virginia, 6 Wheat. 264.

It is the opinion of this court that the judgment of the superior court for the county of Gwinnett, in the state of Georgia, condemning Samuel A. Worcester to hard labour, in the penitentiary of the state of Georgia, for four years, was pronounced by that court under colour of a law which is void, as being repugnant to the constitution, treaties, and laws of the United States, and ought, therefore, to be reversed and annulled.

✣ *D O C U M E N T   5*

South Carolina Nullifies the Tariff, 1832

An Ordinance to Nullify Certain Acts of the Congress of the United States, Purporting to Be Laws Laying Duties and Imposts on the Importation of Foreign Commodities

Whereas the Congress of the United States, by various acts, purporting to be acts laying duties and imposts on foreign imports, but in reality intended for the protection of domestic manufactures, and the giving of bounties to classes and individuals engaged in particular employments, at the expense and to the injury and oppression of other classes and individuals, and by wholly exempting from taxation certain foreign commodities, such as are not produced or manufactured in the United States, to afford a pretext for imposing higher and excessive duties on articles similar to those intended to be protected, hath exceeded its just powers under the Constitution, which confers on it no authority to afford such protection, and hath violated the true meaning and intent of the Constitution, which provides for equality in imposing the burthens of taxation upon the several States and portions of the Confederacy: *And whereas* the said Congress, exceeding its just power to impose taxes and collect revenue for the purpose of effecting and accomplishing the specific objects and purposes which the Constitution of the United States authorizes it to effect and accomplish, hath raised and collected unnecessary revenue for objects unauthorized by the Constitution:—

We, therefore, the people of the State of South Carolina in Convention assembled, do declare and ordain, ... That the several acts and parts of acts of the Congress of the United States, purporting to be laws for the imposing of duties and imposts on the importation of foreign commodities, ... and, more especially, ... [the tariff acts of 1828 and 1832] ... , are unauthorized by the Constitution of the United States, and violate the true meaning and intent thereof, and are null, void, and no law, nor binding upon this State, its officers or citizens; and all promises, contracts, and coligations, made or entered into, or to be made or entered into, with purpose to secure the duties imposed by the said acts, and all judicial proceedings which shall be hereafter had in affirmance thereof, are and shall be held utterly null and void.

And it is further Ordained, That it shall not be lawful for any of the constituted authorities, whether of this State or of the United States, to enforce the payment of duties imposed by the said acts within the limits of this State; but it shall be the duty of the Legislature to adopt such measures and pass such acts as may be necessary to give full effect to this Ordinance, and to prevent the enforcement and arrest the operation of the said acts and parts of acts of the Congress of the United States within the limits of this State, from and after the 1st day of February next, ...

And it is further Ordained, That in no case of law or equity, decided in the courts of this State, wherein shall be drawn in question the authority of this ordinance, or the validity of such act or acts of the Legislature as may be passed for the purpose of giving effect thereto, or the validity of the aforesaid acts of Congress, imposing duties, shall any appeal be taken or allowed to the Supreme Court of the United States, nor shall any copy of the record be printed or allowed for that purpose; and if any such appeal shall be attempted to be taken, the courts of this State shall proceed to execute and enforce their judgments, according to the laws and usages of the State, without reference to such attempted appeal, and the person or persons attempting to take such appeal may be dealt with as for a contempt of the court.

And it is further Ordained, That all persons now holding any office of honor, profit, or trust, civil or military, under this State, (members of the Legislature excepted), shall, within such time, and in such manner as the Legislature shall prescribe, take an oath well and truly to obey, execute, and enforce, this Ordinance, and such act or acts of the Legislature as may be passed in pursuance thereof, according to the true intent and meaning of the same; and on the neglect or omission of any such person or persons so to do, his or their office or offices shall be forthwith vacated, ... and no person hereafter elected to any office of honor, profit, or trust, civil or military, (members of the Legislature excepted), shall, until the Legislature shall otherwise provide and direct, enter on the execution of his office, ... until he shall, in like manner, have taken a similar oath; and no juror shall be empannelled in any of the courts of this State, in any cause in which shall be in question this Ordinance, or any act of the Legislature passed in pursuance thereof, unless he shall first, in addition to the usual oath, have taken an oath that he will well and truly obey, execute, and enforce this Ordinance, and such act or acts of the Legislature as may be passed to carry the same into operation and effect, according to the true intent and meaning thereof.

And we, the People of South Carolina, to the end that it may be fully understood by the Government of the United States, and the people of the co-States, that we are determined to maintain this, our Ordinance and Declaration, at every hazard, *Do further Declare* that we will not submit to the application of force, on the part of the Federal Government, to reduce this State to obedience; but that we will consider the passage, by Congress, of any act ... to coerce the State, shut up her ports, destroy or harass her commerce, or to enforce the acts hereby declared to be null and void, otherwise than through the civil tribunals of the country, as inconsistent with the longer continuance of South Carolina in the Union: and that the people of this State will thenceforth hold themselves absolved from all further obligation to maintain or preserve their political connexion with the people of the other States, and will forthwith proceed to organize a separate Government, and do all other acts and things which sovereign and independent States may of right to do.

✠ *D O C U M E N T   6*

Jackson Threatens South Carolina, 1832

Whereas a convention assembled in the State of South Carolina have passed an ordinance by which they declare "that the several acts and parts of acts of the Congress of the United States purporting to be laws for the imposing of duties and imposts on the importation of foreign commodities, ... are unauthorized by the Constitution of the United States, and violate the true meaning and intent thereof, and are null and void and no law," nor binding on the citizens of that State or its officers; and by the said ordinance it is further declared to be unlawful for any of the constituted authorities of the State or of the United States to enforce the payment of the duties imposed by the said acts within the same State, and that it is the duty of the legislature to pass such laws as may be necessary to give full effect to the said ordinance ...

The ordinance is founded, not on the indefeasible right of resisting acts which are plainly unconstitutional and too oppressive to be endured, but on the strange position that any one State may not only declare an act of Congress void, but prohibit its execution; that they may do this consistently with the Constitution; that the true construction of that instrument permits a State to retain its place in the Union and yet be bound by no other of its laws than those it may choose to consider as constitutional. It is true, they add, that to justify this abrogation of a law it must be palpably contrary to the Constitution; but it is evident that to give the right of resisting laws of that description, coupled with the uncontrolled right to decide what laws deserve that character, is to give the power of resisting all laws; for as by the theory there is no appeal, the reasons alleged by the State, good or bad, must prevail. If it should be said that public opinion is a sufficient check against the abuse of this power, it may be asked why it is not deemed a sufficient guard against the passage of an unconstitutional act by Congress? There is, however, a restraint in this last case which makes the assumed power of a State more indefensible, and which does not exist in the other. There are two appeals from an unconstitutional act passed by Congress—one to the judiciary, the other to the people and the States. There is no appeal from the State decision in theory, and the practical illustration shows that the courts are closed against an application to review it, both judges and jurors being sworn to decide in its favor. But reasoning on this subject is superfluous when our social compact, in express terms, declares that the laws of the United States, its Constitution, and treaties made under it are the supreme law of the land, and, for greater caution, adds "that the judges in every State shall be bound thereby, anything in the constitution or laws of any State to the contrary notwithstanding." And it may be asserted without fear of refutation that no federative government could exist without a similar provision. Look for a moment to the consequence. If South Carolina considers the revenue laws unconstitutional and has a right to prevent their execution in the port of Charleston, there would be a clear constitutional objection to their collection in every other port; and no revenue could be collected anywhere, for all imposts must be equal. It is no answer to repeat that an unconstitutional law is no law so long as the question of its legality is to be decided by the State itself, for every law operating injuriously upon any local interest will be perhaps thought, and certainly represented, as unconstitutional, and, as has been shown, there is no appeal.

If this doctrine had been established at an earlier day, the Union would have been dissolved in its infancy. The excise law in Pennsylvania, the embargo and nonintercourse law in the Eastern States, the carriage tax in Virginia, were all deemed unconstitutional, and were more unequal in their operation than any of the laws now complained of; but, fortunately, none of those States discovered that they had the right now claimed by South Carolina. The war into which we were forced to support the dignity of the nation and the rights of our citizens might have ended in defeat and disgrace, instead of victory and honor, if the States who supposed it a ruinous and unconstitutional measure had thought they possessed the right of nullifying the act by which it was declared and denying supplies for its prosecution. Hardly and unequally as those measures bore upon several members of the Union, to the legislatures of none did this efficient and peaceable remedy, as it is called, suggest itself. The discovery of this important feature in our Constitution was reserved to the present day. To the statesmen of South Carolina belongs the invention, and upon the citizens of that State will unfortunately fall the evils of reducing it to practice.

If the doctrine of a State veto upon the laws of the Union carries with it internal evidence of its impracticable absurdity, our constitutional history will also afford abundant proof that it would have been repudiated with indignation had it been proposed to form a feature in our Government.

Our present Constitution was formed … in vain if this fatal doctrine prevails. It was formed for important objects that are announced in the preamble, made in the name and by the authority of the people of the United States, whose delegates framed and whose conventions approved it. The most important among these objects—that which is placed first in rank, on which all the others rest—is "*to form a more perfect union.*" Now, is it possible that even if there were no express provision giving supremacy to the Constitution and laws of the United States over those of the States, can it be conceived that an instrument made for the purpose of "*forming a more perfect union*" than that of the Confederation could be so constructed by the assembled wisdom of our country as to substitute for that Confederation a form of government dependent for its existence on the local interest, the party spirit, of a State, or of a prevailing faction in a State? Every man of plain, unsophisticated understanding who hears the question will give such an answer as will preserve the Union. Metaphysical subtlety, in pursuit of an impracticable theory, could alone have devised one that is calculated to destroy it.

I consider, then, the power to annul a law of the United States, assumed by one State, *incompatible with the existence of the Union, contradicted expressly by the letter of the Constitution, unauthorized by its spirit, inconsistent with every principle on which it was founded, and destructive of the great object for which it was formed....*

The States severally have not retained their entire sovereignty. It has been shown that in becoming parts of a nation, not members of a league, they surrendered many of their essential parts of sovereignty. The right to make treaties, declare war, levy taxes, exercise exclusive judicial and legislative powers, were all of them functions of sovereign power. The States, then, for all these important purposes were no longer sovereign.... How, then, with all these proofs that under all changes of our position we had, for designated purposes and with defined powers, created national governments, how is it that the most perfect of those several modes of union should now be considered as a mere league that may be dissolved at pleasure? It is from an abuse of terms. Compact is used as synonymous with league, although the true term is not employed, because it would at once show the fallacy of the reasoning. It would not do to say that our Constitution was only a league, but it is labored to prove it a compact (which in one sense it is) and then to argue that as a league is a compact every compact between nations must of course be a league, and that from such an engagement every sovereign power has a right to recede. But it has been shown that in this sense the States are not sovereign, and that even if they were, and the national Constitution had been formed by compact, there would be no right in any one State to exonerate itself from its obligations.

This, then, is the position in which we stand: A small majority of the citizens of one State in the Union have elected delegates to a State convention; that convention has ordained that all the revenue laws of the United States must be repealed, or that they are no longer a member of the Union. The governor of that State has recommended to the legislature the raising of an army to carry the secession into effect, and that he may be empowered to give clearances to vessels in the name of the State. No act of violent opposition to the laws has yet been committed, but such a state of things is hourly apprehended. And it is the intent of this instrument to *proclaim*, not only that the duty imposed on me by the Constitution "to take care that the laws be faithfully executed" shall be performed to the extent of the powers already vested in me by law, or of such others as the wisdom of Congress shall devise and intrust to me for that purpose, but to warn the citizens of South Carolina who have been deluded into an opposition to the laws of the danger they will incur by obedience to the illegal and disorganizing ordinance of the convention; to exhort those who have refused to support it to persevere in their determination to uphold the Constitution and laws of their country; and to point out to all the perilous situation into which the good people of that State have been led, and that the course they are urged to pursue is one of ruin and disgrace to the very State whose rights they affect to support. ...

If your leaders could succeed in establishing a separation, what would be your situation? Are you united at home? Are you free from the apprehension of civil discord, with all its fearful consequences? Do our neighboring republics, every day suffering some new revolution or contending with some new insurrection, do they excite your envy? But the dictates of a high duty oblige me solemnly to announce that you can not succeed. The laws of the United States must be executed. I have no discretionary power on the subject; my duty is emphatically pronounced in the Constitution. Those who told you that you might peaceably prevent their execution deceived you; they could not have been deceived themselves. They know that a forcible opposition could alone prevent the execution of the laws, and they know that such opposition must be repelled. Their object is disunion. But be not deceived by names. Disunion by armed force is *treason*. Are you really ready to incur its guilt? If you are, on the heads of the instigators of the act be the dreadful consequences; on their heads be the dishonor, but on yours may fall the punishment. On your unhappy State will inevitably fall all the evils of the conflict you force upon the Government of your country. It can not accede to the mad project of disunion, of which you would be the first victims. Its First Magistrate can not, if he would, avoid the performance of his duty. The consequence must be fearful for you, distressing to your fellow-citizens here and to the friends of good government throughout the world. Its enemies have beheld our prosperity with a vexation they could not conceal; it was a standing refutation of their slavish doctrines, and they will point to our discord with the triumph of malignant joy. It is yet in your power to disappoint them. ...

Fellow-citizens of the United States, the threat of unhallowed disunion, the names of those once respected by whom it is uttered, the array of military force to support it, denote the approach of a crisis in our affairs on which the continuance of our unexampled prosperity, our political existence, and perhaps that of all free governments may depend. The conjuncture demanded a free, a full, and explicit enunciation, not only of my intentions, but of my principles of action; and as the claim was asserted of a right by a State to annul the laws of the Union, and even to secede from it at pleasure, a frank exposition of my opinions in relation to the origin and form of our Government and the construction I give to the instrument by which it was created seemed to be proper. Having the fullest confidence in the justness of the legal and constitutional opinion of my duties which has been expressed, I rely with equal confidence on your undivided support in my determination to execute the laws, to preserve the Union by all constitutional means, to arrest, if possible, by moderate and firm measures the necessity of a recourse to force; and if it be the will of Heaven that the recurrence of its primeval curse on man for the shedding of a brother's blood should fall upon our land, that it be not called down by any offensive act on the part of the United States.

Fellow-citizens, the momentous case is before you. On your undivided support of your Government depends the decision of the great question it involves—whether your sacred Union will be preserved and the blessing it secures to us as one people shall be perpetuated. No one can doubt that the unanimity with which that decision will be expressed will be such as to inspire new confidence in republican institutions, and that the prudence, the wisdom, and the courage which it will bring to their defense will transmit them unimpaired and invigorated to our children.

May the Great Ruler of Nations grant that the signal blessings with which He has favored ours may not, by the madness of party or personal ambition, be disregarded and lost; and may His wise providence bring those who have produced this crisis to see the folly before they feel the misery of civil strife, and inspire a returning veneration for that Union which, if we may dare to penetrate His designs, He has chosen as the only means of attaining the high destinies to which we may reasonably aspire.

✥ *E S S A Y S*

Jill Norgren, an emerita professor of government and political science at John Jay College of Criminal Justice, examines the immediate aftermath and non-enforcement of the *Worcester* decision. She shows how the politics of nullification and concern over disunion played a critical role in the resolution of the matter. In this account, immediate events determined the courses pursued by both Jackson and the Cherokee.

Gerard N. Magliocca, a law professor at Indiana University–Indianapolis, interprets *Worcester* and Jackson's response from a wider perspective—as exemplifying fundamental constitutional conflict, which, he argues, regularly occurs in generational cycles. According to Magliocca, *Worcester* was a "preemptive opinion" that sought to affirm Cherokee rights and promote national supremacy. With the constitutional stakes raised, Jackson responded with an equally strong view of the Constitution in his veto of the bill re-chartering the Second National Bank.

Worcester and the Politics of the Nullification Crisis

JILL NORGREN

The decision of the Court was welcomed by the Cherokee, but could it be enforced? Many people involved in the appeal expressed the opinion that Georgia and Jackson would ignore a ruling favoring the missionaries. Justice [Joseph] Story openly voiced his concern to a friend only days after Marshall handed down the *Worcester v. Georgia* decision:

> We have just decided the Cherokee case.... The decision produced a very strong sensation.... Georgia is full of anger and violence. What she will do, it is difficult to say. Probably she will resist the execution of our judgment, and if she does, I do not believe the President will interfere, unless public opinion among the religious of the Eastern and Western and Middle States, should be brought to bear strong upon him. The rumor is, that he had told the Georgians he will do nothing.

Story was wise to worry, as events immediately after *Worcester* amply demonstrate the limits on the enforcement of judicial decisions. Real victory—as opposed to theoretical victory—for the missionaries and the Cherokee depended on enforcement of the Supreme Court's decision. Here they each lost, with devastating results for the Cherokee.

Two days after the justices read their opinions, the Court issued a mandate to the Georgia superior court—carried from Washington by Elisha Chester—ordering it to reverse its decision and free [Samuel] Worcester and [Elizur] Butler. Governor [Wilson] Lumpkin responded that he would hang the missionaries rather than "submit to this decision made by a few superannuated *life estate* Judges." Officials of the Georgia superior court said that the U.S. Supreme Court had exceeded its authority and refused to reverse the conviction of the missionaries. The two men's sentences were affirmed, and Butler and Worcester continued to be held in the state penitentiary. In the view of local officials, Georgia had to stand firm against a renegade national court that, they suggested, might soon attempt to assert its jurisdiction over *another* issue—African slavery.

In Boston, David Greene knew none of this when he forwarded $500 to John Sergeant and congratulated him on the happy result at court. Sergeant had returned to Philadelphia, and Wirt to Baltimore. The Cherokee delegation in Washington stayed on to monitor events while awaiting word from Chester on the actions of the superior court. A month passed with no message from the attorney. Chester already knew Governor Lumpkin and the superior court's response and, on Wirt's prior instructions, was preparing a letter asking Lumpkin to intercede and order the discharge of the prisoners. The same week a messenger in Georgia, knowing of the superior court's denial, rushed to Washington to get the new Supreme Court decree needed to authorize a federal marshal to free the prisoners. The Supreme Court, possibly to avoid further confrontation, had adjourned on March 17 without waiting to hear whether Georgia had obeyed its mandate and freed the missionaries.

In fact, the whole business revealed a larger unresolved legal problem in the United States. General law governing federal judicial and executive power over the states was unclear and, for some, inadequate. As a result, technical legal issues provided a smoke screen for President Jackson, who invoked them as his reason for not enforcing the Court's decision in *Worcester*. Although some historians believe that the President would have enforced the decision if the law had absolutely required it, Jackson was known to be pleased by the Court's inability to "coerce Georgia."

Even Wirt and Sergeant disagreed about whether a federal judge could issue the necessary writ of habeas corpus (order to produce the prisoner) after the refusal of a state court to execute a federal court decree. Responding to an inquiry from Congressman William Lewis, Wirt argued that nothing more could be done for the missionaries until Georgia put its refusal to free them in writing, something the governor's officials deliberately avoided doing until Superior Judge Charles Dougherty acquiesced and permitted the necessary affidavits to be prepared. Even after Dougherty's concession, Wirt wrote that there were legal obstacles and went on to argue the need for new federal legislation. Such a law, he said, would give federal judges the power to issue the writs necessary to free prisoners held under state laws that were declared unconstitutional by the U.S. Supreme Court. Wirt also recommended changes in the Militia Act of 1795, a statute that authorized presidential use of the militia to enforce national law. Wirt wanted the act amended to *require* that the President take action.

Wirt believed that if he was correct, there was little the Supreme Court could do until Congress made these legislative changes. Two months after the Court's decision, however, he continued to counsel the possibility of resolving the problem by directly petitioning Jackson and the Congress. Wirt had not given up the fight and was displeased to hear that other Americans had advised the missionaries to admit their crime and accept a pardon. Influential "friends of the Cherokee" who only weeks before had considered the policy of Indian removal a contemptible violation of rights suddenly found the idea reasonable and necessary. Only six weeks after the *Worcester* decision, Senator Theodore Frelinghuysen, with whom Evarts had earlier worked out an antiremoval strategy, wrote David Greene at the American Board that the Cherokee ought to seek a liberal treaty of removal and leave. Supreme Court Justice John McLean acted more directly. He asked the Cherokee delegation still living in the capital to meet with him and proceeded to argue the futility of continued litigation. He urged them to sign a removal treaty by which the Cherokee Nation would become a territory with a patent in fee simple and a delegate in Congress. A small number of Cherokee leaders, Boudinot and John Ridge among them, had been reported to be ready to "surrender their country finding no faith is to be placed in the treaties, constitution or laws of the U. States." If all this was so, Wirt concluded to Lewis, "the state of Georgia is likely to be victorious [and] ... the constitution, treaties, and laws of the U.S. ... are to be prostrated with impunity."

The new supporter of removal for whom John Ross had the most biting words was Worcester's local attorney, Elisha Chester. After failing to win release of the missionaries, Chester had returned to Washington. Still in the employ of the Cherokee and the American Board, Chester nevertheless met with U.S. officials at the War Department and in mid-May let himself be hired as a special agent of that department. His job was to present the government's new proposal of removal to his client, the Cherokee National Council. In this capacity, Chester visited Wirt, Sergeant, and the officers of the American Board, urging them all to renounce their position on removal and support the government's proposal. In spite of other defections and pressure, none of these men showed any interest in Chester's message.

The missionaries also received visits from individuals who urged them to apply for pardons. David Greene heard about the visits and wrote the two prisoners that the decision on a pardon rested solely with them. He believed, however, that since they had been judged not guilty by the Supreme Court, they should not bear "the stigma of being pardoned culprits." Throughout May and for the next six months, Butler and Worcester, who had long since expected to be free men, remained firmly opposed to the idea of a pardon: "If we now yield ... who will hereafter venture to place any reliance on the Supreme Court of the United States for protection against laws however unconstitutional?"

Not put off by his poor reception in the North, Chester returned to the Cherokee Nation in early June, ready to outline the new removal proposition to Chief Ross. It was the first Ross knew of Chester's defection. Shortly afterward, a bitter John Ross wrote to Wirt, saying that Chester had strongly denied deserting the Cherokee for

Jackson and had "boldly declared that he was acting under the special advice and influence of sincere friends of the Cherokees in Congress." Chester had warned Ross that the "vulgar populace" on the Georgia frontier could not be restrained from aggression against the Cherokee and that removal was the only hope. Ross replied sarcastically that a sergeant's command under the authority of the United States would be sufficient to make that vulgar populace submit to the laws of Congress.

The Supreme Court remained out of session. Marshall's schedule did not call for the Court to reconvene for several months. Beyond some powerful new words from the justices, the only chance for "the sergeant's command" that Ross sought lay in the possibility of Henry Clay's defeat of Jackson in the presidential election. Clay, along with Daniel Webster, had been a leading supporter of a pro-Cherokee policy in Congress. While banking, economics, and opportunities for common people were the main issues in the 1832 campaign, Indian politics also figured in the debates and in voters' considerations. To the extent that the November election represented a mandate on *Worcester*, however, the Cherokee and the Marshall Court lost when Jackson trounced Clay and remained in the White House. American voters rejected Clay's candidacy and criticism of Jackson's Indian policy. The outcome of the presidential election, however, was not the only national political factor contributing to Jackson's final refusal to enforce the *Worcester* decision. In the same month, November 1832, the passage of a Nullification Ordinance in South Carolina created a significant new problem for the government in Washington. Although it could not have been predicted, the rebellion in South Carolina contributed directly to the defeat of the missionaries and the Cherokee.

The long-simmering states' rights rebellion in South Carolina exploded in the autumn of 1832. Since 1816, tension had been building between the southern states, which opposed a national tariff policy that they felt favored northern economic interests, and the federal government. Antitariff sentiment ran particularly high in South Carolina. In other southern states—Alabama, Georgia, Mississippi, and Tennessee—Jackson's support for Indian removal had lessened antipathy toward the tariff and diminished the power of the common cause involving states' rights. South Carolina, however, held firm in its opposition. On November 23, 1832, the sixth day of a state convention called to consider the legality of the tariff, South Carolina delegates declared the federal tax null and void. There was talk of civil war.

Surprising some Americans, President Jackson came out strongly against the Nullification Ordinance and those who would destroy the nation. Jackson's position might have helped the Cherokee. When South Carolina threatened military resistance to the tariff, there was talk that Jackson would ask Congress for legislation to meet state force with national force, laws that also might have been used, as Ross and Wirt had suggested, against Georgia. Few American friends of the Cherokee, however, spoke of this possibility. Indeed, many of the American politicians who had served as factotums for the Cherokee cause quickly broke ranks with Ross and the missionaries, fearing that agitation over the Cherokee would add to the danger of civil dissension in the United States. In some quarters there was a political excitement bordering on panic, with the missionaries being urged to save their country by renouncing their position and accepting a pardon. The missionaries, of course, were critical to the enforcement of the *Worcester* decision since they, not the Cherokee

Nation, were the legal parties to the case. If Butler and Worcester accepted a pardon, the case would end with the legal, but not the political, affirmation of Cherokee rights. Despite *Worcester*'s text, Georgia would win, and in almost all respects the Cherokee would be no better off than before.

Initially the imprisoned men resisted the pressure put on them "to save their nation." They had their lawyers file papers to have the Supreme Court consider a new writ for their release at the January 1833 session. The attorneys maintained a reserved stance. Writing about the nullification crisis to his son-in-law in early December, William Wirt said, "I cannot help thinking it will pass off without any serious consequences." Wirt's reception of Georgia Senator Forsythe just before Christmas reflected the same air of professional calm. Forsythe threatened that Butler and Worcester would have to serve out their terms if Wirt did not advise them to withdraw the new motion before the Supreme Court. Wirt responded that he had no authority to change the direction of the case unless he was instructed to do so by the two missionaries or the American Board. Four days later Wirt wrote the missionary William Potter that he and Sergeant would make no decision with regard to the motion filed at the Supreme Court, since such a decision had to be made by the missionaries and the Board. His wish was "to remain merely in the professional character I have hitherto borne towards them. ... " Wirt, however, still believed, as he had in the spring, that there would be difficulties because of "deficiencies in the state of the law." Wirt's letters in this period, proper in tone, seek to avoid an advisory role and are virtually devoid of any reference to the Cherokee or the effect a pardon could have on their cause. Wirt had become chiefly concerned with whether the authority of the Supreme Court would be vindicated.

Wirt and Sergeant did not have to wait long for instructions from their clients. During December, Butler and Worcester had second thoughts about the wisdom of another Supreme Court appeal: They feared its effect on the Union and doubted, for reasons that are unclear, that the Cherokee had anything more to gain from the case. Worcester wrote to the American Board to voice these concerns and asked for the view of the governing board. Its Prudential Committee, without waiting for advice from Wirt and Sergeant, met late in December 1832 and resolved "that, in view of the changes of circumstances, it is, in the opinion of the Committee, inexpedient for Messrs. Worcester & Butler to prosecute their case further before the Supreme Court of the United States." Among those present, only David Greene, heir to Evarts's work, thought that there was any wisdom in carrying on with the case.

The missionaries received the text of the Prudential Committee's resolution on January 7, 1833. The next day, they wrote to Wirt and Sergeant, saying that they wished their Supreme Court appeal to be withdrawn. After a battle of wills with Governor Lumpkin over the tone of the required letter requesting pardons, the two men acknowledged the "magnanimity" of the state. The governor responded with a release order

> taking into consideration the earnest solicitude for the release of these individuals ... taking into view the triumphant ground which the state finally occupies in relation to this subject, in the eyes of the Nation, as has been sufficiently attested through various channels, especially in the recent overwhelming re-election of President Jackson ... being assured ... that the State is free from the menace of any pretended power whatever, to

infringe upon her rights, or control her will in relation to this subject. ... I therefore, as the organ of the State, feel bound to sustain the generous and liberal character of her people.

Whatever may have been the errors of these individuals—whatever embarrassments and heart-burnings they may have been instrumental in creating—however mischievous they may have been in working evil to the State, to themselves, and the still more unfortunate Cherokees. ... They shall go free.

As directed, the warden freed Worcester and Butler on January 14, 1833. With their release, the third test case of Cherokee sovereignty had ended in a manner thoroughly at odds with Jeremiah Evarts's earlier predictions.

Early in 1831 Evarts had written to Worcester to encourage civil disobedience that would lead to a further test of Georgia's laws. He told the young missionary that standing up to Georgia would do much for the Cherokee cause. But, he said, as a race, the Cherokee did not have the heart to keep using the law as a weapon against oppression: "Courage is the thing they want ... long continued courage or fortitude; it is the very point, in my judgment, where they will lose their country and their earthly all. ... I have always feared for them on this point. I have often said, 'White men, in a high state of civilization, are alone competent and expect deliverance by the slow process of law.'" Legal action does demand time and patience. The great irony is that Evarts was so wrong about who could stay the course: Ross and the Cherokee Council remained committed to the promise and honor of a nation under law and to the belief that American courts could be fair and neutral and that the U.S. Congress would respond favorably to memorials. For several reasons—not the least of which was to save themselves from removal—the Cherokee leadership had internalized the myths of liberal constitutionalism. It was the white man in his "high state of civilization" who could not, or would not, live by the slow process of law.

Worcester and Butler composed a long letter in February 1833 giving the reasons for their capitulation. The statement emphasized that the oath and license law had been repealed late in December 1832 but neglected to mention that all of Georgia's other anti-Indian jurisdiction laws remained in force. Thus, they could claim that the "*utmost* we could expect [were] mandates of the court ... [to] effect our release from confinement, *without benefitting the Cherokee Nation*." The larger notion of a test case in its fullest meaning, including enforcement, was dismissed because the "political aspect" of the United States had changed. The missionaries knew the physical and economic injury sustained daily by the Cherokee. For the two men, the possible injury to be sustained by "our public [the United States] ... by the prosecution of our appeal" outweighed the ongoing real abuse of the Cherokee and ultimately determined their decision. Once pardoned, however, their politics took different turns. Worcester and the officers of the American Board joined Boudinot, Ridge, and others in support of a removal treaty. Butler continued to support Ross and the right of the Cherokee to remain on their own land and bitterly condemned Worcester's betrayal in joining the proremoval camp.

Wirt and Sergeant continued to be involved in the Cherokee cause. In January, commenting on the link between the missionaries' pardon and efforts to contain South Carolina, Wirt wrote that it was a "mournful" omen of the strength and durability of the Union that it could be kept together only by "means like these." Nevertheless, in a short letter dated February 26, 1833, he counseled the Cherokee to delay bringing a new Supreme Court case because "as the missionaries have buried the hatchet from the patriotic desire not to involve Georgia with Carolina in a united resistance to the Union, it may be worthy of your consideration whether a better time than the present moment may not be chosen for making the question you contemplate." The lawyer's loyalties were torn. He loved his country and had come to believe that the Cherokee cause could harm the Union. However, lawyers are paid to give advice. It is not unreasonable that Wirt should have advised delay out of strategic legal concern. This does not mean that either he or Sergeant had abandoned the Cherokee cause. Even as he counseled delay in his February 26 letter, Wirt wrote that he was willing to write a legal opinion on request. Several months later—after Wirt's death—Sergeant agreed to litigate several new appeals for the Cherokee.

John Ross was scornful of the missionaries' decision to withdraw the appeal to the Supreme Court in January 1833 and end the case. As an indirect party to the litigation, the Cherokee National Council was left powerless to pursue enforcement of the Court's decision as it applied to the broad question of Georgia's jurisdiction over the Cherokee. However, the irrepressible Ross was not without hope. During the nullification crisis Ross maintained that President Jackson's proclamation of the supremacy of the constitution and laws of the United States, along with new congressional legislation, might make it impossible for the President to avoid enforcing *Worcester* and relevant treaties. Ross's logic was impeccable. Unfortunately for the Cherokee, the U.S. Congress, the only body that could create the political pressure to force Jackson's hand, did not have the will to do so.

The sacrifice of the Cherokee cause to nullification politics bitterly disappointed the Cherokee, and in the opinion of many Americans, the concessions made to South Carolina failed to save the political honor of the Union. In Congress, Clay negotiated compromise legislation, the Tariff Bill of 1833, which Jackson signed into law. John Marshall's biographer later wrote, "South Carolina was mollified. For the time the storm subsided; but the net result was that Nullification triumphed—a National law had been modified at the threat of a State which was preparing to back up that threat by force." South Carolina officials spared no one; they even criticized Georgia "for sneaking out of a fight."

Jackson, *Worcester*, and Generational Change

GERARD N. MAGLIOCCA

Those who lived through 1832 thought they were seeing a turning point in constitutional law that rivaled the Founding. The first act of that dramatic year came in February, when the Court heard argument in *Worcester v. Georgia*. Once again, the State displayed its unwillingness to obey the Court by boycotting the session. Law and politics were on display, for while Wirt was making Worcester's plea he was also preparing a third-party bid for the White House. In this charged atmosphere, Chief Justice Marshall issued his famous opinion striking down the Cherokee Codes and declaring that Tribes "had always

From Gerard N. Magliocca, *Andrew Jackson and the Constitution: The Rise and Fall of Generational Regimes*, University Press of Kansas, 2007. Reproduced with permission of the publisher.

been considered as distinct, independent, political communities, retaining their original natural rights, as the undisputed possessors of the soil, from time immemorial."

The conventional wisdom is that *Worcester* was a model of judicial integrity for reversing the missionaries' conviction in the teeth of intense political pressure. Justice Hugo Black stated the Court's official position on the case in an opinion during the 1950s, calling *Worcester* "one of [Marshall's] most courageous and eloquent opinions." In *Bush v. Gore*, Justice Stephen Breyer's dissent cited Marshall's defense of the Cherokees as a shining example of law transcending politics. Academic commentary is just as complimentary, with one leading Indian law scholar stating that "to emulate Chief Justice Marshall in *Worcester* requires many things, including judicial courage."

These tributes are misleading because they assume that the chief justice was merely restating existing doctrine, when in fact he was engaged in an act of massive resistance to the rising generation that I call a "preemptive opinion." This form of aggressive response is founded on the Court's willingness to create new doctrine that is specifically targeted at the reformers' agenda. In a preemptive case, the justices generally reach conclusions that are valid under existing precedent but restate those tenets in a grossly exaggerated manner that is more about negating the views of the rising generation than honestly evaluating the legal authorities. Naturally, these opinions are rare since they occur only when intergenerational tensions are at their peak; but when they do happen a fascinating mix of legal and political considerations comes into play.

Preemptive cases are the pinnacle of conservative resistance in the judicial branch, but they also mark the point where the escalation in the generational battle begins to warp the constitutional fabric. To achieve their sweeping political goals, preemptive opinions use three unusual tactics. First, the justices strain to decide every issue in the case rather than avoid ones that are unnecessary. Needless to say, decisive intervention and judicial restraint are not good partners. Second, the Court distorts the principles of the established generation in a way that hurts the opposition as much as possible. At this point, the justices throw off their blindfolds and actively join the political resistance. An opinion capable of accomplishing these goals, however, is hard to pull off because precedent generally (and thankfully) does not support such expansive and partisan reasoning. Thus, the third facet of a preemptive case is the development of some new theory of equality or fairness that can overcome this obstacle. All of these elements would be present in *Worcester*—the Supreme Court's first preemptive opinion.

Deciding Unnecessary Issues

Reading *Worcester* for the first time, its most striking feature is Marshall's disregard for the issues on appeal. Although the case was about the oath statute, the Court focused its opinion—over twenty pages—on "an elaborate argument for Cherokee independence." Only at the end did the chief justice add a few paragraphs about the missionaries' plight. In that brief analysis, though, he managed to hold all of the Cherokee Codes unconstitutional. Moreover, the Court used this as a *third* ground for reversal after concluding that the state statutes were preempted by federal law and by treaties with the Tribe.

Despite this extraordinary effort to reach the constitutional issues, Marshall claimed that he had no choice because "those who fill the judicial department have no discretion in selecting the subjects to be brought before them." This statement was false. The Court had at least three ways to avoid declaring that the Georgia laws were unconstitutional. For one thing, the petitioners did not get the lower court record properly certified—a pleading defect that could well have led to a dismissal of the suit if the Court was so inclined. Next, the 1802 compact between the United States and Georgia stated that no person could enter Cherokee land without a federal license. By adding conditions for entry, the State was impeding federal policy and violating the compact. Third, the Treaty of Hopewell said the Cherokees were "under the protection of the United States, and of no other sovereign whatsoever" and had the right to punish trespassers "as they might think proper." This language did not contemplate a State playing a role in regulating the Tribe, and thus the Court could also have rested its judgment on that ground. All of this leads to an important point— there is no doubt that the conclusion in *Worcester* was correct. The problem was how the Court got there.

Chief Justice Marshall did not stop with these reasons because such a narrow holding would not have had an impact on the broader constitutional debate. The Court wanted to turn public opinion against the Removal Act, not just against the Cherokee Codes. Moreover, Marshall wanted to counter the Jacksonian argument that the Tribes had no sovereign rights and that the States should have the primary role in setting Native American policy. As the Court stated, "The Cherokees acknowledge themselves to be under the protection of the United States, and of no other power. Protection does not imply the destruction of the protected."

Reactive Legal Reasoning

After brushing aside the prudential concerns that counseled against deciding the sensitive issues, the chief justice proceeded to articulate a sweeping view of federal authority and tribal sovereignty that could not be squared with traditional principles but did respond to the new generation's critique. The most remarkable example was at the end of Marshall's opinion. He wrote that "according to the settled principles of our constitution," control of tribal relations "are committed exclusively to the government of the Union." This was the broadest assertion ever made by a Court that was always eager to proclaim federal supremacy. Holding that Congress had exclusive power over commerce with the Tribes was reasonable. Expanding that rationale to cover all interactions with Native Americans was not. Marshall's critics pointed out that the Commerce Clause, which was the only fount of authority available, could not provide Congress power over all noncommercial affairs with the Tribes when it did not grant such a police power elsewhere.

The problem with the chief justice's emphatic (and distorted) assertion of federal authority is that it enhanced the credibility of the Removal Act, which explains why the rest of *Worcester* discussed the otherwise tangential issue of Cherokee rights. Mounting an effective challenge to the Jacksonian generation required the Court to explain why it was improper for Congress to use its exclusive power to pursue removal. Marshall's answer was to develop what were later characterized as "platonic notions of Indian sovereignty" that were unprecedented. While Knox held that the national government should recognize some tribal rights, the Supreme Court said that Washington must respect Native American sovereignty in virtually all matters.

Once again, this expansive interpretation was a fine political riposte to the Jacksonian assertion that the Tribes had no rights, but Marshall's legal position was weak. For instance, Marshall asserted that the European powers never claimed sovereignty over the Tribes, contending that "the extravagant and absurd idea, that the feeble settlements made on the sea-coast, or the companies under whom they were made, acquired legitimate power by them to govern the [Tribes] ... did not enter the mind of any man." The problem is that the Europeans did make this claim, as the concurring justices in *Cherokee Nation* pointed out. Likewise, Marshall said that prior to the American Revolution the Crown respected the Tribes' sovereignty and "never coerced a surrender" of their land. That claim was hard to sustain given the many brutal wars that had previously led to cessions of tribal land. ...

A New Understanding of Equality

Since traditional precepts did not provide a firm basis for resisting Jacksonian Democracy, the chief justice changed the rules and fashioned a new constitutional principle of equality. He contended that the adverse text in the Treaty of Hopewell should be interpreted narrowly because the Tribe was a disadvantaged class. He asked if it was "reasonable to suppose, that the Indians, who could not write, and most probably could not read, who certainly were not critical judges of our language, should distinguish the word 'allotted' from the words 'marked out.'" Since "no chief was capable of signing his name," the Court said it was "probable the treaty was interpreted to them ... [and that] it may very well be supposed, that they might not understand the term [allotted]." The chief justice added that language giving Congress the right to manage Cherokee affairs should not be read as a relinquishment of sovereignty because it was "inconceivable that they could have supposed themselves, by a phrase thus slipped into an article ... to have divested themselves of the right of self-government. ... Had such a result been intended, it would have been openly avowed."

Continuing in this vein, Marshall stressed that the treaties between the Tribes and the United States dealt in the "language of equality." For instance, the Court cited the first treaty ever made between Native Americans and the United States and said that "the language of equality in which it is drawn, evinces the temper with which the negotiation was undertaken, and the opinion which then prevailed in the United States." In the Cherokee treaties, the chief justice emphasized that in most cases the rights and duties imposed by these agreements were the same for each side. From these facts, the Court argued that "the only inference to be drawn ... is, that the United States considered the Cherokees a nation." Accordingly, he concluded that the Tribe must have sovereignty similar to that of the United States and could not be subjected to the discrimination of the Georgia statutes or (implicitly) the Removal Act.

Viewed from a modern perspective, *Worcester* was the first case to state a crude equal protection principle in which the courts apply heightened scrutiny to laws because of their impact on an aggrieved minority. Not surprisingly, the nascent abolitionist movement was thrilled by Marshall's ruling and saw it as a beacon for the future. To the extent that *Worcester* marks the birth of antidiscrimination law in this country, though, there are two rather surprising aspects to the opinion. One is that Native Americans, not

African Americans, were the subject of the Court's first great pronouncement on equality. The other was that Marshall did not rest his analysis on the violation of individual rights. Although the Cherokee Codes and the Removal Act discriminated against individuals, he chose to base his opinion on the injury to the collective rights of the Tribe.

Marshall's creation of an equality principle in *Worcester*, along with the debate over religious liberty discussed earlier, drives home a recurring theme of this study. Many of the constitutional principles that are now considered fundamental began as nothing more than offshoots of a generational conflict. The great engine of legal creativity is the primal desire to win. As a result, leaders caught up in the emotions unleashed by a fight for power often reach for unorthodox solutions to attract support. Innovations introduced in the heat of battle often become pillars of the constitutional order over time. This is nothing more than the common-law process at work, where intuitions drive the results and the deeper justifications come later....

Not surprisingly, Georgia refused to obey the federal mandate to release the prisoners, but the State came up with a clever solution to the problem posed by Marshall's opinion. Obviously, rejecting an order from the Supreme Court posed a big risk. To the extent that the establishment was trying to portray the reformers as a bunch of wild-eyed radicals, blatant obstruction by local authorities would aid that effort. Instead of affirmatively refusing to obey, the state court with jurisdiction over the missionaries simply did nothing. This presented a dilemma for Jackson's opponents because the Judiciary Act of 1789 said that the Supreme Court could order federal marshals to enforce a judgment only if the state court put its objections to the judgment in writing. This form of passive resistance by the state had two implications, one of which is well known. The other, however, remains underappreciated.

First, notwithstanding the myth that Jackson said, "John Marshall has made his decision; now let him enforce it," in reality there was nothing to enforce. One could say the president had a moral obligation to persuade Georgia to obey, with one congressman grumbling that "Jackson could by a nod of the head or a crook of the finger induce Georgia to submit to the law." But the president had no legal duty to act. His supporters stressed this point, with one pamphlet noting that "when the Supreme Court assemble, and are officially informed that obedience to their mandate has been refused by the Court of Georgia, they must adopt some ulterior measure to enforce it.... Until they do decide, the President has no authority." The problem was that even if Georgia put its refusal in writing, the Supreme Court was not in session and hence could not issue another order until it reconvened. As a result, historians who study this era agree that Jackson was right when he told a friend that "the decision of the supreme court has fell still born" and that no federal action was required.

There is a second feature of this episode, though, that receives less attention. Why would Chief Justice Marshall and his colleagues issue an opinion without taking measures to ensure it would be obeyed? Since Georgia boycotted the oral argument in *Worcester* and *Cherokee Nation*, there could be little doubt that they would not accept the judgment. The justices may not have anticipated the decision of the state court to omit its objections from the record on remand, but by recessing for the year they left themselves in no position to act no matter what Georgia did. In this moment of constitutional drama, the casual air with which Marshall issued his opinion and then left town is perplexing. Unless, of course, the chief justice did not want to see his opinion enforced before the election.

The hidden element of *Worcester* is that it was an advisory opinion that affected no concrete rights at all. Through his artful stratagem of doing nothing to enforce the ruling, the chief justice avoided the embarrassing prospect of having the president refuse to carry out the judgment. That kind of open resistance would create a precedent that could have permanently harmed the judicial branch. Instead, the Court gave voters a chance to consider *Worcester's* indictment of the Jacksonian agenda and to change the political dynamic. The beauty of Marshall's trick is that *Worcester* looks like a real case rather than an advisory opinion that is, after all, prohibited under Article Three, Section Two, of the Constitution. Courts have cited *Worcester* many times since then without realizing that they are relying on what was in reality an improper election manifesto.

All of this demonstrates that the chief justice developed an elegant solution to the problem posed when courts join the resistance to reform. In *Worcester*, and to a lesser degree in *Cherokee Nation*, the justices offered a defense of tradition while minimizing the Court's institutional exposure. Georgia's refusal to put its resistance on the record only helped Marshall's cause. As long as the State took this position, the Court would not have to enforce its order and suffer the indignity of seeing its authority flouted by the president. Of course, this state of affairs could not be maintained indefinitely, because at some point it would be clear to all concerned that the Court was helpless.

In the meantime, the chief losers were the Cherokees and the members of Congress who wanted *Worcester* enforced. Once it was clear that Georgia would not acknowledge the judgment, the Tribe's sympathizers introduced another petition seeking "the most speedy and effectual measures to enforce the judgment of the Supreme Court of the United States, in the case of the missionaries Worcester and Butler, imprisoned under a judgment of a State court in Georgia." A congressman outlined the State's unprecedented opposition and said that "surely the House will never consent to suffer the public justice to be defeated by such a trick as this." Nevertheless, the petition was tabled and Jackson's supporters began to sense a change in the political momentum. A leading member of Georgia's congressional delegation countered: "Whenever a law or a judicial decision is of such a character that it does not receive the sanction of the moral feeling of the country, it is vain to hope to enforce it. ... Sir, I may be permitted, without exhibiting an air of unbecoming triumph, to refer to the late decision of the Supreme Court as completely illustrative of these ideas." With the fate in *Worcester* in doubt, generational tensions were near their peak. And the president was about to raise the stakes. ...

The spiral of escalation that drives the law in these transitional moments, however, was pushing both sides into a more extreme posture as the election neared. Marshall's preemptive opinion in *Worcester* articulated an extraordinary view of Federalism that shattered traditional principles in an attempt to discredit the new generation's policies. Now the president would act in kind with the most consequential veto of all time—a rejection of the National Bank that took out a central pillar of the old Constitution. Casting aside his prior caution, Jackson offered the bold vision of limited federal power free from corruption that was the wellspring of his movement. ...

Following its rejection of legislative authority, the president addressed the relevance (or lack thereof) of *M'Culloch*. Jackson said that the opinion "ought not to control the coordinate authorities of this Government. The Congress, the Executive, and the Court must each for itself be guided by its own opinion of the Constitution." In contrast to the analysis of tradition, which got lots of attention from contemporaries but is barely noticed now, the statement about the Court got relatively little notice from Jackson's peers but is the focus of modern analysts. Part of this is due to our fixation on the Supreme Court. In Jackson's day, it was accepted that all branches of government could make their own constitutional judgments. After all, the concept of legislative precedent would have been hollow if the justices could trump that consensus whenever they wanted. Moreover, Jackson noted that *M'Culloch* held that Congress could conclude that a Bank was a "necessary" means to execute its power, not that a president was required to concur.

This discussion of the relationship between the Court and the president had a subtext that was not lost on contemporary observers. Read as a reply to *Worcester* rather than to *M'Culloch*, the Bank Veto takes on a different cast. In essence, Jackson was offering a justification for his refusal to back the justices on the Cherokee issue while laying the foundation for a more drastic step to not enforce the judgment in *Worcester* if he was called upon to do so. The president did not go that far yet, but many in that era picked up on this coded message that each branch must "be guided by its own opinion of the Constitution."

This was not an isolated example of lawlessness but represents a broader pattern of presidential response during a generational shift. The rise of the executive branch as the driving force for constitutional reform, which was contrary to the expectation of the Framers, is one of the most important institutional developments during the last two centuries. Jefferson was the first to experiment with using his office as a focal point of the popular will, which explains why leaders in the 1830s often invoked his acts as a precedent for Jackson's decisions. But Jefferson always publicly proclaimed his deference to Congress. What makes Jackson unique is that he was the first president to declare that he was the tribune of the people and could assert an independent constitutional vision on their behalf. Webster typified the conservative reaction to this claim when he asked where "is the authority for saying that the President is *the direct representative of the People*? I hold this...to be mere assumption, and dangerous assumption. Yet other presidents would follow Jackson's example when confronted by judicial resistance....

The Bank Veto not only dismissed *M'Culloch* as irrelevant; it attacked the chief justice's reasoning supporting implied federal power. For example, the Court asserted that the Constitution did not restrict the means that Congress could use to carry out its power. The president disagreed. He explained that "on two subjects only does the Constitution recognize in Congress the power to grant exclusive privileges or monopolies.... Out of this express delegation of power have grown our laws of patents and copyrights." Since Article One, Section Eight, said that this means was authorized only to support these ends, Jackson concluded that "it is consistent with the fair rules of construction to conclude that such a power was not intended to be granted as a means of accomplishing any other end." That view oozed with bias against federal action. One could easily see Marshall taking the same text as proof that Congress was given this means and that it was not specifically withheld elsewhere....

Submitting to the Verdict of the People

Although the parties in every transitional period escalate their demands out of an urge to win, the net effect of these escalations is to crystallize the constitutional issues for the electorate. As each camp is pushed into a more radical position, the voters get a clearer picture of the paths they must choose between. Thus, almost every generational collision is marked by a series of increasingly polarized elections that focus on first principles. In each of these moments, the people truly are the masters of their fate.

During the 1832 campaign, the dueling sides were represented by their respective texts—*Worcester* for traditionalists and the Bank Veto for reformers. Not coincidentally, these two great documents of state focused on the two lead issues of the campaign. The Bank's director, Nicholas Biddle, thought that Jackson's message was such a blunder that he paid for its distribution to the public. Later, he realized his mistake and started sending out Webster's Reply to the Veto. While the Bank issue was more important during the campaign, the Cherokee Removal drew considerable attention as well. Senator Clay, Jackson's presidential foe, opened his campaign by discussing *Worcester* first and the Bank second, stating that "the Supreme Court is paralyzed, and the missionaries retained in prison in contempt of its authority, and in defiance of numerous treaties and laws of the United States ... [and] that the veto has been applied to the Bank of the United States." Hostile papers often ran debates on the issues side by side because in both cases Jackson "refused to recognize the supremacy of the Constitution as interpreted by the Supreme Court."

Conservatives thought one path to victory involved splitting the rising generation through an appeal to religious voters upset by Georgia's imprisonment of the missionaries. The keynote address at the convention that nominated Clay for president pounded on this angle, stating that "few examples can be found, even in the history of barbarous communities, in which the sacred character of a minister of religion has furnished so slight a protection against disrespect and violence to the persons invested with it." Indeed, the "inhuman and unconstitutional outrages committed under the authority of Georgia" motivated Van Buren's own niece to lecture him on the controversy when he was on a campaign swing through New York. A paper asked whether "the Christian people of the United States [would] give their sanction ... to the conduct of a President who treats the ministers of the Christian religion with open outrage ... [and] commits them in defiance of law like common criminals to the penitentiary."

Jackson's supporters sensed the danger and continued their impassioned defense against the charge that they were oppressing religious practice by allowing Georgia to jail Worcester and Butler. One Democratic pamphlet argued that "to connect the subject of the missionaries, now confined in the State of Georgia, with the election of the President, was altogether unwarranted. But as our opponents have chosen to do so—as they have assailed him for not having interfered and liberated them from their confinement" a reply was warranted. The substance of their answer, once again, was that the missionaries had violated a neutral law that applied to everyone and thus it was wrong to say that ministers were being targeted or that they had any right to refuse the loyalty oath. In the president's view, "neither to him nor to any man does it belong, in this country, to step beyond the limits assigned by the laws, and to assume a power connected with religious concerns, not assigned nor authorized by our great constitutional charter."

As the election results began to dribble in—in those days there was no national election day—the trend in Jackson's favor was unmistakable. The president carried the country with a clear margin, defeating Clay in the Electoral College 219 to 49 and winning 55 percent of the popular vote. Jacksonians also seized control of the House of Representatives, bringing one more organ of federal power under their thumb. Marshall fell into a gloomy mood and told Story that "I yield slowly and reluctantly to the conviction that our Constitution cannot last.... The union has been prolonged thus far by miracles. I fear they cannot continue." The chief justice was right in a sense. His generation was passing away, and "our Constitution" would now belong to Jacksonian Democracy....

✠ *F U R T H E R   R E A D I N G*

Brands, H.W. *Andrew Jackson: His Life and Times* (2005).

Brown, Richard H. "The Missouri Crisis, Slavery, and the Politics of Jacksonianism," *South Atlantic Quarterly*, 65 (Winter 1966): 55–72.

Cole, Donald B. *The Presidency of Andrew Jackson* (1993).

Ellis, Richard E. *The Union at Risk: Jacksonian Democracy, States' Rights, and the Nullification Crisis* (1989).

Ely, James W. Jr., ed. *A History of the Tennessee Supreme Court* (2002).

Freehling, William W. *Prelude to Civil War: The Nullification Crisis in South Carolina, 1816–1836* (1965).

Garrison, Tim Alan. *The Legal Ideology of Removal: The Southern Judiciary and the Sovereignty of Native American Nations* (2002).

Hall, Kermit L. "Andrew Jackson and the Judiciary: The Michigan Territorial Judiciary as a Test Case, 1828–1832," *Michigan History*, 59 (Fall 1975): 177–186.

Hershberger, Mary. "Mobilizing Women, Anticipating Abolition: The Struggle against Indian Removal in the 1830s," *Journal of American History*, 86 (1999): 15–40.

Hofstadter, Richard. *The American Political Tradition and the Men Who Made It* (1948).

Huebner, Timothy S. "Divided Loyalties: Justice William Johnson and the Rise of Disunion in South Carolina, 1822–1834," *Journal of Supreme Court History* (1995): 19–30.

Kateb, George. "The Majority Principle: Calhoun and His Antecedents," *Political Science Quarterly*, 84 (1969): 583–605.

Latner, Richard B. "The Nullification Crisis and Republican Subversion," *Journal of Southern History*, 43 (1977): 19–38.

———. *The Presidency of Andrew Jackson: White House Politics, 1829–1837* (1979).

Miles, Edwin A. "After John Marshall's Decision: *Worcester v. Georgia* and the Nullification Crisis," *Journal of Southern History*, 39 (1973): 519–544.

Nagel, Paul C. *One Nation Indivisible: The Union in American Thought* (1964).

Norgren, Jill. *Cherokee Cases: Two Landmark Federal Decisions in the Fight for Sovereignty* (2004).

Remini, Robert V. *Andrew Jackson and the Bank War: A Study in the Growth of Presidential Power* (1967).

———. *The Legacy of Andrew Jackson: Essays on Democracy, Indian Removal, and Slavery* (1988).

———. *The Presidency of Andrew Jackson* (1967).

Rogin, Michael Paul. *Fathers and Children: Andrew Jackson and the Subjugation of the American Indian* (1975).

Satz, Ronald. *American Indian Policy in the Jacksonian Era* (1975).

Schlesinger, Jr., Arthur. *The Age of Jackson* (1945).

Stewart, James B. "A Great Talking and Eating Machine: Patriarchy, Mobilization and the Dynamics of Nullification in South Carolina," *Civil War History*, 27 (1981): 197–220.

Wallace, Anthony F.C. *The Long, Bitter Trail: Andrew Jackson and the Indians* (1993).

Watson, Harry. *Liberty and Power: The Politics of Jacksonian America* (2006).

Wilentz, Sean. *Andrew Jackson* (2005).

CHAPTER

6

Abraham Lincoln, Slavery, and the Civil War

By the middle of the nineteenth century, the slavery issue threatened to destroy the Union. The founders had neglected to act definitively on the matter, never mentioning the institution by name, yet providing for its continued existence through the Three-Fifths and Fugitive Slave Clauses of the Constitution. Over the next several decades, the federal government's mostly hands-off policy with regard to slavery, moreover, had allowed the states to pursue their own paths of social and economic development. What little slavery had existed in the North all but disappeared by the early nineteenth century, and in the meantime immigration and industrialization resulted in dramatic population growth and economic expansion, particularly in the Northeast. With the numbers of factories, laborers, canals, and railroads all on the rise, the North was becoming an increasingly diverse and prosperous region of the country. While the South too witnessed its share of prosperity, economic growth in the southern states took a different form. The South came more and more to rely upon black slave labor, which made possible the production of a variety of cash crops, particularly cotton. As agricultural profits and production increased, so did white southerners' commitment to slavery.

During the late 1840s and 1850s, the debate over slavery involved two main issues: the extension of slavery to new territories and the return of fugitive slaves to their masters in the southern states. The Constitution provided little clarity on either question, and continued conflict over state sovereignty only complicated matters. Did Congress have the power to legislate on—or even exclude—slavery in the territories, based on its constitutional authority in Article IV to make "needful rules and regulations respecting the territory or other property belonging to the United States"? Or did the people who settled new territories possess this power? Did the national government have an obligation to oversee the rendition of fugitive slaves, based on the existence of the Constitution's Fugitive Slave Clause, or did states possess the power to stymie federal efforts in this area? Did "southern rights" to own and transport slave property throughout the country override whatever powers the national government or territorial governments possessed in this regard?

In Dred Scott v. Sandford *(1857), Chief Justice Roger B. Taney, joined by pro-slavery colleagues, attempted to solve these problems with a single, definitive judicial decision. Taney adopted the southern rights position, by ruling that the Constitution's Fifth Amendment guarantee of property rights prevented Congress from passing any legislation interfering with slavery in the territories. Because the decision clearly put the national government on the side of slaveholders, leaders of the recently formed Republican Party claimed that the ruling represented a dangerous step toward the nationalization of slavery. When Republican Abraham Lincoln—an avowed opponent of the spread of slavery—won the presidency in 1860, southern leaders feared that the rights affirmed by the Supreme Court were no longer safe. Because the continued growth of the northern population foreshadowed increased northern power in Congress, white southerners feared that slavery faced an uncertain future. During the 7 months after Lincoln's election, 11 southern states seceded and formed the Confederate States of America.*

Lincoln viewed the Union as indivisible. When the new president indicated his intention to supply Fort Sumter, one of the last remaining federal forts in the South, the Confederates attacked and the Civil War began. During the first few months of the war, with Congress out of session, Lincoln took a series of unprecedented steps to save the republic. With Confederate sympathizers in abundance in Maryland, Lincoln suspended the writ of habeas corpus between Philadelphia and Washington, thus giving power to the military to arrest and imprison suspected traitors without formal proceedings. (He later applied the order to the whole country.) In addition, Lincoln blockaded southern ports and censored the mail. Most dramatically, in 1863 he issued the Emancipation Proclamation, which claimed to liberate 3 million slaves in the Confederate States. Although Congress eventually supported all of these policies, Lincoln's tremendous expansion of the powers of his office drew criticism in both the North and South. Despite the controversy surrounding the president's actions, only northern victory on the battlefield ensured the survival of the Union and the demise of slavery. The war ended in April 1865, after 4 years of fighting that left more than 600,000 Americans dead. Later that year, the Thirteenth Amendment abolished slavery throughout the nation.

The debate over the constitutional aspects of the Civil War focuses on the issues of slavery, presidential powers, and civil liberties. Was the Constitution a pro-slavery document? If so, was Taney's pro-slavery decision in Dred Scott a faithful interpretation of the founders' intentions, or did the ruling represent a perversion of the Constitution's true meaning with regard to slavery? Did Lincoln exceed his constitutional authority as chief executive, or did the exigencies of war and the fate of the Union justify his unprecedented actions? Was the Civil War a constitutional watershed?

✠ D O C U M E N T S

The great constitutional debate of the 1840s and 1850s was over whether the Constitution was pro-slavery or antislavery. Even abolitionists were split on the issue. William Lloyd Garrison, one of the most powerful voices among those morally opposed to slavery, believed that the Constitution was a pro-slavery compact. He routinely described the nation's charter as a "covenant with death and an agreement with hell." Although the former-slave-turned-abolitionist Frederick Douglass originally sided with Garrison, by 1852 Douglass had changed his position. Document 1, taken from his speech, "What to the Slave is the Fourth of July," is a spirited defense of the Constitution. However much they disagreed over the morality of slavery, Chief Justice Taney and Garrison agreed about slavery's constitutional status.

In *Dred Scott v. Sandford*, Document 2, Taney held that the Constitution conferred no rights on slaves or free blacks. The case involved a Missouri slave, owned by an army surgeon, who had traveled with his master and lived in the free territory of Wisconsin and the free state of Illinois for about 2 years. Scott filed suit for his freedom, based on the principle that his residence in free territory had made him a free man. In a 7-2 decision, Taney and the majority concluded that at the time of the founding, black people, whether slave or free, "had no rights that the white man was bound to respect." Having denied Scott his freedom and citizenship to African Americans, Taney took on the thorny issue of slavery in the territories and ruled definitely in favor of slaveholders.

After leading the fight against *Dred Scott* in his debates with Senator Stephen Douglas in 1858, Abraham Lincoln won election to the presidency in 1860. Disunion quickly followed. Delegates from the first seven southern states to secede wrote the Confederate Constitution, excerpted here as Document 3. Although it closely resembled the Constitution of the United States, the Confederacy's founding document contained a number of distinctive features. Lincoln recognized the legitimacy of neither secession nor the Confederacy. In his First Inaugural Address of March 4, 1861, Document 4, the new president attempted to stick to his principles, while striking a conciliatory tone in an attempt to avoid war.

Once the war began, Lincoln moved swiftly to preserve the Union. His suspension of the writ of habeas corpus met with considerable opposition, and in *Ex parte Merryman*, a federal circuit case involving a wealthy Marylander arrested for drilling Confederate troops, Chief Justice Taney issued a stinging rebuke to the president. (Taney heard the case in his capacity as a federal judge of the Maryland circuit.) The opinion in *Merryman*, Document 5, challenged Lincoln's constitutional authority to suspend the writ. Even more controversial was the Emancipation Proclamation, Document 6, issued on January 1, 1863. Lincoln viewed emancipation as a military measure that would assist the Union in undermining the Confederacy, and the Proclamation declared an end to slavery in the Confederacy. Although limited in its reach and famously described by one historian as having "all the moral grandeur of a bill of lading," the Proclamation unleashed the forces that eventually culminated in the complete abolition of slavery with the ratification of the Thirteenth Amendment. Lincoln defended his wartime military authority in his June 12, 1863, Letter to Erastus Corning, Document 7, written in response to a set of resolutions drafted at a meeting in Albany, New York.

✤ D O C U M E N T   1

Abolitionist Frederick Douglass Describes the Constitution as Anti–Slavery, 1852

But it is answered in reply to all this, that precisely what I have now denounced is, in fact, guaranteed and sanctioned by the Constitution of the United States; that the right to hold and to hunt slaves is a part of that Constitution framed by the illustrious Fathers of this Republic.

Then, I dare to affirm, notwithstanding all I have said before, your fathers stooped, basely stooped

From Blassingame, John W., Editor. *The Frederick Douglass Papers, Series One: Speeches, Debates, and Interviews, Volume 2: 1847–54.* Copyright © 1982 by Yale University Press. Reproduced with permission of the publisher.

"To palter with us in a double sense:
And keep the word of promise to the ear,
But break it to the heart."

And instead of being the honest men I have before declared them to be, they were the veriest imposters that ever practised on mankind. *This* is the inevitable conclusion, and from it there is no escape. But I differ from those who charge this baseness on the framers of the Constitution of the United States. *It is a slander upon their memory*, at least, so I believe. ...

Fellow-citizens! there is no matter in respect to which, the people of the North have allowed themselves to be so ruinously imposed upon, as that of the pro-slavery character of the Constitution. In *that* instrument I hold there is neither warrant, license, nor sanction of the hateful thing; but, interpreted as it *ought* to be interpreted, the Constitution is a GLORIOUS LIBERTY DOCUMENT. Read its preamble, consider its purposes. Is slavery among them? Is it at the gateway? or is it in the temple? It is neither. While I do not intend to argue this question on the present occasion, let me ask, if it be not somewhat singular that, if the Constitution were intended to be, by its framers and adopters, a slave-holding instrument, why neither *slavery, slaveholding*, nor *slave* can anywhere be found in it. What would be thought of an instrument, drawn up, *legally* drawn up, for the purpose of entitling the city of Rochester to a track of land, in which no mention of land was made? Now, there are certain rules of interpretation, for the proper understanding of all legal instruments. These rules are well established. They are plain, common-sense rules, such as you and I, and all of us, can understand and apply, without having passed years in the study of law. I scout the idea that the question of the constitutionality or unconstitutionality of slavery is not a question for the people. I hold that every American citizen has a right to form an opinion of the constitution, and to propagate that opinion, and to use all honorable means to make his opinion the prevailing one. Without this right, the liberty of an American citizen would be as insecure as that of a Frenchman. Ex-Vice-President Dallas tells us that the constitution is an object to which no American mind can be too attentive, and no American heart too devoted. He further says, the constitution, in its words, is plain and intelligible, and is meant for the home-bred, unsophisticated understandings of our fellow-citizens. Senator Berrien tells us that the Constitution is the fundamental law, that which controls all others. The charter of our liberties, which every citizen has a personal interest in understanding thoroughly. The testimony of Senator Breese, Lewis Cass, and many others that might be named, who are everywhere esteemed as sound lawyers, so regard the constitution. I take it, therefore, that it is not presumption in a private citizen to form an opinion of that instrument.

Now, take the constitution according to its plain reading, and I defy the presentation of a single pro-slavery clause in it. On the other hand it will be found to contain principles and purposes, entirely hostile to the existence of slavery.

I have detained my audience entirely too long already. At some future period I will gladly avail myself of an opportunity to give this subject a full and fair discussion.

Allow me to say, in conclusion, notwithstanding the dark picture I have this day presented of the state of the nation, I do not despair of this country. There are forces in operation, which must inevitably work the downfall of slavery. *"The arm of the Lord is not shortened,*" and the doom of slavery is certain. I, therefore, leave off where I began, with *hope*. While drawing encouragement from the Declaration of Independence, the great principles it contains, and the genius of American Institutions, my spirit is also cheered by the obvious tendencies of the age. Nations do not now stand in the same relation to each other that they did ages ago. No nation can now shut itself up from the surrounding world, and trot round in the same old path of its fathers without interference. The time *was* when such could be done. Long established customs of hurtful character could formerly fence themselves in, and do their evil work with social impunity. Knowledge was then confined and enjoyed by the privileged few, and the multitude walked on in mental darkness. But a change has now come over the affairs of mankind. Walled cities and empires have become unfashionable. The arm of commerce has borne away the gates of the strong city. Intelligence is penetrating the darkest corners of the globe. It makes its pathway over and under the sea, as well as on the earth. Wind, steam, and lightning are its chartered agents. Oceans no longer divide, but link nations together. From Boston to London is now a holiday excursion. Space is comparatively annihilated. Thoughts expressed on one side of the Atlantic are distinctly heard on the other.

The far off and almost fabulous Pacific rolls in grandeur at our feet. The Celestial Empire, the mystery of ages, is being solved. The fiat of the Almighty, "*Let there be Light,*" has not yet spent its force. No abuse, no outrage whether in taste, sport or avarice, can now hide itself from the all-pervading light. ...

✥ D O C U M E N T   2

Dred Scott v. Sandford, 1857

Mr. Chief Justice Taney delivered the opinion of the Court. The question is simply this: Can a negro, whose ancestors were imported into this country, and sold as slaves, become a member of the political community formed and brought into existence by the constitution of the United States, and as such become entitled to all the rights, and privileges, and immunities, guaranteed by that instrument to the citizen? One of which rights is the privilege of suing in a court of the United States in the case specified in the constitution.

It will be observed, that the plea applies to that class of persons only whose ancestors were negroes of the African race, and imported into this country, and sold and held as slaves. The only matter in issue before the court, therefore, is, whether the descendants of such slaves, when they shall be emancipated, or who are born of parents who had become free before their birth, are citizens of a State, in the sense in which the word citizen is used in the constitution of the United States. And this being the only matter in dispute on the pleadings, the court must be understood as speaking in this opinion of that class only, that is, of those persons who are the descendants of Africans who were imported into this country, and sold as slaves. ...

The words "people of the United States" and "citizens" are synonymous terms, and mean the same thing. They both describe the political body who, according to our republican institutions, form the sovereignty, and who hold the power and conduct the government through their representatives. They are what we familiarly call the "sovereign people," and every citizen is one of this people, and a constituent member of this sovereignty. The question before us is, whether the class of persons described in the plea in abatement compose a portion of this people, and are constituent members of this sovereignty? We think they are not, and that they are not included, and were not intended to be included, under the word "citizens" in the constitution, and can therefore claim none of the rights and privileges which that instrument provides for and secures to citizens of the United States. On the contrary, they were at that time considered as a subordinate and inferior class of beings, who had been subjugated by the dominant race, and, whether emancipated or not, yet remained subject to their authority, and had no rights or privileges but such as those who held the power and the government might choose to grant them.

It is not the province of the court to decide upon the justice or injustice, the policy or impolicy, of these laws. The decision of that question belonged to the political or law-making power; to those who formed the sovereignty and framed the constitution. The duty of the court is, to interpret the instrument they have framed, with the best lights we can obtain on the subject, and to administer it as we find it, according to its true intent and meaning when it was adopted.

In discussing this question, we must not confound the rights of citizenship which a State may confer within its own limits, and the rights of citizenship as a member of the Union. It does not by any means follow, because he has all the rights and privileges of a citizen of a State, that he must be a citizen of the United States. He may have all of the rights and privileges of the citizen of a State, and yet not be entitled to the rights and privileges of a citizen in any other State. For, previous to the adoption of the constitution of the United States, every State had the undoubted right to confer on whomsoever it pleased the character of citizen, and to endow him with all its rights. But this character of course was confined to the boundaries of the State, and gave him no rights or privileges in other States beyond those secured to him by the laws of nations and the comity of States. Nor have the several States surrendered the power of conferring these rights and privileges by adopting the constitution of the United States. . . .

It is very clear, therefore, that no State can, by any act or law of its own, passed since the adoption of the constitution, introduce a new member into the political community created by the constitution of the United States. It cannot make him a member of this community by making him a member of its own. And for the same reason it cannot introduce any person, or description of persons, who were not intended to be embraced in this new political family, which the constitution brought into existence, but were intended to be excluded from it.

The question then arises, whether the provisions of the constitution, in relation to the personal rights and privileges to which the citizen of a State should be entitled, embraced the negro African race, at that time in this country, or who might afterwards be imported, who had then or should afterwards be made free in any State; and to put it in the power of a single State to make him a citizen of the United States, and endue him with the full rights of citizenship in every other State without their consent? Does the constitution of the United States act upon him whenever he shall be made free under the laws of a State, and raised there to the rank of a citizen, and immediately clothe him with all the privileges of a citizen in every other State, and in its own courts?

The court think the affirmative of these propositions cannot be maintained. And if it cannot, the plaintiff in error could not be a citizen of the State of Missouri, within the meaning of the constitution of the United States, and, consequently, was not entitled to sue in its courts.

It is true, every person, and every class and description of persons, who were at the time of the adoption of the constitution recognized as citizens in the several States, became also citizens of this new political body; but none other; it was formed by them, and for them and their posterity, but for no one else. And the personal rights and privileges guaranteed to citizens of this new sovereignty were intended to embrace those only who were then members of the several State communities, or who should afterwards by birthright or otherwise become members, according to the provisions of the constitution and the principles on which it was founded. ...

In the opinion of the court, the legislation and histories of the times, and the language used in the declaration of independence, show, that neither the class of persons who had been imported as slaves, nor their descendants, whether they had become free or not, were then acknowledged as a part of the people, nor intended to be included in the general words used in that memorable instrument. ...

They had for more than a century before been regarded as beings of an inferior order, and altogether unfit to associate with the white race, either in social or political relations; and so far inferior, that they had no rights which the white man was bound to respect; and that the negro might justly and lawfully be reduced to slavery for his benefit. ...

The legislation of the different colonies furnishes positive and indisputable proof of this fact. ...

The language of the declaration of independence is equally conclusive. ...

But it is too clear for dispute, that the enslaved African race were not intended to be included, and formed no part of the people who framed and adopted this declaration; for if the language, as understood in that day, would embrace them, the conduct of the distinguished men who framed the declaration of independence would have been utterly and flagrantly inconsistent with the principles they asserted; and instead of the sympathy of mankind, to which they so confidently appealed, they would have deserved and received universal rebuke and reprobation. ...

This state of public opinion had undergone no change when the constitution was adopted, as is equally evident from its provisions and language. ...

But there are two clauses in the constitution which point directly and specifically to the negro race as a separate class of persons, and show clearly that they were not regarded as a portion of the people or citizens of the government then formed.

One of these clauses reserves to each of the thirteen States the right to import slaves until the year 1808, if it thinks proper. ... And by the other provision the States pledge themselves to each other to maintain the right of property of the master, by delivering up to him any slave who may have escaped from his service, and be found within their respective territories. ...

The only two provisions which point to them and include them, treat them as property, and make it the duty of the government to protect it; no other power, in relation to this race, is to be found in the constitution; and as it is a government of special, delegated, powers, no authority beyond these two provisions can be constitutionally exercised. The government of the United States had no right to interfere for any other purpose but that of protecting the rights of the owner, leaving it altogether with the several States to deal with this race, whether emancipated or not, as each State may think justice, humanity, and the interests and safety of society, require. The States evidently intended to reserve this power exclusively to themselves. ...

[U]pon a full and careful consideration of the subject, the court is of opinion, that, upon the facts stated ..., Dred Scott was not a citizen of Missouri within the meaning of the constitution of the United States, and not entitled as such to sue in its courts; and, consequently, that the circuit court had no jurisdiction of the case, and that the judgment on the plea in abatement is erroneous. ...

We proceed ... to inquire whether the facts relied on by the plaintiff entitled him to his freedom. ...

The act of Congress, upon which the plaintiff relies, declares that slavery and involuntary servitude, except as a punishment for crime, shall be forever prohibited in all that part of the territory ceded by France, under the name of Louisiana, which lies north of thirty-six degrees thirty minutes north latitude and not included within the limits of Missouri. And the difficulty which meets us at the threshold of this part of the inquiry is whether Congress was authorized to pass this law under any of the powers granted to it by the Constitution; for, if the authority is not given by that instrument, it is the duty of this Court to declare it void and inoperative and incapable of conferring freedom upon anyone who is held as a slave under the laws of any one of the states.

The counsel for the plaintiff has laid much stress upon that article in the Constitution which confers on Congress the power "to dispose of and make all needful rules and regulations respecting the territory or other property belonging to the United States"; but, in the judgment of the Court, that provision has no bearing on the present controversy, and the power there given, whatever it may be, is confined, and was intended to be confined, to the territory which at that time belonged to, or was claimed by, the United States and was within their boundaries as settled by the treaty with Great Britain and can have no influence upon a territory afterward acquired from a foreign government. It was a special provision for a known and particular territory, and to meet a present emergency, and nothing more. ...

All we mean to say on this point is that, as there is no express regulation in the Constitution defining the power which the general government may exercise over the person or property of a citizen in a territory thus acquired, the Court must necessarily look to the provisions and principles of the Constitution, and its distribution of powers, for the rules and principles by which its decision must be governed.

Taking this rule to guide us, it may be safely assumed that citizens of the United States who migrate to a territory belonging to the people of the United States cannot be ruled as mere colonists, dependent upon the will of the general government, and to be governed by any laws it may think proper to impose. The principle upon which our governments rest, and upon which alone they continue to exist, is the union of states, sovereign and independent within their own limits in their internal and domestic concerns, and bound together as one people by a general government, possessing certain enumerated and restricted powers, delegated to it by the people of the several states, and exercising supreme authority within the scope of the powers granted to it, throughout the dominion of the United States. A power, therefore, in the general government to obtain and hold colonies and dependent territories, over which they might legislate without restriction, would be inconsistent with its own existence in its present form. Whatever it acquires, it acquires for the benefit of the people of the several states who created it. It is their trustee acting for them and charged with the duty of promoting the interests of the whole people of the Union in the exercise of the powers specifically granted....

But the power of Congress over the person or property of a citizen can never be a mere discretionary power under our Constitution and form of government. The powers of the government and the rights and privileges of the citizen are regulated and plainly defined by the Constitution itself. And, when the territory becomes a part of the United States, the federal government enters into possession in the character impressed upon it by those who created it. It enters upon it with its powers over the citizen strictly defined and limited by the Constitution, from which it derives its own existence, and by virtue of which alone it continues to exist and act as a government and sovereignty. It has no power of any kind beyond it; and it cannot, when it enters a territory of the United States, put off its character and assume discretionary or despotic powers which the Constitution has denied to it. It cannot create for itself a new character separated from the citizens of the United States and the duties it owes them under the provisions of the Constitution. The territory, being a part of the United States, the government and the citizen both enter it under the authority of the Constitution, with their respective rights defined and marked out; and the federal government can exercise no power over his person or property, beyond what that instrument confers, nor lawfully deny any right which it has reserved....

These powers, and others, in relation to rights of person, which it is not necessary here to enumerate, are, in express and positive terms, denied to the general government; and the rights of private property have been guarded with equal care. Thus the rights of property are united with the rights of person and placed on the same ground by the Fifth Amendment to the Constitution, which provides that no person shall be deprived of life, liberty, and property without due process of law. And an act of Congress which deprives a citizen of the United States of his liberty or property, without due process of law, merely because he came himself or brought his property into a particular territory of the United States, and who had committed no offense against the laws, could hardly be dignified with the name of due process of law....

The powers over person and property of which we speak are not only not granted to Congress but are in express terms denied, and they are forbidden to exercise them. And this prohibition is not confined to the states, but the words are general and extend to the whole territory over which the Constitution gives it power to legislate, including those portions of it remaining under territorial government as well as that covered by states....

It seems, however, to be supposed that there is a difference between property in a slave and other property and that different rules may be applied to it in expounding the Constitution of the United States. And the laws and usages of nations, and the writings of eminent jurists upon the relation of master and slave and their mutual rights and duties, and the powers which governments may exercise over it, have been dwelt upon in the argument.

But, in considering the question before us, it must be borne in mind that there is no law of nations standing between the people of the United States and their government and interfering with their relation to each other. The powers of the government and the rights of the citizen under it are positive and practical regulations plainly written down. The people of the United States have delegated to it certain enumerated powers and forbidden it to exercise others. It has no power over the person or property of a citizen but what the citizens of the United States have granted. And no laws or usages of other nations, or reasoning of statesmen or jurists upon the relations of master and slave, can enlarge the powers of the government or take from the citizens the rights they have reserved. And if the Constitution recognizes the right of property of the master in a slave, and makes no distinction between that description of property and other property owned by a citizen, no tribunal, acting under the authority of the United States, whether it be legislative, executive, or judicial, has a right to draw such a distinction or deny to it the benefit of the provisions and guarantees which have been provided for the protection of private property against the encroachments of the government.

Now, as we have already said in an earlier part of this opinion, upon a different point, the right of property in a slave is distinctly and expressly affirmed in the Constitution. The right to traffic in it, like an ordinary article of merchandise and property, was guaranteed to the citizens of the United States, in every state that might desire it, for twenty years. And the government in express terms is pledged to protect it in all future time if the slave escapes from his owner. That is done in plain words—too plain to be misunderstood. And no word can be found in the Constitution which gives Congress a greater power over slave property or which entitles property of that kind to less protection than property of any other description. The only power conferred is the power coupled with the duty of guarding and protecting the owner in his rights.

Upon these considerations it is the opinion of the Court that the act of Congress which prohibited a citizen from holding and owning property of this kind in the territory of the United States north of the line therein mentioned is not warranted by the Constitution and is therefore void; and that neither Dred Scott himself, nor any of his family, were made free by being carried into this territory; even if they had been carried there by the owner with the intention of becoming a permanent resident. ...

✠ *D O C U M E N T   3*

The Confederacy Writes a Constitution, 1861

We, the people of the Confederate States, each State acting in its sovereign and independent character, in order to form a permanent federal government, establish justice, insure domestic tranquillity, and secure the blessings of liberty to ourselves and our posterity—invoking the favor and guidance of Almighty God—do ordain and establish this Constitution for the Confederate States of America.

Article I

Section 7. (2)...The President may approve any appropriation and disapprove any other appropriation in the same bill. In such case he shall, in signing the bill, designate the appropriations disapproved; and shall return a copy of such appropriations, with his objections, to the House in which the bill shall have originated; and the same proceedings shall then be had as in case of other bills disapproved by the President. ...

Section 8. The Congress shall have power—

(1) To lay and collect taxes, duties, imposts, and excises, for revenue necessary to pay the debts, provide for the common defence, and carry on the Government of the Confederate States; but no bounties shall be granted from the treasury; nor shall any duties or taxes on importations from foreign nations be laid to promote or foster any branch of industry; and all duties, imposts, and excises shall be uniform throughout the Confederate States. ...

(3) To regulate commerce with foreign nations, and among the several States, and with the Indian tribes; but neither this, nor any other clause contained in the Constitution shall be construed to delegate the power to Congress to appropriate money for any internal improvement intended to facilitate commerce; except for the purpose of furnishing lights, beacons, and buoys, and other aids to navigation upon the coasts, and the improvement of harbors, and the removing of obstructions in river navigation, in all which cases, such duties shall be laid on the navigation facilitated thereby, as may be necessary to pay the costs and expenses thereof.

(4) To establish uniform laws of naturalization, and uniform laws on the subject of bankruptcies throughout the Confederate States, but no law of Congress shall discharge any debt contracted before the passage of the same. ...

(7) To establish post-offices and post-routes; but the expenses of the Post-office Department, after the first day of March, in the year of our Lord eighteen hundred and sixty-three, shall be paid out of its own revenues. ...

Section 9. (1) The importation of negroes of the African race, from any foreign country, other than the slaveholding States or Territories of the United States of America, is hereby forbidden; and Congress is required to pass such laws as shall effectually prevent the same.

(2) Congress shall also have power to prohibit the introduction of slaves from any State not a member of, or Territory not belonging to, this Confederacy. ...

(4) No bill of attainder, or *ex post facto* law, or law denying or impairing the right of property in negro slaves shall be passed. ...

(6) No tax or duty shall be laid on articles exported from any State, except by a vote of two-thirds of both Houses.

(7) No preference shall be given by any regulation of commerce or revenue to the ports of one State over those of another. ...

(9) Congress shall appropriate no money from the treasury except by a vote of two-thirds of both Houses, taken by yeas and nays, unless it be asked and estimated for by some one of the heads of departments, and submitted to Congress by the President; or for the purpose of paying its own expenses and contingencies; or for the payment of claims against the Confederate States, the justice of which shall have been judicially declared by a tribunal for the investigation of claims against the Government, which it is hereby made the duty of Congress to establish.

(10) All bills appropriating money shall specify in federal currency the exact amount of each appropriation and the purposes for which it is made; and Congress shall grant no extra compensation to any public contractor, officer, agent, or servant, after such contract shall have been made or such service rendered. ...

[Paragraphs 12 through 19 incorporate the first 8 amendments to the U.S. Constitution.]

(20) Every law, or resolution having the force of law, shall relate to but one subject, and that shall be expressed in the title.

Section 10. (3) No State shall, without the consent of Congress, lay any duty on tonnage, except on sea-going vessels, for the improvement of its rivers and harbors navigated by the said vessels; but such duties shall not conflict with any treaties of the Confederate States with foreign nations; and any surplus of revenue, thus derived, shall, after making such improvement, be paid into the common treasury; nor shall any State keep troops or ships of war in time of peace, enter into any agreement or compact with another State, or with a foreign power, or engage in war, unless actually invaded, or in such imminent danger as will not admit of delay. But when any river divides or flows through two or more States, they may enter into compacts with each other to improve the navigation thereof.

Article II

Section 1. (1) The Executive power shall be vested in a President of the Confederate States of America. He and the Vice-President shall hold their offices for the term of six years; but the President shall not be reeligible. ...

[Paragraph 3 incorporates the twelfth amendment.]

(7) No person except a natural born citizen of the Confederate States, or a citizen thereof, at the time of the adoption of this Constitution, or a citizen thereof born in the United States prior to the 20th December, 1860, shall be eligible to the office of President. ...

Article IV

Section 2. (1) The citizens of each State shall be entitled to all the privileges and immunities of citizens of the several States, and shall have the right of transit and sojourn in any State of this Confederacy, with their slaves and other property; and the right of property in said slaves shall not be thereby impaired. ...

(3) No slave or other person held to service or labor in any State or Territory of the Confederate States, under the laws thereof, escaping or unlawfully carried into another, shall, in consequence of any law or regulation therein, be discharged from such service or labor; but shall be delivered up on claim of the party to whom such slave belongs, or to whom such service or labor may be due.

Section 3. (1) Other States may be admitted into this Confederacy by a vote of two-thirds of the whole House of Representatives, and two-thirds of the Senate, the Senate voting by States. ...

(2) The Congress shall have power to dispose of and make all needful rules and regulations concerning the property of the Confederate States, including the lands thereof.

(3) The Confederate States may acquire new territory; and Congress shall have power to legislate and provide governments for the inhabitants of all territory belonging to the Confederate States, lying without the limits of the several States, and may permit them, at such times, and in such manner as it may by law provide, to form

States to be admitted into the Confederacy. In all such territory, the institution of negro slavery, as it now exists in the Confederate States, shall be recognized and protected by Congress and by the territorial government; and the inhabitants of the several Confederate States and Territories shall have the right to take to such territory any slaves lawfully held by them in any of the States or Territories of the Confederate States....

✦ D O C U M E N T   4

President Abraham Lincoln Rejects Secession and Criticizes the Supreme Court, 1861

Fellow-Citizens of the United States:

. . . A disruption of the Federal Union, heretofore only menaced, is now formidably attempted.

I hold that, in contemplation of universal law and of the Constitution, the Union of these States is perpetual. Perpetuity is implied, if not expressed, in the fundamental law of all national governments. It is safe to assert that no government proper ever had a provision in its organic law for its own termination. Continue to execute all the express provisions of our national Constitution, and the Union will endure forever—it being impossible to destroy it except by some action not provided for in the instrument itself.

Again, if the United States be not a government proper, but an association of States in the nature of contract merely, can it as a contract be peaceably unmade by less than all the parties who made it? One party to a contract may violate it—break it, so to speak; but does it not require all to lawfully rescind it? ←

Descending from these general principles, we find the proposition that in legal contemplation the Union is perpetual confirmed by the history of the Union itself. The Union is much older than the Constitution. It was formed, in fact, by the Articles of Association in 1774. It was matured and continued by the Declaration of Independence in 1776. It was further matured, and the faith of all the then thirteen States expressly plighted and engaged that it should be perpetual, by the Articles of Confederation in 1778. And, finally, in 1787 one of the declared objects for ordaining and establishing the Constitution was "to form a more perfect Union."

But if the destruction of the Union by one or by a part only of the States be lawfully possible, the Union is less perfect than before the Constitution, having lost the vital element of perpetuity.

→ It follows from these views that no State upon its own mere motion can lawfully get out of the Union; that resolves and ordinances to that effect are legally void; and that acts of violence, within any State or States, against the authority of the United States, are insurrectionary or revolutionary, according to circumstances.

I therefore consider that, in view of the Constitution and the laws, the Union is unbroken; and to the extent of my ability I shall take care, as the Constitution itself expressly enjoins upon me, that the laws of the Union be faithfully executed in all the States. Doing this I deem to be only a simple duty on my part; and I shall perform it so far as practicable, unless my rightful masters, the American people, shall withhold the requisite means, or in some authoritative manner direct the contrary. I trust this will not be regarded as a menace, but only as the declared purpose of the Union that it will constitutionally defend and maintain itself.

In doing this there needs to be no bloodshed or violence; and there shall be none, unless it be forced upon the national authority. The power confided to me will be used to hold, occupy, and possess the property and places belonging to the Government, and to collect the duties and imposts; but beyond what may be necessary for these objects, there will be no invasion, no using of force against or among the people anywhere....

All profess to be content in the Union if all constitutional rights can be maintained. Is it true, then, that any right, plainly written in the Constitution, has been denied? I think not. Happily the human mind is so constituted that no party can reach to the audacity of doing this. Think, if you can, of a single instance in which a plainly written provision of the Constitution has ever been denied. If by the mere force of numbers a majority should deprive a minority of any clearly written constitutional right, it might, in a moral point of view, justify revolution—certainly would if such a right were a vital one. But such is not our case. All the vital rights of minorities and of individuals are so plainly assured to them by affirmations and negations, guarantees and prohibitions, in the Constitution, that controversies never arise concerning them. But no organic law can ever be framed with a provision specifically applicable to every question which may occur in practical administration. No foresight can anticipate, nor any document of reasonable length contain, express provision for all possible questions. Shall fugitives from labor be surrendered by national or by State authority? The Constitution does not expressly say. *May* Congress prohibit slavery in the Territories? The Constitution does not expressly say. *Must* Congress protect slavery in the Territories? The Constitution does not expressly say.

From questions of this class spring all our constitutional controversies, and we divide upon them into majorities and minorities. If the minority will not acquiesce, the majority must, or the Government must cease. There is no other alternative; for continuing the Government is acquiescence on one side or the other.

If a minority in such case will secede rather than acquiesce, they make a precedent which in turn will divide and ruin them; for a minority of their own will secede from them whenever a majority refuses to be controlled by such minority. For instance, why may not any portion of a new confederacy a year or two hence arbitrarily secede again, precisely as portions of the present Union now claim to secede from it? All who cherish disunion sentiments are now being educated to the exact temper of doing this.

Is there such perfect identity of interests among the States to compose a new Union as to produce harmony only, and prevent renewed secession?

Plainly, the central idea of secession is the essence of anarchy. A majority held in restraint by constitutional checks and limitations, and always changing easily with deliberate changes of popular opinions and sentiments, is the only true sovereign of a free people. Whoever rejects it does, of necessity, fly to anarchy or to despotism. Unanimity is impossible; the rule of a minority, as a permanent arrangement, is wholly inadmissible; so that, rejecting the majority principle, anarchy or despotism in some form is all that is left.

I do not forget the position assumed by some, that constitutional questions are to be decided by the Supreme Court; nor do I deny that such decisions must be binding, in any case, upon the parties to a suit, as to the object of that suit, while they are also entitled to a very high respect and consideration in all parallel cases by all other departments of the government. And, while it is obviously possible that such decision may be erroneous in any given case, still the evil effect following it, being limited to that particular case, with the chance that it may be overruled and never became a precedent for other cases, can better be borne than could the evils of a different practice. At the same time, the candid citizen must confess that if the policy of the government, upon vital questions affecting the whole people, is to be irrevocably fixed by the decisions of the Supreme Court, the instant they are made, in ordinary litigation between parties in personal actions, the people will have ceased to be their own rulers, having to that extent practically resigned the government into the hands of that eminent tribunal. Nor is there in this view any assault upon the court or the judges. It is a duty from which they may not shrink to decide cases properly brought before them, and it is no fault of theirs if others seek to turn their decisions to political purposes.

One section of our country believes slavery is right, and ought to be extended, while the other believes it is wrong, and ought not to be extended. This is the only substantial dispute. The fugitive slave clause of the Constitution and the law for the suppression of the foreign slave trade are each as well enforced, perhaps, as any law can ever be in a community where the moral sense of the people imperfectly supports the law itself. The great body of the people abide by the dry legal obligation in both cases, and a few break over in each. This, I think, cannot be perfectly cured; and it would be worse in both cases after the separation of the sections than before. The foreign slave trade, now imperfectly suppressed, would be ultimately revived, without restriction, in one section, while fugitive slaves, now only partially surrendered, would not be surrendered at all by the other.

Physically speaking, we cannot separate. We cannot remove our respective sections from each other, nor build an impassable wall between them. A husband and wife may be divorced and go out of the presence and beyond the reach of each other; but the different parts of our country cannot do this. They cannot but remain face to face, and intercourse, either amicable or hostile, must continue between them. Is it possible, then, to make that intercourse more advantageous or more satisfactory after separation than before? Can aliens make treaties easier than friends can make laws? Can treaties be more faithfully enforced between aliens than laws can among friends? Suppose you go to war, you cannot fight always; and when, after much loss on both sides, and no gain on either, you cease fighting, the identical old questions as to terms of intercourse are again upon you. ...

In your hands, my dissatisfied fellow-countrymen, and not in mine, is the momentous issue of civil war. The government will not assail you. You can have no conflict without being yourselves the aggressors. You have no oath registered in heaven to destroy the government, while I shall have the most solemn one to "preserve, protect, and defend" it.

I am loath to close. We are not enemies, but friends. We must not be enemies. Though passion may have strained, it must not break, our bonds of affection. The mystic chords of memory, stretching from every battlefield and patriot grave to every living heart and hearthstone all over this broad land, will yet swell the chorus of the Union when again touched, as surely they will be, by the better angels of our nature.

✳ D O C U M E N T   5

Ex Parte Merryman, 1861

. . . **Before the Chief Justice of the Supreme Court of the United States, at Chambers.**

The application in this case for a writ of *habeas corpus* is made to me under the 14th section of the Judiciary Act of 1789, which renders effectual for the citizen the constitutional privilege of the *habeas corpus*. That act gives to the Courts of the United States, as well as to each Justice of the Supreme Court, and to every District Judge, power to grant writs of *habeas corpus* for the purpose of an inquiry into the cause of commitment. The petition was presented to me at Washington, under the impression that I would order the prisoner to be brought before me there, but as he was confined in Fort McHenry, at the city of Baltimore, which is in my circuit, I resolved to hear it in the latter city, as obedience to the writ, under such circumstances, would not withdraw Gen. Cadwalader, who had him in charge, from the limits of his military command. . . .

But being thus officially notified that the privilege of the writ has been suspended under the orders and by the authority of the President, and believing as I do that the President has exercised a power which he does not possess under the Constitution, a proper respect for the high office he fills requires me to state plainly and fully the grounds of my opinion, in order to show that I have not ventured to question the legality of this act without a careful and deliberate examination of the whole subject.

The clause in the Constitution which authorizes the suspension of the privilege of the writ of *habeas corpus* is in the ninth section of the first article.

This article is devoted to the Legislative Department of the United States, and has not the slightest reference to the Executive Department. It begins by providing "that all legislative powers therein granted shall be vested in a Congress of the United States, which shall consist of a Senate and House of Representatives." And after prescribing the manner in which these two branches of the legislative department shall be chosen, it proceeds to enumerate specifically the legislative powers which it thereby grants, and legislative powers which it expressly prohibits, and, at the conclusion of this specification, a clause is inserted giving Congress "the power to make all laws which may be necessary and proper for carrying into execution the foregoing powers, and all other powers vested by this Constitution in the Government of the United States or in any department or office thereof."

The power of legislation granted by this latter clause is by its word carefully confined to the specific objects before enumerated. But as this limitation was unavoidably somewhat indefinite, it was deemed necessary to guard more effectually certain great cardinal principles essential to the liberty of the citizen and to the rights and equality of the States by denying to Congress, in express terms, any power of legislation over them. It was apprehended, it seems, that such legislation might be attempted under the pretext that it was necessary and proper to carry into execution the powers granted; and it was determined that there should be no room to doubt, where rights of such vital importance were concerned, and, accordingly this clause is immediately followed by an enumeration of certain subjects to which the powers of legislation shall not extend; and the great importance which the framers of the Constitution attached to the privilege of the writ of *habeas corpus*, to protect the liberty of the citizen, is proved by the fact that its suspension, except in cases of invasion and rebellion, is first in the list of prohibited powers; and even in these cases the power is denied and its exercise prohibited unless the public safety shall require it. It is true that in the cases mentioned Congress is of necessity the judge of whether the public safety does or does not require it; and its judgment is conclusive. But the introduction of these words is a standing admonition to the legislative body of the danger of suspending it and of the extreme caution they should exercise before they give the Government of the United States such power over the liberty of a citizen.

It is the second article of the Constitution that provides for the organization of the Executive Department, and enumerates the powers conferred on it, and prescribes its duties. And if the high power over the liberty of the citizens now claimed was intended to be conferred on the President, it would undoubtedly be found in plain words in this article. But there is not a word in it that can furnish the slightest ground to justify the exercise of the power....

So, too, his powers in relation to the civil duties and authority necessarily conferred on him are carefully restricted, as well as those belonging to his military character. He cannot appoint the ordinary officers of Government, nor make a treaty with a foreign nation or Indian tribe without the advice and consent of the Senate, and cannot appoint even inferior officers unless he is authorized by an act of Congress to do so. He is not empowered to arrest any one charged with an offence against the United States, and whom he may, from the evidence before him, believe to be guilty; nor can he authorize any officer, civil or military, to exercise this power, for the fifth article of the amendments to the Constitution expressly provides that no person "shall be deprived of life, liberty, or property without due process of law;" that is, judicial process. And even if the privilege of the writ of *habeas corpus* was suspended by act of Congress, and a party not subject to the rules and articles of war was afterwards arrested and imprisoned by regular judicial process, he could not be detained in prison or brought to trial before a military tribunal, for the article in the Amendments to the Constitution immediately following the one above referred to—that is, the sixth article—provides that, "In all criminal prosecutions, the accused shall enjoy the right to a speedy and public trial by an impartial jury of the State and district wherein the crime shall have been committed, which district shall have been previously ascertained by law; and to be informed of the nature and cause of the accusation; to be confronted with the witnesses against him; to have compulsory process for obtaining witnesses in his favor, and to have the assistance of counsel for his defence."

And the only power, therefore, which the President possesses, where the "life, liberty, or property" of a private citizen is concerned, is the power and duty prescribed in the third section of the second article, which requires "that he shall take care that the laws be faithfully executed." He is not authorized to execute them himself, or through agents or officers, civil or military, appointed by himself, but he is to take care that they be faithfully carried into execution as they are expounded and adjudged by the coordinate branch of the Government to which that duty is assigned by the Constitution. It is thus made his duty to come in aid of the judicial authority, if it shall be resisted by a force too strong to be overcome without the assistance of the Executive arm. But in exercising this power, he acts in subordination to judicial authority, assisting it to execute its process and enforce its judgments.

With such provisions in the Constitution, expressed in language too clear to be misunderstood by any one, I can see no ground whatever for supposing that the President, in any emergency or in any state of things, can authorize the suspension of the privilege of the writ of *habeas corpus*, or arrest a citizen, except in aid of the judicial power. He certainly does not faithfully execute the laws if he takes upon himself legislative power by suspending the writ of *habeas corpus*—and the judicial power, also, by arresting and imprisoning a person without due process of law. Nor can any argument be drawn from the nature of sovereignty, or the necessities of government for self-defense, in times of tumult and danger. The Government of the United States is one of delegated and limited powers. It derives it existence and authority altogether from the Constitution, and neither of its branches—executive, legislative or judicial—can exercise any of the powers of government beyond those specified and granted. For the tenth article of the amendments to the Constitution, in express terms, provides that "the powers not delegated to the United States by the Constitution, nor prohibited by it to the States, are reserved to the States, respectively, or to the people." ...

The right of the subject to the benefit of the writ of *habeas corpus*, it must be recollected, was one of the great points in controversy during the long struggle in England between arbitrary government and free institutions, and must therefore have strongly attracted the attention of statesmen engaged in framing a new and, as they supposed, a freer government than the one which they had thrown off by the Revolution. For, from the earliest history of the common law, if a person was imprisoned—no matter by what authority—he had a right to the writ of *habeas corpus*, to bring his case before the King's Bench, and, if no specific offence was charged against him in the warrant of commitment, he was entitled to be forthwith discharged; and if an offence was charged which was bailable in its character the court was bound to set him at liberty on bail. And the most exciting contests between the Crown and the people of England from the time of *Magna Charta* were in relation to the privilege of this writ, and they continued until the passage of the statute of 31st Charles 2d, commonly known as the great *habeas corpus* act.

This statute put an end to the struggle, and finally and firmly secured the liberty of the subject against the usurpation and oppression of the executive branch of the Government. It nevertheless conferred no new right upon the subject, but only secured a right already existing; for, although the right could not justly be denied, there was often no effectual remedy against its violation. Until the statute of 13 William III., the judges held their offices at the pleasure of the King, and the influence which he exercised over timid, time—serving and partisan judges, often induced them, upon some pretext or other, to refuse to discharge the party, although entitled by law to his discharge, or delayed their decision, from time to time, so as to prolong the imprisonment of persons who were obnoxious to the King for their political opinions, or had incurred his resentment in any other way. ...

But I am not left to form my judgment upon this great question from analogies between the English Government and our own, or the commentaries of English jurists, or the decisions of English courts, although upon this subject they are entitled to the highest respect, and are justly regarded and received as authoritative by our courts of justice. To guide me to a right conclusion, I have the *Commentaries on the Constitution of the United States* of the late Mr. Justice Story, not only one of the most eminent jurists of the age, but for a long time one of the brightest ornaments of the Supreme Court of the United States, and also the clear and authoritative decision of that Court itself, given more than half a century since, and conclusively establishing the principles I have above stated. Mr. Justice Story, speaking in his *Commentaries*, of the *habeas corpus* clause in the Constitution, says:

(3 Story, Comm. Const. section 1336): ...

Hitherto no suspension of the writ has ever been authorized by Congress since the establishment of the Constitution. It would seem, as the power is given to Congress to suspend the writ of *habeas corpus* in cases of rebellion or invasion, that the right to judge whether the exigency had arisen must exclusively belong to that body."
—3 Story's Com. on the Constitution, section 1,336.

And Chief Justice Marshall, in delivering the opinion of the Supreme Court in the case *ex parte* Bollman and Swartwout, uses this decisive language: ...

"If at any time the public safety should require the suspension of the powers vested by this act in the courts of the United States, it is for the Legislature to say so. That question depends on political considerations, on which the Legislature is to decide. Until the legislative will be expressed, this court can only see its duty, and must obey the laws."

I can add nothing to these clear and emphatic words of my great predecessor.

But the documents before me show that the military authority in this case has gone far beyond the mere suspension of the privilege of the writ of *habeas corpus*. It has, by force of arms, thrust aside the judicial authorities and officers to whom the Constitution has confided the power and duty of interpreting and administering the laws, and substituted a military government in its place, to be administered and executed by military officers. For at the time these proceedings were had against John Merryman, the District Judge of Maryland—the commissioner appointed under the act of Congress—the District Attorney and the Marshal, all resided in the city of Baltimore, a few miles only from the home of the prisoner. Up to that time there had never been the slightest resistance or obstruction to the process of any Court or judicial officer of the United States in Maryland, except by the military authority. And if a military officer, or any other person, had reason to believe that the prisoner had committed any offence against the laws of the United States, it was his duty to give information of the fact and the evidence to support it to the District Attorney, and it would then have become the duty of that officer to bring the matter before the District Judge or Commissioner, and if there was sufficient legal evidence to justify his arrest, the Judge or Commissioner would have issued his warrant to the Marshal to arrest him, and, upon the hearing of the party, would have held him to bail, or committed him for trial, according to the character of the offense as it appeared in the testimony, or would have discharged him immediately if there was not sufficient evidence to support the accusation. There was no danger of any obstruction or resistance to the action of the civil authorities, and therefore no reason whatever for the interposition of the military. And yet, under these circumstances, a military officer, stationed in Pennsylvania, without giving any information to the District Attorney, and without any application to the judicial authorities, assumes to himself the judicial power in the District of Maryland; undertakes to decide what constitutes the crime of treason or rebellion; what evidence (if, indeed, he required any) is sufficient to support the accusation and justify the commitment; and commits the party, without having a hearing even before himself, to close custody in a strongly garrisoned fort, to be there held, it would seem, during the pleasure of those who committed him.

The Constitution provides, as I have before said, that "no person shall be deprived of life, liberty, or property, without due process of law." It declares that "the right of the people to be secure in their persons, houses, papers, and effects against unreasonable searches and seizures shall not be violated, and no warrant shall issue but upon probable cause, supported by oath or affirmation, and particularly describing the place to be searched and the persons or things to be seized." It provides that the party accused shall be entitled to a speedy trial in a court of justice.

And these great and fundamental laws, which Congress itself could not suspend, have been disregarded and suspended, like the writ of *habeas corpus*, by a military order, supported by force of arms. Such is the case now before me; and I can only say that if the authority which the Constitution has confided to the judiciary department and judicial officers may thus upon any pretext or under any circumstances be usurped by the military power at its discretion, the people of the United States are no longer living under a Government of laws, but every citizen holds life, liberty, and property at the will and pleasure of the army officer in whose military district he may happen to be found. ...

R. B. Taney,
Chief Justice of the Supreme Court of the United States.

✠ D O C U M E N T   6

Lincoln Emancipates Slaves in the Confederacy, 1863

Whereas, on the twenty-second day of September, in the year of our Lord one thousand eight hundred and sixty-two, a proclamation was issued by the President of the United States, containing, among other things, the following, to wit:

"That on the first day of January, in the year of our Lord one thousand eight hundred and sixty-three, all persons held as slaves within any State or designated part of a State, the people whereof shall then be in rebellion against the United States, shall be then, thenceforward, and forever free; and the Executive Government of the United States, including the military and naval authority thereof, will recognize and maintain the freedom of such persons, and will do no act or acts to repress such persons, or any of them, in any efforts they may make for their actual freedom.

"That the Executive will, on the first day of January aforesaid, by proclamation, designate the States and parts of States, if any, in which the people thereof, respectively, shall then be in rebellion against the United States; and the fact that any State, or the people thereof, shall on that day be, in good faith, represented in the Congress of the United States by members chosen thereto at elections wherein a majority of the qualified voters of such State shall have participated, shall, in the absence of strong countervailing testimony, be deemed conclusive evidence that such State, and the people thereof, are not then in rebellion against the United States."

Now, therefore, I, Abraham Lincoln, President of the United States, by virtue of the power in me vested as Commander-in-Chief, of the Army and Navy of the United States in time of actual armed rebellion against the authority and government of the United States, and as a fit and necessary war measure for suppressing said rebellion, do, on this first day of January, in the year of our Lord one thousand eight hundred and sixty-three, and in accordance with my purpose so to do publicly proclaimed for the full period of one hundred days, from the day first above mentioned, order and designate as the States and parts of States wherein the people thereof respectively, are this day in rebellion against the United States, the following, to wit:

Arkansas, Texas, Louisiana, (except the Parishes of St. Bernard, Plaquemines, Jefferson, St. John, St. Charles, St. James Ascension, Assumption, Terrebonne, Lafourche, St. Mary, St. Martin, and Orleans, including the City of New Orleans) Mississippi, Alabama, Florida, Georgia, South Carolina, North Carolina, and Virginia, (except the forty-eight counties designated as West Virginia, and also the counties of Berkley, Accomac, Northampton, Elizabeth City, York, Princess Ann, and Norfolk, including the cities of Norfolk and Portsmouth), and which excepted parts, are for the present, left precisely as if this proclamation were not issued.

And by virtue of the power, and for the purpose aforesaid, I do order and declare that all persons held as slaves within said designated States, and parts of States, are, and henceforward shall be free; and that the Executive government of the United States, including the military and naval authorities thereof, will recognize and maintain the freedom of said persons.

And I hereby enjoin upon the people so declared to be free to abstain from all violence, unless in necessary self-defence; and I recommend to them that, in all cases when allowed, they labor faithfully for reasonable wages.

And I further declare and make known, that such persons of suitable condition, will be received into the armed service of the United States to garrison forts, positions, stations, and other places, and to man vessels of all sorts in said service.

And upon this act, sincerely believed to be an act of justice, warranted by the Constitution, upon military necessity, I invoke the considerate judgment of mankind, and the gracious favor of Almighty God.

In witness whereof, I have hereunto set my hand and caused the seal of the United States to be affixed.

Done at the City of Washington, this first day of
January, in the year of our Lord one thousand eight
hundred and sixty three, and of the Independence of the
United States of America the eighty-seventh.

By the President: ABRAHAM LINCOLN
WILLIAM H. SEWARD, Secretary of State.

Lincoln Defends His Suspension of the Writ of Habeas Corpus, 1863

Ours is a case of Rebellion—so called by the resolutions before me—in fact, a clear, flagrant, and gigantic case of Rebellion; and the provision of the constitution that "The previlege of the writ of Habeas Corpus shall not be suspended, unless when in cases of Rebellion or Invasion, the public Safety may require it" is *the* provision which specially applies to our present case. This provision plainly attests the understanding of those who made the constitution that ordinary courts of justice are inadequate to "cases of Rebellion"—attests their purpose that in such cases, men may be held in custody whom the courts acting on ordinary rules, would discharge. Habeas Corpus, does not discharge men who are proved to be guilty of defined crime; and its suspension is allowed by the constitution on purpose that, men may be arrested and held, who can not be proved to be guilty of defined crime, "when, in cases of Rebellion or Invasion the public Safety may require it." This is precisely our present case—a case of Rebellion, wherein the public Safety does require the suspension. Indeed, arrests by process of courts, and arrests in cases of rebellion, do not proceed altogether upon the same basis. The former is directed at the small per centage of ordinary and continuous perpetration of crime; while the latter is directed at sudden and extensive uprisings against the government, which, at most, will succeed or fail, in no great length of time. In the latter case, arrests are made, not so much for what has been done, as for what probably would be done. The latter is more for the preventive, and less for the vindictive, than the former. In such cases the purposes of men are much more easily understood, than in cases of ordinary crime. The man who stands by and says nothing, when the peril of his government is discussed, can not be misunderstood. If not hindered, he is sure to help the enemy. Much more, if he talks ambiguously—talks for his country with "buts" and "ifs" and "ands." Of how little value the constitutional provision I have quoted will be rendered, if arrests shall never be made until defined crimes shall have been committed, may be illustrated by a few notable examples. Gen. John C. Breckienridge, Gen. Robert E. Lee, Gen. Joseph E. Johnston, Gen. John B. Magruder, Gen. William B. Preston, Gen. Simon B. Buckner, and Comodore [Franklin] Buchanan, now occupying the very highest places in the rebel war service, were all within the power of the government since the rebellion began, and were nearly as well known to be traitors then as now. Unquestionably if we had seized and held them, the insurgent cause would be much weaker. But no one of them had then committed any crime defined in the law. Every one of them if arrested would have been discharged on Habeas Corpus, were the writ allowed to operate. In view of these and similar cases, I think the time not unlikely to come when I shall be blamed for having made too few arrests rather than too many.

By the third resolution the meeting indicate their opinion that military arrests may be constitutional in localities where rebellion actually exists; but that such arrests are unconstitutional in localities where rebellion, or insurrection, does not actually exist. They insist that such arrests shall not be made "outside of the lines of necessary military occupation, and the scenes of insurrection." In asmuch, however, as the constitution itself makes no such distinction, I am unable to believe that there is any such constitutional distinction. I concede that the class of arrests complained of, can be constitutional only when, in case of Rebellion or Invasion, the public Safety may require them; and I insist that in such cases, they are constitutional *wherever* the public safety does require them—as well in places to which they may prevent the rebellion extending, as in those where it may be already prevailing—as well where they may restrain mischievous interference with the raising and supplying of armies, to suppress the rebellion, as where the rebellion may actually be—as well where they may restrain the enticing men out of the army, as where they would prevent mutiny in the army—equally constitutional at all places where they will conduce to the public Safety, as against the dangers of Rebellion or Invasion. ...

I understand the meeting, whose resolutions I am considering, to be in favor of suppressing the rebellion by military force—by armies. Long experience has shown that armies can not be maintained unless desertion shall be punished by the severe penalty of death. The case requires, and the law and the constitution, sanction this punishment. Must I shoot a simple-minded soldier boy who deserts, while I must not touch a hair of a wiley agitator who induces him to desert? This is none the less injurious when effected by getting a father, or brother, or friend, into a public meeting, and there working upon his feelings, till he is persuaded to write the soldier boy, that he is fighting in a bad cause, for a wicked administration of a contemptable government, too weak to arrest and punish him if he shall desert. I think that in such a case, to silence the agitator, and save the boy, is not only constitutional, but, withal, a great mercy.

If I be wrong on this question of constitutional power, my error lies in believing that certain proceedings are constitutional when, in cases of rebellion or Invasion, the public Safety requires them, which would not be constitutional when, in absence of rebellion or invasion, the public Safety does not require them—in other words, that the constitution is not in it's application in all respects the same, in cases of Rebellion or invasion, involving the public Safety, as it is in times of profound peace and public security. The constitution itself makes the distinction; and I can no more be persuaded that the government can constitutionally take no strong measure in time of rebellion, because it can be shown that the same could not be lawfully taken in time of peace, than I can be persuaded that a particular drug is not good medicine for a sick man, because it can be shown to not be good food for a well one. Nor am I able to appreciate the danger, apprehended by the meeting, that the American people will, by means of military arrests during the rebellion, lose the right of public discussion, the liberty of speech and the press, the law of evidence, trial by jury, and Habeas corpus, throughout the indefinite peaceful future which I trust lies before them, any more than I am able to believe that a man could contract so strong an appetite for emetics during temporary illness, as to persist in feeding upon them through the remainder of his healthful life. ...

✣ E S S A Y S

Historians have long debated Lincoln's actions during wartime. In the first essay, Daniel Farber, a professor of law at the University of Minnesota, discusses Lincoln's record with regard to emancipation, the suspension of the writ of habeas corpus, and the use of military trials in the North. With the perspective of a constitutional lawyer, Farber examines the developments of the Civil War era alongside more recent cases involving presidential power and individual rights during wartime. Farber believes that Lincoln exceeded his authority in some areas but acted justifiably in others.

James McPherson, a retired professor of history at Princeton University and the leading authority on the American Civil War, takes a very different approach. McPherson places Lincoln firmly in the context of his times. According to McPherson, Lincoln accomplished nothing less than the transformation of the concept of liberty. Although the founders believed that power was the enemy of liberty, Lincoln believed in a more expansive notion that viewed governmental power as the protector of rights.

Lincoln's Mixed Record on Individual Rights

DANIEL FARBER

Individual rights were undoubtedly curtailed during the Civil War. Having said that, the exact extent of the instrusions on individual rights is hard to determine. According to the best recent estimate, at least thirteen thousand civilians were held under military arrest during the course of the war. Most of these arrests involved suspected deserters or draft dodgers, citizens of the Confederacy, possible blockade runners, or individuals trading with the enemy. Some were arrested purely for disloyal speech. Some arrestees, such as the deserters and possibly the draft evaders, were properly under military jurisdiction. Others may have been wrongfully deprived of their right to a jury trial and other procedural protections. Property rights were also impaired. As the Union armies moved through the South, they destroyed or seized property such as cotton, imposed military rule, and (eventually) freed slaves. Some of these actions had precedents of one kind or another, but certainly nothing on a similar scale has ever happened in American history....

Merryman and Habeas

William H. Seward, the secretary of state, was in charge of military arrests until February 1862, when control was transferred to the War Department. He reputedly told the British ambassador that he had more power than the British monarch and could order the arrest of a citizen anywhere in the country by ringing a little bell on his desk. But under Seward's supervision, the government arrested fewer than nine hundred civilians, a small percentage of the wartime total. Seward was busy with other pressing matters like keeping England out of the war. He also lacked any administrative apparatus for making these arrests. Besides, most disloyal Americans were out of the government's reach at that time. Of those who were arrested, many were in effect enemy aliens—residents of the Confederacy. Only around a hundred of the prisoners lived above the border states in uncontested Union territory.

The eventual number of arrests was in the thousands. After Secretary of War Edwin M. Stanton suspended the writ of habeas corpus in August 1862, apparently under Lincoln's direction, the ensuing arrests were undertaken by petty officials under weak central control. But it was in the South, as the Union began to regain territory, or in the contested portions of border states such as Missouri, that military arrests were most rampant. The number of prisoners who can be identified as Northern (non-border state) residents ran in the hundreds, though they were still a small percentage of the total. Most were probably suspected draft evaders or deserters. Lincoln often intervened on the side of clemency in such cases as reached his desk, but these cases were only the tip of the iceberg.

Detention of the prisoners without any judicial hearing was made possible by the suspension of habeas corpus. Habeas is the traditional common-law writ used to test the legality of detention. The suspension clause (Article I, section 9) provides: "The Privilege of the Writ of Habeas Corpus shall not be suspended, unless when in Cases of Rebellion or Invasion the public safety may require it." Whether or not the military could legally impose punishment on disloyal citizens, the suspension of habeas made it possible at least to detain them for preventive purposes.

The major constitutional issue was whether Congress or the president had the power to suspend the writ. After Congress eventually approved the suspension, this issue was moot. But Lincoln was responsible for the initial suspension of habeas. Until Congress acted to ratify his actions, controversy raged over the existence of any presidential control over habeas. . . .

[O]n April 27, Lincoln issued an order suspending the writ of habeas corpus (or rather, authorizing General Scott to do so) along the military line between Philadelphia and Washington. On May 25, John Merryman was arrested for allegedly drilling troops to aid the Confederacy, thus setting the stage for the confrontation with Chief Justice Taney.

The chief justice mounted a powerful challenge to Lincoln's power to suspend the writ. He made three major points. First the suspension clause is found in Article I, devoted mostly to the legislative power, not in Article II, devoted to the executive power. This placement seemed unlikely for a constraint on the president. Second, after long struggles on behalf of liberty, the English monarch had been completely deprived of the power to suspend the writ. Would the Framers have given the president more draconian powers than those possessed by George III? Third, eminent judicial authorities and commentators such as Chief Justice Marshall and Justice Story had described the suspension power as congressional. Thus, Lincoln's actions contradicted the accepted reading of the clause.

In his July 4 special message to Congress, Lincoln responded to these arguments. It was here that he made his famous argument of necessity, asking whether "all the laws *but one*" were to go unexecuted, "and the government itself go to pieces, lest that one be violated?" But, he went on to say, "it was not believed that this question was presented," for it was "not believed that any law was violated." The Constitution is silent about who has the power to suspend. To vest the suspension power solely in Congress, Lincoln said, would be imprudent: "[A]s the provision was plainly made for a dangerous emergency, it cannot be believed the framers of the instrument intended, that in every case, the danger should run its course, until Congress could be called together; the very assembling of which might be prevented, as was intended in this case, by the rebellion." For the benefit of anyone who remained in doubt, Lincoln added that the attorney general would furnish a more complete analysis in due course.

The attorney general obliged with an opinion filed the next day. Not surprisingly, he upheld the president's power to suspend. Bates argued that under the oath clause as well as the militia act, the president was required to suppress insurrections by use of the militia, the army, and the navy. He must use his discretion in meeting the threat. "If the insurgents assail the nation with an army, he may find it best to meet them with an army, and suppress the insurrection in the field of battle." But "if they employ spies and emissaries, to gather information, to forward rebellion, he may find it both prudent and humane to arrest and imprison them," either to bring them to trial or to hold them in custody until the emergency is past. As to the suspension clause, Bates admitted, "learned persons have differed widely about the meaning of this short sentence, and I am by no means confident that I fully understand it myself." But when the judiciary is unable to maintain public order, the president must step in to deal with the emergency. When the president has called out the military, Bates maintained, it would be absurd to say he must send captured soldiers or spies before any judge who chooses to issue a writ.

Congress ultimately settled the dispute in March 1863 with a statute declaring that the president did have the power to suspend the writ. Under the statute, a military officer could respond to the writ merely by certifying that the person was detained by authority of the president. This language was carefully ambiguous about whether Congress was conferring the power to suspend the writ or merely recognizing its existence in the hands of the president. In the meantime, Lincoln issued a whole series of suspension orders, gradually expanding the scope of the authorization until it covered the entire nation. He was apparently not very enthusiastic about these measures. In a memo on May 17, he said, "Unless the *necessity* for these arbitrary arrests is *manifest*, and *urgent*, I prefer they should cease."

Lincoln's actions, though extraordinary, were not completely unprecedented. In 1777, the Continental Congress had recommended that disloyal persons in Delaware and Pennsylvania be taken into custody. Only later did the Pennsylvania legislature pass a statute approving the measure and indemnifying the state executive. In the meantime, the prisoners had obtained a writ of habeas, which was ignored by their custodian. In a better-known incident, as commanding general in New Orleans, Andrew Jackson had suspended the writ. Not only that, but he imprisoned the judge who had issued it. And when the U.S. attorney went to another judge to secure the first judge's release, Jackson had them arrested as well. When the first judge was finally released, he held Jackson in contempt of court and fined him one thousand dollars, which "Old Hickory" paid out of his own pocket. Years later, Congress ordered the fine repaid with interest, but with no clear indication whether this was an endorsement of his actions or just a charitable act toward an aging hero.

In contrast, on other notable occasions when the writ was suspended, the action was taken by the legislature. This was true in Shays's Rebellion, an uprising that helped prompt the drive toward the 1787 Philadelphia convention. Similarly, it was the state legislature that suspended habeas in the Rhode Island uprising that gave rise to *Luther v. Borden*. But suspending access to civilian courts had been a rare event in American history, and the sparse precedents were relatively uninformative. ...

There are three possible interpretations of the suspension power. It either belongs exclusively to Congress or to the president, or concurrently to both. The least plausible of these possibilities is that the president has exclusive power. That view is at least in tension with the constitutional text and with our admittedly limited evidence regarding the original understanding. The location of the clause, in Article I rather than Article II, suggests at least some congressional role. Except for its brief sojourn in the judiciary article, which left the source of the suspension power completely ambiguous, everything else about the drafting and ratification history suggests a connection between Congress and the suspension power. So does the long English struggle to move the power to the legislature, recounted by Taney (but validated by more objective historians). Moreover, the Framers were suspicious of unchecked power. They would have been unlikely to give the president the exclusive, final word about his own power to deprive citizens of their liberty without legal process. This leaves us with the other two possibilities, exclusive congressional power or concurrent power.

A concurrent presidential power would require some source in Article II. If the president does have some constitutional power to suspend habeas, where does he get it? The suspension clause itself limits the power to suspend to certain circumstances rather than serving as a source of suspension authority. It is a "thou shalt not," rather than a "thou mayest." Plainly, suspending habeas would not have been considered an inherent part of the "executive power" granted by the vesting clause of Article II (assuming the vesting clause actually is an independent source of power). The whole thrust of English history had been to move the power to Parliament; it was not a power the king possessed at the time of American independence. Where else? The only plausible answers are the same clauses that authorized Lincoln to take military action against the rebellion—in particular, the power to use military force in response to sudden attacks. If he can supplement the congressional power to declare war by making war on his own in certain circumstances, he presumably can also take other emergency measures needed to meet the same threat, such as declaring martial law or suspending habeas. Or at least he should be able to do so when Congress has not spoken to the contrary in advance of the emergency. Thus, the president's power to make war in response to "sudden attack" is the most plausible source of his authority to suspend habeas in the theater of the ensuing war.

In any event, if prior congressional authorization was needed, it probably did exist. In the special session called by Lincoln, Congress ratified all of his orders relating to the militia or armed forces. Since Lincoln's suspension directive took the form of an authorization to General Scott, this may well have ratified at least his past suspension in cases like *Merryman*. But, even before the special session, Lincoln already probably had whatever congressional authorization he needed, at least for the initial emergency suspension in *Merryman*. This source of authority was the militia act. This theory was adopted in *Ex parte Field*, where the federal circuit court held that the statutes empowering Lincoln to call out the militia also implicitly authorized him to declare martial law, and hence to suspend habeas.

The circuit court's view in *Ex parte Field* was upheld, in effect, in the Supreme Court's later opinion in *Moyer v. Peabody*...Although not directly concerned with presidential power, the Court provided a crucial interpretation of the federal statute authorizing the state governor to call out the national guard. The Court emphasized that this statute necessarily allowed him to use deadly force if needed, and therefore also allowed him to detain prisoners if needed to suppress the insurrection. Perhaps not coincidentally, the author of the opinion was Holmes, who had been wounded repeatedly in action during the Civil War. Although it is usually said that the Supreme Court never ruled on the legality of Lincoln's habeas suspension, *Moyer* was the next best thing to a direct holding on point, though delivered years after the fact. In the spring and summer of 1861, the area of insurrection might be said to include Maryland. If so, under *Moyer*, Lincoln clearly would have been empowered to use deadly force to suppress the insurrection. It is hard to quarrel with Holmes's conclusion that the power to detain dangerous individuals goes along with the power to use deadly military force against them.

Thus, emergency habeas suspension, in the face of sudden attack, may well have been implicitly authorized by statute. At worst, it seems to fall in the "twilight zone" of concurrent power under the three-part analysis discussed in the last chapter. Justice Holmes's reasoning in *Moyer*, though addressed to a statutory issue, would apply with equal force to the president's constitutional power as commander in chief. Under the rationale of *Moyer*, that power presumptively includes the ability to suspend habeas where required by military necessity, when the president has congressional authorization to use military force to quell insurrection. Prior interactions between the branches do not speak clearly to the question. But as in the Iranian hostage case, the fact of subsequent congressional approval supports the legality of Lincoln's actions. Once again, later decisions like the hostage case obviously do not prove that Lincoln's actions were valid under the constitutional doctrine of the time. They do show, however, that his views are consistent with our current views of legitimate executive power.

Thus, although the constitutional issue can hardly be considered free from doubt, on balance Lincoln's use of habeas in areas of insurrection or actual war should be considered constitutionally appropriate, at least in the absence of any contrary action by Congress. When the war broke out, given the riots in Baltimore and the threat of secession by Maryland, that state could be considered a site of insurrection, particularly given its proximity to enemy territory and its control over access to Washington. Consequently, suspension of habeas could be justified as an emergency military measure....

Vallandigham and Free Speech

A small percentage, but still a disturbing number, of Civil War actions taken under military authority impinged on freedom of speech. These actions might have occurred anyway, but were probably encouraged by the absence of the usual procedural safeguards, not to mention the ingrained military attitude toward insubordination and disloyalty.

Free speech issues arose early in the war. Prisoners' records in the early days referred to "treasonable language" and "disloyalty" as grounds for arrest, along with "threatening Unionists" or "inducing desertion." In Cincinnati, a man was arrested for selling stationery with Confederate mottoes. A general in Tennessee enforced a ban on similar items. A dozen of the individuals arrested without legal process were identified as newspaper editors or reporters. One general in Indiana prohibited any criticism of statutes such as those creating the draft or the income tax. Lincoln's proclamation of September 1862 authorized military trials for persons discouraging enlistments. A year later, though, he wrote a Missouri general to caution him against suppressing newspapers or assemblies except "when they may be working *palpable injury* to the Military in your charge."

Lincoln played only a secondary role in the most famous instance of inter-ference with free speech, the *Vallandigham* case. The case arose from an 1863 order by General Burnside, an incompetent whose men had been slaughtered at Fredericksburg. To get him out of the way before any more of his troops were butchered, he was made commanding general of the Department of Ohio. The move did not improve the soundness of his judgment. Burnside's General Order No. 38 proclaimed that the "habit of declaring sympathies for the enemy will not be allowed in this Department." Treason, "express or implied," would not be toler-ated. That spring, over a hundred Union soldiers arrived at the house of Clement Vallandigham in the middle of the night, forced their way into the house, and arrested him for violating Burnside's order. Vallandigham was a well-known national figure, a former congressman who (like Milligan) was a Peace Democrat. The basis for Vallandigham's arrest was a speech he had given a few days earlier. In that speech, he had called the war "wicked, cruel, and unnecessary," a war fought for abolition-ism rather than to save the Union. He allegedly said, however, that he would not counsel "resistance to military or civil law; that was not needed." Instead, he called upon his audience to use the ballot box to hurl "King Lincoln" from his throne. The military commission found him guilty and ordered his confinement for the duration of the war. This blunder was a great embarrassment to the administration, and Lincoln ultimately ordered Vallandigham expelled into Confederate territory instead of imprisoning him.

In response to protests against Vallandigham's conviction, Lincoln defended the general policy of military arrests in an open letter to some prominent New York Democrats. He defended the policy on the basis of public necessity. Early interven-tion was needed to restrain dangerous individuals before they could commit actual crimes. If this policy had been pursued earlier, he pointed out, Lee would never have had the chance to join the Confederate army. And, said Lincoln, "he who dissuades one man from volunteering, or induces one soldier to desert, weakens the Union cause as much as he who kills a union soldier in battle." As to Vallandigham, the arrest was not for criticizing the administration or General Burnside, which Lincoln conceded would be wrong. Instead, Vallandigham "avows his hostility to the war on the part of the Union; and his arrest was made because he was laboring, with some effect, to prevent the raising of troops; to encourage desertions from the army, and to leave the rebellion without an adequate military force to suppress it." "Must I shoot a simple-minded soldier boy who deserts," asked Lincoln, "while I must not touch a hair of a wiley agitator who induces him to desert?"

Did Vallandigham's conviction violate the First Amendment? This is a difficult question to answer because views of the First Amendment have changed so much over the years. Unlike separation-of-powers doctrine, current First Amendment doctrine has not merely evolved since the Civil War; it has essentially sprung into existence out of a legal void. Before and during the Civil War, freedom of speech was vigorously debated and had strong defenders. But the Supreme Court did not seriously confront First Amendment issues until about fifty years later, during World War I and its aftermath. . . .

If the question instead is whether Lincoln was "right" about the First Amendment in some objective sense, it is hard to know how to answer. What is the one true meaning of the First Amendment? The text and original intent are both unhelpful here. For one thing, the text only says that "Congress shall make no law," and Lincoln claimed to be acting under his own war powers, not those of Congress. The amendment forbids any abridgement of "the freedom of speech." But unless that term is implausibly taken to mean the unlimited right to communicate anything at all under any circumstances—the right to engage in false advertising or price-fixing agreements, for instance—its meaning is hardly self-defining. And as to the original understanding, little is clear except perhaps a desire to go beyond Blackstone's definition (which banned only prior censorship, not punishment after the fact for harmful speech). Persuasive arguments can be made that the Court's current approach is most consistent with the needs of a free society. But those arguments are based in part on information (like the World War I experience and the excesses of the McCarthy era) unavailable to Lincoln. And even today, in circumstances as dire as those of the Civil War, who can be sure what the courts would do?

Some other restrictions on speech involved clearer constitutional violations. These incidents involved military orders that shut down newspapers, at least temporarily. The most notorious incident involved the *New York World*. Two journalists forged an Associated Press story about a bogus presidential call for drafting four hundred thousand men. (As a signal of desperation by the president, this "news" was supposed to drive up the price of gold, allowing the two men to make a quick profit.) The *World* fell for the stunt and published the story. Suspecting a Confederate plot, Lincoln ordered the arrest of the editors and publishers, as well as the seizure of the premises. This put the newspaper out of business until the order was countermanded. ...

These Civil War intrusions on speech seem excessive. Because interference with free speech during the Civil War was sporadic, it did not damage American liberty nearly as much as it might have. But the very infrequency and arbitrariness of cases like *Vallandigham* strongly suggest that these actions were not truly necessary. This conclusion is reinforced by Lincoln's own misgivings about these actions, even when he felt compelled to defend them. By and large, the army got along just fine without suppressing dissident Northern politicians or newspapers, even during the worst of the Civil War. By comparison, later periods like World War I seem to have involved more systematic, though equally unnecessary, forms of censorship. Lincoln's intuition that free speech should be suppressed only under imperative circumstances was correct, but he failed to effectively hold his subordinates to that standard. In defending them in his letter to Corning, he went too far in condoning invasions of civil liberties.

The verdict on the Lincoln administration's civil liberties record is mixed. Many of the acts denounced as dictatorial—the suspension of habeas at the beginning of the war, emancipation, military trials of civilians in contested or occupied territory—seem in retrospect to have reasonably good constitutional justifications under the war power. Other leaders, faced with half the country in open rebellion, would have gone much farther than Lincoln did. But there were clear excesses, like the treatment of ... Vallandigham, and the *New York World*. Such actions were generally not taken at Lincoln's initiative, but as president, he retained ultimate accountability.

Abraham Lincoln and the Transformation of American Liberty

JAMES M. McPHERSON

...To us, today, it seems self-evident that the emancipation of four million slaves from bondage was a great triumph of liberty. But for a majority of white Americans in the Civil War era—until almost the end of the war—this accomplishment represented the antithesis of liberty. This majority of white Americans included most southerners and more than two-fifths of the northerners—the Democrats, who opposed emancipation to the bitter end. It was the outcome of the war that transformed and expanded the concept of liberty to include abolition of slavery, and it was Lincoln who was the principal agent of this transformation.

Lincoln's complaint that the world had never had a good definition of liberty was well founded. The problem is that there are too many definitions. The *Oxford English Dictionary* has eight major definitions of liberty, with historical illustrations. One historian of ideas has recorded some two hundred definitions that run the gamut from natural liberty, civil liberties, intellectual freedom, religious liberty, to toleration of eccentricities or of deviant personal behavior, freedom of the will, and equality of voting rights in republican self-government. The foremost philosopher of liberty in Lincoln's time—perhaps of all time—was John Stuart Mill, who defined liberty as "protection against the tyranny of the political rulers," a concept that involved the limitation "of the power which can be legitimately exercised by the society over the individual." The leading American political scientist of Lincoln's generation, Francis Lieber, defined liberty as "a high degree of untrammeled political action in the citizen, and an acknowledgment of his dignity and his important rights by the government." A modern historian has pointed out that from the beginning Americans have "associated liberty primarily with their rejection of coercive authority," especially the authority of government. The classic statement of American liberty—the Magna Charta of the United States, as it were—is the Declaration of Independence. "All men are created equal," wrote Thomas Jefferson, and "endowed by their Creator with certain unalienable rights," including "life, liberty, and the pursuit of happiness." Governments are instituted "to secure these rights," but they derive "their just powers from the consent of the governed," so that "whenever any form of government becomes destructive of these ends, it is the right of the people to alter or abolish it."...

Many of the founding fathers were preoccupied with the threat of government to liberty. They tended to see all political history, back at least as far as classical Greece and Rome, as a conflict between liberty and power, with liberty usually losing in the end to the aggrandizement of centralized power by a Caesar, a tyrant, an emperor, a king. Republics based on the liberties and equal rights of citizens under law had been fragile and usually short-lived experiments. Eternal vigilance against the aggressions of government was indeed the price of liberty. At great cost, Englishmen from the days of the Magna Charta down to the Glorious Revolution of 1688 had carved out

From McPherson, James M., *Abraham Lincoln and the Second American Revolution*. Reproduced with permission of Oxford University Press.

an enlarged sphere of liberty and self-government through their representatives in Parliament, curtailing the powers of the crown in the process. It was these rights and liberties of Englishmen that Americans fought for in their revolution of 1776. It was this fragile experiment in republicanism that they sought to protect against the threat of excessive power, by adopting a bill of rights, by instituting a series of checks and balances and a division of powers within the national government, and by creating a federal system that fragmented power among national, state, and local governments....

Lincoln rejected the notion that the rights of liberty and the pursuit of happiness were confined to the white race. He was not the only American to challenge this dogma, of course. From the beginning of their movement, abolitionists had insisted that black people were equal to whites in the sight of God and equally entitled to liberty in this world. Indeed, the abolitionists and the radical wing of the Republican party went further than Lincoln in maintaining the principle of equal rights for all people. But because of his prominence as a Republican party leader after 1858 and his power as president of the United States after 1860, Lincoln's were the opinions that mattered most and that are of most interest to us.

Lincoln had always considered slavery an institution "founded on both injustice and bad policy," as he told the Illinois legislature in 1837. But he nevertheless indulged in the American habit of describing the United States as a "freecountry" that enjoyed more "civil and religious liberty," more "human liberty, human right" than any other people in the history of the world. Even as late as 1861 Lincoln could refer to "the free institutions which we have unceasingly enjoyed for three-quarters of a century." But a decade earlier Lincoln had begun to question just how free those institutions were, so long as slavery existed in this otherwise free country. The "monstrous injustice of slavery," he said in 1854, "deprives our republican example of its just influence in the world—enables the enemies of free institutions, with plausibility, to taunt us as hypocrites." In the 1850s Lincoln began to insist, contrary to the belief of perhaps two-thirds of white Americans, that the Declaration of Independence was not merely "the white-man's charter of freedom." "The negro is included in the word 'men' used in the Declaration," he maintained. This "is the great fundamental principle upon which our free institutions rest," and "negro slavery is violative of that principle" because the black man is "entitled to ... the right to life, liberty, and the pursuit of happiness. I hold that he is as much entitled to these as the white man. I agree with Judge Douglas he is not my equal in many respects"—here Lincoln stopped short of the abolitionist affirmation of full equality—but, Lincoln continued, "in the right to eat the bread, without leave of anybody else, which his own hand earns, he is my equal and the equal of Judge Douglas, and the equal of every living man."

Lincoln did not consider this a new definition of liberty. He believed that Thomas Jefferson and the other founders had meant to include the Negro in the phrase "all men are created equal," even though many of the founders owned slaves, for they were stating a principle that they hoped would eventually become a reality. Douglas maintained that, on the contrary, Jefferson had not meant "all men" to include blacks— nor for that matter any race except Caucasians. "This government was made by white men, for the benefit of white men and their posterity forever, and should never be administered by any except white men," insisted Douglas over and over again.

"The signers of the Declaration had no reference to the negro whatever when they declared all men to be created equal. They ... [meant] white men, men of European birth and European descent and had no reference either to the negro, the savage Indians, the Fejee, the Malay, or any other inferior and degraded race."

If a national referendum could have been held on these two definitions of liberty—Lincoln's inclusive one and Douglas's definition exclusive of all but white men—Douglas's position would have won. But Lincoln persisted against the odds, denouncing Douglas's argument as representing a disastrous declension from the faith of the fathers, a declension that if it went much further would extinguish the light of liberty in America. ...

It was Lincoln's eloquent definition—or redefinition—of liberty that the South most feared. So when he won the presidency, southern states seceded in the name of their own liberties of property and state sovereignty, in the name of their right proclaimed by the Declaration of Independence to "alter or abolish" the form of government if it became destructive of the purpose of protecting their property. Southerners, said an Alabama newspaper in 1861, were a "liberty loving people," and therefore "the same spirit of freedom and independence that impelled our Fathers to the separation from the British Government" would inspire the South's fight for independence from a tyrannical and oppressive government dominated by Black Republican Yankees. A Georgia secessionist declared that southerners would be "either *slaves in the Union or freemen out of it*." One of four brothers from Texas who enlisted in the Confederate army said that like their forefathers of 1776, he and his brothers "are now enlisted in 'The Holy Cause of Liberty and Independence.' " Another Texan called for all true sons of the Lone Star State to rally "to the standard of Liberty and Equality for white men" against "our Abolition enemies who are pledged to prostrate the white freemen of the South down to equality with negroes." And Jefferson Davis appealed to his people to "renew such sacrifices as our fathers bequeathed to us" from "the tyranny of an unbridled majority, the most odious ... form of despotism." ...

Slavery was not the only problem that involved the question of liberty during the Civil War. In any war the civil liberties of citizens are liable to become victims of the passions or necessities of the conflict. ... The Civil War posed an even greater potential threat to civil liberties. By its very nature a civil war produces a more intense concern with internal security than a foreign war. Martial law prevails over large parts of a country wracked by civil war; newspapers and other media of communication are often muzzled; enemy partisans and sympathizers are arbitrarily arrested and jailed, sometimes tortured and murdered.

Both sides in the American Civil War experienced an erosion of civil liberties during the conflict. One of Lincoln's first wartime orders as commander in chief was to suspend the privilege of the writ of habeas corpus in portions of Maryland wracked by guerrilla activities and mob attacks on Union forces. If the Confederates gained control of Maryland by such actions, the national capital would be surrounded by enemy territory and the North would lose the war before it had fairly started. Union soldiers arrested numerous pro-southern citizens in Maryland, including the mayor and police chief of Baltimore and thirty-one members of the state legislature, and clapped them in prison for months and in a few cases for more than a year without trial. Lincoln eventually extended the suspension of the writ of habeas corpus to the whole country in cases of what he defined as "disloyal persons [who] are not adequately restrained by the ordinary processes of law from ... giving aid and comfort in various ways to the insurrection." By the time the war was over, Union soldiers had arrested and detained in prison without charge at least fifteen thousand civilians, while military courts had tried and convicted hundreds of others....

One of the most notorious wartime violations of civil liberties occurred in Ohio where a military court convicted Democratic gubernatorial candidate Clement L. Vallandigham of treason for speaking out against the war. Lincoln commuted the sentence from imprisonment to banishment, and Vallandigham went to Canada, from where he conducted his unsuccessful campaign for governor of Ohio....

There was no shortage of such rebukes during the Civil War itself. In fact, northern Democrats made this issue the central theme in their attacks on Lincoln as a despot, a tyrant bent on snuffing out the liberties of white men in a calamitous and unconstitutional crusade to liberate black slaves. Countless Democratic speeches and editorials, especially at the time of Vallandigham's arrest, condemned Lincoln for suppressing "the right of the people to assemble and discuss the affairs of government, the liberty of speech and of the press, the right of trial by jury," for violating "the rights of the States and the liberties of the citizen," and for "establishing a despotism." Was the government, asked a group of New York Democrats in 1863, trying to suppress rebellion in the South or "to destroy free institutions in the North"? A Democratic pamphlet published in 1863 portrayed Lincoln as standing trial before the founding fathers. They find him guilty. "You were born in the freest country under the sun," they tell the sixteenth president, "but you have converted it into a despotism. [We] now leave you, with the brand of TYRANT upon your brow."

Is this how we, too, should leave Lincoln? Perhaps we should first let him speak in his own defense. Hear him on the suspension of the writ of habeas corpus, for example. By protecting individuals from arbitrary arrest and imprisonment without indictment and trial, this writ has been the safeguard of Anglo-American civil liberties for centuries. The United States Constitution specifies that the privilege of the writ of habeas corpus "shall not be suspended, except when in cases of rebellion or invasion the public safety may require it." But this rebellion, said Lincoln in 1861, was precisely the kind of exceptional crisis the framers had in mind. Chief Justice Taney—author of the Dred Scott decision—insisted that only Congress, and not the president acting in executive capacity, had the power to suspend the writ. Lincoln disagreed, and many constitutional scholars then and since have supported his position. Suspension of the writ was an emergency power; only the executive could act quickly enough in a crisis, especially if Congress was not in session. The very life of the nation was at stake, Lincoln maintained. The survival of that nation "conceived in liberty and dedicated to the proposition that all men are created equal," was the central purpose of the war. If the nation died, so did the fragile experiment in republican liberty launched in 1776. Thus the temporary suspension of habeas corpus, said Lincoln in his first message to Congress on July 4, 1861, was a small price to pay for the preservation of that larger framework of liberty, the nation itself. "Are all the laws but one [habeas corpus] to go unexecuted," asked Lincoln rhetorically, "and the government itself go to pieces, lest that one be violated?" ...

In any event, said Lincoln, most of the military arrests of civilians were for military crimes such as sabotage, espionage, and guerrilla bushwhacking. "Under cover of 'liberty of speech,' 'liberty of the press,' and 'Habeas corpus,'" he continued, the rebels "hoped to keep on foot amongst us a most efficient corps of spies, informers, suppliers, and aiders and abettors of their cause." As for the few conspicuous cases of arrests of politicians like Vallandigham or of newspaper editors for speaking out against the war or the draft, Lincoln argued that their speeches and editorials discouraged enlistment in the army or encouraged desertions from it, thereby "damaging the army, upon the existence and vigor of which the life of the nation depends." In a rhetorical question that became one of the most famous of Lincoln's utterances, he asked: "Must I shoot a simpleminded soldier boy who deserts, while I must not touch a hair of a wily agitator who induces him to desert?... I think that in such a case to silence the agitator and save the boy is not only constitutional, but withal a great mercy"...

But there is a larger question involved here—nothing less than a transformation in the concept of liberty itself. To illustrate this point, let us turn to the definitions offered by the British philosopher Isaiah Berlin in a famous essay, "Two Concepts of Liberty." The two concepts are Negative Liberty and Positive Liberty. The idea of negative liberty is perhaps more familiar. It can be defined as the absence of restraint, a freedom from interference by outside authority with individual thought or behavior. A law requiring motorcyclists to wear a helmet would be, under this definition, to prevent them from enjoying the freedom to go bareheaded if they wish. Negative liberty, therefore, can be described as freedom *from*. Positive liberty can best be understood as freedom *to*. It is not necessarily incompatible with negative liberty, but has a different focus or emphasis: Freedom of the press is generally viewed as a negative liberty—freedom from interference with what a writer writes or a reader reads. But an illiterate person suffers from a denial of positive liberty; he is unable to enjoy the freedom to write or read whatever he pleases, not because some authority prevents him from doing so, but because he cannot read or write anything. He suffers not the absence of a negative liberty—freedom from—but of a positive liberty—freedom *to* read and write. The remedy lies not in removal of restraint but in achievement of the capacity to read and write.

Another way of defining the distinction between these two concepts of liberty is to describe their relation to power. Negative liberty and power are at opposite poles; power is the enemy of liberty, especially power concentrated in the hands of a central government. That is the kind of power that many of the founding fathers feared most; that is why they fragmented power in the Constitution and the federal system; that is why they wrote a bill of rights to restrain the power of the national government to interfere with individual liberty. The Bill of Rights is an excellent example of negative liberty. Nearly all of the first ten amendments to the Constitution apply the phrase "shall not" to the federal government. In fact, eleven of the first twelve amendments placed limitations on the power of the national government. But beginning with the Thirteenth Amendment in 1865—the Amendment that abolished slavery—six of the next seven amendments radically expanded the power of the federal government at the expense of the states. The very language of these amendments illustrates the point: instead of applying the phrase "shall not" to the national government, every one of them grants significant new powers to the government with the phrase that "Congress *shall have* the power to enforce this article" (italics added).

These six amendments did not all necessarily enlarge the sphere of liberty. The Sixteenth authorized a federal income tax and the Eighteenth prohibited the manufacture and sale of alcoholic beverages. Some of their supporters regarded these amendments as expanding the sphere of positive liberty, by increasing the potential of the federal government to redistribute income and provide social welfare, thereby improving the condition of the poor, and by ending the "enslavement" of millions of Americans to liquor. Whatever the validity of these arguments, the other four constitutional amendments do offer examples of positive liberty. They nicely illustrate the relationship between positive liberty and power. Power in these cases expanded liberty instead of repressing it; power and liberty were allies, not enemies. The emphasis was not on freedom from, but freedom to. These four amendments represent a positive expansion of liberty in another respect as well. They define *into* the population enjoying certain rights and liberties large groups that had been previously defined *out*: black people and women. The Thirteenth, Fourteenth, and Fifteenth Amendments freed the slaves and granted blacks equal civil and political rights; the Nineteenth granted women equal political rights.

Abraham Lincoln played a crucial role in this historic shift of emphasis from negative to positive liberty. Those southerners who seceded from the Union in the name of preserving their liberties and rights—including the right to own slaves—and those northerners who denounced the Lincoln administration for violating their civil liberties, were acting in the tradition of negative liberty. . . .

Positive liberty is an open-ended concept. It has the capacity to expand toward notions of equity, justice, social welfare, equality of opportunity. For how much liberty does a starving person enjoy, except the liberty to starve? How much freedom of the press can exist in a society of illiterate people? How free is a motorcyclist who is paralyzed for life by a head injury that might have been prevented if he had worn a helmet? With the "new birth of freedom" proclaimed in the Gettysburg Address and backed by a powerful army, Lincoln helped to move the nation toward an expanded and open-ended concept of positive liberty. "On the side of the Union," he said on another occasion, this war "is a struggle for maintaining in the world, that form, and substance of government, whose leading object is, to elevate the condition of men—to lift artificial weights from all shoulders—to clear the paths of laudable pursuit for all"—black as well as white—"to afford all, an unfettered start, and a fair chance, in the race of life." In "giving freedom to the slave," declared Lincoln, "we *assure* freedom to the *free*."

✢ *F U R T H E R   R E A D I N G*

Allen, Austin. *Origins of Dred Scott: Jacksonian Jurisprudence and the Supreme Court, 1837–1857* (2006).

Bestor, Jr., Arthur. "The Civil War as a Constitutional Crisis," *American Historical Review*, 69 (1964): 327–352.

——. "State Sovereignty and Slavery: A Reinterpretation of Proslavery Constitutional Doctrine, 1846–1860," *Journal of the Illinois State Historical Society*, 54 (1961): 117–180.

Carnaham, Burrus M. *Act of Justice: Lincoln's Emancipation Proclamation and the Law of War* (2007).

Colaiaco, James A. *Frederick Douglass and the Fourth of July* (2006).

Fehrenbacher, Don E. *Constitutions and Constitutionalism in the Slaveholding South* (1989).

——. *The Dred Scott Case: Its Significance in American Law and Politics* (1978).

——. *The Slaveholding Republic: An Account of the United States Government's Relations to Slavery* (2001).

Finkelman, Paul. *Dred Scott v. Sandford: A Brief History with Documents* (1997).

——. "'Hooted Down the Page of History': Reconsidering the Greatness of Chief Justice Taney," *Journal of Supreme Court History* (1994): 83–102.

——. *An Imperfect Union: Slavery, Federalism, and Comity* (1981).

——. "*Prigg v. Pennsylvania* and Northern State Courts: Anti-Slavery Use of a Pro-Slavery Opinion," *Civil War History*, 25 (March 1979): 5–35.

Freehling, William. *The Road to Disunion, vol. 2: Secessionists Triumphant, 1854–1861* (2007).

Gara, Larry. "The Fugitive Slave Law: A Double Paradox," *Civil War History*, 10 (September 1964): 229–240.

Graber, Mark. *Dred Scott and the Problem of Constitutional Evil* (2006).

Guelzo, Allen C. *Lincoln's Emancipation Proclamation: The End of Slavery in America* (2004).

Hamilton, Holman. *Prologue to Conflict: Crisis and the Compromise of 1850* (1964).

Holzer, Harold, Edna Greene Medford, and Frank J. Williams, *The Emancipation Proclamation: Three Views—Social, Political, Iconographic* (2006).

Huebner, Timothy S. *The Southern Judicial Tradition: State Judges and Sectional Distinctiveness, 1790–1890* (1999).

——. *The Taney Court: Justices, Rulings, and Legacy* (2003).

Hyman, Harold M. *A More Perfect Union: The Impact of the Civil War and Reconstruction on the Constitution* (1973).

Hyman, Harold M. and William M. Wiecek, *Equal Justice Under Law: Constitutional Development, 1835–1875* (1982).

Lee, Charles R. *The Confederate Constitution* (1963).

Maltz, Jr., Earl. Dred Scott *and the Politics of Slavery* (2007).

McGinty, Brian. *Lincoln and the Court* (2008).

Neely, Jr., Mark E. *The Fate of Liberty: Abraham Lincoln and Civil Liberties* (1991).

——. *Southern Rights: Political Prisoners and the Myth of Confederate Constitutionalism* (1999).

Newmyer, R. Kent. *Supreme Court Justice Joseph Story: Statesman of the Old Republic* (1985).

——. *The Supreme Court under Marshall and Taney*, 2nd ed. (2006).

Potter, David M. *The Impending Crisis, 1848–1861* (1976).

Russell, Robert R. "Constitutional Doctrines with Regard to Slavery in the Territories," *Journal of Southern History*, 32 (November 1966): 466–486.

Saunders, Jr., Robert. *John Archibald Campbell: Southern Moderate, 1811–1889* (1997).

Simon, James F. *Lincoln and Chief Justice Taney: Slavery, Secession, and the President's War Powers* (2006).

Smiley, David L. "Revolutionary Origins of the South's Constitutional Defenses," *North Carolina Historical Review*, 44 (1967): 256–269.

Stampp, Kenneth M. *And the War Came: The North and the Secession Crisis, 1860–1861* (1950).

Swisher, Carl B. *History of the Supreme Court of the United States, vol. 5: The Taney Period, 1836–1864* (1974).

Wiecek, William M. "Slavery and Abolition before the United States Supreme Court, 1820–1860," *Journal of American History*, 65 (June 1978): 34–59.

——. *The Sources of Antislavery Constitutionalism in America, 1760–1848* (1977).

Wooster, Ralph A. *The Secession Conventions of the South* (1962).

Reconstruction and the Fourteenth Amendment

The Civil War obliterated the institution of slavery, as well as the doctrines of state sovereignty and secession that supported it. Such sweeping changes forced a wholesale reexamination of federalism and civil rights that lasted for almost a quarter-century. Politics played a critical role in the process. The Republican Party, which controlled Congress throughout the Reconstruction period, viewed the Confederacy's collapse as an opportunity to build a new political following in the South. To secure the political support of the more than 4 million newly freed slaves, the Republicans hoped to transform the South's social order. That social revolution, in turn, depended on a redefinition of the federal government's responsibility for civil rights.

Former Confederates and their northern Democratic allies, in the meantime, had their own agenda. White southerners, while defeated militarily, clung proudly to their traditions, including white social and political control. Much to Republicans' consternation, ex-Confederates immediately assumed prominent positions of authority in southern state governments, which swiftly passed black codes restricting the rights of former slaves. The efforts of the ex-Confederates received the blessing of President Andrew Johnson, a Democrat from Tennessee, who believed deeply in state sovereignty and sought to forge alliances with former rebels. Johnson's resistance to Republican initiatives eventually brought about his impeachment.

Greater attention to African Americans' civil rights coincided with increasing concern for the constitutional and legal status of women. Antebellum American culture had consigned women to the "private sphere" of home and family, while men were to occupy the "public sphere" of business and politics. Consequently, women lacked equality in state and federal law. The struggle for women's rights evolved largely out of the antislavery movement. As abolitionist Abby Kelly remarked, women "had good cause to be grateful to the slave," for in "striving to strike his irons off, we found most surely that we were manacled ourselves." The "woman question" became a major source of division within antislavery ranks. Nowhere was this debate over women's place more apparent than at a world antislavery convention in London in 1840. Forced to sit behind a curtain apart from the male delegates, Elizabeth Cady Stanton and Lucretia Mott determined to organize a women's rights movement in America. In 1848, about one hundred *women, led by Stanton and Mott, assembled in Seneca Falls, New York, where they issued a "Declaration of Sentiments." Modeled after the Declaration of Independence, the Seneca Falls Declaration proclaimed that "all men and women were created equal" and resolved, among other things, women's duty "to secure to themselves their sacred right to the elective franchise." Yet, women abolitionists often felt the need to choose one reform over the other, and, believing that abolition was the great reform of the age, at times sacrificed their cause for the sake of anti-slavery. But when the war ended and abolition triumphed, women's rights activists pressed for reform.*

Even with the demise of state sovereignty as a constitutional theory, expanding civil rights for African Americans and women raised difficult issues about the nature of American federalism. During Reconstruction, Congress for the first time passed a civil rights law, as well as the Thirteenth, Fourteenth, and Fifteenth Amendments to the Constitution. Of these, the Fourteenth was potentially the most far reaching, as some claimed that it revolutionized the relationship between the national government and the states. Before its passage, the states possessed almost total control over civil rights. In Barron v. Baltimore *(1833), the U.S. Supreme Court had held that the Bill of Rights applied only to the national government—not the states. The Fourteenth Amendment, however, contained a "state action" clause, which empowered the national government to scrutinize states' actions based on due process of law, equal protection of the laws, and the privileges and immunities accorded to U.S. citizens. Scholars have long debated whether the framers of the Fourteenth Amendment intended to incorporate all of the guarantees of the Bill of Rights into the amendment, thereby making those rights apply to the states.*

While Congress took the lead in advancing civil rights during this period, a number of cases involving congressional legislation and the Reconstruction amendments eventually made it to the Supreme Court. In the final analysis, the justices ruled that the amendments offered few rights to African Americans or women.

⊕ *D O C U M E N T S*

After the Thirteenth Amendment abolished slavery, southern state governments moved quickly to confirm white control over the lives of freed African Americans. States enacted black codes, which in addition to outlining new rights accorded freedpeople (the right to marry and own property, for example) severely limited their economic opportunities through some form of coerced labor. These codes also usually included provisions that criminalized interracial sexual relationships and either banned or taxed blacks' ownership of guns. In order to overturn such laws, Congress debated the passage of the Fourteenth Amendment. Because the debates (Document 1) touched on critical issues—including whether its framers wanted the Bill of Rights to apply to the states—scholars study these records as closely as those of the Philadelphia convention. The Fourteenth Amendment was ratified in 1868.

Over the next three decades, the Supreme Court had numerous opportunities to interpret the meaning of the new amendment. The *Slaughterhouse Cases* (Document 2) was the first such instance, although it had nothing to do with African Americans or women. Instead, it involved a Louisiana state regulation that so improved the sanitary conditions of New Orleans's slaughterhouse business that many butchers lost their jobs. The butchers sued, claiming that they had been denied rights in violation of the Privileges and Immunities Clause of the Fourteenth Amendment. The justices split 5-4. Justice Samuel F. Miller's majority opinion held that the protection of most privileges and immunities fell to the states. Therefore, the Court upheld the law and granted no relief to the beleaguered butchers. Justice Stephen J. Field issued a notable dissent.

Within a short time, the Court heard two cases pertaining to the rights of women. The day after the justices announced the decision in *Slaughterhouse*, they decided the fate of Myra Bradwell, who sought admission to the bar in Illinois. The Illinois Supreme Court denied her admission on the basis of her gender, and she appealed to the U.S. Supreme Court. In an 8-1 decision in *Bradwell v. Illinois* (Document 3), the Court held, as in *Slaughterhouse*, that the Privileges and Immunities Clause of the Fourteenth Amendment did not embrace the right to practice a profession. Justice Miller again wrote the opinion. A few years later, women activists led by Susan B. Anthony brought another case to the Court, this one involving suffrage. Women's rights advocates had been outraged when the Fourteenth Amendment, in a provision relating to voting rights and representation in Congress, included the word "male." This was the first reference to gender in the Constitution, and suffragists feared that its inclusion meant that it would take another amendment to accomplish the enfranchisement of women. When efforts to add the word "sex" to the Fifteenth Amendment's prohibition on voting restrictions based on "race, color, or previous condition of servitude" failed, women pressed their cause in court. Much to their disappointment, in *Minor v. Happersett* (Document 4), the Court denied that women's status as citizens necessarily conferred a right to vote. Chief Justice Morrison Waite wrote the unanimous opinion.

Over the next two decades, the Court offered a similarly narrow construction of the Fourteenth Amendment in cases involving African Americans. In the *Civil Rights Cases* (Document 5), Justice Joseph Bradley's majority opinion overturned the Civil Rights Act of 1875, which had prohibited racial discrimination in public accommodations. Justice John Marshall Harlan issued a powerful dissent. In *Plessy v. Ferguson* (Document 6), the justices let stand a Louisiana statute that established "equal but separate" accommodations in railway cars as a valid exercise of the state's police powers. Again, only Justice Harlan dissented from the majority. The *Plessy* decision prompted a flood of state legislative enactments that eventually segregated by race nearly every aspect of life in the South.

✤ *D O C U M E N T   1*
_____

Congress Debates the Fourteenth Amendment, 1866

February 27, 1866

Mr. Hale. What is the effect of the amendment which the committee on reconstruction propose for the sanction of this House and the States of the Union? I submit that it is in effect a provision under which all State legislation, in its codes of civil and criminal jurisprudence and procedure, affecting the individual citizen, may be overridden, may be repealed or abolished, and the law of Congress established instead. I maintain that in this respect it is an utter departure from every principle ever dreamed of by the men who framed our Constitution.

Mr. Stevens. Does the gentleman mean to say that, under this provision, Congress could interfere in any case where the legislation of a State was equal, impartial to all?

Or is it not simply to provide that, where any State makes a distinction in the same law between different classes of individuals, Congress shall have power to correct such discrimination and inequality? Does this proposition mean anything more than that?

Mr. Hale. I will answer the gentleman. In my judgment it does go much further than the remarks of the gentleman would imply: but even if it goes no further than that—and I will discuss this point more fully before I conclude—it is still open to the same objection, that it proposes an entire departure from the theory of the Federal Government in meddling with these matters of State jurisdiction at all.

Now, I say to the gentleman from Pennsylvania [Mr. Stevens] that reading the language in its grammatical and legal construction it is a grant of the fullest and most ample power to Congress to make all laws "necessary and proper to secure to all persons in the several States protection in the rights of life, liberty, and property," with the simple proviso that such protection shall be equal. It is not a mere provision that when the States undertake to give protection which is unequal Congress may equalize it: it is a grant of power in general terms—a grant of the right to legislate for the protection of life, liberty and property, simply qualified with the condition that it shall be equal legislation. That is my construction of the proposition as it stands here. It may differ from that of other gentlemen.

Mr. Eldridge. Mr. Speaker, let me go a little further here. If it be true that the construction of this amendment, which I understand to be claimed by the gentlemen from Ohio, [Mr. Bingham] who introduced it, and which I infer from his question is claimed by the gentleman from Pennsylvania. [Mr. Stevens:] if it be true that that is the true construction of this article, is it not even then introducing a power never before intended to be conferred upon Congress. For we all know it is true that probably every State in this Union fails to give equal protection to all persons within its borders in the rights of life, liberty, and property. It may be a fault in the States that they do not do it. A reformation may be desirable, but by the doctrines of the school of politics in which I have been brought up, and which I have been taught to regard was the best school of political rights and duties in this Union, reforms of this character should come from the States, and not be forced upon them by the centralized power of the Federal Government.

Take a single case by way of illustration, and I take it simply to illustrate the point, without expressing any opinion whatever on the desirability or undesirability of a change in regard to it. Take the case of the rights of married women: did any one ever assume that Congress was to be invested with the power to legislate on that subject, and to say that married women, in regard to their rights of property, should stand on the same footing with men and unmarried women? There is not a State in the Union where disability of married women in relation to the rights of property does not to a greater or less extent still exist. Many of the States have taken steps for the partial abolition of that distinction in years past, some to a greater extent and others to a less. But I apprehend there is not to-day a State in the Union where there is not a distinction between the rights of married women, as to property, and the rights of *femmes sole* and men.

Mr. Stevens. If I do not interrupt the gentleman I will say a word. When a distinction is made between two married people or two *femmes sole*, then it is unequal legislation: but where all of the same class are dealt with in the same way then there is no pretense of inequality.

Mr. Hale. The gentleman will pardon me: his argument seems to me to be more specious than sound. The language of the section under consideration gives to *all persons* equal protection. Now, if that means you shall extend to one married woman the same protection you extend to another, and not the same you extend to unmarried women or men, then by parity of reasoning it will be sufficient if you extend to one negro the same rights you do to another, but not those you extend to a white man. I think, if the gentleman from Pennsylvania claims that the resolution only intends that all of a certain class shall have equal protection, such class legislation may certainly as easily satisfy the requirements of this resolution in the case of the negro as in the case of the married woman. The line of distinction is, I take it, quite as broadly marked between negroes and white men as between married and unmarried women.

Mr. Hale. It is claimed that this constitutional amendment is aimed simply and purely toward the protection of "American citizens of African descent" in the States lately in rebellion. I understand that to be the whole intended practical effect of the amendment.

Mr. Bingham. It is due to the committee that I should say that it is proposed as well to protect the thousands and tens of thousands and hundreds of thousands of loyal white citizens of the United States whose property, by State legislation, has been wrested from them under confiscation, and protect them also against banishment.

Mr. Hale. I trust that when the gentlemen comes to reply, he will give me as much of his time as he takes of mine. As he has the reply, I do not think he ought to interject his remarks into my speech. I will modify my statement and say that this amendment is intended to apply solely to the eleven States lately in rebellion, so far as any practical benefit to be derived from it is concerned. The gentleman from Ohio can correct me if I am again in error.

Mr. Bingham. It is to apply to other States also that have in their constitutions and laws to-day provisions in direct violation of every principle of our Constitution.

Mr. Rogers. I suppose this gentleman refers to the State of Indiana!

Mr. Bingham. I do not know: it may be so. It applies unquestionably to the State of Oregon.

Mr. Hale. Then I will again modify my correction and say that it is intended to apply to every State which, in the judgment of the honorable member who introduced this measure, has failed to provide equal protection to life, liberty, and property. And here we come to the very thing for which I denounce this proposition, that it takes away from these States the right to determine for themselves what their institutions shall be.

February 28, 1866

Mr. Bingham. Excuse me. Mr. Speaker, we have had some most extraordinary arguments against the adoption of the proposed amendment.

But, say the gentleman, if you adopt this amendment you give to Congress the power to enforce all the rights of married women in the several States. I beg the gentleman's pardon. He need not be alarmed at the condition of married women. Those rights which are universal and independent of all local State legislation belong, by the gift of God, to every woman, whether married or single. The rights of life and liberty are theirs whatever States may enact. But the gentleman's concern is as to the right of property in married women.

Although this word property has been in your bill of rights from the year 1789 until this hour, who ever heard it intimated that anybody could have property protected in any State until he owned or acquired property there according to its local law or according to the law of some other State which he may have carried thither? I undertake to say no one.

As to real estate, every one knows that its acquisition and transmission under every interpretation ever given to the word property, as used in the Constitution of the country, are dependent exclusively upon the local law of the States, save under a direct grant of the United States. But suppose any person has acquired property not contrary to the laws of the State, but in accordance with its law, are they not to be equally protected in the enjoyment of it, or are they to be denied all protection? That is the question, and the whole question, so far as that part of the case is concerned.

Mr. Speaker. I speak in behalf of this amendment in no party spirit, in no spirit of resentment toward any State or the people of any State or the people of any State, in no spirit of innovation, but for the sake of a violated Constitution and a wronged and wounded country whose heart is now smitten with a strange, great sorrow. I urge the amendment for the enforcement of these essential provisions of your Constitution, divine in their justice, sublime in their humanity, which declare that all men are equal in the rights of life and liberty before the majesty of American law.

Representatives, to you I appeal, that hereafter, by your act and the approval of the loyal people of this country, every man in every State of the Union, in accordance with the written words of your Constitution, may, by the national law, be secured in the equal protection of his personal rights. Your Constitution provides that no man, no matter what his color, no matter beneath what sky he may have been born, no matter in what disastrous conflict or by what tyrannical hand his liberty may have been cloven down, no matter how poor, no matter how friendless, no matter how ignorant, shall be deprived of life or liberty or property without due process of law—law in its highest sense, that law which is the perfection of human reason, and which is impartial, equal, exact justice; that justice which requires that every man shall have his right: that justice which is the highest duty of nations as it is the imperishable attribute of the God of nations. . . .

May 8, 1866

Mr. Stevens. Let us now refer to the provisions of the proposed amendment.

The first section prohibits the States from abridging the privileges and immunities of citizens of the United States, or unlawfully depriving them of life, liberty, or property, or of denying to any person within their jurisdiction the "equal" protection of the laws.

I can hardly believe that any person can be found who will not admit that every one of these provisions is just. They are all asserted, in some form or other, in our DECLARATION or organic law.—But the Constitution limits only the action of Congress, and is not a limitation on the States. This amendment supplies that defect, and allows Congress to correct the unjust legislation of the States, so far that the law which operates upon one man shall operate *equally* upon all. Whatever law punishes a white man for a crime shall punish the black man precisely in the same way and to the same degree. Whatever law protects the white man shall afford "equal" protection to the black man. Whatever law allows the white man to testify in court shall allow the man of color to do the same. These are great advantages over their present codes. Now different degrees of punishment are inflicted, not on account of the magnitude of the crime, but according to the color of the skin. Now color disqualifies a man from testifying in courts, or being tried in the same way as white men. I need not enumerate these partial and oppressive laws. Unless the Constitution should restrain them those States will all, I fear, keep up this discrimination, and crush to death the hated freedmen. Some answer, "Your civil rights bill secures the same things." That is party true, but a law is repealable by a majority. And I need hardly say that the first time that the South with their copperhead allies obtain the command of Congress it will be repealed. The veto of the President and their votes on the bill are conclusive evidence of that. . . .

May 10, 1866

Mr. Bingham. The necessity for the first section of this amendment to the Constitution, Mr. Speaker, is one of the lessons that have been taught to your committee and taught to all the people of this country by the history of the past four years of terrific conflict—that history in which God is, and in which He teaches the profoundest lessons to men and nations. There was a want hitherto, and there remains a want now, in the Constitution of our country, which the proposed amendment will supply. What is that? It is the power in the people, the whole people of the United States, by express authority of the Constitution to do that by congressional enactment which hitherto they have not had the power to do, and have never even attempted to do; that is, to protect by national law the privileges and immunities of all the citizens of the Republic and the inborn rights of every person within its jurisdiction whenever the same shall be abridged or denied by the unconstitutional acts of any State.

Allow me, Mr. Speaker, in passing, to say that this amendment takes from no State any right that ever pertained to it. No State ever had the right, under the forms of law or otherwise, to deny to any freeman the equal protection of the laws or to abridge the privileges or immunities of any citizen of the Republic, although many of them have assumed and exercised the power, and that without remedy. The amendment does not give, as the second section shows, the power to Congress of regulating suffrage in the several States. . . .

May 23, 1866

Mr. Howard. The first clause of this section relates to the privileges and immunities of citizens of the United States as such, and as distinguished from all other persons not citizens of the United States.

It would be a curious question to solve what are the privileges and immunities of citizens of each of the States in the several States. I do not propose to go at any length into that question at this time. It would be a somewhat barren discussion. But it is certain the clause was inserted in the Constitution for some good purpose. It has in view some results beneficial to the citizens of the several States, or it would not be found there; yet I am not aware that the Supreme Court have ever undertaken to define either the nature or extent of the privileges and immunities thus guaranteed. Indeed, if my recollection serves me, that court, on a certain occasion not many years since, when this question seemed to present itself to them, very modestly declined to go into a definition of them, leaving questions arising under the clause to be discussed and adjudicated when they should happen practically to arise. But we may gather some intimation of what probably will be the opinion of the judiciary by referring to a case adjudged many years ago in one of the circuit courts of the United States by Judge Washington: and I will trouble the Senate but for a moment by reading what that very learned and excellent judge says about these privileges and immunities of the citizens of each State in the several States. It is the case of *Corfield v. Coryell.*

Such is the character of the privileges and immunities spoken of in the second section of the fourth article of the Constitution. To these privileges and immunities, whatever they may be—for they are not and cannot be fully defined in their entire extent and precise nature—to these should be added the personal rights guaranteed and secured by the first eight amendments of the Constitution; such as the freedom of speech and of the press; the right of the people peaceably to assemble and petition the Government for a redress of grievances, a right appertaining to each and all the people; the right to keep and to bear arms; the right to be exempted from the quartering of soldiers in a house without the consent of the owner; the right to be exempt from unreasonable searches and seizures, and from any search or seizure except by virtue of a warrant issued upon a formal oath or affidavit: the right of an accused person to be informed of the nature of the accusation against him, and his right to be tried by an impartial jury of the vicinage; and also the right to be secure against excessive bail and against cruel and unusual punishments.

Now, sir, here is a mass of privileges, immunities, and rights, some of them secured by the second section of the fourth article of the Constitution, which I have recited, some by the first eight amendments of the Constitution; and it is a fact well worthy of attention that the course of decision of our courts and the present settled doctrine is, that all these immunities, privileges, rights, thus guaranteed by the Constitution or recognized by it, are secured to the citizen solely as a citizen of the United States and as a party in their courts. They do not operate in the slightest degree as a restraint or prohibition upon State legislation. States are not affected by them, and it has been repeatedly held that the restriction contained in the Constitution against the taking of private property for public use without just compensation is not a restriction upon State legislation, but applies only to the legislation of Congress.

Now, sir, there is no power given in the Constitution to enforce and to carry out any of these guarantees. They are not powers granted by the Constitution to Congress, and of course do not come within the sweeping clause of the Constitution authorizing Congress to pass all laws necessary and proper for carrying out the foregoing or granted powers, but they stand simply as a bill of rights in the Constitution, without power on the part of Congress to give them full effect; while at the same time the States are not restrained from violating the principles embraced in them except by their own local constitutions, which may be altered from year to year. The great object of the first section of this amendment is, therefore, to restrain the power of the

States and compel them at all times to respect these great fundamental guarantees. How will it be done under the present amendment? As I have remarked, they are not powers granted to Congress, and therefore it is necessary, if they are to be effectuated and enforced, as they assuredly ought to be, that additional power should be given to Congress to that end. This is done by the fifth section of this amendment, which declares that "the Congress shall have power to enforce by appropriate legislation the provisions of this article." Here is a direct affirmative delegation of power to Congress to carry out all the principles of all these guarantees, a power not found in the Constitution.

The last two clauses of the first section of the amendment disable a State from depriving not merely a citizen of the United States, but any person, whoever he may be, of life, liberty, or property without due process of law, or from denying to him the equal protection of the laws of the State. This abolishes all class legislation in the States and does away with the injustice of subjecting one caste of persons to a code not applicable to another. It prohibits the hanging of a black man for a crime for which the white man is not to be hanged. It protects the black man in his fundamental rights as a citizen with the same shield which it throws over the white man. Is it not time, Mr. President, that we extend to the black man, I had almost called it the poor privilege of the equal protection of the law? Ought not the time to be now passed when one measure of justice is to be meted out to a member of one caste while another and a different measure is meted out to the member of another caste, both castes being alike citizens of the United States, both bound to obey the same laws, to sustain the burdens of the same Government, and both equally responsible to justice and to God for the deeds done in the body?

But, sir, the first section of the proposed amendment does not give to either of these classes the right of voting. The right of suffrage is not, in law, one of the privileges or immunities thus secured by the Constitution. It is merely the creature of law. It has always been regarded in this country as the result of positive local law, not regarded as one of those fundamental rights lying at the basis of all society and without which a people cannot exist except as slaves, subject to a despotism.

As I have already remarked, section one is a restriction upon the States, and does not, of itself, confer any power upon Congress. The power which Congress has, under this amendment, is derived, not from that section, but from the fifth section, which gives it authority to pass laws which are appropriate to the attainment of the great object of the amendment. I look upon the first section, taken in connection with the fifth, as very important. It will, if adopted by the States, forever disable every one of them from passing laws trenching upon those fundamental rights and privileges which pertain to citizens of the United States, and to all persons who may happen to be within their jurisdiction. It establishes equality before the law, and it gives to the humblest, the poorest, the most despised of the race the same rights and the same protection before the law as it gives to the most powerful, the most wealthy, or the most haughty. That, sir, is republican government, as I understand it, and the only one which can claim the praise of a just Government. Without this principle of equal justice to all men and equal protection under the shield of the law, there is no republican government and none that is really worth maintaining.

✤ D O C U M E N T   2

The Slaughterhouse Cases, 1873

Justice Miller for the Court. ... It cannot be denied that the statute under consideration is aptly framed to remove from the more densely populated part of the city, the noxious slaughter-houses, and large and offensive collections of animals necessarily incident to the slaughtering business of a large city, and to locate them where the convenience, health, and comfort of the people require they shall be located. And it must be conceded that the means adopted by the act for this purpose are appropriate, are stringent, and effectual. But it is said that in creating a corporation for this purpose, and conferring upon it exclusive privileges—privileges which it is said constitute a monopoly—the legislature has exceeded its power. If this statute had imposed on the city of New Orleans precisely the same duties, accompanied by the same privileges, which it has on the corporation which it created, it is believed that no question would have been raised as to its constitutionality. In that case the effect on the butchers in pursuit of their occupation and on the public would have been the same as it is now. Why cannot the legislature confer the same powers on another corporation, created for a lawful and useful public object, that it can on the municipal corporation already existing? That wherever a legislature has the right to accomplish a certain result, and that result is best attained by means of a corporation, it has the right to create such a corporation, and to endow it with the powers necessary to effect the desired and lawful purpose, seems hardly to admit of debate. ...

It may, therefore, be considered as established, that the authority of the legislature of Louisiana to pass the present statute is ample, unless some restraint in the exercise of that power be found in the constitution of that State or in the amendments to the Constitution of the United States, adopted since the date of the decisions we have already cited.

If any such restraint is supposed to exist in the constitution of the State, the Supreme Court of Louisiana having necessarily passed on that question, it would not be open to review in this court.

The plaintiffs in error accepting this issue, allege that the statute is a violation of the Constitution of the United States in these several particulars:

That it creates an involuntary servitude forbidden by the thirteenth article of amendment;

That it abridges the privileges and immunities of citizens of the United States;

That it denies to the plaintiffs the equal protection of the laws; and,

That it deprives them of their property without due process of law; contrary to the provisions of the first section of the fourteenth article of amendment.

This court is thus called upon for the first time to give construction to these articles. ...

The first section of the fourteenth article, to which our attention is more specially invited, opens with a definition of citizenship—not only citizenship of the United States, but citizenship of the States. No such definition was previously found in the Constitution, nor had any attempt been made to define it by act of Congress. It had been the occasion of much discussion in the courts, by the executive departments, and in the public journals. It had been said by eminent judges that no man was a citizen of the United States, except as he was a citizen of one of the States composing the Union. Those, therefore, who had been born and resided always in the District of Columbia or in the Territories, though within the United States, were not citizens. Whether this proposition was sound or not had never been judicially decided. But it had been held by this court, in the celebrated Dred Scott case, only a few years before the outbreak of the civil war, that a man of African descent, whether a slave or not, was not and could not be a citizen of a State or of the United States. This decision, while it met the condemnation of some of the ablest statesmen and constitutional lawyers of the country, had never been overruled; and if it was to be accepted as a constitutional limitation of the right of citizenship, then all the negro race who had recently been made freemen, were still, not only not citizens, but were incapable of becoming so by anything short of an amendment to the Constitution.

To remove this difficulty primarily, and to establish a clear and comprehensive definition of citizenship which should declare what should constitute citizenship of the United States, and also citizenship of a State, the first clause of the first section was framed.

"All persons born or naturalized in the United States, and subject to the jurisdiction thereof, are citizens of the United States and of the State wherein they reside." ...

[T]he distinction between citizenship of the United States and citizenship of a State is clearly recognized and established. Not only may a man be a citizen of the United States without being a citizen of a State, but an important element is necessary to convert the former into the latter. He must reside within the State to make him a citizen of it, but it is only necessary that he should be born or naturalized in the United States to be a citizen of the Union.

It is quite clear, then, that there is a citizenship of the United States, and a citizenship of a State, which are distinct from each other, and which depend upon different characteristics or circumstances in the individual.

We think this distinction and its explicit recognition in this amendment of great weight in this argument, because the next paragraph of this same section, which is the one mainly relied on by the plaintiffs in error, speaks only of privileges and immunities of citizens of the United States, and does not speak of those of citizens of the several States. The argument, however, in favor of the plaintiffs rests wholly on the assumption that the citizenship is the same, and the privileges and immunities guaranteed by the clause are the same.

The language is, "No State shall make or enforce any law which shall abridge the privileges or immunities of citizens of *the United States.*" It is a little remarkable, if this clause was intended as a protection to the citizen of a State against the legislative power of his own State, that the word citizen of the State should be left out when it is so carefully used, and used in contradistinction to citizens of the United States, in the very sentence which precedes it. It is too clear for argument that the change in phraseology was adopted understandingly and with a purpose.

Of the privileges and immunities of the citizen of the United States, and of the privileges and immunities of the citizen of the State, and what they respectively are, we will presently consider; but we wish to state here that it is only the former which are placed by this clause under the protection of the Federal Constitution, and that the latter, whatever they may be, are not intended to have any additional protection by this paragraph of the amendment.

If, then, there is a difference between the privileges and immunities belonging to a citizen of the United States as such, and those belonging to the citizen of the State as such, the latter must rest for their security and protection where they have heretofore rested; for they are not embraced by this paragraph of the amendment....

In the Constitution of the United States, which superseded the Articles of Confederation, the corresponding provision is found in section two of the fourth article, in the following words: "The citizens of each State shall be entitled to all the privileges and immunities of citizens of the several States."

There can be but little question that the purpose of both these provisions is the same, and that the privileges and immunities intended are the same in each. In the article of the Confederation we have some of these specifically mentioned, and enough perhaps to give some general idea of the class of civil rights meant by the phrase.

Fortunately we are not without judicial construction of this clause of the Constitution. The first and the leading case on the subject is that of *Corfield v. Coryell*, decided by Mr. Justice Washington in the Circuit Court for the District of Pennsylvania in 1823.

"The inquiry," he says, "is, what are the privileges and immunities of citizens of the several States? We feel no hesitation in confining these expressions to those privileges and immunities which are *fundamental*; which belong of right to the citizens of all free governments, and which have at all times been enjoyed by citizens of the several States which compose this Union, from the time of their becoming free, independent, and sovereign. What these fundamental principles are, it would be more tedious than difficult to enumerate. They may all, however, be comprehended under the following general heads: protection by the government, with the right to acquire and possess property of every kind, and to pursue and obtain happiness and safety, subject, nevertheless, to such restraints as the government may prescribe for the general good of the whole." ...

It would be the vainest show of learning to attempt to prove by citations of authority, that up to the adoption of the recent amendments, no claim or pretence was set up that those rights depended on the Federal government for their existence or protection, beyond the very few express limitations which the Federal Constitution imposed upon the States—such, for instance, as the prohibition against ex post facto laws, bills of attainder, and laws impairing the obligation of contracts. But with the exception of these and a few other restrictions, the entire domain of the privileges and immunities of citizens of the States, as above defined, lay within the constitutional and legislative power of the States, and without that of the Federal government. Was it the purpose of the fourteenth amendment, by the simple declaration that no State should make or enforce any law which shall abridge the privileges and immunities of *citizens of the United States*, to transfer the security and protection of all the civil rights which we have mentioned, from the States to the Federal government? And where it is declared that Congress shall have the power to enforce that article, was it intended to bring within the power of Congress the entire domain of civil rights heretofore belonging exclusively to the States?

All this and more must follow, if the proposition of the plaintiffs in error be sound. For not only are these rights subject to the control of Congress whenever in its discretion any of them are supposed to be abridged by State legislation, but that body may also pass laws in advance, limiting and restricting the exercise of legislative power by the States, in their most ordinary and usual functions, as in its judgment it may think proper on all such subjects. And still further, such a construction followed by the reversal of the judgments of the Supreme Court of Louisiana in these cases, would constitute this court a perpetual censor upon all legislation of the States, on the civil rights of their own citizens, with authority to nullify such as it did not approve as consistent with those rights, as they existed at the time of the adoption of this amendment. The argument we admit is not always the most conclusive which is drawn from the consequences urged against the adoption of a particular construction of an instrument. But when, as in the case before us, these consequences are so serious, so far-reaching and pervading, so great a departure from the structure and spirit of our institutions; when the effect is to fetter and degrade the State governments by subjecting them to the control of Congress, in the exercise of powers heretofore universally conceded to them of the most ordinary and fundamental character; when in fact it radically changes the whole theory of the relations of the State and Federal governments to each other and of both these governments to the people; the argument has a force that is irresistible, in the absence of language which expresses such a purpose too clearly to admit of doubt.

We are convinced that no such results were intended by the Congress which proposed these amendments, nor by the legislatures of the States which ratified them.

Having shown that the privileges and immunities relied on in the argument are those which belong to citizens of the States as such, and that they are left to the State governments for security and protection, and not by this article placed under the special care of the Federal government, we may hold ourselves excused from defining the privileges and immunities of citizens of the United States which no State can abridge, until some case involving those privileges may make it necessary to do so.

But lest it should be said that no such privileges and immunities are to be found if those we have been considering are excluded, we venture to suggest some which owe their existence to the Federal government, its National character, its Constitution, or its laws.

One of these is well described in the case of *Crandall v. Nevada*. It is said to be the right of the citizen of this great country, protected by implied guarantees of its Constitution, "to come to the seat of government to assert any claim he may have upon that government, to transact any business he may have with it, to seek its protection, to share its offices, to engage in administering its functions. He has the right of free access to its seaports, through which all operations of foreign commerce are conducted, to the subtreasuries, land offices, and courts of justice in the several States." ...

Another privilege of a citizen of the United States is to demand the care and protection of the Federal government over his life, liberty, and property when on the high seas or within the jurisdiction of a foreign government. Of this there can be no doubt, nor that the right depends upon his character as a citizen of the United States. The right to peaceably assemble and petition for redress of grievances, the privilege of the writ of *habeas corpus*, are rights of the citizen guaranteed by the Federal Constitution. The right to use the navigable waters of the United States, however they may penetrate the territory of the several States, all rights secured to our citizens by treaties with foreign nations, are dependent upon citizenship of the United States, and not citizenship of a State. One of these privileges is conferred by the very article under consideration. It is that a citizen of the United States can, of his own volition, become a citizen of any State of the Union by a *bonâfide* residence therein, with the same rights as other citizens of that State. To these may be added the rights secured by the thirteenth and fifteenth articles of amendment, and by the other clause of the fourteenth, next to be considered.

But it is useless to pursue this branch of the inquiry, since we are of opinion that the rights claimed by these plaintiffs in error, if they have any existence, are not privileges and immunities of citizens of the United States within the meaning of the clause of the fourteenth amendment under consideration. ...

In the early history of the organization of the government, its statesmen seem to have divided on the line which should separate the powers of the National government from those of the State governments, and though this line has never been very well defined in public opinion, such a division has continued from that day to this.

The adoption of the first eleven amendments to the Constitution so soon after the original instrument was accepted, shows a prevailing sense of danger at that time from the Federal power. And it cannot be denied that such a jealousy continued to exist with many patriotic men until the breaking out of the late civil war. It was then discovered that the true danger to the perpetuity of the Union was in the capacity of the State organizations to combine and concentrate all the powers of the State, and of contiguous States, for a determined resistance to the General Government.

Unquestionably this has given great force to the argument, and added largely to the number of those who believe in the necessity of a strong National government.

But, however pervading this sentiment, and however it may have contributed to the adoption of the amendments we have been considering, we do not see in those amendments any purpose to destroy the main features of the general system. Under the pressure of all the excited feeling growing out of the war, our statesmen have still believed that the existence of the States with powers for domestic and local government, including the regulation of civil rights—the rights of person and of property—was essential to the perfect working of our complex form of government, though they have thought proper to impose additional limitations on the States, and to confer additional power on that of the Nation. ...

Mr. Justice Field, dissenting: I am unable to agree with the majority of the court in these cases. ...

The question presented is, therefore, one of the gravest importance, not merely to the parties here, but to the whole country. It is nothing less than the question whether the recent amendments to the Federal Constitution protect the citizens of the United States against the deprivation of their common rights by State legislation. In my judgment the fourteenth amendment does afford such protection, and was so intended by the Congress which framed and the States which adopted it. ...

What, then, are the privileges and immunities which are secured against abridgment by State legislation?

In the first section of the Civil Rights Act Congress has given its interpretation to these terms, or at least has stated some of the rights which, in its judgment, these terms include; it has there declared that they include the right "to make and enforce contracts, to sue, be parties and give evidence, to inherit, purchase, lease, sell, hold, and convey real and personal property, and to full and equal benefit of all laws and proceedings for the security of person and property." That act, it is true, was passed before the fourteenth amendment, but the amendment was adopted, as I have already said, to obviate objections to the act, or, speaking more accurately, I should say, to obviate objections to legislation of a similar character, extending the protection of the National government over the common rights of all citizens of the United States. Accordingly, after its ratification, Congress re-enacted the act under the belief that whatever doubts may have previously existed of its validity, they were removed by the amendment.

The terms, privileges and immunities, are not new in the amendment; they were in the Constitution before the amendment was adopted. They are found in the second section of the fourth article, which declares that "the citizens of each State shall be entitled to all privileges and immunities of citizens in the several States," and they have been the subject of frequent consideration in judicial decisions. In *Corfield v. Coryell*, Mr. Justice Washington said he had "no hesitation in confining these expressions to those privileges and immunities which were, in their nature, fundamental; which belong of right to citizens of all free governments, and which have at all times been enjoyed by the citizens of the several States which compose the Union, from the time of their becoming free, independent, and sovereign"; and, in considering what those fundamental privileges were, he said that perhaps it would be more tedious than difficult to enumerate them, but that they might be "all comprehended under the following general heads: protection by the government; the enjoyment of life and liberty, with the right to acquire and possess property of every kind, and to pursue and obtain happiness and safety, subject, nevertheless, to such restraints as the government may justly prescribe for the general good of the whole." This appears to me to be a sound construction of the clause in question. The privileges and immunities designated are those *which of right belong to the citizens of all free governments*. Clearly among these must be placed the right to pursue a lawful employment in a lawful manner, without other restraint than such as equally affects all persons. ...

The privileges and immunities designated in the second section of the fourth article of the Constitution are, then, according to the decision cited, those which of right belong to the citizens of all free governments, and they can be enjoyed under that clause by the citizens of each State in the several States upon the same terms and conditions as they are enjoyed by the citizens of the latter States. ...

✢ *D O C U M E N T   3*

Bradwell v. Illinois, 1873

Mr. Justice Miller delivered the opinion of the Court. The record in this case is not very perfect, but it may be fairly taken that the plaintiff asserted her right to a license on the grounds, among others, that she was a citizen of the United States, and that having been a citizen of Vermont at one time, she was, in the State of Illinois, entitled to any right granted to citizens of the latter State.

The court having overruled these claims of right founded on the clauses of the Federal Constitution before referred to, those propositions may be considered as properly before this court.

As regards the provision of the Constitution that citizens of each State shall be entitled to all the privileges and immunities of citizens in the several States, the plaintiff in her affidavit has stated very clearly a case to which it is inapplicable.

The protection designed by that clause, as has been repeatedly held, has no application to a citizen of the State whose laws are complained of. If the plaintiff was a citizen of the State of Illinois, that provision of the Constitution gave her no protection against its courts or its legislation.

The plaintiff seems to have seen this difficulty, and attempts to avoid it by stating that she was born in Vermont.

While she remained in Vermont that circumstance made her a citizen of the State. But she states, at the same time, that she is a citizen of the United States, and that she is now, and has been for many years past, a resident of Chicago, in the State of Illinois.

The fourteenth amendment declares that citizens of the United States are citizens of the State within which they reside; therefore the plaintiff was, at the time of making her application, a citizen of the United States and a citizen of the State of Illinois.

We do not here mean to say that there may not be a temporary residence in one State, with intent to return to another, which will not create citizenship in the former. But the plaintiff states nothing to take her case out of the definition of citizenship of a State as defined by the first section of the fourteenth amendment.

In regard to that amendment counsel for the plaintiff in this court truly says that there are certain privileges and immunities which belong to a citizen of the United States as such; otherwise it would be nonsense for the fourteenth amendment to prohibit a State from abridging them, and he proceeds to argue that admission to the bar of a State of a person who possesses the requisite learning and character is one of those which a State may not deny.

In this latter proposition we are not able to concur with counsel. We agree with him that there are privileges and immunities belonging to citizens of the United States, in that relation and character, and that it is these and these alone which a State is forbidden to abridge. But the right to admission to practice in the courts of a State is not one of them. This right in no sense depends on citizenship of the United States. It has not, as far as we know, ever been made in any State, or in any case, to depend on citizenship at all. Certainly many prominent and distinguished lawyers have been admitted to practice, both in the State and Federal courts, who were not citizens of the United States or of any State. But, on whatever basis this right may be placed, so far as it can have any relation to citizenship at all, it would seem that, as to the courts of a State, it would relate to citizenship of the State, and as to Federal courts, it would relate to citizenship of the United States.

The opinion just delivered in the *Slaughter-House Cases* renders elaborate argument in the present case unnecessary; for, unless we are wholly and radically mistaken in the principles on which those cases are decided, the right to control and regulate the granting of license to practice law in the courts of a State is one of those powers which are not transferred for its protection to the Federal government, and its exercise is in no manner governed or controlled by citizenship of the United States in the party seeking such license.

It is unnecessary to repeat the argument on which the judgment in those cases is founded. It is sufficient to say they are conclusive of the present case.

Judgment affirmed.

✣ D O C U M E N T   4

Minor v. Happersett, 1875

Chief Justice Waite for the Court. The question is presented in this case, whether, since the adoption of the fourteenth amendment, a woman, who is a citizen of the United States and of the State of Missouri, is a voter in that State, notwithstanding the provision of the constitution and laws of the State, which confine the right of suffrage to men alone. ...

It is contended that the provisions of the constitution and laws of the State of Missouri which confine the right of suffrage and registration therefore to men, are in violation of the Constitution of the United States, and therefore void. The argument is, that as a woman, born or naturalized in the United States and subject to the jurisdiction thereof, is a citizen of the United States and of the State in which she resides, she has the right of suffrage as one of the privileges and immunities of her citizenship, which the State cannot by its laws or constitution abridge. ...

If the right of suffrage is one of the necessary privileges of a citizen of the United States, then the constitution and laws of Missouri confining it to men are in violation of the Constitution of the United States, as amended, and consequently void. The direct question is, therefore, presented whether all citizens are necessarily voters.

The Constitution does not define the privileges and immunities of citizens. For that definition we must look elsewhere. In this case we need not determine what they are, but only whether suffrage is necessarily one of them.

It certainly is nowhere made so in express terms. The United States has no voters in the States of its own creation. The elective officers of the United States are all elected directly or indirectly by State voters. The members of the House of Representatives are to be chosen by the people of the States, and the electors in each State must have the qualifications requisite for electors of the most numerous branch of the State legislature. Senators are to be chosen by the legislatures of the States, and necessarily the members of the legislature required to make the choice are elected by the voters of the State. Each State must appoint in such manner, as the legislature thereof may direct, the electors to elect the President and Vice-President. The times, places, and manner of holding elections for Senators and Representatives are to be prescribed in each State by the legislature thereof; but Congress may at any time, by law, make or alter such regulations, except as to the place of choosing Senators. It is not necessary to inquire whether this power of supervision thus given to Congress is sufficient to authorize any interference with the State laws prescribing the qualifications of voters, for no such interference has ever been attempted. The power of the State in this particular is certainly supreme until Congress acts.

The amendment did not add to the privileges and immunities of a citizen. It simply furnished an additional guarantee for the protection of such as he already had. No new voters were necessarily made by it. Indirectly it may have had that effect, because it may have increased the number of citizens entitled to suffrage under the constitution and laws of the States, but it operates for this purpose, if at all, through the States and the State laws, and not directly upon the citizen.

It is clear, therefore, we think, that the Constitution has not added the right of suffrage to the privileges and immunities of citizenship as they existed at the time it was adopted. This makes it proper to inquire whether suffrage was coextensive with the citizenship of the States at the time of its adoption. If it was, then it may with force be argued that suffrage was one of the rights which belonged to citizenship, and in the enjoyment of which every citizen must be protected. But if it was not, the contrary may with propriety be assumed.

When the Federal Constitution was adopted, all the States, with the exception of Rhode Island and Connecticut, had constitutions of their own. These two continued to act under their charters from the Crown. Upon an examination of those constitutions we find that in no State were all citizens permitted to vote. Each State determined for itself who should have that power. ...

In this condition of the law in respect to suffrage in the several States it cannot for a moment be doubted that if it had been intended to make all citizens of the United States voters, the framers of the Constitution would not have left it to implication. So important a change in the condition of citizenship as it actually existed, if intended, would have been expressly declared.

But if further proof is necessary to show that no such change was intended, it can easily be found both in and out of the Constitution. By Article 4, section 2, it is provided that "the citizens of each State shall be entitled to all the privileges and immunities of citizens in the several States." If suffrage is necessarily a part of citizenship, then the citizens of each State must be entitled to vote in the several States precisely as their citizens are. This is more than asserting that they may change their residence and become citizens of the State and thus be voters. It goes to the extent of insisting that while retaining their original citizenship they may vote in any State. This, we think, has never been claimed. And again, by the very terms of the amendment we have been considering (the fourteenth), "Representatives shall be apportioned among the several States according to their respective numbers, counting the whole number of persons in each State, excluding Indians not taxed. But when the right to vote at any election for the choice of electors for President and Vice-President of the United States, representatives in Congress, the executive and judicial officers of a State, or the members of the legislature thereof, is denied to any of the male inhabitants of such State, being twenty-one years of age and citizens of the United States, or in any way abridged, except for participation in the rebellion, or other crimes, the basis of representation therein shall be reduced in the proportion which the number of such male citizens shall bear to the whole number of male citizens twenty-one years of age in such State." Why this, if it was not in the power of the legislature to deny the right of suffrage to some male inhabitants? And if suffrage was necessarily one of the absolute rights of citizenship, why confine the operation of the limitation to male inhabitants? Women and children are, as we have seen, "persons." They are counted in the enumeration upon which the apportionment is to be made, but if they were necessarily voters because of their citizenship unless clearly excluded, why inflict the penalty for the exclusion of males alone? Clearly, no such form of words would have been selected to express the idea here indicated if suffrage was the absolute right of all citizens.

And still again, after the adoption of the fourteenth amendment, it was deemed necessary to adopt a fifteenth, as follows: "The right of citizens of the United States to vote shall not be denied or abridged by the United States, or by any State, on account of race, color, or previous condition of servitude." The fourteenth amendment had already provided that no State should make or enforce any law which should abridge the privileges or immunities of citizens of the United States. If suffrage was one of these privileges or immunities, why amend the Constitution to prevent its being denied on account of race, &c.? Nothing is more evident than that the greater must include the less, and if all were already protected why go through with the form of amending the Constitution to protect a part?...

As has been seen, all the citizens of the States were not invested with the right of suffrage. In all, save perhaps New Jersey, this right was only bestowed upon men and not upon all of them. Under these circumstances it is certainly now too late to contend that a government is not republican, within the meaning of this guarantee in the Constitution, because women are not made voters.

The same may be said of the other provisions just quoted. Women were excluded from suffrage in nearly all the States by the express provision of their constitutions and laws. If that had been equivalent to a bill of attainder, certainly its abrogation would not have been left to implication. Nothing less than express language would have been employed to effect so radical a change. So also of the amendment which declares that no person shall be deprived of life, liberty, or property without due process of law, adopted as it was as early as 1791. If suffrage was intended to be included within its obligations, language better adapted to express that intent would most certainly have been employed. The right of suffrage, when granted, will be protected. He who has it can only be deprived of it by due process of law, but in order to claim protection he must first show that he has the right. ...

Certainly, if the courts can consider any question settled, this is one. For nearly ninety years the people have acted upon the idea that the Constitution, when it conferred citizenship, did not necessarily confer the right of suffrage. If uniform practice long continued can settle the construction of so important an instrument as the Constitution of the United States confessedly is, most certainly it has been done here. Our province is to decide what the law is, not to declare what it should be.

We have given this case the careful consideration its importance demands. If the law is wrong, it ought to be changed; but the power for that is not with us. The arguments addressed to us bearing upon such a view of the subject may perhaps be sufficient to induce those having the power, to make the alteration, but they ought not to be permitted to influence our judgment in determining the present rights of the parties now litigating before us. No argument as to woman's need of suffrage can be considered. We can only act upon her rights as they exist. It is not for us to look at the hardship of withholding. Our duty is at an end if we find it is within the power of a State to withhold.

Being unanimously of the opinion that the Constitution of the United States does not confer the right of suffrage upon any one, and that the constitutions and laws of the several States which commit that important trust to men alone are not necessarily void, we affirm the judgment.

* D O C U M E N T   5

The Civil Rights Cases, 1883

Justice Bradley delivered the opinion of the Court. The first section of the Fourteenth Amendment (which is the one relied on), after declaring who shall be citizens of the United States, and of the several States, is prohibitory in its character, and prohibitory upon the States. It declares that:

> "No State shall make or enforce any law which shall abridge the privileges or immunities of citizens of the United States; nor shall any State deprive any person of life, liberty, or property without due process of law; nor deny to any person within its jurisdiction the equal protection of the laws."

It is State action of a particular character that is prohibited. Individual invasion of individual rights is not the subject-matter of the amendment. It has a deeper and broader scope. It nullifies and makes void all State legislation, and State action of every kind, which impairs the privileges and immunities of citizens of the United States, or which injures them in life, liberty or property without due process of law, or which denies to any of them the equal protection of the laws. It not only does this, but, in order that the national will, thus declared, may not be a mere *brutum fulmen*, the last section of the amendment invests Congress with power to enforce it by appropriate legislation. To enforce what? To enforce the prohibition. To adopt appropriate legislation for correcting the effects of such prohibited State laws and State acts, and thus to render them effectually null, void, and innocuous. This is the legislative power conferred upon Congress, and this is the whole of it. It does not invest Congress with power to legislate upon subjects which are within the domain of State legislation; but to provide modes of relief against State legislation, or State action, of the kind referred to. It does not authorize Congress to create a code of municipal law for the regulation of private rights; but to provide modes of redress against the operation of State laws, and the action of State officers executive or judicial, when these are subversive of the fundamental rights specified in the amendment. Positive rights and privileges are undoubtedly secured by the Fourteenth Amendment; but they are secured by way of prohibition against State laws and State proceedings affecting those rights and privileges, and by power given to Congress to legislate for the purpose of carrying such prohibition into effect: and such legislation must necessarily be predicated upon such supposed State laws or State proceedings, and be directed to the correction of their operation and effect....

And so in the present case, until some State law has been passed, or some State action through its officers or agents has been taken, adverse to the rights of citizens sought to be protected by the Fourteenth Amendment, no legislation of the United State under said amendment, nor any proceeding under such legislation, can be called into activity: for the prohibitions of the amendment are against State laws and acts done under State authority. Of course, legislation may, and should be, provided in advance to meet the exigency when it arises; but it should be adapted to the mischief and wrong which the amendment was intended to provide against; and that is, State laws, or State action of some kind, adverse to the rights of the citizen secured by the amendment. Such legislation cannot properly cover the whole domain of rights appertaining to life, liberty and property, defining them and providing for their vindication. That would be to establish a code of municipal law regulative of all private rights between man and man in society. It would be to make Congress take the place of the State legislatures and to supersede them. ...

When a man has emerged from slavery, and by the aid of beneficent legislation has shaken off the inseparable concomitants of that state, there must be some stage in the progress of his elevation when he takes the rank of a mere citizen, and ceases to be the special favorite of the laws, and when his rights as a citizen, or a man, are to be protected in the ordinary modes by which other men's rights are protected. There were thousands of free colored people in this country before the abolition of slavery, enjoying all the essential rights of life, liberty and property the same as white citizens; yet no one, at that time, thought that it was any invasion of his personal status as a freeman because he was not admitted to all the privileges enjoyed by white citizens, or because he was subjected to discriminations in the enjoyment of accommodations in inns, public conveyances and places of amusement. Mere discriminations on account of race or color were not regarded as badges of slavery. ...

On the whole we are of opinion, that no countenance of authority for the passage of the law in question can be found in either the Thirteenth or Fourteenth Amendment of the Constitution; and no other ground of authority for its passage being suggested, it must necessarily be declared void, at least so far as its operation in the several States is concerned. ...

Justice Harlan dissenting.

... That there are burdens and disabilities which constitute badges of slavery and servitude, and that the power to enforce by appropriate legislation the Thirteenth Amendment may be exerted by legislation of a direct and primary character, for the eradication, not simply of the institution, but of its badges and incidents, are propositions which ought to be deemed indisputable. They lie at the foundation of the Civil Rights Act of 1866. Whether that act was authorized by the Thirteenth Amendment alone, without the support which it subsequently received from the Fourteenth Amendment, after the adoption of which it was re-enacted with some additions, my brethren do not consider it necessary to inquire. But I submit, with all respect to them, that its constitutionality is conclusively shown by their opinion. They admit, as I have said, that the Thirteenth Amendment established freedom; that these are burdens and disabilities, the necessary incidents of slavery, which constitute its substance and visible form; that Congress, by the act of 1866, passed in view of the Thirteenth Amendment, before the Fourteenth was adopted, undertook to remove certain burdens and disabilities, the necessary incidents of slavery, and to secure to all citizens of every race and color, and without regard to previous servitude, those fundamental rights which are the essence of civil freedom, namely, the same right to make and enforce contracts, to sue, be parties, give evidence, and to inherit, purchase, lease, sell, and convey property as is enjoyed by white citizens; that under the Thirteenth Amendment, Congress has to do with slavery and its incidents; and that legislation, so far as necessary or proper to eradicate all forms and incidents of slavery and involuntary servitude, may be direct and primary, operating upon the acts of individuals, whether sanctioned by State legislation or not. ... Congress, therefore, under its express power to enforce that amendment, by appropriate legislation, may enact laws to protect that people against the deprivation, *because of their race*, of any civil rights granted to other freemen in the same State; and such legislation may be of a direct and primary character, operating upon States, their officers and agents, and, also, upon, at least, such individuals and corporations as exercise public functions and wield power and authority under the State....

Congress has not, in these matters, entered the domain of State control and supervision. It does not, as I have said, assume to prescribe the general conditions and limitations under which inns, public conveyances, and places of public amusement, shall be conducted or managed. It simply declares, in effect, that since the nation has established universal freedom in this country, for all time, there shall be no discrimination, based merely upon race or color, in respect of the accommodations and advantages of public conveyances, inns, and places of public amusement.

I am of the opinion that such discrimination practised by corporations and individuals in the exercise of their public or quasi-public functions is a badge of servitude the imposition of which Congress may prevent under its power, by appropriate legislation, to enforce the Thirteenth Amendment; and, consequently, without reference to its enlarged power under the Fourteenth Amendment, the act of March 1, 1875, is not, in my judgment, repugnant to the Constitution.

It remains now to consider these cases with reference to the power Congress has possessed since the adoption of the Fourteenth Amendment. Much that has been said as to the power of Congress under the Thirteenth Amendment is applicable to this branch of the discussion, and will not be repeated.

Before the adoption of the recent amendments, it had become, as we have seen, the established doctrine of this court that negroes, whose ancestors had been imported and sold as slaves, could not become citizens of a State, or even of the United States, with the rights and privileges guaranteed to citizens by the national Constitution; further, that one might have all the rights and privileges of a citizen of a State without being a citizen in the sense in which that word was used in the national Constitution, and without being entitled to the privileges and immunities of citizens of the several States. Still, further, between the adoption of the Thirteenth Amendment and the proposal by Congress of the Fourteenth Amendment, on June 16, 1866, the statute books of several of the States, as we have seen, had become loaded down with enactments which, under the guise of Apprentice, Vagrant, and Contract regulations, sought to keep the colored race in a condition, practically, of servitude. It was openly announced that whatever might be the rights which persons of that race had, as freemen, under the guarantees of the national Constitution, they could not become citizens of a State, with the privileges belonging to citizens, except by the consent of such State; consequently, that their civil rights, as citizens of the State, depended entirely upon State legislation. To meet this new peril to the black race, that the purposes of the nation might not be doubted or defeated, and by way of further enlargement of the power of Congress, the Fourteenth Amendment was proposed for adoption....

But what was secured to colored citizens of the United States—as between them and their respective States—by the national grant to them of State citizenship? With what rights, privileges, or immunities did this grant invest them? There is one, if there be no other—exemption from race discrimination in respect of any civil right belonging to citizens of the white race in the same State. That, surely, is their constitutional privilege when within the jurisdiction of other States. And such must be their constitutional right, in their own State, unless the recent amendments be splendid baubles, thrown out to delude those who deserved fair and generous treatment at the hands of the nation. Citizenship in this country necessarily imports at least equality of civil rights among citizens of every race in the same State. It is fundamental in American citizenship that, in respect of such rights, there shall be no discrimination by the State, or its officers, or by individuals or corporations exercising public functions or authority, against any citizen because of his race or previous condition of servitude....

But if it were conceded that the power of Congress could not be brought into activity until the rights specified in the act of 1875 had been abridged or denied by some State law or State action, I maintain that the decision of the court is erroneous....

In every material sense applicable to the practical enforcement of the Fourteenth Amendment, railroad corporations, keepers of inns, and managers of places of public amusement are agents or instrumentalities of the State, because they are charged with duties to the public, and are amenable, in respect of their duties and functions, to governmental regulation....

My brethren say, that when a man has emerged from slavery, and by the aid of beneficent legislation has shaken off the inseparable concomitants of that state, there must be some stage in the progress of his elevation when he takes the rank of a mere citizen, and ceases to be the special favorite of the laws, and when his rights as a citizen, or a man, are to be protected in the ordinary modes by which other men's rights are protected. It is, I submit, scarcely just to say that the colored race has been the special favorite of the laws. The statute of 1875, now adjudged to be unconstitutional, is for the benefit of citizens of every race and color. What the nation, through Congress, has sought to accomplish in reference to that race, is—what had already been done in every State of the Union for the white race—to secure and protect rights belonging to them as freemen and citizens; nothing more. It was not deemed enough "to help the feeble up, but to support him after." The one underlying purpose of congressional legislation has been to enable the black race to take the rank of mere citizens. The difficulty has been to compel a recognition of the legal right of the black race to take the rank of citizens, and to secure the enjoyment of privileges belonging, under the law, to them as a component part of the people for whose welfare and happiness government is ordained....

✤ DOCUMENT 6

Plessy v. Ferguson, 1896

Mr. Justice Brown ... delivered the opinion of the Court.

This case turns upon the constitutionality of an act of the General Assembly of the State of Louisiana, passed in 1890, providing for separate railway carriages for the white and colored races....

The first section of the statute enacts "that all railway companies carrying passengers in their coaches in this State, shall provide equal but separate accommodations for the white, and colored races, by providing two or more passenger coaches for each passenger train, or by dividing the passenger coaches by a partition so as to secure separate accommodations: *Provided*, That this section shall not be construed to apply to street railroads. No person or persons, shall be admitted to occupy seats in coaches, other than, the ones, assigned, to them on account of the race they belong to." ...

The constitutionality of this act is attacked upon the ground that it conflicts both with the Thirteenth Amendment of the Constitution, abolishing slavery, and the Fourteenth Amendment, which prohibits certain restrictive legislation on the part of the States.

1. That it does not conflict with the Thirteenth Amendment, which abolished slavery and involuntary servitude, except as a punishment for crime, is too clear for argument. Slavery implies involuntary servitude—a state of bondage; the ownership of mankind as a chattel, or at least the control of the labor and services of one man for the benefit of another, and the absence of a legal right to the disposal of his own person, property and services. ...

A statute which implies merely a legal distinction between the white and colored races—a distinction which is founded in the color of the two races, and which must always exist so long as white men are distinguished from the other race by color—has no tendency to destroy the legal equality of the two races, or reëstablish a state of involuntary servitude. Indeed, we do not understand that the Thirteenth Amendment is strenuously relied upon by the plaintiff in error in this connection.

2. By the Fourteenth Amendment, all persons born or naturalized in the United States, and subject to the jurisdiction thereof, are made citizens of the United States and of the State wherein they reside; and the States are forbidden from making or enforcing any law which shall abridge the privileges or immunities of citizens of the United States, or shall deprive any person of life, liberty or property without due process of law, or deny to any person within their jurisdiction the equal protection of the laws.

The proper construction of this amendment was first called to the attention of this court in the *Slaughter-house cases* ..., which involved, however, not a question of race, but one of exclusive privileges. The case did not call for any expression of opinion as to the exact rights it was intended to secure to the colored race, but it was said generally that its main purpose was to establish the citizenship of the negro; to give definitions of citizenship of the United States and of the States, and to protect from the hostile legislation of the States the privileges and immunities of citizens of the United States, as distinguished from those of citizens of the States.

The object of the amendment was undoubtedly to enforce the absolute equality of the two races before the law, but in the nature of things it could not have been intended to abolish distinctions based upon color, or to enforce social, as distinguished from political equality, or a commingling of the two races upon terms unsatisfactory to either. Laws permitting, and even requiring, their separation in places where they are liable to be brought into contact do not necessarily imply the inferiority of either race to the other, and have been generally, if not universally, recognized as within the competency of the state legislatures in the exercise of their police power. The most common instance of this is connected with the establishment of separate schools for white and colored children, which has been held to be a valid exercise of the legislative power even by courts of States where the political rights of the colored race have been longest and most earnestly enforced. ...

While we think the enforced separation of the races, as applied to the internal commerce of the State, neither abridges the privileges or immunities of the colored man, deprives him of his property without due process of law, nor denies him the equal protection of the laws, within the meaning of the Fourteenth Amendment, we are not prepared to say that the conductor, in assigning passengers to the coaches according to their race, does not act at his peril, or that the provision of the second section of the act, that denies to the passenger compensation in damages for a refusal to receive him into the coach in which he properly belongs, is a valid exercise of the legislative power. ...

So far, then, as a conflict with the Fourteenth Amendment is concerned, the case reduces itself to the question whether the statute of Louisiana is a reasonable regulation, and with respect to this there must necessarily be a large discretion on the part of the legislature. In determining the question of reasonableness it is at liberty to act with reference to the established usages, customs and traditions of the people, and with a view to the promotion of their comfort, and the preservation of the public peace and good order. Gauged by this standard, we cannot say that a law which authorizes or even requires the separation of the two races in public conveyances is unreasonable, or more obnoxious to the Fourteenth Amendment than the acts of Congress requiring separate schools for colored children in the District of Columbia, the constitutionality of which does not seem to have been questioned, or the corresponding acts of state legislatures.

We consider the underlying fallacy of the plaintiff's argument to consist in the assumption that the enforced separation of the two races stamps the colored race with a badge of inferiority. If this be so, it is not by reason of anything found in the act, but solely because the colored race chooses to put that construction upon it. The argument necessarily assumes that if, as has been more than once the case, and is not unlikely to be so again, the colored race should become the dominant power in the state legislature, and should enact a law in precisely similar terms, it would thereby relegate the white race to an inferior position. We imagine that the white race, at least, would not acquiesce in this assumption. The argument also assumes that social prejudices may be overcome by legislation, and that equal rights cannot be secured to the negro except by an enforced commingling of the two races. We cannot accept this proposition. If the two races are to meet upon terms of social equality, it must be the result of natural affinities, a mutual appreciation of each other's merits and a voluntary consent of individuals. ... Legislation is powerless to eradicate racial instincts or to abolish distinctions based upon physical differences, and the attempt to do so can only result in accentuating the difficulties of the present situation. If the civil and political rights of both races be equal one cannot be inferior to the other civilly or politically. If one race be inferior to the other socially, the Constitution of the United States cannot put them upon the same plane.

It is true that the question of the proportion of colored blood necessary to constitute a colored person, as distinguished from a white person, is one upon which there is a difference of opinion in the different States, some holding that any visible admixture of black blood stamps the person as belonging to the colored race ...; others that it depends upon the preponderance of blood ...; and still others that the predominance of white blood must only be in the proportion of three fourths. ... But these are questions to be determined under the laws of each State and are not properly put in issue in this case. Under the allegations of his petition it may undoubtedly become a question of importance whether, under the laws of Louisiana, the petitioner belongs to the white or colored race.

The judgment of the court below is, therefore, *Affirmed.*

Mr. Justice Harlan dissenting.

... In respect of civil rights, common to all citizens, the Constitution of the United States does not, I think, permit any public authority to know the race of those entitled to be protected in the enjoyment of such rights. Every true man has pride of race, and under appropriate circumstances when the rights of others, his equals before the law, are not to be affected, it is his privilege to express such pride and to take such action based upon it as to him seems proper. But I deny that any legislative body or judicial tribunal may have regard to the race of citizens when the civil rights of those citizens are involved. Indeed, such legislation, as that here in question, is inconsistent not only with that equality of rights which pertains to citizenship, National and State, but with the personal liberty enjoyed by every one within the United States.

The Thirteenth Amendment does not permit the withholding or the deprivation of any right necessarily inhering in freedom. It not only struck down the institution of slavery as previously existing in the United States, but it prevents the imposition of any burdens or disabilities that constitute badges of slavery or servitude. It decreed universal civil freedom in this country. This court has so adjudged. But that amendment having been found inadequate to the protection of the rights of those who had been in slavery, it was followed by the Fourteenth Amendment, which added greatly to the dignity and glory of American citizenship, and to the security of personal liberty, by declaring that "all persons born or naturalized in the United States, and subject to the jurisdiction thereof, are citizens of the United States and of the State wherein they reside," and that "no State shall make or enforce any law which shall abridge the privileges or immunities of citizens of the United States; nor shall any State deprive any person of life, liberty or property without due process of law, nor deny to any person within its jurisdiction the equal protection of the laws." These two amendments, if enforced according to their true intent and meaning, will protect all the civil rights that pertain to freedom and citizenship....

These notable additions to the fundamental law were welcomed by the friends of liberty throughout the world. They removed the race line from our governmental systems. They had, as this court has said, a common purpose, namely, to secure "to a race recently emancipated, a race that through many generations have been held in slavery, all the civil rights that the superior race enjoy." They declared, in legal effect, this court has further said, "that the law in the States shall be the same for the black as for the white; that all persons, whether colored or white, shall stand equal before the laws of the States, and, in regard to the colored race, for whose protection the amendment was primarily designed, that no discrimination shall be made against them by law because of their color." ...

The white race deems itself to be the dominant race in this country. And so it is, in prestige, in achievements, in education, in wealth and in power. So, I doubt not, it will continue to be for all time, if it remains true to its great heritage and holds fast to the principles of constitutional liberty. But in view of the Constitution, in the eye of the law, there is in this country no superior, dominant, ruling class of citizens. There is no caste here. Our Constitution is color-blind, and neither knows nor tolerates classes among citizens. In respect of civil rights, all citizens are equal before the law. The humblest is the peer of the most powerful. The law regards man as man, and takes no account of his surroundings or of his color when his civil rights as guaranteed by the supreme law of the land are involved. It is, therefore, to be regretted that this high tribunal, the final expositor of the fundamental law of the land, has reached the conclusion that it is competent for a State to regulate the enjoyment by citizens of their civil rights solely upon the basis of race.

In my opinion, the judgment this day rendered will, in time, prove to be quite as pernicious as the decision made by this tribunal in the *Dred Scott case*....

✥ *E S S A Y S*

Scholars have vigorously debated the extent to which the framers of the Reconstruction amendments sought to alter the existing relationship between the national government and the states. In the first essay, Akhil Reed Amar, a professor at Yale Law School, characterizes the Reconstruction amendments as revolutionary. Only during Reconstruction did the first ten amendments to the Constitution take on the label and the status of a self-contained "Bill of Rights," he argues, thanks largely to Ohio Congressman John A. Bingham's efforts. Bingham and the other framers of the Fourteenth Amendment, Amar believes, transformed existing notions of federalism and individual rights. In the second selection, Michael Les Benedict, an emeritus professor of history at Ohio State University, takes a more skeptical view of Republicans' intentions. Benedict argues that, although they brought about a social revolution through abolition, Republicans were concerned about "outrunning public opinion" on the issue of civil rights. They thus sought to preserve the essential features of the federal system. Finally, Joan Hoff, an emeritus professor of history at Montana State University, shows the utter unresponsiveness of the Supreme Court to the rights of women, even in light of the passage of the Fourteenth Amendment. Traditional notions of federalism and gender combined to thwart the efforts of women activists in court.

Reconstruction and the Birth of the Bill of Rights

AKHIL REED AMAR

Clause by clause, amendment by amendment, the Bill of Rights was refined and strengthened in the crucible of the 1860s. Indeed, the very phrase *bill of rights* as a description of the first ten (or nine, or eight) amendments was forged anew in these years.

Here, then, is a remarkable fact: before the adoption of the Fourteenth Amendment, the Supreme Court never—not once—referred to the 1791 decalogue as "the" or "a" "bill of rights." Yet within a few years of John Bingham's odes to the Bill, the Court began to adopt Bingham's terminology. Contrarians like Bingham helped change the vocabulary of legal discourse—and ultimately changed its substance and structure.

The 1807 Supreme Court case of *Ex parte Burford* epitomized High Court terminology in the *Barron* era. Note the obvious contrast of language as Chief Justice Marshall quoted warrant-limiting clauses from the Virginia and federal Constitutions, respectively: "By the 10th article of the *bill of rights* of Virginia it is declared [quotation].... By the [original] 6th [that is, our 4th] *article of amendments to the Constitution of the United States*, it is declared [quotation]." In the 1833 case of *Livingston v. Moore*, which applied *Barron*'s rule to the Fourth and Seventh Amendments, the Supreme Court likewise referred to the "ninth article of the amendments of the Constitution of the United States and the sixth section of the Pennsylvania bill of rights." Antebellum state court usage often followed a similar pattern: when in 1841 the Massachusetts Supreme Judicial Court unselfconsciously referred to "the bill of rights," it obviously meant the *state's* bill.

When the antebellum Supreme Court discussed the first ten amendments as a set, if often did so in ways that emphasized their protections of states' rights. Consider, for example, two cases reaffirming *Barron: Fox v. Ohio* and *Withers v. Buckley*. In *Fox*, decided in 1847, the Court reaffirmed that the initial "*amendments* to the constitution ... were not designed as limits on the State governments. ... They are exclusively restrictions upon *federal* power, intended to prevent interference with *the rights of the States*, and of their citizens." *Withers*, decided a decade later, echoed all this, stylistically and substantively: "The *amendments* thus adopted were designed to be modifications of the powers vested in the *Federal* Government [only. ... The Fifth Amendment] was applicable to the Federal Government alone, and not to the States, *except so far as it was designed for their security against Federal power*." In 1841, an attorney before the Court did use the phrase *bill of rights*, but he, too, linked the early amendments to states' rights: "[Antifederalists criticized the] want of a bill of rights, similar to that subsequently adopted by the ten amendments to the constitution, and *especially the tenth*. ..."

Rhetoric and substance mutually reinforced. If one saw Amendments I-X as largely sounding in federalism, deeply protective of states' rights, and thus inapplicable against state governments, these amendments really weren't like state bills of rights protecting citizens. Conversely, to a contrarian, the amendments declared fundamental freedoms of all Americans, and the set thus *was* like a state bill of rights, and thus *did* apply (in a suitably refined way) against states.

These are precisely the rhetorical battle lines that shaped debate over the anti-*Barron* amendment in the Thirty-ninth Congress. Contrarians repeatedly appealed to "the bill of rights"—a phrase that John Bingham invoked more than a dozen times in a single day. And here are the words of Bingham's fellow Republican Robert Hale: "Now, what are these amendments to the Constitution, numbered from one to ten, one of which is the fifth article in question? ... They constitute the bill of rights, a bill of rights for the protection of the citizen, and defining and limiting the power of Federal and State legislation." In a similar vein, leading contrarians like Representatives James Wilson and William Lawrence and Senator Jacob Howard all spoke of "the" or "a" "bill of rights."

Opponents spoke a very different language. Democrat Michael Kerr cited both *Barron* and *Fox* and twice referred to "the first eleven amendments," which he defined as "limitations upon the power of Congress and not upon the powers of the States. They are not guarantees at all, except to protect the States against the usurpations of Congress and the General Government. They simply say that Congress shall not invade the rights of the States. ..." Likewise, Democratic Representative Andrew Jackson Rogers, after paraphrasing *Barron* and its progeny, refrained from calling the amendments a bill of rights and instead labeled them "clauses of the Constitution of the United States."

When we move outside Congress, we see a similar rhetorical pattern among Reconstruction commentators. Contrarian commentator Timothy Farrar described the initial amendments as "in the nature of a bill of rights," and his fellow contrarian and treatise writer John Norton Pomeroy referred even less self-consciously to "our national bill of rights."

Apparently all this Republican "bill of rights" talk in the air in 1866–68 began to waft in the direction of the Supreme Court. ... By the 1890s, this rhetorical trickle had swelled into a steady stream of references to the "first ten amendments ... in the nature of a bill of rights" to protect "persons and property" and "unalienable rights", to "provisions in the nature of a Bill of Rights" "securing to every individual" "rights of the citizen," some of which traced back to "the days of Magna Charta"; to "the first ten amendments to the Constitution, commonly known as the Bill of Rights," which "embod[ied] certain guaranties and immunities which we had inherited from our English ancestors"; to "the earliest amendments to the Constitution of the United States, in the nature of a Bill of Rights"; and so on. In 1900, we find the phrase, "the National Bill of Rights," appearing no fewer than four times in a single opinion—Justice Harlan's great dissent in *Maxwell v. Dow*. Gone was the view, publicly expressed by Supreme Court Justice Samuel F. Miller as late as 1880, that "our Constitution, unlike most modern ones, does not contain any formal declaration or bill of rights." ...

The conventional narrative focuses on those present at the Creation—on the hasty oversights and omissions in the last days of a hot summer in Philadelphia; on the centrality of the (absence of a) Bill of Rights in ratification debates; and on the quick repair worked by the First Congress, fixing in place the keystone of the arch of liberty. And we all lived happily ever after.

There is some truth in this stock story so far as it goes, but it doesn't go far enough. Most dramatically, it ignores all the ways in which the Reconstruction generation—not their Founding fathers or grandfathers—took a crumbling and somewhat obscure edifice, placed it on new, high ground, and remade it so that it truly would stand as a temple of liberty and justice for all.

We would do well to remember that a separate Bill of Rights was no part of Madison's carefully conceived original plan at Philadelphia. To some extent, his ultimate sponsorship of the Bill must be seen as a sop—a peace offering—to Anti-Federalists, and many in the First Congress were relatively uninterested in the Bill, finding it a "nauseous" distraction. John Bingham, by contrast, placed the Bill of Rights at the center of his thinking about constitutionalism; his speeches in the Thirty-ninth Congress are far more inspired, and perhaps more inspiring, than Madison's in the First.

Mid-twentieth-century skeptics worried aloud that incorporation would ultimately weaken the Bill of Rights. If the Bill were to be applied against the states, the argument went, it would need to be watered down to take account of the considerable diversity of state practice; and then in turn, the federal government would be held to only this watered-down version. In a couple of doctrinal corners, this fear has been borne out. For example, in a series of preincorporation dissents, Justices Black and Douglas insisted that federal criminal contempt, as then defined, could not be deemed a "petty" offense unprotected by the Constitution's twin jury commands (in Article III and the Sixth Amendment). But the very day the Sixth Amendment was incorporated against states in *Duncan v. Louisiana*, Black and Douglas seemed to pull their punches in a companion case, arising out of a *state* criminal contempt prosecution; they now joined a Court opinion that recognized a sizable "petty crime" exception to jury trial. *Duncan* itself explicitly signaled the possible causal link between incorporation and watering-down with the following ominous observation: "It seems very unlikely to us that our decision today will require widespread changes in state criminal processes. First, our decisions interpreting the Sixth Amendment are always subject to reconsideration." The upshot of all this became clear over the next decade when the Court, responding to the variety of state jury practice, implausibly held that the Sixth Amendment did not really require twelve-person juries—a view that cut against a near-universal assumption of every justice who had addressed the issue prior to *Duncan*.

But to dwell on the few doctrinal corners where the anti-incorporation Cassandras proved right is to miss the much larger story on the other side: extension of the Bill of Rights against the states has, in general, dramatically strengthened the Bill, not weakened it, in both legal doctrine and popular consciousness. Unused muscles atrophy, while those that are regularly put to use grow strong. In the first century of our nation's existence, the Bill of Rights played a surprisingly trivial role: only once before 1866 was it used by the Supreme Court to invalidate federal action, and that one use was *Dred Scott's* highly implausible and strikingly casual claim that the Fifth Amendment due-process clause invalidated free-soil territory laws like the Northwest Ordinance and the Missouri Compromise. In a review of newspapers published in 1841, Dean Robert Reinstein could find not a single fiftieth anniversary celebration of the Bill of Rights.

In area after area, incorporation enabled judges first to invalidate state and local laws—and then, with this doctrinal base thus built up, to begin to keep Congress in check. Countless examples could be offered, but our First Amendment is perhaps the best. Before 1925, when the Court began in earnest the process of First Amendment incorporation, free speech had never prevailed against a repressive statute in the United States Supreme Court. (And although no case ever reached the Supreme Court, we should recall that no federal judge in the 1790s ever invalidated the infamous Sedition Act of 1798.) Within a few years of incorporation, however, freedom of expression and religion began to win in cases involving states like Kansas (*Fiske*, 1927), California (*Stromberg*, 1931), Minnesota (*Near*, 1931), and Connecticut (*Cantwell*, 1940). These and other cases began to build up a First Amendment tradition, in and out of court, and that tradition could then be used against even federal officials. Not until 1965 did the Supreme Court strike down an act of Congress on First Amendment grounds, and when it did so, it relied squarely on doctrine built up in earlier cases involving states. Consider also the more recent flag-burning cases. The Supreme Court laid down the requisite doctrine in a 1989 case involving a Texas statute and then, in 1990, stood its ground on precisely that doctrine to strike down an act of Congress.

This swelling body of legal doctrine has spilled out of courtrooms and soaked into the vocabulary and worldview of law students, journalists, activists, and ultimately the citizenry at large. But without incorporation, and the steady flow of cases created by state and local laws, the Supreme Court would have had far fewer opportunities to be part of the ongoing American conversation about liberty. Here, too, we see that the central role of the Bill of Rights today owes at least as much to the Reconstruction as to the Creation.

In both legal and popular culture, notions of individual and minority rights loom large today. Conventional wisdom attributes these themes to the Founders' Bill; but as we have seen, this conventional story misreads the Creation and misses the Reconstruction. James Madison did believe in strong individual rights; in many ways, however, he was ahead of his time, and the First Congress did not always share his vision. Bingham and the Thirty-ninth Congress did embrace individualism, but the conventional narrative uses Madison as an anachronistic trope in lieu of Bingham. Congressman Madison first proposed a "No State shall" Fourteenth Amendment, so we tend to slight the later Congressman who actually got his own "No State shall" Fourteenth Amendment enacted. Madison was antiestablishment, so the original First Amendment was too, we tell ourselves. Madison thought that property rights were central, so the takings clause was paradigmatic of the Founding era, we think. Madison stressed federal protection of minority rights in *The Federalist* No. 10, so this now-classic text must always have been canonical, we suppose. Madison spoke of the role of judges, so the original Bill of Rights was judge-centric, we assume. On all these points, and many others, we might do well to study John Bingham more, and lift some of the load from James Madison's stooped shoulders.

A further point: modern academic discourse about the Bill of Rights is unreflectively clausebound. Yet this discourse ignores the ways in which the Bill is, well, a *bill*—a set of interconnected provisions. There is some irony here. Madison stressed the didactic role that a bill of rights could play, yet his original planned amendments would have scattered various provisions throughout the original document. Only late in the process—and over Madison's objections—were his proposed amendments recast into a single set to be placed together at the end of the original Constitution. When, providentially, only ten amendments were ratified in the 1790s, the ultimate effect was to create a kind of decalogue—ten commandments—whose whole was greater than the sum of its parts. In real estate, the three most important things are location, location, and location; a nice house gains value when it sits next to other nice houses. So, too, each clause of the early amendments gains by its proximity to the others. No one understood this better than John Bingham and his fellow contrarians. Whereas others spoke of discrete "articles of amendment," he and they holistically insisted on the centrality of the "*Bill* of Rights," exemplifying a unified theory of liberty.

The modern notion of a self-contained federal bill of rights thus derives at least as much from Bingham as from Madison. The federal Constitution contains no explicit caption introducing a "bill of rights"—unlike many early state constitution, which feature a self-styled "declaration of rights" preceding an explicit "frame of government." And because the first ten federal amendments ultimately came in as appendixes rather than as a preface, still later amendments had the effect of pushing the early amendments to the middle—ten early postscripts before later post-postscripts. It was Bingham's generation that in effect added a closing parenthesis after the first eight (or nine, or ten) amendments, distinguishing *these* amendments from all others. As a result, Americans today can lay claim to a federal "*Bill* of Rights" set apart from everything else, and symbolically first even if textually middling.

This brings us to our last point; for Bingham and others also insisted that the early amendments were largely a "Bill of *Rights*"—of persons, not states. Today's conventional wisdom sharply distinguishes between structural issues and rights issues. Here, too, this distinction is attributed to the Founders—their Constitution delineated structure; their Bill, rights. But once again this conventional account misreads the Founding and misses the Reconstruction. Structure and rights tightly intertwined in the original Constitution and in the original Bill, which themselves tightly intertwined. The basic need to separate rights from structure comes from the Fourteenth Amendment itself—from the need for a suitable filter that enables incorporation to mine and refine rights from the mixed ore in which these rights were initially embedded in the Founders' quarry. Although incorporation does require us to separate rights from structure for some purposes, it does not require us to ignore the subtle interplay between them for other purposes; indeed, a suitably refined model should highlight this interplay. . . .

Even as we celebrate the Founders, we must ponder the sobering words of Charles Cotesworth Pinckney in the 1788 South Carolina ratifying debates: "Another reason weighed particularly, with the members from this state, against the insertion of a bill of rights. Such bills generally begin with declaring that all men are by nature born free. Now, we should make that declaration with a very bad grace, when a large part of our property consists in men who are actually born slaves."

But the Reconstruction Amendment did begin with an affirmation of the freedom, and citizenship, of all. Those who birthed it renounced the Slave Power and all its works. These midwives were women alongside men, blacks alongside whites. After their mighty labors, more work did remain to be done—more work always remains to be done, if all are to be free and equal. But because of these men and women, our Bill of Rights was reborn.

The Conservative Basis of Radical Reconstruction

MICHAEL LES BENEDICT

[T]he Republican Party's rise to dominance in the northern states and its victory in the presidential election of 1860 portended a constitutional revolution—an effort to transform the slaveholding republic to one consistent with the Declaration's promise of liberty and equality. Southerners were fully aware of the significance of the change. They seceded from a Union whose constitution promised to be radically transformed from the one they had known. The Civil War both speeded the process and made it even more radical than it would have been had southerners resisted within the system. No longer accommodating slavery, with the Thirteenth Amendment the Constitution became a document of freedom. Not content simply to reinterpret its existing language in light of this transformation, Republicans explicitly incorporated the change into the document itself through the Fourteenth and Fifteenth Amendments. It was a profound transformation that changed the nature of the republic.

Yet African Americans were denied the equal rights of citizenship for another century, and other racial disparities persist to this day. Historians have wondered what went wrong. What emerged from the Civil War era was not racial justice, much less racial equality. . . .

From Michael Les Benedict, *Preserving the Constitution: Essays on Politics and the Constitution in the Reconstruction Era.* Reproduced with permission of Fordham University Press.

Historians offer two not inconsistent explanations for the failure to carry the transformation to its logical fruition: (1) persistent racism in the North undermined commitment to a new racially egalitarian order, and (2) a conservative reaction against northern working-class militancy undermined support for black workers and their political representatives in the South. But while these factors were important, historians of Reconstruction have tended to slight another crucial element. This factor was a persistent concern with federalism—maintaining a proper balance between the responsibilities of the state and federal governments—and a corresponding reluctance to arm the federal government with the powers necessary to protect the rights now guaranteed to all.

Legal and constitutional historians have paid more attention to this factor than other historians have, but they have attributed this concern with federalism primarily to the justices of the Supreme Court, whose perverse commitment to state rights, if not to white supremacy, subverted the radical constitutional transformation Republicans had tried to bring about. It was, as one has written, the most "striking instance in American constitutional history of outright judicial disregard for congressional intent."

This understanding is based on a conviction that Republican Reconstruction legislation reflected a popular, or at least congressional, commitment to a transformation of federalism as part of the longer transformation from a slaveholding to a free republic. ... But while Republicans knew that abolition had radically altered the constitutional system by rededicating the nation to freedom, they were deeply ambivalent about the implications of what they had done and were plainly worried about outrunning public opinion. Having transformed American constitutionalism—and indeed American society—they wanted to retain the essentials of the federal system. Their problem was how to do so and at the same time protect the rights of the people they had freed from slavery.

Facing this dilemma, Republicans opted to expand national power to protect rights whenever events forced them to. But they did so reluctantly and still attempting to preserve the traditional constitutional order of federalism as much as possible. Their rhetoric indicates that they understood the political danger of doing otherwise. They were not merely acting on their own preferences, but the preferences of the people they represented. No matter how radical it was culturally and socially, from a constitutional perspective, Negro suffrage was conservative.

Persisting commitment to federalism helps explain why Reconstruction failed to achieve its goals and why so many Republicans appeared so quickly to abandon the struggle after 1869.

Republicans' constitutional justification for their Reconstruction program indicates that it is an oversimplification to accuse them of abandoning Reconstruction. The reluctance of many Republicans to interfere in the South was manifest in their program itself. They insisted on guarantees for the security of loyal whites and blacks; they passed laws and constitutional amendments that delegated power to the national government to secure basic rights. But most Republicans did not want to displace state and local governments as the primary protectors of the ordinary rights of their citizens. Coping with a revolutionary situation, Republicans framed the most limited Reconstruction they could and still secure meaningful freedom in the South. Until 1868, Republicans adhered to the position that their legislation was merely a temporary aberration in the federal system. They hoped to alter both southern politics and federal law in such a way as to minimize the need for continued federal action to protect rights. When persistent violence forced Republicans to advocate long-term federal action to protect rights, most still tried to limit its scope, and some refused to make this new departure at all.

Suggesting that Republicans were concerned with maintaining the traditional federal system is controversial, because the understanding of those who framed the Reconstruction-era constitutional amendments and civil rights legislation has implications for present-day constitutional law. The understanding or intention with which Americans framed and ratified constitutional amendments and the intent of legislators when they enact statutes is a significant source of legal authority for their interpretation. Indeed, some constitutional theorists argue that original intent is determinative. Suggesting that Republicans were less than fully committed to transferring the primary responsibility for protecting rights to the federal government provides ammunition for those trying to limit the federal role today.

Because of the legal implications, a number of legal analysts researching Reconstruction have done so primarily to divine the original intent or understanding of the Fourteenth Amendment. Of course, they have reached widely disparate conclusions. Academic historians are hardly surprised. Historical actors are rarely as clear about their own intentions and understandings as legal analysts would like, and historical evidence does not lend itself to interpretative certainty. Historians take complexity and ambiguity as the norm; they expect legal interpretations of legislation to be contested and resolved over time. Interrogating history for the purpose of discovering an "original intent" or "original understanding" requires the investigator to reduce complexity and arrive at a best answer. This purpose can significantly influence research methods, making them quite different from those of academic historians.

Playing for high present-day stakes, legal analysts who stress the radicalism of Reconstruction-era civil rights legislation tend to concentrate on the logical implications of the Civil War constitutional transformation, often ignoring Republicans' efforts to reassure their constituents of their moderation. Measured against the antebellum, proslavery Constitution, the Republican effort to reshape southern society and protect the rights of American citizens—indeed recognizing African Americans as citizens at all—*was* radical, and everyone knew it. The question was, how far would the old landmarks be obliterated? Engaged in a great constitutional transformation, Republicans sought to reassure their constituents of their continued commitment to constitutionalism and the federal system. . . .

The desire to preserve the federal system's prewar balance weighed heavily on the minds of leading Republicans. As early as 1861, a worried Republican Senator James W. Grimes wrote fellow Senator Lyman Trumbull, "We are gradually surrendering all the rights of the states & functions & shall soon be incapable of resuming them." Five years later, as one of the respected members of the prestigious Joint Committee of Fifteen on Reconstruction, Grimes was insisting that "During the prevalence of the war we drew to ourselves here as the Federal Government authority which had been considered doubtful by all and denied by many of the statesmen of this country. That time, it seems to me, has ceased and ought to case. Let us go back to the original condition of things, and allow the States to take care of themselves as they have been in the habit of taking care of themselves."

This kind of constitutional conservatism left Republicans ill prepared to cope with the complex problems of Reconstruction, which so clearly called at minimum for long-term national protection of citizens' rights. By 1865 Republicans had become so committed to the proposition that the national government's power would shrink to prewar dimensions at war's end that an immediate recognition of continued southern statehood upon the surrender of the rebel armies would have restored prewar state rights virtually intact, rendering the national government powerless to secure any guarantees of loyalty from the South. Because during the war Republicans had refused to acquiesce in a permanent expansion of national power at the expense of the states, in 1865 and 1866 they were forced to deny that the southern political organizations were as yet entitled to the rights of states. Therefore, the great controversy between President Andrew Johnson and his supporters and the Republican Party centered on the constitutional issue of the status of the former southern states. ...

Having defined the status of the rebel states in a way that denied them immediate restoration to prewar rights, Republicans turned to three sources of national power over them. Stevens enunciated one alternative, suggesting that "as there are no symptoms that the people of these provinces will be prepared to participate in constitutional government for some years, I know of no arrangement so proper for them as territorial governments." "They would be held in a territorial condition until they are fit to form State Constitutions, republican in fact not in form only, and ask admission into the Union as new States," he suggested. ...

Although many radicals preferred Stevens's territorial policy to establish congressional control over the South, his program met with such a negative response from more centrist Republicans that when he presented a Reconstruction bill to the House in 1867 it bore no resemblance to his earlier suggestion.

Republicans discerned a second source of congressional power over Reconstruction in Congress's war powers. Building consciously on the legal-constitutional justifications for expanded national power developed during the war, these Republicans suggested that although peace would indeed restore the sway of peacetime constitutional limitations, it was up to the government to decide precisely when peace had arrived. In this case, the government might demand that the rebel states meet certain conditions in return for recognition that peace was restored. This view was popularized by the conservative Richard Henry Dana in a speech delivered in Boston's Faneuil Hall on June 21, 1865: "The conquering party may hold the other in the grasp of war until it has secured whatever it has a right to acquire," he maintained. This theory was received with favor in Boston. Ohio's new governor, Jacob D. Cox; House speaker Schuyler Colfax; William Pitt Fessenden, Republican leader in the Senate and the chairman of the Joint Committee on Reconstruction; Representative George S. Boutwell, also named to the Reconstruction Committee; Representative William Lawrence of the House Judiciary Committee, and the influential German Republican leader Carl Schurz all expressed views similar to Dana's. ...

So, like Stevens's territorial scheme, the grasp-of-war policy gave no permanent power to Congress. Dana's friend John Bigelow, American minister to France, recognized the weakness of the theory immediately: There was nothing to prevent a southern state from reneging on its agreements once restored to normal relations in the Union. Dana acknowledged the danger but believed it was the best the North could do. Dana had proposed a consciously conservative program. As he wrote to

Charles Francis Adams Jr. immediately after his speech, "It would be an irreparable mischief for Congress to assume civil and political authority in state matters, but it is not an irreparable mischief for the general government to continue the exercise of such war powers as are necessary until the people of those States do what we in conscience think necessary for the reasonable security of the republic." ...

Republicans found a third source of congressional power in the duty the Constitution imposed on the national government to guarantee republican forms of government to the states. Republicans who argued that the southern states had ceased to exist during the war particularly favored this theory. If there were no state governments at all in the South, then "manifestly, the first step after the war ended was for someone to establish a local government there." And this duty the Guarantee Clause placed on the national government.

This was the only constitutional basis for Reconstruction that could promise the national government permanent power after the rebel states were restored to normal relations. Some Republicans felt it assumed a standard of republicanism and gave the national government power to enforce that standard whenever a state—any state— fell short of it. But few Republicans endorsed such a radical expansion of national power. In 1867 the House of Representatives agreed to a resolution instructing the Judiciary Committee to investigate "whether the States of Kentucky, Maryland, and Delaware now have State governments republican in form." Such resolutions normally passed without Republican opposition as they embodied no actual legislation, but on this occasion twenty-two Republicans joined Democrats in opposition. The committee took testimony and evidence but let the matter die. Several Republicans proposed bills based on the Guarantee Clause in efforts to extend universal male suffrage and protect its exercise throughout the Union, but none passed or even won endorsement by a committee.

Although Republicans regularly pointed to the Guarantee Clause as somehow sanctioning their Reconstruction policy in campaign speeches, they were reluctant to base their actual legislation on it. Instead they referred to the clause as setting a standard that southern states had to meet to be released from the grasp of war. Most Republicans relied on the grasp-of-war doctrine to justify their Reconstruction legislation, and in so doing they employed the narrowest, most conservative theory of the three available—the one that virtually sanctified "the federal system as it was."

Republicans twice formulated conditions for the southern states to meet before Congress would recognize their restoration. Each time they conditioned restoration on the voluntary passage of state legislation, stolidly preserving the states as the primary authors of legislation, firmly refusing to force compliance through exercise of national power. And southern reaction demonstrated that this "voluntarism" was more than illusory. ...

Only as the Reconstruction process neared completion did many Republicans finally realize its essential weakness. As southerners met Congress's conditions and pressed for restoration in 1868, Republicans suspected that their compliance with the Reconstruction Acts was more apparent than real. "You are hastening back States where rebelism is pervading them from end to end," complained an outspoken radical. The grasp-of-war theory had worked too well, perhaps. In many states southerners had met the conditions set forth in the Reconstruction acts not out of reawakened loyalty or a new commitment to racial justice but out of a simple desire to be rid of the national presence. Radicals who recognized the weakness of the loyal forces in the South urged delay in restoration. In reality, "there are not ten men in this Senate who believe it is a safe thing to do at this time," Timothy Otis Howe warned. Other radical Republicans agreed, but political necessities required readmission.

Realizing the futility of trying to delay restoration, many Republicans finally decided on an effort to guarantee permanence to the new political order in the South. As a new fundamental condition, Republicans insisted southern states agree never to alter the basis of suffrage in their new constitutions, moving to insert the requirement in the legislation restoring most of the southern states to normal relations. This time they eschewed the constraining grasp-of-war theory as a justification. Hoping to establish a basis for ongoing federal power to fasten black suffrage on the South, some turned to the Guarantee Clause for constitutional authority. The power to guarantee republican forms of government to the states was "plenary and absolute," insisted Senator George F. Edmunds. Therefore Congress clearly had the authority "to put that government in such a form that it shall 'stay put.'" But the Guarantee Clause justification implied a sweeping alteration in national-state relations. Illinois Senator Richard Yates made clear just how sweeping when he argued that it made Congress the final arbiter of voting qualifications:

> When the question arises whether a constitution is republican in form, who decides it? Congress. May not Congress say that no constitution is republican in form which excludes any large class of people from voting ... ?
>
> If New York excludes any portion of her citizens who bear arms and pay taxes from the right of suffrage, here is not, according to our republican theory, a government republican in form. Congress, not the States, decide that question.

Worried that Democrats would charge Republicans with intending to impose black suffrage on the North, most Republicans recoiled from so radical a proposition. William M. Stewart, the second-ranking Republican on the Senate Judiciary Committee, drew a parallel between the restoration of the southern states and the admission of new states. Congress had regularly exacted concessions from petitioning territories in return for grants of statehood, he pointed out. But would Congress be authorized to take action if a state repudiated such a condition? In the end, even Stewart had to concede that it would not. "I do not pretend to say that the insertion of this declaration in the bill [to restore the southern states] will alter either the constitution of the State or of the General Government." It was merely "a declaration of principle, which has generally been respected."

This timorous attempt to provide permanent national power to protect rights precipitated the first of the series of intra-Republican confrontations on constitutional questions that would mark Reconstruction legislation of the post-1868 era. Conservative constitutionalists in the Republican Party, including Fessenden, Trumbull, and Conkling, the very architects of congressional Reconstruction, were unprepared to cooperate in this new attempt to limit state prerogatives....

Surveying the wreckage of Republican Reconstruction policy in the late 1870s, ex-President Ulysses S. Grant concluded that, after all, "the wisest thing would have been to continue for some time the military rule" over the South. "I am clear now it would have been better for the North to have postponed suffrage, reconstruction, State governments, for ten years and held the South in a territorial condition." But despite radicals' advocacy of that course, it had never really been an option. "Our people did not like it. It was not in accord with our institutions." Quoting Grant's insight, historian Brooks Simpson points out the immutable fact: Republicans were limited by "Americans' commitment to civil government and federalism." "For many people, 'reconstruction' was primarily the restoration of loyal civil government, pure and simple. However much one wants to debate the extent to which congressional proposals were conservative or revolutionary, they all looked to this end, one way or another. In turn, that restricted what one could do to protect black rights."

Yet the constitutional conservatism of Republican Reconstruction should not be overstated. Whatever their desire to maintain the contours of the traditional federal system, Republican civil right legislation and the Fourteenth and Fifteenth Amendments made clear that the Constitution created a republic dedicated to freedom, not slavery. Republicans undermined their own efforts by their dedication to federalism, and the Supreme Court went even further in doing so. But it was these decisions that ultimately proved anomalous in a freedom-loving republic. It took nearly a century, but present-day advocates of broad national power to protect rights may exaggerate the degree to which Republicans were committed to a "revolutionary constitutionalism," but they are right that the bolder steps that radical Republicans advocated would have been consistent with the constitutional transformation of the Civil War era—more consistent than those actually undertaken. And that may be the true lesson for Americans today.

The Supreme Court's Denial of the Rights of Women

JOAN HOFF

... For the first time beginning in the early 1870s, women systematically tried to obtain constitutional equality and full citizenship from the courts by challenging the remaining common-law restrictions on them. While this rights-consciousness campaign of the First Feminists did not succeed, their attempts in retrospect are significant for a number of reasons. First, the major female reconstruction cases indicate that women altered not only the texts but also the contexts of legal discourse in their briefs and legislative appeals to be included as part of "We, the people." They found judges and elected officials unresponsive to their awakened sense of constitutionalism not only because it threatened their patriarchal hegemony, but also because it exposed the inherent contradictions in liberal legalism that had relegated women to second-class citizenship since the American Revolution. Second, judicial patterns or preferences that emerged by 1900 from these negative reconstruction decisions lingered for many years—some down to the present. Third, as I first pointed out in 1976, there was also a subtle interaction (and potential contradiction) between the collective political and individualistic legal activities of women reformers during this period, which new scholarship since then has helped to disentangle.

From Hoff, *Law, Gender, and Injustice: A Legal History of U.S. Women.* Published by New York University Press, 2001. Reproduced with permission of the publisher.

It is now possible to trace how these two types of activity on the part of women varied *according to the intensity of their legal-rights consciousness at any given time.* In fact, it can be argued that to the degree that the courts discouraged women from pursuing full citizenship through constitutional equality, they took political action as a form of compensation. Such compensatory political actions, although better organized and orchestrated than some of their legal initiatives, were often more typically conservative in nature than their court cases appeared to be. However, the litigation of these early feminists in behalf of specific individual rights also represented a compromise with the male legal system, rather than a frontal attack on it. A similar, but possibly less obvious, seesaw relationship between political and legal action continues to exist today because women have still to find acceptance for a feminist jurisprudence that does not require their assimilation as a group in return for equality as individual citizens. Reconstruction provided the first opportunity for women to try to reconcile the "inherited libertarian rhetoric" of "possessive individualism" with "collective organization and collective identities." In retrospect, their failure is not as much a surprise as is the degree to which they succeeded in reviving the First Women's movement and in laying a legal discursive foundation from which to argue for their own equality.

The legal system in this ... period of constitutional discrimination successfully thwarted the newly articulated rights struggle on the part of post—Civil War feminists by simply refusing to address the central issue: to what extent should women be regarded as persons and, therefore, full citizens in the eyes of the Constitution? Instead, judges evaded this legal determination by handing down decisions based on traditional pre- and postrevolutionary stereotypes about women. Supreme Court decisions following the Civil War specifically classified women as other than full citizens of the United States and cast serious doubt on their legal capacities as persons. ...

From 1865 to 1908, only two cases involving the exclusion of women from the practice of law reached the Supreme Court of the United States. The best known was Bradwell v. Illinois, ... Myra Colby Bradwell, an avowed suffragist and champion of women's legal rights, had studied law under her husband, Judge James B. Bradwell, and passed the Illinois bar examination in 1869 only to be denied admission to that bar because she was married. Myra Bradwell specifically sought redress through the benefit of the privileges-and-immunities clause of the first section of the Fourteenth Amendment. Despite the precedent that had been set earlier in the year by the *Mansfield* case in Iowa, courts in Illinois based their refusal to allow her to practice law on Blackstone's idea that a married woman was not competent to perform such duties as making contracts, which an attorney would have to do. This argument about her common-law disabilities was totally inapplicable because Myra Bradwell had been making contracts and acting in other official, legal capacities as president of a publishing company in Illinois and as founder and editor of the most important legal publication in the West and Midwest, the *Chicago Legal News*. In fact, the state had granted her a special charter to engage in such legal activities. Yet, the Illinois Supreme Court said she was not qualified to act in a similar capacity as a lawyer.

When the case came before the Supreme Court of the United States, Justice Miller, writing for the majority, ignored the lower-court opinions about her common-law disabilities as a married woman and held that the right to practice law was not a privilege and immunity of citizenship. (This, of course, was the same argument that would later be used against female voting rights.) He based his position on the well-known Slaughter-House Cases, 16 Wall 36 (1873), a decision delivered the day before, on 14 April 1873. Miller's decision placed such severe limitations on the scope and meaning of the privileges-and-immunities clause of the Fourteenth Amendment that it has been virtually unused since. While this majority opinion was bad enough as far as Bradwell's right to practice law was concerned, the concurring opinion of Justice Bradley was even more damaging because of the overtly sexist language and attitudes it contained based on common-law precedent. In the Blackstone tradition, Bradley insisted that women had no legal existence separate from their husbands despite the passage of a number of Married Women's Property Acts. His opinion stated:

> ... the civil law, as well as nature herself, has always recognized a wide difference in the respective spheres and destinies of man and woman. Man is, or should be, woman's protector and defender. The natural and proper timidity and delicacy which belongs to the female sex evidently unfits it for many of the occupations of civil life. The constitution of the family organization, which is founded in the divine ordinance, as well as in the nature of things, indicates the domestic sphere as that which properly belongs to the domain and functions of womanhood. The harmony, not to say identity, of interests and views which belong or should belong to the family institution is repugnant to the idea of a woman adopting a distinct and independent career from that of her husband. So firmly fixed was this sentiment in the founders of the common law that it became a maxim of that system of jurisprudence that a woman had no legal existence separate from her husband, who was regarded as her head and representative in the social state.

Bradley conceded that some women remained single and not affected by any of the duties, complications, and incapacities arising from marriage, but these were exceptions to the general rule. "The paramount destiny and mission of women [was] to fulfill the noble and benign offices of wife and mother," according to Bradley. "This is the law of the Creator. And the rules of civil society must be adapted to the general constitution of things, and cannot be based upon exceptional cases."

Bradley heartily supported women's participation in those reform movements that opened up avenues for their advancement into occupations that he assumed were suitable for their legal condition and gendered societal functions. But he was not prepared to say that women had the fundamental right and privilege to be admitted into every office and position, including those requiring highly special qualifications and demanding special responsibilities. In the nature of things, Bradley argued, not every citizen of every age, sex, and condition was qualified for every calling and position. It was the prerogative of the legislator to prescribe regulations founded on nature, reason, and experience for the due admission of qualified persons to professions and callings demanding special skill and confidence. Thus, he concluded:

> This fairly belongs to the police power of the state; and, in my opinion, in view of the peculiar characteristics, destiny, and mission of woman, it is within the province of the legislature to ordain what offices, positions, and callings shall be filled and discharged by men, and shall receive the benefit of those energies and responsibilities, and that decision and firmness which are presumed to predominate in the sterner sex.

While Bradley's often-quoted concurring sexist remarks did not decide the case in *Bradwell* because the ruling on law in the *Slaughter-House Cases* prevailed, his words remain a classic example of "false paternalism," according to Frances Olsen. His opinion was not benignly paternalistic, as is usually claimed, because Bradley was not trying "to promote Myra Bradwell's true best interests." Instead, Olsen argues that Bradley was being "disingenuous" by claiming that for Bradwell and other women to practice as lawyers would somehow "harm" them as women. When demystifying Bradley's (and countless other jurists') detrimental or false paternalism, it is also necessary to project what would be "good" for women in a particular time period in order to take collective action in behalf of women. Thus, Olsen uses *Bradwell* to caution contemporary feminists who similarly do not distinguish false paternalism (or, to use my term, false protection) from beneficial paternalism (protection) under the law. ...

Justice Bradley's position on these two cases is also noteworthy. In his concurring opinion, he argued *against* Myra Bradwell's right of choice of occupation, but he was not in the majority when he argued *for* the butchers having that same right. In his dissenting opinion in the *Slaughter-House Cases*, Bradley said that "a law which prohibits a large class of citizens from adopting a lawful employment ... does deprive them of liberty as well as property, without due process of law. Their right of choice is a portion of their liberty; their occupation is their property. Such a law also deprives those citizens of the equal protection of the laws." He held to a diametrically opposed viewpoint in *Bradwell*.

Matthew Carpenter, one of the best-known advocates of the day, also took similarly irreconcilable positions in these two cases. He was, unlike Bradley, arguing *against* the butchers and *for* Bradwell as her attorney and a family friend. His positions were as inconsistent as Bradley's, albeit for different legal reasons. Nonetheless, both men used standard sexist arguments. Carpenter, for example, tried in *Bradwell* to trade the right to follow an occupation for the right to vote. He assured the Court that if they granted women their choice of profession it would not lead to granting them suffrage, for this was simply a political right that could be infringed or abridged while an occupation was a right of citizenship. Furthermore, he assured the Court of this by noting that "female suffrage ... would overthrow Christianity, defeat the ends of modern civilization and upturn the world," and no one wanted this—except Myra Bradwell and her feminist supporters.

Such inconsistencies on the part of Carpenter and Bradley were never seriously questioned by the Court or by any lawyer or legal historian until recently. Was the *Bradwell* case simply considered less important because of prevailing "natural-male-dominance" theories of the time? Did the general political climate of the Reconstruction play a more important role than sexism or capitalism in the *Bradwell* and *Slaughter-House Cases* decisions? It should be remembered that this was a time of political and constitutional uncertainty as Northern Republicans tried to assert federal authority over Southern Democrats and the power of individual states in general. The Supreme Court ended up the referee in this sectional and constitutional struggle between congressional and state power. Both decisions asserted that the Court "knew" what the original intent was. Both decisions also ostensibly upheld state legislation, but often in surprising and contradictory ways. For example, in

Bradwell the decision second-guessed (thus expanded) what Illinois legislators had "intended"; in the *Slaughter-House Cases*, the decision exercised judicial restraint that favored a wealthy minority of businessmen over a powerful group of independent butchers by accepting (thus restricting) the "original intent" of the drafters of the Fourteenth Amendment.

Thus federalism, in the form of states' rights, and judicial restraint versus judicial activism were clearly issues—at least in the *Slaughter-House Cases*. If instead of exercising restraint the Supreme Court had countered the arguments of the four dissenting justices who wanted to protect citizens from legislative threats to such basic rights as the one to work, it would have had to have based its decision on a broad, activist interpretation of state police power. Since the state's defense rested in part on the argument that it created the Slaughter-House corporate monopoly as a health measure, had the justices used this approach in the butchers' case they could have possibly reached a decision favoring Myra Bradwell since Illinois could not argue as Louisiana did that its discriminatory legislation was motivated by health considerations. Instead, they simply applied their narrow interpretation of the privileges-and-immunities clause in the *Slaughter-House Cases* to *Bradwell* without having to compare or rethink anything about the police power of states. Thus, Carpenter's victory as an attorney in the former seems to have set the stage for defeat in the latter. Logically, the four dissenting justices in the *Slaughter-House Cases* should have supported Bradwell's right to practice law as they had supported the butchers' right to work where they wanted, but only one did—Chief Justice Salmon P. Chase. Moreover, three of these four justices were a part of the majority on the Court later in *Minor v. Happersett* (discussed later): Noah Swayne, Joseph Bradley, and Stephen J. Field (Chase having died was replaced by Waite.) Still later when these four justices again found themselves in the majority, they began to use their belief in basic individual rights to strike down early reform legislation of the Progressive Era. This is a classic example of where judicial activism as represented by the dissenters in the *Slaughter-House Cases* did not promote liberal reform when it became the majority position of the Supreme Court....

The only case to reach the Supreme Court out of all the attempts women made to vote in the 1870s was *Minor v. Happersett.*... Virginia Minor tried to vote at the same time that Anthony did in the fall of 1872. Unlike Anthony, however, she was not even allowed to register in St. Louis, Missouri, and so never did cast a ballot. Also unlike the Anthony trial, Minor's was a civil, not a criminal, case. Finally, as a married woman she could not sue independently under Missouri law, as Anthony had been able to do in New York as a single woman. Instead, she and her husband, as co-plaintiff and counsel, first filed suit against the local registrar, Reese Happersett; they then appealed the case to the Missouri Supreme Court and finally to the United States Supreme Court in 1874....

The Minors' Supreme Court brief began with an elaborate political and constitutional argument that "there can be no half-way citizenship" under the Constitution. This was dismissed by the Court out of hand, as were the arguments about female disfranchisement being a bill of attainder and, therefore, a violation of due process. The Court entertained only those arguments based on the rights of citizens to vote under the First Amendment (voting was a form of free expression), the Thirteenth Amendment (not voting was a form of involuntary servitude), and the Fourteenth

Amendment (voting for officials of the federal government was a privilege and immunity of national citizenship rather than simply state citizenship because these offices would not exist to vote for if the federal government did not). Of these arguments, the Supreme Court chose only to consider whether voting was a privilege and immunity of citizenship. It most noticeably failed to address the question of why voting for *national* officers did not constitute a form of *national* citizenship that could not be abridged arbitrarily by individual states.

Writing for a unanimous court, Chief Justice Morrison Waite began by noting that "disputes have arisen as to whether or not *certain persons or certain classes of persons* were part of the people at the time [of the adoption of the Constitution of 1787]" (emphasis added), concluding that there was never any question of their being citizens. Since the Court had already held that "there is no doubt that women may be citizens because sex has never been made one of the elements of citizenship in the United States," it concluded that in this respect "men have never had an advantage over women." Chief Justice Waite argued that women, like children, were also legally "persons" because they were counted as part of the total population. Then, the Court presented a simplistic historical summary to prove that it had never been the "intent" of the framers of the federal or state constitutions to enfranchise women, despite the fact that they were *both* "citizens" and "persons." "For nearly ninety years the people have acted upon the idea that the Constitution when it conferred citizenship did not necessarily confer the right of suffrage…. Our province is to decide what the law is, not to declare what it should be."

Rather than simply relying on the narrow constitutional precedent set in the *Slaughter-House Cases* about national citizenship under the Fourteenth Amendment, as the Court had in *Bradwell*, Chief Justice Waite proceeded to discuss the political implications of the sweeping charge of despotism made by the Minors in their brief. Although the unanimous opinion of the Supreme Court ignored most of the legitimate constitutional questions raised in the Minors' brief, it could not afford to let the one political challenge to republican government go unanswered. This is why half of the fourteen-page decision consists of a historical recitation demonstrating that the framers of the Constitution did *not* intend "to make all citizens of the United States voters." Therefore, "women were excluded from suffrage in nearly all the States by the express provision of their constitutions and laws."

Chief Justice Waite and his colleagues were clearly disturbed by the idea that their "common understanding" about women as second-class citizens might somehow be construed as unrepublican or that female disfranchisement was somehow antirepublican. While the Court summarily dismissed most of the constitutional arguments of the Minors, the justices seemed compelled by their political arguments to engage in a debate over what constituted citizenship and republicanism in Victorian America. Like all women who sued in the courts over political or professional discrimination following the Civil War, Virginia Minor through here attorneys had been forced to adopt masculine language about individual rights to argue for national citizenship under the Fourteenth Amendment. In turn, the justices of the Supreme Court were forced into a discussion about why women had never been accorded full citizenship. Gendered constitutional discourse changed with this decision in October 1874, despite the fact the constitutional specialists have yet to accord *Minor v. Happersett* such jurisprudential importance.

Using parallel reasoning to the *Dred Scott* decision, the *Minor* decision declared that historically women constituted a special category of citizens whose inability to vote did not infringe upon their rights as citizens or persons. Thus, it avoided the constitutional question raised by the Minors of whether voting for national officials was a privilege and immunity of national citizenship. The *Minor* decision, like the *Dred Scott* one twenty years before, could only be overruled by constitutional amendment. In other words, it took the Thirteenth Amendment to abolish the special category of slavehood for African-Americans by granting them citizenship, and it finally took the Nineteenth Amendment to abolish in part the special category of citizenship for women by granting them the right to vote....

The passage of the Fourteenth and Fifteenth amendments figuratively as well as literally separated the rights of women and the rights of African-Americans and contributed to the split within the women's movement in 1869. Indeed, the rights of these two legally inferior groups had been separate political issues all along, even though they were logically and morally similar. After all, the existence of slavery had caused a Civil War; the women's question was never accorded such status or intensity of feeling in the nineteenth century except on a personal, private level. It was one thing for Northern male abolitionists to free southern slaves—little would change in their personal lives as a result, especially if black civil rights were not forced on the former Confederate states. It was entirely another matter for them to free their own women from common-law and other socioeconomic restraints.

The constitutionalism that the First Feminists began to develop then (and that feminists continue to use today) to try to overcome these disabilities was not radical to the degree that it was safely within the paradigm of legal discourse of their respective time periods. Constitutionalism has seldom been a lever for radical social change in the United States, despite claims of some constitutional specialists to the contrary. Radicals always start out appealing to "higher laws" of God, or nature, or technology but usually end up tailoring their original demands to meet the requirements of liberal constitutionalism. That post–Civil War women reformers fell into this familiar pattern is not surprising. By taking their cause to the courts, however, they forced a change in legal discourse that makes these late nineteenth-century decisions sound hopelessly gendered and obsolete in retrospect....

✣ *F U R T H E R   R E A D I N G*

Belz, Herman. *Emancipation and Equal Rights: Politics and Constitutionalism in the Civil War Era* (1978).

Benedict, Michael Les. *A Compromise of Principle: Congressional Republicans and Reconstruction* (1974).

Berger, Raoul. *Government by Judiciary: The Transformation of the Fourteenth Amendment* (1977).

Curtis, Michael Kent. *No State Shall Abridge: The Fourteenth Amendment and the Bill of Rights* (1986).

Cushman, Claire, ed. *Supreme Court Decisions and Women's Rights* (2001).

DuBois, Ellen Carol. "Outgrowing the Compact of the Fathers: Equal Rights, Woman Suffrage, and the United States Constitution, 1820–1878," *Journal of American History*, 74 (1987): 836–862.

Edwards, Laura. *Gendered Strife and Confusion: The Political Culture of Reconstruction* (1997).

Fairman, Charles. *Reconstruction and Reunion, 1864–1888* (Part One), vol. 6 of *History of the Supreme Court of the United States*, P. Freund, ed. (1971).

Foner, Eric. *Reconstruction: America's Unfinished Revolution, 1863–1877* (1988).

Goldman, Robert M. *Reconstruction and Black Suffrage: Losing the Vote in Reese and Cruikshank* (2001).

Hyman, Harold M. *A More Perfect Union: The Impact of the Civil War and Reconstruction on the Constitution* (1973).

———. *The Reconstruction Justice of Salmon P. Chase: In re Turner and Texas v. White* (1997).

Hyman, Harold M. and William M. Wiecek, *Equal Justice Under Law: Constitutional Development, 1835–1875* (1982).

James, Joseph B. *The Ratification of the Fourteenth Amendment* (1984).

Kaczorowski, Robert J. *The Politics of Judicial Interpretation: The Federal Courts, Department of Justice and Civil Rights, 1866–1876* (1985).

———. "To Begin the Nation Anew: Congress, Citizenship, and Civil Rights after the Civil War," *American Historical Review*, 92 (1987): 45–68.

Kutler, Stanley I. *Judicial Power and Reconstruction Politics* (1968).

Labbe, Ronald M. and Jonathan Lurie, *The Slaughterhouse Cases: Regulation, Reconstruction, and the Fourteenth Amendment* (2003).

Lofgren, Charles A. *The Plessy Case: A Legal-Historical Interpretation* (1987).

Lurie, Jonathan. *The Chase Court: Justices, Rulings, and Legacy* (2004).

Nelson, William E. *The Fourteenth Amendment: From Political Principle to Judicial Doctrine* (1988).

Nieman, Donald G. *Promises to Keep: African-Americans and the Constitutional Order, 1776 to the Present* (1991).

Paludan, Phillip S. *A Covenant with Death: The Constitution, Law, and Equality in the Civil War Era* (1975).

Przybyszewski, Linda. *The Republic according to John Marshall Harlan* (1999).

Ross, Michael A. *Justice of Shattered Dreams: Samuel Freeman Miller and the Supreme Court during the Civil War Era* (2003).

Scaturro, Frank J. *The Supreme Court's Retreat from Reconstruction: A Distortion of Constitutional Jurisprudence* (2000).

Stephenson, Jr., Donald Grier. *The Waite Court: Justices, Rulings, and Legacy* (2003).

Ten Broek, Jacobus. *The Antislavery Origins of the Fourteenth Amendment* (1951).

Williams, Lou F. *The Great South Carolina Ku Klux Klan Trials* (1996).

Protective Legislation and the Liberty to Contract

During the late nineteenth and early twentieth centuries, the United States under-
went a series of social and economic changes, the likes of which the nation had never
seen. Advances in technology and transportation dramatically increased agricultural
output, and as farm production outpaced demand, prices for agricultural products
dropped steadily. Farmers faced dire financial consequences. The growth of railroads
and an abundance of natural resources, meanwhile, abetted the rise of a new industrial order. Millions flocked to American cities, including a wave of European immigrants, in order to fill the jobs created by the expanding economy. For the first time in
U.S. history, women surged into the labor force, and by 1900 they accounted for 17%
of all manufacturing employees.

    Rapid economic expansion brought with it a host of social and economic ills.
Industrial workers routinely labored long hours for low wages under dangerous
and unhealthy conditions. Cities became home to slums and tenements, where poor
sanitation bred chronic illness and disease. Poverty, violence, prostitution, alcoholism,
and child labor all plagued urban society. Agricultural depression and urban unrest
led to the creation of two great social reform movements—Populism and Progressivism.
Although Populists sought to assist ailing farmers and Progressives aimed to alleviate
the problems associated with urban life, both advocated a greater role for government
in regulating markets and redistributing resources. Most reform measures arose
initially at the state level, as legislatures exercised their police powers to pass legislation
in the interest of the health, safety, and welfare of the public. In response, conservative
legal commentators supported business leaders in opposing any use of government
power that threatened their economic interests. This opposition took constitutional
expression in the doctrines of substantive due process of law and liberty to contract.

    For most of the nineteenth century, due process had been defined in one way—as
procedural. The due process provisions in state constitutions and the Fifth and
Fourteenth Amendments to the U.S. Constitution provided that every person, if accused
of a crime, was entitled to an orderly proceeding that afforded an opportunity to be
heard and to have one's rights protected. After the Civil War, due process also acquired
a substantive meaning that derived from the doctrine of vested rights. Substantive due
process meant that each individual possessed an irreducible sum of rights with which

[handwritten margin note: why regulation was necessary]

the government could not arbitrarily interfere. In short, there were substantive—not just procedural—limitations on the government's exercise of its powers.

By the mid-1890s, the doctrine of substantive due process emerged full-blown. State and federal courts held that certain kinds of regulatory legislation could so affect property as to amount to a violation of individual—or corporate—rights. But when courts overturned such legislation, they *invariably favored the wealthy over the poor and capital over labor.* Substantive due process had another dimension as well. The courts viewed special, or class, legislation—measures that clearly favored one group over another—as also *violating due process rights.* Many of these decisions involved businesses competing with one another, rather than poor individuals fighting to resist the rich and powerful.

Substantive due process reinforced the concept of the liberty to contract, which had its roots in the free labor ideology of the antebellum North. Before the Civil War, northern Republicans championed the idea that individuals should be free to work where and for whom they wanted, free to seek the best wages and working conditions they could attain, and free to move wherever they wished. Substantive due process of law turned one's labor into a property *right to make* whatever arrangements one wanted *with an employer, without interference* from government. Such a "right," however, presumed a degree of equality in bargaining between employer and employee that simply did not exist in an economic order dominated by capitalists. In many cases, in other words, judges claimed to protect workers' "rights" by invalidating state laws that aimed to ensure workers' health and safety.

Liberty to contract also had implications for contemporary notions about gender. Nineteenth-century Americans assumed women to be physically inferior to men and, as the mothers of future generations, in need of special protection. Antebellum free labor ideology excluded women, of course, but their subsequent entry into the industrial workforce stirred debate about their status. If the state protected them but not men, then the assumptions behind liberty to contract were suspect. If lawmakers treated women as men's equals, however, they threatened the cultural assumptions on which gender relations rested. Debates among feminists over protective legislation laid bare the divisions within their ranks over the best way to advance the cause of women.

The attempts of the constitutional order to accommodate the rapid social changes wrought by the rise of industrialism raise a number of questions for students of constitutional history. Did the Supreme Court support big business interests during this era, or were the justices adhering to constitutional principles? How did debates over protective legislation and the liberty to contract contribute to new ways of thinking about the place of government and the role of law in American society? Did progressive reform measures help women, or did such laws simply embody and confirm the sexist attitudes of the time? In a larger sense, was paternalism or reform at the heart of progressive thinking about the law?

✤ *D O C U M E N T S*

During the late nineteenth century, legal thinkers increasingly emphasized the notion of property rights and laissez faire at the same time that workers and farmers began organizing to advocate government intervention in the economy. Christopher J. Tiedeman, a professor of law at the University of Missouri at the time, emerged as a doctrinaire critic of the states' police powers. In *A Treatise on the Limitations of Police Power in the United States*, excerpted as Document 1, Tiedeman urged judges to construe that power narrowly. Populists possessed a radically different vision. The People's Party, which grew out of the agrarian movement of the 1870s and 1880s, ran its first presidential candidate in 1892. By the mid-1890s, Populists were a force to be reckoned with on the national scene. Their 1896 platform, Document 2, reflected their concern that financial interests in Europe and America held such a tight grip on the system that "the people" needed to act. Notably, the Populists attacked the courts for using injunctions to break strikes, and they particularly criticized the Supreme Court for declaring unconstitutional the recently enacted federal income tax law, a key piece of the populist reform program.

In a series of decisions between the 1890s and 1920s, the Supreme Court grappled with the tensions between state protective legislation and the notion of liberty to contract. In 1905 the Court issued its most famous opinion invalidating a state regulatory measure. In *Lochner v. New York*, Document 3, the justices split 5–4 in striking down a progressive-backed New York law that limited the number of hours that bakers could work, in order to protect their health and safety. The majority opinion, written by Justice Rufus W. Peckham, found "no reasonable ground" for interfering with the liberty to contract in this instance, which provoked Justice Oliver Wendell Holmes Jr. to issue one of the Court's most famous dissents. Because the justices had been skeptical of the health and safety aspects of the New York law, attorneys and activists pursued an innovative strategy in defending the next major piece of protective legislation to come before the Court. Louis Brandeis, with the help of Florence Kelley and Josephine Goldmark of the National Consumer's League, prepared a new kind of legal brief—one that stressed the social, psychological, and economic necessity of legislation. Excerpted as Document 4, Brandeis's almost one-hundred-page brief included reams of social science evidence—and very little law—to defend an Oregon statute that established a 10-hour workday for women. In *Muller v. Oregon*, Document 5, a unanimous Court upheld the measure. Justice David J. Brewer's opinion in the case added a thick layer of paternalism to Brandeis's brief.

During the early twentieth century, some scholars began to advocate a theory of law that emphasized the social and economic consequences of judicial decisions. Roscoe Pound, the Dean of Harvard Law School from 1916 to 1936, coined the term "sociological jurisprudence" to describe this view, and one of his essays from the *Yale Law Journal* is excerpted as Document 6. With the Brandeis Brief, the *Muller* decision, and sociological jurisprudence all indicating that the constitutional winds were shifting away from the notion of liberty to contract, the Court nevertheless clung to the doctrine. In *Adkins v. Children's Hospital*, Document 7, the Court struck down a minimum wage law for women. Justice George Sutherland, writing for a 5-3 majority, not only rested his decision on the Due Process Clause of the Fifth Amendment (a federal law was at issue, which implicated the Fifth Amendment, rather than the Fourteenth) but drew strength from the recent passage of the Nineteenth Amendment, which granted women the vote. Protective legislation like that in the District of Columbia, Sutherland reasoned, undermined the freedom of women. Sutherland proclaimed that freedom of contract in the economic arena was a corollary to political equality.

✤ D O C U M E N T   1

Legal Scholar Christopher G. Tiedeman Advocates a Limited Police Power, 1886

. . . The private rights of the individual, apart from a few statutory rights, which when compared with the whole body of private rights are insignificant in number, do not rest upon the mandate of municipal law as a source. They belong to man in a state of nature; they are natural rights, rights recognized and existing in the law of reason. But the individual, in a state of nature, finds in the enjoyment of his own rights that he transgresses the rights of others. Nature wars upon nature, when subjected to no spiritual or moral restraint. The object of government is to impose that degree of restraint upon human actions, which is necessary to the uniform and reasonable conservation and enjoyment of private rights. Government and municipal law protect and develop, rather than create, private rights. The conservation of private rights is attained by the imposition of a wholesome restraint upon their exercise, such a restraint as will prevent the infliction of injury upon others in the enjoyment of them; it involves a provision of means for enforcing the legal maxim, which enunciates the fundamental rule of both the human and the natural law, *sic utere tuo, ut alienum non lædas* [use your own property in such a way as not to injure another's]. The power of the government to impose this restraint is called POLICE POWER. By this "general police power of the State, persons and property are subjected to all kinds of restraints and burdens, in order to secure the general comfort, health and prosperity of the State; of the perfect right in the legislature to do which no question ever was or upon acknowledged general principles ever can be made, so far as natural persons are concerned." Blackstone defines the police power to be "the due regulation and domestic order of the kingdom, whereby the inhabitants of a State, like members of a well-governed family, are bound to conform their general behavior to the rules of propriety, good neighborhood and good manners, and to be decent, industrious and inoffensive in their respective stations." ... The continental jurists include, under the term *Police Power*, not only those restraints upon private rights which are imposed for the general welfare of all, but also all the governmental institutions, which are established with public funds for the better promotion of the public good, and the alleviation of private want and suffering. Thus they would include the power of the government to expend the public moneys in the construction and repair of roads, the establishment of hospitals and asylums and colleges, in short, the power to supplement the results of individual activity with what individual activity can not accomplish. "The governmental provision for the public security and welfare in its daily necessities, that provision which establishes the needful and necessary, and therefore appears as a bidding and forbidding power of the State, is the scope and character of the police." But in the present connection, as may be gathered from the American definitions heretofore given, the term must be confined to the imposition of restraints and burdens upon persons and property. The power of the government to embark in enterprises of public charity and benefit can only be limited by the restrictions upon the power of taxation, and to that extent alone can these subjects in American law be said to fall within the police power of the State.

It is to be observed, therefore, that the police power of the government, as understood in the constitutional law of the United States, is simply the power of the government to establish provisions for the enforcement of the common as well as civil-law maxim, *sic utere tuo, ut alienum non lædas*.... Any law which goes beyond that principle, which undertakes to abolish rights, the exercise of which does not involve an infringement of the rights of others, or to limit the exercise of rights beyond what is necessary to provide for the public welfare and the general security, cannot be included in the police power of the government. It is a governmental usurpation, and violates the principles of abstract justice, as they have been developed under our republican institutions. ...

30. Personal Liberty—How Guaranteed

It is altogether needless in this connection to indulge in a panegyric upon the blessings of guaranteed personal liberty. The love of liberty, of freedom from irksome and unlawful restraints, is implanted in every human breast. In the American Declaration of Independence, and in the bills of rights of almost every State constitution, we find that personal liberty is expressly guaranteed to all men equally. But notwithstanding the existence of these fundamental and constitutional guaranties of personal liberty, the astounding anomaly of the slavery of an entire race in more than one-third of the States of the American Union, during three-fourths of a century of national existence, gave the lie to their own constitutional declarations, that "*all* men are endowed by their Creator, with certain inalienable rights, among which are the right to life, liberty, and the pursuit of happiness." But, happily, this contradiction is now a thing of the past, and in accordance with the provisions of the thirteenth amendment to the constitution of the United States, it is now the fundamental and practically unchangeable law of the land, that "neither slavery nor involuntary servitude, except as a punishment for crime whereof the party shall have been duly convicted, shall exist within the United States, or any place subject to their jurisdiction."

But to a practical understanding of the effect of these constitutional guaranties, a clear idea of what personal liberty consists is necessary. It is not to be confounded with a license to do what one pleases. Liberty, according to Montesquieu, consists "only in the power of doing what we ought to will, and in not being constrained to do what we ought not to will." No man has a right to make such a use of his liberty as to commit an injury to the rights of others. His liberty is controlled by the oft quoted maxim, *sic utere tuu, ut alienum non lædas*. Indeed liberty is that amount of personal freedom, which is consistent with a strict obedience to this rule.... While liberty does not consist in a paucity of laws, still it is only consistent with a limitation of the restrictive laws to those which exercise a wholesome restraint. "That man is free who is protected from injury," and his protection involves necessarily the restraint of other individuals from the commission of the injury. In the proper balancing of the contending interests of individuals, personal liberty is secured and developed; any further restraint is unwholesome and subversive of liberty. As Herbert Spencer has expressed it, "every man may claim the fullest liberty to exercise his faculties compatible with the possession of like liberty by every other man."

The constitutional guaranties are generally unqualified, and a strict construction of them would prohibit all limitations upon liberty, if any other meaning but the limited one here presented were given to the word. But these guaranties are to be liberally construed, so that the object of them may be fully attained. They do not prohibit the exercise of police power in restraint of licentious trespass upon the rights of others, but the restrictive measures must be kept within these limits. "Powers, which can be justified only on this specific ground (that they are police regulations), and which would otherwise be clearly prohibited by the constitution, can be such only as are so clearly necessary to the safety, comfort and well-being of society, or so imperatively required by the public necessity, as to lead to the rational and satisfactory conclusion that the framers of the constitution could not, as men of ordinary prudence and foresight, have intended to prohibit their exercise in the particular case, notwithstanding the language of the prohibition would otherwise include it."

✠ *D O C U M E N T   2*

The People's Party Announces its Agenda for Reform, 1896

The People's Party, assembled in National Convention, reaffirms its allegiance to the principles declared by the founders of the Republic, and also to the fundamental principles of just government as enunciated in the platform of the party in 1892.

We recognize that through the connivance of the present and preceding Administrations the country has reached a crisis in its National life, as predicted in our declaration four years ago, and that prompt and patriotic action is the supreme duty of the hour.

We realize that, while we have political independence, our financial and industrial independence is yet to be attained by restoring to our country the Constitutional control and exercise of the functions necessary to a people's government, which functions have been basely surrendered by our public servants to corporate monopolies. The influence of European moneychangers has been more potent in shaping legislation than the voice of the American people. Executive power and patronage have been used to corrupt our legislatures and defeat the will of the people, and plutocracy has thereby been enthroned upon the ruins of democracy. To restore the Government intended by the fathers, and for the welfare and prosperity of this and future generations, we demand the establishment of an economic and financial system which shall make us masters of our own affairs and independent of European control, by the adoption of the following declaration of principles:

The Finances

1. We demand a National money, safe and sound, issued by the General Government only, without the intervention of banks of issue, to be a full legal tender for all debts, public and private; a just, equitable, and efficient means of distribution, direct to the people, and through the lawful disbursements of the Government.

2. We demand the free and unrestricted coinage of silver and gold at the present legal ratio of 16 to 1, without waiting for the consent of foreign nations.

3. We demand that the volume of circulating medium be speedily increased to an amount sufficient to meet the demand of the business and population, and to restore the just level of prices of labor and production.

4. We denounce the sale of bonds and the increase of the public interest-bearing debt made by the present Administration as unnecessary and without authority of law, and demand that no more bonds be issued, except by specific act of Congress.

5. We demand such legislation as will prevent the demonetization of the lawful money of the United States by private contract.

6. We demand that the Government, in payment of its obligation, shall use its option as to the kind of lawful money in which they are to be paid, and we denounce the present and preceding Administrations for surrendering this option to the holders of Government obligations.

7. We demand a graduated income tax, to the end that aggregated wealth shall bear its just proportion of taxation, and we regard the recent decision of the Supreme

Court relative to the income-tax law as a misinterpretation of the Constitution and an invasion of the rightful powers of Congress over the subject of taxation. ...

Railroads and Telegraphs

1. Transportation being a means of exchange and a public necessity, the Government should own and operate the railroads in the interest of the people and on a non-partisan basis, to the end that all may be accorded the same treatment in transportation, and that the tyranny and political power now exercised by the great railroad corporations, which result in the impairment, if not the destruction of the political rights and personal liberties of the citizens, may be destroyed. Such ownership is to be accomplished gradually, in a manner consistent with sound public policy. ...

4. The telegraph, like the Post Office system, being a necessity for the transmission of news, should be owned and operated by the Government in the interest of the people.

The Public Lands

1. True policy demands that the National and State legislation shall be such as will ultimately enable every prudent and industrious citizen to secure a home, and therefore the land should not be monopolized for speculative purposes. All lands now held by railroads and other corporations in excess of their actual needs should by lawful means be reclaimed by the Government and held for actual settlers only, and private land monopoly, as well as alien ownership, should be prohibited.

2. We condemn the land grant frauds by which the Pacific railroad companies have, through the connivance of the Interior Department, robbed multitudes of *bona-fide* settlers of their homes and miners of their claims, and we demand legislation by Congress which will enforce the exemption of mineral land from such grants after as well as before the patent.

3. We demand that *bona-fide* settlers on all public lands be granted free homes, as provided in the National Homestead Law, and that no exception be made in the case of Indian reservations when opened for settlement, and that all lands not now patented come under this demand.

The Referendum

We favor a system of direct legislation through the initiative and referendum, under proper Constitutional safeguards.

Direct Election of President and Senators by the People

We demand the election of President, Vice-President, and United States Senators by a direct vote of the people. ...

The Territories

We favor home rule in the Territories and the District of Columbia, and the early admission of the Territories as States.

Public Salaries

All public salaries should be made to correspond to the price of labor and its products.

Employment to Be Furnished by Government

In times of great industrial depression, idle labor should be employed on public works as far as practicable.

Arbitrary Judicial Action

The arbitrary course of the courts in assuming to imprison citizens for indirect contempt and ruling by injunction should be prevented by proper legislation....

The Financial Question: "The Pressing Issue"

While the foregoing propositions constitute the platform upon which our party stands, and for the vindication of which its organization will be maintained, we recognize that the great and pressing issue of the pending campaign, upon which the present election will turn, is the financial question, and upon this great and specific issue between the parties we cordially invite the aid and co-operation of all organizations and citizens agreeing with us upon this vital question.

✣ *D O C U M E N T   3*

Lochner v. New York, 1905

Mr. Justice Peckham ... delivered the opinion of the Court.

The indictment, it will be seen, charges that the plaintiff in error violated the one hundred and tenth section of article 8, chapter 415, of the Laws of 1897, known as the labor law of the State of New York, in that he wrongfully and unlawfully required and permitted an employé working for him to work more than sixty hours in one week. There is nothing in any of the opinions delivered in this case, either in the Supreme Court or the Court of Appeals of the State, which construes the section, in using the word "required," as referring to any physical force being used to obtain the labor of an employé. It is assumed that the word means nothing more than the requirement arising from voluntary contract for such labor in excess of the number of hours specified in the statute. There is no pretense in any of the opinions that the statute was intended to meet a case of involuntary labor in any form. All the opinions assume that there is no real distinction, so far as this question is concerned, between the words "required" and "permitted." The mandate of the statute that "no employé shall be required or permitted to work," is the substantial equivalent of an enactment that "no employé shall contract or agree to work," more than ten hours per day, and as there is no provision for special emergencies the statute is mandatory in all cases. It is not an act merely fixing the number of hours which shall constitute a legal day's work, but an absolute prohibition upon the employer, permitting, under any circumstances, more than ten hours work to be done in his establishment. The employé may desire to earn the extra money, which would arise from his working more than the prescribed time, but this statute forbids the employer from permitting the employé to earn it.

The statute necessarily interferes with the right of contract between the employer and employés, concerning the number of hours in which the latter may labor in the bakery of the employer. The general right to make a contract in relation to his business is part of the liberty of the individual protected by the Fourteenth Amendment of the Federal Constitution. *Allgeyer v. Louisiana.* ... Under that provision no State can deprive any person of life, liberty or property without due process of law. The right to purchase or to sell labor is part of the liberty protected by this amendment, unless there are circumstances which exclude the right. There are, however, certain powers, existing in the sovereignty of each State in the Union, somewhat vaguely termed police powers the exact description and limitation of which have not been attempted by the courts. Those powers, broadly stated and without, at present, any attempt at a more specific limitation, relate to the safety, health, morals and general welfare of the public. Both property and liberty are held on such reasonable conditions as may be imposed by the governing power of the State in the exercise of those powers, and with such conditions the Fourteenth Amendment was not designed to interfere. ...

The State, therefore, has power to prevent the individual from making certain kinds of contracts, and in regard to them the Federal Constitution offers no protection. If the contract be one which the State, in the legitimate exercise of its police power, has the right to prohibit, it is not prevented from prohibiting it by the Fourteenth Amendment. Contracts in violation of a statute, either of the Federal or state government, or a contract to let one's property for immoral purposes, or to do any other unlawful act, could obtain no protection from the Federal Constitution, as coming under the liberty of person or of free contract. Therefore, when the State, by its legislature, in the assumed exercise of its police powers, has passed an act which seriously limits the right to labor or the right of contract in regard to their means of livelihood between persons who are *sui juris* (both employer and employé), it becomes of great importance to determine which shall prevail—the right of the individual to labor for such time as he may choose, or the right of the State to prevent the individual from laboring or from entering into any contract to labor, beyond a certain time prescribed by the State ...

It must, of course, be conceded that there is a limit to the valid exercise of the police power by the State. There is no dispute concerning this general proposition. Otherwise the Fourteenth Amendment would have no efficacy and the legislatures of the States would have unbounded power, and it would be enough to say that any piece of legislation was enacted to conserve the morals, the health or the safety of the people; such legislation would be valid, no matter how absolutely without foundation the claim might be. The claim of the police power would be a mere pretext—become another and delusive name for the supreme sovereignty of the State to be exercised free from constitutional restraint. This is not contended for. In every case that comes before this court, therefore, where legislation of this character is concerned and where the protection of the Federal Constitution is sought, the question necessarily arises: Is this a fair, reasonable and appropriate exercise of the police power of the State, or is it an unreasonable, unnecessary and arbitrary interference with the right of the individual to his personal liberty or to enter into those contracts in relation to labor which may seem to him appropriate or necessary for the support of himself and his family? Of course the liberty of contract relating to labor includes both parties to it. The one has as much right to purchase as the other to sell labor.

This is not a question of substituting the judgment of the court for that of the legislature. If the act be within the power of the State it is valid, although the judgment of the court might be totally opposed to the enactment of such a law. But the question would still remain: Is it within the police power of the State? and that question must be answered by the court.

The question whether this act is valid as a labor law, pure and simple, may be dismissed in a few words. There is no reasonable ground for interfering with the liberty of person or the right of free contract, by determining the hours of labor, in the occupation of a baker. There is no contention that bakers as a class are not equal in intelligence and capacity to men in other trades or manual occupations, or that they are not able to assert their rights and care for themselves without the protecting arm of the State, interfering with their independence of judgment and of action. They are in no sense wards of the State. Viewed in the light of a purely labor law, with no reference whatever to the question of health, we think that a law like the one before us involves neither the safety, the morals nor the welfare of the public, and that the interest of the public is not in the slightest degree affected by such an act. The law must be upheld, if at all, as a law pertaining to the health of the individual engaged in the occupation of a baker. It does not affect any other portion of the public than those who are engaged in that occupation. Clean and wholesome bread does not depend upon whether the baker works but ten hours per day or only sixty hours a week. The limitation of the hours of labor does not come within the police power on that ground.

It is a question of which of two powers or rights shall prevail—the power of the State to legislate or the right of the individual to liberty of person and freedom of contract. The mere assertion that the subject relates though but in a remote degree to the public health does not necessarily render the enactment valid. The act must have a more direct relation, as a means to an end, and the end itself must be appropriate and legitimate, before an act can be held to be valid which interferes with the general right of an individual to be free in his person and in his power to contract in relation to his own labor. ...

We think the limit of the police power has been reached and passed in this case. There is, in our judgment, no reasonable foundation for holding this to be necessary or appropriate as a health law to safeguard the public health or the health of the individuals who are following the trade of a baker. If this statute be valid, and if, therefore, a proper case is made out in which to deny the right of an individual, *sui juris*, as employer or employé, to make contracts for the labor of the latter under the protection of the provisions of the Federal Constitution, there would seem to be no length to which legislation of this nature might not go. The case differs widely, as we have already stated, from the expressions of this court in regard to laws of this nature, as stated in *Holden v. Hardy*....

We think that there can be no fair doubt that the trade of a baker, in and of itself, is not an unhealthy one to that degree which would authorize the legislature to interfere with the right to labor, and with the right of free contract on the part of the individual, either as employer or employé. In looking through statistics regarding all trades and occupations, it may be true that the trade of a baker does not appear to be as healthy as some other trades, and is also vastly more healthy than still others. To the common understanding the trade of a baker has never been regarded as an unhealthy one. Very likely physicians would not recommend the exercise of that or of any other trade as a remedy for ill health. Some occupations are more healthy than others, but we think there are none which might not come under the power of the legislature to supervise and control the hours of working therein, if the mere fact that the occupation is not absolutely and perfectly healthy is to confer that right upon the legislative department of the Government. It might be safely affirmed that almost all occupations more or less affect the health. There must be more than the mere fact of the possible existence of some small amount of unhealthiness to warrant legislative interference with liberty....

It is also urged, pursuing the same line of argument, that it is to the interest of the State that its population should be strong and robust, and therefore any legislation which may be said to tend to make people healthy must be valid as health laws, enacted under the police power. If this be a valid argument and a justification for this kind of legislation, it follows that the protection of the Federal Constitution from undue interference with liberty of person and freedom of contract is visionary, wherever the law is sought to be justified as a valid exercise of the police power. Scarcely any law but might find shelter under such assumptions, and conduct, properly so called, as well as contract, would come under the restrictive sway of the legislature. Not only the hours of employés, but the hours of employers, could be regulated, and doctors, lawyers, scientists, all professional men, as well as athletes and artisans, could be forbidden to fatigue their brains and bodies by prolonged hours of exercise, lest the fighting strength of the State be impaired. We mention these extreme cases because the contention is extreme. We do not believe in the soundness of the views which uphold this law. On the contrary, we think that such a law as this, although passed in the assumed exercise of the police power, and as relating to the public health, or the health of the employés named, is not within that power, and is invalid. The act is not, within any fair meaning of the term, a health law, but is an illegal interference with the rights of individuals, both employers and employés, to make contracts regarding labor upon such terms as they may think best, or which they may agree upon with the other parties to such contracts. Statutes of the nature of that under review, limiting the hours in which grown and intelligent men may labor to earn their living, are mere meddlesome interferences with the rights of the individual, and they are not saved from condemnation by the claim that they are passed in the exercise of the police power and upon the subject of the health of the individual whose rights are interfered with, unless there be some fair ground, reasonable in and of itself, to say that there is material danger to the public health or to the health of the employés, if the hours of labor are not curtailed. If this be not clearly the case the individuals, whose rights are thus made the subject of legislative interference, are under the protection of the Federal Constitution regarding their liberty of contract as well as of person; and the legislature of the State has no power to limit their right as proposed in this statute. ...

It was further urged on the argument that restricting the hours of labor in the case of bakers was valid because it tended to cleanliness on the part of the workers, as a man was more apt to be cleanly when not overworked, and if cleanly then his "output" was also more likely to be so. What has already been said applies with equal force to this contention. We do not admit the reasoning to be sufficient to justify the claimed right of such interference. The State in that case would assume the position of a supervisor, or *pater familias*, over every act of the individual, and its right of governmental interference with his hours of labor, his hours of exercise, the character thereof, and the extent to which it shall be carried would be recognized and upheld. In our judgment it is not possible in fact to discover the connection between the number of hours a baker may work in the bakery and the healthful quality of the bread made by the workman. The connection, if any exists, is too shadowy and thin to build any argument for the interference of the legislature. If the man works ten hours a day it is all right, but if ten and a half or eleven his health is in danger and his bread may be unhealthful, and, therefore, he shall not be permitted to do it. This, we think, is unreasonable and entirely arbitrary. ...

It is manifest to us that the limitation of the hours of labor as provided for in this section of the statute under which the indictment was found, and the plaintiff in error convicted, has no such direct relation to and no such substantial effect upon the health of the employé, as to justify us in regarding the section as really a health law. It seems to us that the real object and purpose were simply to regulate the hours of labor between the master and his employés (all being men, *sui juris*), in a private business, not dangerous in any degree to morals or in any real and substantial degree, to the health of the employés. Under such circumstances the freedom of master and employé to contract with each other in relation to their employment, and in defining the same, cannot be prohibited or interfered with, without violating the Federal Constitution. ...

Mr. Justice Holmes dissenting.

. . . This case is decided upon an economic theory which a large part of the country does not entertain. If it were a question whether I agreed with that theory, I should desire to study it further and long before making up my mind. But I do not conceive that to be my duty, because I strongly believe that my agreement or disagreement has nothing to do with the right of a majority to embody their opinions in law. It is settled by various decisions of this court that state constitutions and state laws may regulate life in many ways which we as legislators might think as injudicious or if you like as tyrannical as this, and which equally with this interfere with the liberty to contract. Sunday laws and usury laws are ancient examples. A more modern one is the prohibition of lotteries. The liberty of the citizen to do as he likes so long as he does not interfere with the liberty of others to do the same, which has been a shibboleth for some well-known writers, is interfered with by school laws, by the Post Office, by every state or municipal institution which takes his money for purposes thought desirable, whether he likes it or not. The Fourteenth Amendment does not enact Mr. Herbert Spencer's Social Statics. The other day we sustained the Massachusetts vaccination law. *Jacobson v. Massachusetts.* ... United States and state statutes and decisions cutting down the liberty to contract by way of combination are familiar to this court. *Northern Securities Co. v. United States.* ... Two years ago we upheld the prohibition of sales of stock on margins or for future delivery in the constitution of California. *Otis v. Parker.* ... The decision sustaining an eight hour law for miners is still recent. *Holden v. Hardy.* ... Some of these laws embody convictions or prejudices which judges are likely to share. Some may not. But a constitution is not intended to embody a particular economic theory, whether of paternalism and the organic relation of the citizen to the State or of *laissez faire.* It is made for people of fundamentally differing views, and the accident of our finding certain opinions natural and familiar or novel and even shocking ought not to conclude our judgment upon the question whether statutes embodying them conflict with the Constitution of the United States.

General propositions do not decide concrete cases. The decision will depend on a judgment or intuition more subtle than any articulate major premise. But I think that the proposition just stated, if it is accepted, will carry us far toward the end. Every opinion tends to become a law. I think that the word liberty in the Fourteenth Amendment is perverted when it is held to prevent the natural outcome of a dominant opinion, unless it can be said that a rational and fair man necessarily would admit that the statute proposed would infringe fundamental principles as they have been understood by the traditions of our people and our law. ...

✚ D O C U M E N T   4

Reformers Louis D. Brandeis and Josephine Goldmark Document the Hardships Faced by Women Industrial Workers, 1908

VII. Laundries

The specific prohibition in the Oregon Act of more than ten hours' work in laundries is not an arbitrary discrimination against that trade. Laundries would probably not be included under the general terms of "manufacturing" or "mechanical establishments"; and yet the special dangers of long hours in laundries, as the business is now conducted, present strong reasons for providing a legal limitation of the hours of work in that business. ...

B. Bad Effect upon Health.   *Report of British Chief Inspector of Factories and Workshops, 1900.*

The whole work of a laundry is done standing, and the practice of so apportioning the legal "sixty hours a week" that on three or four days in the week the women have to work from 8 A.M. to 10 or 11 at night—a practice which could be, and where there is proper organization often is, rendered needless—has its natural result in the form of disease to which laundry workers are extremely liable. It is well known that they suffer much from varicose veins, and terrible ulcers on the legs; but the extraordinary extent to which they are afflicted is, I think, not generally known. In many other trades standing is a necessary condition, and it is difficult to account for the far greater prevalence of this disease among laundry workers than among others of the same class engaged in ordinary factory occupations, except on the ground of the long and irregular hours. ...

With a view to arriving, if possible, at some definite knowledge of the position of laundry workers as compared with other women of their class and situation, in regard to the question of health, I have this year devoted some time to inquiring into the subject in the districts under my charge and in neighboring localities. ... By the kindness of the superintendents of the two first infirmaries (Islesworth, and Wandsworth and Clapham) I have been able to examine the carefully kept records of the number, ages, occupations, and diseases of the patients. ...

D. Bad Effect upon Morals.   *Report of British Chief Inspector of Factories and Workshops, 1900.*

One of the most unsatisfactory results of the present system or lack of system of working hours in laundries is the unfortunate moral effect on the women and girls of this irregularity. The difficulty of securing steady regular work from employees and of insuring punctual attendance is complained of on all sides, and the more intelligent employers are beginning to see that this is the natural result of the irregularity in working hours, which is still too readily fostered by many who do not realize its mischievous effect. Women who are employed at arduous work till far into the night are not likely to be early risers nor given to punctual attendance in the mornings, and workers who on one or two days in the week are dismissed to idleness or to other occupations, while on the remaining days they are expected to work for abnormally long hours, are not rendered methodical, industrious, or dependable workers by such an unsatisfactory training. The self-control and good habits engendered by a regular and definite period of moderate daily employment, which affords an excellent training for the young worker in all organized industries, is sadly lacking, and, instead, one finds periods of violent over-work alternating with hours of exhaustion. The result is the establishment of a kind of "vicious circle"; bad habits among workers make compliance by their employers with any regulation as to hours very difficult, while a lack of loyal adherence to reasonable hours of employment by many laundry occupiers increases the difficulty for those who make the attempt in real earnestness. ...

Dangerous Trades. Thomas Oliver, M.D., *Medical Expert to Dangerous Trades Committee of the Home Office. 1902.* The ten minutes or quarter-hour "lunch" of "beer" is common, and the "beer-man" who goes his rounds at 10 A.M. and 6 or 7 P.M. to all the laundries, delivering his cans of beer from the nearest public house, is an institution which is, I believe, unknown in any other trade. Imagine the amazement of the master of a mill or weaving factory if his employees were to stop in a body for a quarter of an hour twice a day between meals to drink beer! Yet in many laundries the beer is kept on the premises for the purpose, and it is certain that as long as time thus wasted (to put it on the lowest grounds) can be made up by each separate woman "working it out" at the end of the day, irregular dawdling and intemperate habits will be encouraged. On the other hand, a woman who is expected on Thursdays or Fridays to be in the laundry from 8 or 8:30 in the morning till 9 or 10 or 11 at night may claim with some show of reason that only by some kind of spur can she keep her over-tired body from flagging. ...

Conclusion

We submit that in view of the facts above set forth and of legislative action extending over a period of more than sixty years in the leading countries of Europe, and in twenty of our States, it cannot be said that the Legislature of Oregon had no reasonable ground for believing that the public health, safety, or welfare did not require a legal limitation on women's work in manufacturing and mechanical establishments and laundries to ten hours in one day. ...

✣ *D O C U M E N T   5*

Muller v. Oregon, 1908

Mr. Justice Brewer delivered the opinion of the Court.

... We held in *Lochner v. New York* ... that a law providing that no laborer shall be required or permitted to work in bakeries more than sixty hours in a week or ten hours in a day was not as to men a legitimate exercise of the police power of the State, but an unreasonable, unnecessary, and arbitrary interference with the right and liberty of the individual to contract in relation to his labor, and as such was in conflict with, and void under, the Federal Constitution. That decision is invoked by plaintiff in error as decisive of the question before us. But this assumes that the difference between the sexes does not justify a different rule respecting a restriction of the hours of labor.

In patent cases counsel are apt to open the argument with a discussion of the state of the art. It may not be amiss, in the present case, before examining the constitutional question, to notice the course of legislation as well as expressions of opinion from other than judicial sources. In the brief filed by Mr. Louis D. Brandeis, for the defendant in error, is a very copious collection of all these matters. ...

The legislation and opinions referred to ... may not be, technically speaking, authorities, and in them is little or no discussion of the constitutional question presented to us for determination, yet they are significant of a widespread belief that woman's physical structure, and the functions she performs in consequence thereof, justify special legislation restricting or qualifying the conditions under which she should be permitted to toil. Constitutional questions, it is true, are not settled by even a consensus of present public opinion, for it is the peculiar value of a written constitution that it places in unchanging form limitations upon legislative action, and thus gives a permanence and stability to popular government which otherwise would be lacking. At the same time, when a question of fact is debated and debatable, and the extent to which a special constitutional limitation goes is affected by the truth in respect to that fact, a widespread and long continued belief concerning it is worthy of consideration. We take judicial cognizance of all matters of general knowledge.

It is undoubtedly true, as more than once declared by this court, that the general right to contract in relation to one's business is part of the liberty of the individual, protected by the Fourteenth Amendment to the Federal Constitution; yet it is equally well settled that this liberty is not absolute and extending to all contracts, and that a State may, without conflicting with the provisions of the Fourteenth Amendment, restrict in many respects the individual's power of contract. Without stopping to discuss at length the extent to which a State may act in this respect, we refer to the following cases in which the question has been considered: ..., *Holden v. Hardy* ..., *Lochner v. New York.* ...

That woman's physical structure and the performance of maternal functions place her at a disadvantage in the struggle for subsistence is obvious. This is especially true when the burdens of motherhood are upon her. Even when they are not, by abundant testimony of the medical fraternity continuance for a long time on her feet at work, repeating this from day to day, tends to injurious effects upon the body, and as healthy mothers are essential to vigorous offspring, the physical well-being of woman becomes an object of public interest and care in order to preserve the strength and vigor of the race.

Still again, history discloses the fact that woman has always been dependent upon man. He established his control at the outset by superior physical strength, and this control in various forms, with diminishing intensity, has continued to the present. As minors, though not to the same extent, she has been looked upon in the courts as needing especial care that her rights may be preserved. Education was long denied her, and while now the doors of the school-room are opened and her opportunities for acquiring knowledge are great, yet even with that and the consequent increase of capacity for business affairs it is still true that in the struggle for subsistence she is not an equal competitor with her brother. Though limitations upon personal and contractual rights may be removed by legislation, there is that in her disposition and habits of life which will operate against a full assertion of those rights. She will still be where some legislation to protect her seems necessary to secure a real equality of right. Doubtless there are individual exceptions, and there are many respects in which she has an advantage over him; but looking at it from the viewpoint of the effort to maintain an independent position in life, she is not upon an equality. Differentiated by these matters from the other sex, she is properly placed in a class by herself, and legislation designed for her protection may be sustained, even when like legislation is not necessary for men and could not be sustained. It is impossible to close one's eyes to the fact that she still looks to her brother and depends upon him. Even though all restrictions on political, personal, and contractual rights were taken away, and she stood, so far as statutes are concerned, upon an absolutely equal plane with him, it would still be true that she is so constituted that she will rest upon and look to him for protection; that her physical structure and a proper discharge of her maternal functions—having in view not merely her own health, but the well-being of the race—justify legislation to protect her from the greed as well as the passion of man. The limitations which this statute places upon her contractual powers, upon her right to agree with her employer as to the time she shall labor, are not imposed solely for her benefit, but also largely for the benefit of all. Many words cannot make this plainer. The two sexes differ in structure of body, in the functions to be performed by each, in the amount of physical strength, in the capacity for long-continued labor, particularly when done standing, the influence of vigorous health upon the future well-being of the race, the self-reliance which enables one to assert full rights, and in the capacity to maintain the struggle for subsistence. This difference justifies a difference in legislation and upholds that which is designed to compensate for some of the burdens which rest upon her. ...

For these reasons, and without questioning in any respect the decision in *Lochner v. New York*, we are of the opinion that it cannot be adjudged that the act in question is in conflict with the Federal Constitution, so far as it respects the work of a female in a laundry, and the judgment of the Supreme Court of Oregon is *Affirmed.*

✣ *D O C U M E N T   6*

Legal Scholar Roscoe Pound Criticizes the Liberty to Contract, 1909

"The right of a person to sell his labor," says Mr. Justice Harlan, "upon such terms as he deems proper, is in its essence, the same as the right of the purchaser of labor to prescribe the conditions upon which he will accept such labor from the person offering to sell it. So the right of the employee to quit the service of the employer, for whatever reason, is the same as the right of the employer, for whatever reason, to dispense with the services of such employee. ... In all such particulars the employer and the employee have equality of right, and any legislation that disturbs that equality is an arbitrary interference with the liberty of contract, which no government can legally justify in a free land." With this positive declaration of a lawyer, the culmination of a line of decisions now nearly twenty-five years old, a statement which a recent writer on the science of jurisprudence has deemed so fundamental as to deserve quotation and exposition at an unusual length, as compared with his treatment of other points, let us compare the equally positive statement of a sociologist:

"Much of the discussion about 'equal rights' is utterly hollow. All the ado made over the system of contract is surcharged with fallacy."

To everyone acquainted at first hand with actual industrial conditions the latter statement goes without saying. Why, then do courts persist in the fallacy? Why do so many of them force upon legislation an academic theory of equality in the face of practical conditions of inequality? Why do we find a great and learned court in 1908 taking the long step into the past of dealing with the relation between employer and employee in railway transportation, as if the parties were individuals—as if they were farmers haggling over the sale of a horse? Why is the legal conception of the relation of employer and employee so at variance with the common knowledge of mankind? The late President has told us that it is because individual judges project their personal, social and economic views into the law. A great German publicist holds that it is because the party bent of judges has dictated decisions. But when a doctrine is announced with equal vigor and held with equal tenacity by courts of Pennsylvania and of Arkansas, of New York and of California, of Illinois and of West Virginia, of Massachusetts and of Missouri, we may not dispose of it so readily. Surely the sources of such a doctrine must lie deeper. Let us inquire then, what further and more potent causes may be discovered, how these causes have operated to bring about the present state of the law as to freedom of contract, what the present doctrine of the courts is upon that subject, and how far we may expect amelioration thereof in the near future. ...

. . . [O]ur ideal of justice has been to let every force play freely and exert itself completely, limited only by the necessity of avoiding friction. As a result, and as a result of our legal history, we exaggerate the importance of property and of contract, as an incident thereof. A leader of the bar, opposing the income tax, argues that a fundamental object of our polity is "preservation of the rights of private property." Text writers tell us of the divine origin of property. The Supreme Court of Wisconsin tells us that the right to take property by will is an absolute and inherent right, not depending upon legislation. The absolute certainty which is one of our legal ideals, an ideal responsible for much that is irritatingly mechanical in our legal system, is demanded chiefly to protect property. And our courts regard the right to contract, not as a phase of liberty—a sort of freedom of mental motion and locomotion—but as a phase of property, to be protected as such. A further result is to exaggerate private right at the expense. Blackstone's proposition that "the public good is in nothing more essentially interested than in the protection of every individual's private rights," has been quoted in more than one American decision; and one of these is a case often cited in support of extreme doctrines of liberty of contract. It is but a corollary that liberty of contract cannot be restricted merely in the interest of a contracting party. His right to contract freely is to yield only to the safety, health, or moral welfare of the public. Still another result is that bench and bar distrust and object to legislation. ... Suffice it to say here that the doctrine as to liberty of contract is bound up in the decisions of our courts with a narrow view of what constitutes special or class legislation that greatly limits effective law-making. If we can only have laws of wide generality of application, we can have only a few laws; for the wider their application the more likelihood there is of injustice in concrete cases. But from the individualist standpoint a minimum of law is desirable. The common law antipathy to legislation sympathizes with this, and in consequence we find courts saying that it is not necessary to consider the reasons that led up to the type of legislation they condemn and that the maxim that the government governs best which governs least is proper for courts to bear in mind in expounding the Constitution.

   The second cause [is] mechanical jurisprudence. ... The effect of all system is apt to be petrifaction of the subject systematized. Legal science is not exempt from this tendency. Legal systems have their periods in which system decays into technicality, in which a scientific jurisprudence becomes a mechanical jurisprudence. In a period of growth through juristic speculation and judicial decision, there is little danger of this. But whenever such a period has come to an end, when its work has been done and its legal theories have come to maturity, jurisprudence tends to decay. Conceptions are fixed. The premises are no longer to be examined. Everything is reduced to simple deduction from them. Principles cease to have importance. The law becomes a body of rules. ...

   Survival of a purely juristic notion of the state and of economics and politics, in contrast with the social conception of the present, the third cause suggested, can be looked at but briefly. Formerly the juristic attitude obtained in religion, in morals, and in politics as well as in law. This fundamentally juristic conception of the world, due possibly to Roman law being the first subject of study in the universities, which gave a form of legality even to theology, has passed away elsewhere. But it lingers in the courts. Jurisprudence is the last in the march of the sciences away from the method of deduction from predetermined conceptions. The sociological movement in jurisprudence, the movement for pragmatism as a philosophy of law, the movement for the adjustment of principles and doctrines to the human conditions they are to govern rather than to assumed first principles, the movement for putting the human factor in the central place and relegating logic to its true position as an instrument, has scarcely shown itself as yet in America. Perhaps the dissenting opinion of Mr. Justice Holmes in *Lochner v. New York*, is the best exposition of it we have.

Another factor of no mean importance in producing the line of decisions we are considering is the training of lawyers and judges in eighteenth century theories of natural law.... Until a comparatively recent date, all legal education, whether in school or in office, began with the study of Blackstone. Probably all serious office study begins with Blackstone or some American imitator to-day. Many schools make Blackstone the first subject of instruction to-day, and in others Blackstone is a subject of examination for admission or of prescribed reading after admission, or there are courses on elementary law in which texts reproducing the theories of the introduction to and the first book of the *Commentaries* are the basis of instruction. A student who is college-trained may have had a course or courses that brought him in contact with modern thought. It is quite as likely he has not, or if he has, the natural law theories which are a matter of course in all our law books are not unlikely to persuade him that what he learned in college is immaterial in the domain of law. Constitutional law is full of natural law notions. For one thing, there is the doctrine that apart from constitutional restrictions there are individual rights resting on a natural basis, to which courts must give effect "beyond the control of the state." In the judicial discussions of liberty of contract this idea has been very prominent. ... These natural law ideas are carried to an extreme by the Supreme Court of Illinois in *Ritchie* v. *People*, in which case it is announced that women have a natural equality with men and that no distinction may be drawn between them with respect to power of engaging to labor....

Not only, however, is natural law the fundamental assumption of our elementary books and of professional philosophy, but we must not forget that it is the theory of our bills of rights. Not unnaturally, therefore, courts have clung to it as being the orthodox theory of our constitutions. But the fact that the framers held that theory by no means demonstrates that they intended to impose the theory upon us for all time. It is contrary to their principles to assume that they intended to dictate philosophical or juristic beliefs and opinions to those who were to come after them. What they did intend was the *practical* securing of each individual against arbitrary and capricious governmental acts. They intended to protect the people against their rulers, not against themselves. They laid down principles, not rules, and rules can only be illustrations of those principles so long as facts and opinions remain what they were when the rules were announced....

The attitude of many of our courts on the subject of liberty of contract is so certain to be misapprehended, is so out of the range of ordinary understanding, the decisions themselves are so academic and so artificial in their reasoning, that they cannot fail to engender such feelings. Thus, those decisions do an injury beyond the failure of a few acts. These acts can be replaced as legislatures learn how to comply with the letter of the decisions and to evade the spirit of them. But the lost respect for courts and law cannot be replaced. The evil of those cases will live after them in impaired authority of the courts long after the decisions themselves are forgotten.

✤ *D O C U M E N T   7*

Adkins v. Children's Hospital, 1923

Mr. Justice Sutherland delivered the opinion of the Court.

. . . The statute now under consideration is attacked upon the ground that it authorizes an unconstitutional interference with the freedom of contract included within the guaranties of the due process clause of the Fifth Amendment. That the right to contract about one's affairs is a part of the liberty of the individual protected by this clause, is settled by the decisions of this Court and is no longer open to question. . . .

Within this liberty are contracts of employment of labor. In making such contracts, generally speaking, the parties have an equal right to obtain from each other the best terms they can as the result of private bargaining. . . .

There is, of course, no such thing as absolute freedom of contract. It is subject to a great variety of restraints. But freedom of contract is, nevertheless, the general rule and restraint the exception; and the exercise of legislative authority to abridge it can be justified only by the existence of exceptional circumstances. Whether these circumstances exist in the present case constitutes the question to be answered. It will be helpful to this end to review some of the decisions where the interference has been upheld and consider the grounds upon which they rest.

(1) *Those dealing with statutes fixing rates and charges to be exacted by businesses impressed with a public interest. . . .*

(2) *Statutes relating to contracts for the performance of public work. . . .*

(3) *Statutes prescribing the character, methods and time for payment of wages.*

(4) *Statutes fixing hours of labor.* It is upon this class that the greatest emphasis is laid in argument and therefore, and because such cases approach most nearly the line of principle applicable to the statute here involved, we shall consider them more at length. In some instances the statute limited the hours of labor for men in certain occupations and in others it was confined in its application to women. No statute has thus far been brought to the attention of this Court which by its terms, applied to all occupations. In *Holden v. Hardy . . .* , the Court considered an act of the Utah legislature, restricting the hours of labor in mines and smelters. This statute was sustained as a legitimate exercise of the police power, on the ground that the legislature had determined that these particular employments, when too long pursued, were injurious to the health of the employees, and that, as there were reasonable grounds for supporting this determination on the part of the legislature, its decision in that respect was beyond the reviewing power of the federal courts.

That this constituted the basis of the decision is emphasized by the subsequent decision in *Lochner v. New York . . .* , reviewing a state statute which restricted the employment of all persons in bakeries to ten hours in any one day. The Court referred to *Holden v. Hardy, supra,* and, declaring it to be inapplicable, held the statute unconstitutional as an unreasonable, unnecessary and arbitrary interference with the liberty of contract and therefore void under the Constitution. . . .

Subsequent cases in this Court have been distinguished from that decision [*Lochner*], but the principles therein stated have never been disapproved. ...

The essential characteristics of the statute now under consideration, which differentiate it from the laws fixing hours of labor, will be made to appear as we proceed. It is sufficient now to point out that the latter ... deal[s] with incidents of the employment having no necessary effect upon the heart of the contract, that is, the amount of wages to be paid and received. A law forbidding work to continue beyond a given number of hours leaves the parties free to contract about wages and thereby equalize whatever additional burdens may be imposed upon the employer as a result of the restrictions as to hours, by an adjustment in respect of the amount of wages. Enough has been said to show that the authority to fix hours of labor cannot be exercised except in respect of those occupations where work of long continued duration is detrimental to health. This Court has been careful in every case where the question has been raised, to place its decision upon this limited authority of the legislature to regulate hours of labor and to disclaim any purpose to uphold the legislation as fixing wages, thus recognizing an essential difference between the two. It seems plain that these decisions afford no real support for any form of law establishing minimum wages.

If now, in the light furnished by the foregoing exceptions to the general rule forbidding legislative interference with freedom of contract, we examine and analyze the statute in question, we shall see that it differs from them in every material respect. It is not a law dealing with any business charged with a public interest or with public work, or to meet and tide over a temporary emergency. It has nothing to do with the character, methods or periods of wage payments. It does not prescribe hours of labor or conditions under which labor is to be done. It is not for the protection of persons under legal disability or for the prevention of fraud. It is simply and exclusively a price-fixing law, confined to adult women (for we are not now considering the provisions relating to minors), who are legally as capable of contracting for themselves as men. It forbids two parties having lawful capacity—under penalties as to the employer—to freely contract with one another in respect of the price for which one shall render service to the other in a purely private employment where both are willing, perhaps anxious, to agree, even though the consequence may be to oblige one to surrender a desirable engagement and the other to dispense with the services of a desirable employee. The price fixed by the board need have no relation to the capacity or earning power of the employee, the number of hours which may happen to constitute the day's work, the character of the place where the work is to be done, or the circumstances or surroundings of the employment; and, while it has no other basis to support its validity than the assumed necessities of the employee, it takes no account of any independent resources she may have. It is based wholly on the opinions of the members of the board and their advisers—perhaps an average of their opinions, if they do not precisely agree—as to what will be necessary to provide a living for a woman, keep her in health and preserve her morals. It applies to any and every occupation in the District, without regard to its nature or the character of the work. ...

The feature of this statute which, perhaps more than any other, puts upon it the stamp of invalidity is that it exacts from the employer an arbitrary payment for a purpose and upon a basis having no causal connection with his business, or the contract or the work the employee engages to do. The declared basis, as already pointed out, is not the value of the service rendered, but the extraneous circumstance that the employee needs to get a prescribed sum of money to insure her subsistence, health and morals. The ethical right of every worker, man or woman, to a living wage may be conceded. One of the declared and important purposes of trade organizations is to secure it. And with that principle and with every legitimate effort to realize it in fact, no one can quarrel; but the fallacy of the proposed method of attaining it is that it assumes that every employer is bound at all events to furnish it. The moral requirement implicit in every contract of employment, viz., that the amount to be paid and the service to be rendered shall bear to each other some relation of just equivalence, is completely ignored. The necessities of the employee are alone considered and these arise outside of the employment, are the same when there is no employment, and as great in one occupation as in another. Certainly the employer by paying a fair equivalent for the service rendered, though not sufficient to support the employee, has neither caused nor contributed to her poverty. On the contrary, to the extent of what he pays he has relieved it. In principle, there can be no difference between the case of selling labor and the case of selling goods. If one goes to the butcher, the baker or grocer to buy food, he is morally entitled to obtain the worth of his money but he is not entitled to more. If what he gets is worth what he pays he is not justified in demanding more simply because he needs more; and the shopkeeper, having dealt fairly and honestly in that transaction, is not concerned in any peculiar sense with the question of his customer's necessities. Should a statute undertake to vest in a commission power to determine the quantity of food necessary for individual support and require the shopkeeper, if he sell to the individual at all, to furnish that quantity at not more than a fixed maximum, it would undoubtedly fall before the constitutional test. The fallacy of any argument in support of the validity of such a statute would be quickly exposed. The argument in support of that now being considered is equally fallacious, though the weakness of it may not be so plain. A statute requiring an employer to pay in money, to pay at prescribed and regular intervals, to pay the value of the services rendered, even to pay with fair relation to the extent of the benefit obtained from the service, would be understandable. But a statute which prescribes payment without regard to any of these things and solely with relation to circumstances apart from the contract of employment, the business affected by it and the work done under it, is so clearly the product of a naked, arbitrary exercise of power that it cannot be allowed to stand under the Constitution of the United States.

We are asked, upon the one hand, to consider the fact that several States have adopted similar statutes, and we are invited, upon the other hand, to give weight to the fact that three times as many States, presumably as well informed and as anxious to promote the health and morals of their people, have refrained from enacting such legislation. We have also been furnished with a large number of printed opinions approving the policy of the minimum wage, and our own reading has disclosed a large number to the contrary. These are all proper enough for the consideration of the lawmaking bodies, since their tendency is to establish the desirability or undesirability of the legislation; but they reflect no legitimate light upon the question of its validity, and that is what we are called upon to decide. The elucidation of that question cannot be aided by counting heads.

It is said that great benefits have resulted from the operation of such statutes, not alone in the District of Columbia but in the several States, where they have been in force. A mass of reports, opinions of special observers and students of the subject, and the like, has been brought before us in support of this statement, all of which we have found interesting but only mildly persuasive. That the earnings of women now are greater than they were formerly and that conditions affecting women have become better in other respects may be conceded, but convincing indications of the logical relation of these desirable changes to the law in question are significantly lacking. They may be, and quite probably are, due to other causes. We cannot close our eyes to the notorious fact that earnings everywhere in all occupations have greatly increased—not alone in States where the minimum wage law obtains but in the country generally—quite as much or more among men as among women and in occupations outside the reach of the law as in those governed by it. No real test of the economic value of the law can be had during periods of maximum employment, when general causes keep wages up to or above the minimum; that will come in periods of depression and struggle for employment when the efficient will be employed at the minimum rate while the less capable may not be employed at all.

Finally, it may be said that if, in the interest of the public welfare, the police power may be invoked to justify the fixing of a minimum wage, it may, when the public welfare is thought to require it, be invoked to justify a maximum wage. The power to fix high wages connotes, by like course of reasoning, the power to fix low wages. If, in the face of the guaranties of the Fifth Amendment, this form of legislation shall be legally justified, the field for the operation of the police power will have been widened to a great and dangerous degree. If, for example, in the opinion of future lawmakers, wages in the building trades shall become so high as to preclude people of ordinary means from building and owning homes, an authority which sustains the minimum wage will be invoked to support a maximum wage for building laborers and artisans, and the same argument which has been here urged to strip the employer of his constitutional liberty of contract in one direction will be utilized to strip the employee of his constitutional liberty of contract in the opposite direction. A wrong decision does not end with itself: it is a precedent, and, with the swing of sentiment, its bad influence may run from one extremity of the arc to the other.

It has been said that legislation of the kind now under review is required in the interest of social justice, for whose ends freedom of contract may lawfully be subjected to restraint. The liberty of the individual to do as he pleases, even in innocent matters, is not absolute. It must frequently yield to the common good, and the line beyond which the power of interference may not be pressed is neither definite nor unalterable but may be made to move, within limits not well defined, with changing need and circumstance. Any attempt to fix a rigid boundary would be unwise as well as futile. But, nevertheless, there are limits to the power, and when these have been passed, it becomes the plain duty of the courts in the proper exercise of their authority to so declare. To sustain the individual freedom of action contemplated by the Constitution, is not to strike down the common good but to exalt it; for surely the good of society as a whole cannot be better served than by the preservation against arbitrary restraint of the liberties of its constituent members ...

For decades, scholars studying this period in U.S. constitutional history stressed the Supreme Court's conservative nature. Laissez-faire ideology, according to this perspective, permeated the Court and gave the justices an intellectual hook on which to hang their conservative economic views. Paul Kens, a professor of political science at Texas State University, writes within this vein in his examination of *Lochner v. New York*. Kens emphasizes the ideology of individual justices and places particular weight on the dissent of Justice Holmes, who criticized his colleagues for supposedly writing economic theory into constitutional law.

Julie Novkov, a professor of political science and women's studies at the University at Albany, State University of New York, sheds a different light on debates over economic regulation. Novkov demonstrates that courts upheld protective legislation more often than not and that courts were much more likely to uphold protective legislation in cases involving women. Judges and legal thinkers, she contends, began to focus on women as a specific category of laborers rather than on the type of labor that they performed. Ideas about gender, in short, significantly influenced judicial thinking about the scope of police powers and the meaning of liberty to contract.

The *Lochner* Court and Judicial Conservatism

PAUL KENS

. . . The *Lochner* case afforded [Justice Rufus W.] Peckham an opportunity to express disdain for what he perceived to be a trend toward paternalistic legislation. "It is impossible for us to shut our eyes to the fact that many laws of this character, while passed under what is claimed to be the police power for the purpose of protecting the public health or welfare, are, in reality, passed for other motives," he explained. Peckham did not explain what improper motives he had in mind, but he proclaimed that the state had to show more than a vague link to health and safety. Otherwise any type of regulation would be possible. Directing attention to the extremes, he projected that the work hours not only of employees but also of employers might be limited. Artisans, scientists, doctors, and even lawyers could be forbidden to fatigue their brains and bodies by prolonged hours of exercise. The rights of all individuals to do what they want with the fruit of their labor would be at the mercy of legislative majorities.

"This is not a question of substituting the judgment of the Court for that of the legislature," Peckham explained. But of course that is exactly what he was doing. The Bakeshop Act had been passed not once, but twice, by the legislature of the state of New York. Both times the vote had been unanimous, and amendments to the ten-hour workday provision were specifically at issue in the second vote. At the very least it could be said that one hundred nineteen legislators had voted in favor of the ten-hour ceiling.

Although some studies indicated that the trade was not unusually dangerous, there was ample statistical support for the contention that baking was an unhealthy occupation. A study conducted by the state labor commissioner one year before the Bakeshop Act was passed had reached that conclusion, and it was supported by a substantial portion of the scientific and medical opinion of the time. Attorney General

From Paul Kens, *Lochner v. New York: Economic Regulation on Trial,* University Press of Kansas, 1999. Reproduced with permission of the publisher.

Mayer had not emphasized this in his brief, but Judge Vann had done so in a concurring opinion that was available to the justices as part of the record of the case.

All of the justices who heard Joseph Lochner's appeal had been sitting on the Court two years earlier when, in *Atkin v. Kansas*, they ruled that legislative enactments should be recognized and enforced "unless they are plainly and palpably, beyond all question, in violation of the fundamental law of the Constitution." According to that standard, when the validity of a statute was being questioned, the burden of proof fell upon those who asserted that it was unconstitutional. John Harlan, who wrote Atkin for a 6 to 3 majority, argued this point often and vehemently. For him, that there was room for debate and for an honest difference of opinion should have put an end to the case. Even if a statute seemed unwise or unjust, Harlan believed the responsibility for making that determination belonged to the legislature.

If the Court had remained true to this part of the *Atkin* decision, the New York Bakeshop Act would have been upheld. But Peckham shifted the burden. Taking a weight from the shoulders of Weismann and Field, he presented the attorney general, the legislature, or anyone else who might want to defend the statute with a duty to clearly demonstrate that there was some fair ground to say that the public health or the health of bakers would suffer if the hours of labor were not shortened.

The vote was close – so close that historical rumor has it that the case was at first decided the other way and that Harlan initially prepared a draft that was to be the opinion of the Court. Nevertheless when the final vote was taken, a 5 to 4 majority of the Court agreed that the ten-hour limitation on the workday of New York bakers was unconstitutional. At some point Harlan had lost two votes. Justices Henry Billings Brown and Joseph McKenna, who had stood with him in *Atkin*, switched. Gone with their votes was the principle that an act of a state legislature was presumed to be valid.

Gone too was any doubt about how the Court intended to define the police power in cases involving state "experimentation" with labor regulations. "There is no contention that bakers as a class are not equal in intelligence and capacity to men in other trades or manual occupations, or that they are not able to assert their rights and care for themselves without the protecting arm of the state," wrote Peckham. The term "public welfare" appeared in Peckham's text, but the majority plainly had agreed that the only valid justification for such legislation was its relationship to health and safety. Six years after Justice Stephen J. Field's death, the Court had finally adopted his view of a limited police power....

"The Fourteenth Amendment does not enact Mr. Herbert Spencer's *Social Statics*." With this one sentence, explained his friend Harold Laski, Justice Holmes exposed the inarticulate major premise of the *Lochner* majority. His terse two-page dissent elucidated reformers' misgivings about the decision and more. Oliver Wendell Holmes Jr. had been sitting on the Supreme Court for less than two years when *Lochner* was decided, but he was hardly an unknown. He had been a justice of the Massachusetts Supreme Court for twenty years when Theodore Roosevelt nominated him for the nation's highest court in 1902. By then Holmes had long established his reputation as a legal scholar. Early in his career as a practicing lawyer he edited the prestigious *American Law Review*, and in 1881 he wrote a classic legal treatise entitled *The Common Law*. One year later a new chair was established for him at Harvard Law School, where he taught for a year before assuming his position on the Massachusetts high court.

Born in 1841 into a family that was part of the "Brahmin caste" of New England, Holmes's circumstances were marked by pedigree and privilege. But this elite class of New Englanders prided itself on intellectual prowess as well, and in the late nineteenth century it was experiencing a renaissance. Holmes's father, a well-known physician and author, was associated with a literary group called the Saturday Club. Its members included Ralph Waldo Emerson, Henry Wadsworth Longfellow, Richard Henry Dana, and Harvard professors Louis Agassiz, James Russell Lowell, and Benjamin Peirce. As a youth, Holmes had the opportunity to associate with these great thinkers of his time, and he was even close to some. Emerson, for example, critiqued a youthful essay on Plato, and Holmes sought his advice before embarking on a career in law.

Throughout his life Holmes formed and maintained friendships with people of intellectual distinction. In the field of American law, Felix Frankfurter, Louis Brandeis, Roscoe Pound, and Learned Hand come to mind. Outside of the profession, Henry Adams, William and Henry James, and A. G. Segwick are some that might be remembered today. The point is that Holmes's proclivities were toward the historical, literary, and philosophical disciplines; and these carried over to his legal writings and judicial opinions, which at times bore the stamp of an essayist and philosopher.

This may explain in part why no justice of the Supreme Court has attracted more attention or been the subject of more comment with more fervor than has Holmes. Over time he has become as much legend as judge. And as is often the case with legendary figures, those who study him are not in agreement about the value of his contribution, nor for that matter about just what his philosophy entailed. Various commentators have placed Holmes into widely disparate categories—positivist, cynic, social Darwinist, liberal, legal realist, relativist. Such attempts to categorize and even to assess the long-term impact of the justice's career lend themselves to dispute. But certain aspects of Holmes's thinking are unmistakable.

Interestingly, Holmes had little sympathy for reform. He never expressed a systematic theory of economics, but he did lean toward the classic doctrines of nineteenth-century laissez faire. Harold Laski recalled that "the basis of Holmes' economic faith would have been rejected neither by Adam Smith nor Ricardo." Private ownership and self-interest made up its foundation, and he distrusted what he deemed to be the futile if not mischievous economic tinkering of welfare legislation.

Although he did not join reformers in rejecting laissez-faire economics, Holmes was plainly with them and with Roscoe Pound in disliking the legal method of reasoning that deduced conclusions from a priori principles. In an 1897 speech presented at Boston University School of Law, Holmes argued that the legal method suffered from a "fallacy of logical form." It perceived the universe in terms of a fixed quantitative relation between every phenomenon and its antecedents and consequences, he continued. Thus it operated from the notion that a legal system could be worked out like mathematics from general axioms of conduct. This mode of thinking was entirely natural for lawyers, in part because of their training, but also because "it flatters a longing for certainty." But certainty, he warned, is an illusion. "No concrete proposition is self evident, no matter how ready we may be to accept it." Reflected in this conclusion was the nucleus of Holmes's thinking—his well-known skepticism. "When I say that a thing is true I mean that I can't help believing it—and nothing more," he explained. "But as I observe that the cosmos is not always limited by my 'can't helps' I don't bother about absolute truth or even inquire whether there is such a thing, but define the truth as the system of my limitations."

The uncertainty reflected in Holmes's description of his "can't helps" should not be confused with timidity. Observing that Holmes was the least hesitant of men, one of his critics, Yosal Rogat, later noted that it was difficult to think of anyone who expressed fewer qualifications or occupied fewer halfway positions. What then did this skepticism mean? Rogat thought that it could be translated into crude relativism: might makes right. He argued that Holmes was too detached from the consequences of his decisions and too fatalistic in his attitude toward power. Rogat's argument seems convincing, but it fails to recognize that one can act on a belief without insisting that it is universal or immutable law.

Holmes did not distrust his own principles or beliefs. Rather, he distrusted dogma. If the search for truth was subject to ever-changing human limitations and personal prejudices, as he believed, the best approximation of truth would be reached through the free play of ideas. The meaning of all this has been the subject of considerable debate. What is important, however, is that Holmes's uncertainty, his "can't helps," his skepticism ultimately boil down to a suspicion of first principles. Principles elevated to a level of immutable law posed the greatest danger to a free exchange of ideas. Holmes believed that rather than providing truth, they limited the search for the truth.

Skepticism carried over into Holmes's ideas about the role of judges. In 1913 he told a Harvard Law School audience that "all law embodies beliefs that have triumphed in the battle of ideas and then have translated themselves into action." So long as there is still doubt and opposite convictions continue to battle, he said, "it is a mistake if a judge reads his conscious or unconscious sympathy with one side or the other prematurely into law, and forgets that what seems to him to be first principles are believed by half of his fellow men to be wrong."

The impact his beliefs would have on his opinions from the bench of the United States Supreme Court was made clear in his first written opinion. "Considerable latitude must be allowed for differences of view," he wrote in *Otis v. Parker*. "Otherwise a constitution, instead of embodying only relatively fundamental rules of right, as generally understood by all English-speaking communities, would become the partisan of a particular set of ethical or economical opinions which by no means are held *semper ubique et ab omnibus*."

It is popular today to speak of the Supreme Court as the "forum of principle." Principle, as distinguished from policy, is said to be "a standard observed, not because it will advance or secure an economic, political, or social situation deemed desirable, but because it is a requirement of justice or fairness or some other dimension of morality." Because it is appointed, life tenured, and thus insulated from the pressures of politics, the federal judiciary is thought to be the institution best suited to determine such matters of principle. Michael J. Perry, for example, maintains that "the Court is ordained by tradition to serve as the forum for the subtle dialectical interplay of complex, principled ethical discourse." He and others believe that of the branches of government, the politically insulated Court is the most likely to shed the sediment of old moralities and move toward moral evolution. At the very least, judicial review is said to encourage and increase dialogue and thereby move us more certainly in the direction of truth.

Modern scholars have not forgotten the *Lochner* case, but their memory of it has been selective. The decision has come to be known as an instance of the Court mistakenly dabbling in matters of economic policy. When the background of the case is recalled, however, it is readily apparent that it involved something more: it was a dispute between competing principles. Holmes recognized this and pointed out the implications in his short dissent. "A constitution is not intended to embody a particular economic theory," he wrote. "It is made for people of fundamentally differing views, and the accident of our finding certain opinions natural and familiar or novel or even shocking ought not to conclude our judgment upon the question whether statutes embodying them conflict with the Constitution of the United States."

Several years later, Learned Hand wondered why the validity of the bakeshop law ever became a matter of health in the first place. His answer was predictable. The crucial aspect of *Lochner* was that the majority had finally adopted Field's definition of the police power. It had embraced a laissez-faire-social Darwinian interpretation of the Constitution. This did not mean that a complete absence of state involvement in the economy was assured. Some regulation might be acceptable under this interpretation, but only so long as it fit within the laissez-faire framework.

The word "interpretation" should be emphasized. Laissez faire-social Darwinism is not part of the Constitution of the United States. The Court took two large steps away from that document to reach the conclusion that states were confined to that framework in managing their internal affairs. Initially mutation of the Fourteenth Amendment's due process guarantee provided the means by which the Court was able to review the substance of laws dealing with a state's management of its internal affairs. Then liberty of contract provided an extra constitutional theory upon which the laissez-faire boundary was erected around a state's police power.

Almost anywhere else Rufus Peckham could have spoken his mind with little harm done. But the American system of government tends to give the Supreme Court the final word on what is and what is not constitutional. Its decisions therefore often represent much more than a final determination in a specific dispute between competing parties. They become part of the nation's fundamental law. As such they carry an air of immutability, of being first principles upon which all other laws should be based. This was the implication of the *Lochner* decision that most concerned Justice Holmes. ...

The symbolic importance of *Lochner v. New York* is beyond question. For more than thirty years it served reformers as evidence of the conservative nature of the judiciary and as a striking example of its usurpation of political power. Even today this historical period marked by judicial interference with reform is referred to as "the *Lochner* Era," and the terms "lochnerism" and "lochnerian" can be found in legal writings. The Holmes dissent added fuel to this legacy, but it also explained how the timeless significance of the decision goes beyond symbolism. Holmes recognized that the Court's impact on the public conscience in defining the parameters of moral and philosophical debate, although intangible, was very real. To understand this is to understand why a case so trivial in terms of its direct result has become such an important part of constitutional history.

Gender, Law, and Labor in the Progressive Era

JULIE NOVKOV

In the years between the Supreme Court's decision in *Holden v. Hardy* and the Court's decision in *Adkins v. Children's Hospital*, the legitimacy of protective labor legislation was a major question for both state and federal courts. ...

In the entire group of opinions, courts tended to uphold protective labor legislation more frequently than they struck it down (64 percent and 36 percent, respectively). Looking at the cases divided by whether they dealt with statutes specifically limiting women's work, however, provides a modified picture. Fifty-nine percent of the general cases upheld protective legislation, as compared to over 80 percent of the cases dealing with protective legislation specifically aimed at women.

The most famous case of this time was undoubtedly *Lochner v. New York*; of the ten cases heard on the federal level, three struck down protective labor legislation using the kind of reasoning made famous (or infamous) by the Court in *Lochner*. As *Lochner* demonstrated and the outcomes of other cases confirm, plenty of controversy still existed with regard to cases involving general legislation. Two of the federal cases—*Muller v. Oregon* and *Cronin v. Adams*—upheld legislation directed at women. The remaining eight cases upheld various general regulations in the workplace.

This period was busy for the state courts. They participated actively in the process of judicial intervention into progressive legislation; often their decisions prefigured those of the federal courts. While not as hostile to protective labor legislation as they had been previously, state courts still struck down over 37 percent of the legislation they considered in reported opinions. As on the federal level, though, the difference gender makes is evident. State courts were much more willing to uphold laws affecting women. Once the nine cases involving explicitly gender-based legislation are placed in their own category, the rate of striking down general protective laws in reported opinions rises to 42 percent. The state courts were particularly amenable to upholding such legislation for women: only two cases resulted in the reversal of a protective measure for women.

As discussed below, the courts were particularly willing to uphold protective labor legislation directed at minors. Eight of the twenty-five state cases that upheld protective legislation between 1898 and 1910 dealt with laws designed to limit children's participation in the workforce. When the cases involving such legislation

Decisions in All Cases Involving Protective Labor Legislation, 1898–1910

	Upheld Protective Legislation	Struck Down Protective Legislation	Total
All cases	32 (64%)	18 (36%)	50
General cases	23 (59%)	16 (41%)	39
Cases involving women	9 (82%)	2 (18%)	11

From Novkov, Julie, *Constituting Workers, Protecting Women: Gender, Law, and Labor in the Progressive Era and New Deal Years.* University of Michigan Press, 2004. Reproduced with permission of the publisher.

Decisions in State Cases Involving Protective Labor Legislation, 1898–1910

	Upheld Protective Legislation	Struck Down Protective Legislation	Total
All cases	25 (62.5%)	15 (37.5%)	40
General cases	18 (58%)	13 (42%)	31
Cases involving women	7 (78%)	2 (22%)	9

are excluded on the state level, the difference between courts' attitudes toward general protective legislation and protective legislation for women increases. Here, while the rate of striking down statutes relating to women remains at only 22 percent, the rate of striking down protective legislative enactments not related to women reaches 58 percent.

The courts thus upheld women's protective legislation more frequently than general protective legislation on the whole, at the federal level, and at the state level. When cases involving children are excluded from the analysis, the strongest contrast emerges, with courts being notably hostile to most forms of general protective legislation while strongly supporting such legislation for women. While this record may not suggest an overwhelming ideological opposition to the progressive agenda, it does show that legislative attempts to regulate the terms and conditions of men's labor ran into significant roadblocks in both state and federal courts.

Brief Overview of Nodes and Litigation in the Period of Specific Balancing

The major nodes of conflict during this period arose directly from the emerging battles of the previous decades. The discussions about liberty, property, and police power now grew into full-fledged nodes of conflict, provoking responses in jurisdictions throughout the country both within and outside of the legal community. As the central legal questions became increasingly tightly defined, attention began to shift toward developing and expressing the facts as effectively as possible. This led the legal community to engage in specific, rather than generalized, balancing, weighing the factual content of the legal categories established in the previous period. Attorneys during these years began to work more directly with reformers, using the information reformers had developed to advance their legal arguments.

Attention centered around liberty and its role but in a more concrete fashion. The legal community further articulated the relationship between the due process clause and liberty of contract in a grounded way, analyzing closely the guarantees of liberty and property. The earlier period had confirmed the default normative position that regulation was improper; special justifications relating to the type of work or worker were needed to justify statutory protection. At this point, interpretations of liberty in cases involving women's protective legislation began to diverge from interpretations in cases addressing general legislation. With regard to general protective labor legislation, the legal community focused on liberty and its role, continuing

Decisions in State Cases, Excluding Cases Dealing with Children, Involving Protective Labor Legislation, 1898–1910

	Upheld Protective Legislation	Struck Down Protective Legislation	Total
All cases	17 (53%)	15 (47%)	32
General cases	10 (43%)	13 (57%)	23
Cases involving women	7 (78%)	2 (22%)	9

to rely upon a conception of a male subject of the guarantee of liberty. As reformers began to convince courts that protective legislation for women was constitutionally acceptable, the terms of the discussion about liberty in cases involving legislation regulating women's work began to shift. This gradually led to a situation in which liberty did not play a central role in such cases. The focus of these cases instead became women's relationship to liberty and labor, leading to an increasing emphasis on police power.

Police power, particularly in its relationship to public interest, also provoked major conflicts during these years, and analyses of its impact on general and female-oriented protective labor legislation began to diverge. With regard to general legislation, the legal community sought to delimit the scope of the state's authority to regulate, focusing on the meaning of health regulations. The touchstone was whether the regulation of a particular industry could validly be said to serve the public's interest. In these battles, the arguments were largely disputes about how the facts of particular cases fit into the legal frameworks developed in the earlier period. In light of the decisions made before the turn of the century, legislatures and attorneys seeking to validate limits knew that they could not prevail without a strong argument regarding police power; increasingly they argued that the statutes they supported addressed a particular kind of labor that was subject to regulation.

In cases involving women, the legal community began to consider the laborer in question more closely than the nature of the labor. Questions about police power quickly became questions about the state's capacity to regulate in favor of morality and in favor of women's reproductive health. Drawing on the outcomes and interpretive frameworks of the earlier cases, reformers worked to develop factual information linking regulation to the goals of the state, and some members of the legal community began to use this information to achieve their goal of legitimating state policies limiting women's work. The maternalist conception of the primacy of women's civic duties of childbearing and child rearing proved powerful as a justification for regulating feminine labor in the interest of the state as a whole. Throughout, arguments increasingly came to address the state's authority to limit women because of their status as problematic laborers due to their physical and emotional characteristics, thereby relying on and reinforcing the implicit male norm of the worker. These shifts in the focal points for analysis and the success of women's protective labor legislation would lead to the next stage of development in which considerations of statutes addressing women's work would come to the forefront of the debate.

The period of specific balancing began with the Supreme Court's ruling in *Holden v. Hardy* that a limitation that Utah placed on the number of hours per day that miners could work was a permissible exercise of the state's police powers. This case confirmed that the arguments about protective labor legislation were shifting toward the analysis of the types of labor and laborers who could be regulated, contrasting with the earlier abstract arguments about the scope and nature of the constitutional guarantees of due process and equal protection. Between 1898 and 1910, cases involving general limits on the terms and conditions of labor dominated the landscape of litigation. While some notable cases involved legislation intended to benefit women, the discussions within the legal community focused on general legislation. The idea that women's legislation required additional independent analysis slowly began to take hold during these years as the reasoning in cases involving general legislation evolved, resulting ultimately in the shift of emphasis from general legislation to women's legislation that would prevail after 1910.

With regard to general legislation, the Supreme Court's ruling in *Lochner* sculpted the federal landscape, confirming the basic thrust of many earlier state cases. Decided in 1905, this case invalidated New York's law limiting bakers to sixty-hour work weeks (*Lochner v. New York*, 198 U.S. 45 (1905)). Nonetheless during these years, the Supreme Court upheld a similar limitation on miners in *Holden v. Hardy* in 1898 (169 U.S. 366); a law preventing barbers from working on Sundays (*Petit v. Minnesota*, 177 U.S. 164 (1900)); a congressional statute limiting federal construction workers to eight hours of labor per day (*Ellis v. U.S.*, 206 U.S. 246 (1906)); and an Arkansas statute regulating payment of employees in the mining industry (*McLean v. Arkansas*, 211 U.S. 539 (1909)). While *Lochner* is at the center of many other analyses of the period, in this interpretation it comes in the middle of the period and simply confirmed argumentative trends that were taking place among attorneys and in the state courts. ...

Hours of Labor and the Special Risks of Female Workers

While the state courts developed reasoning concerning the relationship between police power and morality, in the period of specific balancing the legal community also addressed limits on women's hours of labor. These cases continued the trend established in the litigation over women's capacity to serve alcohol, focusing on women's special needs and relationship to the state. ...

The most noted arguments regarding women's differences were those constructed by Goldmark and Brandeis in their companion brief to persuade the Supreme Court to uphold Oregon's ten-hour-per-day limit on female laundry workers. Like the attorney arguing for the limit on hours at issue in *Lochner*, Goldmark and Brandeis sought to persuade the Court through the use of empirical data. Unlike the New York attorney, however, they focused on female workers rather than on the particular hazards associated with laundry work. Relying on the reams of information collected by the National Consumers' League over the years and additional studies from overseas, they built an argument based in police power that justified regulating women's labor by differentiating women from men in two ways. First, they expressed the general understanding that women, unlike men, had a particularly important role not only in bearing but also in rearing the next generation of citizens. Second, they argued that women's physical structure was different from men's, rendering women's reproductive capacities more vulnerable to damage from overwork. The lengthy brief was devoted mostly to demonstrating the physical differences, allowing the brief for the State of Oregon (of which Brandeis was also a coauthor) to draw the connection between these differences and the legitimate exercise of police power by the state. Their maternalist emphasis derived both from their connections to the National Consumers' League and from their belief that these arguments would most effectively convince the Court to depart from its ruling in *Lochner* only three years earlier.

Relying on evidence from the medical community, Goldmark and Brandeis documented the threats of overwork to women's delicate and complicated reproductive systems. Women whose line of work required them to stay on their feet were at particular risk: "The long hours of standing, which are required in many industries, are universally denounced by physicians as the cause of pelvic disorders". Even if a woman stopped working upon marriage, her reproductive system was not safe from the ravages of overwork (and thus was not safe for the developing citizens in her womb), since "The evil effect of overwork before as well as after marriage upon childbirth is marked and disastrous". Limiting women's hours of labor would thus help to prevent damage to their ability to bear children successfully.

The physical differences that Goldmark and Brandeis cataloged went beyond the reproductive organs. Again relying on evidence from physicians and information developed by the National Consumers' League, they argued that due to women's special structure and function as mothers, they had less natural endurance than men:

> Besides these anatomical and physiological differences, physicians are agreed that women are fundamentally weaker than men in all that makes for endurance: in muscular strength, in nervous energy, in the powers of persistent attention and application. Overwork, therefore, which strains endurance to the utmost, is more disastrous to the health of women than of men, and entails upon them more lasting injury.

Women's lack of endurance, they asserted, made women far more prone to suffer a variety of workplace injuries when they worked too long. Therefore, the state would be justified in providing special protection for them for the same reasons that the Court had upheld the protective statute for miners at issue in *Holden v. Hardy*. The need for protection, however, was rooted in women's bodies rather than in the labor itself....

Ultimately, all of these differences and particular potential harms related to women's connection to children. The substantial risks of harm to women alone were bad enough, threatening to initiate a period of decline in the physical, mental, and moral state of the entire community. The real harm, though, was that this deterioration would persist in the next generation, passed on by the overworked and damaged women of the current generation. Goldmark and Brandeis warned that when women were consistently permitted to work too long, "Infant mortality rises, while the children of married working-women, who survive, are injured by inevitable neglect. The overwork of future mothers thus directly attacks the welfare of the nation". The inevitable conclusion was that the state had the authority, if not the duty, to protect itself against the impending catastrophe.

In the brief for the state, the attorneys summarized Brandeis and Goldmark's extensive array of factual information, claiming that arguments in favor of women's freedom of contract were revealed as "mere sophistry" when balanced against the factual record of difference. The attorneys went on to paint a picture of women as marginal and strained workers who deserved the protection of the state. The state's ability to exercise police power to protect the public interest, they argued, clearly included the authority to regulate women's work. Given the particular risks that women ran when they overworked and given women's vital role in reproducing and raising the next generation, the state ridiculed the idea that a law limiting women's hours "is not a law involving the safety, the morals, nor the welfare of the public". Throughout this analysis, the brief's authors focused consistently on women and their physical risks; an uninformed reader would have had some difficulty discerning that the case was about laundry work.

Attorneys for Curt Muller, the laundry owner, attempted to counter this onslaught of factual evidence. They sought to use the strategy that had succeeded in *Lochner*, claiming that laundry work was not particularly dangerous to women's health, and that the statute rested instead on the illegitimate theory that women were in need of special protection solely on account of sex. They argued that in addition to resting on inaccurate assumptions regarding women's differences from men, the ultimate result of the statute in question would be to injure women's ability to succeed in the labor market by making them unable to compete effectively with unregulated men. Much of their argument, as discussed above, rested on the assertion that women were men's equals in their capacity to work and make contracts and on an expansive understanding of women's liberty under the ruling in *Lochner*. In doing so, they constructed women as holders of the abstract right to contract endorsed by the legal community in the period of generalized balancing. ...

The significance of the attorneys' debate was that it confirmed the shift in analysis for women's cases, both in terms of the focus and of the approach. The briefs all centered around women as laborers rather than the nature of laundry work and its particular hazards, following the patterns of litigation developed in the state courts, where judges and attorneys initiated the focus on female laborers in the context of the cases addressing alcohol servers. Goldmark and Brandeis's brief also forced the opponents of the law to respond to a dense factual debate, confirming that scientific evidence and factual arguments, rather than formal legal categories, would be the interpretive battleground for this case and for future cases.

The arguments against the limit on women's hours were ultimately unconvincing to the Supreme Court, which adopted Brandeis and Goldmark's arguments practically wholesale. The Court summarized the amicus brief quickly, citing the "abundant testimony of the medical fraternity" to support its assertion that the state had the authority to limit women's labor in order to protect its interest in "preserv[ing] the strength and vigor of the race" (*Muller v. Oregon*, 413). Reiterating the arguments made on the state's side, Justice Brewer went on to explain that regulating women's work benefited the entire populace and not only the women thus limited (421). The discussion of public health relied equally on the health of individual women as potential child bearers and rearers and the health of the body politic through its continuation in the next generation (421). It further confirmed the public significance of women and of their bodies particularly.

Following the trend already established on the state level, the Court further endorsed the idea that with regard to protective statutes addressing women's work, the laborer herself was the significant factor. The justices explained, "Differentiated by these matters from the other sex, she is properly placed in a class by herself, and legislation designed for her protection may be sustained, even when like legislation is not necessary for men, and could not be sustained" (*Muller v. Oregon*, 422). Here and in its explicit statement that its decision in no way raised questions about *Lochner*'s status, the Court demonstrated its implicit determination that male labor was the norm and female labor was a significant exception that warranted its own rules and ultimately its own jurisprudence. Such statements confirmed the move toward developing arguments specifically addressing women's situation rather than continuing to apply reasoning developed with regard to male-centered legislation like that at issue in either *Holden v. Hardy* or *Lochner v. New York*.

The outcome and reasoning in *Muller* were notable for their national significance, not for their novelty. The state courts, through their analysis of whether women's legislation automatically constituted illegitimate class legislation, had already moved toward considering women's position in the labor market in order to justify upholding limits on women's work. With increasing frequency, courts permitted the exercise of legislative control over women's work by articulating a state interest in women's health. Whether the courts upheld or struck down legislation, they mostly argued over whether women were in need of special protection, leaving the basis of discussion as the laborer rather than the restricted labor. Likewise, judges increasingly framed their opinions in terms of their beliefs about women's concrete capacities and the relationship between these capacities and the state. To make these kinds of claims, they relied on the scientific and social scientific evidence developed specifically for the cases. . . .

The two leading Supreme Court cases of the era, *Lochner v. New York* and *Muller v. Oregon*, highlighted the tensions of this period and demonstrated the split between cases involving general legislation and cases involving protection for women. Both involved challenges to state statutes limiting the hours of workers—New York had limited (male) bakers to sixty-hour work weeks, and Oregon prevented female laundry employees from working more than ten hours in a day—and *Muller* was decided only three years after *Lochner*. Nonetheless, the Supreme Court invalidated New York's statute and upheld Oregon's. The gender of the limited workers was the most obvious difference between the cases, but a closer look shows that the analyses in the two cases diverged on other grounds as well. These differences rested upon each case's position within different nodes of conflict.

Lochner is justifiably famous for establishing nationally the primacy of freedom of contract and thus the doctrinal and political significance of substantive due process. Within the development of nodes of conflict, *Lochner* was significant because it confirmed particular trends, not because it established them. The New York legislature, responding to the developing rule that protective measures had to be based on broadly defined threats to public health, ensured that they based the statute explicitly on the hazards of the baking industry to individual bakers and on the health risks that the general public faced from eating bread produced by unhealthy bakers. In doing so, the legislature relied on factual elaborations of two emerging legal principles: that some types of private labor were dangerous enough to the workers to warrant intervention and that some types of private labor had sufficient public significance to allow regulation. The Supreme Court confirmed that the threshold for justification under both of these principles was high indeed.

Muller was a key moment in the period of negotiation, but its significance went beyond the national establishment of the principle that measures protecting women were constitutionally valid despite the ruling in *Lochner*. The case marked the Supreme Court's public endorsement of legal realist reasoning through the justices' reliance on a factual brief submitted by a noted progressive attorney and reformer and an officer of a national group seeking protection for workers. The success of Louis Brandeis and Josephine Goldmark in convincing the Supreme Court to uphold Oregon's limit on the hours of female laundry employees confirmed that reformers could have a significant role in the legal process, contributing to the further development of vigorously contested nodes of conflict. In future years, support for challenged protective measures would not come solely from the attorneys general who defended them on the states' and Congress's behalf. Furthermore, the line between legal advocacy and political advocacy would continue to blur as activist attorneys became more involved in efforts to validate protective measures.

These developments would shape the next phase of the period of negotiation. After 1910, cases involving women's legislation came to the fore as general legislation faded into the background. Activists, lawyers, and judges all reacted quickly to the success of the National Consumers' League in *Muller v. Oregon*, gearing up for a pitched battle over women's legislation, a battle to be fought with extensive factual information rather than with legal rhetoric.

✥ F U R T H E R   R E A D I N G

Baer, Judith. *The Chains of Protection: The Judicial Response to Women's Labor Legislation* (1978).

Benedict, Michael Les. "A Re-Evaluation of the Meaning and Origins of Laissez-Faire Constitutionalism," *Law and History Review*, 3 (1985): 293–331.

Beth, Loren. *The Development of the American Constitution, 1877–1917* (1971).

Cohen, Nancy. *The Reconstruction of American Liberalism, 1865–1914* (2002).

Ely, Jr., James W. *The Chief Justiceship of Melville W. Fuller, 1888–1910* (1995).

_____. *The Guardian of Every Other Right: A Constitutional History of Property Rights*, 3rd ed. (2008).

_____. *The Fuller Court: Justices, Rulings, and Legacy* (2003).

Fiss, Owen. *Troubled Beginnings of the Modern State, 1888–1910* (1993).

Foner, Eric. *Free Soil, Free Labor, Free Men: The Ideology of the Republican Party before the Civil War* (1995).

Gillman, Howard. *The Constitution Besieged: The Rise and Demise of Locnher Era Police Powers Jurisprudence* (1993).

Hofstadter, Richard. *The Age of Reform* (1955).

Horwitz, Morton J. *The Transformation of American Law, 1870–1960* (1992).

Jacobs, Clyde E. *Law Writers and the Courts: The Influence of Thomas M. Cooley, Christopher Tiedeman, and John F. Dillon upon American Constitutional Law* (1954).

Lipschultz, Sybil. "Social Feminism and Legal Discourse, 1908–1923," *Yale Journal of Law and Feminism*, 2 (1989): 131–160.

Mason, Alpheus T. "The Case of the Overworked Laundress," in J. Garraty, ed., *Quarrels That Have Shaped the Constitution* (1975): 176–190.

McCurdy, Charles W. "The Roots of Liberty of Contract Reconsidered," *Yearbook of the Supreme Court Historical Society*, 20 (1984): 20–33.

Nelson, William E. *The Fourteenth Amendment: From Political Principle to Judicial Doctrine* (1988).

Paul, Arnold. *Conservative Crisis and the Rule of Law: Attitudes of Bar and Bench, 1887– 1895* (1960).

Phillips, Michael J. *The Lochner Court, Myth and Reality: Substantive Due Process from the 1890s to the 1930s* (2001).

Pratt, Jr., Walter F. *The Supreme Court under Edward Douglass White, 1910–1921* (1999).

Semonche, John. *Charting the Future: The Supreme Court Responds to a Changing Society, 1890–1920* (1978).

Shoemaker, Rebecca S. *The White Court: Justices, Rulings, and Legacy* (2004).

Swindler, William F. *Court and Constitution in the Twentieth Century: The Old Legality, 1889–1932* (1968).

Tomlins, Christopher L. *The State and the Unions: Labor Relations, Law, and the Organized Labor Movement, 1880–1960* (1985).

Urofsky, Melvin I. *A Mind of One Piece: Brandeis and American Reform* (1971).

——. "State Courts and Protective Legislation during the Progressive Era: A Reevaluation," *Journal of American History*, 72 (1985): 63–91.

Wiecek, William M. *The Lost World of Classical Legal Thought: Law and Ideology in America, 1886–1937* (1998).

Wikander, Ulla, Alice Kesler-Harris, and Jane Lewis, eds. *Protecting Women: Labor Legislation in Europe, the United States, and Australia, 1880–1920* (1995).

Woloch, Nancy. *Muller v. Oregon: A Brief History with Documents* (1996).

Total War and the Emergence
of Modern Civil Liberties

Rampant nativism, combined with fever-pitch patriotism, resulted in serious violations of civil liberties during and immediately after World War I. In the American
scheme of government, the notion of civil liberties has a distinctly political connotation. The Bill of Rights, especially the First Amendment, set forth individuals' rights
to take political action—to speak, publish, petition the government, and associate
with one another—without governmental interference. For the first 130 years of
American history—despite controversies surrounding the Alien and Sedition Acts in
the 1790s and the suspension of the writ of habeas corpus during the Civil War—
little federal case law existed in the area of civil liberties. World War I marked the
turning point. The expansion of the national government during the progressive era
served as a rehearsal for the even more rapid centralization of power brought about
by American entry into the war. Congress enacted significant legislation to regulate
economic production, nationalize railroad transportation, initiate a propaganda
campaign—and limit free speech. The Espionage Act in particular imposed severe
limits on criticism of the government, the nation, and the war effort.

The post-World War I era proved even more unfriendly to the freedom of
speech. With the rise of Bolshevism in Russia, the formation of a communist party
in the United States, and the deployment of American troops in Russia's civil war,
the United States initiated a crackdown on a variety of alleged radicals and labor
organizers, most of them recent immigrants. In 1918, in the immediate aftermath
of the peace settlement, A. Mitchell Palmer, the attorney general under President
Woodrow Wilson, established an antiradical division in the Department of Justice
and assigned a young attorney, J. Edgar Hoover, to oversee its operation. Based on
intelligence gathered by Hoover, Palmer in late 1919 and 1920 carried out raids that
resulted in the arrest of more than 6,000 alleged radicals and the deportations of
hundreds more. State governments followed suit, by passing antiradical and antila-
bor laws to blunt the growing force of union organizing.

Although restrictions on speech had wide popular support, some Americans
strongly opposed the measures and challenged their constitutionality. As interest
groups formed to advance the cause of civil liberties, for the first time in its history
the Supreme Court heard cases implicating the speech and press clauses of the First

*Amendment. The Court initially gave a cool reception to the free speech claims of
dissenters. Eventually, however, as the war receded into memory and the postwar
Red Scare subsided, the justices became increasingly sensitive to the arguments of free
speech advocates. Significantly, the Court also began to embrace the notion of incorporation, the idea that the due process clause of the Fourteenth Amendment "incorporated" the guarantees of freedom of speech and press against state action. This
process of nationalizing the Bill of Rights—of extending the protections of the Bill of
Rights against state action through the Fourteenth Amendment—occurred gradually, incrementally, but inexorably. These early years of the development of First
Amendment law laid the foundation for the dramatic expansion of civil liberties that
occurred during the 1950s and 1960s.*

*   The historical debate surrounding civil liberties during World War I revolves
around questions that are specific to this time period, as well as larger issues in
American constitutional history. Did the restrictions on freedom of speech in wartime
constitute a wholesale subversion of the rule of law, or were these measures a legitimate attempt to preserve the nation during a time of war? Should free speech and
other civil liberties be protected as vigilantly in wartime as in peace time? Why did
the Supreme Court refuse to invalidate the Espionage Act? Did the justices share the
nativism and patriotism of their fellow Americans, or was the lack of guiding legal
precedent in the area of free speech a determinative factor? Given the lack of precedent, how critical should we be of the slow pace at which the Supreme Court began
to protect individual liberties? Why did the Court ultimately protect the freedom of
speech? Was it responding more to popular pressure or to changes within the legal
community? Given that judges often both reflect and respond to majority opinion,
can courts adequately protect minority rights?*

✤ D O C U M E N T S

The Great War, as it was known at the time, began in 1914 and resulted from years of
nationalistic and economic rivalries, as well as an alliance system that bound nations
to side with each other in the event of war. Although the United States stayed out of
Europe's war for 3 years, Germany's policy of unrestricted submarine warfare increasingly provoked American outrage. On April 2, 1917, President Woodrow Wilson
asked Congress to declare war on Germany, and within a few days Congress gave
nearly unanimous approval to war resolutions. With war declared, Wilson immediately proclaimed alien enemy regulations, which governed the behavior of German
immigrant males, 14 years and older, who had not been naturalized. Those regulations
are excerpted here as Document 1. A few months later, at Wilson's urging, Congress
enacted the Espionage Act, portions of which are included here as Document 2. The
Espionage Act, particularly after being amended the following year, contained the most
far-reaching restrictions on speech and expression in American history. In *Schenck v.
United States*, Document 3, Justice Oliver Wendell Holmes Jr. wrote the opinion for a
unanimous Court upholding the act.

    Such blatant restrictions on speech prompted the formation of opposition groups
such as the Civil Liberties Bureau of the American Union Against Militarism, which
later evolved into the American Civil Liberties Union. More significant for the short-
term development of free speech law, though, were discussions within the community of
legal scholars. Zechariah Chafee Jr., a professor at Harvard Law School and one of the
most influential writers on First Amendment issues during the twentieth century, wrote

"Freedom of Speech in War Time," Document 4, which argued for a balancing test that would take account of both the public interest and individual rights. Chafee's views seemed to have a particular influence on Holmes . Some scholars, in fact, partially attribute Holmes's evolving position on free speech to his association with Chafee. Some months after the *Schenck* decision, in *Abrams v. United States,* Document 5, the Court again sustained the constitutionality of the act. This time, Holmes, joined by Justice Louis Brandeis, issued an eloquent dissent.

During the postwar Red Scare, antiradical hysteria also surfaced in the states, which passed various criminal anarchy statues that curbed free speech. In *Gitlow v. New York*, Document 6, the justices voted 7-2 (Holmes and Brandeis dissenting) to sustain the conviction of Benjamin Gitlow, a member of the American Communist Party and publisher of a "Left-Wing Manifesto." Still, Justice Edward T. Sanford's majority opinion accepted the idea that the due process clause of the Fourteenth Amendment incorporated fundamental rights such as freedom of speech and freedom of the press. The Court, therefore, put itself in the position of holding state laws affecting free speech and press up to First Amendment standards. (The justices, of course, had already reached the conclusion, through the use of substantive due process, that property could be protected against state action.) The implications of this new approach became clear in 1931, when the Court in *Stromberg v. California* and *Near v. Minnesota*, Document 7, struck down state laws curbing speech and press, respectively. *Near*, decided by a 5–4 vote, was the first great press censorship case to come before the Supreme Court.

✣ *D O C U M E N T   1*

President Woodrow Wilson Announces Regulations Governing Alien Enemies, 1917

…I, Woodrow Wilson, President of the United States of America, do hereby proclaim to all whom it may concern that a state of war exists between the United States and the Imperial German Government; …

And pursuant to the authority vested in me, I hereby declare and establish the following regulations, which I find necessary in the premises and for the public safety: …

(5) An alien enemy shall not write, print, or publish any attack or threats against the Government or Congress of the United States, or either branch thereof, or against the measures or policy of the United States, or against the person or property of any person in the military, naval, or civil service of the United States, or of the States or Territories, or of the District of Columbia, or of the municipal governments therein;

(6) An alien enemy shall not commit or abet any hostile act against the United States, or give information, aid, or comfort to its enemies;

(7) An alien enemy shall not reside in or continue to reside in, to remain in, or enter any locality which the President may from time to time designate by Executive Order as a prohibited area in which residence by an alien enemy shall be found by him to constitute a danger to the public peace and safety of the United States, except by permit from the President and except under such limitations or restrictions as the President may prescribe;

(8) An alien enemy whom the President shall have reasonable cause to believe to be aiding or about to aid the enemy, or to be at large to the danger of the public peace or safety of the United States, or to have violated or to be about to violate any of these regulations, shall remove to any location designated by the President by Executive Order, and shall not remove therefrom without a permit, or shall depart from the United States if so required by the President;

(9) No alien enemy shall depart from the United States until he shall have received such permit as the President shall prescribe, or except under order of a court, judge, or justice, under Sections 4069 and 4070 of the Revised Statutes;

(10) No alien enemy shall land in or enter the United States, except under such restrictions and at such places as the President may prescribe;

(11) If necessary to prevent violations of these regulations, all alien enemies will be obliged to register;

(12) An alien enemy whom there may be reasonable cause to believe to be aiding or about to aid the enemy, or who may be at large to the danger of the public peace or safety, or who violates or attempts to violate, or of whom there is reasonable ground to believe that he is about to violate, any regulation duly promulgated by the President, or any criminal law of the United States, or of the States or Territories thereof, will be subject to summary arrest by the United States Marshal, or his deputy, or such other officer as the President shall designate, and to confinement in such penitentiary, prison, jail, military camp, or other place of detention as may be directed by the President.

This proclamation and the regulations herein contained shall extend and apply to all land and water, continental or insular, in any way within the jurisdiction of the United States. ...

⊹ *D O C U M E N T   2*

The Espionage Act Restricts Speech in Wartime, 1917/1918

Be it enacted, That section three of the Act ... approved June 15, 1917, be ... amended so as to read as follows:

"Sec. 3. Whoever, when the United States is at war, shall wilfully make or convey false reports or false statements with intent to interfere with the operation or success of the military or naval forces of the United States, or to promote the success of its enemies, or shall wilfully make or convey false reports, or false statements, or say or do anything except by way of bona fide and not disloyal advice to an investor ... with intent to obstruct the sale by the United States of bonds ... or the making of loans by or to the United States, or whoever, when the United States is at war, shall wilfully cause ... or incite ... insubordination, disloyalty, mutiny, or refusal of duty, in the military or naval forces of the United States, or shall wilfully obstruct ... the recruiting or enlistment service of the United States, and whoever, when the United States is at war, shall wilfully utter, print, write, or publish any disloyal, profane, scurrilous, or abusive language about the form of government of the United States, or the Constitution of the United States, or the military or naval forces of the United States, or the flag ... of the uniform of the Army or Navy of the United States, or any language intended to bring the form of government ... or the Constitution ... or the military or naval forces ... or the flag ... of the United States into contempt, scorn, contumely, or disrepute ... or shall wilfully display the flag of any foreign enemy, or shall wilfully ... urge, incite, or advocate any curtailment of production in this country of any thing or things ... necessary or essential to the prosecution of the war ... and whoever shall wilfully advocate, teach, defend, or suggest the doing of any of the acts or things in this section enumerated and whoever shall by word or act support or favor the cause of any country with which the United States is at war or by word or act oppose the cause of the United States therein, shall be punished by a fine of not more than $10,000 or imprisonment for not more than twenty years, or both. ...

⊞ *D O C U M E N T   3*

Schenck v. United States, 1919

Mr. Justice Holmes delivered the opinion of the Court.

This is an indictment in three counts. The first charges a conspiracy to violate the Espionage Act of June 15, 1917, c. 30, § 3, 40 Stat. 217, 219, by causing and attempting to cause insubordination, &c., in the military and naval forces of the United States, and to obstruct the recruiting and enlistment service of the United States, when the United States was at war with the German Empire, to-wit, that the defendants wilfully conspired to have printed and circulated to men who had been called and accepted for military service under the Act of May 18, 1917, a document set forth and alleged to be calculated to cause such insubordination and obstruction. ... The defendants were found guilty on all the counts. They set up the First Amendment to the Constitution forbidding Congress to make any law abridging the freedom of speech, or of the press, and bringing the case here on that ground have argued some other points also of which we must dispose. ...

The document in question upon its first printed side recited the first section of the Thirteenth Amendment, said that the idea embodied in it was violated by the Conscription Act and that a conscript is little better than a convict. In impassioned language it intimated that conscription was despotism in its worst form and a monstrous wrong against humanity in the interest of Wall Street's chosen few. It said "Do not submit to intimidation," but in form at least confined itself to peaceful measures such as a petition for the repeal of the act. The other and later printed side of the sheet was headed "Assert Your Rights." It stated reasons for alleging that any one violated the Constitution when he refused to recognize "your right to assert your opposition to the draft," and went on "If you do not assert and support your rights, your are helping to deny or disparage rights which it is the solemn duty of all citizens and residents of the United States to retain." It described the arguments on the other side as coming from cunning politicians and a mercenary capitalist press, and even silent consent to the conscription law as helping to support an infamous conspiracy. It denied the power to send our citizens away to foreign shores to shoot up the people of other lands, and added that words could not express the condemnation such cold-blooded ruthlessness deserves, &c., &c., winding up "You must do your share to maintain, support and uphold the rights of the people of this country." Of course the document would not have been sent unless it had been intended to have some effect, and we do not see what effect it could be expected to have upon persons subject to the draft except to influence them to obstruct the carrying of it out. The defendants do not deny that the jury might find against them on this point.

But it is said, suppose that that was the tendency of this circular, it is protected by the First Amendment to the Constitution. Two of the strongest expressions are said to be quoted respectively from well-known public men. It well may be that the prohibition of laws abridging the freedom of speech is not confined to previous restraints, although to prevent them may have been the main purpose. ... We admit that in many places and in ordinary times the defendants in saying all that was said in the circular would have been within their constitutional rights. But the character of every act depends upon the circumstances in which it is done. ... The most stringent protection of free speech would not protect a man in falsely shouting fire in a theatre and causing a panic. It does not even protect a man from an injunction against uttering words that may have all the effect of force. ... The question in every case is whether the words used are used in such circumstances and are of such a nature as to create a clear and present danger that they will bring about the substantive evils that Congress has a right to prevent. It is a question of proximity and degree. When a nation is at war many things that might be said in time of peace are such a hindrance to its effort that their utterance will not be endured so long as men fight and that no Court could regard them as protected by any constitutional right. It seems to be admitted that if an actual obstruction of the recruiting service were proved, liability for words that produced that effect might be enforced. The statute of 1917 in § 4 punishes conspiracies to obstruct as well as actual obstruction. If the act, (speaking, or circulating a paper,) its tendency and the intent with which it is done are the same, we perceive no ground for saying that success alone warrants making the act a crime. ... Indeed that case might be said to dispose of the present contention if the precedent covers all *media concludendi.* But as the right to free speech was not referred to specially, we have thought fit to add a few words.

It was not argued that a conspiracy to obstruct the draft was not within the words of the Act of 1917. The words are "obstruct the recruiting or enlistment service," and it might be suggested that they refer only to making it hard to get volunteers. Recruiting heretofore usually having been accomplished by getting volunteers the word is apt to call up that method only in our minds. But recruiting is gaining fresh supplies for the forces, as well by draft as otherwise. It is put as an alternative to enlistment or voluntary enrollment in this act. The fact that the Act of 1917 was enlarged by the amending Act of May 16, 1918, c. 75, 40 Stat. 553, of course, does not affect the present indictment and would not, even if the former act had been repealed. ... *Judgments affirmed.*

Legal Scholar Zechariah Chafee, Jr., Advocates Freedom of Speech, 1919

Freedom of Speech in War Time

Never in the history of our country, since the Alien and Sedition Laws of 1798, has the meaning of free speech been the subject of such sharp controversy as to-day. Over two hundred prosecutions and other judicial proceedings during the war, involving speeches, newspaper articles, pamphlets, and books, have been followed since the armistice by a widespread legislative consideration of bills punishing the advocacy of extreme radicalism. It is becoming increasingly important to determine the true limits of freedom of expression, so that speakers and writers may know how much they can properly say, and governments may be sure how much they can lawfully and wisely suppress. The United States Supreme Court has recently handed down several decisions upon the Espionage Act, which put us in a much better position than formerly to discuss the wartime aspects of the general problem of liberty of speech, and this article will approach the general problem from that side. At some later day it may be possible to discuss the proper limits of radical agitation in peace, and also to make a detailed historical examination of the events and documents leading up to the free speech clauses in our state and federal constitutions. For the present it is not feasible to do more than consider the application of those clauses to the treatment of opposition to war. . . .

Clearly, the problem of the limits of freedom of speech in war time is no academic question. On the one side, thoughtful men and journals are asking how scores of citizens can be imprisoned under this constitution only for their disapproval of the war as irreligious, unwise, or unjust. On the other, federal and state officials point to the great activities of German agents in our midst and to the unprecedented extension of the business of war over the whole nation, so that in the familiar remark of Ludendorff, wars are no longer won by armies in the field, but by the *morale* of the whole people. The widespread Liberty Bond campaigns, and the shipyards, munition factories, government offices, training camps, in all parts of the country, are felt to make the entire United States a theater of war, in which attacks upon our cause are as dangerous and unjustified as if made among the soldiers in the rear trenches. The government regards it as inconceivable that the Constitution should cripple its efforts to maintain public safety. Abstaining from countercharges of disloyalty and tyranny, let us recognize the issue as a conflict between two vital principles, and endeavor to find the basis of reconciliation between order and freedom.

At the outset, we can reject two extreme views in the controversy. First, there is the view that the Bill of Rights is a peacetime document and consequently freedom of speech may be ignored in war. This view has been officially repudiated. At the opposite pole is the belief of many agitators that the First Amendment renders unconstitutional any Act of Congress without exception "abridging the freedom of speech, or of the press," that all speech is free, and only action can be restrained and punished. This view is equally untenable. The provisions of the Bill of Rights cannot be applied with absolute literalness but are subject to exceptions. . . . The difficulty, of course, is to define the principle on which the implied exceptions are based, and an effort to that end will be made subsequently.

Since it is plain that the true solution lies between these two extreme views, and that even in war time freedom of speech exists subject to a problematical limit, it is necessary to determine where the line runs between utterance which is protected by the Constitution from governmental control and that which is not....

We can, of course, be sure that certain forms of utterance, which have always been crimes or torts at common law, are not within the scope of the free speech clauses. The courts in construing such clauses have, for the most part, done little more than place obvious cases on this or that side of the line. They tell us, for instance, that libel and slander are actionable, or even punishable, that indecent books are criminal, that it is contempt to interfere with pending judicial proceedings, and that a permit can be required for street meetings; and on the other hand, that some criticism of the government must be allowed, that a temperate examination of a judge's opinion is not contempt, and that honest discussion of the merits of a painting causes no liability for damages. But when we ask where the line actually runs and how they know on which side of it a given utterance belongs, we find no answer in their opinions. Justice Holmes in his Espionage Act decisions had a magnificent opportunity to make articulate for us that major premise, under which judges ought to classify words as inside or outside the scope of the First Amendment. He, we hoped, would concentrate his great abilities on fixing the line. Instead, like the other judges, he has told us that certain plainly unlawful utterances are, to be sure, unlawful.

"The First Amendment ... obviously was not intended to give immunity for every possible use of language.... We venture to believe that neither Hamilton nor Madison, nor any other competent person then or later, ever supposed that to make criminal the counselling of a murder ... would be an unconstitutional interference with free speech."

"The most stringent protection of free speech would not protect a man in falsely shouting fire in a theatre and causing a panic."

How about the man who gets up in a theater between the acts and informs the audience honestly but perhaps mistakenly that the fire exits are too few or locked? He is a much closer parallel to Schenck or Debs. How about James Russell Lowell when he counseled, not murder, but the cessation of murder, his name for war? The question whether such perplexing cases are within the First Amendment or not cannot be solved by the multiplication of obvious examples, but only by the development of a rational principle to mark the limits of constitutional protection....

The true meaning of freedom of speech seems to be this. One of the most important purposes of society and government is the discovery and spread of truth on subjects of general concern. This is possible only through absolutely unlimited discussion, for, as Bagehot points out, once force is thrown into the argument, it becomes a matter of chance whether it is thrown on the false side or the true, and truth loses all its natural advantage in the contest. Nevertheless, there are other purposes of government, such as order, the training of the young, protection against external aggression. Unlimited discussion sometimes interferes with these purposes, which must then be balanced against freedom of speech, but freedom of speech ought to weigh very heavily in the scale. The First Amendment gives binding force to this principle of political wisdom.

Or to put the matter another way, it is useless to define free speech by talk about rights. The agitator asserts his constitutional right to speak, the government asserts its constitutional right to wage war. The result is a deadlock. Each side takes the position of the man who was arrested for swinging his arms and hitting another in the nose, and asked the judge if he did not have a right to swing his arms in a free country. "Your right to swing your arms ends just where the other man's nose begins." To find the boundary line of any right, we must get behind rules of law to human facts. In our problem, we must regard the desires and needs of the individual human being who wants to speak and those of the great group of human beings among whom he speaks. That is, in technical language, there are individual interests and social interests, which must be balanced against each other, if they conflict, in order to determine which interest shall be sacrificed under the circumstances and which shall be protected and become the foundation of a legal right. It must never be forgotten that the balancing cannot be properly done unless all the interests involved are adequately ascertained, and the great evil of all this talk about rights is that each side is so busy denying the other's claim to rights that it entirely overlooks the human desires and needs behind that claim. . . .

The First Amendment protects two kinds of interests in free speech. There is an individual interest, the need of many men to express their opinions on matters vital to them if life is to be worth living, and a social interest in the attainment of truth, so that the country may not only adopt the wisest course of action but carry it out in the wisest way. This social interest is especially important in war time. Even after war has been declared there is bound to be a confused mixture of good and bad arguments in its support, and a wide difference of opinion as to its objects. Truth can be sifted out from falsehood only if the government is vigorously and constantly cross-examined, so that the fundamental issues of the struggle may be clearly defined, and the war may not be diverted to improper ends, or conducted with an undue sacrifice of life and liberty, or prolonged after its just purposes are accomplished. Legal proceedings prove that an opponent makes the best cross-examiner. Consequently it is a disastrous mistake to limit criticism to those who favor the war. Men bitterly hostile to it may point out evils in its management like the secret treaties, which its supporters have been too busy to unearth. The history of the last five years shows how the objects of a war may change completely during its progress, and it is well that those objects should be steadily reformulated under the influence of open discussion not only by those who demand a military victory but by pacifists who take a different view of the national welfare. Further argument for the existence of this social interest becomes unnecessary if we recall the national value of the opposition in former wars.

The great trouble with most judicial construction of the Espionage Act is that this social interest has been ignored and free speech has been regarded as merely an individual interest, which must readily give way like other personal desires the moment it interferes with the social interest in national safety. The judge who has done most to bring social interests into legal thinking said years ago, "I think that the judges themselves have failed adequately to recognize their duty of weighing considerations of social advantage. The duty is inevitable, and the result of the often proclaimed judicial aversion to deal with such considerations is simply to leave the very ground and foundation of judgments inarticulate and often unconscious." The failure of the courts in the past to formulate any principle for drawing a boundary line around the right of free speech has not only thrown the judges into the difficult questions of the Espionage Act without any well-considered standard of criminality, but has allowed some of them to impose standards of their own and fix the line at a point which makes all opposition to this or any future war impossible....

The true boundary line of the First Amendment can be fixed only when Congress and the courts realize that the principle on which speech is classified as lawful or unlawful involves the balancing against each other of two very important social interests, in public safety and in the search for truth. Every reasonable attempt should be made to maintain both interests unimpaired, and the great interest in free speech should be sacrificed only when the interest in public safety is really imperiled, and not, as most men believe, when it is barely conceivable that it may be slightly affected. In war time, therefore, speech should be unrestricted by the censorship or by punishment, unless it is clearly liable to cause direct and dangerous interference with the conduct of the war.

Thus our problem of locating the boundary line of free speech is solved. It is fixed close to the point where words will give rise to unlawful acts. ... There is a similar balancing in the determination of what is "due process of law." And we can with certitude declare that the First Amendment forbids the punishment of words merely for their injurious tendencies. The history of the Amendment and the political function of free speech corroborate each other and make this conclusion plain.

The Espionage Act of 1917 seems on its face constitutional under this interpretation of the First Amendment, but it may have been construed so extremely as to violate the Amendment. Furthermore, freedom of speech is not only a limit on Congressional power, but a policy to be observed by the courts in applying constitutional statutes to utterance....

Justice Holmes seems to discuss the constitutionality of the Espionage Act of 1917 rather than its construction. There can be little doubt that it is constitutional under any test if construed naturally, but it has been interpreted in such a way as to violate the free speech clause and the plain words of the statute, to say nothing of the principle that criminal statutes should be construed strictly. If the Supreme Court test had been laid down in the summer of 1917 and followed in charges by the District Courts, the most casual perusal of the utterances prosecuted makes it sure that there would have been many more acquittals. Instead, bad tendency has been the test of criminality, a test which this article has endeavored to prove wholly inconsistent with freedom of speech, or any genuine discussion of public affairs.

Furthermore, it is regrettable that Justice Holmes did nothing to emphasize the social interest behind free speech, and show the need of balancing even in war time. The last sentence of the passage quoted from the Schenck case seems to mean that the Supreme Court will sanction any restriction of speech that has military force behind it, and reminds us that the Justice used to say when he was young, "that truth was the majority vote of that nation that could lick all others." His liberalism seems held in abeyance by his belief in the relativity of values. It is not by giving way to force and the majority that truth has been won. Hard it may be for a court to protect those who oppose the cause for which men are dying in France, but others have died in the past for freedom of speech....

✠ *D O C U M E N T* 5

Abrams v. United States, 1919

Mr. Justice Clarke delivered the opinion of the Court.

... It was charged in each count of the indictment that it was a part of the conspiracy that the defendants would attempt to accomplish their unlawful purpose by printing, writing and distributing in the City of New York many copies of a leaflet or circular, printed in the English language, and of another printed in the Yiddish language, copies of which, properly identified, were attached to the indictment.

All of the five defendants were born in Russia. They were intelligent, had considerable schooling, and at the time they were arrested they had lived in the United States terms varying from five to ten years, but none of them had applied for naturalization. Four of them testified as witnesses in their own behalf and of these, three frankly avowed that they were "rebels," "revolutionists," "anarchists," that they did not believe in government in any form, and they declared that they had no interest whatever in the Government of the United States. The fourth defendant testified that he was a "socialist" and believed in "a proper kind of government, not capitalistic," but in his classification the Government of the United States was "capitalistic."

It was admitted on the trial that the defendants had united to print and distribute the described circulars and that five thousand of them had been printed and distributed about the 22d day of August, 1918. The group had a meeting place in New York City, in rooms rented by defendant Abrams, under an assumed name, and there the subject of printing the circulars was discussed about two weeks before the defendants were arrested. The defendant Abrams, although not a printer, on July 27, 1918, purchased the printing outfit with which the circulars were printed and installed it in a basement room where the work was done at night. The circulars were distributed some by throwing them from a window of a building where one of the defendants was employed and others secretly, in New York City.

The defendants pleaded "not guilty," and the case of the Government consisted in showing the facts we have stated, and in introducing in evidence copies of the two printed circulars attached to the indictment, a sheet entitled "Revolutionists Unite for Action," written by the defendant Lipman, and found on him when he was arrested, and another paper, found at the headquarters of the group, and for which Abrams assumed responsibility.

Thus the conspiracy and the doing of the overt acts charged were largely admitted and were fully established.

On the record thus described it is argued, somewhat faintly, that the acts charged against the defendants were not unlawful because within the protection of that freedom of speech and of the press which is guaranteed by the First Amendment to the Constitution of the United States, and that the entire Espionage Act is unconstitutional because in conflict with that Amendment.

This contention is sufficiently discussed and is definitely negatived in *Schenck v. United States.* ...

It will not do to say, as is now argued, that the only intent of these defendants was to prevent injury to the Russian cause. Men must be held to have intended, and to be accountable for, the effects which their acts were likely to produce. Even if their primary purpose and intent was to aid the cause of the Russian Revolution, the plan of action which they adopted necessarily involved, before it could be realized, defeat of the war program of the United States, for the obvious effect of this appeal, if it should become effective, as they hoped it might, would be to persuade persons of character such as those whom they regarded themselves as addressing, not to aid government loans and not to work in ammunition factories, where their work would produce "bullets, bayonets, cannon" and other munitions of war, the use of which would cause the "murder" of Germans and Russians. . . .

[E]xcerpts sufficiently show, that while the immediate occasion for this particular outbreak of lawlessness, on the part of the defendant alien anarchists, may have been resentment caused by our Government sending troops into Russia as a strategic operation against the Germans on the eastern battle front, yet the plain purpose of their propaganda was to excite, at the supreme crisis of the war, disaffection, sedition, riots, and, as they hoped, revolution, in this country for the purpose of embarrassing and if possible defeating the military plans of the Government in Europe. A technical distinction may perhaps be taken between disloyal and abusive language applied to the *form* of our government or language intended to bring the *form* of our government into contempt and disrepute, and language of like character and intended to produce like results directed against the President and Congress, the agencies through which that form of government must function in time of war. But it is not necessary to a decision of this case to consider whether such distinction is vital or merely formal, for the language of these circulars was obviously intended to provoke and to encourage resistance to the United States in the war, as the third count runs, and, the defendants, in terms, plainly urged and advocated a resort to a general strike of workers in ammunition factories for the purpose of curtailing the production of ordnance and munitions necessary and essential to the prosecution of the war as is charged in the fourth count. Thus it is clear not only that some evidence but that much persuasive evidence was before the jury tending to prove that the defendants were guilty as charged in both the third and fourth counts of the indictment and under the long established rule of law hereinbefore stated the judgment of the District Court must be *Affirmed.*

Mr. Justice Holmes dissenting.

. . . The first . . . says that the President's cowardly silence about the intervention in Russia reveals the hypocrisy of the plutocratic gang in Washington. . . .

The other leaflet, headed "Workers—Wake Up," with abusive language says that America together with the Allies will march for Russia to help the Czecko-Slovaks in their struggle against the Bolsheviki, and that this time the hypocrites shall not fool the Russian emigrants and friends of Russia in America. It tells the Russian emigrants that they now must spit in the face of the false military propaganda by which their sympathy and help to the prosecution of the war have been called forth and says that with the money they have lent or are going to lend "they will make bullets not only for the Germans but also for the Workers Soviets of Russia," and further, "Workers in the ammunition factories, you are producing bullets, bayonets, cannon, to murder not only the Germans, but also your dearest, best, who are in Russia and are fighting for freedom." It then appeals to the same Russian emigrants at some length not to consent to the "inquisitionary expedition to Russia," and says that the destruction of the Russian revolution is "the politics of the march to Russia." The leaflet winds up by saying "Workers, our reply to this barbaric intervention has to be a general strike!," and after a few words on the spirit of revolution, exhortations not to be afraid, and some usual tall talk ends "Woe unto those who will be in the way of progress. Let solidarity live! The Rebels."

No argument seems to me necessary to show that these pronunciamentos in no way attack the form of government of the United States, or that they do not support either of the first two counts. What little I have to say about the third count may be postponed until I have considered the fourth. With regard to that it seems too plain to be denied that the suggestion to workers in the ammunition factories that they are producing bullets to murder their dearest, and the further advocacy of a general strike, both in the second leaflet, do urge curtailment of production of things necessary to the prosecution of the war within the meaning of the Act of May 16, 1918.... But to make the conduct criminal that statute requires that it should be "with intent by such curtailment to cripple or hinder the United States in the prosecution of the war." It seems to me that no such intent is proved.

I am aware of course that the word intent as vaguely used in ordinary legal discussion means no more than knowledge at the time of the act that the consequences said to be intended will ensue. Even less than that will satisfy the general principle of civil and criminal liability. A man may have to pay damages, may be sent to prison, at common law might be hanged, if at the time of his act he knew facts from which common experience showed that the consequences would follow, whether he individually could foresee them or not. But, when words are used exactly, a deed is not done with intent to produce a consequence unless that consequence is the aim of the deed. It may be obvious, and obvious to the actor, that the consequence will follow, and he may be liable for it even if he regrets it, but he does not do the act with intent to produce it unless the aim to produce it is the proximate motive of the specific act, although there may be some deeper motive behind.

It seems to me that this statute must be taken to use its words in a strict and accurate sense. They would be absurd in any other. A patriot might think that we were wasting money on aeroplanes, or making more cannon of a certain kind than we needed, and might advocate curtailment with success, yet even if it turned out that the curtailment hindered and was thought by other minds to have been obviously likely to hinder the United States in the prosecution of the war, no one would hold such conduct a crime. I admit that my illustration does not answer all that might be said but it is enough to show what I think and to let me pass to a more important aspect of the case. I refer to the First Amendment to the Constitution that Congress shall make no law abridging the freedom of speech.

I never have seen any reason to doubt that the questions of law that alone were before this Court in the cases of *Schenck, Frohwerk* and *Debs* ... were rightly decided. I do not doubt for a moment that by the same reasoning that would justify punishing persuasion to murder, the United States constitutionally may punish speech that produces or is intended to produce a clear and imminent danger that it will bring about forthwith certain substantive evils that the United States constitutionally may seek to prevent. The power undoubtedly is greater in time of war than in time of peace because war opens dangers that do not exist at other times.

But as against to dangers peculiar to war, as against others, the principle of the right to free speech is always the same. It is only the present danger of immediate evil or an intent to bring it about that warrants Congress in setting a limit to the expression of opinion where private rights are not concerned. Congress certainly cannot forbid all effort to change the mind of the country. Now nobody can suppose that the surreptitious publishing of a silly leaflet by an unknown man, without more, would present any immediate danger that its opinions would hinder the success of the government arms or have any appreciable tendency to do so. Publishing those opinions for the very purpose of obstructing however, might indicate a greater danger and at any rate would have the quality of an attempt. So I assume that the second leaflet if published for the purposes alleged in the fourth count might be punishable. But it seems pretty clear to me that nothing less than that would bring these papers within the scope of this law. An actual intent in the sense that I have explained is necessary to constitute an attempt, where a further act of the same individual is required to complete the substantive crime. . . . It is necessary where the success of the attempt depends upon others because if that intent is not present the actor's aim may be accomplished without bringing about the evils sought to be checked. An intent to prevent interference with the revolution in Russia might have been satisfied without any hindrance to carrying on the war in which we were engaged.

I do not see how anyone can find the intent required by the statute in any of the defendants' words. The second leaflet is the only one that affords even a foundation for the charge, and there, without invoking the hatred of German militarism expressed in the former one, it is evident from the beginning to the end that the only object of the paper is to help Russia and stop American intervention there against the popular government—not to impede the United States in the war that it was carrying on. To say that two phrases taken literally might import a suggestion of conduct that would have interference with the war as an indirect and probably undesired effect seems to me by no means enough to show an attempt to produce that effect. . . .

Persecution for the expression of opinions seems to me perfectly logical. If you have no doubt of your premises or your power and want a certain result with all your heart your naturally express your wishes in law and sweep away all opposition. To allow opposition by speech seems to indicate that you think the speech impotent, as when a man says that he has squared the circle, or that you do not care wholeheartedly for the result, or that you doubt either your power or your premises. But when men have realized that time has upset many fighting faiths, they may come to believe even more than they believe the very foundations of their own conduct that the ultimate good desired is better reached by free trade in ideas—that the best test of truth is the power of the thought to get itself accepted in the competition of the market, and that truth is the only ground upon which their wishes safely can be carried out. That at any rate is the theory of our Constitution. It is an experiment, as all life is an experiment. Every year if not every day we have to wager our salvation upon some prophecy based upon imperfect knowledge. While that experiment is part of our system I think that we should be eternally vigilant against attempts to check the expression of opinions that we loathe and believe to be fraught with death, unless they so imminently threaten immediate interference with the lawful and pressing purposes of the law that an immediate check is required to save the country. I wholly disagree with the argument of the Government that the First Amendment left the common law as to seditious libel in force. History seems to me against the notion. I had conceived that the United States through many years had shown its repentance for the Sedition Act of 1798, by repaying fines that it imposed. Only the emergency that makes it immediately dangerous to leave the correction of evil counsels to time warrants making any exception to the sweeping command, "Congress shall make no law ... abridging the freedom of speech." Of course I am speaking only of expressions of opinion and exhortations, which were all that were uttered here, but I regret that I cannot put into more impressive words my belief that in their conviction upon this indictment the defendants were deprived of their rights under the Constitution of the United States.

Mr. Justice Brandeis concurs with the foregoing opinion.

✣ *D O C U M E N T   6*

Gitlow v. New York, 1925

Mr. Justice Sanford delivered the opinion of the Court.

Benjamin Gitlow was indicted in the Supreme Court of New York, with three others, for the statutory crime of criminal anarchy. New York Penal Laws, §§ 160, 161. He was separately tried, convicted, and sentenced to imprisonment. The judgment was affirmed by the Appellate Division and by the Court of Appeals.... The case is here on writ of error to the Supreme Court, to which the record was remitted.

The contention here is that the statute by its terms and as applied in this case, is repugnant to the due process clause of the Fourteenth Amendment....

The following facts were established on the trial by undisputed evidence and admissions: The defendant is a member of the Left Wing Section of the Socialist Party, a dissenting branch or faction of that party formed in opposition to its dominant policy of "moderate Socialism." Membership in both is open to aliens as well as citizens. The Left Wing Section was organized nationally at a conference in New York City in June, 1919, attended by ninety delegates from twenty different States. The conference elected a National Council, of which the defendant was a member, and left to it the adoption of a "Manifesto." This was published in The Revolutionary Age, the official organ of the Left Wing. The defendant was on the board of managers of the paper and was its business manager. He arranged for the printing of the paper and took to the printer the manuscript of the first issue which contained the Left Wing Manifesto, and also a Communist Program and a Program of the Left Wing that had been adopted by the conference. Sixteen thousand copies were printed, which were delivered at the premises in New York City used as the office of the Revolutionary Age and the headquarters of the Left Wing, and occupied by the defendant and other officials. These copies were paid for by the defendant, as business manager of the paper. Employees at this office wrapped and mailed out copies of the paper under the defendant's direction; and copies were sold from this office. It was admitted that the defendant signed a card subscribing to the Manifesto and Program of the Left Wing, which all applicants were required to sign before being admitted to membership; that he went to different parts of the State to speak to branches of the Socialist Party about the principles of the Left Wing and advocated their adoption; and that he was responsible for the Manifesto as it appeared, that "he knew of the publication, in a general way and he knew of its publication afterwards, and is responsible for its circulation."

There was no evidence of any effect resulting from the publication and circulation of the Manifesto....

The specification of the errors relied on relates solely to the specific rulings of the trial court in the matters hereinbefore set out. The correctness of the verdict is not questioned, as the case was submitted to the jury. The sole contention here is, essentially, that as there was no evidence of any concrete result flowing from the publication of the Manifesto or of circumstances showing the likelihood of such result, the statute as construed and applied by the trial court penalizes the mere utterance, as such, of "doctrine" having no quality of incitement, without regard either to the circumstances of its utterance or to the likelihood of unlawful sequences; and that, as the exercise of the right of free expression with relation to government is only punishable "in circumstances involving likelihood of substantive evil," the statute contravenes the due process clause of the Fourteenth Amendment. The argument in support of this contention rests primarily upon the following propositions: 1st, That the "liberty" protected by the Fourteenth Amendment includes the liberty of speech and of the press; and 2nd, That while liberty of expression "is not absolute," it may be restrained "only in circumstances where its exercise bears a causal relation with some substantive evil, consummated, attempted or likely," and as the statute "takes no account of circumstances," it unduly restrains this liberty and is therefore unconstitutional.

The precise question presented, and the only question which we can consider under this writ of error, then is, whether the statute, as construed and applied in this case by the state courts, deprived the defendant of his liberty of expression in violation of the due process clause of the Fourteenth Amendment.

The statute does not penalize the utterance or publication of abstract "doctrine" or academic discussion having no quality of incitement to any concrete action. It is not aimed against mere historical or philosophical essays. It does not restrain the advocacy of changes in the form of government by constitutional and lawful means. What it prohibits is language advocating, advising or teaching the overthrow of organized government by unlawful means. These words imply urging to action....

The Manifesto, plainly, is neither the statement of abstract doctrine nor, as suggested by counsel, mere prediction that industrial disturbances and revolutionary mass strikes will result spontaneously in an inevitable process of evolution in the economic system. It advocates and urges in fervent language mass action which shall progressively foment industrial disturbances and through political mass strikes and revolutionary mass action overthrow and destroy organized parliamentary government. It concludes with a call to action in these words: "The proletariat revolution and the Communist reconstruction of society—*the struggle for these*—is not indispensible....The Communist International calls the proletariat of the world to the final struggle!" This is not the expression of philosophical abstraction, the mere prediction of future events; it is the language of direct incitement.

The means advocated for bringing about the destruction of organized parliamentary government, namely, mass industrial revolts usurping the functions of municipal government, political mass strikes directed against the parliamentary state, and revolutionary mass action for its final destruction, necessarily imply the use of force and violence, and in their essential nature are inherently unlawful in a constitutional government of law and order. That the jury were warranted in finding that the Manifesto advocated not merely the abstract doctrine of overthrowing organized government by force, violence and unlawful means, but action to that end, is clear.

For present purposes we may and do assume that freedom of speech and of the press—which are protected by the First Amendment from abridgment by Congress—are among the fundamental personal rights and "liberties" protected by the due process clause of the Fourteenth Amendment from impairment by the States. We do not regard the incidental statement in *Prudential Ins. Co. v. Cheek*... that the Fourteenth Amendment imposes no restrictions on the States concerning freedom of speech, as determinative of this question.

It is a fundamental principle, long established, that the freedom of speech and of the press which is secured by the Constitution, does not confer an absolute right to speak or publish, without responsibility, whatever one may choose, or an unrestricted and unbridled license that gives immunity for every possible use of language and prevents the punishment of those who abuse this freedom.... Reasonably limited.... this freedom is an inestimable privilege in a free government; without such limitation, it might become the scourge of the republic.

That a State in the exercise of its police power may punish those who abuse this freedom by utterances inimical to the public welfare, tending to corrupt public morals, incite to crime, or disturb the public peace, is not open to question....

Thus it was held by this Court in the *Fox Case,* that a State may punish publications advocating and encouraging a breach of its criminal laws; and, in the *Gilbert Case,* that a State may punish utterances teaching or advocating that its citizens should not assist the United States in prosecuting or carrying on war with its public enemies.

And, for yet more imperative reasons, a State may punish utterances endangering the foundations of organized government and threatening its overthrow by unlawful means. These imperil its own existence as a constitutional State. Freedom of speech and press... does not protect disturbances to the public peace or the attempt to subvert the government. It does not protect publications or teachings which tend to subvert or imperial the government or to impede or hinder it in the performance of its governmental duties.... It does not protect publications prompting the overthrow of government by force; the punishment of those who publish articles which tend to destroy organized society being essential to the security of freedom and the stability of the State.... And a State may penalize utterances which openly advocate the overthrow of the representative and constitutional form of government of the United States and the several States, by violence or other unlawful means.... In short this freedom does not deprive a State of the primary and essential right of self preservation; which, so long as human governments endure, they cannot be denied....

By enacting the present statute the State has determined, through its legislative body, that utterances advocating the overthrow of organized government by force, violence and unlawful means, are so inimical to the general welfare and involve such danger of substantive evil that they may be penalized in the exercise of its police power. That determination must be given great weight. Every presumption is to be indulged in favor of the validity of the statute.... And the case is to be considered "in the light of the principle that the State is primarily the judge of regulations required in the interest of public safety and welfare"; and that its police "statutes may only be declared unconstitutional where they are arbitrary or unreasonable attempts to exercise authority vested in the State in the public interest." ... That utterances inciting to the overthrow of organized government by unlawful means, present a sufficient danger of substantive evil to bring their punishment within the range of legislative discretion, is clear. Such utterances, by their very nature, involve danger to the public peace and to the security of the State. They threaten breaches of the peace and ultimate revolution. And the immediate danger is none the less real and substantial, because the effect of a given utterance cannot be accurately foreseen. The State cannot reasonably be required to measure the danger from every such utterance in the nice balance of a jeweler's scale. A single revolutionary spark may kindle a fire that, smouldering for a time, may burst into a sweeping and destructive conflagration. It cannot be said that the State is acting arbitrarily or unreasonably when in the exercise of its judgement as to the measures necessary to protect the public peace and safety, it seeks to extinguish the spark without waiting until it has enkindled the flame or blazed into the conflagration. It cannot reasonably be required to defer the adoption of measures for its own peace and safety until the revolutionary utterances lead to actual disturbances of the public peace or imminent and immediate danger of its own destruction; but it may, in the exercise of its judgment, suppress the threatened danger in its incipiency. ...

We cannot hold that the present statute is an arbitrary or unreasonable exercise of the police power of the State unwarrantably infringing the freedom of speech or press; and we must and do sustain its constitutionality.

This being so it may be applied to every utterance—not too trivial to be beneath the notice of the law—which is of such a character and used with such intent and purpose as to bring it within the prohibition of the statute. ... In other words, when the legislative body has determined generally, in the constitutional exercise of its discretion, that utterances of a certain kind involve such danger of substantive evil that they may be punished, the question whether any specific utterance coming within the prohibited class is likely, in and of itself, to bring about the substantive evil, is not open to consideration. It is sufficient that the statute itself be constitutional and that the use of the language comes within its prohibition. ...

And finding, for the reasons stated, that the statute is not in itself unconstitutional, and that it has not been applied in the present case in derogation of any constitutional right, the judgment of the Court of Appeals is *Affirmed.*

Mr. Justice Holmes, dissenting.

Mr. Justice Brandeis and I are of opinion that this judgment should be reversed. The general principle of free speech, it seems to me, must be taken to be included in the Fourteenth Amendment, in view of the scope that has been given to the word "liberty" as there used, although perhaps it may be accepted with a somewhat larger latitude of interpretation than is allowed to Congress by the sweeping language that governs or ought to govern the laws of the United States. If I am right, then I think that the criterion sanctioned by the full Court in *Schenck v. United States* ... applies. "The question in every case is whether the words used are used in such circumstances and are of such a nature as to create a clear and present danger that they will bring about the substantive evils that [the State] has a right to prevent." It is true that in my opinion this criterion was departed from in *Abrams* v. *United States* ..., but the convictions that I expressed in that case are too deep for it to be possible for me as yet to believe that it [has] settled the law. If what I think the correct test is applied, it is manifest that there was no present danger of an attempt to overthrow the government by force on the part of the admittedly small minority who shared the defendant's views. It is said that this manifesto was more than a theory, that it was an incitement. Every idea is an incitement. It offers itself for belief and if believed it is acted on unless some other belief outweighs it or some failure of energy stifles the movement at its birth. The only difference between the expression of an opinion and an incitement in the narrower sense is the speaker's enthusiasm for the result. Eloquence may set fire to reason. But whatever may be thought of the redundant discourse before us it had no chance of starting a present conflagration. If in the long run the beliefs expressed in proletarian dictatorship are destined to be accepted by the dominant forces of the community, the only meaning of free speech is that they should be given their chance and have their way.

If the publication of this document had been laid as an attempt to induce an uprising against government at once and not at some indefinite time in the future it would have presented a different question. The object would have been one with which the law might deal, subject to the doubt whether there was any danger that the publication could produce any result, or in other words, whether it was not futile and too remote from possible consequences. But the indictment alleges the publication and nothing more.

✴ D O C U M E N T 7

Near v. Minnesota, 1931

Chief Justice Hughes delivered the opinion of the Court.

This statute, for the suppression as a public nuisance of a newspaper or periodical, is unusual, if not unique, and raises questions of grave importance transcending the local interests involved in the particular action. It is no longer open to doubt that the liberty of the press, and of speech, is within the liberty safeguarded by the due process clause of the Fourteenth Amendment from invasion by state action....

In maintaining this guaranty, the authority of the State to enact laws to promote the health, safety, morals and general welfare of its people is necessarily admitted. The limits of this sovereign power must always be determined with appropriate regard to the particular subject of its exercise.... Liberty of speech, and of the press, is also not an absolute right, and the State may punish its abuse.... Liberty, in each of its phases, has its history and connotation and, in the present instance, the inquiry is as to the historic conception of the liberty of the press and whether the statute under review violates the essential attributes of that liberty....

If we cut through more details of procedure, the operation and effect of the statute in substance is that public authorities may bring the owner or publisher of a newspaper or periodical before a judge upon a charge of conducting a business of publishing scandalous and defamatory matter—in particular that the matter consists of charges against public officers of official dereliction—and unless the owner or publisher is able and disposed to bring competent evidence to satisfy the judge that the charges are true and are published with good motives and for justifiable ends, his newspaper or periodical is suppressed and further publication is made punishable as a contempt. This is of the essence of censorship.

The question is whether a statute authorizing such proceedings in restraint of publication is consistent with the conception of the liberty of the press as historically conceived and guaranteed. In determining the extent of the constitutional protection, it has been generally, if not universally, considered that it is the chief purpose of the guaranty to prevent previous restraints upon publication. The struggle in England, direct against the legislative power of the licenser, resulted in renunciation of the censorship of the press. . . .

[P]unishment for the abuse of the liberty accorded to the press is essential to the protection of the public, and . . . the common law rules that subject the libeler to responsibility for the public offense, as well as for the private injury, are not abolished by the protection extended in our constitutions. . . . In the present case, we have no occasion to inquire as to the permissible scope of subsequent punishment. For whatever wrong the appellant has committed or may commit, by his publications, the State appropriately affords both public and private redress by its libel laws. As has been noted, the statue in question does not deal with punishments; it provided for no punishment, except in case of contempt for violation of the court's order, but for suppression and injunction, that is, for restraint upon publication. . . .

The exceptional nature of its limitations places in a strong light the general conception that liberty of the press, historically considered and taken up by the Federal Constitution, has meant, principally although not exclusively, immunity from previous restraints or censorship. The conception of the liberty of the press in this country had broadened with the exigencies of the colonial period and with the efforts to secure freedom from oppressive administration. That liberty was especially cherished for the immunity it afforded from previous restraint of the publication of censure of public officers and charges of official misconduct. . . .

The importance of this immunity has not lessened. While reckless assaults upon public men, and efforts to bring obloquy upon those who are endeavoring faithfully to discharge official duties, exert a baleful influence and deserve the severest condemnation in public opinion, it cannot be said that this abuse is greater, and it is believed to be less, than that which characterized the period in which our institutions took shape. Meanwhile, the administration of government has become more complex, the opportunities for malfeasance and corruption have multiplied, crime has grown to most serious proportions, and the danger of its protection by unfaithful officials and of the impairment of the fundamental security of life and property by criminal alliances and official neglect, emphasizes the primary need of a vigilant and courageous press, especially in great cities. The fact that the liberty of the press may be abused by miscreant purveyors of scandal does not make any the less necessary the immunity of the press from previous restraint in dealing with official misconduct. Subsequent punishment for such abuses as may exist is the appropriate remedy, consistent with constitutional privilege.

The statute in question cannot be justified by reason of the fact that the publisher is permitted to show, before injunction issues, that the matter published is true and is published with good motives and for justifiable ends. If such a statute, authorizing suppression and injunction on such a basis, is constitutionally valid, it would be equally permissible for the legislature to provide that at any time the publisher of any newspaper could be brought before a court, or even an administrative officer (as the constitutional protection may not be regarded as resting on mere procedural details) and required to produce proof of the truth of his publication, or of what he intended to publish, and of his motives, or stand enjoined. If this can be done, the legislature may provide machinery for determining in the complete exercise of its discretion what are justifiable ends and restrain publication accordingly. And it would be but a step to a complete system of censorship. The recognition of authority to impose previous restraint upon publication in order to protect the community against the circulation of charges of misconduct, and especially of official misconduct, necessarily would carry with it the admission of the authority of the censor against which the constitutional barrier was erected. The preliminary freedom, by virtue of the very reason for its existence, does not depend, as this Court has said, on proof of truth. . . .

For these reasons we hold the statute . . . to be an infringement of the liberty of the press guaranteed by the Fourteenth Amendment. We should add that this decision rests upon the operation and effect of the statute, without regard to the question of the truth of the charges contained in the particular periodical. . . .

✣ *E S S A Y S*

These selections provide insights into different parts of the story of the emergence of civil liberties during World War I. David A. Rabban, a professor at the University of Texas School of Law and one of the leading experts on free speech, provides an analysis of the most important Supreme Court cases of the immediate postwar era, focusing on Holmes's opinions in *Schenck* and *Abrams*. Rabban argues that a clear change in Justice Holmes's thinking occurred, which brought about a significant shift in the legal terrain in the area of free speech.

The second essay is by Samuel Walker, a retired professor of criminal justice at the University of Nebraska at Omaha, who has written a comprehensive history of the American Civil Liberties Union. Walker's essay details the rise of the Civil Liberties Bureau of the American Union Against Militarism (AUAM), which later evolved into the American Civil Liberties Union. Portraying the work of the Civil Liberties Bureau as key to the development of modern notions of free speech, Walker's account brings to light the early work of one of the most important interest groups of the twentieth century. Together, these essays show how both Supreme Court justices and interest groups have a role in shaping constitutional interpretation.

Oliver Wendell Holmes and the Judicial Transformation of the First Amendment

DAVID M. RABBAN

. . . The same factors that transformed many progressives into civil libertarians probably influenced Holmes and Brandeis as well. During the period between March and November, debate over the Versailles Peace Treaty prompted many Americans to realize that the war had failed to achieve the idealistic goals that justified their

From Rabban, David M., *Free Speech in Its Forgotten Years* (Cambridge: Cambridge University Press, 1997). Reproduced with permission of Cambridge University Press.

initial support of American intervention. These same months also marked the height of the postwar repression of radical speech, which horrified many people previously uninterested in free speech issues. Moreover, in June 1919, the *Harvard Law Review* published Chafee's "Freedom of Speech in War Time," which Holmes and Chafee discussed in July.

The dissent by Justice Holmes in *Abrams* relied heavily on Chafee's article. Holmes recognized the strategic possibilities of Chafee's misconstruction of Holmes's original use of the phrase *clear and present danger* in *Schenck*. He accepted as his own the protective meaning Chafee had erroneously read into that phrase. Holmes was thus able to express his changed views while claiming that the majority in *Abrams*, which closely followed the reasoning of his own unanimous Espionage Act opinions the previous March, had deviated from precedent.

Although the *Abrams* dissent marked the transformation of Holmes and Brandeis into defenders of free speech, they developed their new approach to the First Amendment in opinions throughout the 1920s. By the end of the Warren Court in the late 1960s, the mostly dissenting positions of Holmes and Brandeis in the 1920s had become the dominant perspective of the Supreme Court majority. Tracing judicial analysis of the First Amendment since 1920 reveals the content and ramifications of the "worthy tradition" begun by the postwar civil libertarians. It also provides the historical background for understanding more recent attacks on judicial interpretation of the First Amendment by critics who believe that this "worthy tradition" has become perverted by Supreme Court decisions during the past two decades.

From Holmes's dissent in *Abrams* through Brandeis's 1927 concurrence in *Whitney v. California*, Holmes and Brandeis elevated clear and present danger to constitutional significance and clung to it as the doctrinal peg for the protective interpretation of the First Amendment it did not express when Holmes first used the phrase in *Schenck*. The two justices frequently dissented together in First Amendment cases during the 1920s, but Brandeis wrote most of the opinions after *Abrams*. Unlike Holmes, Brandeis cited Chafee directly while relying on him more heavily. Building on Chafee and Holmes, Brandeis elaborated and extended the meaning of clear and present danger to provide increasing protection for speech.

Despite their joint dissents in many cases, Holmes and Brandeis developed substantially different justifications for protecting speech. Holmes invoked the economic metaphor of the free market as his model to defend the free competition of ideas unrestrained by the state. By contrast, Brandeis emphasized the role of free speech in developing the individual character traits essential to the proper operation of a democratic society. His focus on free speech as part of the mutual and potentially reinforcing relationship between the individual and society closely resembled Dewey's postwar analysis of free speech, as Dewey himself recognized. For Brandeis, as for Dewey, by protecting free speech the state liberates individuals, who in turn contribute to society.

Although there were important differences between the competitive market model of Holmes and the democratic citizenship model of Brandeis, both justices challenged together the traditional judicial hostility to free speech claims that the Supreme Court majority extended through the 1920s. This challenge did not rely on the major prewar approaches to the defense of free speech. Holmes and Brandeis did not invoke either the core commitment to individual autonomy of the libertarian radicals, or the more traditional individualism represented most clearly by [Thomas] Cooley's view that the "constitutional limitations" on government power extend to both personal and economic liberties. Using Chafee as their primary scholarly guide made it easier for Holmes and Brandeis to neglect prewar discussion of free speech.…

The defendants in *Abrams* were Russian immigrants who had published and distributed leaflets in English and Yiddish. These leaflets castigated President Wilson for sending American troops into Russia after the Bolshevik Revolution and urged a general strike in protest. The defendants had been charged and convicted under the 1918 amendments to the Espionage Act for attempting to harm the prosecution of the war. Justice Clarke conceded that the "primary purpose and intent" of these "defendant alien anarchists" might have been "to aid the cause of the Russian Revolution," an activity not proscribed by any law. Yet just as Holmes had held that Debs's "general program" could not protect his speech if even an "incidental" and "indirect" part tended to encourage the obstruction of recruitment, Clarke determined that Abrams could be punished for the "obvious effect" of his language – "defeat of the war program of the United States." Holmes had said that the use of "words tending to obstruct the recruiting service" was evidence that Debs "meant that they should have that effect." According to Clarke, "[m]en must be held to have intended, and to be accountable for, the effects which their acts were likely to produce."

The other majority opinions in the 1920s reiterated these familiar themes. Interlacing legal analysis with emotional outbursts, the opinions used the bad tendency doctrine as the means to punish radicals who had made a "travesty" of the First Amendment by invoking its provisions "to justify the activities of anarchy or of the enemies of the United States." …

In *Abrams*, as in *Schenck*, Holmes still viewed speech as a category of attempt and continued to rely on his thinking about the general law of criminal attempts. The circumstances in which speech is uttered, including the proximity and seriousness of the threatened danger as well as the intent of the speaker, remained important. In *Abrams*, however, Holmes infused new elements into his restatement of clear and present danger that emphasized the importance of a very close relationship between speech and crime. He used variations of "immediate" and "imminent" with remarkable frequency throughout his dissent, and even appended "forthwith" and "pressing" for additional emphasis.

Subtle variations in language in *Abrams* also indicated that Holmes was less willing than he was in *Schenck* to defer to legislative judgments of what constitutes the "substantive evils" that justify the punishment of speech threatening their occurrence. In *Schenck*, Holmes referred to "the substantive evils that Congress has a right to prevent" without anywhere indicating the limits of congressional power. By contrast, in *Abrams* Holmes rephrased this passage in words that significantly modified its meaning: "certain substantive evils that the United States constitutionally may seek to prevent." By adding the word *certain*, Holmes allowed that even some admittedly substantive evils cannot be invoked to restrict freedom of expression. Holmes may also have included *constitutionally*, modifying *seek*, in order to stress that the Constitution limits the government's right to prevent evil. Moreover, by substituting *the United States* for *Congress*, Holmes suggested that these constitutional limitations apply to all branches of government, thereby insinuating a justification for judicial review of congressional legislation without announcing a new standard that would have seemed inconsistent with the great deference manifested by his prewar and Espionage Act decisions. He now stressed that "Congress certainly cannot forbid all effort to change the mind of the country," and, for the first time, referred to the First Amendment as a "sweeping command." Perhaps Holmes no longer firmly believed that the majority could legitimately exercise whatever power it deemed efficient to obtain desired results.

Holmes also appeared to identify in *Abrams* the distinction between "public" and "private" speech stressed by prewar scholarly commentary on the First Amendment. In restating the clear and present danger test, Holmes implied that "where private rights are not concerned," Congress has less power to punish speech, a point he did not make in *Schenck, Frohwerk*, or *Debs*. Holmes seems to have accepted, as he had not in the past, that speech on matters of public affairs deserves added protection and cannot be viewed in the same manner as a simple solicitation to do a private wrong. Moreover, he now rejected as historically inaccurate the government's claim that the First Amendment did not abolish the common-law crime of seditious libel, a claim he had ignored the previous March.

Holmes's concluding paragraph in his *Abrams* dissent, which contains the most eloquent and best remembered passages in this famous opinion, suggests that he himself recognized the vast change in his views on free speech during the eight months since he wrote *Schenck, Frohwerk*, and *Debs*.

> Persecution for the expression of opinions seems to me perfectly logical. If you have no doubt of your premises or your power and want a certain result with all your heart you naturally express your wishes in law and sweep away all opposition. To allow opposition by speech seems to indicate that you think the speech impotent, as when a man says that he has squared the circle, or that you do not care whole-heartedly for the result, or that you doubt either your power or your premises. But when men have realized that time has upset many fighting faiths, they may come to believe even more than they believe the very foundations of their own conduct that the ultimate good desired is better reached by free trade in ideas – that the best test of truth is the power of the thought to get itself accepted in the competition of the market, and that truth is the only ground upon which their wishes safely can be carried out. That at any rate is the theory of our Constitution. It is an experiment, as all life is an experiment. Every year if not every day we have to wager our salvation upon some prophecy based upon imperfect knowledge.

It is remarkable that this paragraph, which includes a stirring defense of free speech, opens with a sentence that declares, "Persecution for the expression of opinions seems to me perfectly logical." The "but" that introduces Holmes's protective language comes only in the fourth sentence. Moreover, the second and third sentences bear a remarkable similarity to the contents of Holmes's private correspondence defending his decisions in *Schenck, Frohwerk*, and *Debs*, and to *The Common Law*. The text beginning with the word *but*, the most general and least technical portion of the entire dissent, seems as much a confession of personal conversion as a statement of constitutional law. Holmes, perhaps unselfconsciously, appears to be commenting on himself and those of his contemporaries who came to a belated appreciation of the value of free speech. The phrase *fighting faith* may well refer more specifically to the American support of World War I, a faith that was "upset" in the aftermath of the war when many, including Holmes's good friends at *The New Republic*, began to doubt "the very foundations of their own conduct." Only with the disillusionment that followed the war did these men begin to believe, above all, "that the ultimate good desired is better reached by free trade in ideas." Holmes here acknowledged that "the best test of truth" is not "the majority vote of that nation that can lick all others," as he had previously written to Hand, but "the power of the thought to get itself accepted in the competition of the market."

Despite these important protective innovations, however, Holmes retained in *Abrams* significant vestiges of his lifelong beliefs. He reapplied rather than abandoned his Social Darwinism. He tested truth by the "power" of thought to prevail in the "competition of the market" of ideas, and did not specify the value of free speech to the individual or to society. He also did not conceive of the First Amendment as the legal expression of democratic political theory. He still believed in the survival of the fittest, but he was now willing to let ideas battle each other rather than brute force. Holmes's dissent in *Abrams* did not constitute a complete transformation of his prior thought. In contrast to his admittedly summary treatment of the First Amendment in the initial Espionage Act cases, however, Holmes strove in *Abrams* to develop meaningful protection for free speech. He even concluded his dissent, in an uncharacteristic display of modesty, by stating, "I regret that I cannot put into more impressive words my belief that in their conviction upon this indictment the defendants were deprived of their rights under the Constitution of the United States."

What led Justice Holmes to change his views on free speech so dramatically between his opinions for a unanimous Supreme Court in *Schenck, Frohwerk,* and *Debs* and his dissent in *Abrams* just eight months later? This question is difficult to answer with precision, largely because there were so many factors that might have influenced him. Certain factual differences between *Abrams* and the first Espionage Act cases might have prompted Holmes to write his dissent. Current events during those eight months might have alerted Holmes, as they alerted many others, to the importance of freedom of expression. Psychological needs for approval from the postwar civil libertarians as well as his reading of books that condemned the repression of speech could have influenced Holmes. More specifically, the criticisms of his earlier Espionage Act decisions, particularly from men as prominent and respected as Chafee, Freund, and Hand, could have affected his thinking in *Abrams,* even in ways which Holmes himself might not have recognized.

As Holmes pointed out in his dissent in *Abrams,* the indictment under which the defendants were convicted alleged that they intended their publications to encourage resistance to American participation in World War I. After reviewing the texts of the defendants' leaflets, Holmes maintained that their only object was "to help Russia and stop American intervention there against the popular government—not to impede the United States in the war that it was carrying on." "An intent to prevent interference with the revolution in Russia," Holmes remarked, "might have been satisfied without any hindrance to carrying on the war in which we were engaged." ...

More generally, the opposition to the war expressed by the defendants in *Schenck, Frohwerk,* and *Debs* might have seemed much more threatening to Holmes than did the objections by the defendants in *Abrams* to American interference in the Russian Revolution. Holmes characterized the facts of *Abrams* as involving "the surreptitious publishing of a silly leaflet by an unknown man" and later described various pamphlets as "poor and puny anonymities." In such circumstances, Holmes maintained, no reasonable person could detect "any immediate danger" or "appreciable ten-dency" to hinder the war effort. By contrast, Schenck was an important official of the Socialist Party, and Debs was the most famous socialist in the United States. Though Frohwerk, like Abrams, was an unknown, Holmes, like much of the legal community, viewed *Schenck, Frohwerk,* and *Debs* as an interconnected trilogy, which probably made it difficult for him to consider *Frohwerk* on its own facts. *Abrams*, the only Espionage Act case decided the following fall, provided a better context than *Frohwerk* for Holmes to recognize and point out that less risk existed than in *Schenck* or *Debs*. It is also possible that Holmes, writing in dissent, felt able to express his personal opinions on freedom of expression more freely than when he wrote on behalf of all the justices, many of whom had more restrictive views on the subject.

Contemporary developments, many of which collectively formed part of the "Red Scare" of 1919–20, might also have made Holmes more sensitive to the value of free speech by November 1919 than he had been the previous March. The national debate over the Versailles Peace Treaty, which reached its peak in the summer and early fall of 1919, convinced many, perhaps including Holmes, that their enthusiasm for the war had been misplaced. Retrospective doubts about the wisdom of the war might have made the opposition voiced earlier by defendants in Espionage Act cases seem less threatening to the national interest. At the same time, the popular mood of repression that contributed to the convictions of the Espionage Act defendants had culminated in the hysteria of the "Red Scare" in the months between *Schenck* and *Abrams*. The creation of the Communist Third International in March 1919, designed to encourage worldwide proletarian revolutions, intensified the preexisting domestic fear of radicals and greatly assisted the efforts of American business interests and patriotic societies to identify postwar labor conflicts with communist activity.

Widespread industrial unrest, which began in January 1919 with a general strike in Seattle, culminated in the Boston Police Strike in September, the nation-wide steel strike, also in September, and the nationwide coal strike in November. The violence that accompanied these strikes was exaggerated and sensationally reported by the national news media. The strikes and the publicity they gener-ated further identified labor with radicalism. A series of unsuccessful attempted bombings around May Day, 1919, an apparently coordinated effort directed at a variety of prominent Americans, including Justice Holmes, and explosions within an hour of each other in eight different cities about a month later, also encour-aged popular alarm about radicals. By the fall of 1919, virtually anyone who did not succumb to the prevailing hysteria ran the risk of being labeled a radical. For example, Frankfurter and Chafee were under pressure to resign from the Harvard Law School during this period.

The events that made many of his friends and contemporaries more sensitive to the value of free speech probably affected Justice Holmes as well. His letters rarely referred to the hysteria, perhaps because he considered it unworthy of his interest. But when Holmes heard that Frankfurter's position at Harvard might be in jeopardy because influential people considered him too radical, he promptly wrote President Lowell praising Frankfurter for contributing to "the ferment which is more valuable than an endowment." Indeed, in his own book on Holmes, Frankfurter later main-tained that this "period of hysteria undoubtedly focused the attention of Mr. Justice Holmes on the practical consequences of a relaxed attitude toward" free speech.

Psychological needs as well as current events may have motivated Holmes. Edmund Wilson surmised that Holmes, long lonely for intellectual companionship, found it through his friendship with the postwar liberals. These liberals "stimulated and entertained him as well as gave him the admiration he craved." Wilson believed that they may have "counted for something with Holmes in his opinions after the first World War in cases in which the issue of free speech was involved. G. Edward White has suggested more recently that Holmes's "unfulfilled career expectations made him more receptive to the ideas" of the influential circle who wrote in *The New Republic*. ...

It also seems probable that the criticisms of his earlier Espionage Act decisions by Chafee, Freund, and Hand contributed to the more protective approach Holmes took in *Abrams*. The impact of Chafee on Holmes is easiest to trace. Harold Laski, who was well acquainted with Chafee and Holmes, invited both men to tea in late July 1919, midway between *Schenck* and *Abrams*. Laski, who had given Holmes a copy of "Freedom of Speech in War Time" before this meeting, wrote Chafee that "we must fight on it." Unfortunately, no record of this meeting appears to exist. In a letter to Judge Amidon the following September, however, Chafee commented on his summer conversation with Holmes. Chafee came away from this encounter with the impression that he did not convince Holmes about several key points in his article. Although Chafee was certain that Holmes, as a juror, would have voted to acquit Debs, Chafee reported that Holmes "is inclined to allow a very wide latitude to Congressional discretion in the carrying on of the war" and "further thinks that he could not have gone behind the jury verdict in the Debs case."

Holmes, although apparently not converted by his initial reading of "Freedom of Speech in War Time" or by his summer meeting with Chafee, soon began to agree with him. Holmes's dissent in *Abrams,* written less than four months after this talk, provides the best evidence of Chafee's influence. It is most striking that after omitting any reference to clear and present danger in *Frohwerk* and *Debs*, Holmes reformulated this phrase in *Abrams* in ways indicating that he now interpreted these words more as Chafee had misconstrued and glorified them than as he himself had originally used them in *Schenck*.

The *Abrams* dissent incorporated other views of the First Amendment advocated by Chafee, Hand, and Freund, but missing from Holmes's own prior decisions. Holmes emphasized in *Abrams* the relationship between free speech and the search for truth, recognized its importance even during a war, and conceded that the First Amendment is inconsistent with the common law of seditious libel. Although Holmes required "specific intent" in *Debs* as well as *Abrams,* his stress in *Abrams* on a "strict" construction of intent responded to the concerns of Chafee, Hand and Freund about employing vague standards to evaluate the legality of speech. It is perhaps most important that Holmes accepted in *Abrams* the independent judicial role they all had advocated. For the first time, Holmes indicated that he had abandoned his reflexive deference to legislative or jury determinations affecting the exercise of speech. He no longer treated the Espionage Act cases as ordinary criminal appeals, and seemed instead to appreciate their constitutional dimension.

It is impossible to determine which of these plausible influences actually contributed to the protective innovations Holmes introduced in his *Abrams* dissent. Holmes himself did not help to solve this puzzle. He never directly acknowledged that he had altered his interpretation of the First Amendment between his initial Espionage Act decisions and *Abrams*. In fact, many of his statements indicate that he considered his dissent in *Abrams* to be a logical extension of *Schenck, Frohwerk,* and *Debs.* The language of the dissent, however, contradicts Holmes's claims to consistency. All or some of these factors, consciously or unconsciously, might have helped change his views. Though the reasons remain uncertain, the significant transformation in Holmes's approach to freedom of expression is evident.

The Civil Liberties Bureau and the Origins of the Fight for Free Speech

SAMUEL WALKER

...While Wilson delivered his war message to Congress, Crystal Eastman convened an emergency meeting of the AUAM Executive Committee in New York. Since 1914 the committee had led the fight against the United States' entry into the war, and it was devastated by the prospect of war. Rev. John Haynes Holmes recalled the shock of discovering "that America is no longer, probably never was, the country that we loved." Many felt personally betrayed by Wilson, whom they had supported for reelection in 1916 because he had "kept the country out of war." He had encouraged their efforts and even met with them in the White House. Ben Huebsch recalled a debonair Wilson "smiling and greeting everybody" in the AUAM delegation. Max Eastman led a desperate last-minute effort on February 28, 1917, when they again met with Wilson in the Oval Office. But all their efforts were for naught, as Congress subsequently declared war.

But Crystal Eastman was undaunted. The energetic AUAM executive secretary already had an ambitious "war time program" of opposition to the draft, assistance to conscientious objectors, and support for "A Just and Lasting Peace." Her hopes of success, furthermore, were not unreasonable. The AUAM was a respected organization, with many friends in the Wilson administration. Cochairs Lillian Wald and Paul U. Kellogg were prominent Progressive reformers with a substantial record of influencing national policy. Wald's settlement house on Henry Street was a nerve center of Progressive Era social reform, and Kellogg was the editor of *The Survey,* virtually a house organ for social work reformers. They had successfully lobbied two presidents to create the federal Industrial Relations Commission, a broad-ranging government inquiry into labor–management conflict. The previous summer Eastman had organized a bold "people's diplomacy" campaign that helped stop American intervention in Mexico.

Eastman was joined by Roger Baldwin, who had just arrived from St. Louis. The two were remarkably similar in outlook, talent, and temperament. They shared a broad vision of social reform, believing that the promise of democracy could be achieved only if good people put their talents to the task. Both had boundless energy and a particular genius for organization building. Eastman had written a detailed investigation, *Work Accidents and the Law,* in 1910, and Baldwin had coauthored the

From Walker, Samuel, *In Defense of American Liberties: A History of the ACLU.* Reproduced with permission of Oxford University Press.

leading book on the juvenile court. Both charmed nearly everyone they met. Eastman was as strikingly beautiful as her brother Max was handsome: Poet Claude McKay called her the most beautiful white woman he ever met. And Baldwin maintained a twinkle in his eye until he died at age ninety-seven. Their energy, charm, and infectious enthusiasm helped give birth to the ACLU.

Baldwin's and Eastman's immediate task was to stop Congress from creating a military draft. They regarded conscription as a violation of democratic principles: If people would not volunteer to fight, the country should not go to war. England, they pointed out, had fought for two years without a draft. Over 2.5 million of the 4.6 million eligible men had voluntarily enlisted. Conscription was also contrary to the Christian principles on which American society was based and violated the "sacred liberty of conscience" implicit in the Bill of Rights. This was a novel and untested legal argument, for no one knew for sure whether the First Amendment's guarantee of religious freedom included exemption from military service. But the AUAM's arguments fell on deaf ears, and on May 18 Congress overwhelmingly passed the Selective Service Act. ...

By mid-June Eastman and Baldwin realized they faced a far more serious crisis than the draft. The mounting wartime furor threatened fundamental rights of freedom of speech, press, and assembly. They warned President Wilson that the proposed Espionage Act "may easily lend itself to the suppression of free speech, free assemblage, [and] popular discussion and criticism." They begged him "to make an impressive statement" about upholding "our constitutional rights and liberties." Wilson said nothing. AUAM Washington lobbyists Charles T. Hallinan, Harry Weinberger, and Jane Addams lobbied against the Espionage bill, but without success. Congress enacted the law on June 15 by an overwhelming majority.

The AUAM was suddenly uncertain about its own legal status. Did the Espionage Act's prohibition of "willfully obstruct[ing]" the draft include advising young men about conscientious objection? An AUAM pamphlet warned prophetically that "a district attorney or court might construe almost any activity in favor of peace or in criticism of the Government's war policies as coming within its provision." The AUAM's Executive Committee anxiously asked Weinberger for his opinion about "the legality of our present and proposed activities."

AUAM cochairs Wald and Kellogg were particularly upset by Eastman's and Baldwin's activities. Although staunch pacifists, they accepted Wilson's argument that the declaration of war settled the issue. They had hoped to influence the eventual peace settlement of this war to end all wars, but such influence required credibility in Washington, which in turn meant avoiding even the appearance of opposition. Wald and Kellogg and their allies in the AUAM faced a crucial choice: Would they defend civil liberties principles, regardless of the cost to their influence, or would they ignore them in the hope of gaining influence on other issues? They chose the latter course, and the resulting split with Eastman and Baldwin marked the birth of the civil liberties fight. ...

The dispute that had produced the Civil Liberties Bureau defined the basic terms of the free speech fight. The principled defense of civil liberties was a two-sided struggle: It fought the suppression of free speech by government officials and conservative superpatriots, but at the same time, it rejected liberal pragmatism. The temptation to ignore violations of civil liberties in the name of pursuing some other worthy social objective was a constant theme in ACLU history.

Wald's and Kellogg's position was a product of their reformist ideals. They were instinctively attracted to Wilson's rhetoric about making the world safe for democracy and his call for an international peacekeeping agency. Like many other prewar reformers, they were seduced by the opportunities for social change created by the enormous expansion of government regulation in the war effort. The National War Labor Board recognized collective bargaining, imposed a minimum wage and the eight-hour workday, and improved working conditions for women and children. The Shipping Board and the Department of Labor sponsored the first public housing units. Mary Van Kleeck, a major ACLU figure in the 1930s, drafted War Labor Board standards for women. And the 1917 Military and Naval Insurance Act included an experimental social security program.

The opportunity to wield power was an intoxicating experience. As some historians have argued, the war represented not a contradiction but the fulfillment of Progressive reform. Prewar reformers implicitly assumed that the welfare of the individual and the interests of the state were synonymous. They saw no fundamental conflict between state intervention and individual rights.

Liberal intellectuals offered elaborate rationalizations for the war effort. A *New Republic* editorial welcomed it as a historic opportunity for the "remarking of the life of the world" and "the creation of a united America." Philosopher John Dewey wrote that "some surrenders and abandonments of the liberties of peace time are inevitable." Many of these liberals were swept up by the wartime patriotic fervor and welcomed the common national purpose. Randolph Bourne, a maverick Progressive, answered Dewey with a devastating attack on liberal pragmatism. "It has been a bitter experience," he wrote, "to see the unanimity with which the American intellectuals have thrown their support to the use of war-technique." Like their European counterparts, they willingly put their talents in the service of the most undemocratic forces and ceased to think critically. In a stinging indictment of Wald, Kellogg, and the *New Republic* editors, Bourne argued that their "pragmatism" came to this: "If we obstruct, we surrender all power for influence. If we responsibly approve, we then retain our power for guiding." The price of responsible approval meant overlooking the systematic suppression of all political dissent. Bourne's essay, "The War and the Intellectuals," became an American classic and reappeared during World War II and the Vietnam War when the question of the responsibility of intellectuals in wartime arose again.

The members of the NCLB's Executive Committee came from three groups: Eastman and Baldwin were social workers who saw the free speech fight as a logical extension of prewar social reform activities. Largely oblivious to civil liberties considerations before the war, the wartime crisis forced them to abandon both their faith in the inevitability of social progress and their majoritarian view of democracy. They now began to see that majority rule and liberty were not necessarily synonymous and thus discovered the First Amendment as a new principle for advancing human freedom.

The second group were Protestant clergy, inspired by the reform ideas of the social gospel. Norman Thomas served a Presbyterian church in a poor section of New York City, and John Haynes Holmes led a Unitarian church. Harry F. Ward taught social ethics at Union Theological Seminary and was a prolific writer on social questions. The wartime crisis shattered their old faith and pushed them toward a secular, civil libertarian outlook: Thomas abandoned religion for the Socialist party. Holmes severed his formal ties with Unitarianism, renamed his church the Community church, and transformed it into a nonsectarian community center. Ward eventually became a Marxist.

Conservative lawyers comprised the third group. They idealized the Constitution and were outraged by the violations of free speech and due process. L. Hollingsworth Wood, a successful New York attorney, was also moved by Quaker pacifism. Albert DeSilver, an outspoken, prowar patriot, declared that "my law-abiding neck gets very warm under its law-abiding collar these days at the extraordinary violations of fundamental laws which are being put over." Independently wealthy, he dropped his private law practice, assisted Morris Hillquit in the *Masses* case, and then worked nearly full time with the NCLB, using his war bonds to post bail for defendants in free speech cases.

Over the next seventy years, this mixture of liberal social reformism and conservative faith in the promises of the Constitution remained the basic ingredient in the ACLU....

From the moment it was born, the AUAM Civil Liberties Bureau was overwhelmed by the assault on dissent. The first crisis in early July was the U.S. Postal Service's suppression of the antiwar press. Baldwin convened an emergency meeting of nearly one hundred editors and journalists and urged his AUAM contacts around the country to send protests to the president. He led a delegation to Washington to seek a meeting with Wilson "in order to bring to his personal attention this violation of one of America's most precious rights." On July 16, he, Oswald Garrison Villard, Clarence Darrow, and Amos Pinchot met with Postmaster General Burleson. Darrow used "all his folksy talents of persuasion," but to no avail. Neither Postal Service nor Justice Department officials would define the limits of permissible discussion of the war. One even bluntly told them to "cut out war criticism."

The Postal Service seized all the Civil Liberties Bureau's mail in mid-July. Baldwin met with postal officials and fired off another protest to the president. But eventually, over twelve pamphlets were banned as "unmailable," including *War's Heretics, The Truth About the IWW*, and an account of the nearlynching of Rev. Bigelow. Such an action was unexpected, as Baldwin had taken great pains to clear in advance his publications with the government, sending the Justice Department copies of all AUAM pamphlets in June and explaining that "we are exceedingly careful not to print anything which is likely to be questioned in the slightest." He also had asked postal officials whether *War's Heretics* "might lawfully be transmitted through the United States mails." Despite initial assurances, the post office seized all 3,500 copies. Quiet negotiations failed, and the NCLB eventually sued to obtain release of their material. The case dragged on for over a year until another suit secured release of all the seized mail....

The government's assault on dissent also included gross violations of due process of law. Federal agents—often private citizens working through the American Protective League—descended, without warrants, on private homes and the offices of political groups, seizing records and arresting virtually everyone in sight. The government seized and eventually burned all of the records of the Industrial Workers of the World (IWW). There were seven raids on the International Bible Students' Association in March 1918 alone, with officials seizing nearly 100,000 of the sect's pamphlets. The NCLB called for fair trials for all Espionage Act defendants, but with little effect: Virtually all war critics were convicted and sentenced to long prison terms.

The government directed its heaviest attacks against the Socialist party and the IWW, neither of which regained its prewar strength. The Socialist party was crippled through the Postal Service's ban on virtually all of its publications and the prosecution of many of its top leaders. The government's attack on the IWW was even more systematic. Prompted by business interests and government officials who feared the Wobblies' radical brand of unionism, the Justice Department staged a coordinated series of raids on every IWW office in the country on September 5, 1917. Hundreds of suspected members were indiscriminately arrested. Eventually 169 of the top leaders, including Big Bill Haywood, were indicted under the Espionage Act.

Baldwin sprang to the IWW's defense, writing to President Wilson, Secretary of Labor William B. Wilson, and Frankfurter to demand the indictments be dropped. In private meetings he suggested to Justice Department attorney John Lord O'Brian and presidential adviser Joseph Tumulty that "wholesale prosecutions were about the most unfortunate methods which could be devised of dealing with radical organizations in America." The NCLB demanded a fair trial and helped raise legal defense funds for the IWW. Baldwin began a long and stormy relationship with IWW member Elizabeth Gurley Flynn, whose own indictment had been dropped. (Flynn helped found the ACLU in 1920 but was expelled from the ACLU board in 1940 in one of the most controversial episodes in ACLU history.)

The NCLB's defense of the IWW finally brought down the wrath of the government. Administration hard-liners saw this as conclusive proof that the rhetoric of free speech was merely a smoke screen for revolutionary radicalism. Both military intelligence and the federal Bureau of Investigation began spying on the NCLB. Prominent liberals drew back in fear. As a result, the *New Republic*, the *Atlantic Monthly*, and the *Outlook* refused to publish NCLB ads defending the rights of the IWW. Max and Crystal Eastman also were cowed. The *Liberator*, which they founded in 1918 to replace the suppressed *Masses*, deliberately refrained from criticizing the government. Max explained that they "would have to temper [their] speech to the taste of the Postmaster General." In this political climate the outcome of the IWW trials was a foregone conclusion. Big Bill Haywood and thirteen other defendants received twenty-year prison sentences; thirty-three others were sentenced to ten years. Judge Kenesaw Mountain Landis explained bluntly, "You have a legal right to oppose, by free speech, preparations for war. But once war is declared, that right ceases."

In 1919, the Supreme Court finally addressed the question of free speech in wartime, four months after the war had ended. The result was a devastating defeat for civil liberties.

The first of the three major 1919 decisions involved Socialist party General Secretary Charles T. Schenck, convicted for mailing antiwar and antidraft leaflets to draft-age men. . . . On March 3, 1919, the Court unanimously upheld Schenck's conviction. . . .

The implications of *Schenck* became clear a week later when the Court unanimously upheld the conviction of Eugene Debs. In a June 16, 1918, speech to a Socialist party convention in Canton, Ohio, Debs had condemned war and capitalism but had carefully refrained from advocating any illegal conduct. "I abhor war," he declared.

"I would oppose the war if I stood alone." While government agents took notes, he asserted that the courts, the press, and the entire political system were controlled by the rich. Acutely aware of possible prosecution, he commented, "I realize that, in speaking to you this afternoon there are certain limitations placed upon the right of free speech. I must be exceedingly careful, prudent, as to what I say, and even more careful and prudent as to how I say it." He stressed the importance of political activity and labor organization: "Political action and industrial action must supplement and sustain each other. ... Vote as you strike and strike as you vote." Despite his disclaimer, the Court upheld his conviction. *Debs* was a shocking indication of how elastic the clear and present danger test could be. Schenck's pamphlets urged resistance to the draft and might be interpreted as counseling illegal action, but Debs's Canton speech was an abstract discussion of war and politics.

The *Abrams* decision five months later marked an important change on the Court. ...

In a sharp and unexpected break with their position in *Schenck* and *Debs*, Justices Holmes and Louis Brandeis dissented. Holmes wrote an impassioned defense of the "sweeping command" of the First Amendment. History, he argued, taught the importance of tolerance for unpopular ideas. Truth was best "reached by free trade in ideas," and "the best test of truth is the power of the thought to get itself accepted in the competition of the market." Freedom of speech, he concluded, "is the theory of our Constitution. It is an experiment, as all life is an experiment. ... While that experiment is part of our system I think that we should be eternally vigilant against attempts to check the expression of opinions that we loathe." Holmes revised his own clear and present danger test to add the element of imminent harm. Speech could be punished only in case of an "emergency that makes it immediately dangerous to leave the correction of evil counsel to time."

Holmes's *Abrams* dissent marks the beginning of modern First Amendment theory. He gave judicial notice to the idea, expressed two years earlier by Norman Thomas, that free speech was the basis of democratic self-government. The distinguished legal scholar John Henry Wigmore replied by restating the majoritarian view that "the moral right of the majority to enter upon the war imports the moral right to secure success by suppressing public agitation against completion of the struggle." There was no right to dissent from a democratically determined goal. Holmes's change of heart between *Schenck* and *Abrams* may have been stimulated by a summer meeting with Harvard law professor Zechariah Chafee, author of two important articles on free speech in wartime in the *New Republic* and the *Harvard Law Review*. ...

The prewar posture of the Supreme Court on free speech was consistent with long-standing American practice. Roger Baldwin and others in the NCLB attacked the wartime suppression of free speech as a violation of "old fashioned American liberties," but this was a highly romanticized view of American history. There was no tradition of free speech before World War I, in either legal doctrine or public tolerance for unpopular views. The glittering phrases of the First Amendment were an empty promise to the labor movement, immigrants, unorthodox religious sects, and political radicals. Intolerance began with the first English settlers who attempted to suppress religious heresy. The Puritans may have come to the new world seeking religious freedom for themselves, but they had no intention of granting it to others in their own communities. Through the end of the nineteenth century, American society was a set of "island communities," each a "closed enclave," intolerant of the ideas or behavior it disliked. For most, liberty meant economic freedom, the right to engage in economic pursuits free from government restraint. The geographic expanse of the country allowed dissident religious groups to set themselves apart, effectively postponing the question of tolerance in a pluralistic community.

Democratic theory justified the suppression of unpopular ideas and groups. Majority rule meant the right to suppress anything threatening or distasteful. Throughout the nineteenth century, the courts scarcely functioned in many frontier communities. The majority imposed swift and certain justice through vigilante action. The anti-Catholic mob that burned the Charlestown Convent in 1834 was led by pillars of the community. The northern mobs that attacked and, in some cases, killed abolitionists were composed of "gentlemen of property and standing." In 1856, the San Francisco Vigilance Committee, representing powerful business interests, staged a political coup d'état in city government.

The new aspect of the World War I assault on unpopular ideas was its national scope and the role of the federal government. Vigilantism had previously been a local and ad hoc phenomenon. But the war then nationalized the repression of unpopular ideas and institutionalized the machinery of the national security state. This in turn spurred an organized movement to defend free speech. Most of the wartime advocates of free speech—Baldwin, De-Silver, Nelles, Thomas, and Chafee—were from wealthy families or comfortably respectable Protestant backgrounds. They had no personal experience of the intolerance and suppression visited upon immigrants, labor unions, Catholics, minor religious sects, black Americans, and political radicals, and the wartime violations of free speech shattered their comfortable illusions about American liberty. The trauma of the war years exposed the First Amendment as an empty promise and galvanized this small group into the defense of free speech. In 1920 the old National Civil Liberties Bureau became the American Civil Liberties Union.

✢ *F U R T H E R   R E A D I N G*

Anderson, Alexis J. "The Formative Period of First Amendment Theory, 1870–1915," *American Journal of Legal History*, 24 (1980): 56–75.

Auerbach, Jerold S. "The Patrician as Libertarian: Zechariah Chafee, Jr., and Freedom of Speech," *New England Quarterly*, 24 (December 1969): 511–531.

Berns, Walter F. *The First Amendment and the Future of American Democracy* (1976).

Bogen, David. "The Free Speech Metamorphosis of Mr. Justice Holmes," *Hofstra Law Review*, 11 (1982): 97–189.

Capozzola, Christopher. *Uncle Sam Wants You: World War I and the Making of the Modern American Citizen* (2008).

Cortner, Richard C. *The Kingfish and the Constitution: Huey Long, the First Amendment, and the Emergence of Modern Press Freedom in America* (1996).

——. *The Supreme Court and the Second Bill of Rights: The Fourteenth Amendment and the Nationalization of the Bill of Rights* (1981).

Curtis, Michael Kent. *Free Speech, "The People's Darling Privilege": Struggles for Freedom of Expression in American History* (2000).

Ferrell, Robert H. *Woodrow Wilson and World War I, 1917–1921* (1985).

Kornweibel, Jr., Theodore. *"Investigate Everything": Federal Efforts to Compel Black Loyalty During World War I* (2002).

Murphy, Paul L. *The Meaning of Freedom of Speech: First Amendment Freedoms from Wilson to FDR* (1972).

——. *"Near v. Minnesota* in the Context of Historical Developments," *Minnesota Law Review*, 66 (1981): 95–160.

——. *World War I and the Origin of Civil Liberties in the United States* (1979).

Murray, Robert K. *Red Scare: A Study in National Hysteria, 1919–1920* (1955).

Polenberg, Richard. *Fighting Faiths: The Abrams Case, the Supreme Court, and Free Speech* (1987).

Pratt, Walter F., Jr. *The Supreme Court under Edward Douglass White, 1910–1921* (1999).

Rabban, David M. "The Emergence of Modern First Amendment Doctrine," *University of Chicago Law Review*, 50 (1983): 1207–1355.

Ragan, Fred D. "Justice Oliver Wendell Homes, Jr., Zechariah Chafee, Jr., and the Clear and Present Danger Test for Free Speech: The First Year, 1919," *Journal of American History* 58 (June 1971): 24–45.

Renstrom, Peter G. *The Taft Court: Justices, Rulings, and Legacy* (2003).

Schaffer, Ronald. *America in the Great War: The Rise of the War Welfare State* (1991).

Scheiber, Harry N. *The Wilson Administration and Civil Liberties, 1917–1921* (1960).

Shoemaker, Rebecca S. *The White Court: Justices, Rulings, and Legacy* (2004).

Smith, Donald L. *Zechariah Chafee, Jr.: Defender of Liberty and Law* (1986).

Steele, Richard W. *Free Speech in the Good War* (1999).

Strong, Frank R. "Fifty Year of 'Clear and Present Danger': From *Schenck* to *Brandenburg*– and Beyond," *Supreme Court Review* (1969): 41–80.

Tyack, David B. "The Perils of Pluralism: The Background of the *Pierce* Case," *American Historical Review*, 74 (October 1968): 74–98.

Vaughn, Stephen. "First Amendment Liberties and the Committee on Public Information," *American Journal of Legal History* 23 (1979): 95–119.

Zieger, Robert H. *America's Great War: World War I and the American Experience* (2000).

Franklin Roosevelt, the Depression, and the New Deal

The rapid expansion and rampant speculation of the 1920s gave way to a swift and severe economic downturn during the 1930s. After the stock market crashed in 1929, businesses failed in record numbers, levels of production and trade plummeted, and more and more Americans found themselves out of work and out of luck. By 1932, with about one-third of the nation's workforce unemployed, the United States settled into a prolonged depression. Republican President Herbert Hoover's half-hearted attempts to deal with the crisis neither promoted economic recovery nor advanced his political fortunes. Millions of Americans began to question the highly individualistic assumptions of laissez-faire constitutionalism, while demanding that government provide more of a collective social-welfare approach to economic hardship. Democratic presidential candidate Franklin D. Roosevelt responded directly to these popular concerns. After soundly defeating Hoover in the 1932 election, the incoming president proposed an ambitious "New Deal" to promote recovery and reform. Roosevelt's reforms, although they enjoyed widespread public support, arguably departed from decades of legal precedent regarding the role of the federal government in the economy. Led by four conservative justices who adhered strictly to constitutional orthodoxy (known derisively as the "Four Horsemen of the Apocalypse"), the Supreme Court struck down many of the early New Deal measures. After winning re-election in a landslide, in February 1937 Roosevelt pushed back by proposing a far-reaching judicial reform proposal, which provided for the appointment of additional judges to all the federal courts. With regard to the Supreme Court, he proposed that once a justice reached age 70, he would have 6 months to retire. If the justice failed to do so, the president would be permitted to appoint an additional justice, with a maximum of six new appointees. At the time FDR proposed the bill, six justices would have qualified, including the four staunch conservatives. The so-called Court-packing scheme ultimately failed, partly because Congress, the justices, and the public viewed it with suspicion and partly because the Court itself sensed that its continued opposition to the New Deal might ultimately undermine its own legitimacy. In early 1937, the justices began to sustain several pieces of state and federal regulatory legislation designed to relieve the hardships of the Depression.

The New Deal era constitutes one of the most significant periods in American constitutional history. Was the Court articulating sound constitutional principles when it invalidated several New Deal measures during Roosevelt's first term in office, or were the justices attempting to further a conservative economic agenda? Was Roosevelt's proposal to add new justices to the Supreme Court a necessary reform measure, or a blatant attempt to pack the Court with those who would uphold his legislative program? Did the Court-packing episode and its aftermath demonstrate the triumph of the rule of law, or the overtly political nature of the constitutional order? How different was the post-1937 constitutional order from the pre-1937 era? Did the New Deal period constitute a revolution in American constitutional history?

✠ D O C U M E N T S

As a presidential candidate and in his first inaugural address, Roosevelt offered few specifics about his program for economic recovery, as he chose instead to refer vaguely to the need for "action." FDR held no unified vision of economic policy, and during his first few years in office his legislative agenda embodied a number of different approaches to restoring the nation's economic health. The centerpiece of Roosevelt's initial plan for economic recovery was the National Industrial Recovery Act (NIRA), excerpted here as Document 1. The act gave considerable leeway to business leaders to draw up codes regulating competition and labor practices, while giving to the president the power to approve these regulations. Assisting farmers also became one of the top priorities of the administration. The Agricultural Adjustment Act (AAA) imposed a tax on agricultural processors to help fund a program of subsidies for farmers, who for decades had suffered from falling prices. The AAA is excerpted below as Document 2.

Both of these measures came before the Supreme Court and, according to the justices, ran afoul of the Constitution. In a unanimous decision written by Chief Justice Charles Evans Hughes, the Court struck down the NIRA in *Schechter v. the United States*, Document 3, where both the delegation of legislative authority to the president and the provisions of the "Live Poultry Code" were at issue. The decision occurred on May 27, 1935, "Black Monday," so called because on that same day the Court declared several other pieces of New Deal legislation unconstitutional. Roosevelt's luck with the Supreme Court worsened before it improved. The following year, the justices invalidated the Agricultural Adjustment Act in *United States v. Butler*, Document 4. The 6-3 decision, written by Justice Owen Roberts, focused on the law's establishment of a tax on agricultural processors.

After his reelection, FDR proposed his plan to expand the federal judiciary. On March 9, 1937, less than a week after his inauguration, Roosevelt gave a "fireside chat" radio address, Document 5, in which he explained his reasons for sponsoring the Judicial Reform Act of 1937. The speech reveals Roosevelt's beliefs about the place of the Supreme Court in the American constitutional order. Barely a month later, as debate continued over the proposal, the Court issued a number of opinions upholding New Deal measures and reform legislation in general. In *National Labor Relations Board v. Jones and Laughlin Steel Corporation*, Document 6, a 5-4 majority sustained the National Labor Relations Act, which guaranteed the right of workers to organize. In *West Coast Hotel v. Parrish*, Document 7, the same five justices voted to sustain a Washington state minimum wage law for women, thus dealing a death blow to the notion of substantive due process. Chief Justice Hughes—one of the Court's "swing justices" during this era—wrote the majority opinion in both instances. Within 4 years of these decisions, all four of the Court's most conservative members left the bench. Because he served three full terms in office, FDR went on to appoint nine justices, more than any president in American history except for George Washington. While Roosevelt lost the battle for the judiciary act, he clearly won the larger war over the direction of the Supreme Court.

✣ D O C U M E N T   1

The National Recovery Act Attempts to Bring the Nation Out of the Depression, 1933

(U. S. Statutes at Large, Vol. XLVIII, p. 195)

⸨ *An Act to encourage national industrial recovery, to foster fair competition, and to provide for the construction of certain useful public works, and for other purposes.*

Title I—Industrial Recovery

Declaration of Police.   Sec. 1. A national emergency productive of widespread unemployment and disorganization of industry, which burdens interstate and foreign commerce, affects the public welfare, and undermines the standards of living of the American people, is hereby declared to exist. It is hereby declared to be the policy of Congress to remove obstructions to the free flow of interstate and foreign commerce which tend to diminish the amount thereof; and to provide for the general welfare by promoting the organization of industry for the purpose of cooperative action among trade groups, to induce and maintain united action of labor and management under adequate governmental sanctions and supervision, to eliminate unfair competitive practices, to promote the fullest possible utilization of the present productive capacity of industries, to avoid undue restriction of production (except as may be temporarily required), to increase the consumption of industrial and agricultural products by increasing purchasing power, to reduce and relieve unemployment, to improve standards of labor, and otherwise to rehabilitate industry and to conserve natural resources.

Administrative Agencies.   Sec. 2.... (c) This title shall cease to be in effect and any agencies established hereunder shall cease to exist at the expiration of two years after the date of enactment of this Act, or sooner if the President shall by proclamation or the Congress shall by joint resolution declare that the emergency recognized by section 1 has ended.

Codes of Fair Competition.   Sec. 3. (a) Upon the application to the President by one or more trade or industrial associations or groups, the President may approve a code or codes of fair competition for the trade or industry or subdivision thereof, represented by the applicant or applicants, if the President finds (1) that such associations or groups impose no inequitable restrictions on admission to membership therein and are truly representative of such trades or industries or subdivisions thereof, and

(2) that such code or codes are not designed to promote monopolies or to eliminate or oppress small enterprises and will not operate to discriminate against them, and will tend to effectuate the policy of this title: *Provided,* That such code or codes shall not permit monopolies or monopolistic practices: *Provided further,* That where such code or codes affect the services and welfare of persons engaged in other steps of the economic process, nothing in this section shall deprive such persons of the right to be heard prior to approval by the President of such code or codes. The President may, as a condition of his approval of any such code, impose such conditions (including requirements for the making of reports and the keeping of accounts) for the protection of consumers, competitors, employees, and others, and in furtherance of the public interest, and may provide such exceptions to and exemptions from the provisions of such code, as the President in his discretion deems necessary to effectuate the policy herein declared.

(b) After the President shall have approved any such code, the provisions of such code shall be the standards of fair competition for such trade or industry or subdivision thereof. Any violation of such standards in any transaction in or affecting interstate or foreign commerce shall be deemed an unfair method of competition in commerce within the meaning of the Federal Trade Commission Act, as amended; but nothing in this title shall be construed to impair the powers of the Federal Trade Commission under such Act, as amended....

(d) Upon his own motion, or if complaint is made to the President that abuses inimical to the public interest and contrary to the policy herein declared are prevalent in any trade or industry or subdivision thereof, and if no code of fair competition therefor has theretofore been approved by the President, the President, after such public notice and hearing as he shall specify, may prescribe and approve a code of fair competition for such trade or industry or subdivision thereof, which shall have the same effect as a code of fair competition approved by the President under subsection (a) of this section....

Agreements and Licenses.   Sec. 4. (a) The President is authorized to enter into agreements with, and to approve voluntary agreements between and among, persons engaged in a trade or industry, labor organizations, and trade or industrial organizations, associations, or groups, relating to any trade or industry, if in his judgment such agreements will aid in effectuating the policy of this title with respect to transactions in or affecting interstate or foreign commerce, and will be consistent with the requirements of clause (2) of subsection (a) of section 3 for a code of fair competition.

(b) Whenever the President shall find that destructive wage or price cutting or other activities contrary to the policy of this title are being practiced in any trade or industry or any subdivision thereof, and, after such public notice and hearing as he shall specify, shall find it essential to license business enterprises in order to make effective a code of fair competition or an agreement under this title or otherwise to effectuate the policy of this title, and shall publicly so announce, no person shall, after a date fixed in such announcement, engage in or carry on any business, in or affecting interstate or foreign commerce, specified in such announcement, unless he shall have first obtained a license issued pursuant to such regulations as the President shall prescribe. The President may suspend or revoke any such license, after due notice and opportunity for hearing, for violations of the terms or conditions thereof. Any order of the President suspending or revoking any such license shall be final if in accordance with law. ...

Sec. 5. While this title is in effect ... and for sixty days thereafter, any code, agreement, or license approved, prescribed, or issued and in effect under this title, and any action complying with the provisions thereof taken during such period, shall be exempt from the provisions of the antitrust laws of the United States.

Nothing in this Act, and no regulation thereunder, shall prevent an individual from pursuing the vocation of manual labor and selling or trading the products thereof; nor shall anything in this Act, or regulation thereunder, prevent anyone from marketing or trading the produce of his farm.

Limitations upon Application of Title.   Sec. 6. (a) No trade or industrial association or group shall be eligible to receive the benefit of the provisions of this title until it files with the President a statement containing such information relating to the activities of the association or group as the President shall by regulation prescribe. ...

Sec. 7. (a) Every code of fair competition, agreement, and license approved, prescribed, or issued under this title shall contain the following conditions: (1) That employees shall have the right to organize and bargain collectively through representatives of their own choosing, and shall be free from the interference, restraint, or coercion of employers of labor, or their agents, in the designation of such representatives or in self-organization or in other concerted activities for the purpose of collective bargaining or other mutual aid or protection; (2) that no employee and no one seeking employment shall be required as a condition of employment to join any company union or to refrain from joining, organizing, or assisting a labor organization of his own choosing; and (3) that employers shall comply with the maximum hours of labor, minimum rates of pay, and other conditions of employment, approved or prescribed by the President.

(b) The President shall, so far as practicable, afford every opportunity to employers and employees in any trade or industry or subdivision thereof with respect to which the conditions referred to in clauses (1) and (2) of subsection (a) prevail, to establish by mutual agreement, the standards as to the maximum hours of labor, minimum rates of pay, and such other conditions of employment as may be necessary in such trade or industry or subdivision thereof to effectuate the policy of this title; and the standards established in such agreements, when approved by the President, shall have the same effect as a code of fair competition. ...

(c) Where no such mutual agreement has been approved by the President he may investigate the labor practices, policies, wages, hours of labor, and conditions of employment in such trade or industry or subdivision thereof; and upon the basis of such investigations, and after such hearings as the President finds advisable, he is authorized to prescribe a limited code of fair competition fixing such maximum hours of labor, minimum rates of pay, and other conditions of employment in the trade or industry or subdivision thereof investigated as he finds to be necessary to effectuate the policy of this title, which shall have the same effect as a code of fair competition approved by the President under subsection (a) of section 3. The President may differentiate according to experience and skill of the employees affected and according to the locality of employment; but no attempt shall be made to introduce any classification according to the nature of the work involved which might tend to set a maximum as well as a minimum wage.

(d) As used in this title, the term "person" includes any individual, partnership, association, trust, or corporation; ...

✠ *D O C U M E N T   2*

The Agricultural Adjustment Act Provides Subsidies for Farmers, 1933 d

(*U. S. Statutes at Large,* Vol. XLVIII, P. 31)

An Act to relieve the existing national economic emergency by increasing agricultural purchasing power, ... to provide for the orderly liquidation of joint-stock land banks, and for other purposes.

Title I—Agricultural Adjustment

Declaration of Emergency. That the present acute economic emergency being in part the consequence of a severe and increasing disparity between the prices of agricultural and other commodities, which disparity has largely destroyed the purchasing power of farmers for industrial products, has broken down the orderly exchange of commodities, and has seriously impaired the agricultural assets supporting the national credit structure, it is hereby declared that these conditions in the basic industry of agriculture have affected transactions in agricultural commodities with a national public interest, have burdened and obstructed the normal currents of commerce in such commodities, and render imperative the immediate enactment of title I of this Act....

Sec. 6. (a) The Secretary of Agriculture is hereby authorized to enter into option contracts with the producers of cotton to sell to any such producer an amount of cotton to be agreed upon not in excess of the amount of reduction in production of cotton by such producer below the amount produced by him in the preceding crop year, in all cases where such producer agrees in writing to reduce the amount of cotton produced by him in 1933, below his production in the previous year, by not less than 30 per centum, without increase in commercial fertilization per acre.

(b) To any such producer so agreeing to reduce production the Secretary of Agriculture shall deliver a nontransferable-option contract agreeing to sell to said producer an amount, equivalent to the amount of his agreed reduction, of the cotton in the possession and control of the Secretary.

(c) The producer is to have the option to buy said cotton at the average price paid by the Secretary for the cotton procured under section 3, and is to have the right at any time up to January 1, 1934, to exercise his option, upon proof that he has complied with his contract and with all the rules and regulations of the Secretary of Agriculture with respect thereto, by taking said cotton upon payment by him of his option price and all actual carrying charges on such cotton; or the Secretary may sell such cotton for the account of such producer, paying him the excess of the market price at the date of sale over the average price above referred to after deducting all actual and necessary carrying charges: *Provided*, That in no event shall the producer be held responsible or liable for financial loss incurred in the holding of such cotton or on account of the carrying charges therein: *Provided further*, That such agreement to curtail cotton production shall contain a further provision that such cotton producer shall not use the land taken out of cotton production for the production for sale, directly or indirectly, of any other nationally produced agricultural commodity or product....

Part 2—Commodity Benefits

General Powers.   Sec. 8. In order to effectuate the declared policy, the Secretary of Agriculture shall have power—

(1) To provide for reduction in the acreage or reduction in the production for market, or both, of any basic agricultural commodity, through agreements with producers or by other voluntary methods, and to provide for rental or benefit payments in connection therewith or upon that part of the production of any basic agricultural commodity required for domestic consumption, in such amounts as the Secretary deems fair and reasonable, to be paid out of any moneys available for such payments....

(2) To enter into marketing agreements with processors, associations of producers, and others engaged in the handling, in the current of interstate or foreign commerce of any agricultural commodity or project thereof, after due notice and opportunity for hearing to interested parties. The making of any such agreement shall not be held to be in violation of any of the antitrust laws of the United States, and any such agreement shall be deemed to be lawful....

Processing Tax.   Sec. 9. (a) To obtain revenue for extraordinary expenses incurred by reason of the national economic emergency, there shall be levied processing taxes as hereinafter provided. When the Secretary of Agriculture determines that rental or benefit payments are to be made with respect to any basic agricultural commodity, he shall proclaim such determination, and a processing tax shall be in effect with respect to such commodity from the beginning of the marketing year therefor next following the date of such proclamation. The processing tax shall be levied, assessed, and collected upon the first domestic processing of the commodity, whether of domestic production or imported, and shall be paid by the processor....

(b) The processing tax shall be at such rate as equals the difference between the current average farm price for the commodity and the fair exchange value of the commodity; except that if the Secretary has reason to believe that the tax at such rate will cause such reduction in the quantity of the commodity or products thereof domestically consumed as to result in the accumulation of surplus stocks of the commodity or products thereof or in the depression of the farm price of the commodity, then he shall cause an appropriate investigation to be made and afford due notice and opportunity for hearing to interested parties. If thereupon the Secretary finds that such result will occur, then the processing tax shall be at such rate as will prevent such accumulation of surplus stocks and depression of the farm price of the commodity....

(c) For the purposes of part 2 of this title, the fair exchange value of a commodity shall be the price therefor that will give the commodity the same purchasing power, with respect to articles farmers buy, as such commodity had during the base period specified in section 2.…

(d) As used in part 2 of this title—

(1) In case of wheat, rice, and corn, the term "processing" means the milling or other processing (except cleaning and drying) of wheat, rice, or corn for market, including custom milling for toll as well as commercial milling, but shall not include the grinding or cracking thereof not in the form of flour for feed purposes only.

(2) In case of cotton, the term "processing" means the spinning, manufacturing, or other processing (except ginning) of cotton; and the term "cotton" shall not include cotton linters.

(3) In case of tobacco, the term "processing" means the manufacturing or other processing (except drying or converting into insecticides and fertilizers) of tobacco.

(4) In case of hogs, the term "processing" means the slaughter of hogs for market.

(5) In the case of any other commodity, the term "processing" means any manufacturing or other processing involving a change in the form of the commodity or its preparation for market, as defined by regulations of the Secretary of Agriculture; and in prescribing such regulations the Secretary shall give due weight to the customs of the industry.

(e) When any processing tax, or increase or decrease therein, takes effect in respect of a commodity the Secretary of Agriculture, in order to prevent pyramiding of the processing tax and profiteering in the sale of the products derived from the commodity, shall make public such information as he deems necessary regarding (1) the relationship between the processing tax and the price paid to producers of the commodity, (2) the effect of the processing tax upon prices to consumers of products of the commodity, (3) the relationship, in previous periods, between prices paid to the producers of the commodity and prices to consumers of the products thereof, and (4) the situation in foreign countries relating to prices paid to producers of the commodity and prices to consumers of the products thereof.…

✥ *D O C U M E N T   3*
_____

Schechter v. United States, 1935

Mr. Chief Justice Hughes delivered the opinion of the Court.

Petitioners in No. 854 were convicted in the District Court of the United States for the Eastern District of New York on eighteen counts of an indictment charging violations of what is known as the "Live Poultry Code," and on an additional count for conspiracy to commit such violations. By demurrer to the indictment and appropriate motions on the trial, the defendants contended (1) that the Code had been adopted pursuant to an unconstitutional delegation by Congress of legislative power; (2) that it attempted to regulate intrastate transactions which lay outside the authority of Congress; and (3) that in certain provisions it was repugnant to the due process clause of the Fifth Amendment. ...

First. Two preliminary points are stressed by the Government with respect to the appropriate approach to the important questions presented. We are told that the provision of the statute authorizing the adoption of codes must be viewed in the light of the grave national crisis with which Congress was confronted. Undoubtedly, the conditions to which power is addressed are always to be considered when the exercise of power is challenged. Extraordinary conditions may call for extraordinary remedies. But the argument necessarily stops short of an attempt to justify action which lies outside the sphere of constitutional authority. Extraordinary conditions do not create or enlarge constitutional power. The Constitution established a national government with powers deemed to be adequate, as they have proved to be both in war and peace, but these powers of the national government are limited by the constitutional grants. Those who act under these grants are not at liberty to transcend the imposed limits because they believe that more or different power is necessary. Such assertions of extra-constitutional authority were anticipated and precluded by the explicit terms of the Tenth Amendment—"The powers not delegated to the United States by the Constitution, nor prohibited by it to the States, are reserved to the States respectively, or to the people."

The further point is urged that the national crisis demanded a broad and intensive coöperative effort by those engaged in trade and industry, and that this necessary coöperation was sought to be fostered by permitting them to initiate the adoption of codes. But the statutory plan is not simply one for voluntary effort. It does not seek merely to endow voluntary trade or industrial associations or groups with privileges or immunities. It involves the coercive exercise of the law-making power. The codes of fair competition which the statute attempts to authorize are codes of laws. If valid, they place all persons within their reach under the obligation of positive law, binding equally those who assent and those who do not assent. Violations of the provisions of the codes are punishable as crimes.

Second. The question of the delegation of legislative power. We recently had occasion to review the pertinent decisions and the general principles which govern the determination of this question. *Panama Refining Co. v. Ryan.* ... The Constitution provides that "All legislative powers herein granted shall be vested in a Congress of the United States, which shall consist of a Senate and House of Representatives." Art. I, § 1. And the Congress is authorized "To make all laws which shall be necessary and proper for carrying into execution" its general powers. Art. I, § 8, par. 18. The Congress is not permitted to abdicate or to transfer to others the essential legislative functions with which it is thus vested. We have repeatedly recognized the necessity of adapting legislation to complex conditions involving a host of details with which the national legislature cannot deal directly. We pointed out in the *Panama Company* case that the Constitution has never been regarded as denying to Congress the necessary resources of flexibility and practicality, which will enable it to perform its function in laying down policies and establishing standards, while leaving to selected instrumentalities the making of subordinate rules within prescribed limits and the determination of facts to which the policy as declared by the legislature is to apply. But we said that the constant recognition of the necessity and validity of such provisions, and the wide range of administrative authority which has been developed by means of them, cannot be allowed to obscure the limitations of the authority to delegate, if our constitutional system is to be maintained. ...

Accordingly, we look to the statute to see whether Congress has overstepped these limitations—whether Congress in authorizing "codes of fair competition" has itself established the standards of legal obligation, thus performing its essential legislative function, or, by the failure to enact such standards, has attempted to transfer that function to others. ...

In providing for codes, the National Industrial Recovery Act dispenses with this administrative procedure and with any administrative procedure of an analogous character. But the difference between the code plan of the Recovery Act and the scheme of the Federal Trade Commission Act lies not only in procedure but in subject matter. We cannot regard the "fair competition" of the codes as antithetical to the "unfair methods of competition" of the Federal Trade Commission Act. The "fair competition" of the codes has a much broader range and a new significance. The Recovery Act provides that it shall not be construed to impair the powers of the Federal Trade Commission, but, when a code is approved, its provisions are to be the "standards of fair competition" for the trade or industry concerned, and any violation of such standards in any transaction in or affecting interstate or foreign commerce is to be deemed "an unfair method of competition" within the meaning of the Federal Trade Commission Act. § 3 (b). ...

The Government urges that the codes will "consist of rules of competition deemed fair for each industry by representative members of that industry—by the persons most vitally concerned and most familiar with its problems." Instances are cited in which Congress has availed itself of such assistance; as *e.g.*, in the exercise of its authority over the public domain, with respect to the recognition of local customs or rules of miners as to mining claims, or, in matters of a more or less technical nature, as in designating the standard height of drawbars. But would it be seriously contended that Congress could delegate its legislative authority to trade or industrial associations or groups so as to empower them to enact the laws they deem to be wise and beneficent for the rehabilitation and expansion of their trade or industries? Could trade or industrial associations or groups be constituted legislative bodies for that purpose because such associations or groups are familiar with the problems of their enterprises? And, could an effort of that sort be made valid by such a preface of generalities as to permissible aims as we find in section 1 of title I? The answer is obvious. Such a delegation of legislative power is unknown to our law and is utterly inconsistent with the constitutional prerogatives and duties of Congress.

The question, then, turns upon the authority which § 3 of the Recovery Act vests in the President to approve or prescribe. If the codes have standing as penal statutes, this must be due to the effect of the executive action. But Congress cannot delegate legislative power to the President to exercise an unfettered discretion to make whatever laws he thinks may be needed or advisable for the rehabilitation and expansion of trade or industry. ...

Accordingly we turn to the Recovery Act to ascertain what limits have been set to the exercise of the President's discretion. *First*, the President, as a condition of approval, is required to find that the trade or industrial associations or groups which propose a code, "impose no inequitable restrictions on admission to membership" and are "truly representative." That condition, however, relates only to the status of the initiators of the new laws and not to the permissible scope of such laws. *Second*, the President is required to find that the code is not "designed to promote monopolies or to eliminate or to eliminate or oppress small enterprises, and will not operate to discriminate against them." And, to this is added a proviso that the code "shall not permit monopolies or monopolistic practices." But these restrictions leave virtually untouched the field of policy envisaged by section one, and, in that wide field of legislative possibilities, the proponents of a code, refraining from monopolistic designs, may roam at will and the President may approve or disapprove their proposals as he may see fit. . . .

Nor is the breadth of the President's discretion left to the necessary implications of this limited requirement as to his findings. As already noted, the President in approving a code may impose his own conditions, adding to or taking from what is proposed, as "in his discretion" he thinks necessary "to effectuate the policy" declared by the Act. Of course, he has no less liberty when he prescribes a code on his own motion or on complaint, and he is free to prescribe one if a code has not been approved. The Act provides for the creation by the President of administrative agencies to assist him, but the action or reports of such agencies, or of his other assistants—their recommendations and findings in relation to the making of codes— have no sanction beyond the will of the President, who may accept, modify or reject them as he pleases. Such recommendations or findings in no way limit the authority which § 3 undertakes to vest in the President with no other conditions than those there specified. And this authority relates to a host of different trades and industries, thus extending the President's discretion to all the varieties of laws which he may deem to be beneficial in dealing with the vast array of commercial and industrial activities throughout the country.

Such a sweeping delegation of legislative power finds no support in the decisions upon which the Government especially relies. . . .

To summarize and conclude upon this point: Section 3 of the Recovery Act is without precedent. It supplies no standards for any trade, industry or activity. It does not undertake to prescribe rules of conduct to be applied to particular states of fact determined by appropriate administrative procedure. Instead of prescribing rules of conduct, it authorizes the making of codes to prescribe them. For that legislative undertaking, § 3 sets up no standards, aside from the statement of the general aims of rehabilitation, correction and expansion described in section one. In view of the scope of that broad declaration, and of the nature of the few restrictions that are imposed, the discretion of the President in approving or prescribing codes and thus enacting laws for the government of trade and industry throughout the country, is virtually unfettered. We think that the code-making authority thus conferred is an unconstitutional delegation of legislative power.

Third. The question of the application of the provisions of the Live Poultry Code to intrastate transactions. . . .

The undisputed facts thus afford no warrant for the argument that the poultry handled by defendants at their slaughterhouse markets was in a "*current*" or "*flow*" of interstate commerce and was thus subject to congressional regulation. The mere fact that there may be a constant flow of commodities into a State does not mean that the flow continues after the property has arrived and has become commingled with the mass of property within the State and is there held solely for local disposition and use. So far as the poultry here in question is concerned, the flow in interstate commerce had ceased. The poultry had come to a permanent rest within the State. It was not held, used, or sold by defendants in relation to any further transactions in interstate commerce and was not destined for transportation to other States. Hence, decisions which deal with a stream of interstate commerce—where goods come to rest within a State temporarily and are later to go forward in interstate commerce—and with the regulations of transactions involved in that practical continuity of movement, are not applicable here. ...

(2) Did the defendants' transactions directly "*affect*" interstate commerce so as to be subject to federal regulation? The power of Congress extends not only to the regulation of transactions which are part of interstate commerce, but to the protection of that commerce from injury. It matters not that the injury may be due to the conduct of those engaged in intrastate operations. Thus, Congress may protect the safety of those employed in interstate transportation "no matter what may be the source of the dangers which threaten it." ...

In determining how far the federal government may go in controlling intrastate transactions upon the ground that they "affect" interstate commerce, there is a necessary and well-established distinction between direct and indirect effects. The precise line can be drawn only as individual cases arise, but the distinction is clear in principle. Direct effects are illustrated by the railroad cases we have cited, as *e.g.*, the effect of failure to use prescribed safety appliances on railroads which are the highways of both interstate and intrastate commerce, injury to an employee engaged in interstate transportation by the negligence of an employee engaged in an intrastate movement, the fixing of rates for intrastate transportation which unjustly discriminate against interstate commerce. But where the effect of intrastate transactions upon interstate commerce is merely indirect, such transactions remain within the domain of state power. If the commerce clause were construed to reach all enterprises and transactions which could be said to have an indirect effect upon interstate commerce, the federal authority would embrace practically all the activities of the people and the authority of the State over its domestic concerns would exist only by sufferance of the federal government. ...

It is not the province of the Court to consider the economic advantages or disadvantages of such a centralized system. It is sufficient to say that the Federal Constitution does not provide for it. Our growth and development have called for wide use of the commerce power of the federal government in its control over the expanded activities of interstate commerce, and in protecting that commerce from burdens, interferences, and conspiracies to restrain and monopolize it. But the authority of the federal government may not be pushed to such an extreme as to destroy the distinction, which the commerce clause itself establishes, between commerce "among the several States" and the internal concerns of a State. The same answer must be made to the contention that is based upon the serious economic situation which led to the passage of the Recovery Act—the fall in prices, the decline in wages and employment, and the curtailment of the market for commodities. Stress is laid upon the great importance of maintaining wage distributions which would provide the necessary stimulus in starting "the cumulative forces making for expanding commercial activity." Without in any way disparaging this motive, it is enough to say that the recuperative efforts of the federal government must be made in a manner consistent with the authority granted by the Constitution.

We are of the opinion that the attempt through the provisions of the Code to fix the hours and wages of employees of defendants in their intrastate business was not a valid exercise of federal power....

✢ *D O C U M E N T   4*

United States v. Butler, 1936

Mr. Justice Roberts delivered the opinion of the Court.

In this case we must determine whether certain provisions of the Agricultural Adjustment Act, 1933, conflict with the federal Constitution....

There should be no misunderstanding as to the function of this court in such a case. It is sometimes said that the court assumes a power to overrule or control the action of the people's representatives. This is a misconception. The Constitution is the supreme law of the land ordained and established by the people. All legislation must conform to the principles it lays down. When an act of Congress is appropriately challenged in the courts as not conforming to the constitutional mandate the judicial branch of the Government has only one duty—to lay the article of the Constitution which is invoked beside the statute which is challenged and to decide whether the latter squares with the former. All the court does, or can do, is to announce its considered judgment upon the question. The only power it has, if such it may be called, is the power of judgment. This court neither approves nor condemns any legislative policy. Its delicate and difficult office is to ascertain and declare whether the legislation is in accordance with, or in contravention of, the provisions of the Constitution; and, having done that, its duty ends.

The question is not what power the federal Government ought to have but what powers in fact have been given by the people. It hardly seems necessary to reiterate that ours is a dual form of government; that in every state there are two governments,—the state and the United States. Each State has all governmental powers save such as the people, by their Constitution, have conferred upon the United States, denied to the States, or reserved to themselves. The federal union is a government of delegated powers. It has only such as are expressly conferred upon it and such as are reasonably to be implied from those granted. In this respect we differ radically from nations where all legislative power, without restriction or limitation, is vested in a parliament or other legislative body subject to no restrictions except the discretion of its members.

Article I, § 8, of the Constitution vests sundry powers in the Congress. But two of its clauses have any bearing upon the validity of the statute under review.

The third clause endows the Congress with power "to regulate Commerce ... among the several States." Despite a reference in its first section to a burden upon, and an obstruction of the normal currents of commerce, the act under review does not purport to regulate transactions in interstate or foreign commerce. Its stated purpose is the control of agricultural production, a purely local activity, in an effort to raise the prices paid the farmer. Indeed, the Government does not attempt to uphold the validity of the act on the basis of the commerce clause, which, for the purpose of the present case, may be put aside as irrelevant.

The clause thought to authorize the legislation,—the first,—confers upon the Congress power "to lay and collect Taxes, Duties, Imposts and Excises, to pay the Debts and provide for the common Defence and general Welfare of the United States...." It is not contended that this provision grants power to regulate agricultural production upon the theory that such legislation would promote the general welfare. The Government concedes that the phrase "to provide for the general welfare" qualifies the power "to lay and collect taxes."...

Nevertheless the Government asserts that warrant is found in this clause for the adoption of the Agricultural Adjustment Act. The argument is that Congress may appropriate and authorize the spending of moneys for the "general welfare;" that the phrase should be liberally construed to cover anything conducive to national welfare; that decision as to what will promote such welfare rests with Congress alone, and the courts may not review its determination; and finally that the appropriation under attack was in fact for the general welfare of the United States.

The Congress is expressly empowered to lay taxes to provide for the general welfare. Funds in the Treasury as a result of taxation may be expended only through appropriation. (Art. I, § 9, cl. 7.) They can never accomplish the objects for which they were collected unless the power to appropriate is as broad as the power to tax. The necessary implication from the terms of the grant is that the public funds may be appropriated "to provide for the general welfare of the United States." These words cannot be meaningless, else they would not have been used. The conclusion must be that they were intended to limit and define the granted power to raise and to expend money....

As elsewhere throughout the Constitution the section in question lays down principles which control the use of the power, and does not attempt meticulous or detailed directions. Every presumption is to be indulged in favor of faithful compliance by Congress with the mandates of the fundamental law. Courts are reluctant to adjudge any statute in contravention of them. But, under our frame of government, no other place is provided where the citizen may be heard to urge that the law fails to conform to the limits set upon the use of a granted power. When such a contention comes here we naturally require a showing that by no reasonable possibility can the challenged legislation fall within the wide range of discretion permitted to the Congress. How great is the extent of that range, when the subject is the promotion of the general welfare of the United States, we need hardly remark. But, despite the breadth of the legislative discretion, our duty to hear and to render judgment remains. If the statute plainly violates the stated principle of the Constitution we must so declare.

We are not now required to ascertain the scope of the phrase "general welfare of the United States" or to determine whether an appropriation in aid of agriculture falls within it. Wholly apart from that question, another principle embedded in our Constitution prohibits the enforcement of the Agricultural Adjustment Act. The act invades the reserved rights of the states. It is a statutory plan to regulate and control agricultural production, a matter beyond the powers delegated to the federal government. The tax, the appropriation of the funds raised, and the direction for their disbursement, are but parts of the plan. They are but means to an unconstitutional end.

From the accepted doctrine that the United States is a government of delegated powers, it follows that those not expressly granted, or reasonably to be implied from such as are conferred, are reserved to the states or to the people. To forestall any suggestion to the contrary, the Tenth Amendment was adopted. The same proposition, otherwise stated, is that powers not granted are prohibited. None to regulate agricultural production is given, and therefore legislation by Congress for that purpose is forbidden. ...

If the taxing power may not be used as the instrument to enforce a regulation of matters of state concern with respect to which the Congress has no authority to interfere, may it, as in the present case, be employed to raise the money necessary to purchase a compliance which the Congress is powerless to command? The Government asserts that whatever might be said against the validity of the plan, if compulsory, sit is constitutionally sound because the end is accomplished by voluntary cooperation. There are two sufficient answers to the contention. The regulation is not in fact voluntary. The farmer, of course, may refuse to comply, but the price of such refusal is the loss of benefits. The amount offered is intended to be sufficient to exert pressure on him to agree to the proposed regulation. The power to confer or withhold unlimited benefits is the power to coerce or destroy. If the cotton grower elects not to accept the benefits, he will receive less for his crops; those who receive payments will be able to undersell him. The result may well be financial ruin. The coercive purpose and intent of the statute is not obscured by the fact that it has not been perfectly successful. ...

But if the plan were one for purely voluntary co-operation it would stand no better so far as federal power is concerned. At best it is a scheme for purchasing with federal funds submission to federal regulation of a subject reserved to the states. ...

But it is said that there is a wide difference in another respect, between compulsory regulation of the local affairs of a state's citizens and the mere making of a contract relating to their conduct; that, if any state objects, it may declare the contract void and thus prevent those under the state's jurisdiction from complying with its terms. The argument is plainly fallacious. The United States can make the contract only if the federal power to tax and to appropriate reaches the subject matter of the contract. If this does reach the subject matter, its exertion cannot be displaced by state action. To say otherwise is to deny the supremacy of the laws of the United States; to make them subordinate to those of a State. This would reverse the cardinal principle embodied in the Constitution and substitute one which declares that Congress may only effectively legislate as to matters within federal competence when the States do not dissent.

Congress has no power to enforce its commands on the farmer to the ends sought by the Agricultural Adjustment Act. It must follow that it may not indirectly accomplish those ends by taxing and spending to purchase compliance. The Constitution and the entire plan of our government negative any such use of the power to tax and to spend as the act undertakes to authorize. It does not help to declare that local conditions throughout the nation have created a situation of national concern; for this is but to say that whenever there is a widespread similarity of local conditions, Congress may ignore constitutional limitations upon its own powers and usurp those reserved to the states. If, in lieu of compulsory regulation of subjects within the states' reserved jurisdiction, which is prohibited, the Congress could invoke the taxing and spending power as a means to accomplish the same end, clause 1 of § 8 of Article I would become the instrument for total subversion of the governmental powers reserved to the individual states. ...

✤ *D O C U M E N T   5*

President Franklin D. Roosevelt Advocates Judicial Reform, 1937

... Tonight, sitting at my desk in the White House, I make my first radio report to the people in my second term of office. ...

The American people have learned from the depression. For in the last three national elections an overwhelming majority of them voted a mandate that the Congress and the President begin the task of providing ... protection—not after long years of debate, but now.

The courts, however, have cast doubts on the ability of the elected Congress to protect us against catastrophe by meeting squarely our modern social and economic conditions. ...

I want to talk with you very simply about the need for present action in this crisis—the need to meet the unanswered challenge of one-third of a nation ill-nourished, ill-clad, ill-housed.

Last Thursday I described the American form of government as a three-horse team provided by the Constitution to the American people so that their field might be plowed. The three horses are, of course, the three branches of government—the Congress, the executive, and the courts. Two of the horses are pulling in unison today; the third is not. Those who have intimated that the President of the United States is trying to drive that team overlook the simple fact that the President, as Chief Executive, is himself one of the three horses.

It is the American people themselves who are in the driver's seat.

It is the American people themselves who want the furrow plowed.

It is the American people themselves who expect the third horse to pull in unison with the other two.

I hope that you have reread the Constitution of the United States. Like the Bible, it ought to be read again and again.

It is an easy document to understand when you remember that it was called into being because the Articles of Confederation under which the Original Thirteen States tried to operate after the Revolution showed the need of a National Government with power enough to handle national problems. In its preamble the Constitution states that it was intended to form a more perfect Union and promote the general welfare; and the powers given to the Congress to carry out those purposes can be best described by saying that they were all the powers needed to meet each and every problem which then had a national character and which could not be met by merely local action.

But the framers went further. Having in mind that in succeeding generations many other problems then undreamed of would become national problems, they gave to the Congress the ample broad powers "to levy taxes ... and provide for the common defense and general welfare of the United States."

That, my friends, is what I honestly believe to have been the clear and underlying purpose of the patriots who wrote a Federal Constitution to create a National Government with national power, intended as they said, "to form a more perfect union ... for ourselves and our posterity."

For nearly 20 years there was no conflict between the Congress and the Court. Then, in 1803, ... [t]he Court claimed the power to declare it [a statute] unconstitutional and did so declare it. But a little later the Court itself admitted that it was an extraordinary power to exercise and through Mr. Justice Washington laid down this limitation upon it: "It is but a decent respect due to the wisdom, the integrity, and the patriotism of the legislative body, by which any law is passed, to presume in favor of its validity until its violation of the Constitution is proved beyond all reasonable doubt."

But since the rise of the modern movement for social and economic progress through legislation, the Court has more and more often and more and more boldly asserted a power to veto laws passed by the Congress and State legislatures in complete disregard of this original limitation.

In the last 4 years the sound rule of giving statutes the benefit of all reasonable doubt has been cast aside. The Court has been acting not as a judicial body, but as a policy-making body.

When the Congress has sought to stabilize national agriculture, to improve the conditions of labor, to safeguard business against unfair competition, to protect our national resources, and in many other ways to serve our clearly national needs, the majority of the Court has been assuming the power to pass on the wisdom of these acts of the Congress—and to approve or disapprove the public policy written into these laws....

In the case holding the A.A.A. unconstitutional, Justice Stone said of the majority opinion that it was a "tortured construction of the Constitution." And two other Justices agreed with him.

In the case holding the New York Minimum Wage Law unconstitutional, Justice Stone said that the majority were actually reading into the Constitution their own "personal economic predilections," and that if the legislative power is not left free to choose the methods of solving the problems of poverty, subsistence, and health of large numbers in the community, then "government is to be rendered impotent." And two other Justices agreed with him.

In the face of these dissenting opinions, there is no basis for the claim made by some members of the Court that something in the Constitution has compelled them regretfully to thwart the will of the people.

In the face of such dissenting opinions, it is perfectly clear that as Chief Justice Hughes has said, "We are under a Constitution, but the Constitution is what the judges say it is."

The Court in addition to the proper use of its judicial functions has improperly set itself up as a third House of the Congress—a superlegislature, as one of the Justices has called it—reading into the Constitution words and implications which are not there, and which were never intended to be there.

We have, therefore, reached the point as a Nation where we must take action to save the Constitution from the Court and the Court from itself. We must find a way to take an appeal from the Supreme Court to the Constitution itself. We want a Supreme Court which will do justice under the Constitution—not over it. In our courts we want a government of laws and not of men.

I want—as all Americans want—an independent judiciary as proposed by the framers of the Constitution. That means a Supreme Court that will enforce the

Constitution as written—that will refuse to amend the Constitution by the arbitrary exercise of judicial power—amendment by judicial say-so. It does not mean a judiciary so independent that it can deny the existence of facts universally recognized.

How, then, could we proceed to perform the mandate given us? It was said in last year's Democratic platform, "If these problems cannot be effectively solved within the Constitution, we shall seek such clarifying amendment as will assure the power to enact those laws, adequately to regulate commerce, protect public health and safety, and safeguard economic security." In other words, we said we would seek an amendment only if every other possible means by legislation were to fail.

When I commenced to review the situation with the problem squarely before me, I came by a process of elimination to the conclusion that short of amendments the only method which was clearly constitutional, and would at the same time carry out other much-needed reforms, was to infuse new blood into all our courts. We must have men worthy and equipped to carry out impartial justice. But at the same time we must have judges who will bring to the courts a present-day sense of the Constitution—judges who will retain in the courts the judicial functions of a court and reject the legislative powers which the courts have today assumed.

In 45 out of 48 States of the Union, judges are chosen not for life but for a period of years. In many States judges must retire at the age of 70. Congress has provided financial security by offering life pensions at full pay for Federal judges on all courts who are willing to retire at 70. In the case of Supreme Court Justices, that pension is $20,000 a year. But all Federal judges, once appointed, can, if they choose, hold office for life no matter how old they may get to be.

What is my proposal? It is simply this: Whenever a judge or justice of any Federal court has reached the age of 70 and does not avail himself of the opportunity to retire on a pension, a new member shall be appointed by the President then in office, with the approval, as required by the Constitution, of the Senate of the United States.

That plan has two chief purposes: By bringing into the judicial system a steady and continuing stream of new and younger blood, I hope, first, to make the administration of all Federal justice speedier and therefore less costly; secondly, to bring to the decision of social and economic problems younger men who have had personal experience and contact with modern facts and circumstances under which average men have to live and work. This plan will save our National Constitution from hardening of the judicial arteries.

The number of judges to be appointed would depend wholly on the decision of present judges now over 70 or those who would subsequently reach the age of 70.

If, for instance, any one of the six Justices of the Supreme Court now over the age of 70 should retire as provided under the plan, no additional place would be created. Consequently, although there never can be more than 15, there may be only 14, or 13, or 12, and there may be only 9.

There is nothing novel or radical about this idea. It seeks to maintain the Federal bench in full vigor. It has been discussed and approved by many persons of high authority ever since a similar proposal passed the House of Representatives in 1869.

Why was the age fixed at 70? Because the laws of many States, the practice of the civil service, the regulations of the Army and Navy, and the rules of many of our universities and of almost every great private business enterprise commonly fix the retirement age at 70 years or less.

The statute would apply to all the courts in the Federal system. There is general approval so far as the lower Federal courts are concerned. The plan has met opposition only so far as the Supreme Court of the United States itself is concerned. If such a plan is good for the lower courts, it certainly ought to be equally good for the highest court, from which there is no appeal.

Those opposing this plan have sought to arouse prejudice and fear by crying that I am seeking to "pack" the Supreme Court and that a baneful precedent will be established.

What do they mean by the words "packing the Court"?

Let me answer this question with a bluntness that will end all honest misunderstanding of my purposes.

If by that phrase "packing the Court" it is charged that I wish to place on the bench spineless puppets who would disregard the law and would decide specific cases as I wished them to be decided, I make this answer: That no President fit for his office would appoint, and no Senate of honorable men fit for their office would confirm, that kind of appointees to the Supreme Court.

But if by that phrase the charge is made that I would appoint and the Senate would confirm Justices worthy to sit beside present members of the Court who understand those modern conditions; that I will appoint Justices who will not undertake to override the judgment of the Congress on legislative policy; that I will appoint Justices who will act as Justices and not as legislators—if the appointment of such Justices can be called "packing the Courts"—then I say that I, and with me the vast majority of the American people, favor doing just that thing—now.

Is it a dangerous precedent for the Congress to change the number of the Justices? The Congress has always had, and will have, that power. The number of Justices has been changed several times before—in the administrations of John Adams and Thomas Jefferson, both signers of the Declaration of Independence, Andrew Jackson, Abraham Lincoln, and Ulysses S. Grant....

We think it so much in the public interest to maintain a vigorous judiciary that we encourage the retirement of elderly judges by offering them a life pension at full salary. Why then should we leave the fulfillment of this public policy to chance or make it dependent upon the desire or prejudice of any individual Justice?

It is the clear intention of our public policy to provide for a constant flow of new and younger blood into the judiciary. Normally, every President appoints a large number of district and circuit judges and a few members of the Supreme Court. Until my first term practically every President of the United States had appointed at least one member of the Supreme Court. President Taft appointed five members and named a Chief Justice; President Wilson three; President Harding four, including a Chief Justice; President Coolidge one; President Hoover three, including a Chief Justice.

Such a succession of appointments should have provided a court well balanced as to age. But chance and the disinclination of individuals to leave the Supreme Bench have now given us a Court in which five Justices will be over 75 years of age before next June and one over 70. Thus a sound public policy has been defeated.

I now propose that we establish by law an assurance against any such ill-balanced Court in the future. I propose that hereafter, when a judge reaches the age of 70, a new and younger judge shall be added to the Court automatically. In this way I propose to enforce a sound public policy by law instead of leaving the composition of our

Federal courts, including the highest, to be determined by chance or the personal decision of individuals.

If such a law as I propose is regarded as establishing a new precedent, is it not a most desirable precedent?

Like all lawyers, like all Americans, I regret the necessity of this controversy. But the welfare of the United States, and indeed of the Constitution itself, is what we all must think about first. Our difficulty with the Court today rises not from the Court as an institution but from human beings within it. But we cannot yield our constitutional destiny to the personal judgment of a few men who, being fearful of the future, would deny us the necessary means of dealing with the present.

This plan of mine is no attack on the Court; it seeks to restore the Court to its rightful and historic place in our system of constitutional government and to have it resume its high task of building anew on the Constitution "a system of living law."

I have thus explained to you the reasons that lie behind our efforts to secure results by legislation within the Constitution. I hope that thereby the difficult process of constitutional amendment may be rendered unnecessary....

I am in favor of action through legislation—

First, because I believe that it can be passed at this session of the Congress.

Second, because it will provide a reinvigorated, liberal-minded judiciary necessary to furnish quicker and cheaper justice from bottom to top.

Third, because it will provide a series of Federal courts willing to enforce the Constitution as written, and unwilling to assert legislative powers by writing into it their own political and economic policies.

During the past half century the balance of power between the three great branches of the Federal Government has been tipped out of balance by the courts in direct contradiction of the high purposes of the framers of the Constitution. It is my purpose to restore that balance. You who know me will accept my solemn assurance that in a world in which democracy is under attack I seek to make American democracy succeed.

✥ D O C U M E N T   6

National Labor Relations Board v. Jones and Laughlin Steel Corporation, 1937

Mr. Chief Justice Hughes delivered the opinion of the Court.

In a proceeding under the National Labor Relations Act of 1935, the National Labor Relations Board found that the respondent, Jones & Laughlin Steel Corporation, had violated the Act by engaging in unfair labor practices affecting commerce.... The unfair labor practices charged were that the corporation was discriminating against members of the union with regard to hire and tenure of employment, and was coercing and intimidating its employees in order to interfere with their self-organization. The discriminatory and coercive action alleged was the discharge of certain employees.

The National Labor Relations Board, sustaining the charge, ordered the corporation to cease and desist from such discrimination and coercion, to offer reinstatement to ten of the employees named, to make good their losses in pay, and to post for thirty days notices that the corporation would not discharge or discriminate against members, or those desiring to become members, of the labor union. As the corporation failed to comply, the Board petitioned the Circuit Court of Appeals to enforce the order. The court denied the petition, holding that the order lay beyond the range of federal power. . . .

The corporation is organized under the laws of Pennsylvania and has its principal office at Pittsburgh. It is engaged in the business of manufacturing iron and steel in plants situated in Pittsburgh and nearby Aliquippa, Pennsylvania. It manufactures and distributes a widely diversified line of steel and pig iron, being the fourth largest producer of steel in the United States. With its subsidiaries—nineteen in number—it is a completely integrated enterprise, owning and operating ore, coal and limestone properties, lake and river transportation facilities and terminal railroads located at its manufacturing plants. It owns or controls mines in Michigan and Minnesota. It operates four ore steamships on the Great Lakes, used in the transportation of ore to its factories. It owns coal mines in Pennsylvania. It operates towboats and steam barges used in carrying coal to its factories. It owns limestone properties in various places in Pennsylvania and West Virginia. It owns the Monongahela connecting railroad which connects the plants of the Pittsburgh works and forms an interconnection with the Pennsylvania, New York Central and Baltimore and Ohio Railroad systems. It owns the Aliquippa and Southern Railroad Company which connects the Aliquippa works with the Pittsburgh and Lake Erie, part of the New York Central system. Much of its product is shipped to its warehouses in Chicago, Detroit, Cincinnati and Memphis,—to the last two places by means of its own barges and transportation equipment. In Long Island City, New York, and in New Orleans it operates structural steel fabricating shops in connection with the warehousing of semi-finished materials sent from its works. Through one of its wholly-owned subsidiaries it owns, leases and operates stores, warehouses and yards for the distribution of equipment and supplies for drilling and operating oil and gas mills and for pipe lines, refineries and pumping stations. It has sales offices in twenty cities in the United States and a wholly-owned subsidiary which is devoted exclusively to distributing its product in Canada. Approximately 75 per cent. of its product is shipped out of Pennsylvania.

Summarizing these operations, the Labor Board concluded that the works in Pittsburgh and Aliquippa "might be likened to the heart of a self-contained, highly integrated body. They draw in the raw materials from Michigan, Minnesota, West Virginia, Pennsylvania in part through arteries and by means controlled by the respondent; they transform the materials and then pump them out to all parts of the nation through the vast mechanism which the respondent has elaborated." . . .

The Act is challenged in its entirety as an attempt to regulate all industry, thus invading the reserved powers of the States over their local concerns. It is asserted that the references in the Act to interstate and foreign commerce are colorable at best; that the Act is not a true regulation of such commerce or of matters which directly affect it but on the contrary has the fundamental object of placing under the compulsory supervision of the Federal government all industrial labor relations within the nation. . . .

We think it clear that the National Labor Relations Act may be construed so as to operate within the sphere of constitutional authority. The jurisdiction conferred upon the Board, and invoked in this instance, is found in § 10 (a), which provides:

"Sec. 10 (a). The Board is empowered, as hereinafter provided, to prevent any person from engaging in any unfair labor practice (listed in § 8) affecting commerce."

The critical words of this provision, prescribing the limits of the Board's authority in dealing with the labor practices, are "affecting commerce." The Act specifically defines the "commerce" to which it refers (§ 2 (6)):

"The term 'commerce' means trade, traffic, commerce, transportation, or communication among the several States, or between the District of Columbia or any Territory of the United States and any State or other Territory, or between any foreign country and any State, Territory, or the District of Columbia, or within the District of Columbia or any Territory, or between points in the same State but through any other State or any Territory or the District of Columbia or any foreign country."

There can be no question that the commerce thus contemplated by the Act (aside from that within a Territory or the District of Columbia) is interstate and foreign commerce in the constitutional sense. The Act also defines the term "affecting commerce" (§ 2 (7)):

"The term 'affecting commerce' means in commerce, or burdening or obstructing commerce or the free flow of commerce, or having led or tending to lead to a labor dispute burdening or obstructing commerce or the free flow of commerce."

This definition is one of exclusion as well as inclusion. The grant of authority to the Board does not purport to extend to the relationship between all industrial employees and employers. Its terms do not impose collective bargaining upon all industry regardless of effects upon interstate or foreign commerce. It purports to reach only what may be deemed to burden or obstruct that commerce and, thus qualified, it must be construed as contemplating the exercise of control within constitutional bounds. It is a familiar principle that acts which directly burden or obstruct interstate or foreign commerce, or its free flow, are within the reach of the congressional power. ...

Giving full weight to respondent's contention with respect to a break in the complete continuity of the "stream of commerce" by reason of respondent's manufacturing operations, the fact remains that the stoppage of those operations by industrial strife would have a most serious effect upon interstate commerce. In view of respondent's farflung activities, it is idle to say that the effect would be indirect or remote. It is obvious that it would be immediate and might be catastrophic. We are asked to shut our eyes to the plainest facts of our national life and to deal with the question of direct and indirect effects in an intellectual vacuum. Because there may be but indirect and remote effects upon interstate commerce in connection with a host of local enterprises throughout the country, it does not follow that other industrial activities do not have such a close and intimate relation to interstate commerce as to make the presence of industrial strife a matter of the most urgent national concern. When industries organize themselves on a national scale, making their relation to interstate commerce the dominant factor in their activities, how can it be maintained that their industrial labor relations constitute a forbidden field into which Congress may not enter when it is necessary to protect interstate commerce from the paralyzing consequences of industrial war? We have often said that interstate commerce itself is a practical conception. It is equally true that interferences with that commerce must be appraised by a judgment that does not ignore actual experience.

Experience has abundantly demonstrated that the recognition of the right of employees to self-organization and to have representatives of their own choosing for the purpose of collective bargaining is often an essential condition of industrial peace. Refusal to confer and negotiate has been one of the most prolific causes of strife. This is such an outstanding fact in the history of labor disturbances that it is a proper subject of judicial notice and requires no citation of instances.

Our conclusion is that the order of the Board was within its competency and that the Act is valid as here applied.

✣ *D O C U M E N T   7*

West Coast Hotel v. Parrish, 1937

... Mr. Chief Justice Hughes delivered the opinion of the Court.

This case presents the question of the constitutional validity of the minimum wage law of the State of Washington. ...

The principle which must control our decision is not in doubt. The constitutional provision invoked is the due process clause of the Fourteenth Amendment governing the States, as the due process clause invoked in the *Adkins* case governed Congress. In each case the violation alleged by those attacking minimum wage regulation for women is deprivation of freedom of contract. What is this freedom? The Constitution does not speak of freedom of contract. It speaks of liberty and prohibits the deprivation of liberty without due process of law. In prohibiting that deprivation the Constitution does not recognize an absolute and uncontrollable liberty. Liberty in each of its phases has its history and connotation. But the liberty safeguarded is liberty in a social organization which requires the protection of law against the evils which menace the health safety, morals and welfare of the people. Liberty under the Constitution is thus necessarily subject to the restraints of due process, and regulation which is reasonable in relation to its subject and is adopted in the interests of the community is due process.

This essential limitation of liberty in general governs freedom of contract in particular. More than twenty-five years ago we set forth the applicable principle in these words, after referring to the cases where the liberty guaranteed by the Fourteenth Amendment had been broadly described. ...

This power under the Constitution to restrict freedom of contract has had many illustrations. That it may be exercised in the public interest with respect to contracts between employer and employee is undeniable. ...

The point that has been strongly stressed that adult employees should be deemed competent to make their own contracts was decisively met nearly forty years ago in *Holden v. Hardy* ..., where we pointed out the inequality in the footing of the parties. ...

It is manifest that this established principle is peculiarly applicable in relation to the employment of women in whose protection the State has a special interest. That phase of the subject received elaborate consideration in *Muller v. Oregon* (1908) ..., where the constitutional authority of the State to limit the working hours of women was sustained. We emphasized the consideration that "woman's physical structure and the performance of maternal functions place her at a disadvantage in the struggle for subsistence" and that her physical well being "becomes an object of public interest and care in order to preserve the strength and vigor of the race." We emphasized the need of protecting women against oppression despite her possession of contractual rights. We said that "though limitations upon personal and contractual rights may be removed by legislation, there is that in her disposition and habits of life which will operate against a full assertion of those rights. She will still be where some legislation to protect her seems necessary to secure a real equality of right." Hence she was "properly placed in a class by herself, and legislation designed for her protection may be sustained even when like legislation is not necessary for men and could not be sustained." We concluded that the limitations which the statute there in question "placed upon her contractual powers, upon her right to agree with her employer as to the time she shall labor" were "not imposed solely for her benefit, but also largely for the benefit of all." ...

The minimum wage to be paid under the Washington statute is fixed after full consideration by representatives of employers, employees and the public. It may be assumed that the minimum wage is fixed in consideration of the services that are performed in the particular occupations under normal conditions. Provision is made for special licenses at less wages in the case of women who are incapable of full service. The statement of Mr. Justice Holmes in the *Adkins* case is pertinent: "This statute does not compel anybody to pay anything. It simply forbids employment at rates below those fixed as the minimum requirement of health and right living. It is safe to assume that women will not be employed at even the lowest wages allowed unless they earn them, or unless the employer's business can sustain the burden. In short the law in its character and operation is like hundreds of so-called police laws that have been upheld." ...

We think that the views thus expressed are sound and that the decision in the *Adkins* case was a departure from the true application of the principles governing the regulation by the State of the relation of employer and employed. ...

With full recognition of the earnestness and vigor which characterize the prevailing opinion in the *Adkins* case, we find it impossible to reconcile that ruling with these well-considered declarations. What can be closer to the public interest than the health of women and their protection from unscrupulous and overreaching employers? And if the protection of women is a legitimate end of the exercise of state power, how can it be said that the requirement of the payment of a minimum wage fairly fixed in order to meet the very necessities of existence is not an admissible means to that end? The legislature of the State was clearly entitled to consider the situation of women in employment, the fact that they are in the class receiving the least pay, that their bargaining power is relatively weak, and that they are the ready victims of those who would take advantage of their necessitous circumstances. The legislature was entitled to adopt measures to reduce the evils of the "sweating system," the exploiting of workers at wages so low as to be insufficient to meet the bare cost of living, thus making their very helplessness the occasion of a most injurious competition. The legislature had the right to consider that its minimum wage requirements would be an important aid in carrying out its policy of protection. The adoption of similar requirements by many States evidences a deep-seated conviction both as to the presence of the evil and as to the means adopted to check it. Legislative response to that conviction cannot be regarded as arbitrary or capricious, and that is all we have to decide. Even if the wisdom of the policy be regarded as debatable and its effects uncertain, still the legislature is entitled to its judgment. ...

The community may direct its law-making power to correct the abuse which springs from their selfish disregard of the public interest. The argument that the legislation in question constitutes an arbitrary discrimination, because it does not extend to men, is unavailing. This Court has frequently held that the legislative authority, acting within its proper field, is not bound to extend its regulation to all cases which it might possibly reach....

Our conclusion is that the case of *Adkins v. Children's Hospital,* ... should be, and it is, overruled. The judgment of the Supreme Court of the State of Washington is *Affirmed.*

✣ E S S A Y S

Jim Powell, a senior fellow at the Cato Institute, takes a dim view of the New Deal and portrays the conservative members of the Court as heroic advocates of economic liberty. To Powell, FDR's economic program represented an ill-advised divergence from longstanding constitutional principles. Cass R. Sunstein, a professor of law at the University of Chicago, offers a completely different interpretation. Sunstein sees the Constitution as a flexible document, which allows for adjustment and experimentation in order to meet changing social needs. The New Deal—although it altered some of the nation's constitutional arrangements—in his view, never violated constitutional principles.

The "Four Horsemen" Were Right: The New Deal Was Unconstitutional

JIM POWELL

The early 1930s saw powerful political pressures to suppress economic liberty, as the New Deal promoted price fixing and cartels that benefited producer interests at the expense of consumers. But for three years, the U.S. Supreme Court defended economic liberty and struck down one New Deal law after another.

New Deal historians long blamed these adverse Supreme Court decisions on the "Four Horsemen of Reaction," meaning Justices Willis Van Devanter, James C. McReynolds, Pierce Butler, and George Sutherland. The four were sometimes joined by others, particularly Chief Justice Charles Evans Hughes and Justice Owen Roberts....

The "Four Horsemen of Reaction" gained support on the Court as FDR increasingly asserted arbitrary power via executive orders, rather than going through the legislative process. The Congressional Research Service reported, "During his first 15 months in office, President Roosevelt signed 674 executive orders.... Many of these administrative regulations were needed to implement statutory policy. In its first year, the National Recovery Administration (NRA) approved hundreds of codes and released 2,998 administrative orders that approved or modified the codes. Almost 6,000 NRA press releases, some of them having a legislative effect, were issued during this period. So many orders were issued that departmental officials were often unaware of their own regulations. At one point the government discovered that it had brought an indictment and taken an appeal to the Supreme Court without realizing that the portion of the regulation on which the proceeding was based had been eliminated by an executive order."

FDR's continued assaults on economic liberty began to alarm Chief Justice Hughes, and he wrote the majority opinion in *Panama Refining Co. v. Ryan,* ... (1935). State and federal regulations restricted the quantities of petroleum that could be produced, and on July 11, 1933, FDR issued Executive Order 6199, which banned the interstate shipment of any excess production. Three days after this executive order, FDR issued Executive Order 6204, which authorized the secretary of the interior to carry out 6199. Anyone convicted of violating these orders could be hit with a $1,000 fine and/or a six-month prison sentence. These and subsequent executive orders were related to the National Industrial Recovery Act, which had become law on June 16.

The regulations harmed many people. Panama Refining Company, which had oil and gas leases in Texas, filed a lawsuit claiming that the regulations amounted to an unconstitutional delegation of power from Congress to the executive. Amazon Petroleum filed a similar lawsuit.

Justice Hughes agreed that the delegation of power violated the Constitution. He observed that the executive orders didn't offer any findings to justify the delegation of power. He didn't see any reason to assume that a president would always use this power to serve the public good. Accordingly, he concluded the power was unconstitutional.

The challenge to the National Industrial Recovery Act came from the most unlikely source, a chicken producer. Joseph Schechter operated Schechter Poultry Company, and Martin, Alex, and Alan Schechter operated A.L.A. Schechter Company, both of which were slaughterhouses selling chickens to kosher markets in New York City. Schechter was convicted of violating the Code of Fair Competition for the Live Poultry Industry of the Metropolitan Area in and about the City of New York, in the District Court of the United States for the Eastern District of New York. On April 13, 1934, FDR had issued his executive order authorizing this code.

There were two key issues. First, Schechter conducted its business entirely within New York State. The company purchased chickens in New York State and sold them in New York State. Schechter wasn't involved with interstate commerce.

In the *unanimous* decision, written by Chief Justice Hughes, he noted that the Constitution's commerce clause (Article 1, section 8, clause 3) provides that "Congress shall have the power ... to regulate commerce ... among the several States." This had long been interpreted as a limitation on the power of the states, but all the justices believed it was also a limitation on the power of Congress, barring it from interfering with business that didn't involve interstate commerce.

The second key issue involved the delegation of legislative power to a president. Hughes wrote, "The President in approving a code may impose his own conditions, adding to or taking from what is proposed, as 'in his discretion' he thinks necessary 'to effectuate the policy' declared by the Act. Of course, he has no less liberty when he prescribes a code on his own motion or on complaint, and he is free to prescribe one if a code has not been approved. The Act provides for the creation by the

President of administrative agencies to assist him, but the action or reports of such agencies, or of his other assistants—their recommendations and findings in relation to the making of codes—have no sanction beyond the will of the President, who may accept, modify or reject them as he pleases ... the discretion of the President in approving or prescribing codes, and thus enacting laws for the government of trade and industry throughout the country, is virtually unfettered."

This violated the constitutional principle of delegated, enumerated powers, the principle that the branches of the federal government had only such powers as were specifically delegated to them. As Hughes explained, "These powers of the national government are limited by the constitutional grants. Those who act under these grants are not at liberty to transcend the imposed limits because they believe that more or different power is necessary. Such assertions of extra-constitutional authority were anticipated and precluded by the explicit terms of the Tenth Amendment,—'The powers not delegated to the United States by the Constitution, nor prohibited by it to the States, are reserved to the States respectively, or to the people.' ... We think that the code-making authority thus conferred is an unconstitutional delegation of legislative power."

Hughes rejected claims that the NRA operated on the basis of voluntary cooperation: "It involves the coercive exercise of the law-making power. The codes of fair competition which the statute attempts to authorize are codes of laws. If valid, they place all persons within their reach under the obligation of positive law, binding equally those who assent and those who do not assent. Violations of the provisions of the codes are punishable as crimes. ...

"It is not the province of the Court to consider the economic advantages or disadvantages of such a centralized system," Hughes wrote. "It is sufficient to say that the Federal Constitution does not provide for it."

So, on May 27, 1935, the NIRA was struck down, and the NRA was out of business. After the Supreme Court *Schechter* decision had been published, Justice Brandeis met with two of FDR's advisers, lawyers Benjamin V. Cohen and Thomas G. Corcoran, and explained: "They change everything. The Court was unanimous. ... The President has been living in a fool's paradise."

At a press conference, FDR complained, "The whole tendency over these years has been to view the interstate commerce clause in the light of present-day civilization. The country was in the horse-and-buggy age when that clause was written and if you go back to the debates on the Federal Constitution you will find in 1787 that one of the impelling motives for putting in that clause was this: There wasn't much interstate commerce at all—probably 80 or 90 percent of the human beings in the thirteen original States were completely self-supporting within their own communities."

The *Schechter* decision was a blow to FDR, but as things turned out, it was a boon for the economy. As economists Richard K. Vedder and Lowell E. Gallaway explained, "The [1935–1936] job expansion coincided with a leveling-off in the sharp money-wage growth observed in 1933 and 1934. This was probably because one wage-increasing piece of legislation, the National Industrial Recovery Act, was found unconstitutional, and a second such piece of legislation, the National Labor Relations Act of 1935, had not yet had any real effect, as its constitutionality was still uncertain."

Before the Supreme Court ruled on the NIRA, Congress passed the Bituminous Coal Conservation Act, known as the Guffey Act—which was much like the NIRA, except that it applied to coal mining. It aimed to maintain high coal prices and high wages amidst the depression. Under the act, the National Bituminous Coal Commission was established to issue a Bituminous Coal Code for enforcing coal mining cartels. The act divided the coal mining industry into twenty-three districts, each ruled by three commissioners who had the power to restrict mining output and fix minimum coal prices, minimum wages, and maximum working hours. The commissioners, working with the biggest producers, set policies that presumably served the interests of these producers, even though other producers might be harmed. Every coal mining company would be subject to a 15 percent excise tax, and those that went along with the cartel would get a 90 percent rebate. Thus, any company refusing to go along would be hit with the full 15 percent tax and be at a potentially ruinous competitive disadvantage.

The board of directors of Carter Coal, a Kentucky company, voted to join the government cartel so the 15 percent punitive tax could be avoided, but principal stockholder James Carter filed suit in an effort to stay out of the cartel and honor existing contracts. The Roosevelt administration defended the Guffey Act by saying that coal mining had an impact on interstate commerce and accordingly federal regulation was justified by the Constitution's commerce clause.

Justice Sutherland wrote the 5–4 majority opinion, with Justices Butler, McReynolds, Roberts, and Van Devanter concurring. The "firmly established principle is that the powers which the general government may exercise are only those specifically enumerated in the Constitution and such implied powers as are necessary and proper to carry into effect the enumerated powers," the court said in its decision, announced on May 18, 1936. "The supremacy of the Constitution as law is declared without qualification. That supremacy is absolute; the supremacy of a statute enacted by Congress is not absolute, but conditioned upon its being made in pursuance of the Constitution."

Sutherland rejected the Roosevelt administration's claim that the Bituminous Coal Conservation Act was sanctioned by the Constitution's commerce clause. Mining is a local business, he observed, and the law restricted it before the products (coal) entered interstate commerce, which meant that the law couldn't be justified on the basis of the commerce clause. By contrast, in the *Schechter* case, the National Industrial Recovery Act was found to be unconstitutional because it regulated products after they left interstate commerce.

Sutherland considered the tax illegitimate: "It is very clear that the 'excise tax' is not imposed for revenue, but exacted as a penalty to compel compliance with the regulatory provisions of the act. The whole purpose of the exaction is to coerce what is called an agreement—which, of course, it is not, for it lacks the essential element of consent. One who does a thing in order to avoid a monetary penalty does not agree; he yields to compulsion precisely the same as though he did so to avoid a term in jail."

Sutherland was especially concerned about the power of a majority to harm a minority: "This is legislative delegation in its most obnoxious form, for it is not even delegation to an official or an official body, presumptively disinterested, but to private persons whose interests may be and often are adverse to the interests of others in the same business. The record shows that the conditions of competition differ among the various localities. In some, coal dealers compete among themselves. In other localities, they also compete with the mechanical production of electrical energy and of natural gas. Some coal producers favor the Code; others oppose it, and the record clearly indicates that this diversity of view arises from their conflicting and even antagonistic interests."

Although the text of the Bituminous Coal Conservation Act said that if one part of it were found unconstitutional, this shouldn't invalidate the entire law, Sutherland believed that the section fixing high prices and the section fixing high wages couldn't be separated. They worked together. Consequently, since there were so many problems with the price-fixing section (the wage-fixing section hadn't yet gone into effect), the entire law must be struck down.

In his dissenting opinion, with which Justices Brandeis, Cardozo, and Stone concurred, Chief Justice Hughes agreed that a key provision of the Bituminous Coal Conservation Act, restricting production, was invalid because "It attempts a broad delegation of legislative power to fix hours and wages without standards or limitation.... (2) The provision permits a group of producers and employees, according to their own views of expediency, to make rules as to hours and wages for other producers and employees who were not parties to the agreement. Such a provision, apart from the mere question of the delegation of legislative power, is not in accord with the requirement of due process of law which under the Fifth Amendment dominates the regulations which Congress may impose. (3) The provision goes beyond any proper measure of protection of interstate commerce, and attempts a broad regulation of industry within the State." Having acknowledged all this, Hughes didn't think the case should be thrown out: "If, in fixing prices, due process is violated by arbitrary, capricious or confiscatory action, judicial remedy is available."

The next big Supreme Court case involved the Agricultural Adjustment Act, which New Dealers considered as important for reviving agriculture as the National Industrial Recovery Act was thought to be for industry.... [T]he idea was to tax food processors and channel the proceeds to farmers who destroyed crops, thereby reducing supplies and maintaining farm prices. Raising farm prices was viewed as the way to raise farmers' income, much as high wage rates were supposed to raise the incomes of industrial workers.

When the government billed Hoosac Mills, a bankrupt food processor, for taxes under the Agricultural Adjustment Act, the receivers disregarded them. The district court ruled the taxes were valid, the court of appeals reversed this ruling, and the case went before the Supreme Court.

The Roosevelt administration claimed that the tax was just another tax, and taxpayers couldn't refuse to pay because they disagreed with the way it was spent. But Justice Roberts, in his majority opinion, observed that the sole purpose of this tax was to pay farmers who reduced their cultivated acreage and destroyed crops, which meant it wasn't a legitimate tax: "A tax, in the general understanding of the term, and as used in the Constitution, signifies an exaction for the support of the Government. The word has never been thought to connote the expropriation of money from one group for the benefit of another."

Roberts continued, "The question is not what power the Federal Government ought to have, but what powers, in fact, have been given by the people.... The federal union is a government of delegated powers. It has only such as are expressly conferred upon it and such as are reasonably to be implied from those granted. In this respect, we differ radically from nations where all legislative power, without restriction or limitation, is vested in a parliament or other legislative body subject to no restrictions except the discretion of its members."

Did the Constitution delegate to the federal government power over agricultural production? Since agricultural production was a local activity, it couldn't be covered by the commerce clause. Nor was such power implied in the clause about enacting taxes for the "common Defense and general Welfare of the United States." The phrase "general welfare" couldn't reasonably be invoked when a tax benefits particular people (like farmers) rather than the general population. Roberts insisted that if "general welfare" were applied to whatever the government wanted to spend money on, it would gain unlimited power, and the primary purpose of the Constitution was to protect liberty by limiting government power.

To underscore the absurdity of the Agricultural Adjustment Act, Roberts considered how it would apply to other industries: "Assume that too many shoes are being manufactured throughout the nation; that the market is saturated, the price depressed, the factories running half-time, the employes suffering. Upon the principle of the statute in question, Congress might authorize the Secretary of Commerce to enter into contracts with shoe manufactures providing that each shall reduce his output, and that the United States will pay him a fixed sum proportioned to such reduction, the money to make the payments to be raised by a tax on all retail shoe dealers or their customers.

"Suppose that there are too many garment workers in the large cities; that this results in dislocation of the economic balance. Upon the principle contended for, an excise might be laid on the manufacture of all garments manufactured, and the proceeds paid to those manufactures who agree to remove their plants to cities having not more than a hundred thousand population. Thus, through the asserted power of taxation, the federal government, against the will of individual states, might completely redistribute the industrial population....A possible result of sustaining the claimed federal power would be that every business group which thought itself underprivileged might demand that a tax be laid on its vendors or vendees, the proceeds to be appropriated to the redress of its deficiency of income."

Roberts concluded: "From the accepted doctrine that the United States is a government of delegated powers, it follows that those not expressly granted, or reasonably to be implied from such as are conferred, are reserved to the states, or to the people. To forestall any suggestion to the contrary, the Tenth Amendment was adopted. The some proposition, otherwise stated, is that powers not granted are prohibited. None to regulate agricultural production is given, and therefore legislation by Congress for that purpose is forbidden." ...

Justices Sutherland, McReynolds, Van Devanter, and Butler, sometimes joined by Hughes, Roberts, and others, did a splendid job articulating vital principles of economic liberty in the worst of times. Very few authors of any era have done better. These justices faced enormous political pressure from a popular president with commanding majorities in Congress, so they deserve credit for displaying the courage of their convictions. Subsequent experience has made clear that the purported New Deal "reform" measures that these justices struck down were, in fact, prolonging the

Great Depression. The economic liberty they defended, criticized as an obstacle to recovery, has been vindicated as the mainspring of human progress.

The New Deal Shows the Flexibility—and Genius— of the Constitution

CASS R. SUNSTEIN

In an astonishingly short period, the national government was dramatically expanded and reformed with the addition of a remarkable range of new programs and agencies. No fewer than five agencies were created in 1933 to give people jobs: the Civil Works Administration, the Civilian Conservation Corps, the Federal Emergency Relief Administration, the Public Works Administration, and the Tennessee Valley Authority. Of the several new laws designed to protect workers, the most important was the National Labor Relations Act, enacted in 1935, which gave workers the right to organize and provided a range of protections to unions and union organizers. The Fair Labor Standards Act, enacted in 1938, created minimum wage and maximum hour protections. A number of statutes, including most significantly the 1935 Social Security Act, were designed to provide assistance for the nonworking poor.

The blizzard of activity had a wide range of diverse themes. The "first New Deal" is sometimes distinguished from the "second New Deal." On the conventional view, the Roosevelt administration sought from 1933 to 1935 to promote cooperative action within industry to prevent falling prices and increase employment. It also sought to provide multiple forms of short-term economic relief, sometimes through jobs, sometimes through financial assistance. Many of the early agencies—most notably the Civilian Conservation Corps, the Federal Emergency Relief Administration, and the Works Progress Administration—were attempts to provide employment and economic assistance to those who most needed it.

The second New Deal, from 1935 to 1937, largely abandoned the effort to promote industry cooperation and emphasized antitrust policy instead. Between 1935 and 1937, the goal was to provide long-term protection for the vulnerable through larger reforms. Here the New Dealers were more ambitious, as reflected in Harry Hopkins's suggestion after the 1934 elections: "Boys, this is our hour. We've got to get everything we want—a works program, social security, wages and hours, everything—now or never. Get your minds to work on developing a complete ticket to provide security for all the folks of this country up and down and across the board." An early step was the Emergency Relief Appropriation Act, which gave the Works Progress Administration $4.8 billion, at the time the highest peace-time allocation in the nation's history. Subsequent measures included not only the Social Security Act and National Labor Relations Act but also the Wealth Tax Act (aimed mostly at the very rich) and the Banking Act, creating the Federal Reserve Board.

There was no simple or consistent theme to Roosevelt's domestic policies. In the words of Robert Jackson, one of Roosevelt's close advisers, "The New Deal was not a reform movement. It was an assembly of movements—sometimes inconsistent with each other." As the historian Ellis Hawley explains, "The New Deal began

The Second Bill of Rights: FDR's Unfinished Revolution and why we Need It More Than Ever. Reprinted with permission of BASIC BOOKS 2004, a member of Perseus Books Group.

with government sponsorship of cartels and business planning; it ended with the antitrust campaign and the attack on rigid prices; and along the way, it engaged in minor excursions into socialism, public utility regulation, and the establishment of 'government yardsticks.'" After 1937 there were further shifts, with an interest in new regulatory strategies and especially in the use of fiscal policy to stabilize the economy. Roosevelt was an experimenter, a pragmatist interested in results and solutions rather than theories and themes. "Take a method and try it. If it fails admit it frankly and try another. But above all, try something."

This willingness to experiment should not obscure the broader effects of Roosevelt's presidency. He challenged the framework of government in three different ways, first and most importantly with a new conception of rights. The New Dealers viewed the preexisting understanding of rights as including both too much and too little—excessive protection of established property interests and insufficient protection of the interests of the poor, the elderly, and the unemployed. In his speech accepting the Democratic presidential nomination in 1936, for instance, he argued that although the constitutional framers were concerned only with political rights, new circumstances required the recognition of economic rights as well because "freedom is no half-and-half affair." Hence the New Deal reformers called for substantial changes that would recognize new interests as entitlements and redistribute resources. With respect to the enlarged conception of freedom, Roosevelt's means shifted, but his ends did not.

The second element of Roosevelt's challenge focused on the separation of powers. According to the New Dealers, a system of sharply separated functions prevented the government from reacting flexibly and rapidly to stabilize the economy and protect the disadvantaged from fluctuations in the market. In addition, the distribution of powers among the three branches of government created political struggles that disabled officials in the executive branch from responding to serious problems on its own. A more unified set of powers was necessary to allow dramatic and frequent governmental action. Moreover, the complicated character of modern regulation vastly increased the need for technical expertise and specialization in making governmental decisions. Hence the New Dealers argued (successfully in both cases) for enhanced presidential authority and new regulatory agencies able to provide both work and security. The New Deal conception of administration regarded regulatory agencies as politically insulated, self-starting, and technically sophisticated. Roosevelt himself proclaimed that "the day of enlightened administration has come."

The third element in the New Deal challenge resulted in a shift in the relationship between the federal government and the states, greatly expanding the power of the former. Competition among the states sometimes produced paralysis on problems that called for a uniform national remedy. States were often arenas for factional strife and parochialism. The dominance of well-organized private groups in the states made it difficult to accept the traditional belief that state autonomy really served local self-determination. To the New Dealers, the states were weak and ineffectual, unable to protect rights or deal with serious social problems; they seemed too large to provide a forum for genuine self-determination. The time-honored idea that the states would check the federal government appeared perverse in light of the need for national action. Most of all, the newly recognized rights catalogued by the second bill could not be guaranteed at the state level. In these circumstances, the call for a dramatic increase in the exercise of federal regulatory power was quite natural.

Many previous efforts at reform relied on state and local institutions, in part because of the tenacity of the Jeffersonian belief in an engaged citizenry operating through something like face-to-face democracy. By contrast, the New Dealers made the presidency, rather than states and localities, the focal point for self-government. In so doing, the New Deal reformers in a single stroke linked Alexander Hamilton's belief in an energetic national government with Thomas Jefferson's endorsement of citizen self-determination. Roosevelt thus democratized Hamiltonian notions of energetic government through a new conception of the presidency and administration.

But all this is far too abstract. What did the new agencies actually do? In a message to Congress in 1934, Roosevelt explained the goals of his programs:

> These three great objectives—the security of the home, the security of a livelihood, and the security of social insurance—are, it seems to me, a minimum of the promise that we can offer to the American people. They constitute a right which belongs to every individual and every family willing to work. They are the essential fulfillment of measures already taken toward relief, recovery, and reconstruction.

Under Roosevelt, the national government largely attempted to promote work and security. His method was deliberately and self-consciously experimental. As individual programs succeeded or failed throughout the 1930s, agencies were created, altered, and dismantled. ...

Roosevelt was singularly unenthusiastic about welfare as such, which he disparaged as "the dole." Believing that government handouts were demoralizing and contrary to national ideals, he sought to find ways to provide relief to the masses of the unemployed that did not compromise the recipients' pride and self-respect. "The Federal Government," he said, "has no intention or desire to force either upon the country or the unemployed themselves a system of relief which is repugnant to American ideals of individual self-reliance." In his 1935 State of the Union address, he argued that "continued dependence upon relief induces a spiritual disintegration fundamentally destructive to the national fiber. To dole out relief in this way is to administer a narcotic, a subtle destroyer of the human spirit. ... Work must be found for able-bodied but destitute workers."

Employment relief, although often more costly than cash payments, was preferred by the administration and recipients alike. Thus the New Dealers "expected government jobs programmes and social insurance to banish forever the degrading spectre of public assistance based on a means test." They wanted to ensure against mass unemployment with work programs and to protect, through specific programs, "against the ordinary insecurities of age, disability, ill-health, and joblessness." ...

The 1930s saw an intense struggle between the Supreme Court and the Roosevelt administration. Before Roosevelt assumed office, the Court had erected a series of barriers to the kinds of initiatives Roosevelt hoped to undertake. First, the Court ruled that the power of Congress under the commerce clause of the Constitution was sharply limited, in a way that would make it difficult for the national government to do much of what Roosevelt sought to do: forbid child labor, impose maximum hour and minimum wage laws, and take steps to govern labor-management relations. Second, the Court had suggested that Congress could not "delegate" its power to the president and federal agencies, thus indicating that much of New Deal legislation would be in grave constitutional difficulty if it authorized the president and regulatory institutions to exercise discretion to solve the problems at hand. Third, the Court held (e.g., in the *Adkins* decisions ...) that the Constitution protected "liberty of contract" and thus would not allow government, whether state or federal, to regulate the relationship between employers and employees.

Taken as a whole, these rulings put the New Deal on shaky constitutional ground, as the Court repeatedly ruled in the early years of Roosevelt's administration. When the New Deal suffered a set of large defeats in the Court, Roosevelt concocted his infamous "court-packing" plan, which would allow him to add an additional member to the Court for each justice who had reached the age of seventy, thus gaining a sympathetic majority.

It was only in 1937, in *West Coast Hotel*, that the Court capitulated to Roosevelt amid the threat of a genuine constitutional crisis. We have seen that *West Coast Hotel* rejected the Court's previous protection of freedom of contract. Since that decision, the Court has *never* struck down federal action on the ground that it interferes with that freedom. Two other developments were crucial. The first involved the increased power of the president. After signaling that it might discipline "delegations" of congressional authority from Congress to the president, the Court promptly retreated. It concluded that as long as Congress set out an "intelligible principle," it could give the president and his agencies a great deal of discretion to set regulations as they saw fit. In modern government, both the president and federal agencies are often permitted to choose policy under vague laws, saying, for example, that regulation of telecommunications should be in "the public interest" and that controls on occupational hazards should be imposed "to the extent feasible." Since the New Deal, the Supreme Court has permitted Congress to grant quite open-ended power to the executive branch.

The final development expanded the powers of Congress itself. In short order, the Court ruled that the national government had broad authority to regulate the economy under the commerce clause. Accepting Roosevelt's own arguments, the Court emphasized that because of interdependencies in the national economy, problems in one state are highly likely to affect interstate commerce. For example, a strike in one state would likely affect others, and hence the national government could reasonably decide that national protection of labor-management relations was necessary to protect interstate commerce. Going even further, the Court ruled that compaines whose economic activities are apparently limited to one state might be taken to have interstate effects, if only because they tend to purchase products from elsewhere. As a result, the Court refused to strike down *any* exercise of congressional power as beyond the commerce clause for nearly sixty years. Not until 1995 did the Court invalidate congressional action under the commerce clause, when it invalidated a congressional effort to ban the possession of firearms near schools.

How should we assess these changes in constitutional understanding? Did Roosevelt actually violate or amend the Constitution? When the Court capitulated to Roosevelt, did it allow a kind of unwritten constitutional amendment, akin to the written ones that followed the *Civil War*? This is the view of some of Roosevelt's greatest admirers—and critics. Yale law professor Bruce Ackerman, for example, argues that the United States has had three "constitutional moments": the founding, the Civil War, and the New Deal. In Ackerman's view, each of these moments stimulated a large-scale rethinking of the nation's commitments in a way that fundamentally altered the basic design and goal of the Constitution. The New Deal was unique among the three periods in that it did not involve any textual change in the Constitution. But Ackerman believes that by 1937, the meaning of the Constitution had changed greatly from its meaning in 1932. He argues that the change came from a massive popular movement that did the same work as a literal constitutional change. Because the New Deal was ratified by the public, no less than the Civil War had been, Ackerman believes that it was entirely legitimate.

Other people agree with Ackerman's assessment of what happened but do not share his approval. In their view, the New Deal was an illegitimate departure from the constitutional framework, giving the national government unprecedented powers, allowing Congress to delegate those powers, and intruding on constitutionally protected liberty. This view is widely held today and helps explain some of the work of the Supreme Court under Chief Justice William Rehnquist, which has, in some respects, attempted to reinvigorate the pre–New Deal constitution. In its most extreme form, this view suggests that there is a "Constitution in Exile"—a real document that the Court abandoned when it capitulated to Roosevelt. Douglas H. Ginsburg, an especially able, fair-minded, and distinguished appellate judge, writes that "respect for the text of the Constitution was the norm ... through the first third of the twentieth century," but that the "great Depression and the determination of the Roosevelt Administration placed the Supreme Court's commitment to the Constitution as written under severe strain in the 1930s, and it was then that the wheels began to come off." Judge Ginsburg challenges a number of decisions in which the Court allowed the Roosevelt administration to do what it wanted; he singles out the Court's decision to uphold the National Labor Relations Act as a legitimate exercise of congressional power.

Many critics believe it is both possible and important to restore the true Constitution. Less radically, numerous current American judges appear to believe that the courts should make incremental movements toward restoring the constitutional understandings that preceded Roosevelt. In their view, Roosevelt's Constitution lacks full constitutional legitimacy.

This view also exists outside of the judiciary. In fact the early twenty-first century has witnessed a remarkable shift in conservative legal thought. In the 1980s, conservative legal scholars reacted against the liberal decisions of the Warren Court by urging a principle of judicial restraint. They wanted courts to back off—to allow restrictions on abortion, aggressive practices by the police, and a degree of public assistance to religious organizations. These criticisms of the Warren Court were founded on an understandable desire to let the people rule themselves, with limited judicial oversight. But there is no question that among some contemporary Republicans, the New Deal has now become a principal target. For them, Roosevelt is the villain, not Earl Warren, and they find it appropriate to attack Roosevelt's initiatives through politics and law, in courts as well as legislatures. For some of these people, Roosevelt's proudest accomplishments (e.g., the Social Security Act) are nothing to celebrate. One of their major goals is to move toward the constitutional system that preceded Roosevelt—a system with a weaker federal government, fewer regulatory agencies, and a narrower conception of rights. The administrations of

Ronald Reagan, George H. W. Bush, and George W. Bush have included many who are skeptical of the New Deal. ...

In my view, Roosevelt's admirers and antagonists are quite wrong to suggest that his initiatives were unconstitutional. Judge Ginsburg misreads both constitutional history and the Constitution as written. To be sure, the Supreme Court issued a series of decisions protecting freedom of contract. But those decisions were illegitimate, lacking any basis in the nation's founding document. The Constitution was not in the least offended by New Deal initiatives that attempted to protect workers from some of the pressures of the marketplace. It was the Court, not Roosevelt, that was acting in violation of the Constitution. Nor does the Constitution forbid Congress from giving a degree of discretion to the president. It is true that under the Constitution, Congress makes the laws. But nothing in the Constitution forbids Congress to "make" a law that allows the president a wide range of choices.

Contrary to a widely held view, regulatory agencies are hardly foreign to the American constitutional framework. Major departments, including those at the cabinet level, existed from the beginning. It is true that the federal government has limited powers and that Congress cannot regulate whatever topics it chooses. But Congress does have the power to regulate "commerce among the several states," to tax, and to spend. Most of the New Deal legislation fit comfortably within these authorities. In our highly interdependent economy, acts in Texas might well affect people in California and New York. It follows that the power to regulate "commerce" among the states naturally allows more federal action than it did when states were more like separate islands. Labor–management strife in one state is very likely to affect interstate commerce. Contrary to Judge Ginsburg's suggestion, the Court was entirely right to uphold the National Labor Relations Act; this was not even a difficult question.

There is an additional consideration. In a democratic system, courts are not our rulers. Judges owe the elected branches of government a large measure of deference and respect. In the face of reasonable doubt, courts should accept any plausible claim that an action is within the constitutional authority of Congress and the president. At least this is the best general rule. Before the New Deal, the Court repeatedly violated that rule, rejecting wholly reasonable judgments by the states and the national government. The most serious acts of unconstitutionality came not from the Roosevelt administration, but from the decisions of the early-twentieth-century Supreme Court, striking down minimum wage and maximum hour legislation and narrowly limiting the power of Congress under the commerce clause.

I do not deny that Roosevelt and the New Deal had a massive effect on the nation's understanding of what the president and Congress could legitimately do. Ackerman's claim that the New Deal was a "constitutional moment" is plausible for one reason: In 1937 American government was dramatically different from what it was in 1932. A large part of my goal here has been to capture the nature of these differences. But the transformation involved no violation of constitutional principles. The American Constitution is a flexible instrument, one that allows for a great deal of change over time. It does not forbid experiment and adjustment. To some extent, it allows for new understandings of rights. It permits changes in institutional arrangements. This is part of its genius.

✤ *FURTHER READING*

Ackerman, Bruce. *We the People: Transformations* (1998).

Baker, Leonard. *Back to Back: The Duel Between FDR and the Supreme Court* (1967).

Chambers, John W. "The Big Switch: Justice Roberts and the Minimum Wage Cases," *Labor History*, 10 (1969): 44–73.

Cortner, Richard. *The Jones & Laughlin Case* (1970).

Cushman, Barry. *Rethinking the New Deal Court: The Structure of a Constitutional Revolution* (1998).

Friedel, Frank. "The Sick Chicken Case," in J. Garraty, *Quarrels That Have Shaped the Constitution* (1975): 191–209.

Hawley, Ellis. *The New Deal and the Problem of Monopoly* (1966).

Irons, Peter. *The New Deal Lawyers* (1982).

Jackson, Robert H. *The Struggle for Judicial Power* (1949).

Kalman, Laura. *The Strange Career of Legal Liberalism* (1996).

Keller, Morton. *Regulating a New Economy* (1990).

Leonard, Charles A. *A Search for a Judicial Philosophy: Mr. Justice Roberts and the Constitutional Revolution of 1937* (1971).

Leuchtenburg, William E. *The Supreme Court Reborn: The Constitutional Revolution in the Age of Roosevelt* (1995).

Mettler, Suzanne. *Dividing Citizens: Gender and Federalism in New Deal Public Policy* (1998).

Milkis, Sidney M. and Jerome M. Mileur. *The New Deal and the Triumph of Liberalism* (2002).

Murphy, Paul L. *The Constitution in Crisis Times, 1918–1969* (1972).

Nelson, Michael. "The President and the Court: Reinterpreting the Court-Packing Episode of 1937," *Political Science Quarterly*, 103 (Summer 1988): 267–293.

Parrish, Michael E. *The Hughes Court: Justices, Rulings, and Legacy* (2002).

Ross, William G. *The Chief Justiceship of Charles Evans Hughes, 1930–1941* (2007).

Schlesinger, Jr., Arthur M. *The Crisis of the Old Order, 1919–1933* (1957).

——. *The Politics of Upheaval* (1960).

Swindler, William F. *Court and Constitution in the Twentieth Century: The New Legality, 1932–1968* (1970).

Tomlins, Christopher. *The State and the Unions* (1985).

White, G. Edward. *The Constitution and the New Deal* (2000).

Race and Civil Rights in the Cold War Era

For decades, racial segregation held the American South in a stranglehold. Ever since 1896, when the Supreme Court gave judicial sanction to the practice by sustaining "equal but separate" railway cars in Plessy v. Ferguson, segregation had been a fact of life in the southern states, where most of the nation's African American population lived. Despite the rhetoric of equality associated with segregation laws, rarely did states or municipalities provide truly equal facilities and opportunities for blacks and whites. Nowhere did this prove more apparent than in public education, where African–American children routinely attended school in decaying buildings and learned from dated textbooks. Although the National Association for the Advancement of Colored People (NAACP), founded in 1909, fought hard against racial injustice during the first half of the twentieth century, not until mid-century did the organization make significant headway against the constitutional underpinnings of segregation. Little by little, in cases pertaining to segregation in higher education, the Supreme Court came closer to making the "equal" part of "equal but separate" a reality.

Eventually, the NAACP's Legal Defense Fund attacked public school segregation head-on, by arguing that separate was inherently unequal. In 1954, in Brown v. Board of Education, the Court agreed. Led by a new chief justice, Earl Warren of California, the Court issued a unanimous opinion that firmly declared the end of segregation in American public schools. As recent scholarship has shown, the Cold War context proved decisive in the struggle against segregation in America. Locked in an ideological battle with the Soviet Union and wanting to sway world opinion to the justness and superiority of the American way of life, the U.S. government viewed the end of legal segregation as key to combating the criticism coming from Soviet propaganda. However helpful the Court's opinion in Brown was to the nation's image abroad, it provoked considerable controversy at home. White southerners viewed the justices as meddling with the region's well-established racial customs. Delay and resistance on the part of the white South made Brown difficult to implement, while persistent economic inequality between the races and de facto residential segregation complicated matters even further. By the mid-1970s, after an all but failed experiment with busing to achieve racial balance in public schools, desegregation of public education faded from the national agenda. In recent years, in fact, scholars have begun to highlight the re-segregation of American public schools.

Brown *and its aftermath remain topics of heated debate. Initially, the deci-sion provoked popular opposition because of the justices' reliance on social science evidence and the ruling's interference with state prerogatives. Critics thus viewed the decision as an example of judicial activism. Recent debates, particularly among scholars and judges, have centered more on the meaning of the decision, as well as on the question of whether the Court's subsequent desegregation rulings adhered to the spirit of the original opinion. In essence, conservatives have argued that* Brown *enshrined the principle of a color-blind Constitution, while liberals have claimed that the ruling justified the formulation of race-conscious remedies such as busing and affirmative action.* Brown *itself, moreover, has come under withering criticism from some liberals, who argue that the decision rested on racist assumptions and that the implementation decision,* Brown, II, *let the white South off the hook too easily. Were* Brown I *and* Brown II *correctly decided? Were the decisions helpful or harmful to race relations? What has been the legacy of* Brown? *What role can and should the Supreme Court play in correcting the nation's social ills?*

✣ D O C U M E N T S

Beginning in the 1930s, the NAACP waged a campaign to equalize higher education for blacks and whites. Led by African American lawyers Charles Hamilton Houston and Thurgood Marshall, the NAACP's Legal Defense Fund won victories such as *Missouri ex rel. Gaines v. Canada* (1938), where the Court held that a state would have to provide equal educational opportunities for blacks, rather than paying for them to attend out-of-state institutions. In *Sweatt v. Painter*, Document 1, the Court went a step further, by holding that intangible factors such as reputation would need to be taken into account in evaluating whether higher educational opportunities were truly equal. Chief Justice Fred Vinson wrote the opinion for a unanimous Court in that case. By 1953, with international pressure exposing American hypocrisy on race relations and domestic pressure in the form of the NAACP's legal campaign, the time was ripe for a reconsideration of the principle of separate but equal. The U.S. Department of Justice filed an amicus curiae ("friend of the Court") brief, in which it made clear its desire for legal segregation to come to an end. Portions of the brief are reprinted as Document 2.

After the initial arguments in *Brown v. Board of Education*, Chief Justice Vinson died unexpectedly in the fall of 1953, and President Dwight D. Eisenhower appointed Earl Warren as his replacement. Warren's political skills served him well, as he per-suaded a few fence-sitting colleagues to join in a brief, unanimous opinion authored by the chief justice. The decision, excerpted here as Document 3, declared separate but equal public schools to be "inherently unequal" and in violation of the Fourteenth Amendment's Equal Protection Clause. In so concluding, the justices drew upon social scientific data that indicated that segregation by race damaged the self-esteem of black children. The following year, the Court issued a second decision regarding the implementation of desegregation. *Brown v. Board, II*, Document 4, arguably gave the South a bit more room to circumvent—or at least delay—desegregation. By 1956, at which point virtually no desegregation of public schools had actually taken place in the South, 101 white southern members of Congress affixed their names to the "Southern

Declaration of Constitutional Principles," Document 5, also known as the Southern Manifesto. In defiance of the decision, white southerners challenged the Court's power, while championing regional autonomy.

In 1964, a full decade after *Brown*, Congress enacted a far-reaching civil rights law that brought an end to racial discrimination in, most notably, public educational institutions, employment, and public accommodations. Excerpted as Document 6, the law owed its passage in large part to the support of President Lyndon B. Johnson. Realizing that the Civil Rights Act and Voting Rights Act that followed could not solve the income inequalities between the races, Johnson pledged his administration's support to further federal efforts to end poverty and injustice in his June 4, 1965, commencement speech at Howard University. Portions of the address, "To Fulfill These Rights," constitute Document 7.

✤ D O C U M E N T   1

Sweatt v. Painter, 1950

... Mr. Chief Justice Vinson delivered the opinion of the Court.

... In the instant case, petitioner filed an application for admission to the University of Texas Law School for the February, 1946 term. His application was rejected solely because he is a Negro. Petitioner thereupon brought this suit for mandamus against the appropriate school officials, respondents here, to compel his admission. At that time, there was no law school in Texas which admitted Negroes.

The State trial court recognized that the action of the State in denying petitioner the opportunity to gain a legal education while granting it to others deprived him of the equal protection of the laws guaranteed by the Fourteenth Amendment. The court did not grant the relief requested, however, but continued the case for six months to allow the State to supply substantially equal facilities. At the expiration of the six months, in December, 1946, the court denied the writ on the showing that the authorized university officials had adopted an order calling for the opening of a law school for Negroes the following February. While petitioner's appeal was pending, such a school was made available, but petitioner refused to register therein. The Texas Court of Civil Appeals set aside the trial court's judgment and ordered the cause "remanded generally to the trial court for further proceedings without prejudice to the rights of any party to this suit."

On remand, a hearing was held on the issue of the equality of the educational facilities at the newly established school as compared with the University of Texas Law School. Finding that the new school offered petitioner "privileges, advantages, and opportunities for the study of law substantially equivalent to those offered by the State to white students at the University of Texas," the trial court denied mandamus. The Court of Civil Appeals affirmed.... Petitioner's application for a writ of error was denied by the Texas Supreme Court. We granted certiorari, ... because of the manifest importance of the constitutional issues involved.

The University of Texas Law School, from which petitioner was excluded, was staffed by a faculty of sixteen full-time and three part-time professors, some of whom are nationally recognized authorities in their field. Its student body numbered 850.

The library contained over 65,000 volumes. Among the other facilities available to the students were a law review, moot court facilities, scholarship funds, and Order of the Coif affiliation. The school's alumni occupy the most distinguished positions in the private practice of the law and in the public life of the State. It may properly be considered one of the nation's ranking law schools. . . .

Since the trial of this case, respondents report the opening of a law school at the Texas State University for Negroes. It is apparently on the road to full accreditation. It has a faculty of five full-time professors; a student body of 23; a library of some 16,500 volumes serviced by a full-time staff; a practice court and legal aid association; and one alumnus who has become a member of the Texas Bar.

Whether the University of Texas Law School is compared with the original or the new law school for Negroes, we cannot find substantial equality in the educational opportunities offered white and Negro law students by the State. In terms of number of the faculty, variety of courses and opportunity for specialization, size of the student body, scope of the library, availability of law review and similar activities, the University of Texas Law School is superior. What is more important, the University of Texas Law School possesses to a far greater degree those qualities which are incapable of objective measurement but which make for greatness in a law school. Such qualities, to name but a few, include reputation of the faculty, experience of the administration, position and influence of the alumni, standing in the community, traditions and prestige. It is difficult to believe that one who had a free choice between these law schools would consider the question close.

Moreover, although the law is a highly learned profession, we are well aware that it is an intensely practical one. The law school, the proving ground for legal learning and practice, cannot be effective in isolation from the individuals and institutions with which the law interacts. Few students and no one who has practiced law would choose to study in an academic vacuum, removed from the interplay of ideas and the exchange of views with which the law is concerned. The law school to which Texas is willing to admit petitioner excludes from its student body members of the racial groups which number 85% of the population of the State and include most of the lawyers, witnesses, jurors, judges and other officials with whom petitioner will inevitably be dealing when he becomes a member of the Texas Bar. With such a substantial and significant segment of society excluded, we cannot conclude that the education offered petitioner is substantially equal to that which he would receive if admitted to the University of Texas Law School. . . .

. . . Petitioner may claim his full constitutional right: legal education equivalent to that offered by the State to students of other races. Such education is not available to him in a separate law school as offered by the State. We cannot, therefore, agree with respondents that the doctrine of *Plessy v. Ferguson*, requires affirmance of the judgment below. Nor need we reach petitioner's contention that *Plessy v. Ferguson* should be reexamined in the light of contemporary knowledge respecting the purposes of the Fourteenth Amendment and the effects of racial segregation.

We hold that the Equal Protection Clause of the Fourteenth Amendment requires that petitioner be admitted to the University of Texas Law School. The judgment is reversed and the cause is remanded for proceedings not inconsistent with this opinion.

Reversed.

✦ *D O C U M E N T   2*

An Amicus Brief Filed by the U.S. Government Urges an End to Racial Segregation, 1953

Because of the national importance of the constitutional questions presented in these cases, the United States considers it appropriate to submit this brief as *amicus curiae*. We shall not undertake, however, to deal with every aspect of the issues involved. Comprehensive briefs have been submitted by the parties and other *amici curiae*; and, so far as possible, this brief will avoid repetition of arguments and materials contained in those briefs. We shall try to confine ourselves to those aspects of the cases which are of particular concern to the Government or within its special competence to discuss.

I

The interest of the United States

In recent years the Federal Government has increasingly recognized its special responsibility for assuring vindication of the fundamental civil rights guaranteed by the Constitution. The President has stated: "We shall not ... finally achieve the ideals for which this Nation was founded so long as any American suffers discrimination as a result of his race, or religion, or color, or the land of origin of his forefathers. ... The Federal Government has a clear duty to see that constitutional guaranties of individual liberties and of equal protection under the laws are not denied or abridged anywhere in our Union."

Recognition of the responsibility of the Federal Government with regard to civil rights is not a matter of partisan controversy, even though differences of opinion may exist as to the need for particular legislative or executive action. Few Americans believe that government should pursue a *laissez-faire* policy in the field of civil rights, or that it adequately discharges its duty to the people so long as it does not itself intrude on their civil liberties. Instead, there is general acceptance of an affirmative government obligation to insure respect for fundamental human rights.

The constitutional right invoked in these cases is the basic right, secured to all Americans, to equal treatment before the law. The cases at bar do not involve isolated acts of racial discrimination by private individuals or groups. On the contrary, it is contended in these cases that public school systems established in the states of Kansas, South Carolina, Virginia, and Delaware, and in the District of Columbia, unconstitutionally discriminate against Negroes solely because of their color.

This contention raises questions of the first importance in our society. For racial discriminations imposed by law, or having the sanction or support of government, inevitably tend to undermine the foundations of a society dedicated to freedom, justice, and equality. The proposition that all men are created equal is not mere rhetoric. It implies a rule of law—an indispensable condition to a civilized society—under which all men stand equal and alike in the rights and opportunities secured to them by their government. Under the Constitution every agency of government, national and local, legislative, executive, and judicial, must treat each of our people as an

American, and not as a member of a particular group classified on the basis of race or some other constitutional irrelevancy. The color of a man's skin—like his religious beliefs, or his political attachments, or the country from which he or his ancestors came to the United States—does not diminish or alter his legal status or constitutional rights. "Our Constitution is color-blind, and neither knows nor tolerates classes among citizens."

The problem of racial discrimination is particularly acute in the District of Columbia, the nation's capital. This city is the window through which the world looks into our house. The embassies, legations, and representatives of all nations are here, at the seat of the Federal Government. Foreign officials and visitors naturally judge this country and our people by their experiences and observations in the nation's capital; and the treatment of colored persons here is taken as the measure of our attitude toward minorities generally. The President has stated that "The District of Columbia should be a true symbol of American freedom and democracy for our own people, and for the people of the world." Instead, as the President's Committee on Civil Rights found, the District of Columbia "is a graphic illustration of a failure of democracy." The Committee summarized its findings as follows:

> For Negro Americans, Washington is not just the nation's capital. It is the point at which all public transportation into the South becomes "Jim Crow." If he stops in Washington, a Negro may dine like other men in the Union Station, but as soon as he steps out into the capital, he leaves such democratic practices behind. With very few exceptions, he is refused service at downtown restaurants, he may not attend a downtown movie or play, and he has to go into the poorer section of the city to find a night's lodging. The Negro who decides to settle in the District must often find a home in an overcrowded, substandard area. He must often take a job below the level of his ability. He must send his children to the inferior public schools set aside for Negroes and entrust his family's health to medical agencies which give inferior service. In addition, he must endure the countless daily humiliations that the system of segregation imposes upon the one-third of Washington that is Negro.
>
> . . . The shamefulness and absurdity of Washington's treatment of Negro Americans is highlighted by the presence of many dark-skinned foreign visitors. Capital custom not only humiliates colored citizens, but is a source of considerable embarrassment to these visitors. . . . Foreign officials are often mistaken for American Negroes and refused food, lodging and entertainment. However, once it is established that they are not Americans, they are accommodated.

It is in the context of the present world struggle between freedom and tyranny that the problem of racial discrimination must be viewed. The United States is trying to prove to the people of the world, of every nationality, race, and color, that a free democracy is the most civilized and most secure form of government yet devised by man. We must set an example for others by showing firm determination to remove existing flaws in our democracy.

The existence of discrimination against minority groups in the United States has an adverse effect upon our relations with other countries. Racial discrimination furnishes grist for the Communist propaganda mills, and it raises doubts even among friendly nations as to the intensity of our devotion to the democratic faith. In response to the request of the Attorney General for an authoritative statement of the effects of racial discrimination in the United States upon the conduct of foreign relations, the Secretary of State has written as follows:

> . . . I wrote the Chairman of the Fair Employment Practices Committee on May 8, 1946, that the existence of discrimination against minority groups was having an adverse effect upon our relations with other countries. At that time I pointed out that discrimination against such groups in the United States created suspicion and resentment in other countries, and that we would have better international relations were these reasons for suspicion and resentment to be removed.
>
> During the past six years, the damage to our foreign relations attributable to this source has become progressively greater. The United States is under constant attack in the foreign press, over the foreign radio, and in such international bodies as the United Nations because of various practices of discrimination against minority groups in this country. As might be expected, Soviet spokesmen regularly exploit this situation in propaganda against the United States, both within the United Nations and through radio broadcasts and the press, which reaches all corners of the world. Some of these attacks against us are based on falsehood or distortion; but the undeniable existence of racial discrimination gives unfriendly governments the most effective kind of ammunition for their propaganda warfare. The hostile reaction among normally friendly peoples, many of whom are particularly sensitive in regard to the status of non-European races, is growing in alarming proportions. In such countries the view is expressed more and more vocally that the United States is hypocritical in claiming to be the champion of democracy while permitting practices of racial discrimination here in this country.
>
> The segregation of school children on a racial basis is one of the practices in the United States that has been singled out for hostile foreign comment in the United Nations and elsewhere. Other peoples cannot understand how such a practice can exist in a country which professes to be a staunch supporter of freedom, justice, and democracy. The sincerity of the United States in this respect will be judged by its deeds as well as by its words.
>
> Although progress is being made, the continuance of racial discrimination in the United States remains a source of constant embarrassment to this Government in the day-to-day conduct of its foreign relations; and it jeopardizes the effective maintenance of our moral leadership of the free and democratic nations of the world.

✣ *D O C U M E N T   3*

Brown v. Board of Education, I, 1954

Mr. Chief Justice Warren delivered the opinion of the Court.

These cases come to us from the States of Kansas, South Carolina, Virginia, and Delaware. They are premised on different facts and different local conditions, but a common legal question justifies their consideration together in this consolidated opinion.

In each of the cases, minors of the Negro race, through their legal representatives, seek the aid of the courts in obtaining admission to the public schools of their community on a nonsegregated basis. In each instance, they had been denied admission to schools attended by white children under laws requiring or permitting segregation according to race. This segregation was alleged to deprive the plaintiffs of the equal protection of the laws under the Fourteenth Amendment. In each of the cases other than the Delaware case, a three-judge federal district court denied relief to the plaintiffs on the so-called "separate but equal" doctrine announced by this Court in *Plessy v. Ferguson.* ... Under that doctrine, equality of treatment is accorded when the races are provided substantially equal facilities, even though these facilities be separate. In the Delaware case, the Supreme Court of Delaware adhered to that doctrine, but ordered that the plaintiffs be admitted to the white schools because of their superiority to the Negro schools.

The plaintiffs contend that segregated public schools are not "equal" and cannot be made "equal," and that hence they are deprived of the equal protection of the laws. Because of the obvious importance of the question presented, the Court took jurisdiction. Argument was heard in the 1952 Term, and reargument was heard this Term on certain question propounded by the Court.

Reargument was largely devoted to the circumstances surrounding the adoption of the Fourteenth Amendment in 1868. It covered exhaustively consideration of the Amendment in Congress, ratification by the states, then existing practices in racial segregation, and the views of proponents and opponents of the Amendment. This discussion and our own investigation convince us that, although these sources cast some light, it is not enough to resolve the problem with which we are faced. At best, they are inconclusive. The most avid proponents of the post-War Amendments undoubtedly intended them to remove all legal distinctions among "all persons born or naturalized in the United States." Their opponents, just as certainly, were antagonistic to both the letter and the spirit of the Amendments and wished them to have the most limited effect. What others in Congress and the state legislatures had in mind cannot be determined with any degree of certainty.

An additional reason for the inconclusive nature of the Amendment's history, with respect to segregated schools, is the status of public education at that time. In the South, the movement toward free common schools, supported by general taxation, had not yet taken hold. Education of white children was largely in the hands of private groups. Education of Negroes was almost nonexistent, and practically all of the race were illiterate. In fact, any education of Negroes was forbidden by law in some states. Today, in contrast, many Negroes have achieved outstanding success in the arts and sciences as well as in the business and professional world. It is true that public school education at the time of the Amendment had advanced further in the North, but the effect of the Amendment on Northern States was generally ignored in the congressional debates. Even in the North, the conditions of public education did not approximate those existing today. The curriculum was usually rudimentary; ungraded schools were common in rural areas; the school term was but three months a year in many states; and compulsory school attendance was virtually unknown. As a consequence, it is not surprising that there should be so little in the history of the Fourteenth Amendment relating to its intended effect on public education.

In the first cases in this Court construing the Fourteenth Amendment, decided shortly after its adoption, the Court interpreted it as proscribing all state-imposed discriminations against the Negro race. The doctrine of "separate but equal" did not make its appearance in this Court until 1896 in the case of *Plessy v. Ferguson* ... , involving not education but transportation. American courts have since labored with the doctrine for over half a century. ...

In the instant cases ... , there are findings below that the Negro and white schools involved have been equalized, or are being equalized, with respect to buildings, curricula, qualifications and salaries of teachers, and other "tangible" factors. Our decision, therefore, cannot turn on merely a comparison of these tangible factors in the Negro and white schools involved in each of the cases. We must look instead to the effect of segregation itself on public education.

In approaching this problem, we cannot turn the clock back to 1868 when the Amendment was adopted, or even to 1896 when *Plessy v. Ferguson* was written. We must consider public education in the light of its full development and its present place in American life throughout the Nation. Only in this way can it be determined if segregation in public schools deprives these plaintiffs of the equal protection of the laws.

Today, education is perhaps the most important function of state and local governments. Compulsory school attendance laws and the great expenditures for education both demonstrate our recognition of the importance of education to our democratic society. It is required in the performance of our most basic public responsibilities, even service in the armed forces. It is the very foundation of good citizenship. Today it is a principal instrument in awakening the child to cultural values, in preparing him for later professional training, and in helping him to adjust normally to his environment. In these days, it is doubtful that any child may reasonably be expected to succeed in life if he is denied the opportunity of an education. Such an opportunity, where the state has undertaken to provide it, is a right which must be made available to all on equal terms.

We come then to the question presented: Does segregation of children in public schools solely on the basis of race, even though the physical facilities and other "tangible" factors may be equal, deprive the children of the minority group of equal educational opportunities? We believe that it does.

In *Sweatt v. Painter* ... , in finding that a segregated law school for Negroes could not provide them equal educational opportunities, this Court relied in large part on "those qualities which are incapable of objective measurement but which make for greatness in a law school." In *McLaurin v. Oklahoma State Regents* ... , the Court, in requiring that a Negro admitted to a white graduate school be treated like all other students, again resorted to intangible considerations: "... his ability to study, to engage in discussions and exchange views with other students, and, in general, to learn his profession." Such considerations apply with added force to children in grade and high schools. To separate them from others of similar age and qualifications solely because of their race generates a feeling of inferiority as to their status in the community that may affect their hearts and minds in a way unlikely ever to be undone. The effect of this separation on their educational opportunities was well stated by a finding in the Kansas case by a court which nevertheless felt compelled to rule against the Negro plaintiffs:

Segregation of white and colored children in public schools has a detrimental effect upon the colored children. The impact is greater when it has the sanction of the law; for the policy of separating the races is usually interpreted as denoting the inferiority of the negro group. A sense of inferiority affects the motivation of a child to learn. Segregation with the sanction of law, therefore, has a tendency to [retard] the educational and mental development of negro children and to deprive them of some of the benefits they would receive in a racial[ly] integrated school system.

Whatever may have been the extent of psychological knowledge at the time of *Plessy v. Ferguson*, this finding is amply supported by modern authority. Any language in *Plessy v. Ferguson* contrary to this finding is rejected.

We conclude that in the field of public education the doctrine of "separate but equal" has no place. Separate educational facilities are inherently unequal. Therefore, we hold that the plaintiffs and others similarly situated for whom the actions have been brought are, by reason of the segregation complained of, deprived of the equal protection of the laws guaranteed by the Fourteenth Amendment. This disposition makes unnecessary any discussion whether such segregation also violates the Due Process Clause of the Fourteenth Amendment.

Because these are class actions, because of the wide applicability of this decision, and because of the great variety of local conditions, the formulation of decrees in these cases presents problems of considerable complexity. On reargument, the consideration of appropriate relief was necessarily subordinated to the primary question—the constitutionality of segregation in public education. We have now announced that such segregation is a denial of the equal protection of the laws. In order that we may have the full assistance of the parties in formulating decrees, the cases will be restored to the docket, and the parties are requested to present further argument. ... The Attorney General of the United States is again invited to participate. The Attorneys General of the states requiring or permitting segregation in public education will also be permitted to appear as *amici curiae* upon request to do so by September 15, 1954, and submission of briefs by October 1, 1954. *It is so ordered.*

✤ *D O C U M E N T   4*

Brown v. Board of Education, II, 1955

Mr. Chief Justice Warren delivered the opinion of the Court.

These cases were decided on May 17, 1954. The opinions of that date, declaring the fundamental principle that racial discrimination in public education is unconstitutional, are incorporated herein by reference. All provisions of federal, state, or local law requiring or permitting such discrimination must yield to this principle. There remains for consideration the manner in which relief is to be accorded. Because these cases arose under different local conditions and their disposition will involve a variety of local problems, we requested further argument on the question of relief. In view of the nationwide importance of the decision, we invited the Attorney General of the United States and the Attorneys General of all states requiring or permitting racial discrimination in public education to present their views on that question. The parties, the United States, and the States of Florida, North Carolina, Arkansas, Oklahoma, Maryland, and Texas filed briefs and participated in the oral argument. ...

Full implementation of these constitutional principles may require solution of varied local school problems. School authorities have the primary responsibility for elucidating, assessing, and solving these problems; courts will have to consider whether the action of school authorities constitutes good faith implementation of the governing constitutional principles. Because of their proximity to local conditions and the possible need for further hearings, the courts which originally heard these cases can best perform this judicial appraisal. Accordingly, we believe it appropriate to remand the cases to those courts.

In fashioning and effectuating the decrees, the courts will be guided by equitable principles. Traditionally, equity has been characterized by a practical flexibility in shaping its remedies and by a facility for adjusting and reconciling public and private needs. These cases call for the exercise of these traditional attributes of equity power. At stake is the personal interest of the plaintiffs in admission to public schools as soon as practicable on a nondiscriminatory basis. To effectuate this interest may call for elimination of a variety of obstacles in making the transition to school systems operated in accordance with the constitutional principles set forth in our May 17, 1954, decision. Courts of equity may properly take into account the public interest in the elimination of such obstacles in a systematic and effective manner. But it should go without saying that the vitality of these constitutional principles cannot be allowed to yield simply because of disagreement with them.

While giving weight to these public and private considerations, the courts will require that the defendants make a prompt and reasonable start toward full compliance with our May 17, 1954, ruling. Once such a start has been made, the courts may find that additional time is necessary to carry out the ruling in an effective manner. The burden rests upon the defendants to establish that such time is necessary in the public interest and is consistent with good faith compliance at the earliest practicable date. To that end, the courts may consider problems related to administration, arising from the physical condition of the school plant, the school transportation system, personnel, revision of school districts and attendance areas into compact units to achieve a system of determining admission to the public schools on a nonracial basis, and revision of local laws and regulations which may be necessary in solving the foregoing problems. They will also consider the adequacy of any plans the defendants may propose to meet these problems and to effectuate a transition to a racially nondiscriminatory school system. During this period of transition, the courts will retain jurisdiction of these cases. [L]ower courts are to take such proceedings and enter such orders and decrees consistent with this opinion as are necessary and proper to admit to public schools on a racially nondiscriminatory basis with all deliberate speed the parties to these cases.

✤ *D O C U M E N T* 5

White Southern Members of Congress Declare their Opposition to Brown, 1956

...We regard the decisions of the Supreme Court in the school cases as a clear abuse of judicial power. It climaxes a trend in the Federal Judiciary undertaking to legislate, in derogation of the authority of Congress, and to encroach upon the reserved rights of the States and the people.

The original Constitution does not mention education. Neither does the 14th Amendment nor any other amendment. The debates preceding the submission of the

14th Amendment clearly show that there was no intent that it should affect the system of education maintained by the States.

The very Congress which proposed the amendment subsequently provided for segregated schools in the District of Columbia.

When the amendment was adopted in 1868, there were 37 States of the Union....

Every one of the 26 States that had any substantial racial differences among its people, either approved the operation of segregated schools already in existence or subsequently established such schools by action of the same law-making body which considered the 14th Amendment.

As admitted by the Supreme Court in the public school case (*Brown v. Board of Education*), the doctrine of separate but equal schools "apparently originated in *Roberts v. City of Boston* (1849), upholding school segregation against attack as being violative of a State constitutional guarantee of equality." This constitutional doctrine began in the North, not in the South, and it was followed not only in Massachusetts, but in Connecticut, New York, Illinois, Indiana, Michigan, Minnesota, New Jersey, Ohio, Pennsylvania and other northern states until they, exercising their rights as states through the constitutional processes of local self-government, changed their school systems.

In the case of *Plessy v. Ferguson* in 1896 the Supreme Court expressly declared that under the 14th Amendment no person was denied any of his rights if the States provided separate but equal facilities. This decision has been followed in many other cases. It is notable that the Supreme Court, speaking through Chief Justice Taft, a former President of the United States, unanimously declared in 1927 in *Lum v. Rice* that the "separate but equal" principle is "within the discretion of the State in regulating its public schools and does not conflict with the 14th Amendment."

This interpretation, restated time and again, became a part of the life of the people of many of the States and confirmed their habits, traditions, and way of life. It is founded on elemental humanity and commonsense, for parents should not be deprived by Government of the right to direct the lives and education of their own children.

Though there has been no constitutional amendment or act of Congress changing this established legal principle almost a century old, the Supreme Court of the United States, with no legal basis for such action, undertook to exercise their naked judicial power and substituted their personal political and social ideas for the established law of the land.

This unwarranted exercise of power by the Court, contrary to the Constitution, is creating chaos and confusion in the States principally affected. It is destroying the amicable relations between the white and Negro races that have been created through 90 years of patient effort by the good people of both races. It has planted hatred and suspicion where there has been heretofore friendship and understanding.

Without regard to the consent of the governed, outside mediators are threatening immediate and revolutionary changes in our public schools systems. If done, this is certain to destroy the system of public education in some of the States.

With the gravest concern for the explosive and dangerous condition created by this decision and inflamed by outside meddlers:

We reaffirm our reliance on the Constitution as the fundamental law of the land.

We decry the Supreme Court's encroachment on the rights reserved to the States and to the people, contrary to established law, and to the Constitution.

We commend the motives of those States which have declared the intention to resist forced integration by any lawful means.

We appeal to the States and people who are not directly affected by these decisions to consider the constitutional principles involved against the time when they too, on issues vital to them may be the victims of judicial encroachment.

Even though we constitute a minority in the present Congress, we have full faith that a majority of the American people believe in the dual system of government which has enabled us to achieve our greatness and will in time demand that the reserved rights of the States and of the people be made secure against judicial usurpation.

We pledge ourselves to use all lawful means to bring about a reversal of this decision which is contrary to the Constitution and to prevent the use of force in its implementation.

In this trying period, as we all seek to right this wrong, we appeal to our people not to be provoked by the agitators and troublemakers invading our States and to scrupulously refrain from disorder and lawless acts.

✚ *D O C U M E N T   6*

The Civil Rights Act Forbids Discrimination in Public Education and Employment, 1964

Title IV—Desegregation of Public Education

Survey and Report of Educational Opportunities.   Sec. 402. The Commissioner shall conduct a survey and make a report to the President and the Congress, within two years of the enactment of this title, concerning the lack of availability of equal educational opportunities for individuals by reason of race, color, religion, or national origin in public educational institutions at all levels in the United States, its territories and possessions, and the District of Columbia.

Technical Assistance.   Sec. 403. The Commissioner is authorized, upon the application of any school board, State, municipality, school district, or other governmental unit legally responsible for operating a public school or schools, to render technical assistance to such applicant in the preparation, adoption, and implementation of plans for the desegregation of public schools. Such technical assistance may, among other activities, include making available to such agencies information regarding effective methods of coping with special educational problems occasioned by desegregation, and making available to such agencies personnel of the Office of Education or other persons specially equipped to advise and assist them in coping with such problems. . . .

Grants.   Sec. 405. (a) The Commissioner is authorized, upon application of a school board, to make grants to such board to pay, in whole or in part, the cost of—

    (1) giving to teachers and other school personnel inservice training in deal-
        ing with problems incident to desegregation, and

    (2) employing specialists to advise in problems incident to desegregation.

    (b) In determining whether to make a grant, and in fixing the amount thereof and the terms and conditions on which it will be made, the Commissioner shall take into consideration the amount available for grants under this section and the other applications which are pending before him; the financial condition of the applicant and the other resources available to it; the nature, extent, and gravity of its problems incident to desegregation; and such other factors as he finds relevant. . . .

Title VII—Equal Employment Opportunity

Discrimination Because of Race, Color, Religion, Sex, or National Origin.   Sec. 703. (a) It shall be an unlawful employment practice for an employer—

(1) to fail or refuse to hire or to discharge any individual, or otherwise to discriminate against any individual with respect to his compensation, terms, conditions, or privileges of employment, because of such individual's race, color, religion, sex, or national origin; or

(2) to limit, segregate, or classify his employees in any way which would deprive or tend to deprive any individual of employment opportunities or otherwise adversely affect his status as an employee, because of such individual's race, color, religion, sex, or national origin.

(b) It shall be an unlawful employment practice for an employment agency to fail or refuse to refer for employment, or otherwise to discriminate against, any individual because of his race, color, religion, sex, or national origin, or to classify or refer for employment any individual on the basis of his race, color, religion, sex, or national origin.

(c) It shall be unlawful employment practice for a labor organization—

(1) to exclude or to expel from its membership, or otherwise to discriminate against, any individual because of his race, color, religion, sex, or national origin;

(2) to limit, segregate, or classify its membership, or to classify or fail or refuse to refer for employment any individual, in any way which would deprive or tend to deprive any individual of employment opportunities, or would limit such employment opportunities or otherwise adversely affect his status as an employee or as an applicant for employment, because of such individual's race, color, religion, sex, or national origin; or

(3) to cause or attempt to cause an employer to discriminate against an individual in violation of this section.

(d) It shall be an unlawful employment practice for any employer, labor organization, or joint labor-management committee controlling apprenticeship or other training or retraining, including on-the-job training programs to discriminate against any individual because of his race, color, religion, sex, or national origin in admission to, or employment in, any program established to provide apprenticeship or other training.

(e) Notwithstanding any other provision of this title, (1) it shall not be an unlawful employment practice for an employer to hire and employ employees, for an employment agency to classify, or refer for employment any individual, for a labor organization to classify its membership or to classify or refer for employment any individual, or for an employer, labor organization, or joint labor-management committee controlling apprenticeship or other training or retraining programs to admit or employ any individual in any such program, on the basis of his religion, sex, or national origin in those certain instances where religion, sex, or national origin is a bona fide occupational qualification reasonably necessary to the normal operation of that particular business or enterprise, and (2) it shall not be an unlawful employment practice for a school, college, university, or other educational institution or institution of learning to hire and employ employees of a particular religion if such school, college, university, or other educational institution or institution of learning is, in whole or in substantial part, owned, supported, controlled, or managed by a particular religion or by a particular religious corporation, association, or society, or if the curriculum of such school, college, university, or other educational institution or institution of learning is directed toward the propagation of a particular religion.

(f) As used in this title, the phrase "unlawful employment practice" shall not be deemed to include any action or measure taken by an employer, labor organization, joint labor-management committee, or employment agency with respect to an individual who is a member of the Communist Party of the United States or of any other organization required to register as a Communist-action or Communist-front organization by final order of the Subversive Activities Control Board pursuant to the Subversive Activities Control Act of 1950.

(g) Notwithstanding any other provision of this title, it shall not be an unlawful employment practice for an employer to fail or refuse to hire and employ any individual for any position, for an employer to discharge any individual from any position, or for an employment agency to fail or refuse to refer any individual for employment in any position, or for a labor organization to fail or refuse to refer any individual for employment in any position, if—

(1) the occupancy of such position, or access to the premises in or upon which any part of the duties of such position is performed or is to be performed, is subject to any requirement imposed in the interest of the national security of the United States under any security program in effect pursuant to or administered under any statute of the United States or any Executive order of the President; and

(2) such individual has not fulfilled or has ceased to fulfill that requirement.

(h) Notwithstanding any other provision of this title, it shall not be an unlawful employment practice for an employer to apply different standards of compensation, or different terms, conditions, or privileges of employment pursuant to a bona fide seniority or merit system, or a system which measures earnings by quantity or quality of production or to employees who work in different locations, provided that such differences are not the result of an intention to discriminate because of race, color, religion, sex, or national origin, nor shall it be an unlawful employment practice for an employer to give and to act upon the results of any professionally developed ability test provided that such test, its administration or action upon the results is not designed, intended or used to discriminate because of race, color, religion, sex or national origin. It shall not be an unlawful employment practice under this title for any employer to differentiate upon the basis of sex in determining the amount of the wages or compensation paid or to be paid to employees of such employer if such differentiation is authorized by the provisions of section 6(d) of the Fair Labor Standards Act of 1938, as amended (29 U.S.C. 206(d)).

✤ *D O C U M E N T   7*

President Lyndon Johnson Vows to Fight Injustice and Inequality, 1965

... Our earth is the home of revolution. In every corner of every continent men charged with hope contend with ancient ways in the pursuit of justice. They reach for the newest of weapons to realize the oldest of dreams, that each may walk in freedom and pride, stretching his talents, enjoying the fruits of the earth.

Our enemies may occasionally seize the day of change, but it is the banner of our revolution they take. And our own future is linked to this process of swift and turbulent change in many lands in the world. But nothing in any country touches us more profoundly, and nothing is more freighted with meaning for our own destiny than the revolution of the Negro American.

In far too many ways American Negroes have been another nation: deprived of freedom, crippled by hatred, the doors of opportunity closed to hope.

In our time change has come to this Nation, too. The American Negro, acting with impressive restraint, has peacefully protested and marched, entered the court-rooms and the seats of government, demanding a justice that has long been denied. The voice of the Negro was the call to action. But it is a tribute to America that, once aroused, the courts and the Congress, the President and most of the people, have been the allies of progress.

Thus we have seen the high court of the country declare that discrimination based on race was repugnant to the Constitution, and therefore void. We have seen in 1957, and 1960, and again in 1964, the first civil rights legislation in this Nation in almost an entire century. ...

The voting rights bill will be the latest, and among the most important, in a long series of victories. But this victory—as Winston Churchill said of another triumph for freedom—"is not the end. It is not even the beginning of the end. But it is, per-haps, the end of the beginning."

That beginning is freedom; and the barriers to that freedom are tumbling down. Freedom is the right to share, share fully and equally, in American society—to vote, to hold a job, to enter a public place, to go to school. It is the right to be treated in every part of our national life as a person equal in dignity and promise to all others.

But freedom is not enough. You do not wipe away the scars of centuries by say-ing: Now you are free to go where you want, and do as you desire, and choose the leaders you please.

You do not take a person who, for years, has been hobbled by chains and liberate him, bring him up to the starting line of a race and then say, "you are free to compete with all the others," and still justly believe that you have been completely fair.

Thus it is not enough just to open the gates of opportunity. All our citizens must have the ability to walk through those gates.

This is the next and the more profound stage of the battle for civil rights. We seek not just freedom but opportunity. We seek not just legal equity but human ability, not just equality as a right and a theory but equality as a fact and equality as a result.

For the task is to give 20 million Negroes the same chance as every other American to learn and grow, to work and share in society, to develop their abilities—physical, mental and spiritual, and to pursue their individual happiness.

To this end equal opportunity is essential, but not enough, not enough. Men and women of all races are born with the same range of abilities. But ability is not just the product of birth. Ability is stretched or stunted by the family that you live with, and the neighborhood you live in—by the school you go to and the poverty or the richness of your surroundings. It is the product of a hundred unseen forces playing upon the little infant, the child, and finally the man.

This graduating class at Howard University is witness to the indomitable determination of the Negro American to win his way in American life.

The number of Negroes in schools of higher learning has almost doubled in 15 years. The number of nonwhite professional workers has more than doubled in 10 years. The median income of Negro college women tonight exceeds that of white college women. And there are also the enormous accomplishments of distinguished individual Negroes—many of them graduates of this institution, and one of them the first lady ambassador in the history of the United States.

These are proud and impressive achievements. But they tell only the story of a growing middle class minority, steadily narrowing the gap between them and their white counterparts.

But for the great majority of Negro Americans-the poor, the unemployed, the uprooted, and the dispossessed—there is a much grimmer story. They still, as we meet here tonight, are another nation. Despite the court orders and the laws, despite the legislative victories and the speeches, for them the walls are rising and the gulf is widening.

Here are some of the facts of this American failure.

Thirty-five years ago the rate of unemployment for Negroes and whites was about the same. Tonight the Negro rate is twice as high.

In 1948 the 8 percent unemployment rate for Negro teenage boys was actually less than that of whites. By last year that rate had grown to 23 percent, as against 13 percent for whites unemployed.

Between 1949 and 1959, the income of Negro men relative to white men declined in every section of this country. From 1952 to 1963 the median income of Negro families compared to white actually dropped from 57 percent to 53 percent.

In the years 1955 through 1957, 22 percent of experienced Negro workers were out of work at some time during the year. In 1961 through 1963 that proportion had soared to 29 percent.

Since 1947 the number of white families living in poverty has decreased 27 percent while the number of poorer nonwhite families decreased only 3 percent.

The infant mortality of nonwhites in 1940 was 70 percent greater than whites. Twenty-two years later it was 90 percent greater.

Moreover, the isolation of Negro from white communities is increasing, rather than decreasing as Negroes crowd into the central cities and become a city within a city.

Of course Negro Americans as well as white Americans have shared in our rising national abundance. But the harsh fact of the matter is that in the battle for true equality too many—far too many—are losing ground every day.

We are not completely sure why this is. We know the causes are complex and subtle. But we do know the two broad basic reasons. And we do know that we have to act.

First, Negroes are trapped—as many whites are trapped—in inherited, gateless poverty. They lack training and skills. They are shut in, in slums, without decent medical care. Private and public poverty combine to cripple their capacities.

We are trying to attack these evils through our poverty program, through our education program, through our medical care and our other health programs, and a dozen more of the Great Society programs that are aimed at the root causes of this poverty.

We will increase, and we will accelerate, and we will broaden this attack in years to come until this most enduring of foes finally yields to our unyielding will.

But there is a second cause—much more difficult to explain, more deeply grounded, more desperate in its force. It is the devastating heritage of long years of slavery; and a century of oppression, hatred, and injustice.

For Negro poverty is not white poverty. Many of its causes and many of its cures are the same. But there are differences-deep, corrosive, obstinate differences— radiating painful roots into the community, and into the family, and the nature of the individual. ...

One of the differences is the increased concentration of Negroes in our cities. More than 73 percent of all Negroes live in urban areas compared with less than 70 percent of the whites. Most of these Negroes live in slums. Most of these Negroes live together—a separated people.

Men are shaped by their world. When it is a world of decay, ringed by an invisible wall, when escape is arduous and uncertain, and the saving pressures of a more hopeful society are unknown, it can cripple the youth and it can desolate the men.

There is also the burden that a dark skin can add to the search for a productive place in our society. Unemployment strikes most swiftly and broadly at the Negro, and this burden erodes hope. Blighted hope breeds despair. Despair brings indifferences to the learning which offers a way out. And despair, coupled with indifferences, is often the source of destructive rebellion against the fabric of society.

There is also the lacerating hurt of early collision with white hatred or prejudice, distaste or condescension. Other groups have felt similar intolerance. But success and achievement could wipe it away. They do not change the color of a man's skin. I have seen this uncomprehending pain in the eyes of the little, young Mexican-American schoolchildren that I taught many years ago. But it can be overcome. But, for many, the wounds are always open.

Perhaps most important—its influence radiating to every part of life—is the breakdown of the Negro family structure. For this, most of all, white America must accept responsibility. It flows from centuries of oppression and persecution of the Negro man. It flows from the long years of degradation and discrimination, which have attacked his dignity and assaulted his ability to produce for his family.

This, too, is not pleasant to look upon. But it must be faced by those whose serious intent is to improve the life of all Americans.

Only a minority—less than half—of all Negro children reach the age of 18 having lived all their lives with both of their parents. At this moment, tonight, little less than two-thirds are at home with both of their parents. Probably a majority of all Negro children receive federally-aided public assistance sometime during their childhood.

The family is the cornerstone of our society. More than any other force it shapes the attitude, the hopes, the ambitions, and the values of the child. And when the family collapses it is the children that are usually damaged. When it happens on a massive scale the community itself is crippled.

So, unless we work to strengthen the family, to create conditions under which most parents will stay together—all the rest: schools, and playgrounds, and public assistance, and private concern, will never be enough to cut completely the circle of despair and deprivation.

There is no single easy answer to all of these problems.

Jobs are part of the answer. They bring the income which permits a man to provide for his family.

Decent homes in decent surroundings and a chance to learn—an equal chance to learn—are part of the answer.

Welfare and social programs better designed to hold families together are part of the answer.

Care for the sick is part of the answer.

An understanding heart by all Americans is another big part of the answer.

And to all of these fronts—and a dozen more—I will dedicate the expanding efforts of the Johnson administration. . . .

For what is justice?

It is to fulfill the fair expectations of man.

Thus, American justice is a very special thing. For, from the first, this has been a land of towering expectations. It was to be a nation where each man could be ruled by the common consent of all—enshrined in law given life by institutions, guided by men themselves subject to its rule. And all—all of every station and origin—would be touched equally in obligation and in liberty.

Beyond the law lay the land. It was a rich land, glowing with more abundant promise than man had ever seen. Here, unlike any place yet known, all were to share the harvest.

And beyond this was the dignity of man. Each could become whatever his qualities of mind and spirit would permit—to strive, to seek, and, if he could, to find his happiness.

This is American justice. We have pursued it faithfully to the edge of our imperfections, and we have failed to find it for the American Negro.

So, it is the glorious opportunity of this generation to end the one huge wrong of the American Nation and, in so doing, to find America for ourselves, with the same immense thrill of discovery which gripped those who first began to realize that here, at last, was a home for freedom.

All it will take is for all of us to understand what this country is and what this country must become.

The Scripture promises: "I shall light a candle of understanding in thine heart, which shall not be put out."

Together, and with millions more, we can light that candle of understanding in the heart of all America.

And, once lit, it will never again go out.

Source: *Public Papers of the Presidents of the United States: Lyndon B. Johnson, 1965.* Volume II, entry 301, pp. 635–640. Washington, D. C.: Government Printing Office, 1966.

✢ E S S A Y S

In 2001, a Yale Law School professor invited a group of top legal scholars to re-write the *Brown* decision, and their responses appeared as a collection of "judicial opinions" in *What Brown v. Board of Education Should Have Said*. The book includes Derrick A. Bell's provocative essay, written as a "dissent," in which he argues that the Court should have held states accountable to equalize their separate schools under *Plessy v. Ferguson*. Bell, a professor at New York University Law School, is a leading African American legal scholar and champion of civil rights.

Kermit L. Hall, the late professor of history and president of the University at Albany, State University of New York and the co-editor of this volume, offers a more traditional take on *Brown*. Hall grounds the decision firmly in its historical context, both in the United States and throughout the world, and views the ruling as a landmark in the history of human rights. Still, he acknowledges the limitations of *Brown*, particularly in light of the current challenge of providing equal access to higher education in America.

Brown Was Wrongly Decided

DERRICK A. BELL

BELL, J., dissenting.

I dissent today from the majority's decision in these cases because the detestable segregation in the public schools that the majority finds unconstitutional is a manifestation of the evil of racism the depths and pervasiveness of which this Court fails even to acknowledge, much less address and attempt to correct.

For reasons that I will explain in some detail, I cannot join in a decision that, while serving well the nation's foreign policy and domestic concerns, provides petitioners with no more than a semblance of the racial equality that they and theirs have sought for so long. The Court's long-overdue findings that Negroes are harmed by racial segregation is, regrettably, unaccompanied by an understanding of the economic, political, and psychological advantages whites gain because of that harm.

With some difficulty, the Court finds that *Plessy v. Ferguson*, 163 U.S. 537 (1896), cannot now serve as constitutional justification for segregated schools. *Plessy*, though, is only fortuitously a legal precedent. In actuality, it is a judicial affirmation of an unwritten but no less clearly understood social compact that, older than the Constitution, was incorporated into that document, and has been continually affirmed. Chief Justice Roger Taney's observation in *Dred Scott v. Sandford*, 60 U.S. (19 How.) 393, 407 (1857), that Negroes "had no rights that the white man was bound to respect" was excessive even for its time. The essence of the racial compact, however, is that whites, whatever their status, can view themselves as entitled to privileges and priorities over blacks. Indeed, beyond an appropriate pride in ethnic heritage, this racial compact provides the definitive definition of what it means to be white in America.

From Balkin, Jack M., editor, *What Brown v. Board of Education Should Have Said: The Nation's Top Legal Experts Rewrite America's Landmark Civil Rights Decision*. Published by New York University Press, 2001. Reproduced with permission of the publisher.

Without recognizing and attempting to dismantle this racial compact and in particular the indirect promises made to whites and the surrender of opportunities whites made to gain these racial privileges, today's decision, while viewed as a triumph by Negro petitioners and the class they represent, will be condemned by many whites as a breach of the compact. Their predictable outraged resistance will undermine and eventually negate judicial enforcement efforts, while political support for the Court's decision, like virtually every other racial rights measure adopted basically to serve white interests once those interests have been served, will become irrelevant.

I regret that the Court fails to see in these cases the opportunity to lay bare the simplistic hypocrisy of the "separate but equal" standard, not by overturning *Plessy*, but by ordering its strict enforcement. Respondents' counsel, John W. Davis, a highly respected advocate, urges this Court to uphold "separate but equal" as the constitutionally correct measure of racial status because, as he puts it so elegantly, "somewhere, sometime to every principle comes a moment of repose when it has been so often announced, so confidently relied upon, so long continued, that it passes the limits of judicial discretion and disturbance."

Elegance, though, should not be allowed to trample truth. The "separate" in the "separate but equal" standard has been rigorously enforced. The "equal" has served as a total refutation of equality. Counsel for the Negro children have gone to great lengths to prove what must be obvious to every person who gives the matter even cursory attention: with some notable exceptions, schools provided for Negroes in segregated systems are unequal in facilities—often obscenely so. ...

In their determination to strike down state-mandated segregation, the petitioners ignore the admonishment of W. E. B. DuBois, one of the nation's finest thinkers. "Negro children need neither segregated schools nor mixed schools. What they need is education." The three phases of relief that I will describe below focus attention on what is needed now by the children of both races. It is the only way to avoid a generation or more of strife over an ideal that, while worthwhile, will not achieve the educationally effective education that petitioners' children need and that existing constitutional standards, stripped of their racist understandings, should provide.

The Court has failed to consider three major components of racial segregation that must be addressed in order to provide meaningful relief. They are:

1. Racial segregation furthers societal stability by subordinating Negro Americans, which makes it easier for rich white Americans to dominate poor white Americans.
2. Negro rights are recognized and protected for only so long as they advance the nation's interests.
3. Realistic rather than symbolic relief for segregated schools will require a specific, judicially monitored plan designed primarily to promote educational equity.

I will discuss each of these components in turn:

I.

Racial segregation furthers societal stability by subordinating Negro Americans, which makes it easier for rich white Americans to dominate poor white Americans. ...

A much-neglected history requires the admission that *Plessy v. Ferguson* provided legal confirmation to more than a century of political compromises that diminished the citizenship rights of blacks to the point of invisibility to resolve conflicts among differing groups of whites or further interests deemed important to the nation. Three examples will illustrate the perhaps unconscious but no less pernicious policy.

1. In drafting the Constitution, the framers confronted the already well-established patterns of slavery. While insuring that the foundation of our basic law would recognize rights to life and liberty for every citizen, they knew that America had systematically denied those rights to those of African descent. For the better part of two centuries, the colonies and then the United States developed the country on the labor of literally millions of human beings kidnapped by force from their native Africa and transported under inhuman conditions. The survivors and their progeny were held in a particularly vicious form of human slavery. The war for independence was financed in substantial part out of the profits of slavery....

2. Over time, the friction between free and slave states grew, sparked by scores of lawsuits seeking to utilize the judicial forums of free states to win freedom for slaves who were brought or escaped from slave states. In *Dred Scott v. Sandford*, Chief Justice Roger Taney, as reviled as the framers are revered, attempted to do what they had done. By again refusing to recognize rights for Negroes—whether slave or free—the Court could settle the increasingly divisive slavery issue. The *Dred Scott* decision had the opposite effect, and according to many historians helped precipitate the Civil War.

3. When, hardly a decade after enactment of the Civil War Amendments, it appeared that renewed hostilities might break out following the close and bitterly disputed presidential election of 1876, a congressional commission appointed to resolve the dispute did so through what became known as the Hayes-Tilden compromise. It provided that the Republican, Rutherford B. Hayes, would be deemed to have won the election. For their part of the bargain, southern Democrats received a number of concessions including the promise—devastating to those so recently freed—to withdraw federal troops and leave their fate to the far from tender mercies of those who deemed Negroes fit only for slavery and subjugation....

American racism, though, is not simply a "taint" or "bias." It is the dominant interpretive framework for rendering bodies intelligible. That is to say, racism organizes the American garden's very configuration. Jim Crow was not merely an oppressive legal regime; it consolidated the imaginative lens through which Americans would view race going forward in the future. Jim Crow reaffirmed the binary system through which we (Americans) tend to think of race—i.e., "black" and "white." Jim Crow unceremoniously erased intermediate categories through the biologically ridiculous but politically necessary notion that "one drop" of black blood rendered an individual black. America has not recognized "mulatto," certainly not since post-Reconstruction. The "one drop" concept highlights the rigidity of American racism, and, by virtue of the conceptual currency it continues to enjoy, it makes clear the extent to which Jim Crow segregation was not just a "bad weed." When racism is positioned as a thinking problem (rather than just a "bad weed"), the Court majority's pronouncement can be seen as more a racial provocation than a remedy....

Petitioners, viewing integration with whites as the only means of overthrowing "separate but equal," urge an end to state-mandated racial segregation. Whites, of course, resist any change in the "separate but equal" standard they view as a vested property right. Resistance under these circumstances is a manifestation of white victimization, willing, it is true, but victimization nevertheless. The question for this Court then is not the obvious one of whether racially segregated schools violate the Equal Protection Clause of the Fourteenth Amendment, but how can this Court grant racial relief desired by Negroes, resisted by whites and needed by both? ...

II.

Negro rights are recognized and protected for only so long as they advance the nation's interests.

... While it is nowhere mentioned in the majority's opinion, it is quite clear that a major motivation for the Court to outlaw racial segregation now when it declined to do so in the past is the major boost this decision will provide in our competition with communist governments abroad and our fight to uproot subversive elements at home.

A few examples are illustrative:

The Emancipation Proclamation. Even though he was reluctant to arbitrarily deprive even the rebellious Southerners of their property without due process or compensation, President Lincoln finally issued the document on January 1, 1863, because it would disrupt the labor force in the South and open the way for the enlistment of thousands of former slaves who had left their plantations and were following the union armies. In addition, his declaration that the Civil War was intended to end slavery would serve to mobilize abolitionists in England and France who would prevent their governments from entering the war on the side of the Confederacy. By its terms, of course, the executive order actually freed no slaves for it excluded all slave-owning territories on the Union side and had no legal effect on slavery within the Confederacy.

The Civil War Amendments. The Republicans recognized that unless some action was taken to legitimate the freedmen's status, Southerners would utilize violence to force blacks into slavery, thereby renewing the economic dispute that had led to the Civil War. To avoid this "win the war but lose the peace" result, the Fourteenth and Fifteenth Amendments and Civil Rights Acts of 1870–75 were enacted. They were the work of the Radical Reconstructionists, some of whom were deeply committed to securing the rights of citizenship for the freedmen. For most Republicans, however, a more general motivation was the desire to maintain Republican Party control in the southern states and in Congress.

The Fourteenth Amendment, unpassable as a specific protection for black rights, was enacted finally as a general guarantee of life, liberty, and property of all "persons." Corporations, following a period of ambivalence, were deemed persons under the Fourteenth Amendment, and for several generations received far more protection from the Courts than did Negroes, much of it under a doctrine of "substantive due process" not clearly contained in the amendment's language....

We may regret the pattern in which self-interest is the apparent major motivant in racial remediation policies that are then abandoned when the nation's interest has been served, but we should not ignore this self-interest phenomenon, particularly as it is functioning in the cases now before us. In petitioners' briefs and more particularly in the amicus briefs filed by the Justice Department, the "separate but equal" precedent of *Plessy* is challenged as not only unjust to blacks, but also bad for the country's image, a barrier to development in the South, and harmful to its foreign policy. To make the latter point, the government's brief quoted at some length Secretary of State Dean Acheson, who reported:

> [D]uring the past six years, the damage to our foreign relations attributable to [race discrimination] has become progressively greater. The United States is under constant attack in the foreign press, over the foreign radio, and in such international bodies as the United Nations because of various practices of discrimination against minority groups in this country. ... [t]he undeniable existence of racial discrimination gives unfriendly governments the most effective kind of ammunition for their propaganda warfare. ... [s]chool segregation, in particular, has been singled out for hostile foreign comment in the United States and elsewhere. ... [R]acial discrimination in the United States remains a source of constant embarrassment to this government in the day-to-day conduct of its foreign relations; and it jeopardizes the effective maintenance of our moral leadership of the free and democratic nations of the world.

In addition, this Court is not unaware of the nation's need to protect its national security against those who would exploit our internal difficulties for the benefit of external forces. Justice Frankfurter, while concurring in *Dennis v. United States*, wrote that the Court "may take judicial notice that the communist doctrines which these defendants have conspired to advocate are in the ascendency in powerful nations who cannot be acquitted of unfriendliness to the institutions of this country."

It is likely that not since the Civil War has the need to remedy racial injustice been so firmly aligned with the country's vital interests at home and abroad. The majority's ringing statement will provide a symbolic victory to petitioners and the class of Negroes they represent while, in fact, giving a new, improved face to the nation's foreign policy and responding to charges of blatant racial bias at home, thus furnishing a fresh example of the historic attraction to granting recognition and promising reform of racial injustice when such action converges with the nation's interests. ...

The racial reform-retrenchment pattern so evident here indicates that when the tides of white resentment rise and again swamp the expectations of Negroes in a flood of racial hostility, this Court and likely the country will vacillate. Then, as with the Emancipation Proclamation and the Civil War Amendments, it will rationalize its inability and—let us be honest—its unwillingness to give real meaning to the rights we declare so readily and so willingly sacrifice when our interests turn to new issues, more pressing concerns.

III.

Realistic rather than symbolic relief for segregated schools will require a specific, judicially monitored plan designed primarily to promote educational equity.

While declaring racial segregation harmful to black children, the majority treats these policies as though they descended unwanted from the skies and can now be mopped up like a heavy rainfall and flushed away. The fact is that, as my brief review of the nation's racial history makes clear, a great many white as well as Negro children have been harmed by segregation. Segregation requires school systems to operate duplicate sets of schools that are as educationally inefficient as their gross incompliance with the "separate but equal" *Plessy* mandate makes them constitutionally deficient.

Pressured by this litigation, the school boards assure this Court that they are taking steps to equalize facilities in Negro schools. More important than striking down *Plessy v. Ferguson* is the need to reveal its hypocritical underpinnings by requiring its full enforcement for all children, white as well as black. Full enforcement requires more than either equalizing facilities or, in the case of Delaware because of the inadequacy of the Negro schools, ordering plaintiffs admitted into the white schools. As a primary step toward the disestablishment of the dual school system, I would order relief that must be provided all children in racially segregated districts in three phases:

Phase 1: Equalization. (1) Effective immediately on receipt of this Court's mandate, school officials of the respondent school districts must ascertain through appropriate measures the academic standing of each school district as compared with nationwide norms for school systems of comparable size and financial resources. This data will be published and made available to all patrons of the district. (2) All schools within the district must be fully equalized in physical facilities, teacher training, experience, and salary with the goal that each district as a whole will measure up to national norms within three years.

Phase 2. Representation. The battle cry of those who fought and died to bring this country into existence was "Taxation without representation is tyranny." Effective relief in segregated school districts requires no less than the immediate restructuring of school boards and other policy-making bodies to insure that those formally excluded from representation have persons selected by them in accordance with the percentage of their children in the school system. This restructuring must take effect no later than the start of the 1955–56 school year.

Phase 3. Judicial oversight. To implement these orders efficiently, federal district judges should be instructed to set up three-person monitoring committees, with the Negro and white communities each selecting a monitor and those two agreeing on a third. The monitoring committees will work with school officials to prepare the necessary plans and procedures enabling the school districts to comply with phases 1 and 2. The district courts will oversee compliance and will address firmly any actions intended to subvert or hinder the compliance program.

In my view, the petitioners' goal—the disestablishment of the dual school system—will be more effectively achieved for students, parents, teachers, administrators, and other individuals connected directly or indirectly with the school system by these means than by the majority's ringing order, which I fear will not be effectively enforced and will be vigorously resisted.

In conclusion, I recognize that this dissent comports neither with the hopes of petitioners that we order immediate desegregation nor the pleas of respondent boards that we retain the racial status quo. Our goal, though, should not be to determine winners and losers. It is rather our obligation to unravel the nation's greatest contradiction. ...

Brown Furthered the Cause of Human Rights

KERMIT L. HALL

The purposes of this brief essay are fourfold. The first is to place *Brown* in its appropriate historical perspective, especially in light of the increasingly conflicting judgments about the importance of the decision and what it accomplished. Second, any effort to assess *Brown* today must also take account of the development over the last half-century of the color line in American society. Third, we need to understand the issues surrounding the problem of equality and especially the ways in which, in the past fifty years, the nation's and the Court's understanding of that word has changed. And fourth, and finally, *Brown* must be understood in the context of the much-discussed "racial gap" in learning and educational achievement, not just for K-12, but for higher education as well....

As Paul Finkelman has explained in his insightful analysis of *Brown*, the decision was the most significant action by the High Court in the twentieth century. "When it was decided fifty years ago, *Brown v. Board of Education* seemed like a revolution in law and justice." It ranked, in terms of its impact, along with *Dred Scott v. Sanford*, as the most important decision in the entire history of the Court. Thurgood Marshall, who argued the case for the National Association for the Advancement of Colored People ("NAACP") and later was appointed by President Lyndon Johnson to the High Court, was delighted. Richard Kluger, who has written the best history of the case, reported that when Marshall heard about the result, he stated, "I was so happy I was numb." Today, many scholars rank *Brown* as the single most honored opinion in that institution's history.

Ironically, on this fiftieth anniversary of *Brown*, critics now proclaim the decision a failure. As Finkelman reports, the list of naysayers is impressive. Harvard law professor Charles Ogletree, for example, has reached the "sad conclusion ... that fifty years after *Brown* there is little left to celebrate." Derrick Bell, a former member of the Harvard faculty and a civil rights activist, has gone even further. He concludes that the decision was actually harmful. According to Bell, the Court failed to assert its full power, both in deciding the issues and then demanding implementation, with the result that the decision " 'accomplished ... little.' "

Bell even suggested that the Court should not have overturned the "separate but equal" doctrine set out in *Plessy v. Ferguson*. Instead, the Justices should have demanded that every state—Northern and Southern—enforce fully the "equal" component of "separate but equal." If they had done so, the result would have been more money and better educations for all students, black and white. Bell proposed nothing short of adopting the tactic of John W. Davis, the attorney for the losing school board. Davis argued that the best solution was to pour more money into black schools, not force white and black children to go to school together.

Bell's ideas are given something of a sophisticated and scholarly echo in Michael Klarman's new book, *From Jim Crow to Civil Rights: The Supreme Court and the Struggle for Racial Equality*. Klarman, a law professor at the University of Virginia, claims that the Supreme Court played a limited role a half century ago

From Hall, Kermit L., " 'We've Got to Get Working ... the Clock is Ticking': Equity in Education and the Legacy of Brown v. Board" in Marquette Law Review 89:115, 2005, pp. 115–135. Reproduced with permission of the publisher.

just as it does today in settling matters of race relations. The Justices, according to Klarman, generally reflect prevailing public opinion, and that, as a result, *Brown* was at once a constitutional and social failure. He believes that civil rights advocates were making great progress in the decade before *Brown* and thus argues that "[w]ithout *Brown*, negotiation might have continued to produce gradual change without inciting white violence." While conceding that *Brown* was not "irrelevant" to civil rights, he argues that it led to unnecessary violence, "inspired southern whites to try to destroy the NAACP," and in the end was not central to changing American race relations. According to Klarman, it was not *Brown*, but "deep background forces" that "ensured that the United States would experience a racial reform movement regardless of what the Supreme Court did or did not do."

Klarman's book and the response to it remind us that considerable disagreement exists among scholars about *Brown* and especially how best to assess its impact. My own position is fundamentally different from that of Klarman. *Brown* made a real difference, but we have used it to explain too much and, in the end, raised expectations about it that are far beyond anything that it could ever have delivered. The Supreme Court cannot, and we should not expect it alone to, produce a color-blind society of genuine equality.

Since the critics of *Brown* and the High Court rely on counterfactual arguments to make their case, it seems fair to turn the tables. . . .

As Finkelman observes, "It is not hard to imagine a very different America if the Court had decided *Brown* differently." And, as Finkelman wisely concludes:

> [W]hile [critics of the Brown decision] bemoan the violence against blacks after Brown, it is easy to imagine a much more violent and lethal civil rights movement in the 1950s and 1960s if the Court in Brown and its progeny had not been a stalwart friend and supporter of civil rights.

The arguments of Klarman and others have merit, of course. It would be a mistake, in the end, to attribute too much to the work of the Court. Yet, the appropriate measure of the Court's success is not what it should have done measured against today's standards, but instead what it did during the 1950s and 1960s measured against the standards of that era. When the issues are framed in that much more authentic historical perspective, *Brown* emerges as one of the great milestones in the course of human rights and freedom. Much of the rest of the world has embraced that conclusion. In international human rights law, *Brown* is one of the most, if not the most, respected American cases.

One of the reasons that *Brown* has currency among international human rights lawyers is that it dealt directly with the color line in the United States. In 1903 W.E.B. DuBois correctly predicted that the major problem of the twentieth century would be the color line. One of the underlying arguments about *Brown* is whether it helped to break that color line.

The impact of *Brown* extended beyond school desegregation. Shortly after the decision, federal judges invoked *Brown* in cases challenging different forms of desegregation. These included segregated beaches in Baltimore, golf courses in Atlanta, and public housing in Michigan and Missouri. In doing so, *Brown* helped to break down the status of blacks as the nation's official pariahs. For example, by the early 1980s, at least according to public opinion surveys, the color line was close to disappearing completely. Ninety-four percent of both black and white Americans subscribed to the principle that black and white children should go to the same schools.

Today, save for an extraordinarily few holdouts, racism and the color line that went with it are deemed unacceptable, and racial diversity is viewed as a public good. Corporate America and the military, for example, joined in amicus briefs before the Supreme Court in the recent Michigan affirmative action cases to plead the necessity of just such diversity in elite public institutions of higher education. Such a combination fifty years ago was largely unthinkable.

That said, of course, there is still substantial disagreement about how to achieve diversity and about the grounds on which to use the power of the state to allot some of society's most important rewards and benefits, such as access to a college education. The "how to achieve it" issue is particularly critical, because issues of class and income continue to plague America and to do so along lines often shaped by race as well. We live, today, in a nation where about five percent of all African American men are incarcerated; for black men between ages sixteen and thirty-four, the percentage rises to twelve percent. Black males between ages eighteen and twenty-four are almost ten times more likely than white males of the same age to be the victims of homicide. Black children are far more likely than white children to live in poverty; their parents are far more likely to be unemployed or to earn low incomes.

We are also in the middle of a national trend toward school resegregation. That process has pushed more and more African American and Latino students into those schools with seventy-five percent or more minority children. Gary Orfield, co-director of Harvard University's Civil Rights Project, released a major research report in 2001 that documented this trend. Among other things, the report says, "[t]he data show the emergence of a substantial group of American schools that are virtually all nonwhite, which we call apartheid schools." These trends remind us that the solutions to problems associated with opportunity for those historically denied it depend on more than the law.

Many school systems outside the South are today more racially segregated than they were in 1954. And in the South, the picture is mixed a half century after *Brown*. As Erwin Chemerinsky has observed in drawing on the work of the sociologist Gary Orfield, "nationally, the percentage of African-American students attending majority African-American schools and schools where over 90% of the students are African-American also has increased in the last fifteen years." The percentage of schools where half or more of the student population is African American has been going up since 1986, from 62.9% to 70.2% in 1998–1999. In North Carolina, between 1993 and 2000 the number of African American students attending schools with minority enrollments of eighty percent or more doubled. And in the Charlotte-Mecklenburg School District the percentage of schools that meet the standard definition for diverse has gone down by twenty-five percent.

At the same time, in the University of Michigan affirmative action case of two terms ago, Justice O'Connor was unwilling to invalidate race-based preferences in higher education. In part, her decision reflected the view that having minority faces in historically majority white institutions was a public good. And the faces are there. During the administration of President George W. Bush, for example, African Americans occupy the posts of Secretary of State, the national security advisor to the President, and the Secretary of Education, and Clarence Thomas has followed

Thurgood Marshall on the Supreme Court. Since 1968, there has been an African American on the High Court. Should Thomas leave the High Court, he would almost certainly be replaced by another African American.

These developments were, in 1954, beyond comprehension, and they signal a profound change in American life. Did *Brown* make these developments possible? The answer is clearly yes, although it does not follow that *Brown* alone made them possible.

If we are willing to go back to the period during which the High Court considered *Brown*, it is apparent that the members of the Court viewed the changes taking place then as astounding. Justice Robert Jackson noted privately that the advances made by blacks since the Civil War were among the most impressive in human history. Justice Felix Frankfurter agreed, and he even made the point to his colleagues as they deliberated that, in the end, it was these changes that should prompt the Court to support integration. ...

But *Brown* was strong on rhetoric and weak on implementation, a fact associated with many Supreme Court opinions. In this regard, it is important to remember that there were two *Brown* decisions. The first, in 1954, made broad, equitable assertions about the way American society should function. The second *Brown* decision in 1955 sketched the framework for implementing the broad goals of the first decision. It required that schools be desegregated "with all deliberate speed."

The Justices hedged the moral force and equitable character of the first decision. Implementation became more deliberate than speedy. The Court asserted initially that the Constitution mandates equality, then it backed away nine months later, doing so in the face of political circumstances that it could not control.

Taken together, DuBois' color line remains, but it has been significantly adjusted, and *Brown* played a vital but not conclusive role in that adjustment. The problem today is how to make blacks and other historically under-represented groups successful given the reluctance of the social order to redistribute resources in a way that would facilitate broad change, a point that we will return to at the end. *Brown* at once drew strength from and enhanced the river of change that was running in America. *Brown* clearly deserves credit for beginning the elimination of legally sanctioned segregation. ...

In this sense, *Brown* was all about the meaning of equality. The term, however, has at least two different implications, one legal the other substantive. At the time of the decision, the most important meaning was legal. That is, *Brown* was argued over the question of whether legal segregation should be brought to an end. Race-based discrimination in public education was wrong because it was unequal—all persons should have the *opportunity* to attend schools of similar quality. And, as Chief Justice Warren emphasized in his opinion for the Court, separate but equal was inherently unequal.

Lurking just below the surface, and in some instances reflected in both the briefs and the decision of the Court, was another substantive meaning to equality. That was an equality of social outcomes—educational achievement, not just access to education. This view, by the way, is one of the reasons that countries such as South Africa have taken such a strong, although often ambivalent, interest in the opinion. It has been used by the courts there to insist, as does the South African Constitution, that the State has a positive obligation to make certain that this and other substantive rights—such as income, health care, and a clean environment—are realized.

But *Brown* was, at its heart, a legal and constitutional ruling, although as many commentators have noted, it was far more equitable than it was legal. That is, the decision aimed at doing the fair, fitting thing, not just propounding the law. While the Court demolished the legal basis of segregation, it made clear that the principal reason was that American society would be the better for doing so. In short, the decision operated in two-part harmony. The major chord was the legal destruction of segregation in public schools, but the minor, yet still important one, was to dignify American society by a moral command to end separate but equal.

The distinction is an important one. First, we tend to overload our expectations about laws and courts. There is no doubt, as the early nineteenth century French visitor to America, Alexis de Tocqueville noted, that Americans have been and are uncommonly consumed with the belief that law is the end of government. As a result, Americans tend to attribute an unusual level of authority to the law and to its ability to bring about change.

Second, however, one of the interesting facets of the original Plessy decision was the Court's view in 1896 that law could not change moral beliefs or alter social circumstances to which the majority was committed. Segregation was unstoppable legally, according to Justice Henry Billings *Brown*, because the law could never reshape the way white people felt about black people. In that circumstance, he concluded, legal segregation was acceptable as long as its results were equal.

Third, John W. Davis, the lawyer for the school board in *Brown* and some of the other desegregation cases, adopted just such a position. Davis insisted that it was possible to produce substantive equality while maintaining a bifurcated legal status for whites and black.

Fourth, what is fascinating in all of this is that the NAACP and its Legal Defense Fund agreed on one level with Davis. They were less interested in forcing unwanted social equality, in which the races would be cheek-by-jowl, but instead sought a legal mandate that the state would spend the money to achieve better classrooms, better schools, better principals, and better teachers.

The Supreme Court in general and Chief Justice Earl Warren in particular rejected that approach as itself being discriminatory. Once again, separate but equal, Warren noted, was inherently unequal. As a result, the Court conflated the ideas of legal and substantive equality and left generations to come to read different meanings into what the Justices actually intended to do and, as a result, the significance of what they did. . . .

Over time, . . . the connection between legal equality and substantive equality—these two threads in the *Brown* decision that were wrapped up in the broad concept of equity—began to merge. Legal equality was increasingly viewed as the means by which to reach the end of substantive equality. It seems, in retrospect, hard to believe that the Justices did not articulate this connection more fully, but then the Court achieved its unanimity by avoiding a commitment to specific outcomes and focusing instead on process. And it is also abundantly clear that the NAACP expected substantive results—not just better access to schools, but better schools with better teachers and with graduates who would go on to better lives. Over the next fifteen years, the Justices were forced to come to terms with the broader consequences of the legal sea change they had orchestrated. Just follow the Court's path from *McNeese v. Board of Education* to *Griffin v. County School Board* to *Swann v. Charlotte Mecklenburg Board of Education*, and we can see the Court re-charting its position.

Why did it do so? In short compass, those whom the Justices had expected to obey the law did not do so. Delay was the order of the day; violence emerged as the most dramatic form of resistance. As a result, by 1968 the Justices had moved into the business of requiring action that would produce substantive results and that would also evaluate the efforts of city, county, and state officials on a new scale: whether actual results were achieved. Did blacks attend mixed schools and how many? Were taxpayer dollars being used to achieve improvements in the schools? Was busing of students a workable means of achieving integration? The courts shifted from emphasizing process to measuring outcomes.

This shift helps us understand why commentators today are at odds with one another about the results of *Brown*. It also helps us understand why we continue to overvalue the role of law in promoting social change. There is only so much that courts can do.

These insights are important because both sides of the equation (at least where education was involved) turned out to be badly misguided, if not wrong.

Brown suggested that substantive equality would flow from the equality of educational opportunity produced through the decision. The Justices overestimated the power of law to overcome the pernicious racism that infected twentieth-century America. It also overestimated the power of education alone to counteract that same racism.

The *Brown* decision mustered a great deal of legal will, but it ultimately proved less than successful in mustering what was even more needed—political will. That political will was critical to any effort to allocate the resources necessary to foster substantive equality.

While *Brown*'s consequences flowed in many directions, it was ultimately a decision about education, principally K-12, and its future. According to the Harvard Project on School Desegregation, southern schools are becoming increasingly segregated. That is, the hope that the races in the South would come to learn together is receding. And, perhaps as important, the gap between white and Asian students and the gap between African American and Latino students are growing.

Why, we might ask, after a half-century of *Brown* have things changed so much yet stayed the same? And what is to be done to address these matters? ...

The problem was that many whites did not accept desegregation. There is an old line that the genius of America is the ability of its people to hold contradictory ideas simultaneously. In the 1840s and 1850s, for example, the anti-slavery founders of the Republican Party believed deeply in the idea of free soil and free labor, but they were equally committed to the idea that blacks were inherently inferior and that while they might not deserve the status of slaves, it did not follow that they should be accorded unalloyed liberty.

Much the same is true of many contemporary Americans, who believe that segregation is wrong but are quick to pack the family off to suburbs to escape all of the problems associated with the decline of the city, including black schools. Today, for example, in the city of Chicago, only approximately nine percent of public-school children are white, although the white population of the city is approximately forty-two percent. Indeed, over two-thirds of black children in Illinois attended majority black schools last year. Moreover, forty percent of these black children attend one of the state's 335 schools on academic watch, where students have failed state tests and other standards for four years in a row. Less than one percent of white children attend those schools. In short, in Illinois, separate but equal remains the reality for many black school children fifty years after *Brown*.

Then there is the language of gaps, such as the "learning gap." That term assumes that all students are equally positioned in contemporary public education and that through standardized testing and curricular mandates it becomes possible to close the gap between white and historically under-represented groups. This language is also one of the inheritances of *Brown*—one that comes essentially from John Davis and the school board's perspective. It says that if we simply create better schools and better teachers, no matter the racial make-up, the gap will close.

Today, the problem is even more challenging since we now live in a society in which discrimination based on race is no longer legal. It would seem, then, that the gap should be easier to close with just more hard work and structural changes.

One of the striking features of the *Brown* decision is the faith that it placed in public schooling. In essence, the Court viewed low achievement as primarily a symptom of disfranchisement, rather than a cause. Yet there seems little doubt that closing the learning gap will require something more, and probably something more than the rhetoric of "No Child Left Behind."

We are all hard pressed to object to a public policy aimed at equality. We want children to achieve, and we would be wrong to reject a policy that aims to do just that. Yet the language of leaving no child behind masks some fundamental differences that must be addressed if the structures aimed at eradicating inequality of opportunity are to be widely adopted by those who must implement them.

Fundamentally, the conversation most needed is not merely about structures and tests, but about money—a matter not fully addressed by No Child Left Behind. That means that a meaningful effort to close the gap in learning must be matched by a corresponding effort to close the gap in such areas as housing, hiring, and health care. Education is surely a public good in order to realize a democratic society. To their credit, Davis and the school boards who fought against desegregation realized as much. They made the telling point, lost on us today, that well funded schools were essential to student success. Ironically, they recognized that it is not so much a matter of leaving no child behind as it is making certain that no school is left behind.

But access to education, as the history of *Brown* teaches us, is not a sufficient condition. As Vanessa Siddle Walker reminds us, there remain three powerful facts about the post-*Brown* world in which we live. First, one-third of black children in high-poverty schools are taught by teachers out of field. Second, minority schools are three times as likely to have a teacher with three or fewer years of teaching experience and a teacher absentee rate averaging six to ten percent per day. And third, black children are often in schools with larger class sizes, less technology, greater concerns about safety, and more severe challenges for parental involvement. Acknowledging these inequities might help to transform the debate over the learning gap into a meaningful dialogue about the resource gap.

These same issues echo through public higher education. While affirmative action is an important and logical tool to use in addressing the issues raised by *Brown*, it is clear that admissions policies by themselves do not write the entire text for the future of access and success in higher education. In many states, the fastest growing part of the population is from historically underrepresented groups with little prior experience in higher education. The Supreme Court's recent decision in *Grutter* providing access to a select number of students from these historically underrepresented groups to America's most selective institutions is welcome, but it is far from a solution. That is because, as reports from the American Council on Education ("ACE") regularly make clear, the single greatest barrier to higher education for most students—and minority students especially—is not admissions policies. "Rather, it is the inability of applicants to gain a sufficient financial foothold to enter, persist in, and then graduate from any institution—selective or not." ...

By 2010 the number of qualified students from families with incomes below $50,000 who will not attend four-year colleges within two years of graduating high school will be 4.4 million. The number who will not seek any post-secondary education will total two million. " '[S]mart poor kids go to college at the same rate as stupid rich kids, and that's a tragedy.' "

That is *the* crisis in higher education. And it is the echo, if you will, of the unresolved tension between legal and substantive equality raised in *Brown*. A tension that directly impacts students from historically under-represented groups, lower-income families, and families with little or no experience with higher education. It reminds us that the best way to address the vision of *Brown* is to ensure that every student seeking education—whether K–12 or higher education—can afford it and that the quality of the experience that they receive in less-noted schools and universities is comparable to that showered on students in elite institutions. "At least on the public side, the responsibility to do so rests squarely with the states that are now abandoning the social contract they forged with [public K–12 and] higher education long ago," a contract that carries a codicil. That codicil calls for universities to keep tuition at a level that would not dampen access and in return states would provide subsidies, including direct financial aid.

That contract, however, is quickly dissolving as tough economic times and other demands, notably K–12, force choices that invariably pit higher education against public schools. As a result, higher education institutions that have historically provided access and opportunity increasingly will be unable to fulfill that role and maintain educational quality. Even if the full legacy of *Brown* were realized in the public schools, it is ironically becoming harder to realize in America's universities and colleges.

In the end, *Brown* falls short because it could not and did not address the fundamental problem that levels of income should not determine levels of opportunity; equity and access must be significant components of a successful vision of educational equality. Fifty years after *Brown*, the fate of minority and other students, whether in K–12 or higher education, rests importantly but not conclusively on that decision. Better financial support and greater political—not just legal—will are what is needed to provide educational opportunities that will make the real difference.

✠ F U R T H E R   R E A D I N G

Ball, Howard. Bakke *Case: Race, Education, and Affirmative Action* (2000).
Bartley, Numan. *The Rise of Massive Resistance: Race and Politics in the South Since the 1950s* (1969).
Belknap, Michal R. *Federal Law and Southern Order: Racial Violence and Constitutional Conflict in the Post-Brown South* (1987).
_____. *The Supreme Court under Earl Warren, 1953–1969* (2004).
_____. *The Vinson Court: Justices, Rulings, and Legacy* (2004).
Berman, William C. *The Politics of Civil Rights in the Truman Administration* (1970).
Bickel, Alexander. *The Morality of Consent* (1975).

Brauer, Carl M. *John F. Kennedy and the Second Reconstruction* (1977).

Burk, Robert F. *The Eisenhower Administration and Black Civil Rights, 1953–1961* (1984).

Cottrol, Robert J. *Brown v. Board of Education: Caste, Culture, and the Constitution* (2003).

Dudziak, Mary. *Cold War Civil Rights: Race and the Image of American Democracy* (2000).

Finkelman, Paul. "Civil Rights in Historical Context: In Defense of *Brown*," *Harvard Law Review*, 118 (2005): 973–1029.

Freyer, Tony A., ed. *Defending Constitutional Rights: Frank M. Johnson* (2001).

_____. *Little Rock on Trial: Cooper v. Aaron and School Desegregation* (2007).

Garrow, David J. "'Happy' Birthday, *Brown v. Board of Education*? *Brown*'s Fiftieth Anniversary and the New Critics of Supreme Court Muscularity," *Virginia Law Review*, 90 (2004): 693–729.

Graham, Hugh Davis. *The Civil Rights Era: Origins and Development of National Policy, 1960–1972* (1990).

Klarman, Michael J. *From Jim Crow to Civil Rights: The Supreme Court and the Struggle for Racial Equality* (2004).

Kluger, Richard. *Simple Justice: The History of Brown v. Board of Education and Black America's Struggle for Equality* (1976).

Lawson, Steven F. *Black Ballots: Voting Rights in the South, 1944–1969* (1976).

Martin, Waldo E. Jr. *Brown v. Board of Education: A Brief History with Documents* (1998).

Morsink, Johannes. *The Universal Declaration of Human Rights: Origins, Drafting, Intent* (1999).

Nieman, Donald. *Promises to Keep: African Americans and the Constitutional Order, 1776 to the Present* (1991).

Orfield, Gary, Susan Eaton, and the Harvard Project on School Desegregation, eds. *Dismantling Desegregation: The Quiet Reversal of Brown v. Board of Education* (1996).

Patterson, James T. *Brown v. Board of Education: A Civil Rights Milestone and its Troubled Legacy* (2001).

Perry, Barbara A. *The Michigan Affirmative Action Cases* (2007).

Rosenberg, Gerald N. *The Hollow Hope: Can Courts Bring About Social Change?* (1991).

Schwartz, Bernard. *Behind Bakke: Affirmative Action and the Supreme Court* (1988).

Tushnet, Mark V. *Making Civil Rights Law: Thurgood Marshall and the Supreme Court, 1936–1961* (1994).

_____. *The NAACP's Legal Strategy against Segregated Education, 1925–1950* (1987).

Urofsky, Melvin I. *The Warren Court: Justices, Rulings, and Legacy* (2001).

Wilkinson, J. Harvie. *From Brown to Bakke: The Supreme Court and School Integration, 1954–1978* (1979).

Wolters, Raymond. *The Burden of Brown: Thirty Years of School Desegregation* (1984).

Woodward, C. Vann. *The Strange Career of Jim Crow* (1955).

Zelden, Charles. *Battle for the Black Ballot: Smith v. Allwright and the Defeat of the Texas All-White Primary* (2004).

Abortion Rights: The United States and South Africa Compared

Abortion has been one of the most explosive political and constitutional issues in recent American history. Traditionally, under common law, the practice carried no legal penalties so long as it occurred before "quickening," the period at about 4 or 5 months when the fetus begins to move in the womb. (The term originated during the Middle Ages, when theologians believed that such movement indicated the presence of a soul.) Not until the nineteenth century did American lawmakers take steps to criminalize abortion. With an apparent rise in abortions at mid-century, doctors and religious leaders waged a concerted campaign against the practice. In response, state legislatures imposed a variety of restrictive measures and eliminated the distinction based on quickening. By the beginning of the twentieth century, nearly all abortions in the United States were illegal.

A half century later, three interrelated developments contributed to a dramatic shift in the social and legal landscape with regard to abortion. First, the African–American Civil Rights Movement gave a new boost to a tradition of female activism dating back to the 1848 Declaration of the Seneca Falls Convention. Although women had achieved the right to vote with the adoption of the Nineteenth Amendment, during the 1960s, a revitalized women's movement initiated a new push for constitutional equality. Second, the sexual revolution of that era prompted women to view access to birth control and reproductive freedom as essential components of the women's rights agenda. The climate of social protest and resistance to authority, particularly among the nation's young people, fostered opposition to traditional mores, encouraged sexual freedom, and led to increased numbers of unmarried women. Third, growing out of these social movements, the economic role of women shifted dramatically during the 1960s and 1970s. Women attended college and entered the workforce in huge numbers, so that by 1980, 51.5 percent of all American adult women held jobs outside of the home. All of these developments provide the context for understanding the creation of a constitutional right to privacy and the landmark 1973 decision in Roe v. Wade that followed. The ruling in Roe, of course, set off a fierce political and moral debate over abortion that has yet to subside.

Comparison often serves as a useful form of analysis, and on the matter of abortion, the Republic of South Africa provides an interesting counterpoint to the experience of the United States. In 1994, South Africa ended the practice of apartheid, the strict categorization and segregation of the races that the white minority had imposed in 1948. In a bold break with the past, the new democratically elected government drafted one of the most liberal constitutions in the world with regard to human rights. Under the system of apartheid and customary law that had held sway in South Africa, women had enjoyed few legal protections. The new constitution's lengthy Bill of Rights, in contrast, included clear constitutional language protecting a right to privacy, prohibiting gender discrimination, and affirming "the right to make decisions concerning reproduction." South Africa's drafting of constitutional provisions regarding such matters stands in clear contrast to the experience of the United States, where abortion rights—because they are not mentioned in the constitutional text—have evolved in a more uneven fashion.

An examination of abortion rights in America, in light of the South African experience, poses a variety of questions. Was Roe v. Wade an example of a well-reasoned constitutional decision, or did it represent the excesses of judicial activism? Would the supporters of abortion rights have been better served by seeking an amendment to the constitution—as in South Africa—to enshrine the right to terminate a pregnancy? Why has the abortion controversy in the United States, for the most part, remained a battle in the courts rather than in the Congress? If abortion is a women's rights issue, why did the Equal Rights Amendment (ERA) fail while Roe has survived? What role has American public opinion played in protecting the right to an abortion? What place should the states have, if any, in regulating abortion?

✣ D O C U M E N T S

Griswold v. Connecticut, Document 1, involved an 1879 Connecticut statute prohibiting the use of any drug or device to prevent conception. Two members of the Planned Parenthood League of Connecticut, who had been prosecuted under the statute, challenged the law, and the Supreme Court of Errors of Connecticut upheld their conviction. On appeal to the U.S. Supreme Court, Justice William O. Douglas wrote for a seven-justice majority in overturning the anti-contraception law. In the process, Douglas ignited a firestorm over un-enumerated constitutional rights and the existence of a right to privacy. Justice Hugo Black wrote a notable dissent.

Passage of the Civil Rights Act of 1964 reflected the growing urgency surrounding gender discrimination. Title VII of the act banned discrimination in employment on account of sex. When the federal government balked at enforcing it, activists formed the National Organization for Women (NOW) in 1966. By the early 1970s, feminists achieved overwhelming congressional approval of an Equal Rights Amendment, Document 2. Still, the requisite three-fourths of the states never ratified it. The proposed amendment has been introduced in every Congress since 1982.

The same year that the Equal Rights Amendment went to the states, the Supreme Court decided *Roe v. Wade*, Document 3. In a 7-2 decision, Justice Harry Blackmun's majority opinion, building on the *Griswold* decision, established a limited right to an abortion. Dissenting Justices William Rehnquist and Bryon White argued that the Court had far exceeded its authority in the decision. Opposition to abortion, as well as to the women's movement that supported reproductive rights, soon gained momentum. Antiabortionists and antifeminists—mostly from the ranks of the nation's conservative Christians—voiced grave concerns over the decline of traditional values and changes in gender roles. The views of the Rev. Jerry Falwell, Document 4, represent the fundamentalist Christian strain of antifeminism. In 1979, Falwell founded the Moral Majority, a group that wielded significant influence in national politics for the next decade. With Republicans ascendant during the 1980s, Presidents Ronald Reagan and George H.W. Bush proclaimed their opposition to *Roe* and appointed conservative justices to the Court. In 1992, in *Planned Parenthood of Southeastern Pennsylvania v. Casey*, Document 5, the Court upheld *Roe* by a vote of 5-4 at the same time that it sustained a variety of abortion restrictions enacted by the state of Pennsylvania. In an unusual step, Justices Sandra Day O'Connor, Anthony M. Kennedy, and David H. Souter all wrote the majority opinion, which was joined in part by Justices Blackmun and John Paul Stevens.

After the end of apartheid, the democratically elected government of South Africa wrote a new constitution in 1996, Chapter two of which is a comprehensive Bill of Rights. Several of those rights pertaining to women are reprinted here as Document 6. In 1998, the High Court of South Africa, Transvaal Provincial Division, considered a constitutional challenge to the Choice of Termination of Pregnancy Act of 1996, which had established an unrestricted right to abortion during the first 12 weeks of pregnancy and a limited right to abortion after that point. In *Christian Lawyers Association of South Africa v. Minister of Health*, Document 7, the Court analyzed the act within the context of both the South African Constitution and international law.

✤ D O C U M E N T   1

Griswold v. Connecticut, 1965

Mr. Justice Douglas delivered the opinion of the Court.

... The foregoing cases suggest that specific guarantees in the Bill of Rights have penumbras, formed by emanations from those guarantees that help give them life and substance.... Various guarantees create zones of privacy. The right of association contained in the penumbra of the First Amendment is one, as we have seen. The Third Amendment in its prohibition against the quartering of soldiers "in any house" in time of peace without the consent of the owner is another facet of that privacy. The Fourth Amendment explicitly affirms the "right of the people to be secure in their persons, houses, papers, and effects, against unreasonable searches and seizures." The Fifth Amendment in its Self-Incrimination Clause enables the citizen to create a zone of privacy which government may not force him to surrender to his detriment. The Ninth Amendment provides: "The enumeration in the Constitution, of certain rights, shall not be construed to deny or disparage others retained by the people."

The Fourth and Fifth Amendments were described in *Boyd v. United States*, ..., as protection against all governmental invasions "of the sanctity of a man's home and the privacies of life." We recently referred in *Mapp v. Ohio*, ..., to the Fourth Amendment as creating a "right to privacy, no less important than any other right carefully and particularly reserved to the people." ...

We have had many controversies over these penumbral rights of "privacy and repose." ... These cases bear witness that the right of privacy which presses for recognition here is a legitimate one.

The present case, then, concerns a relationship lying within the zone of privacy created by several fundamental constitutional guarantees. And it concerns a law which, in forbidding the *use* of contraceptives rather than regulating their manufacture or sale, seeks to achieve its goals by means having a maximum destructive impact upon that relationship. Such a law cannot stand in light of the familiar principle, so often applied by this Court, that a "governmental purpose to control or prevent activities constitutionally subject to state regulation may not be achieved by means which sweep unnecessarily broadly and thereby invade the area of protected freedoms." *NAACP v. Alabama,* ... Would we allow the police to search the sacred precincts of marital bedrooms for telltale signs of the use of contraceptives? The very idea is repulsive to the notions of privacy surrounding the marriage relationship.

We deal with a right of privacy older than the Bill of Rights—older than our political parties, older than our school system. Marriage is a coming together for better or for worse, hopefully enduring, and intimate to the degree of being sacred. It is an association that promotes a way of life, not causes; a harmony in living, not political faiths; a bilateral loyalty, not commercial or social projects. Yet it is an association for as noble a purpose as any involved in our prior decisions. ...

Mr. Justice Black, with whom Mr. Justice Stewart joins, dissenting.

... The Court talks about a constitutional "right of privacy" as though there is some constitutional provision or provisions forbidding any law ever to be passed which might abridge the "privacy" of individuals. But there is not. There are, of course, guarantees in certain specific constitutional provisions which are designed in part to protect privacy at certain times and places with respect to certain activities. Such, for example, is the Fourth Amendment's guarantee against "unreasonable searches and seizures." But I think it belittles that Amendment to talk about it as though it protects nothing but "privacy." To treat it that way is to give it a niggardly interpretation, not the kind of liberal reading I think any Bill of Rights provision should be given. The average man would very likely not have his feelings soothed any more by having his property seized openly than by having it seized privately and by stealth. He simply wants his property left alone. And a person can be just as much, if not more, irritated, annoyed and injured by an unceremonious public arrest by a policeman as he is by a seizure in the privacy of his office or home.

One of the most effective ways of diluting or expanding a constitutionally guaranteed right is to substitute for the crucial word or words of a constitutional guarantee another word or words, more or less flexible and more or less restricted in meaning. This fact is well illustrated by the use of the term "right of privacy" as a comprehensive substitute for the Fourth Amendment's guarantee against "unreasonable searches and seizures." "Privacy" is a broad, abstract and ambiguous concept which can easily be shrunken in meaning but which can also, on the other hand, easily be interpreted as a constitutional ban against many things other than searches and seizures. I have expressed the view many times that First Amendment freedoms, for example, have suffered from a failure of the courts to stick to the simple language of the First Amendment in construing it, instead of invoking multitudes of words substituted for those the Framers used. ... For these reasons I get nowhere in this case by talk about a constitutional "right of privacy" as an emanation from one or more constitutional provisions. I like my privacy as well as the next one, but I am nevertheless compelled to admit that government has a right to invade it unless prohibited by some specific constitutional provision. For these reasons I cannot agree with the Court's judgment and the reasons it gives for holding this Connecticut law unconstitutional. ...

✤ *D O C U M E N T   2*

A Proposed Constitutional Amendment Promises Equal Rights for Women, 1972

The Senate and House Joint Resolution containing the proposed Equal Rights Amendment provides as follows:

Resolved by the Senate and House of Representatives of the United States of America in Congress assembled (two-thirds of each House concurring therein), That the following article is proposed as an amendment to the Constitution of the United States, which shall be valid to all intents and purposes as part of the Constitution when ratified by the legislatures of three-fourths of the several States within seven years from the date of its submission by the Congress:

Section 1   Equality of rights under the law shall not be denied or abridged by the United States or by any State on account of sex.

Section 2   The Congress shall have the power to enforce, by appropriate legislation, the provisions of this article.

Section 3   This amendment shall take effect two years after the date of ratification.

✤ *D O C U M E N T   3*

Roe v. Wade, 1973

Mr. Justice Blackmun delivered the opinion of the Court....

We forthwith acknowledge our awareness of the sensitive and emotional nature of the abortion controversy, of the vigorous opposing views, even among physicians, and of the deep and seemingly absolute convictions that the subject inspires. One's philosophy, one's experiences, one's religious training, one's attitudes toward life and family and their values, and the moral standards one establishes and seeks to observe, are all likely to influence and to color one's thinking and conclusions about abortion.

In addition, population growth, pollution, poverty, and racial overtones tend to complicate and not to simplify the problem.

Our task, of course, is to resolve the issue by constitutional measurement, free of emotion and of predilection. We seek earnestly to do this, and, because we do, we have inquired into, and in this opinion place some emphasis upon, medical and medical-legal history and what that history reveals about man's attitudes toward the abortion procedure over the centuries....

V

The principal thrust of appellant's attack on the Texas statutes is that they improperly invade a right, said to be possessed by the pregnant woman, to choose to terminate her pregnancy. Appellant would discover this right in the concept of personal "liberty" embodied in the Fourteenth Amendment's Due Process Clause; or in personal, marital, familial, and sexual privacy said to be protected by the Bill of Rights or its penumbras.... Before addressing this claim, we feel it desirable briefly to survey, in several aspects, the history of abortion, for such insight as that history may afford us, and then to examine the state purposes and interests behind the criminal abortion laws.

VI

It perhaps is not generally appreciated that the restrictive criminal abortion laws in effect in a majority of States today are of relatively recent vintage. Those laws, generally proscribing abortion or its attempt at any time during pregnancy except when necessary to preserve that pregnant woman's life, are not of ancient or even of common-law origin. Instead, they derive from statutory changes effected, for the most part, in the latter half of the nineteenth century....

VIII

The Constitution does not explicitly mention any right of privacy. In a line of decisions, however,... the Court has recognized that a right of personal privacy, or a guarantee of certain areas or zones of privacy, does exist under the Constitution. In varying contexts, the Court or individual Justices have, indeed, found at least the roots of that right in the First Amendment,...; in the Fourth and Fifth Amendments,...; in the penumbras of the Bill of Rights, *Griswold v. Connecticut*,..., in the Ninth Amendment, *id.* at 486 (Goldberg, J., concurring); or in the concept of liberty guaranteed by the first section of the Fourteenth Amendment.... These decisions made it clear that only personal rights that can be deemed "fundamental" or "implicit in the concept of ordered liberty," *Palko v. Connecticut* ... (1937), are included in this guarantee of personal privacy. They also make it clear that the right has some extension to activities relating to marriage....

This right of privacy, whether it be founded in the Fourteenth Amendment's concept of personal liberty and restrictions upon state action, as we feel it is, or, as the District Court determined, in the Ninth Amendment's reservation of rights to the people, is broad enough to encompass a woman's decision whether or not to terminate her pregnancy. The detriment that the State would impose upon the pregnant woman by denying this choice altogether is apparent. Specific and direct harm medically diagnosable even in early pregnancy may be involved. Maternity, or additional offspring, may force upon the woman a distressful life and future. Psychological harm may be imminent. Mental and physical health may be taxed by child care. There is also the distress, for all concerned, associated with the unwanted child and there is the problem of bringing a child into a family already unable psychologically and otherwise, to care for it. In other cases, as in this one the additional difficulties and continuing stigma of unwed motherhood may be involved. All these are factors the woman and her responsible physician necessarily will consider in consultation.

On the basis of elements such as these, appellant and some *amici* argue that the woman's right is absolute and that she is entitled to terminate her pregnancy at whatever time, in whatever way, and for whatever reason she alone chooses. With this we do not agree. Appellant's arguments that Texas either has no valid interest at all in regulating the abortion decision, or no interest strong enough to support any limitation upon the woman's sole determination, are unpersuasive. The Court's decisions recognizing a right of privacy also acknowledge that some regulation in areas protected by that right is appropriate. As noted above, a State may properly assert important interests in safeguarding health, in maintaining medical standards, and in protecting potential life. At some point in pregnancy, these respective interests become sufficiently compelling to sustain regulation of the factors that govern the abortion decision. The privacy right involved, therefore, cannot be said to be absolute. In fact, it is not clear to us that the claim asserted by some *amici* that one has an unlimited right to do with one's body as one pleases bears a close relationship to the right of privacy previously articulated in the Court's decisions. The Court has refused to recognize an unlimited right of this kind in the past. ...

We, therefore, conclude that the right of personal privacy includes the abortion decision, but that this right is not unqualified and must be considered against important state interests in regulation. ... [This] right nonetheless, is not absolute and is subject to some limitations; and ... at some point the state interests as to protection of health, medical standards, and prenatal life, become dominant. ...

Where certain "fundamental rights" are involved, the Court has held that regulation limiting these rights may be justified only by a "compelling state interest," ... and that legislative enactments must be narrowly drawn to express only the legitimate state interests at stake. ...

In the recent abortion cases, ... courts have recognized these principles. Those striking down state laws have generally scrutinized the State's interests in protecting health and potential life, and have concluded that neither interest justified broad limitations on the reasons for which a physician and his pregnant patient might decide that she should have an abortion in the early stages of pregnancy. Courts sustaining state laws have held that the State's determinations to protect health or prenatal life are dominant and constitutionally justifiable.

IX

The District Court held that the appellee failed to meet his burden of demonstrating that the Texas statute's infringement upon Roe's rights was necessary to support a compelling state interest, and that, although the appellee presented "several compelling justifications for state presence in the area of abortions," the statutes outstripped these justifications and swept "far beyond any areas of compelling state interest." ... Appellant and appellee both contest that holding. Appellant, as has been indicated, claims an absolute right that bars any state imposition of criminal penalties in the area. Appellee argues that the State's determination to recognize and protect prenatal life from and after conception constitutes a compelling state interest. As noted above, we do not agree fully with either formulation.

A. The appellee and certain *amici* argue that the fetus is a "person" within the language and meaning of the Fourteenth Amendment. In support of this, they outline at length and in detail the well-known facts of fetal development. If this suggestion of personhood is established, the appellant's case, of course, collapses, for the fetus' right to life would then be guaranteed specifically by the Amendment ... [but] no case [can] be cited that holds that a fetus is a person within the meaning of the Fourteenth Amendment.

The Constitution does not define "person" in so many words. Section 1 of the Fourteenth Amendment contains three references to "person." The first, in defining "citizens," speaks of "persons born or naturalized in the United States." ... "Person" is used in other places in the Constitution. ... But in nearly all these instances, the use of the word is such that it has application only postnatally. None indicates, with any assurance, that it has any possible prenatal application.

All this, together with our observation, ... that throughout the major portion of the nineteenth century prevailing legal abortion practices were far freer than they are today, persuades us that the word "person," as used in the Fourteenth Amendment, does not include the unborn. This is in accord with the results reached in those few cases where the issue has been squarely presented. ...

B. The pregnant woman cannot be isolated in her privacy. She carries an embryo and, later, a fetus. ... The situation therefore is inherently different from marital intimacy, or bedroom possession of obscene material, or marriage, or procreation, or education. ... As we have intimated above, it is reasonable and appropriate for a State to decide that at some point in time another interest, that of health of the mother or that of potential human life, becomes significantly involved. The woman's privacy is no longer sole and any right of privacy she possesses must be measured accordingly.

Texas urges that, apart from the Fourteenth Amendment, life begins at conception and is present throughout pregnancy, and that, therefore, the State has a compelling interest in protecting that life from and after conception. We need not resolve the difficult question of when life begins. When those trained in the respective disciplines of medicine, philosophy, and theology are unable to arrive at any consensus, the judiciary, at this point in the development of man's knowledge, is not in a position to speculate as to the answer. ...

In areas other than criminal abortion, the law has been reluctant to endorse any theory that life, as we recognize it, begins before live birth or to accord legal rights to the unborn except in narrowly defined situations and except when the rights are contingent upon live birth. ...

X

In view of all this, we do not agree that, by adopting one theory of life, Texas may override the rights of the pregnant woman that are at stake. We repeat, however, that the State does have an important and legitimate interest in preserving and protecting the health of the pregnant woman, whether she be a resident of the State or a nonresident who seeks medical consultation and treatment there, and that it has still *another* important and legitimate interest in protecting the potentiality of human life. These interests are separate and distinct. Each grows in substantiality as the woman approaches term and, at a point during pregnancy, each becomes "compelling."

With respect to the State's important and legitimate interest in the health of the mother, the "compelling" point, in the light of present medical knowledge, is at approximately the end of the first trimester. This is so because of the now-established medical fact, referred to above, that until the end of the first trimester mortality in abortion may be less than mortality in normal childbirth. It follows that, from and after this point, a State may regulate the abortion procedure to the extent that the regulation reasonably relates to the preservation and protection of maternal health.

Examples of permissible state regulation in this area are requirements as to the qualifications of the person who is to perform the abortion; as to the licensure of that person; as to the facility in which the procedure is to be performed, that is, whether it must be a hospital or may be a clinic or some other place of less-than-hospital status; as to the licensing of the facility; and the like.

This means, on the other hand, that, for the period of pregnancy prior to this "compelling" point, the attending physician, in consultation with his patient, is free to determine, without regulation by the State, that, in his medical judgment, the patient's pregnancy should be terminated. If that decision is reached, the judgment may be effectuated by an abortion free of interference by the State.

With respect to the State's important and legitimate interest in potential life, the "compelling" point is at viability. This is so because the fetus then presumably has the capability of meaningful life outside the mother's womb. State regulation protective of fetal life after viability thus has both logical and biological justifications. If the State is interested in protecting fetal life after viability, it may go so far as to proscribe abortion during that period, except when it is necessary to preserve the life or health of the mother.

Measured against these standards, Article 1196 of the Texas Penal Code, in restricting legal abortions to those "procured or attempted by medical advice for the purpose of saving the life of the mother," sweeps too broadly. The statute made no distinction between abortions performed early in pregnancy and those performed later, and it limits to a single reason, "saving" the mother's life, the legal justification for the procedure. The statute, therefore, cannot survive the constitutional attack made upon it here....

XI

To summarize and to repeat:

1. A state criminal abortion statute of the current Texas type, that excepts from criminality only a *life-saving* procedure on behalf of the mother, without regard to pregnancy stage and without recognition of the other interests involved, is violative of the Due Process Clause of the Fourteenth Amendment.

   (a) For the stage prior to approximately the end of the first trimester, the abortion decision and its effectuation must be left to the medical judgment of the pregnant woman's attending physician.
   (b) For the stage subsequent to approximately the end of the first trimester, the State, in promoting its interest in the health of the mother, may, if it chooses, regulate the abortion procedure in ways that are reasonably related to maternal health.
   (c) For the stage subsequent to viability, the State in promoting its interest in the potentiality of human life may, if it chooses, regulate, and even proscribe, abortion except where it is necessary, in appropriate medical judgment, for the preservation of the life or health of the mother.

2. The State may define the term "physician," as it has been employed in the preceding paragraphs of this part XI of this opinion, to mean only a physician currently

licensed by the State, and may proscribe any abortion by a person who is not a physician as so defined. ...

Mr. Justice Rehnquist, dissenting. ...

The Court's opinion brings to the decision of this troubling question both extensive historical fact and a wealth of legal scholarship. While the opinion thus commands my respect, I find myself nonetheless in fundamental disagreement with those parts of it that invalidate the Texas statute in question, and therefore dissent.

I

The Court's opinion decides that a State may impose virtually no restriction on the performance of abortions during the first trimester of pregnancy. Our previous decisions indicate that a necessary predicate for such an opinion is a plaintiff who was in her first trimester of pregnancy at some time during the pendency of her lawsuit. While a party may vindicate his own constitutional rights, he may not seek vindication for the rights of others. ... The Court's statement of facts in this case makes clear, however, that the record in no way indicates the presence of such a plaintiff. We know only that plaintiff Roe at the time of filing her complaint was a pregnant woman; for aught that appears in this record, she may have been in her *last* trimester of pregnancy as of the date the complaint was filed.

Nothing in the Court's opinion indicates that Texas might not constitutionally apply its proscription of abortion as written to a woman in that stage of pregnancy. Nonetheless, the Court uses her complaint against the Texas statute as a fulcrum for deciding that States may impose virtually no restrictions on medical abortions performed during the *first* trimester of pregnancy. In deciding such a hypothetical lawsuit, the Court departs from the long-standing admonition that it should never "formulate a rule of constitutional law broader than is required by the precise facts to which it is to be applied." ...

II

Even if there were a plaintiff in this case capable of litigating the issue which the Court decides, I would reach a conclusion opposite to that reached by the Court. I have difficulty in concluding, as the Court does, that the right of "privacy" is involved in this case. Texas, by the statute here challenged, bars the performance of a medical abortion by a licensed physician on a plaintiff such as *Roe*. A transaction resulting in an operation such as this is not "private" in the ordinary usage of the word. Nor is the "privacy" that the Court finds here even a distant relative of the freedom from searches and seizures protected by the Fourth Amendment to the Constitution, which the Court has referred to as embodying a right to privacy. ...

If the Court means by the term "privacy" no more than that the claim of a person to be free from unwanted state regulation of consensual transactions may be a form of "liberty" protected by the Fourteenth Amendment, there is no doubt that similar claims have been upheld in our earlier decisions on the basis of that liberty. I agree with the statement of Mr. Justice Stewart in his concurring opinion that the "liberty," against deprivation of which without due process the Fourteenth Amendment protects, embraces more than the rights found in the Bill of Rights. But that liberty is not guaranteed absolutely against deprivation, only against deprivation without due process of law. The test traditionally applied in the area of social and economic legislation is whether or not a law such as that challenged has a rational relation to a valid state objective. ... The Due Process Clause of the Fourteenth Amendment undoubtedly does place a limit, albeit a broad one, on legislative power to enact laws such as this. If the Texas statute were to prohibit an abortion even where the mother's life is in jeopardy, I have little doubt that such a statute would lack a rational relation to a valid state objective under the test stated in *Williamson*. But the Court's sweeping invalidation of any restrictions on abortion during the first trimester is impossible to justify under that standard, and the conscious weighing of competing factors that the Court's opinion apparently substitutes for the established test is far more appropriate to a legislative judgment than to a judicial one. ...

As in *Lochner* and similar cases applying substantive due process standards to economic and social welfare legislation, the adoption of the compelling state interest standard will inevitably require this Court to examine the legislative policies and pass on the wisdom of these policies in the very process of deciding whether a particular state interest put forward may or may not be "compelling." The decision here to break pregnancy into three distinct terms and to outline the permissible restrictions the State may impose in each one, for example, partakes more of judicial legislation than it does of a determination of the intent of the drafters of the Fourteenth Amendment.

The fact that a majority of the States reflecting, after all, the majority sentiment in those States, have had restrictions on abortions for at least a century is a strong indication, it seems to me, that the asserted right to an abortion is not "so rooted in the traditions and conscience of our people as to be ranked as fundamental.". ... Even today, when society's views on abortion are changing, the very existence of the debate is evidence that the "right" to an abortion is not so universally acceptable as the appellant would have us believe.

To reach its result, the Court necessarily has had to find within the scope of the Fourteenth Amendment a right that was apparently completely unknown to the drafters of the Amendment. As early as 1821, the first state law dealing directly with abortion was enacted by the Connecticut Legislature. ... By the time of the adoption of the Fourteenth Amendment in 1868, there were at least 36 laws enacted by state or territorial legislatures limiting abortion. While many States have amended or updated their laws, 21 of the laws on the books of 1868 remain in effect today. ...

There apparently was no question concerning the validity of this provision or of any of the other state statutes when the Fourteenth Amendment was adopted. The only conclusion possible from this history is that the drafters did not intend to have the Fourteenth Amendment withdraw from the States the power to legislate with respect to this matter.

III

Even if one were to agree that the case that the court decides were here, and that the enunciation of the substantive constitutional law in the Court's opinion were proper, the actual disposition of the case by the Court is still difficult to justify. The Texas statute is struck down in *toto*, even though the Court apparently concedes that at later periods of pregnancy Texas might impose these selfsame statutory limitations on abortion. My understanding of past practice is that a statute found to be invalid as applied to a particular plaintiff, but not unconstitutional as a whole, is not simply "struck down" but is, instead, declared unconstitutional as applied to the fact situation before the Court. ...

For all of the foregoing reasons, I respectfully dissent.

✠ *D O C U M E N T   4*

Fundamentalist Pastor Jerry Falwell Denounces the ERA, 1980

I believe that at the foundation of the women's liberation movement there is a minority core of women who were once bored with life, whose real problems are spiritual problems. Many women have never accepted their God-given roles. They live in disobedience to God's laws and have promoted their godless philosophy throughout our society. God Almighty created men and women biologically different and with differing needs and roles. He made men and women to complement each other and to love each other. Not all the women involved in the feminist movement are radicals. Some are misinformed, and some are lonely women who like being housewives and helpmeets and mothers, but whose husbands spend little time at home and who take no interest in their wives and children. Sometimes the full load of rearing a family becomes a great burden to a woman who is not supported by a man. Women who work should be respected and accorded dignity and equal rewards for equal work. But this is not what the present feminist movement and equal rights movement are all about.

The Equal Rights Amendment is a delusion. I believe that women deserve more than equal rights. And, in families and in nations where the Bible is believed, Christian women are honored above men. Only in places where the Bible is believed and practiced do women receive more than equal rights. Men and women have differing strengths. The Equal Rights Amendment can never do for women what needs to be done for them. Women need to know Jesus Christ as their Lord and Savior and be under His Lordship. They need a man who knows Jesus Christ as his Lord and Savior, and they need to be part of a home where their husband is a godly leader and where there is a Christian family.

The Equal Rights Amendment strikes at the foundation of our entire social structure. If passed, this amendment would accomplish exactly the opposite of its outward claims. By mandating an absolute equality under the law, it will actually take away many of the special rights women now enjoy. ERA is not merely a political issue, but a moral issue as well. A definite violation of holy Scripture, ERA defies the mandate that "the husband is the head of the wife, even as Christ is the head of the church" (Ep. 5:23). In 1 Peter 3:7 we read that husbands are to give their wives honor as unto the weaker vessel, that they are both heirs together of the grace of life. Because a woman is weaker does not mean that she is less important.

✤ D O C U M E N T   5

Planned Parenthood of Southeastern Pennsylvania v. Casey, 1992

At issue in these cases are five provisions of the Pennsylvania Abortion Control Act of 1982, as amended in 1988 and 1989. ... The Act requires that a woman seeking an abortion give her informed consent prior to the abortion procedure, and specifies that she be provided with certain information at least 24 hours before the abortion is performed. §3205. For a minor to obtain an abortion, the Act requires the informed consent of one of her parents, but provides for a judicial bypass option if the minor does not wish to or cannot obtain a parent's consent. §3206. Another provision of the Act requires that, unless certain exceptions apply, a married woman seeking an abortion must sign a statement indicating that she has notified her husband of her intended abortion. §3209. The Act exempts compliance with these three requirements in the event of a "medical emergency," which is defined in §3203 of the Act. See §§3203, 3205(a), 3206(a), 3209(c). In addition to the above provisions regulating the performance of abortions, the Act imposes certain reporting requirements on facilities that provide abortion services. §§3207(b), 3214(a), 3214(f).

Before any of these provisions took effect, the petitioners, who are five abortion clinics and one physician representing himself as well as a class of physicians who provide abortion services, brought this suit seeking declaratory and injunctive relief. Each provision was challenged as unconstitutional on its face. ...

It must be stated at the outset and with clarity that *Roe*'s essential holding, the holding we reaffirm, has three parts. First is a recognition of the right of the woman to choose to have an abortion before viability and to obtain it without undue interference from the State. Before viability, the State's interests are not strong enough to support a prohibition of abortion or the imposition of a substantial obstacle to the woman's effective right to elect the procedure. Second is a confirmation of the State's power to restrict abortions after fetal viability, if the law contains exceptions for pregnancies which endanger the woman's life or health. And third is the principle that the State has legitimate interests from the outset of the pregnancy in protecting the health of the woman and the life of the fetus that may become a child. These principles do not contradict one another; and we adhere to each. ...

Our law affords constitutional protection to personal decisions relating to marriage, procreation, contraception, family relationships, child rearing, and education. *Carey v. Population Services International,* .... Our cases recognize "the right of the *individual,* married or single, to be free from unwarranted governmental intrusion into matters so fundamentally affecting a person as the decision whether to bear or beget a child." *Eisenstadt v. Baird, supra,* .... Our precedents "have respected the private realm of family life which the state cannot enter." *Prince v. Massachusetts,* .... These matters, involving the most intimate and personal choices a person may make in a lifetime, choices central to personal dignity and autonomy, are central to the liberty protected by the Fourteenth Amendment. At the heart of liberty is the right to define one's own concept of existence, of meaning, of the universe, and of the mystery of human life. Beliefs about these matters could not define the attributes of personhood were they formed under compulsion of the State.

These considerations begin our analysis of the woman's interest in terminating her pregnancy but cannot end it, for this reason: though the abortion decision may originate within the zone of conscience and belief, it is more than a philosophic exercise. Abortion is a unique act. It is an act fraught with consequences for others: for the woman who must live with the implications of her decision; for the persons who perform and assist in the procedure; for the spouse, family, and society which must confront the knowledge that these procedures exist, procedures some deem nothing short of an act of violence against innocent human life; and, depending on one's beliefs, for the life or potential life that is aborted. Though abortion is conduct, it does not follow that the State is entitled to proscribe it in all instances. That is because the liberty of the woman is at stake in a sense unique to the human condition and so unique to the law. The mother who carries a child to full term is subject to anxieties, to physical constraints, to pain that only she must bear. That these sacrifices have from the beginning of the human race been endured by woman with a pride that ennobles her in the eyes of others and gives to the infant a bond of love cannot alone be grounds for the State to insist she make the sacrifice. Her suffering is too intimate and personal for the State to insist, without more, upon its own vision of the woman's role, however dominant that vision has been in the course of our history and our culture. The destiny of the woman must be shaped to a large extent on her own conception of her spiritual imperatives and her place in society.

It should be recognized, moreover, that in some critical respects the abortion decision is of the same character as the decision to use contraception, to which *Griswold v. Connecticut, Eisenstadt v. Baird,* and *Carey v. Population Services International* afford constitutional protection. We have no doubt as to the correctness of those decisions. They support the reasoning in *Roe* relating to the woman's liberty because they involve personal decisions concerning not only the meaning of procreation but also human responsibility and respect for it. As with abortion, reasonable people will have differences of opinion about these matters. One view is based on such reverence for the wonder of creation that any pregnancy ought to be welcomed and carried to full term no matter how difficult it will be to provide for the child and ensure its well-being. Another is that the inability to provide for the nurture and care of the infant is a cruelty to the child and an anguish to the parent. These are intimate views with infinite variations, and their deep, personal character underlay our decisions in *Griswold, Eisenstadt,* and *Carey.* The same concerns are present when the woman confronts the reality that, perhaps despite her attempts to avoid it, she has become pregnant.

It was this dimension of personal liberty that *Roe* sought to protect, and its holding invoked the reasoning and the tradition of the precedents we have discussed, granting protection to substantive liberties of the person. *Roe* was, of course, an extension of those cases and, as the decision itself indicated, the separate States could act in some degree to further their own legitimate interests in protecting prenatal life. The extent to which the legislatures of the States might act to outweigh the interests of the woman in choosing to terminate her pregnancy was a subject of debate both in *Roe* itself and in decisions following it.

While we appreciate the weight of the arguments made on behalf of the State in the cases before us, arguments which in their ultimate formulation conclude that *Roe* should be overruled, the reservations any of us may have in reaffirming the central holding of *Roe* are outweighed by the explication of individual liberty we have given combined with the force of *stare decisis*. We turn now to that doctrine. ...

We have seen how time has overtaken some of *Roe*'s factual assumptions: advances in maternal health care allow for abortions safe to the mother later in pregnancy than was true in 1973, ..., and advances in neonatal care have advanced viability to a point somewhat earlier. ... But these facts go only to the scheme of time limits on the realization of competing interests, and the divergences from the factual premises of 1973 have no bearing on the validity of *Roe*'s central holding, that viability marks the earliest point at which the State's interest in fetal life is constitutionally adequate to justify a legislative ban on nontherapeutic abortions. The soundness or unsoundness of that constitutional judgment in no sense turns on whether viability occurs at approximately 28 weeks, as was usual at the time of *Roe*, at 23 to 24 weeks, as it sometimes does today, or at some moment even slightly earlier in pregnancy, as it may if fetal respiratory capacity can somehow be enhanced in the future. Whenever it may occur, the attainment of viability may continue to serve as the critical fact, just as it has done since *Roe* was decided; which is to say that no change in *Roe*'s factual underpinning has left its central holding obsolete, and none supports an argument for overruling it.

The sum of the precedential enquiry to this point shows *Roe*'s underpinnings unweakened in any way affecting its central holding. While it has engendered disapproval, it has not been unworkable. An entire generation has come of age free to assume *Roe*'s concept of liberty in defining the capacity of women to act in society, and to make reproductive decisions; no erosion of principle going to liberty or personal autonomy has left *Roe*'s central holding a doctrinal remnant; *Roe* portends no developments at odds with other precedent for the analysis of personal liberty; and no changes of fact have rendered viability more or less appropriate as the point at which the balance of interests tips. Within the bounds of normal *stare decisis* analysis, then, and subject to the considerations on which it customarily turns, the stronger argument is for affirming *Roe*'s central holding, with whatever degree of personal reluctance any of us may have, not for overruling it. ...

The concept of an undue burden has been utilized by the Court as well as individual Members of the Court, including two of us, in ways that could be considered inconsistent. ... Because we set forth a standard of general application to which we intend to adhere, it is important to clarify what is meant by an undue burden.

A finding of an undue burden is a shorthand for the conclusion that a state regulation has the purpose or effect of placing a substantial obstacle in the path of a woman seeking an abortion of a nonviable fetus. A statute with this purpose is invalid because the means chosen by the State to further the interest in potential life must be calculated to inform the woman's free choice, not hinder it. And a statute which, while furthering the interest in potential life or some other valid state interest, has the effect of placing a substantial obstacle in the path of a woman's choice cannot be considered a permissible means of serving its legitimate ends. To the extent that the opinions of the Court or of individual Justices use the undue burden standard in a manner that is inconsistent with this analysis, we set out what in our view should be the controlling standard. ... In our considered judgment, an undue burden is an unconstitutional burden. ... Understood another way, we answer the question, left open in previous opinions discussing the undue burden formulation, whether a law designed to further the State's interest in fetal life which imposes an undue burden on the woman's decision before fetal viability could be constitutional. ... The answer is no.

Some guiding principles should emerge. What is at stake is the woman's right to make the ultimate decision, not a right to be insulated from all others in doing so. Regulations which do no more than create a structural mechanism by which the State, or the parent or guardian of a minor, may express profound respect for the life of the unborn are permitted, if they are not a substantial obstacle to the woman's exercise of the right to choose. ... Unless it has that effect on her right of choice, a state measure designed to persuade her to choose childbirth over abortion will be upheld if reasonably related to that goal. Regulations designed to foster the health of a woman seeking an abortion are valid if they do not constitute an undue burden. ... We give this summary:

(a) To protect the central right recognized by *Roe v. Wade* while at the same time accommodating the State's profound interest in potential life, we will employ the undue burden analysis as explained in this opinion. An undue burden exists, and therefore a provision of law is invalid, if its purpose or effect is to place a substantial obstacle in the path of a woman seeking an abortion before the fetus attains viability.

(b) We reject the rigid trimester framework of *Roe v. Wade*. To promote the State's profound interest in potential life, throughout pregnancy the State may take measures to ensure that the woman's choice is informed, and measures designed to advance this interest will not be invalidated as long as their purpose is to persuade the woman to choose childbirth over abortion. These measures must not be an undue burden on the right.

(c) As with any medical procedure, the State may enact regulations to further the health or safety of a woman seeking an abortion. Unnecessary health regulations that have the purpose or effect of presenting a substantial obstacle to a woman seeking an abortion impose an undue burden on the right.

(d) Our adoption of the undue burden analysis does not disturb the central holding of *Roe v. Wade*, and we reaffirm that holding. Regardless of whether exceptions are made for particular circumstances, a State may not prohibit any woman from making the ultimate decision to terminate her pregnancy before viability.

(e) We also reaffirm *Roe*'s holding that "subsequent to viability, the State in promoting its interest in the potentiality of human life may, if it chooses, regulate, and even proscribe, abortion except where it is necessary, in appropriate medical judgment, for the preservation of the life or health of the mother." *Roe v. Wade*, ...

These principles control our assessment of the Pennsylvania statute, and we now turn to the issue of the validity of its challenged provisions. ...

[The Court upheld the statute's "informed consent" requirement that, at least 24 hours before performing an abortion, requires a physician to provide information about the procedure and her unborn child. The Court also upheld a requirement that a minor seeking an abortion have the consent of one parent or a judge. The Court invalidated the law's spousal notification requirement as an "undue burden."]

Our Constitution is a covenant running from the first generation of Americans to us and then to future generations. It is a coherent succession. Each generation must learn anew that the Constitution's written terms embody ideas and aspirations that must survive more ages than one. We accept our responsibility not to retreat from interpreting the full meaning of the covenant in light of all of our precedents. We invoke it once again to define the freedom guaranteed by the Constitution's own promise, the promise of liberty.

✦ *D O C U M E N T 6*

South Africa's Constitution Affirms Women's Rights, 1996

...9. Equality

1. Everyone is equal before the law and has the right to equal protection and benefit of the law.
2. Equality includes the full and equal enjoyment of all rights and freedoms. To promote the achievement of equality, legislative and other measures designed to protect or advance persons, or categories of persons, disadvantaged by unfair discrimination may be taken.
3. The state may not unfairly discriminate directly or indirectly against anyone on one or more grounds, including race, gender, sex, pregnancy, marital status, ethnic or social origin, colour, sexual orientation, age, disability, religion, conscience, belief, culture, language and birth.
4. No person may unfairly discriminate directly or indirectly against anyone on one or more grounds in terms of subsection (3). National legislation must be enacted to prevent or prohibit unfair discrimination.
5. Discrimination on one or more of the grounds listed in subsection (3) is unfair unless it is established that the discrimination is fair.

10. Human dignity

Everyone has inherent dignity and the right to have their dignity respected and protected.

11. Life

Everyone has the right to life.

12. Freedom and security of the person

1. Everyone has the right to freedom and security of the person, which includes the right
   a. not to be deprived of freedom arbitrarily or without just cause;
   b. not to be detained without trial;
   c. to be free from all forms of violence from either public or private sources;
   d. not to be tortured in any way; and
   e. not to be treated or punished in a cruel, inhuman or degrading way.

2. Everyone has the right to bodily and psychological integrity, which includes the right
   a. to make decisions concerning reproduction;
   b. to security in and control over their body; and
   c. not to be subjected to medical or scientific experiments without their informed consent.

13. Slavery, servitude and forced labour

No one may be subjected to slavery, servitude or forced labour.

14. Privacy

Everyone has the right to privacy, which includes the right not to have
   a. their person or home searched;
   b. their property searched;
   c. their possessions seized; or
   d. the privacy of their communications infringed.

15. Freedom of religion, belief and opinion

1. Everyone has the right to freedom of conscience, religion, thought, belief and opinion.
2. Religious observances may be conducted at state or state-aided institutions, provided that
   a. those observances follow rules made by the appropriate public authorities;
   b. they are conducted on an equitable basis; and
   c. attendance at them is free and voluntary.
3.
   a. This section does not prevent legislation recognising
      i. marriages concluded under any tradition, or a system of religious, personal or family law; or
      ii. systems of personal and family law under any tradition, or adhered to by persons professing a particular religion.
   b. Recognition in terms of paragraph (a) must be consistent with this section and the other provisions of the Constitution.

16. Freedom of expression

1. Everyone has the right to freedom of expression, which includes
   a. freedom of the press and other media;
   b. freedom to receive or impart information or ideas;
   c. freedom of artistic creativity; and
   d. academic freedom and freedom of scientific research.

2. The right in subsection (1) does not extend to
   a. propaganda for war;
   b. incitement of imminent violence; or
   c. advocacy of hatred that is based on race, ethnicity, gender or religion, and that constitutes incitement to cause harm.

17. Assembly, demonstration, picket and petition

Everyone has the right, peacefully and unarmed, to assemble, to demonstrate, to picket and to present petitions.

✤ *D O C U M E N T   7*

Christian Lawyers Association of South Africa v. Minister of Health, 1998

McCREATH J: The plaintiffs seek an order against the defendants declaring the Choice on Termination of Pregnancy Act 1996 (the Act) to be unconstitutional and that it be struck down in its entirety.

... [T]he plaintiffs rely solely on the provisions of s 11 of the Constitution to substantiate their cause of action. That section provides that 'everyone has the right to life'. A perusal of the Constitution indicates that the terms 'everyone' and 'every person' are used interchangeably. Thus, the bill of rights generally protects 'everyone', but frequently refers to the holders of those rights as 'people' or 'persons'— eg s 7(1), which enshrines the rights of all 'people'; s 38, which confers locus standi on 'everyone listed in this section' to approach the court for relief under the bill of rights but goes on to describe in the list 'the persons' who may do so.

It should be mentioned that in the interim Constitution (the predecessor to the Constitution) a general protection was afforded in the bill of rights forming part thereof to 'every person'. The change to the word 'everyone' was presumably to meet the requirement of Constitutional Principle II that 'everyone shall enjoy all universally accepted fundamental rights, freedoms and civil liberties'. Be that as it may, this change across the board could never, in my judgment, have been intended to introduce a significant new class of rights-bearer. It is inconceivable that any new category could have been introduced by the legislature in this obscure way. The Canadian Charter of Rights confers its protection on 'everyone', 'any person' and 'anyone'. Hogg *Constitutional Law of Canada* (3rd edn, 1992) vol 2, para 34.1(b) says that 'it seems likely that these various terms are synonymous for purposes, of the relevant sections of the Canadian Charter'. There can be no doubt in my mind that, as far as the Republic of South Africa is concerned, the terms 'every person' and 'everyone', as used in the Constitution (and more particularly in s 11 thereof) are synonymous. Counsel for the plaintiffs did not suggest otherwise.

The plaintiffs' cause of action, founded, as it is, solely on s 11 of the Constitution, is therefore dependent for its validity on the question whether 'everyone' or 'every person' applies to an unborn child 'from the moment of the child's conception'. The answer hereto does not depend on medical or scientific evidence as to when the life of a human being commences and the subsequent development of the foetus up to date of birth. Nor is it the function of this court to decide the issue on religious or philosophical grounds. The issue is a legal one to be decided on the proper legal interpretation to be given to s 11....

It is desirable that some consideration be given to the common law status of the foetus. A word of caution should perhaps first be sounded. In the particulars of claim the plaintiffs allege that the foetus qualifies for protection under s 11 because 'the life of a human being starts at conception' and by implication therefore that human beings are from conception a person as envisaged by the said section. This is a non sequitur. As pointed out by Professor Glanville Williams in an article entitled 'The Foetus and the Right to Life' (1994) 33 CLJ 71 at 78 'the question is not whether the conceptus is human but whether it should be given the same legal protection as you and me'.

It is not necessary for me to make any firm decision as to whether an unborn child is a legal persona under the common law. What is important for purposes of interpreting s 11 of the Constitution is that, at best for the plaintiffs, the status of the foetus under the common law may, as at present, be somewhat uncertain.

I proceed to a consideration of the provisions of the Constitution itself. There is no express provision affording the foetus (or embryo) legal personality or protection. It is improbable, in my view, that the drafters of the Constitution would not have made express provision therefor had it intended to enshrine the rights of the unborn child in the bill of rights, in order to cure any uncertainty in the common law and in the light of case law denying the foetus legal personality. One of the requirements of the protection afforded by the nasciturus rule is that the foetus be born alive. There is no provision in the Constitution to protect the foetus pending the fulfilment of that condition. The matter goes further than that. Section 12(2) provides that everyone has the right to make decisions concerning reproduction and to security in and control over their body. Nowhere is a woman's rights in this respect qualified in terms of the Constitution in order to protect the foetus. This does not, of course, mean that the state is prohibited from enacting legislation to restrict and/or regulate abortion. The state may invoke s 36 for that purpose 'to the extent that the limitation is reasonable and justifiable in an open and democratic society based on human dignity, equality and freedom' and taking into account all relevant factors, including those specified in the section.

Had the drafters of the Constitution wished to protect the foetus in the bill of rights at all, one would have expected this to have been done in s 28, which specifically protects the rights of the child. The right of every child to family or parental care (28(1)(b)), to basic nutrition, health care and social services (28(1)(c)), to protection against maltreatment, neglect, abuse or degradation (28(1)(d)), and to legal representation (28(1)(h)), as well as the provision in sub-s (2) that a child's best interests are of paramount importance in every matter concerning the child, would have been particularly apposite to protect the foetus as well. Yet there are clear indications that the safeguards in s 28 do not extend to protect the foetus. A 'child' for purposes of the section is defined in sub-s (3) as a person under the age of eighteen years. Age commences at birth. The protection afforded by sub-ss (1)(f)(i) and (1)(g) (ii) is dependent on the 'child's age'. A foetus is not a 'child' of any 'age'. The rights afforded by s 28(1) are in respect of 'every child'—ie all children. Yet certain of the rights could not have been intended to protect a foetus; para (f) relates to work, para (g) to detention and (i) to armed conflict. The protection afforded in the other paras of sub-s (1) must accordingly also exclude the foetus.

If s 28 of the Constitution, the section specifically designed to protect the rights of the child, does not include the foetus within the ambit of its protection then it can hardly be said that the other provisions of the bill of rights, including s 11, were intended to do so. This conclusion finds further support in the fact that in all the provisions of the bill of rights, other than those in which a specific class of person is singled out for special protection, the rights are conferred on 'everyone'. Yet in many instances it is clear that the term 'everyone' could not have been intended to include the foetus within the scope of its protection. Thus, the right not to be deprived of one's freedom (s 12(1)(a)), not to be detained without trial (s 12(1)(b)), to make decisions concerning reproduction and to security in and control over one's body (s 12(2)(b)), not to be subjected to slavery, servitude or forced labour (s 13), rights relating to privacy and freedom of conscience, religion, thought, belief, opinion, expression, assembly, association and movement (vide ss 14, 15(1), 16(1), 17, 18 and 21) and other rights in regard to language, cultural life, arrest and detention (ss 30 and 35) are all afforded to 'everyone' and clearly do not include a foetus. To include the foetus in the meaning of that term in s 11 would ascribe to it a meaning different from that which it bears everywhere else in the bill of rights. That, in my judgment, is clearly untenable.

Moreover, if s 11 were to be interpreted as affording constitutional protection to the life of a foetus far-reaching and anomalous consequences would ensue. The life of the foetus would enjoy the same protection as that of the mother. Abortion would be constitutionally prohibited even though the pregnancy constitutes a serious threat to the life of the mother. The prohibition would apply even if the pregnancy resulted from rape or incest, or if there were a likelihood that the child to be born would suffer from severe physical or mental abnormality. Abortion in these circumstances has, subject to certain controls, been permissible since 1975, when the Abortion and Sterilisation Act 1975 came into operation. If the plaintiffs' contentions are correct then the termination of a woman's pregnancy would no longer constitute the crime of abortion, but that of murder. In my view, the drafters of the Constitution could not have contemplated such far-reaching results without expressing themselves in no uncertain terms. For the above reasons, and whatever the status of the foetus may be under the common law, I consider that under the Constitution the foetus is not a legal persona.

Counsel for the fourth and fifth defendants have also emphasised the fact that the Constitution is 'primarily and emphatically' an egalitarian Constitution and argue that the transformation of our society along egalitarian lines involves the eradication of systematic forms of domination and disadvantage based on race, gender, class and other grounds of inequality. I agree that proper regard must be had to the rights of women as enshrined in s 9 of the Constitution (the right to equality, which includes the full and actual enjoyment of all rights and freedoms and the protection that the state may not unfairly discriminate against anyone inter alia on the grounds of sex), s 12 (the right to freedom and security of the person, including inter alia the right to make decisions concerning reproduction and the right to security and control over their body) and the rights in respect of human dignity (s 10), life (s 11), privacy (s 14), religion, belief and opinion (s 15) and health and care (s 27), to which I have already referred within another context. I agree also that to afford the foetus the status of a legal persona may impinge, to a greater or lesser extent, on these rights. ...

✤ *E S S A Y S*

The late John Hart Ely, who before his death in 2003 taught law at the University of Miami, published a comment on *Roe* immediately after the decision. His now classic essay asserted that *Roe* represented an inappropriate use of judicial power and made for bad constitutional law. More recently N.E.H. Hull, a law professor at Rutgers University, and Peter Charles Hoffer, a historian at the University of Georgia, have explored *Roe* and the history of the abortion controversy. Situating the case in the larger context of the women's rights movement, they argue that *Roe* has survived because the American public supports the right to reproductive choice.

Roe v. Wade Was a Mistake

JOHN HART ELY

... In *Roe v. Wade*, decided January 22, 1973, the Supreme Court—Justice Blackmun speaking for everyone but Justices White and Rehnquist—held unconstitutional Texas's (and virtually every other state's) criminal abortion statute. The broad outlines of its argument are not difficult to make out:

1. The right to privacy, though not explicitly mentioned in the Constitution, is protected by the Due Process Clause of the Fourteenth Amendment.
2. This right "is broad enough to encompass a woman's decision whether or not to terminate her pregnancy."
3. This right to an abortion is "fundamental" and can therefore be regulated only on the basis of a "compelling" state interest.
4. The state does have two "important and legitimate" interests here, the first in protecting maternal health, the second in protecting the life (or potential life) of the fetus. But neither can be counted "compelling" throughout the entire pregnancy: Each matures with the unborn child.

These interests are separate and distinct. Each grows in substantiality as the woman approaches term and, at a point during pregnancy, each becomes "compelling."

5. During the first trimester of pregnancy, neither interest is sufficiently compelling to justify any interference with the decision of the woman and her physician. Appellants have referred the Court to medical data indicating that mortality rates for women undergoing early abortions, where abortion is legal, "appear to be as low as or lower than the rates for normal childbirth." Thus the state's interest in protecting maternal health is not compelling during the first trimester. Since the interest in protecting the fetus is not yet compelling either, during the first trimester the state can neither prohibit an abortion nor regulate the conditions under which one is performed.

6. As we move into the second trimester, the interest in protecting the fetus remains less than compelling, and the decision to have an abortion thus continues to control. However, at this point the health risks of abortion begin to exceed those of childbirth. "It follows that, from and after this point, a State may regulate the abortion procedure to the extent that the regulation reasonably relates to the preservation and protection of maternal health." Abortion may not be prohibited during the second trimester, however.

"The Wages of Crying Wolf: A Comment on Roe v. Wade" by John Hart Ely *The Yale Law Journal* 82 (1973). Reprinted by permission of The Yale Law Journal Company and Fred B. Rothman & Company from *The Yale Law Journal*, Vol. 82, pp. 920–949.

7. At the point at which the fetus becomes viable the interest in protecting it becomes compelling, and therefore from that point on the state can prohibit abortions *except*—and this limitation is also apparently a constitutional command, though it receives no justification in the opinion—when they are necessary to protect maternal life or health.

I

A number of fairly standard criticisms can be made of *Roe*. A plausible narrower basis of decision, that of vagueness, is brushed aside in the rush toward broader ground. The opinion strikes the reader initially as a sort of guidebook, addressing questions not before the Court and drawing lines with an apparent precision one generally associates with a commissioner's regulations. On closer examination, however, the precision proves largely illusory. Confusing signals are emitted, particularly with respect to the nature of the doctor's responsibilities and the permissible scope of health regulations after the first trimester. The Court seems, moreover, to get carried away on the subject of remedies: Even assuming the case can be made for an unusually protected constitutional right to an abortion, it hardly seems necessary to have banned during the first trimester *all* state regulation of the conditions under which abortions can be performed.

By terming such criticisms "standard," I do not mean to suggest they are unimportant, for they are not. But if they were all that was wrong with *Roe*, it would not merit special comment.

II

The Court' … holds, that after the point of viability (a concept it fails to note will become even less clear than it is now as the technology of birth continues to develop) the interest in protecting the fetus is compelling. Exactly why that is the magic moment is not made clear: Viability, as the Court defines it, is achieved some six to twelve weeks after quickening. (Quickening is the point at which the fetus begins discernibly to move independently of the mother and the point that has historically been deemed crucial—to the extent *any* point between conception and birth has been focused on.) But no, it is *viability* that is constitutionally critical: the Court's defense seems to mistake a definition for a syllogism.

> With respect to the State's important and legitimate interest in potential life, the "compelling" point is at viability. This is so because the fetus then presumably has the capacity of meaningful life outside the mother's womb.

With regard to why the state cannot consider this "important and legitimate interest" prior to viability, the opinion is even less satisfactory. The discussion begins sensibly enough: The interest asserted is not necessarily tied to the question whether the fetus is "alive," for whether or not one calls it a living being, it is an entity with the potential for (and indeed the likelihood of) life. But all of arguable relevance that follows are arguments that fetuses (a) are not recognized as "persons in the whole sense" by legal doctrine generally and (b) are not "persons" protected by the Fourteenth Amendment.

To the extent they are not entirely inconclusive, the bodies of doctrine to which the Court adverts respecting the protection of fetuses under general legal doctrine tend to undercut rather than support its conclusion. And the argument that fetuses (unlike, say, corporations) are not "persons" under the Fourteenth Amendment fares little better. The Court notes that most constitutional clauses using the word "persons"—such as the one outlining the qualifications for the Presidency—appear to have been drafted with postnatal beings in mind. (It might have added that most of them were plainly drafted with *adults* in mind, but I suppose that wouldn't have helped.) In addition, "the appellee conceded on reargument that no case can be cited that holds that a fetus is a person within the meaning of the Fourteenth Amendment." (The other legal contexts in which the question could have arisen are not enumerated.)

The canons of construction employed here are perhaps most intriguing when they are contrasted with those invoked to derive the constitutional right to an abortion. But in any event, the argument that fetuses lack constitutional rights is simply irrelevant. For it has never been held or even asserted that the state interest needed to justify forcing a person to refrain from an activity, *whether or not that activity is constitutionally protected*, must implicate either the life or the constitutional rights of another person. Dogs are not "persons in the whole sense" nor have they constitutional rights, but that does not mean the state cannot prohibit killing them: It does not even mean the state cannot prohibit killing them in the exercise of the First Amendment right of political protest. Come to think of it, draft cards aren't persons either.

Thus even assuming the Court ought generally to get into the business of second-guessing legislative balances, it has picked a strange case with which to begin. Its purported evaluation of the balance that produced anti-abortion legislation simply does not meet the issue: That the life plans of the mother must, not simply may, prevail over the state's desire to protect the fetus simply does not follow from the judgment that the fetus is not a person. Beyond all that, however, the Court has no business getting into that business.

III

Were I a legislator I would vote for a statute very much like the one the Court ends up drafting. I hope this reaction reflects more than the psychological phenomenon that keeps bombardiers sane—the fact that it is somehow easier to "terminate" those you cannot see—and am inclined to think it does: that the mother, unlike the unborn child, has begun to imagine a future for herself strikes me as morally quite significant. But God knows I'm not *happy* with that resolution. Abortion is too much like infanticide on the one hand, and too much like contraception on the other, to leave one comfortable with any answer; and the moral issue it poses is as fiendish as any philosopher's hypothetical.

Of course, the Court often resolves difficult moral questions, and difficult questions yield controversial answers. I doubt, for example, that most people would agree that letting a drug peddler go unapprehended is morally preferable to letting the police kick down his door without probable cause. The difference, of course, is that the Constitution, which legitimates and theoretically controls judicial intervention, has some rather pointed things to say about this choice. There will of course be difficult questions about the applicability of its language to specific facts, but at least the document's special concern with one of the values in conflict is manifest. It simply says nothing, clear or fuzzy, about abortion.

The matter cannot end there, however. The Burger Court, like the Warren Court before it, has been especially soclicitous of the right to travel from state to state, demanding a compelling state interest if it is to be inhibited. Yet nowhere in the Constitution is such a right mentioned. It is, however, as clear as such things can be that this right was one the framers intended to protect, most specifically by the Privileges and Immunities Clause of Article IV. The right is, moreover, plausibly inferable from the system of government, and the citizen's role therein, contemplated by the Constitution. The Court in *Roe* suggests an inference of neither sort—from the intent of the framers, or from the governmental system contemplated by the Constitution—in support of the constitutional right to an abortion.

What the Court does assert is that there is a general right of privacy granted special protection—that is, protection above and beyond the baseline requirement of "rationality"—by the Fourteenth Amendment, and that that right "is broad enough to encompass" the right to an abortion. The general right of privacy is inferred, as it was in *Griswold v. Connecticut*, from various provisions of the Bill of Rights manifesting a concern with privacy, notably the Fourth Amendment's guarantee against unreasonable searches, the Fifth Amendment's privilege against self-incrimination, and the right, inferred from the First Amendment, to keep one's political associations secret.

One possible response is that all this proves is that the things explicitly mentioned are forbidden, if indeed it does not actually demonstrate a disposition *not* to enshrine anything that might be called a general right of privacy. In fact the Court takes this view when it suits its purposes. (One the *same day* it decided *Roe*, the Court held that a showing of reasonableness was not needed to force someone to provide a grand jury with a voice exemplar, reasoning that the Fifth Amendment was not implicated because the evidence was not "testimonial" and that the Fourth Amendment did not apply because there was no "seizure.") But this approach is unduly crabbed. Surely the Court is entitled, indeed I think it is obligated, to seek out the sorts of evils the framers meant to combat and to move against their twentieth century counterparts.

Thus it seems to me entirely proper to infer a general right of privacy, *so long as some care is taken in defining the sort of right the inference will support.* Those aspects of the First, Fourth and Fifth Amendments to which the Court refers all limit the ways in which, and the circumstances under which, the government can go about gathering information about a person he would rather it did not have. *Katz v. United States*, limiting governmental tapping of telephones, may not involve what the framers would have called a "search," but it plainly involves this general concern with privacy. *Griswold* is a long step, even a leap, beyond this, but at least the connection is discernible. Had it been a case that purported to discover in the Constitution a "right to contraception," it would have been *Roe*'s strongest precedent. But the Court in *Roe* gives no evidence of so regarding it, and rightly not. Commentators tend to forget, though the Court plainly has not, that the Court in *Griswold* stressed that it was invalidating only that portion of the Connecticut law that proscribed the *use*, as opposed to the manufacture, sale, or other distribution of contraceptives. That distinction (which would be silly were the right to contraception being constitutionally enshrined) makes sense if the case is rationalized on the ground that the section of the law whose constitutionality was in issue was such that *its enforcement would have been virtually impossible without* the most outrageous sort of governmental prying into the privacy of the home.... Thus even assuming (as the Court surely seemed to) that a state can constitutionally seek to minimize or eliminate the circulation and use of contraceptives, Connecticut had acted unconstitutionally by selecting a means, that is a direct ban on use, that would generate intolerably intrusive modes of data-gathering. No such rationalization is attempted by the Court in *Roe*—and understandably not, for whatever else may be involved, it is not a case about governmental snooping.

The Court reports that some amici curiae argued for an unlimited right to do as one wishes with one's body. This theory holds, for me at any rate, much appeal. However, there would have been serious problems with its invocation in this case. In the first place, more than the mother's own body is involved in a decision to have an abortion; a fetus may not be a "person in the whole sense," but it is certainly not nothing. Second, it is difficult to find a basis for thinking that the theory was meant to be given constitutional sanction: Surely it is no part of the "privacy" interest the Bill of Rights suggests.... Unfortunately, having thus rejected the amici's attempt to define the bounds of the general constitutional right of which the right to an abortion is a part, on the theory that the general right described has little to do with privacy, the Court provides neither an alternative definition nor an account of why *it* thinks privacy is involved. It simply announces that the right to privacy "is broad enough to encompass a woman's decision whether or not to terminate her pregnancy." Apparently this conclusion is thought to derive from the passage that immediately follows it:

> The detriment that the State would impose upon the pregnant woman by denying this choice altogether is apparent. Specific and direct harm medically diagnosable even in early pregnancy may be involved. Maternity, or additional offspring, may force upon the woman a distressful life and future. Psychological harm may be imminent. Mental and physical health may be taxed by child care. There is also the distress, for all concerned, associated with the unwanted child, and there is the problem of bringing a child into a family already unable, psychologically and otherwise, to care for it. In other cases, as in this one, the additional difficulties and continuing stigma of unwed motherhood may be involved.

All of this is true and ought to be taken very seriously. But it has nothing to do with privacy in the Bill of Rights sense or any other the Constitution suggests. I suppose there is nothing to prevent one from using the word "privacy" to mean the freedom to live one's life without governmental interference. But the Court obviously does not so use the term. Nor could it, for such a right is at stake in *every* case. Our life styles are constantly limited, often seriously, by governmental regulation; and while many of us would prefer less direction, granting that desire the status of a preferred constitutional right would yield a system of "government" virtually unrecognizable to us and only slightly more recognizable to our forefathers. The Court's observations concerning the serious, life-shaping costs of having a child prove what might to the thoughtless have seemed unprovable: That even though a human life, or a potential human life, hangs in the balance, the moral dilemma abortion poses is so difficult as to be heartbreaking. What they fail to do is even begin to resolve that dilemma so far as our governmental system is concerned by associating either side of the balance with a value inferable from the Constitution.

But perhaps the inquiry should not end even there. In his famous *Carolene Products* footnote, Justice Stone suggested that the interests to which the Court can responsibly give extraordinary constitutional protection include not only those expressed in the Constitution but also those that are unlikely to receive adequate consideration in the political process, specifically the interests of "discrete and insular minorities" unable to form effective political alliances. There can be little doubt that such considerations have influenced the direction, if only occasionally the rhetoric, of the recent Courts. My repeated efforts to convince my students that sex should be treated as a "suspect classification" have convinced me it is no easy matter to state such considerations in a "principled" way. But passing that problem, *Roe* is not an appropriate case for their invocation.

Compared with men, very few women sit in our legislatures, a fact I believe should bear some relevance—even without an Equal Rights Amendment—to the appropriate standard of review for legislation that favors men over women. But *no* fetuses sit in our legislatures. Of course they have their champions, but so have women. The two interests have clashed repeatedly in the political arena, and had continued to do so up to the date of the opinion, generating quite a wide variety of accommodations. By the Court's lights virtually all of the legislative accommodations had unduly favored fetuses; by its definition of victory, women had lost. Yet in every legislative balance one of the competing interests loses to some extent; indeed usually, as here, they both do. On some occasions the Constitution throws its weight on the side of one of them, indicating the balance must be restruck. And on others—and this is Justice Stone's suggestion—it is at least arguable that, constitutional directive or not, the Court should throw *its* weight on the side of a minority demanding in court more than it was able to achieve politically. But even assuming this suggestion can be given principled content, it was clearly intended and should be reserved for those interests which, *as compared with the interests to which they have been subordinated*, constitute minorities unusually incapable of protecting themselves. Compared with men, women may constitute such a "minority"; compared with the unborn, they do not. I'm not sure I'd know a discrete and insular minority if I saw one, but confronted with a multiple choice question requiring me to designate (a) women or (b) fetuses as one, I'd expect no credit for the former answer.

Of course a woman's freedom to choose an abortion is part of the "liberty" the Fourteenth Amendment says shall not be denied without due process of law, as indeed is anyone's freedom to do what he wants. But "due process" generally guarantees only that the inhibition be procedurally fair and that it have some "rational" connection—though plausible is probably a better word—with a permissible governmental goal. What is unusual about *Roe* is that the liberty involved is accorded a far more stringent protection, so stringent that a desire to preserve the fetus's existence is unable to overcome it—a protection more stringent, I think it fair to say, than that the present Court accords the freedom of the press explicitly guaranteed by the First Amendment. What is frightening about *Roe* is that this super-protected right is not inferable from the language of the Constitution, the framers' thinking respecting the specific problem in issue, any general value derivable from the provisions they included, or the nation's governmental structure. Nor is it explainable in terms of the unusual political impotence of the group judicially protected vis-à-vis the interest that legislatively prevailed over it. And that, I believe—the predictable early reaction to *Roe* notwithstanding ("more of the same Warren-type activism")—is a charge that can responsibly be leveled at no other decision of the past twenty years. At times the inferences the Court has drawn from the values the Constitution marks for special protection have been controversial, even shaky, but never before has its sense of an obligation to draw one been so obviously lacking.

IV

…I am aware the Court cannot simply "lay the Article of the Constitution which is invoked beside the statute which is challenged and…decide whether the latter squares with the former." That is precisely the reason commentators are needed.

> [P]recisely because it is the constitution alone which warrants judicial interference in sovereign operations of the State, the basis of judgment as to the Constitutionality of state action must be a rational one, approaching the text which is the only commission for our power not in a literalistic way, as if we had a tax statute before us, but as the basic charter of our society, setting out in spare but meaningful terms the principles of government.
>
> No matter how imprecise in application to specific modern fact situations, the constitutional guarantees do provide a direction, a goal, an ideal citizen-government relationship. They rule out many alternative directions, goals, and ideals.

And they fail to support the ruling out of others.

Of course that only begins the inquiry. Identification and definition of the values with which the Constitution is concerned will often fall short of indicating with anything resembling clarity the deference to be given those values when they conflict with others society finds important. (Though even here the process is sometimes more helpful than the commentators would allow.) Nor is it often likely to generate, fullblown, the "neutral" principle that will avoid embarrassment in future cases. But though the identification of a constitutional connection is only the beginning of analysis, it is a necessary beginning. The point that often gets lost in the commentary, and obviously got lost in *Roe*, is that *before the Court can get to the "balancing" stage, before it can worry about the next case and the case after that (or even about its institutional position) it is under an obligation to trace its premises to the charter from which it derives its authority*. A neutral and durable principle may be a thing of beauty and a joy forever. But if it lacks connection with any value the Constitution marks as special, it is not a constitutional principle and the Court has no business imposing it. I hope that will seem obvious to the point of banality. Yet those of us to whom it does seem obvious have seldom troubled to say so. And because we have not, we must share in the blame for this decision.

Roe Symbolized an Idea Whose Time Had Come

N.E.H. HULL AND PETER CHARLES HOFFER

The battle over *Roe* goes on and on: new regulations, new challenges, new cases, old protests, old alignments, old arguments, because neither side—and there are only two sides, no middle—can find a way to compromise or quit. Why is there no closure? Perhaps history can explain. ... What does *Roe* tell us about that past? ...

Justice Blackmun's opinion in *Roe* was meant to do justice to all parties—an equitable solution to a complex conflict. The recognition of a fundamental right of reproductive choice did not preclude the state's interest in unborn life. But that interest arose after viability. Blackmun had reached deep into the history of the abortion question, to the old doctrine of quickening, hoping that it still provided a scale in which to balance the competing claims. He did not incorporate the new paradigm of women's voice in the law, instead restating the older, paternalistic, medically driven argument that doctors should be free of state interference in taking care of their pregnant patients. But again, he left open the door that the state could regard the fetus as a legal person at some time in its gestation.

The trimester scheme that embodied that balance of women's fundamental right and states' arising interest survived state challenges through the 1970s and 1980s, but the Court did not deem federal and state limitations on access to public funding and hospital care for abortion an "undue burden" on the right to choose to terminate a pregnancy in its earliest stages. By the end of the 1980s, state requirements of parental notice and the evaluation of fetuses for viability also passed the test of constitutionality. Federal rules barring the discussion of abortion in federally funded facilities similarly gained judicial approval. The Court shifted to the undue burden standard, rather than the trimester formula, to weigh state and federal regulations. *Roe* survived as a concept; the majority of the Court insisted that its core had become an essential part of American constitutional jurisprudence. But its core was gutted. Or was it?

Was this majority right? Or was the dissent—that *Roe* invented rights that the Constitution never mentioned, and gave to courts the power that democratic legislatures were supposed to exercise—better law and wiser policy? Americans have looked to the Court itself for an answer, but *Roe* and its progeny are written in a language that ordinary Americans cannot easily understand. The majority and the minority of the Court certainly had a good deal to say, then and afterward, but their words were part of a specialized, arcane vocabulary that had its own rules of grammar and usage. They intoned the words of appellate law courts, not the words of ordinary people. On occasion, one or another of the justices (usually Brennan or Marshall) made a plea for the Court to hear the voices and see the plight of ordinary people, but that plea was itself part of a complex and highly technical argument. How could it be otherwise? The justices are all skilled lawyers whose job it is to transform the experience of ordinary life into the rarefied language of the law. The court battle over the rights of women to choose abortions and the rights of government to protect fetal life will always be fought in the oxygen-poor altitude of lofty constitutional concepts like due process and equal protection.

From Hull and Hoffer, Roe v. Wade: The Abortion Rights Controversy in American History. Published by University Press of Kansas, 2001. reproduced by the permission of the publisher.

What is more, the choice of one of these constitutional categories often concealed others equally applicable. For example, to treat abortion as a privacy right under the Due Process Clause might deny that abortion rights restrictions were a form of sex discrimination (Ruth Bader Ginsburg's argument). But when the Court shifts to viewing abortion questions as matters of sex discrimination it may well lump together all women instead of looking at the different needs and capacities of rich women and poor women. In other words, emphasis on gender tends to obscure crucial differences in class-based attitudes toward abortion and doctors.

In the same fashion, just looking at the socioeconomic status of women (for example in the funding cases) may blur vital distinctions among women from different ethnic heritages and ancestries. The white upper-class woman may regard her doctor in a different way than does the working-class woman of color—with the result that the doctor's reading of an informed consent message may have a completely different impact on the two women's choice of an abortion. Seen in this light, the categorical thinking of the Court so badly mangles the complex multiplicity of real-life factors in abortion decisions that its holdings on abortion from *Roe* to *Casey* increase rather than allay confusion.

Or it may be that the opinions lack the grit of everyday life because men and women simply do not hear the harmonics of one another's voices when it comes to abortion. In 1968, writing under the pen name Jeffrey Hudson, the novelist Michael Crichton published an abortion murder mystery titled *A Case of Need*. At the end, Crichton, a trained physician, stepped back and listed six reasons for reforming the (then) criminal law of abortion and six reasons to leave the law as it was. Only one of the first six touched women's right to choose or raised questions of reproductive autonomy from a woman's point of view. The last of the twelve, based on controversial evidence about DNA development, summed them all: forming a "commentary on modern man that he must justify his morality on the basis of the molecular mechanisms at work within a single cell of his body." Modern man's body—not a woman's body, and not what happened in her body, but what happened in the body of the fetus—mattered. Crichton was not unsympathetic to the plight of women who wanted or needed abortions, he just did not see it from their point of view or at least adopt their perspective to describe their plight.

Compare his supposedly neutral, objective, dry assessment with another doctor's, an abortionist and general practitioner named Elizabeth Karlin. In the face of escalating violence, she continued to go to her clinic, interview and counsel women, and help, when they were ready, with their abortions. She recalled, "It is very important to me to know that I am not alone doing abortions.…Patients stop for a hug on the way home. Women stop me in the supermarket and, with tears in their eyes, thank me for what I do…and I know, even being hated, that I'm in good company."

To enlarge on Karlin's point: Adrienne Rich, the poet, writes that "some ideas are not really new but keep having to be affirmed from the ground up. Over and over. One of these is the apparently simple idea that women are as intrinsically human as men, that…experience shapes us, randomness shapes us, the stars and the weather, our own accommodations and rebellions, above all, the social order around us." The central fact of that order was the exploitation of women's bodies, as laborers, as "wombs" for a man's children. So Rich can propose, "Procreative choice is for women an equivalent of the demand for the legally limited working day" for men, a statement that is as unlikely to appear in an opinion of the High Court as a volume of her poetry would be in the middle of the United States Code Annotated. It may be that gendered voice matters in court as well: counsel on the briefs of the state and the federal government in favor of curtailment of *Roe* were almost invariably entirely male. Counsel arguing against restriction of the abortion right invariably included men and women, with the latter often addressing the Supreme Court in oral argument.

Crichton assumed that a male doctor was a neutral scientific observer and an aid to the pregnant woman patient, but recent studies of doctors' views of female patients in difficult pregnancies show what Rich intuited: that male doctors are not neutral, and they view their female patients with less than objectivity. A 1987 survey of the heads of programs in fetal medicine revealed that nearly half thought that mothers who wished to carry their labor through without surgical intervention, against the doctor's advice, should be "detained in hospitals or other facilities so that compliance could be ensured." Slightly over one-fourth of these doctors wanted state surveillance of women in the third trimester who stay outside of the hospital system. Keeping women in "other facilities" against their will is a form of "preventive detention" that even the most conservative of state legislatures have not considered.

Another study of male doctors' attitudes toward women patients that brings into question the assumption of their neutrality and objectivity found that doctors regarded poor women and women of color as more likely to be "difficult patients," and such patients were more likely to receive substandard medical care. Some of this can be explained by poverty itself (having a private doctor ensured better care than relying upon the staff of a public hospital), but the responses of the doctors demonstrated that they had opinions closely reacting to their patients' ethnic and economic status, even when the source of payment for the care was not an issue.

Thus *Roe* does not speak to us in either plain or neutral language. We speak to it. We fit it into a historical context. That understood, we need to reframe and enlarge the question, "What does *Roe* tell us?" to make it more supple and realistic. One way to do this is to pose three historical questions. The first is, what made *Roe* and abortion so important in the early 1970s? The second is, why was the debate so bitter and the two sides so intractable? The third is, what do the politics and law of *Roe* reveal about fundamental American values?

Abortion was not a central issue in American politics and abortion cases were not so important in nineteenth- and early-twentieth-century American history because women had little say in lawmaking. The dominant legal paradigm viewed women as inferiors, whose primary function in society was mothering. Women were the virtuous bearers and nurturers of the next generation. The right to abortion challenged those values, but without a say in the law women could not overcome laws passed against abortion.

Over the course of the twentieth century, however, the role and influence of women in society changed. Women entered the professions, amassed wealth, gained the vote, and won government office. At first, despite these gains, the paradigm of women's place in the law remained unchanged. Thus, women had to bring leading male doctors and lawyers into the reproductive rights movement and persuade them that the laws against contraception and abortion were unfair, thereby convincing men to take the lead in "reforming" abortion laws. In the reform movement that men led, abortion was an important but not a defining issue of law. Men aided the women in the fight for control of their own bodies, but it was a battle on the periphery of the law.

It was only when the women's movement of the 1960s emerged and began to formulate a new conception of women's place in the law that abortion became a major national issue. For women reformers saw that the key to legal equality was choice, and the crucial test of choice for women was access to abortion. As the women's movement made abortion rights politically visible, abortion rights advocates added a second strand to the argument for women's rights generally. Abortion rights promoters brought to the courtroom a new, direct, everyday voice. They wove the records of this voice into the dry, technical, formal presentations of law. Abortion rights, absorbing both the ideal of choice and autonomy and the plain style of speaking, became the centerpiece of a new paradigm of women's place in the law. When abortion rights were challenged, narrowed, and endangered, advocates saw an assault not only on a newly won legal right but on the entire system of emancipated feminist thought that right symbolized.

The storm that formed during and after *Roe* was so bitter because both sides saw abortion not as a simple, limited legal issue, but as one that represented two opposing moral worlds. As Justice Breyer wrote in his opinion on partial-birth abortion, pro-life and pro-abortion rights seemed "virtually irreconcilable points of view." We are an intensely moralistic nation. We frame our foreign affairs and our wars, our politics and our economics, in terms of moral precepts. For pro-abortion rights forces, choice was a moral principle that went far beyond abortion rights; for anti-abortion rights groups, fetal life was a moral principle that reached out to the sacred memory of traditional families and motherhood.

Both sides rooted their arguments in older American values. Both sides believed fervently in their cause because they saw themselves as moral preceptors. Their language and their tactics grew more strident because they were radicalized by their participation in the abortion rights wars. Abortion rights rhetoric served as a political litmus test, and entire political campaigns turned on abortion planks.

In the face of the political storm, it was inevitable that the High Court become politicized. Appointment to the federal bench was more and more based on the nominees' views of *Roe*, and debates over *Roe* bent the entire shape of the judiciary in a way similar to abortion rights' impact on local and national elections. The justices of the Supreme Court began to use stronger and stronger language in their opinions, accusing one another of improper purposes and unsound readings of statutes and the Constitution. The polarization of the legal debate and the legal community could hardly be laid to the door of the majority in *Roe*, particularly Justice Blackmun, who tailored his opinion to win the support of all of his colleagues and who wanted *Roe* to take abortion out of politics. But when politics becomes the handmaiden of morality, no branch of government will be safe from political partisanship.

In the courtroom and the convention hall, *Roe* demonstrated that the wall of separation between church and state is translucent if not invisible. This theme too is deeply embedded in our history. Although some religious groups, such as the National Conference of Christians and Jews, supported *Roe*, the opposition to *Roe* was profoundly religious, expressed in religious terms and led by clergymen or those trained for the ministry. In its ability to bring together evangelical and liturgical leaders, pro-life indeed came as close to an ecumenical movement as American history has seen.

Roe also proved that movements for liberal reform and equality in American history, such as the women's movement, are matched against an equally powerful cultural and social conservatism. Had the opposition to *Roe* been all male, one might have ascribed it to the struggle for political and economic power between the sexes. Had it been a quarrel among women, we might attribute it to a deep divide in women's views of their place. In fact, men and women on either side saw abortion as part of a larger scheme, in which change or resistance to change was crucial. Legal issues often become the foci of such free-floating cultural schisms; the creation-evolution controversy is another of them.

Third, the battle over *Roe* proved how powerful the media is and how easily, in some cases, it can manipulate or manufacture opinion. This may seem a cynical judgment on the close tie between democracy and demagoguery, but from the first efforts of the doctors in the 1840s and 1850s to criminalize abortion, through the eugenics movement of the 1920s, to the demonization of abortion providers in the 1990s, the role of mass communication and the unstable emotional currents it unleashes are integral to the abortion rights story.

Finally, *Roe* proved that the course of the law is not linear, making itself pure over time, but loops back and twists and turns. As near as *Roe* has come to extinction, it has survived not because its technical formulas were impervious to criticism. They were not, and no longer suffice. *Roe* still stands because it symbolized an idea whose time had come—the idea that women's bodies belong to women, not men, not doctors, not pressure groups, not Congress, not lobbyists, and certainly not judges and justices in court. In this sense, the symbolic sense, the persistence of *Roe* proves that the arcane tracings of legal language survive only when they conform to larger social and cultural realities.

F U R T H E R   R E A D I N G

Baer, Judith. *Women in American Law: The Struggle Toward Equality from the New Deal to the Present*, 3rd ed. (2002).

Ball, Howard and Phillip J. Cooper. *Of Power and Right: Hugo Black, William O. Douglass, and America's Constitutional Revolution* (1992).

Berry, Mary Frances. *Why the ERA Failed: Politics, Women's Rights and the Amending Process of the Constitution* (1986).

Dworkin, Ronald. *Life's Dominion: An Argument about Abortion, Euthanasia, and Individual Freedom* (1993).

Epstein, Richard A. "Substantive Due Process by Any Other Name: The Abortion Cases," *Supreme Court Review*, (1973): 159–185.

Evans, Sara. *Born for Liberty: A History of Women in America* (1989).

Faux, Marian. *Roe v. Wade: The Untold Story of the Landmark Supreme Court Decision that Made Abortion Legal* (2001).

Garrow, David. *Liberty and Sexuality: The Right to Privacy and the Making of Roe v. Wade* (1994).

Graber, Mark. *Rethinking Abortion: Equal Choice, The Constitution, and Reproductive Politics* (1996).

Held, Allison L., Sheryl L. Herndon, and Danielle M. Stager. "The Equal Rights Amendment: Why the ERA Remains Legally Viable and Properly Before the States," *William and Mary Journal of Women and the Law*, 3 (1997): 113–136.

Hensley, Thomas R. *The Rehnquist Court: Justices, Rulings, and Legacy* (2006).

Johnson, John W. *Griswold v. Connecticut: Birth Control and the Constitutional Right of Privacy* (2005).

Judges, Donald. *Hard Choices, Lost Voices: How the Abortion Conflict has Divided America, Distorted Constitutional Rights, and Damaged the Courts* (1993).

Klug, Heinz. *Constituting Democracy: Law, Globalism and South Africa's Political Reconstruction* (2000).

Maltz, Earl M. *The Chief Justiceship of Warren Burger, 1969–1986* (2000).

Sarkin, Jeremy. "The Drafting of South Africa's Final Constitution from a Human-Rights Perspective," *American Journal of Comparative Law*, 47 (1999): 67–87.

Strum, Phillipa. *Privacy: The Debate in the United States since 1945* (1997).

Tribe, Lawrence H. *Abortion: The Clash of Absolutes* (1990).

Van Burkleo, Sandra. *"Belonging to the World": Women's Rights and American Constitutional Culture* (2001).

Yarbrough, Tinsley E. *The Burger Court: Justices, Rulings, and Legacy* (2000).

CHAPTER
13

Freedom of and Freedom from
Religion

Contradictory themes have pervaded the history of religious freedom in America. Although many Europeans immigrated to the New World in search of religious liberty, most were intolerant of the beliefs of others. Nearly all of the American colonies provided for an "established church," which their citizens were required to attend and pay taxes to support. By the time of the Revolution, the wisdom of such practices came under attack. In Virginia, for example, Thomas Jefferson and James Madison argued for the disestablishment of the Anglican Church. Jefferson insisted that a "wall of separation" between church and state was necessary to guarantee individual religious freedom. Most early state constitutions followed Jefferson's lead, although several states continued to provide direct support to churches. As originally drafted, the U.S. Constitution left open the possibility that the national government could establish a church—a fact which Anti-Federalists sharply criticized. In 1790, James Madison addressed these concerns in the First Amendment: "Congress shall make no law respecting an establishment of religion, or prohibiting the free exercise thereof."

Throughout the first century and a half of American history, the Supreme Court had little occasion to interpret the Constitution's Establishment and Free Exercise Clauses. Because the First Amendment applied explicitly and exclusively to Congress, states retained a free hand to enact legislation regarding religion, provided they acted within the bounds of their own constitutions. The fact that the American population remained overwhelmingly Christian—especially Protestant—for so many decades, moreover, resulted in few federal legal disputes over religion. Not until the 1940s—as the cumulative effects of successive waves of immigration wrought an unprecedented degree of diversity—did religion become a subject of importance to the Supreme Court. In 1947, in Everson v. Board of Education, the Court took two significant steps in its interpretation of the religion clauses. First, it adopted Jefferson's "wall of separation" metaphor as a guiding principle, and second, it held that the First Amendment's prohibition against an establishment of religion applied to the states. In subsequent decades, atheists and religious minorities (including Jews and Jehovah's Witnesses, for example) wanted the justices to sustain this "separationist" stance with regard to the Establishment Clause. They claimed that any attempt by government to require certain religious practices and most efforts to promote religion in the public square breached that wall. Beginning in the 1970s, debates over religious liberty grew increasingly tense, as conservative Christians reacted to the counterculture of the 1960s by pressing for greater government accommodation of religious belief and practice.

As with other recent constitutional controversies, such as school desegregation and abortion, debates over religion have touched on larger issues over the proper role of the Supreme Court and the appropriate means of interpreting the Constitution. The liberal Warren Court embraced the "wall of separation" metaphor and ended such practices as organized prayer and Bible reading in public schools. In doing so, the justices sought to expand and protect the individual rights of religious minorities, despite widespread popular dissatisfaction with such decisions. Some of the more conservative justices on the Burger and Rehnquist Courts relied on a different reading of the nation's history. Adhering to a jurisprudence of original intent, which claims that judges ought to decide cases based on the intentions of those who framed the Constitution, conservatives claimed that the Establishment Clause should be read narrowly as only forbidding the creation of a national church. They argued, moreover, that the clause's authors never intended the First Amendment to be "incorporated" to apply to the states. At the time of the ratification of the amendment, they noted, most states still provided official support to churches. Conservatives, therefore, argued that Everson had led the Court astray—down a path of incorporation and separationism—from which it has never quite diverged.

How should the Constitution's religion clauses be interpreted? Are the Establishment Clause and Free Exercise Clause in tension with each other? Should the individual rights of religious expression outweigh concerns over breeching the "wall of separation" between church and state? Is the "wall" metaphor an effective way of interpreting the First Amendment? To what extent should Jefferson's views—or the views of any of the founders—guide judicial interpretation of the religion clauses? What about when religious practice violates criminal statutes— relating to drug use, for example? What impact will America's increasing religious diversity have on the future interpretation of the religion clauses?

✛ D O C U M E N T S

One of the most controversial Supreme Court decisions of the modern era was *Engel v. Vitale*, Document 1, which invalidated a state-mandated prayer used to open each school day in New York. Justice Hugo Black's majority opinion (in a 7-1 vote) drew heavily on Jefferson's writings, as well as Madison's "Memorial and Remonstrance against Religious Assessments." Justice Potter Stewart's dissent emphasized the role of religious tradition in American public life. President John F. Kennedy weighed in on the issue when asked about it in his news conference of June 27, 1962. His response, Document 2, was that families should devote themselves ever more faithfully to prayer at home. In the immediate aftermath of *Engel*, scores of proposed amendments to the Constitution sought to reverse the Court's school prayer decision. None succeeded.

After the howls of protests against *Engel*, as well as another case the following year that banned organized Bible reading in public schools, the Court attempted to formulate a standard for interpreting the Establishment Clause. In *Lemon v. Kurtzman*, Document 3, the justices considered state laws from Rhode Island and Pennsylvania that allowed for direct state support of salaries for teachers who taught secular subjects in parochial and other nonpublic schools. In striking down the laws, a unanimous Court (7-0) formulated a three-pronged test to evaluate whether a law violated the Establishment Clause. Chief

Justice Warren Burger wrote the opinion. Nearly a decade and a half later, a more conservative Court revisited the school prayer issue in *Wallace v. Jaffree*, Document 4, when considering an Alabama law that provided for a minute of silence for "meditation or voluntary prayer." In a 6-3 ruling, Justice John Paul Stevens applied the so-called *Lemon* test and affirmed the Court's school prayer precedents in declaring the Alabama law unconstitutional. Justice William Rehnquist issued a spirited dissent.

Despite the highly public—and mostly symbolic—debate over school prayer, the Court's decision in *Employment Division v. Smith*, Document 5, has proven more significant from a legal standpoint. The case involved members of the Native American Church, who were fired from their jobs for engaging in the ritual use of peyote, a stimulant. A 5-4 majority, with Justice Antonin Scalia writing the opinion, ruled that the Free Exercise Clause does not require that laws burdening religious practice rest on a "compelling state interest." Their religious beliefs notwithstanding, individuals who violated a state law prohibiting use of peyote could lose their jobs, as well as their unemployment benefits. The *Smith* decision prompted Congress to intervene. In the Religious Freedom Restoration Act, Document 6, lawmakers restored the doctrine that *Smith* had overturned: when enacting laws that burden an individual's free exercise rights, states must prove that they have a "compelling interest" in the legislation. In 1997, the Court overturned the Religious Freedom Restoration Act, in *City of Boerne v. Flores*, as an unconstitutional exercise of congressional authority.

Zelman v. Simmons-Harris, Document 7, involved another controversial issue with implications for the Constitution's religion clauses—school vouchers. To improve educational opportunities in Cleveland, the state of Ohio enacted a plan under which low-income students could use state-funded tuition vouchers to attend participating public and private schools. Nearly all the students ended up in religiously-affiliated schools. Challenged as a violation of the Establishment Clause, a 5-4 majority, with Chief Justice William Rehnquist writing the opinion, upheld the voucher program.

✣ D O C U M E N T   1

Engel v. Vitale, 1962

Mr. Justice Black delivered the opinion of the Court.

The respondent Board of Education of Union Free School District No. 9, New Hyde Park, New York, acting in its official capacity under state law, directed the School District's principal to cause the following prayer to be said aloud by each class in the presence of a teacher at the beginning of each school day:

> Almighty God, we acknowledge our dependence upon Thee, and we beg Thy blessings upon us, our parents, our teachers and our Country.

This daily procedure was adopted on the recommendation of the State Board of Regents, a governmental agency created by the State Constitution to which the New York Legislature has granted broad supervisory, executive, and legislative powers over the State's public school system. ...

We think that by using its public school system to encourage recitation of the Regents' prayer, the State of New York has adopted a practice wholly inconsistent with the Establishment Clause. There can, of course, be no doubt that New York's program of daily classroom invocation of God's blessings as prescribed in the Regents' prayer is a religious activity. It is a solemn avowal of divine faith and supplication for the blessings of the Almighty. The nature of such a prayer has always been religious, none of the respondents has denied this. . . .

It is a matter of history that this very practice of establishing governmentally composed prayers for religious services was one of the reasons which caused many of our early colonists to leave England and seek religious freedom in America. The Book of Common Prayer, which was created under governmental direction and which was approved by Acts of Parliament in 1548 and 1549, set out in minute detail the accepted form and content of prayer and other religious ceremonies to be used in the established, tax-supported Church of England. The controversies over the Book and what should be its content repeatedly threatened to disrupt the peace of that country as the accepted forms of prayer in the established church changed with the views of the particular ruler that happened to be in control at the time. Powerful groups representing some of the varying religious views of the people struggled among themselves to impress their particular views upon the Government and obtain amendments of the Book more suitable to their respective notions of how religious services should be conducted in order that the official religious establishment would advance their particular religious beliefs. Other groups, lacking the necessary political power to influence the Government on the matter, decided to leave England and its established church and seek freedom in America from England's governmentally ordained and supported religion.

It is an unfortunate fact of history that when some of the very groups which had most strenuously opposed the established Church of England found themselves sufficiently in control of colonial governments in this country to write their own prayers into law, they passed laws making their own religion the official religion of their respective colonies. Indeed, as late as the time of the Revolutionary War, there were established churches in at least eight of the thirteen former colonies and established religions in at least four of the other five. But the successful Revolution against English political domination was shortly followed by intense opposition to the practice of establishing religion by law. . . .

By the time of the adoption of the Constitution, our history shows that there was a widespread awareness among many Americans of the dangers of a union of Church and State. These people knew, some of them from bitter personal experience, that one of the greatest dangers to the freedom of the individual to worship in his own way lay in the Government's placing its official stamp of approval upon one particular kind of prayer or one particular form of religious services. They knew the anguish, hardship and bitter strife that could come when zealous religious groups struggled with one another to obtain the Government's stamp of approval from each King, Queen, or Protector that came to temporary power. The Constitution was intended to avert a part of this danger by leaving the government of this country in the hands of the people rather than in the hands of any monarch. But this safeguard was not enough. Our Founders were no more willing to let the content of their prayers and their privilege of praying whenever they pleased be influenced by the ballot box than they were to let these vital matters of personal conscience depend upon the succession of monarchs. The First Amendment was added to the Constitution to stand as a guarantee that neither the power nor the prestige of the Federal Government would be used to control, support or influence the kinds of prayer the American people can say—that the people's religions must not be subjected to the pressures of government for change each time a new political administration is elected to office. Under that Amendment's prohibition against governmental establishment of religion, as reinforced by the provisions of the Fourteenth Amendment, government in this country, be it state or federal, is without power to prescribe by law any particular form of prayer which is to be used as an official prayer in carrying on any program of governmentally sponsored religious activity.

There can be no doubt that New York's state prayer program officially establishes the religious beliefs embodied in the Regents' prayer. The respondents' argument to the contrary, which is largely based upon the contention that the Regents' prayer is "non-denominational" and the fact that the program, as modified and approved by state courts, does not require all pupils to recite the prayer but permits those who wish to do so to remain silent or be excused from the room, ignores the essential nature of the program's constitutional defects. Neither the fact that the prayer may be denominationally neutral nor the fact that its observance on the part of the students is voluntary can serve to free it from the limitations of the Establishment Clause, as it might from the Free Exercise Clause, of the First Amendment, both of which are operative against the States by virtue of the Fourteenth Amendment. Although these two clauses may in certain instances overlap, they forbid two quite different kinds of governmental encroachment upon religious freedom. The Establishment Clause, unlike the Free Exercise Clause, does not depend upon any showing of direct governmental compulsion and is violated by the enactment of laws which establish an official religion whether those laws operate directly to coerce nonobserving individuals or not. This is not to say, of course, that laws officially prescribing a particular form of religious worship do not involve coercion of such individuals. When the power, prestige and financial support of government is placed behind a particular religious belief, the indirect coercive pressure upon religious minorities to conform to the prevailing officially approved religion is plain. But the purposes underlying the Establishment Clause go much further than that. Its first and most immediate purpose rested on the belief that a union of government and religion tends to destroy government and to degrade religion. The history of governmentally established religion, both in England and in this country, showed that whenever government had allied itself with one particular form of religion, the inevitable result had been that it had incurred the hatred, disrespect and even contempt of those who held contrary beliefs. That same history showed that many people had lost their respect for any religion that had relied upon the support of government to spread its faith. The Establishment Clause thus stands as an expression of principle on the part of the Founders of our Constitution that religion is too personal, too sacred, too holy, to permit its "unhallowed perversion" by a civil magistrate. Another purpose of the Establishment Clause rested upon an awareness of the historical fact that governmentally established religions and religious persecutions go hand in hand. ... The New York laws officially prescribing the Regents' prayer are inconsistent both with the purposes of the Establishment Clause and with the Establishment Clause itself.

It has been argued that to apply the Constitution in such a way as to prohibit state laws respecting an establishment of religious services in public schools is to indicate a hostility toward religion or toward prayer. Nothing, of course, could be more wrong. The history of man is inseparable from the history of religion. And perhaps it is not too much to say that since the beginning of that history many people have devoutly believed that

"More things are wrought by prayer than this world dreams of." It was doubtless largely due to men who believed this that there grew up a sentiment that caused men to leave the cross-currents of officially established state religions and religious persecution in Europe and come to this country filled with the hope that they could find a place in which they could pray when they pleased to the God of their faith in the language they chose. And there were men of this same faith in the power of prayer who led the fight for adoption of our Constitution and also for our Bill of Rights with the very guarantees of religious freedom that forbid the sort of governmental activity which New York has attempted here. These men knew that the First Amendment, which tried to put an end to governmental control of religion and of prayer, was not written to destroy either. They knew rather that it was written to quiet well-justified fears which nearly all of them felt arising out of an awareness that governments of the past had shackled men's tongues to make them speak only the religious thoughts that government wanted them to speak and to pray only to the God that government wanted them to pray to. It is neither sacrilegious nor antireligious to say that each separate government in this country should stay out of the business of writing or sanctioning official prayers and leave that purely religious function to the people themselves and to those the people choose to look to for religious guidance.

... To those who may subscribe to the view that because the Regents' official prayer is so brief and general there can be no danger to religious freedom in its governmental establishment, however, it may be appropriate to say in the words of James Madison, the author of the First Amendment:

> [I]t is proper to take alarm at the first experiment on our liberties. ... Who does not see that the same authority which can establish Christianity, in exclusion of all other Religions, may establish with the same ease any particular sect of Christians, in exclusion of all other Sects? That the same authority which can force a citizen to contribute three pence only of his property for the support of any one establishment, may force him to conform to any other establishment in all cases whatsoever?

The judgment of the Court of Appeals of New York is reversed and the cause remanded for further proceedings not inconsistent with this opinion. *Reversed and remanded.*

Mr. Justice Stewart, dissenting.

A local school board in New York has provided that those pupils who wish to do so may join in a brief prayer at the beginning of each school day, acknowledging their dependence upon God and asking His blessing upon them and upon their parents, their teachers, and their country. The Court today decides that in permitting this brief nondenominational prayer the school board has violated the Constitution of the United States. I think this decision is wrong.

The Court does not hold, nor could it, that New York has interfered with the free exercise of anybody's religion. For the state courts have made clear that those who object to reciting the prayer must be entirely free of any compulsion to do so, including any "embarrassments and pressures." ... But the Court says that in permitting school children to say this simple prayer, the New York authorities have established "an official religion."

With all respect, I think the Court has misapplied a great constitutional principle. I cannot see how an "official religion" is established by letting those who want to say a prayer say it. On the contrary, I think that to deny the wish of these school children to join in reciting this prayer is to deny them the opportunity of sharing in the spiritual heritage of our Nation.

The Court's historical review of the quarrels over the Book of Common Prayer in England throws no light for me on the issue before us in this case. England had then and has now an established church. Equally unenlightening, I think, is the history of the early establishment and later rejection of an official church in our own States. For we deal here not with the establishment of a state church, which would, of course, be constitutionally impermissible, but with whether school children who want to begin their day by joining in prayer must be prohibited from doing so. Moreover, I think that the Court's task, in this as in all areas of constitutional adjudication, is not responsibly aided by the uncritical invocation of metaphors like the "wall of separation," a phrase nowhere to be found in the Constitution. What is relevant to the issue here is not the history of an established church in sixteenth century England or in eighteenth century America, but the history of the religious traditions of our people, reflected in countless practices of the institutions and officials of our government.

At the opening of each day's Session of this Court we stand, while one of our officials invokes the protection of God. Since the days of John Marshall our Crier has said, "God save the United States and this Honorable Court." Both the Senate and the House of Representatives open their daily Sessions with prayer. Each of our Presidents, from George Washington to John F. Kennedy, has upon assuming his Office asked the protection and help of God. ...

In 1954 Congress added a phrase to the Pledge of Allegiance to the Flag so that it now contains the words "one Nation *under God,* indivisible, with liberty and justice for all." In 1952 Congress enacted legislation calling upon the President each year to proclaim a National Day of Prayer. Since 1865 the words IN GOD WE TRUST have been impressed on our coins. ...

I do not believe that this Court, or the Congress, or the President has by the actions and practices I have mentioned established an "official religion" in violation of the Constitution. And I do not believe the State of New York has done so in this case. What each has done has been to recognize and to follow the deeply entrenched and highly cherished spiritual traditions of our Nation—traditions which come down to us from those who almost two hundred years ago avowed their "firm Reliance on the Protection of divine Providence" when they proclaimed the freedom and independence of this brave new world.

I dissent.

✣ *D O C U M E N T   2*

President John F. Kennedy Comments on the School Prayer Decision, 1962

... **Q.** Mr. President, in the furor over the Supreme Court's decision on prayer in the schools, some members of Congress have been introducing legislation for constitutional amendments specifically to sanction prayer or religious exercise in the schools. Can you give us your opinion of the decision itself and of these moves of the Congress to circumvent it?

The President. I haven't seen the measures in the Congress and you would have to make a determination of what the language was and what effect it would have on the first amendment. The Supreme Court has made its judgment, and a good many people obviously will disagree with it. Others will agree with it. But I think that it is important for us if we are going to maintain our constitutional principle that we support the Supreme Court decisions even when we may not agree with them.

In addition we have in this case a very easy remedy and that is to pray ourselves. And I would think that it would be a welcome reminder to every American family that we can pray a good deal more at home, we can attend our churches with a good deal more fidelity, and we can make the true meaning of prayer much more important in the lives of all of our children. That power is very much open to us. And I would hope that as a result of this decision that all American parents will intensify their efforts at home, and the rest of us will support the Constitution and the responsibility of the Supreme Court in interpreting it, which is theirs, and given to them by the Constitution....

✤ *D O C U M E N T   3*

Lemon v. Kurtzman, 1971

Chief Justice Burger delivered the opinion of the Court

...In *Everson v. Board of Education,* ... this Court upheld a state statute that reimbursed the parents of parochial school children for bus transportation expenses. There MR. JUSTICE BLACK, writing for the majority, suggested that the decision carried to "the verge" of forbidden territory under the Religion Clauses. *Id.,* at 16. Candor compels acknowledgment, moreover, that we can only dimly perceive the lines of demarcation in this extraordinarily sensitive area of constitutional law.

The language of the Religion Clauses of the First Amendment is at best opaque, particularly when compared with other portions of the Amendment. Its authors did not simply prohibit the establishment of a state church or a state religion, an area history shows they regarded as very important and fraught with great dangers. Instead they commanded that there should be "no law *respecting* an establishment of religion." A law may be one "respecting" the forbidden objective while falling short of its total realization. A law "respecting" the proscribed result, that is, the establishment of religion, is not always easily identifiable as one violative of the Clause. A given law might not *establish* a state religion but nevertheless be one "respecting" that end in the sense of being a step that could lead to such establishment and hence offend the First Amendment.

In the absence of precisely stated constitutional prohibitions, we must draw lines with reference to the three main evils against which the Establishment Clause was intended to afford protection: "sponsorship, financial support, and active involvement of the sovereign in religious activity." *Walz v. Tax Commission,* ...

Every analysis in this area must begin with consideration of the cumulative criteria developed by the Court over many years. Three such tests may be gleaned from our cases. First, the statute must have a secular legislative purpose; second, its principal or primary effect must be one that neither advances nor inhibits religion, *Board of Education v. Allen;* ... finally, the statute must not foster "an excessive government entanglement with religion." ...

Inquiry into the legislative purposes of the Pennsylvania and Rhode Island statutes affords no basis for a conclusion that the legislative intent was to advance religion. On the contrary, the statutes themselves clearly state that they are intended to enhance the quality of the secular education in all schools covered by the compulsory attendance laws. There is no reason to believe the legislatures meant anything else. A State always has a legitimate concern for maintaining minimum standards in all schools it allows to operate. As in *Allen,* we find nothing here that undermines the stated legislative intent; it must therefore be accorded appropriate deference.

In *Allen* the Court acknowledged that secular and religious teachings were not necessarily so intertwined that secular textbooks furnished to students by the State were in fact instrumental in the teaching of religion. ... The legislatures of Rhode Island and Pennsylvania have concluded that secular and religious education are identifiable and separable. In the abstract we have no quarrel with this conclusion.

The two legislatures, however, have also recognized that church-related elementary and secondary schools have a significant religious mission and that a substantial portion of their activities is religiously oriented. They have therefore sought to create statutory restrictions designed to guarantee the separation between secular and religious educational functions and to ensure that State financial aid supports only the former. All these provisions are precautions taken in candid recognition that these programs approached, even if they did not intrude upon, the forbidden areas under the Religion Clauses. We need not decide whether these legislative precautions restrict the principal or primary effect of the programs to the point where they do not offend the Religion Clauses, for we conclude that the cumulative impact of the entire relationship arising under the statutes in each State involves excessive entanglement between government and religion.

In *Walz v. Tax Commission,* ... the Court upheld state tax exemptions for real property owned by religious organizations and used for religious worship. That holding, however, tended to confine rather than enlarge the area of permissible state involvement with religious institutions by calling for close scrutiny of the degree of entanglement involved in the relationship. The objective is to prevent, as far as possible, the intrusion of either into the precincts of the other.

Our prior holdings do not call for total separation between church and state; total separation is not possible in an absolute sense. Some relationship between government and religious organizations is inevitable. ... Fire inspections, building and zoning regulations, and state requirements under compulsory school-attendance laws are examples of necessary and permissible contacts. Indeed, under the statutory exemption before us in *Walz,* the State had a continuing burden to ascertain that the exempt property was in fact being used for religious worship. Judicial caveats against entanglement must recognize that the line of separation, far from being a "wall," is a blurred, indistinct, and variable barrier depending on all the circumstances of a particular relationship.

This is not to suggest, however, that we are to engage in a legalistic minuet in which precise rules and forms must govern. A true minuet is a matter of pure form and style, the observance of which is itself the substantive end. Here we examine the form of the relationship for the light that it casts on the substance.

In order to determine whether the government entanglement with religion is excessive, we must examine the character and purposes of the institutions that are benefited, the nature of the aid that the State provides, and the resulting relationship between the government and the religious authority.... Here we find that both statutes foster an impermissible degree of entanglement....

In *Walz* it was argued that a tax exemption for places of religious worship would prove to be the first step in an inevitable progression leading to the establishment of state churches and state religion. That claim could not stand up against more than 200 years of virtually universal practice imbedded in our colonial experience and continuing into the present.

The progression argument, however, is more persuasive here. We have no long history of state aid to church-related educational institutions comparable to 200 years of tax exemption for churches. Indeed, the state programs before us today represent something of an innovation. We have already noted that modern governmental programs have self-perpetuating and self-expanding propensities. These internal pressures are only enhanced when the schemes involve institutions whose legitimate needs are growing and whose interests have substantial political support. Nor can we fail to see that in constitutional adjudication some steps, which when taken were thought to approach "the verge," have become the platform for yet further steps. A certain momentum develops in constitutional theory and it can be a "downhill thrust" easily set in motion but difficult to retard or stop. Development by momentum is not invariably bad; indeed, it is the way the common law has grown, but it is a force to be recognized and reckoned with. The dangers are increased by the difficulty of perceiving in advance exactly where the "verge" of the precipice lies. As well as constituting an independent evil against which the Religion Clauses were intended to protect, involvement or entanglement between government and religion serves as a warning signal.

Finally, nothing we have said can be construed to disparage the role of church-related elementary and secondary schools in our national life. Their contribution has been and is enormous. Nor do we ignore their economic plight in a period of rising costs and expanding need. Taxpayers generally have been spared vast sums by the maintenance of these educational institutions by religious organizations, largely by the gifts of faithful adherents.

The merit and benefits of these schools, however, are not the issue before us in these cases. The sole question is whether state aid to these schools can be squared with the dictates of the Religion Clauses, Under our system the choice has been made that government is to be entirely excluded from the area of religious instruction and churches excluded from the affairs of government. The Constitution decrees that religion must be a private matter for the individual, the family, and the institutions of private choice, and that while some involvement and entanglement are inevitable, lines must be drawn. ...

✠ *D O C U M E N T   4*

Wallace v. Jaffree, 1985

Mr. Justice Stevens delivered the opinion of the Court

… Our unanimous affirmance of the Court of Appeals' judgment. … makes it unnecessary to comment at length on the District Court's remarkable conclusion that the Federal Constitution imposes no obstacle to Alabama's establishment of a state religion. Before analyzing the precise issue that is presented to us, it is nevertheless appropriate to recall how firmly embedded in our constitutional jurisprudence is the proposition that the several States have no greater power to restrain the individual freedoms protected by the First Amendment than does the Congress of the United States.

As is plain from its text, the First Amendment was adopted to curtail the power of Congress to interfere with the individual's freedom to believe, to worship, and to express himself in accordance with the dictates of his own conscience. Until the Fourteenth Amendment was added to the Constitution, the First Amendment's restraints on the exercise of federal power simply did not apply to the States. But when the Constitution was amended to prohibit any State from depriving any person of liberty without due process of law, that Amendment imposed the same substantive limitations on the States' power to legislate that the First Amendment had always imposed on the Congress' power. This Court has confirmed and endorsed this elementary proposition of law time and time again.

Just as the right to speak and the right to refrain from speaking are complementary components of a broader concept of individual freedom of mind, so also the individual's freedom to choose his own creed is the counterpart of his right to refrain from accepting the creed established by the majority. At one time it was thought that this right merely proscribed the preference of one Christian sect over another, but would not require equal respect for the conscience of the infidel, the atheist, or the adherent of a non-Christian faith such as Mohammedism or Judaism. But when the underlying principle has been examined in the crucible of litigation, the Court has unambiguously concluded that the individual freedom of conscience protected by the First Amendment embraces the right to select any religious faith or none at all. This conclusion derives support not only from the interest in respecting the individual's freedom of conscience, but also from the conviction that religious beliefs worthy of respect are the product of free and voluntary choice by the faithful, and from recognition of the fact that the political interest in forestalling intolerance extends beyond intolerance among Christian sects—or even intolerance among "religions"—to encompass intolerance of the disbeliever and the uncertain. The State of Alabama, no less than the Congress of the United States, must respect that basic truth.

III. … The First Amendment requires that a statute must be invalidated if it is entirely motivated by a purpose to advance religion.

In applying the purpose test, it is appropriate to ask "whether government's actual purpose is to endorse or disapprove of religion." … In this case, the answer to that question is dispositive. For the record not only provides us with an unambiguous affirmative answer, but it also reveals that the enactment … was not motivated by any clearly secular purpose—indeed, the statute had *no* secular purpose.

IV. The sponsor of the bill..., Senator Donald Holmes, inserted into the legislative record—apparently without dissent—a statement indicating that the legislation was an "effort to return voluntary prayer" to the public schools. Later Senator Holmes confirmed this purpose before the District Court. In response to the question whether he had any purpose for the legislation other than returning voluntary prayer to public schools, he stated, "No, I did not have no other purpose in mind." The State did not present evidence of *any* secular purpose....

...The Legislature acted...for the sole purpose of expressing the State's endorsement of prayer activities for one minute at the beginning of each school day. The addition of "or voluntary prayer" indicates that the State intended to characterize prayer as a favored practice. Such an endorsement is not consistent with the established principle that the Government must pursue a course of complete neutrality toward religion.

The importance of that principle does not permit us to treat this as an inconsequential case involving nothing more than a few words of symbolic speech on behalf of the political majority. For whenever the State itself speaks on a religious subject, one of the questions that we must ask is "whether the Government intends to convey a message of endorsement or disapproval of religion." The well-supported concurrent findings of the District Court and the Court of Appeals—that [the statute] was intended to convey a message of State-approval of prayer activities in the public schools—make it unnecessary, and indeed inappropriate, to evaluate the practical significance of the addition of the words "or voluntary prayer" to the statute. Keeping in mind, as we must, "both the fundamental place held by the Establishment Clause in our constitutional scheme and the myriad, subtle ways in which Establishment Clause values can be eroded,"...we conclude that [the statute] violates the First Amendment.

The judgment of the Court of Appeals is affirmed....

Justice Rehnquist, dissenting.

...It is impossible to build sound constitutional doctrine upon a mistaken understanding of constitutional history, but unfortunately the Establishment Clause has been expressly freighted with Jefferson's misleading metaphor for nearly 40 years. Thomas Jefferson was of course in France at the time the constitutional Amendments known as the Bill of Rights were passed by Congress and ratified by the States. His letter to the Danbury Baptist Association was a short note of courtesy, written 14 years after the Amendments were passed by Congress. He would seem to any detached observer as a less than ideal source of contemporary history as to the meaning of the Religion Clauses of the First Amendment....

Notwithstanding the absence of a historical basis for this theory of rigid separation, the wall idea might well have served as a useful albeit misguided analytical concept, had it led this Court to unified and principled results in Establishment Clause cases. The opposite, unfortunately, has been true; in the 38 years since *Everson* our Establishment Clause cases have been neither principled nor unified. Our recent opinions, many of them hopelessly divided pluralities, have with embarrassing candor conceded that the "wall of separation" is merely a "blurred, indistinct, and variable barrier," which "is not wholly accurate" and can only be "dimly perceived." *Lemon v. Kurtzman,...Tilton v. Richardson,...Wolman v. Walter,...Lynch v. Donnelly,....*

Whether due to its lack of historical support or its practical unworkability, the *Everson* "wall" has proved all but useless as a guide to sound constitutional adjudication. It illustrates only too well the wisdom of Benjamin Cardozo's observation that "[m]etaphors in law are to be narrowly watched, for starting as devices to liberate thought, they end often by enslaving it." *Berkey v. Third Avenue R. Co.,* ...

But the greatest injury of the "wall" notion is its mischievous diversion of judges from the actual intentions of the drafters of the Bill of Rights. The "crucible of litigation," ... is well adapted to adjudicating factual disputes on the basis of testimony presented in court, but no amount of repetition of historical errors in judicial opinions can make the errors true. The "wall of separation between church and State" is a metaphor based on bad history, a metaphor which has proved useless as a guide to judging. It should be frankly and explicitly abandoned. ...

✤ *D O C U M E N T   5*

Employment Division, Department of Human Resources of Oregon v. Smith, 1990

Mr. Justice Scalia delivered the opinion of the Court

... The Free Exercise Clause of the First Amendment, which has been made applicable to the States by incorporation into the Fourteenth Amendment, see *Cantwell v. Connecticut,* ..., provides that "Congress shall make no law respecting an establishment of religion, or *prohibiting the free exercise thereof.* ..." U. S. Const., Amdt. 1 (emphasis added). The free exercise of religion means, first and foremost, the right to believe and profess whatever religious doctrine one desires. Thus, the First Amendment obviously excludes all "governmental regulation of religious *beliefs* as such." ...

But the "exercise of religion" often involves not only belief and profession but the performance of (or abstention from) physical acts: assembling with others for a worship service, participating in sacramental use of bread and wine, proselytizing, abstaining from certain foods or certain modes of transportation. It would be true, we think (though no case of ours has involved the point), that a State would be "prohibiting the free exercise [of religion]" if it sought to ban such acts or abstentions only when they are engaged in for religious reasons, or only because of the religious belief that they display. It would doubtless be unconstitutional, for example, to ban the casting of "statues that are to be used for worship purposes," or to prohibit bowing down before a golden calf.

Respondents in the present case, however, seek to carry the meaning of "prohibiting the free exercise [of religion]" one large step further. They contend that their religious motivation for using peyote places them beyond the reach of a criminal law that is not specifically directed at their religious practice, and that is concededly constitutional as applied to those who use the drug for other reasons. They assert, in other words, that "prohibiting the free exercise [of religion]" includes requiring any individual to observe a generally applicable law that requires (or forbids) the performance of an act that his religious belief forbids (or requires).

As a textual matter, we do not think the words must be given that meaning. It is no more necessary to regard the collection of a general tax, for example, as "prohibiting the free exercise [of religion]" by those citizens who believe support of organized government to be sinful, than it is to regard the same tax as "abridging the freedom ... of the press" of those publishing companies that must pay the tax as a condition of staying in business. It is a permissible reading of the text, in the one case as in the other, to say that if prohibiting the exercise of religion (or burdening the activity of printing) is not the object of the tax but merely the incidental effect of a generally applicable and otherwise valid provision, the First Amendment has not been offended. ...

Our decisions reveal that the latter reading is the correct one. We have never held that an individual's religious beliefs excuse him from compliance with an otherwise valid law prohibiting conduct that the State is free to regulate. On the contrary, the record of more than a century of our free exercise jurisprudence contradicts that proposition. As described succinctly by Justice Frankfurter in *Minersville School Dist. Bd. of Ed. v. Gobitis, ...* "Conscientious scruples have not, in the course of the long struggle for religious toleration, relieved the individual from obedience to a general law not aimed at the promotion or restriction of religious beliefs. The mere possession of religious convictions which contradict the relevant concerns of a political society does not relieve the citizen from the discharge of political responsibilities. ..." We first had occasion to assert that principle in *Reynolds v. United States, ...*, where we rejected the claim that criminal laws against polygamy could not be constitutionally applied to those whose religion commanded the practice. "Laws," we said, "are made for the government of actions, and while they cannot interfere with mere religious belief and opinions, they may with practices. ... Can a man excuse his practices to the contrary because of his religious belief? To permit this would be to make the professed doctrines of religious belief superior to the law of the land, and in effect to permit every citizen to become a law unto himself."

Subsequent decisions have consistently held that the right of free exercise does not relieve an individual of the obligation to comply with a "valid and neutral law of general applicability on the ground that the law proscribes (or prescribes) conduct that his religion prescribes (or proscribes)." ...

Respondents argue that even though exemption from generally applicable criminal laws need not automatically be extended to religiously motivated actors, at least the claim for a religious exemption must be evaluated under the balancing test set forth in *Sherbert v. Verner, ...* Under the *Sherbert* test, governmental actions that substantially burden a religious practice must be justified by a compelling governmental interest. ... Applying that test we have, on three occasions, invalidated state unemployment compensation rules that conditioned the availability of benefits upon an applicant's willingness to work under conditions forbidden by his religion. ... We have never invalidated any governmental action on the basis of the *Sherbert* test except the denial of unemployment compensation. Although we have sometimes purported to apply the *Sherbert* test in contexts other than that, we have always found the test satisfied, see *United States v. Lee, ...*; *Gillette v. United States, ...* In recent years we have abstained from applying the *Sherbert* test (outside the unemployment compensation field) at all. In *Bowen v. Roy, ...*, we declined to apply

Sherbert analysis to a federal statutory scheme that required benefit applicants and recipients to provide their Social Security numbers. The plaintiffs in that case asserted that it would violate their religious beliefs to obtain and provide a Social Security number for their daughter. We held the statute's application to the plaintiffs valid regardless of whether it was necessary to effectuate a compelling interest. ... In *Lyng v. Northwest Indian Cemetery Protective Assn.*, ..., we declined to apply *Sherbert* analysis to the Government's logging and road construction activities on lands used for religious purposes by several Native American Tribes, even though it was undisputed that the activities "could have devastating effects on traditional Indian religious practices." In *Goldman v. Weinberger*, ..., we rejected application of the *Sherbert* test to military dress regulations that forbade the wearing of yarmulkes. In *O'Lone v. Estate of Shabazz*, ..., we sustained, without mentioning the *Sherbert* test, a prison's refusal to excuse inmates from work requirements to attend worship services.

Even if we were inclined to breathe into *Sherbert* some life beyond the unemployment compensation field, we would not apply it to require exemptions from a generally applicable criminal law. The *Sherbert* test, it must be recalled, was developed in a context that lent itself to individualized governmental assessment of the reasons for the relevant conduct. As a plurality of the Court noted in *Roy*, a distinctive feature of unemployment compensation programs is that their eligibility criteria invite consideration of the particular circumstances behind an applicant's unemployment: "The statutory conditions [in *Sherbert* and *Thomas*] provided that a person was not eligible for unemployment compensation benefits if, 'without good cause,' he had quit work or refused available work. The 'good cause' standard created a mechanism for individualized exemptions." ... As the plurality pointed out in *Roy*, our decisions in the unemployment cases stand for the proposition that where the State has in place a system of individual exemptions, it may not refuse to extend that system to cases of "religious hardship" without compelling reason. *Bowen v. Roy*, ...

Whether or not the decisions are that limited, they at least have nothing to do with an across-the-board criminal prohibition on a particular form of conduct. Although, as noted earlier, we have sometimes used the *Sherbert* test to analyze free exercise challenges to such laws, see *United States v. Lee, Gillette v. United States*, ... we have never applied the test to invalidate one. We conclude today that the sounder approach, and the approach in accord with the vast majority of our precedents, is to hold the test inapplicable to such challenges. The government's ability to enforce generally applicable prohibitions of socially harmful conduct, like its ability to carry out other aspects of public policy, "cannot depend on measuring the effects of a governmental action on a religious objector's spiritual development." ... To make an individual's obligation to obey such a law contingent upon the law's coincidence with his religious beliefs, except where the State's interest is "compelling"—permitting him, by virtue of his beliefs, "to become a law unto himself," *Reynolds v. United States*, ... —contradicts both constitutional tradition and common sense. ...

✣ D O C U M E N T   6

Congress Overturns *Smith* in the Religious Freedom Restoration Act, 1993

An Act

To protect the free exercise of religion.

Be it enacted by the Senate and House of Representatives of the United States of America in Congress assembled,

Sec. 1. Short Title.   This Act may be cited as the 'Religious Freedom Restoration Act of 1993'.

Sec. 2.   Congressional Findings and Declaration of Purposes.

(a) Findings: The Congress finds that—

(1) the framers of the Constitution, recognizing free exercise of religion as an unalienable right, secured its protection in the First Amendment to the Constitution;

(2) laws 'neutral' toward religion may burden religious exercise as surely as laws intended to interfere with religious exercise;

(3) governments should not substantially burden religious exercise without compelling justification;

(4) in *Employment Division v. Smith*, 494 U.S. 872 (1990) the Supreme Court virtually eliminated the requirement that the government justify burdens on religious exercise imposed by laws neutral toward religion; and

(5) the compelling interest test as set forth in prior Federal court rulings is a workable test for striking sensible balances between religious liberty and competing prior governmental interests.

(b) Purposes: The purposes of this Act are—

(1) to restore the compelling interest test as set forth in *Sherbert v. Verner,* 374 U.S. 398 (1963) and *Wisconsin v. Yoder,* 406 U.S. 205 (1972) and to guarantee its application in all cases where free exercise of religion is substantially burdened; and

(2) to provide a claim or defense to persons whose religious exercise is substantially burdened by government.

Sec. 3.   Free Exercise of Religion Protected.

(a) In General: Government shall not substantially burden a person's exercise of religion even if the burden results from a rule of general applicability, except as provided in subsection (b).

(b) Exception: Government may substantially burden a person's exercise of religion only if it demonstrates that application of the burden to the person—

(1) is in furtherance of a compelling governmental interest; and

(2) is the least restrictive means of furthering that compelling governmental interest.

(c) **Judicial Relief**: A person whose religious exercise has been burdened in violation of this section may assert that violation as a claim or defense in a judicial proceeding and obtain appropriate relief against a government. Standing to assert a claim or defense under this section shall be governed by the general rules of standing under article III of the Constitution....

Sec. 7. Establishment Clause Unaffected.   Nothing in this Act shall be construed to affect, interpret, or in any way address that portion of the First Amendment prohibiting laws respecting the establishment of religion (referred to in this section as the 'Establishment Clause'). Granting government funding, benefits, or exemptions, to the extent permissible under the Establishment Clause, shall not constitute a violation of this Act. As used in this section, the term 'granting', used with respect to government funding, benefits, or exemptions, does not include the denial of government funding, benefits, or exemptions.

✠ *D O C U M E N T   7*

Zelman v. Simmons-Harris, 2002

Chief Justice Rehnquist delivered the opinion of the Court

   ... The Establishment Clause of the First Amendment, applied to the States through the Fourteenth Amendment, prevents a State from enacting laws that have the "purpose" or "effect" of advancing or inhibiting religion. *Agostini v. Felton*, ... ("[W]e continue to ask whether the government acted with the purpose of advancing or inhibiting religion [and] whether the aid has the 'effect' of advancing or inhibiting religion."... There is no dispute that the program challenged here was enacted for the valid secular purpose of providing educational assistance to poor children in a demonstrably failing public school system. Thus, the question presented is whether the Ohio program nonetheless has the forbidden "effect" of advancing or inhibiting religion.

   To answer that question, our decisions have drawn a consistent distinction between government programs that provide aid directly to religious schools, ... and programs of true private choice, in which government aid reaches religious schools only as a result of the genuine and independent choices of private individuals, ... While our jurisprudence with respect to the constitutionality of direct aid programs has "changed significantly" over the past two decades, ... our jurisprudence with respect to true private choice programs has remained consistent and unbroken. Three times we have confronted Establishment Clause challenges to neutral government programs that provide aid directly to a broad class of individuals, who, in turn, direct the aid to religious schools or institutions of their own choosing. Three times we have rejected such challenges.

   In *Mueller*, we rejected an Establishment Clause challenge to a Minnesota program authorizing tax deductions for various educational expenses, including private school tunately flows to religious institutions does so only as a result of the genuinely independent and private choices of aid recipients." ... We further remarked that, as in *Mueller*, "[the] program is made available generally without regard to the sectarian-nonsectarian, or public-nonpublic nature of the institution benefited." ... In light of these factors, we held that the program was not inconsistent with the Establishment Clause....

Five Members of the Court, in separate opinions, emphasized the general rule from *Mueller* that the amount of government aid channeled to religious institutions by individual aid recipients was not relevant to the constitutional inquiry.... Our holding thus rested not on whether few or many recipients chose to expend government aid at a religious school but, rather, on whether recipients generally were empowered to direct the aid to schools or institutions of their own choosing.

Finally, in *Zobrest*, we applied *Mueller* and *Witters* to reject an Establishment Clause challenge to a federal program that permitted sign-language interpreters to assist deaf children enrolled in religious schools. Reviewing our earlier decisions, we stated that "government programs that neutrally provide benefits to a broad class of citizens defined without reference to religion are not readily subject to an Establishment Clause challenge."... Looking once again to the challenged program as a whole, we observed that the program "distributes benefits neutrally to any child qualifying as 'disabled'."... Its "primary beneficiaries," we said, were "disabled children, not sectarian schools."...

We further observed that "[b]y according parents freedom to select a school of their choice, the statute ensures that a government-paid interpreter will be present in a sectarian school only as a result of the private decision of individual parents."... Our focus again was on neutrality and the principle of private choice, not on the number of program beneficiaries attending religious schools.... Because the program ensured that parents were the ones to select a religious school as the best learning environment for their handicapped child, the circuit between government and religion was broken, and the Establishment Clause was not implicated.

Mueller, Witters, and *Zobrest* thus make clear that where a government aid program is neutral with respect to religion, and provides assistance directly to a broad class of citizens who, in turn, direct government aid to religious schools wholly as a result of their own genuine and independent private choice, the program is not readily subject to challenge under the Establishment Clause. A program that shares these features permits government aid to reach religious institutions only by way of the deliberate choices of numerous individual recipients. The incidental advancement of a religious mission, or the perceived endorsement of a religious message, is reasonably attributable to the individual recipient, not to the government, whose role ends with the disbursement of benefits....

It is precisely for these reasons that we have never found a program of true private choice to offend the Establishment Clause.

We believe that the program challenged here is a program of true private choice, consistent with *Mueller, Witters,* and *Zobrest,* and thus constitutional. As was true in those cases, the Ohio program is neutral in all respects toward religion. It is part of a general and multifaceted undertaking by the State of Ohio to provide educational opportunities to the children of a failed school district. It confers educational assistance directly to a broad class of individuals defined without reference to religion, *i.e.*, any parent of a school-age child who resides in the Cleveland City School District. The program permits the participation of *all* schools within the district, religious or nonreligious. Adjacent public schools also may participate and have a financial incentive to do so. Program benefits are available to participating families on neutral terms, with no reference to religion. The only preference stated anywhere in the program is a preference for low-income families, who receive greater assistance and are given priority for admission at participating schools....

✤ *E S S A Y S*

Scholars have vigorously debated the history and meaning of the religion clauses of the Constitution. In the first selection, the late Leonard Levy, a constitutional historian who taught for many years at Claremont Graduate School, provides a powerful defense of the Court's separationist record. Levy criticizes "non-preferentialists"—those who argue that the Establishment Clause allows government aid to religion, so long as no specific religion is given preference. According to Levy, only by maintaining a wall of separation can true religious liberty—both freedom of religion and freedom from religion—be preserved.

   Stephen L. Carter offers a contrary perspective. A professor at Yale Law School and a public intellectual, Carter provides a compelling examination of the concept of church and state separation. In particular, Carter takes issue with the *Lemon* test and argues in support of a vital role for religion in the public sphere.

The Establishment Clause Erects a Wall of Separation

LEONARD W. LEVY

ESTABLISHMENT CLAUSE cases rarely concern acts of the national government. The usual case involves an act of a state, and the usual decision restricts religion in the public schools or government aid to sectarian schools. The First Amendment, as incorporated within the Fourteenth Amendment, operates as a ban against state action, and non-preferentialists hate that fact. They hate the incorporation doctrine. The incorporation doctrine is that the Fourteenth Amendment's due process clause incorporates within its protection of "liberty" most of the provisions of the Bill of Rights, thereby imposing on the states the same limitations imposed by the Bill of Rights on the United States. In the absence of the incorporation doctrine, nothing in the United States Constitution would prevent a state from outlawing an unpopular religious sect, establishing a particular church, storming into private homes without a warrant, imprisoning people who speak their minds in unpopular ways, or taxing local newspapers too critical of the state government. The due process clause of the Fourteenth Amendment, which has been the basis of the incorporation doctrine, states that no state shall deprive any person of life, liberty, or property without due process of law.

   Because the United States has no constitutional power to make laws that directly benefit religion and because under the incorporation doctrine the Fourteenth Amendment imposes upon the states the same limitations as the First Amendment places on the United States, the states have no constitutional power to aid religion directly either. Therefore, nonpreferentialists break a lance against reading the First Amendment's establishment clause into the Fourteenth as a limitation on the states. If the Fourteenth Amendment did not incorporate the First Amendment, the states would be free from the restraints of the United States Constitution and would be able to enact any measure concerning religion, subject only to such limitations as might exist in the individual state constitutions. Some nonpreferentialists and accommodationists therefore advocate the overruling of the incorporation doctrine. In its absence, the establishment clause, said a nonpreferentialist judge, would "not bar the States from establishing a religion."

To expect the Supreme Court to turn back the clock by scrapping the entire incorporation doctrine is so unrealistic as not to warrant consideration. ...

Those who expect a conservative Supreme Court, likely to become more conservative as older liberal Justices are replaced, to overrule the incorporation doctrine with respect to the establishment clause underestimate the political shrewdness of the Court. It does not matter whether liberal or conservative activists dominate the Supreme Court. The precipitous repudiation of entrenched doctrines would appear too obviously the result of subjective choices. Wherever possible the Court has avoided a dramatic overruling of its precedents, and it is likely to continue to do so. In the art of judging, a proper regard for appearances counts. The Court must seem to appreciate the values of coherence, stability, and continuity with the past. Judges, especially conservative ones, prefer to avoid sudden shifts in constitutional law. Any person who reaches the highest court is sophisticated enough to appreciate the strategic and political values of achieving desired results by indirection. Overruling is a device of last resort, employed only when other alternatives are unavailable or unavailing. The Court will not overrule the incorporation doctrine; it will not turn back the clock. But, it is quite likely to reinterpret precedents, distinguishing away some, blunting others, and making new law without the appearance of overruling or disrespecting the past. The Court will nourish the impression that it is for standing pat. It merely refuses to endorse further expansion of rights but faithfully hews to fundamental doctrines.

In a 1985 case the Supreme Court had to reconsider the incorporation doctrine, because a federal district judge in Alabama expressly repudiated it in a bizarre opinion holding that the establishment clause did not bar states from establishing a religion. The Supreme Court, however, serenely continued to employ the doctrine after treating the lower court opinion with something close to the contemptuous disdain it deserved. Not even the reactionary Justice Rehnquist, a loose cannon on the Supreme Court, aimed at the incorporation doctrine. He utterly misconstrued the establishment clause in an interpretation not accepted by any other member of the Court and he grossly distorted history, but he embraced the doctrine, even if reluctantly, when he declared: "Given the 'incorporation' of the Establishment Clause as against the States via the Fourteenth Amendment in *Everson*, States are prohibited as well [as the United States] from establishing a religion or discriminating between sects."

Perhaps the chief reason that the incorporation doctrine will continue undiminished in vitality is that no need exists to overthrow it in order to achieve the results that promote religious interests. One scholar got his history all wrong when he declared that the framers of the First Amendment did not mean to prevent the United States from giving nonpreferential aid to religion if the aid is incidental to the performance of a delegated power, but he stumbled on a truth about the politics of constitutional law. Power that is illegitimately exercised under one constitutional rubric may be valid under another.

Although Congress has no constitutional authority to legislate on religion as such or make it the beneficiary of legislation or other government action, the blunt fact is that regardless of what the Framers intended and regardless of the absence of a power to legislate on religion, the United States does possess constitutional powers to benefit or burden religion as an indirect result of the exercise of delegated powers. For example, the First Congress, in the course of debating the amendments that became the Bill of Rights, recommended a day of national thanksgiving and prayer, and it also reenacted the Northwest Ordinance. Passed in 1787 by the Congress of the Confederation, the Northwest Ordinance included a clause providing that schools and the means of education should be encouraged because religion, like morality and knowledge, is "necessary to good government and the happiness of mankind." And without doubt, religion (Protestantism) constituted an important part of the curriculum at that time. Significantly, however, Congress in 1789 did not reenact the provision of 1787 by which one lot in each township was to be set aside "perpetually for the purposes of religion." "The vast majority of Americans," as Thomas Curry wrote, "assumed that theirs was a Christian, i.e. Protestant country, and they automatically expected that government would uphold the commonly agreed on Protestant ethos and morality. In many instances, they had not come to grips with the implications their belief in the powerlessness of government in religous matters held for a society in which the values, customs and forms of Protestant Christianity thoroughly permeated civil and political life." When the Congress that adopted the First Amendment promoted religion in the Northwest Ordinance or by urging a national day of prayer, it acted unconstitutionally—by later standards. Usually, however, some plausible pretext can be found for the constitutionally of government action. For example, Congress could constitutionally have benefited religion indirectly in the reenactment of the Northwest Ordinance by virtue of an express power to make "needful rules" for the governance of the territories. In a real case the Supreme Court would have a difficult task to explain why territories could not be governed without official encouragement of religion. Few real cases exist, however, and the Court rarely troubles to think seriously about the delegated powers that might be exercised legitimately in a manner benefiting religion. What are those powers?

Under the power to "make rules for the government and regulation" of the armed forces, Congress provided for military and naval chaplains and paid them from public taxes. Under the power to govern its own proceedings, both chambers of Congress have provided for legislative chaplains. Under the power to punish violators of federal laws by imprisonment Congress has built prisons and provided chaplains for the inmates. Congress may close government buildings on the sabbath and on religious holidays, because it controls federal property. Under the power to coin money, Congress has placed a theistic motto on Unted States coins and currency. Under the power to levy taxes, Congress has made exemptions for churches and clergymen. Under the power to raise armies and therefore the power to lay down the terms for conscription, Congress has exempted conscientious objectors and clergymen. By the exercise of the treaty power the government has made treaties with the Indians and has implemented those treaties by appropriations for religion, ostensibly for the purpose of civilizing, Christianizing, and pacifying the Indians. The examples can be extended. However, the Supreme Court does not bother to explain much when it sustains some "accommodation" to religion.

The same authority that can incidentally benefit religion by the exercise of legitimate powers may also injure religion. A power to help is also a power to hinder or harm. Congress could draft conscientious objectors or tax church property, for example. That it does not do so is a matter of politics, not the result of constitutional power. Those who clamor for additional government support of religion should beware of the risks to religion from government entanglements. Those damaging risks are possible, if not likely.

From a constitutional standpoint, however, government can go too far in implementing a spirit of "benevolent neutrality," to use a phrase of Chief Justice Warren Burger, by serving religious needs. Benign "accommodation" is one thing; an implicit alliance with religion or state encouragement or sponsorship of it is another, although the Supreme Court has not distinguished the two in any consistent manner. Congress cannot constitutionally spend tax monies for the erection or maintenance of houses of worship, although it can tax almost as it pleases and spend almost as it pleases for "the common defense and general welfare." Nor can government financially assist a private sectarian school that is integrally a part of the religious mission of the denomination operating that school. The limits on the employment of authorized powers include the proscription against establishments of religion.

The establishment clause is over two centuries old. At the time the First Amendment was framed, government and religion were much closer than they are today, but nothing was clearer than the fact that financial aid to religion or religious establishments constituted an establishment of religion. The establishment clause should be far broader in meaning now than it was when adopted, because the nation is far more religiously pluralistic and is growing ever more so. Then, for all practical purposes religion meant Christianity and Christianity meant Protestantism. But Roman Catholics now compose the largest denomination in the nation, and about 6,000,000 American citizens are Jews. In addition, there are several scores of sects and substantial numbers of adherents to religions that were unknown in 1789, including Mormons, Christian Scientists, Pentecostalists, Jehovah's Witnesses, members of the Unification Church and Hare Krishnas. The number of Muslims, Buddhists, Confuscianists, Hindus, Sikhs, and Taoists is increasing.

We should not want the ban on establishments of religion to mean only what it meant in 1789 or only what its framers intended. Oliver Wendell Holmes said, "historical continuity with the past is not a duty, it is only a necessity." That delphic statement can be construed to mean that we cannot escape history because it has shaped us and guides our policies, but we are not obliged to remain static. Two hundred years of expanding the meaning of democracy should have some constitutional impact. We are not bound by the wisdom of the Framers; we are bound only to consider whether the purposes they had in mind still merit political respect and constitutional obedience. History can only be a guide, not a controlling factor. If we followed the framers of the Constitution blindly, we would be duplicating the method of the *Dred Scott* decision by freezing the meaning of words at the time they became part of the Constitution. Holmes wisely declared that courts—and he might have added scholars—are apt to err by sticking too closely to the words of law when those words "import a policy that goes beyond them." The significance of words, he taught, is vital, not formal, and is to be gathered not simply by taking dictionary definitions "but by considering their origin and the line of their growth." ...

The establishment clause may not be self-defining, but it embodies a policy which time has proved to be best. Despite continuing complaints about the wall of separation between government and religion, that is the policy embodied by the establishment clause. The Constitution erected that wall. If the fact that it is the policy of the Constitution does not satisfy, history helps validate it. A page of history is supposed to be worth a volume of logic, so let us consider a page from Tocqueville. Slightly more than half a century after Independence he wrote that "the religious atmosphere of the country was the first thing that struck me on my arrival in the United States." He expressed "astonishment" because in Europe religion and freedom marched in "opposite directions." Questioning the "faithful of all communions," including clergymen, especially Roman Catholic priests, he found that "they all agreed with each other except about details; all thought that the main reason for the quiet sway of religion over their country was the *complete separation of church and state*. I have no hesitation in stating that throughout my stay in America I met nobody, lay or cleric, who did not agree about that."

Because the domains of religion and government remain separated, religion in the United States, like religious liberty, thrives mightily, far more than it did 200 years ago when the vast majority of Americans were religiously unaffiliated. In a famous letter to the Baptist Association of Danbury, Connecticut, President Jefferson spoke of the "wall of separation." After declaring that religion belonged "solely between man and his God," Jefferson added: "I contemplate with sovereign reverence that act of the whole American people which declared that their legislature should 'make no law respecting an establishment of religion, or prohibiting the free exercise thereof,' thus building a wall of separation between church and state." The usual interpretation of Jefferson's Danbury Baptist letter by those who seek to weaken its force is either to minimize it or to argue that he was here concerned only with the rights of conscience, and that these would "never be endangered by treating all religions *equally* in regard to support" by the government. Neither interpretation is valid.

The rights-of-conscience argument ignores the fact that Jefferson quoted the establishment clause in the very sentence in which he spoke of a wall of separation, indicating that he was concerned with more than protection of the free exercise of religion. In any case, Jefferson most assuredly did believe that government support of all religions violated the rights of conscience. His Statute of Religious Freedom expressly asserts that "even forcing him [any man] to support this or that teacher of his own religious persuasion, is depriving him of the comfortable liberty of giving his contributions ... [No] man shall be compelled to frequent or support any religious worship, place, or ministry whatsoever. ... "

The second technique of robbing the Danbury letter of its clear intent to oppose any government support of religion belittles it as a "little address of courtesy" containing a "figure of speech ... a metaphor." Or, as Edward S. Corwin suggested, the letter was scarcely "deliberate" or "carefully considered"; it was rather "not improbably motivated by an impish desire to heave a brick at the Congregationalist-Federalist hierarchy of Connecticut. ... " Jefferson, however, had powerful convictions on the subject of establishment and religious freedom, and he approached discussion of it with great solemnity. Indeed, on the occasion of writing this letter he was so concerned with the necessity of expressing himself with deliberation and precision that he went out of his way to get the approval of the attorney-general of the United States. ...

Jefferson cared deeply about the rights of conscience, but he cared too for the government's freedom from religion. However, Roger Williams, who cared even more deeply about religion, had spoken of the "wall of separation" more than a century and a half before Jefferson. In 1644 Williams wrote that the wall existed to preserve the integrity of religion by walling out corrupting influences ...

Thus, the wall of separation had the allegiance of a most profound Christian impulse as well as a secular one. To Christian fundamentalists of the Framers' time the wall of separation derived from the biblical injunction that Christ's kingdom is not of this world. The wall of separation ensures the government's freedom from religion and the individual's freedom of religion. The second probably cannot flourish without the first.

Separation has other bountiful results. Government and religion in America are mutually independent of each other, much as Jefferson and Madison hoped they would be. Government maintains a benign neutrality toward religion without promoting or serving religion's interests in any significant way except, perhaps, for the policy of tax exemption. To be sure, government's involvement with religion takes many forms. The joint chiefs of staff supposedly begin their meetings with prayer, as do our legislatures. The incantation, "God save the United States and this honorable Court" and the motto "In God We Trust" and its relatives are of trifling significance in the sense that they have little genuine religious content. Caesar exploits, secularizes, and trivializes, but leaves organized religion alone. Free of government influence, organized religion in turn does not use government for religious ends. Thus, history has made the wall of separation real. The wall is not just a metaphor. It has constitutional existence. Even Chief Justice Burger has approvingly referred to Jefferson's "concept" of a wall as a "useful signpost" to emphasize separateness. Despite its detractors and despite its leaks, cracks, and its archways, the wall ranks as one of the mightiest monuments of constitutional government in this nation. Robert Frost notwithstanding, something there is that loves a wall.

The Establishment Clause was not meant to Establish Public Secularism

STEPHEN L. CARTER

... The courts do indeed enforce a separation of church and state, and it is backed by some very impressive legal philosophy, but one must be careful not to misunderstand what the doctrine and the First Amendment that is said to embody it were designed to do. Simply put, the metaphorical separation of church and state originated in an effort to protect religion from the state, not the state from religion. The religion clauses of the First Amendment were crafted to permit maximum freedom to the religious. In modern, religiously pluralistic America, where, as we have seen, the religions play vital roles as independent sources of meaning for their adherents, this means that the government should neither force people into sectarian religious observances, such as classroom prayer in public schools, nor favor some religions over others, as by erecting a crèche paid for with public funds, nor punish people for their religiosity without a very strong reason other than prejudice. It does not mean, however, that people whose motivations are religious are banned from trying to influence government, nor that the government is banned from listening to them. Understanding this distinction is the key to preserving the necessary separation of church and state without resorting to a philosophical rhetoric that treats religion as an inferior way for citizens to come to public judgment.

Religion is the first subject of the First Amendment. The amendment begins with the Establishment Clause ("Congress shall make no law respecting an establishment of religion . . . ") which is immediately followed by the Free Exercise Clause ("or prohibiting the free exercise thereof"). Although one might scarcely know it from the zeal with which the primacy of the other First Amendment freedoms (free press, free speech) is often asserted, those protections come *after* the clauses that were designed to secure religious liberty, which Thomas Jefferson called "the most inalienable and sacred of all human rights." What this means in practice, however, is often quite complicated.

Consider an example: at a dinner party in New York City a few years ago, I met a Christian minister who told me about a drug-rehabilitation program that he runs in the inner city. His claim—I cannot document it—was that his program had a success rate much higher than other programs. The secret, he insisted, was prayer. It was not just that he and his staff prayed for the drug abusers they were trying to help, he told me, although they naturally did that. But the reason for the program's success, he proclaimed, was that he and his staff taught those who came to them for assistance to pray as well; in other words, they converted their charges, if not to Christianity, then at least to religiosity. But this program, he went on with something close to bitterness, could receive no state funding, because of its religious nature.

Well, all right. To decide that the program should not receive any funds, despite the success of its approach, might seem to be a straightforward application of the doctrine holding that the Constitution sets up a wall of separation between church and state. After all, the program is frankly religious: it uses prayer, and even teaches prayer to its clients. What could be more threatening to the separation of church and state than to provide a government subsidy for it? The Supreme Court has said many times that the government may neither "advance" religion nor engage in an "excessive entanglement" with it. On its face, a program of drug-rehabilitation therapy that relies on teaching people to pray would seem to do both.

It is doubtless frustrating to believe deeply that one has a call from God to do what one does, and then to discover that the secular society often will not support that work, no matter how important it is to the individual. Yet that frustration is itself a sign of the robustness of religious pluralism in America. For the most significant aspect of the separation of church and state is not, as some seem to think, the shielding of the secular world from too strong a religious influence; the principal task of the separation of church and state is to secure religious liberty.

The separation of church and state is one of the great gifts that American political philosophy has presented to the world, and if it has few emulators, that is the world's loss. Culled from the writings of Roger Williams and Thomas Jefferson, the concept of a "wall of separation" finds its constitutional moorings in the First Amendment's firm statement that the "Congress shall make no law respecting any establishment of religion." Although it begins with the word "Congress," the Establishment Clause for decades has been quite sensibly interpreted by the Supreme Court as applying to states as well as to the federal government.

For most of American history, the principal purpose of the Establishment Clause has been understood as the protection of the religious world against the secular government. A century ago, Philip Schaff of Union Seminary in New York celebrated the clause as "the Magna Carta of religious freedom," representing as it did "the first example in history of a government deliberately depriving itself of all legislative control over religion." Note the wording: not religious control over government—government control over religion. Certainly this voluntary surrender of control is an indispensable separation if the religions are to serve as the independent intermediary institutions that Tocqueville envisioned.

Over the years, the Supreme Court has handed down any number of controversial decisions under the Establishment Clause, many of them landmarks of our democratic culture. The best known are the cases in which the Justices struck down the recital of organized prayer in the public school classrooms, decisions that for three decades have ranked (in surveys) as among the most unpopular in our history. But the decisions were plainly right, for if the state is either able to prescribe a prayer to begin the school day or to select a holy book from which a prayer must be taken, it is casting exercising control over the religious aspects of the life of its people—precisely what the Establishment Clause was written to forbid. But although the separation of church and state is essential to the success of a vibrant, pluralistic democracy, the doctrine does not entail all that is done in its name. I have already mentioned the school district in Colorado that thought it the better part of valor to forbid a teacher to add books on Christianity to a classroom library that already included works on other religions. The town of Hamden, Connecticut, where I live, briefly ruled that a church group could not rent an empty schoolhouse for Sunday services. (Cooler heads in the end prevailed.) These rulings were both defended as required by the separation of church and state; so is the intermittent litigation to strike the legend IN GOD WE TRUST from America's coins or the phrase "under God" from the Pledge of Allegiance, an effort, if successful, that would wipe away even the civil religion. In short, it is not hard to understand the frequent complaints that the secular world acts as though the constitutional command is that the nation and its people must keep religion under wraps.

Proponents of the hostility thesis believe that the Supreme Court bears a heavy burden of responsibility for what they see as the disfavored position of religion in America. Justice Hugo Black, in *Everson v. Board of Education* (1947), often is said to have started the ball rolling when he wrote these words: "The First Amendment has erected a wall between church and state. That wall must be kept high and impregnable. We could not approve the slightest breach." A year later, Justice Stanley Reed warned that "a rule of law should not be drawn from a figure of speech." One critic wrote years later that Black had simply penned a few "lines of fiction." The critics are not quite right, but they are not quite wrong, either. There is nothing wrong with the metaphor of a wall of separation. The trouble is that in order to make the Founders' vision compatible with the structure and needs of modern society, the wall has to have a few doors in it.

The embarrassing truth is that the Establishment Clause has no theory; that is, the Supreme Court has not really offered guidance on how to tell when the clause is violated. Since 1971, the Justices have relied on the "*Lemon* test," so named because it was framed (quite awkwardly, one is compelled to add) in the Court's 1971 decision in *Lemon v. Kurtzman*. The case is so often cited that legal scholars tend to forget what it involved: a state program to reimburse all private schools, including religious schools, for expenses of textbooks, materials, and, in part, salaries used to teach non-religious subjects. ... The Court held the program unconstitutional and, in so doing, enunciated the *Lemon* test—a lemon indeed, for it has proved well nigh impossible to apply. In order to pass Establishment Clause muster, the Justices wrote, the statute in question must meet three criteria: "First, the statute must have a secular legislative purpose; second, its principal or primary effect must be one that neither advances nor inhibits religion; finally, the statute must not foster 'an excessive entanglement with religion.'"

Thus conceived, the clause exists less for the benefit of religious autonomy than for the benefit of secular politics; that is, to borrow from the test itself, the Establishment Clause was written to further "a secular legislative purpose," trying to erect around the political process a wall almost impossible to take seriously. It is perhaps needless to add that *Lemon* left the critics in their glory. Did the legislation enacted at the behest of the religiously motivated civil rights movement have a secular purpose? If granting tax relief to parents whose children attend parochial schools advances religion by making the schools cheaper, does refusing to grant them inhibit religion by making the schools more expensive? If competing factions within the same church both seek control of the same church building, does judicial resolution represent an excessive entanglement?

When it promulgates complex multipart tests for constitutional violations, the Supreme Court is almost always luckless, but the *Lemon* test has been extraordinarily unhelpful to the lower courts. Indeed, the courts have reached results that are all over the map—sometimes quite literally, for one of the more interesting cases involved a rather bland "Motorists' Prayer" to God for safety that North Carolina printed on its official state maps. A federal court, missing the significance of America's civil religion, held the practice to be a violation of the Establishment Clause. Another federal court ruled that the clause prohibits religious groups from petitioning the Congress for private laws (available to all other groups) in order to secure copyrights when they are unable to meet the statutory criteria. The list goes on and on—but *Lemon* remains.

The Supreme Court itself has not fared much better than the lower courts in applying its test. The *Lemon* framework might not work too badly, could the courts but take the requirement of a "secular legislative purpose" to mean, as one scholar has proposed, any "political purpose"—that is, any goal the state legitimately is able to pursue. Recently, however, the courts have seemed to fumble this point, confusing the political purpose for which the statute is enacted with the religious sensibilities of legislators or their constituents. ...

The idea that religious motivation renders a statute suspect was never anything but a tortured and unsatisfactory reading of the clause. As one scholar has put the matter, there is good reason to think that "what the religion clauses of the first amendment were designed to do was not to remove religious values from the arena of public debate, but to keep them there." The Establishment Clause by its terms forbids the imposition of religious belief by the state, not statements of religious belief in the course of public dialogue. The distinction is one of more than semantic significance.

Consider the call by Reinhold Niebuhr and others back in the 1920s for the "Christianization" of American industry. Their use of the word "Christianization" did not mean the imposition of ritual and doctrine; it meant, rather, the transformation of industry into a new form that would accord with a principle of respect for the human spirit that Niebuhr and the rest found lacking in industrial organizations of the day. Critics called it socialism, or perhaps communism. But whatever it was, religious faith was plainly at its heart.

Niebuhr struck a chord, not only with any number of left-leaning Protestants, but also with a good number of socialists, many of them Jews, and with other reformers of no religious persuasion. (A well-known support group was Atheists for Niebuhr.) Suppose the response had been greater, that public support had burgeoned; suppose that legislatures had begun enacting programs that matched the socialist spirit of Christianization. This reform legislation would be purely secular in operation and could certainly be justified in secular terms. But under an establishment clause that is read to equate *acting* out of religious motivation with *imposing* religious belief, the programs might be unconstitutional, because both those who proposed them and many of those who voted for them would have done so out of religious conviction.

That should be a deeply troubling result. A rule holding that the religious convictions of the proponents are enough to render a statute constitutionally suspect represents a sweeping rejection of the deepest beliefs of millions of Americans, who are being told, in effect, that their views do not matter. In a nation that prides itself on cherishing religious freedom, it would be something of a puzzle to conclude that the Establishment Clause means that a Communist or a Republican may try to have his or her world view reflected in the nation's law, but a religionist can not. Although some critics fear we are already at that point, the truth is that we have a good long way to go; but we are heading in the wrong direction in our jurisprudence, and if the courts continue to read *Lemon* as they have, the Establishment Clause might well end up not antiestablishment but antireligion.

Recognizing this danger, the Justices, and the scholars who support their Establishment Clause jurisprudence, have simply ignored the rules of *Lemon v. Kurtzman* when applying them might prove too disruptive. In particular, they have tried to tip-toe around many widely accepted practices that seem to run afoul of *Lemon*. But squaring *Lemon*'s rules with the accepted usages of the society's civil religion often requires some fancy footwork. How, for example, does one justify the expenditure of government funds to provide armed forces chaplains, which looks like government sponsorship of religion? Answers one observer; "This is not so much 'setting up a church' as providing access to churches already existing for those removed by government action from their normal communities." Okay, but how to explain the use of public funds during the Christmas season to build and maintain a crèche, which celebrates the nativity of Jesus Christ? The Court itself tackled that one: "The display engenders a friendly community spirit of good will in keeping with the season" and any advancement of particular religions "is indirect, remote and incidental." Oh, really? Well, what about the offering of prayers at the opening of legislative sessions? The Justices had an answer for that one too: "In light of the unambiguous and unbroken history of more than 200 years, there can be no doubt that the practice of opening legislative sessions with prayer has become part of the fabric of our society.

Part of the fabric of our society—it is easy to see why the Court is reluctant to hold that the fabric of society includes some threads of unconstitutionality, but it is difficult to imagine how that can be the right test. Racial segregation was once part of the fabric of our society; so was prohibiting the women's vote, and corrupt patronage politics in the big cities. The idea, for example, that a crèche does not advance religion is ridiculous; the point of the crèche is to celebrate the birth of the Lord. So if the Court is willing to ignore *Lemon* and hold that government funds can pay for one, it is simply not doing its job. If the Justices dare not even follow their own rules, it may be time to find a new way to look at these problems. Yet the Supreme Court, although hinting around the edges, has not yet decided to make a full retreat. ...

[W]hat is most vital, in coming to a sensible understanding of the clause, is to avoid the ahistorical conclusion that its principal purpose is to protect the secular from the religious, an approach that, perhaps inevitably, carries us down the road toward a new establishment, the establishment of religion as a hobby, trivial and unimportant for serious people, not to be mentioned in serious discourse. And nothing could be further from the constitutional, historical, or philosophical truth. ...

Unlike the case of many a constitutional provision, we actually know a great deal about the history of the Establishment Clause and about the development of the ideal of a separated church and state. We know so much, in fact, that it is something of an embarrassment that we so enthusiastically ignore our knowledge in our church-and-state jurisprudence.

In particular, we know that for most members of the Founding Generation the idea of separating church from state meant protecting the church from the state—not the state from the church. ...

James Madison's *Memorial and Remonstrance*, written in 1785 in a successful effort to defeat Patrick Henry's bill to support all churches in Virginia by assessments from the population at large, is often, and correctly, cited as a fundamental document on the separation of church and state. Yet the *Memorial and Remonstrance* is decidedly of a religious, not a secular, cast. For example, the *Memorial* is regularly quoted for the proposition that "the opinions of men, depending only on the evidence contemplated by their own minds, cannot follow the dictates of other men." For Madison, however, this was a defense of the right to hold one's own religion, and his reference was to religious opinion. Indeed Madison proclaimed with some pride that the obligation of man to God was prior to the obligation of man to the state, which meant, he said, that the state was subordinate to God. Similarly, Madison is frequently quoted for the following passage: "Whilst we assert for ourselves a freedom to embrace, to profess and to observe the Religion which we believe to be of divine origin, we cannot deny an equal freedom to those whose minds have not yet yielded to the evidence that has convinced us." But the very next line is striking: "If this freedom be abused, it is an offence against God, not against man."

The point is that the *Memorial and Remonstrance*, although it plainly defends the separation of church and state, frames the argument principally as a protection of the church, not as a protection of the state. Indeed, the entire disestablishment movement in Virginia was a movement to rescue religious freedom from state oppression, not to rescue the state from religious oppression.

Thomas Jefferson is often cited as an exemplar of secular politics, but Jefferson's vision of the relationship between government and religion was strongly shaped by his vision of religion itself, which he considered a matter of individual conscience rather than of corporate worship. Jefferson, a deist, did not think churches important; he thought the individual important. But although Jefferson might therefore be thought to value religion no more than any other aspect of conscience, he did not consider religion an ordinary matter of conscience—rather, religious liberty was for Jefferson "the most inalienable and sacred of all human rights."

... The same spirit animated the drafting of the First Amendment and its twin clauses prohibiting religious establishments and guaranteeing free exercise. It is plain that the Founders conceived of these clauses less as distinct entities than as parts of a coherent whole—and, to the extent that they were distinct, the distinction had nothing to do with the way that we read the clauses today.

The language of the Establishment Clause, of course, prohibits the Congress from making any law "*respecting* an establishment of religion." The evident purpose of this first word was to prevent the Congress from interfering with state establishments of religion. Indeed, there is good reason to think that the principal purpose of the Establishment Clause, and maybe the sole one, was to protect the state religious establishments from disestablishment by the federal government. If the clause is anti-disestablishmentarian in design, however, it makes little sense to speak of applying the Establishment Clause as a limitation on the power of the states, a point noted by Akhil Amar: "To apply the clause against a state government is precisely to eliminate its right to choose whether to establish a religion—a right explicitly confirmed by the establishment clause itself!" Amar would, however, apply the Free Exercise Clause against the states, with the interesting result that each state "would be free to establish one or several churches, but would be obliged to respect the free exercise rights of dissenters to opt out." In fine, there would seem to be nothing odder, from a historical perspective, than the idea that the Establishment Clause prohibits state support for religious institutions. ...

All of which brings us back to the religious drug-treatment program that opened our discussion of the separation of church and state. We are still left with the original question: should the program receive state funding or not?

We have already seen that the Establishment Clause should not be read to prohibit all state support for religion, and, should it be read that way, churches would lose their charitable exemptions. Consequently, one can immediately deduce the rule that religious organizations should be able to compete on the same grounds as other groups for the largess of the welfare state—they should not, on Establishment Clause grounds, be relegated to a second-class status. Consequently, if the program involved no prayer, it would certainly have been eligible for state support: plenty of religious institutions run secular programs that compete for the largess of the welfare state. So the question is whether the fact that the beneficiaries were prayed over—and taught to pray—means that the program should not be eligible.

Many readers might challenge the minister's claim of efficacy, which would make it unnecessary to consider the Establishment Clause claim. However, the claim that the program works well is not wholly implausible. I had no more than a single conversation with the man who runs it, so I honestly do not know whether the program's success rate was unusually good or unusually bad. Drug rehabilitation, unfortunately, is an area in which data are notoriously unreliable. In particular, although claims of this kind are legion, no convincing studies confirm that religiously oriented approaches do a better job than other programs at ending drug habits. I once saw some data suggesting that strongly religious people are less susceptible than others to drug and alcohol dependencies and are more likely to kick the habit once begun—but this is where the scholar must apply a degree of statistical caution. The data do not and cannot reveal whether possession of a strongly religious character is the *reason* that the habit is kicked, or whether the strongly religious character, and the ability to kick the habit, in fact flow independently from some other valuable character trait.

Still, for the sake of argument, suppose that clear and unambiguous data showed, for reasons unknown, that rehabilitation programs involving religious teaching or even conversion were more successful than other drug-treatment programs in helping addicts to return to normal lives. In other words, suppose that this religiously oriented program turns out to be better than the various secular approaches that now receive government aid—with the important distinction that the most successful of its graduates enter with an addiction to drugs and leave with a commitment to God. The program, then, could fairly be described as proselytizing—but, unlike some forms of proselytization, its work is in a secular cause. Should the state then be prepared to fund the program?

Under the *Lemon v. Kurtzman* test, one would probably be forced to conclude that the statistics do not matter, and that assistance to the religiously oriented program, no matter how worthy it might appear, is barred by the "primary effect" test—for, plainly, if the program proselytizes, the effect of the subsidy is to advance the religion in question. But the program might pass muster on some of the alternative tests that have been proposed. For example, support for a drug-treatment program that includes prayer would not involve any coercion, provided that nobody was required to participate. Many observers would surely argue that support for the program involved an endorsement, and therefore it fails Justice O'Connor's test. It is not clear that this is correct, however, for a voluntary drug-treatment program is hardly like the public display of a crèche; besides, if subsidizing a drug-treatment program constitutes an endorsement of religion because the patients learn to pray, the charitable tax deduction for contributions to religious groups would seem to be in terrible jeopardy.

The potential transformation of the Establishment Clause from a guardian of religious liberty into a guarantor of public secularism raises prospects at once dismal and dreadful. The more that the clause is used to disable religious groups from active involvement in the programs of the welfare state, or, for that matter, from active involvement in the public square that is the crucible of public policy, the less the religions will be able to play their proper democratic role of mediating between the individual and the state and the less they will be able to play their proper theological role of protecting the people of God.

The problem does not stop with a silly fight over the rental of a public school building by a religious group or the unhappy order to wipe the Motorist's Prayer from state road maps. We have also seen enthusiastic litigation—so far unsuccessful—that challenges the tax-exempt status of the Roman Catholic Church because of its antiabortion advocacy. And why not? After all, it is a well-understood rule that tax-exempt contributions cannot be used for lobbying or to support or oppose political candidates. Doubtless the same high principles will soon lead the same protesters to demand withdrawal of the tax-exempt status of the church where my wife and I heard the preacher command support for the Sandinistas ..., or, for that matter, to question the tax-exempt status of the many churches where the civil rights movement was nurtured. Or maybe not: maybe there are not any principles involved. Maybe it is just another effort to ensure that intermediate institutions, such as the religions, do not get in the way of the government's will. Perhaps, in short, it is a way of ensuring that only one vision of the meaning of reality—that of the powerful group of individuals called the state—is allowed a political role. Back in Tocqueville's day, this was called tyranny. Nowadays, all too often, but quite mistakenly, it is called the separation of church and state.

✣ *F U R T H E R   R E A D I N G*

Belknap, Michael R. *The Supreme Court under Earl Warren, 1953–1969* (2005).

Cord, Robert L. "Church-State Separation: Restoring the 'No-Preference' Doctrine of the First Amendment," *Harvard Journal of Law and Public Policy*, 9 (1986): 129–172.

Curry, Thomas J. *The First Freedoms: Church and State in America to the Passage of the First Amendment* (1986).

Dierenfield, Bruce J. *Battle over School Prayer: How* Engel v. Vitale *Changed America* (2007).

Dolbeare, Kenneth M. and Phillip E. Hammond. *The School Prayer Decision: From Court Policy to Local Practice* (1971).

Epps, Garrett. "To an Unknown God: The Hidden History of *Employment Division v. Smith*," 30 *Arizona State Law Journal* (1998): 953–1024.

Gaustad, Edwin S. *Faith of the Founders: Religion and the New Nation, 1776–1826* (2004).

——. *Proclaim Liberty Throughout All the Land: A History of Church and State in America* (2003).

Gedicks, Frederick M. *The Rhetoric of Church and State: A Critical Analysis of Religion Clause Jurisprudence* (1995).

Hamburger, Philip. *Separation of Church and State* (2002).

Hensley, Thomas R. *The Rehnquist Court: Justices, Rulings, and Legacy* (2006).

Hitchcock, James. *The Supreme Court and Religion in American Life* (2004).

Holmes, David L. *The Faiths of the Founding Fathers* (2006).

Howe, Mark D. *The Garden and the Wilderness: Religion and Government in American Constitutional History* (1965).

Jeffries, John C. Jr. and James E. Ryan. "A Political History of the Establishment Clause," *Michigan Law Review*, 100 (2001): 279–370.

Long, Carolyn N. *Religious Freedom and Indian Rights: The Case of* Oregon v. Smith (2000).

Manwaring, David R. *Render unto Caesar: The Flag Salute Controversy* (1962).

McConnell, Michael W. "The Origins and Historical Understanding of Free Exercise of Religion," *Harvard Law Review*, 103 (1990): 1409–1517.

——. "Religious Freedom at Crossroads," *University of Chicago Law Review*, 59 (1992): 115–194.

Miller, William L. *The First Liberty: Religion and the American Republic* (1987).

O'Brien, David. *Animal Sacrifice and Religious Freedom: Church of the Lukumi Babalu Aye v. City of Hialeah* (2004).

Peters, Shawn Francis. Yoder *Case: Religious Freedom, Education, and Parental Rights* (2003).

Sorauf, Frank J. *The Wall of Separation: The Constitutional Politics of Church and State* (1976).

Urofsky, Melvin I. *The Warren Court: Justices, Rulings, and Legacy* (2001).

Witte, John Jr. *Religion and the American Constitutional Experiment* (2000).

Federalism and Judicial Review

From the founding of the republic, debates over federalism—the relationship between the national government and the states—have figured prominently in the history of American constitutionalism. The founders' establishment of a federal system arguably stands out as a key contribution in the history of political theory. Prior to 1787, most believed that sovereignty could not be divided—that two governments could not simultaneously maintain authority over the same people. Nevertheless, the framers created a national government with significant powers at the same time that they preserved the existence of state authority. The Tenth Amendment, ratified in 1791, ensured that "the powers not delegated to the United States by the Constitution" were "reserved to the states." Conflict between these competing authorities persisted for much of the early history of the republic—from the introduction of the Virginia and Kentucky Resolutions in the 1790s to the secession crisis and Civil War. After the war, the newly ratified Fourteenth Amendment imposed limitations on the states, while also empowering Congress to protect civil rights.

With the notion of state sovereignty tainted by its association with secession, national power witnessed a slow but inexorable rise. Over the next several decades, unprecedented economic expansion brought increased national regulation, most of which rested on Congress's power under Article I, Section 8 to "regulate commerce . . . among the several states." The Great Depression further invigorated the national government, particularly after the Supreme Court began upholding New Deal legislation. In 1941, for example, the Court announced in United States v. Darby *that the Tenth Amendment had no practical limiting effect on the reach of national regulatory authority. The Tenth Amendment's demise, along with the potent combination of the Commerce Clause and the Fourteenth Amendment, produced a nearly rock-solid constitutional justification for extending the power and influence of national authority into the everyday lives of Americans. From preventing racial discrimination through the Civil Rights Act to imposing federal wage and hours standards on city governments through the Fair Labor Standards Act, congressional legislation almost always received the approval of the justices.*

With conservatism ascendant during the last two decades of the twentieth century, however, the justices became increasingly suspicious of national power. The Rehnquist Court invalidated a series of acts of Congress and, in the process, revitalized the doctrine of state sovereignty and the debate over federalism. As with interpretation of the religion clauses, history and original intent have played a key role in these discussions. Conservatives have championed a return to pre-New Deal notions of federalism, in which the Tenth Amendment held an important place. Liberals, in contrast, have pointed to a different history—the fact that state sovereignty long served as a constitutional cover for racial oppression. What should be the proper relationship between the national government and the states, and what should the Court's role be in determining that relationship? Did Congress go too far during the twentieth century in legislating on matters of local concern, or is congressional action needed to protect public safety and the rights of minorities? Should the Court defer to the legislative branch on such matters, or should it vigorously attempt to uphold the principles of federalism? How important is federalism to the structure of the Constitution?

✤ *D O C U M E N T S*

Wickard v. Filburn, Document 1, stands alongside the *Darby* decision as representing the peak of congressional power under the Commerce Clause. A unanimous Court, in upholding the New Deal's Second Agricultural Adjustment Act, ruled that even wheat that never left the farm and entered the market was subject to congressional regulation. Justice Robert Jackson wrote the opinion.

During subsequent decades, national regulation continued its march, despite some protests. In *The Conscience of a Conservative,* Senator Barry Goldwater, a Republican from Arizona, outlined his belief in the need for a reassertion of state power in the face of an expanding national government. Document 2 is a brief excerpt. Goldwater's ideas helped launch the conservative movement and influenced the thinking of the young William Rehnquist. The Warren Court, meanwhile, upheld a challenge to the Civil Rights Act of 1964 (which Goldwater opposed) in *Heart of Atlanta Motel v. United States,* Document 3. A unanimous Court sustained the law as a valid exercise of the commerce power, with Justice Tom Clark writing the opinion. In his concurrence, Justice William O. Douglas offered a different rationale for federal civil rights legislation.

Congress relied on both the Commerce Clause and the Fourteenth Amendment in enacting the Violence Against Women Act, a part of which is Document 4. This portion of the law established the right of women to file civil damage suits against their attackers. The following year, the Rehnquist Court altered the landscape of federalism with its decision in *United States v. Lopez,* Document 5. With the justices divided 5–4, Rehnquist wrote the majority opinion overturning a law making it a federal offense to possess a firearm in a school zone. Justice Stephen Breyer wrote a dissenting opinion. A few years later, in *Printz v. United States,* Document 6, five justices struck down a provision of the Brady Handgun Violence Prevention Act that required local officials to help conduct background checks on would-be gun owners. Justice Antonin Scalia's majority opinion defended the constitutional centrality of federalism. In *United States v. Morrison,* Document 7, the same five justices who constituted the majority in *Lopez* and *Printz* invalidated the Violence Against Women Act's civil remedy provision. Despite 4 years of congressional hearings that demonstrated the national impact of domestic violence and the states' ineffectiveness in dealing with the problem, the Court held that such violence was beyond Congress's power to regulate under either the Commerce Clause or the Fourteenth Amendment. Rehnquist authored the decision.

✤ D O C U M E N T   1

Wickard v. Filburn, 1942

Mr. Justice Jackson delivered the opinion of the Court.

...The appellee for many years past has owned and operated a small farm in Montgomery County, Ohio, maintaining a herd of dairy cattle, selling milk, raising poultry, and selling poultry and eggs. It has been his practice to raise a small acreage of winter wheat, sown in the Fall and harvested in the following July; to sell a portion of the crop; to feed part to poultry and livestock on the farm, some of which is sold; to use some in making flour for home consumption, and to keep the rest for the following seeding. The intended disposition of the crop here involved has not been expressly stated. In July of 1940, pursuant to the Agricultural Adjustment Act of 1938, as then amended, there were established for the appellee's 1941 crop a wheat acreage allotment of 11.1 acres and a normal yield of 20.1 bushels of wheat an acre. He was given notice of such allotment in July of 1940, before the Fall planting of his 1941 crop of wheat, and again in July of 1941, before it was harvested. He sowed, however, 23 acres, and harvested from his 11.9 acres of excess acreage 239 bushels, which, under the terms of the Act as amended on May 26, 1941, constituted farm marketing excess, subject to a penalty of 49 cents a bushel, or $117.11 in all. The appellee has not paid the penalty, and he has not postponed or avoided it by storing the excess under regulations of the Secretary of Agriculture, or by delivering it up to the Secretary. The Committee, therefore, refused him a marketing card, which was, under the terms of Regulations promulgated by the Secretary, necessary to protect a buyer from liability to the penalty and upon its protecting lien.

    ...It is urged that, under the Commerce Clause of the Constitution, Article I, § 8, clause 3, Congress does not possess the power it has in this instance sought to exercise. The question would merit little consideration, since our decision in *United States v. Darby,* ...sustaining the federal power to regulate production of goods for commerce, except for the fact that this Act extends federal regulation to production not intended in any part for commerce, but wholly for consumption on the farm....

    Hence, marketing quotas not only embrace all that may be sold without penalty, but also what may be consumed on the premises. Wheat produced on excess acreage is designated as "available for marketing" as so defined, and the penalty is imposed thereon. Penalties do not depend upon whether any part of the wheat, either within or without the quota, is sold or intended to be sold. The sum of this is that the Federal Government fixes a quota including all that the farmer may harvest for sale or for his own farm needs, and declares that wheat produced on excess acreage may neither be disposed of nor used except upon payment of the penalty, or except it is stored as required by the Act or delivered to the Secretary of Agriculture.

    Appellee says that this is a regulation of production and consumption of wheat. Such activities are, he urges, beyond the reach of Congressional power under the Commerce Clause, since they are local in character, and their effects upon interstate commerce are, at most, "indirect." In answer, the Government argues that the statute regulates neither production nor consumption, but only marketing, and, in the alternative, that, if the Act does go beyond the regulation of marketing, it is sustainable as a "necessary and proper" implementation of the power of Congress over interstate commerce.

The Government's concern lest the Act be held to be a regulation of production or consumption, rather than of marketing, is attributable to a few dicta and decisions of this Court which might be understood to lay it down that activities such as "production," "manufacturing," and "mining" are strictly "local" and, except in special circumstances which are not present here, cannot be regulated under the commerce power because their effects upon interstate commerce are, as matter of law, only "indirect." Even today, when this power has been held to have great latitude, there is no decision of this Court that such activities may be regulated where no part of the product is intended for interstate commerce or intermingled with the subjects thereof. We believe that a review of the course of decision under the Commerce Clause will make plain, however, that questions of the power of Congress are not to be decided by reference to any formula which would give controlling force to nomenclature such as "production" and "indirect" and foreclose consideration of the actual effects of the activity in question upon interstate commerce....

The Court's recognition of the relevance of the economic effects in the application of the Commerce Clause, exemplified by this statement, has made the mechanical application of legal formulas no longer feasible. Once an economic measure of the reach of the power granted to Congress in the Commerce Clause is accepted, questions of federal power cannot be decided simply by finding the activity in question to be "production," nor can consideration of its economic effects be foreclosed by calling them "indirect."...

Whether the subject of the regulation in question was "production," "consumption," or "marketing" is, therefore, not material for purposes of deciding the question of federal power before us. That an activity is of local character may help in a doubtful case to determine whether Congress intended to reach it. The same consideration might help in determining whether, in the absence of Congressional action, it would be permissible for the state to exert its power on the subject matter, even though, in so doing, it to some degree affected interstate commerce. But even if appellee's activity be local, and though it may not be regarded as commerce, it may still, whatever its nature, be reached by Congress if it exerts a substantial economic effect on interstate commerce, and this irrespective of whether such effect is what might at some earlier time have been defined as "direct" or "indirect."...

The effect of consumption of home-grown wheat on interstate commerce is due to the fact that it constitutes the most variable factor in the disappearance of the wheat crop. Consumption on the farm where grown appears to vary in an amount greater than 20 percent of average production. The total amount of wheat consumed as food varies but relatively little, and use as seed is relatively constant.

The maintenance by government regulation of a price for wheat undoubtedly can be accomplished as effectively by sustaining or increasing the demand as by limiting the supply. The effect of the statute before us is to restrict the amount which may be produced for market and the extent, as well, to which one may forestall resort to the market by producing to meet his own needs. That appellee's own contribution to the demand for wheat may be trivial by itself is not enough to remove him from the scope of federal regulation where, as here, his contribution, taken together with that of many others similarly situated, is far from trivial....

It is well established by decisions of this Court that the power to regulate commerce includes the power to regulate the prices at which commodities in that commerce are dealt in and practices affecting such prices. One of the primary purposes of the Act in question was to increase the market price of wheat, and, to that end, to limit the volume thereof that could affect the market. It can hardly be denied that a factor of such volume and variability as home-consumed wheat would have a substantial influence on price and market conditions. This may arise because being in marketable condition such wheat overhangs the market, and, if induced by rising prices, tends to flow into the market and check price increases. But if we assume that it is never marketed, it supplies a need of the man who grew it which would otherwise be reflected by purchases in the open market. Home-grown wheat in this sense competes with wheat in commerce. The stimulation of commerce is a use of the regulatory function quite as definitely as prohibitions or restrictions thereon. This record leaves us in no doubt that Congress may properly have considered that wheat consumed on the farm where grown, if wholly outside the scheme of regulation, would have a substantial effect in defeating and obstructing its purpose to stimulate trade therein at increased prices....

✤ D O C U M E N T   2

Senator Barry Goldwater Defends The Rights of the States, 1960

The Governor of New York, in 1930, pointed out that the Constitution does not empower the Congress to deal with "a great number of ... vital problems of government, such as the conduct of public utilities, of banks, of insurance, of business, of agriculture, of education, of social welfare, and a dozen other important features." And he added that "Washington must not be encouraged to interfere" in these areas.

Franklin Roosevelt's rapid conversion from Constitutionalism to the doctrine of unlimited government, is an oft-told story. But I am here concerned not so much by the abandonment of States' Rights by the national Democratic Party—an event that occurred some years ago when that party was captured by the Socialist ideologues in and about the labor movement—as by the unmistakable tendency of the Republican Party to adopt the same course. The result is that today *neither* of our two parties maintains a meaningful commitment to the principle of States' Rights. Thus, the cornerstone of the Republic, our chief bulwark against the encroachment of individual freedom by Big Government, is fast disappearing under the piling sands of absolutism....

The Tenth Amendment is *not* "a general assumption," but a prohibitory rule of law. The Tenth Amendment recognizes the States' *jurisdiction* in certain areas. States' Rights means that the States have a right to act or *not to act*, as they see fit, in the areas reserved to them. The States may have duties corresponding to these rights, but the duties are owed to the people of the States, not to the federal government. Therefore, the recourse lies not with the federal government, which is not sovereign, but with the people who are, and who have full power to take disciplinary action. If the people are unhappy with say, their State's disability insurance program, they can bring pressure to bear on their state officials and, if that fails, they can elect a new set of officials. And if, in the unhappy event they should wish to divest themselves of this responsibility, they can amend the Constitution. The Constitution, I repeat, draws a sharp and clear line between federal jurisdiction and state jurisdiction. The federal government's failure to recognize that line has been a crushing blow to the principle of limited government.

But again, I caution against a defensive, or apologetic, appeal to the Constitution. There is a *reason* for its reservation of States' Rights. Not only does it prevent the accumulation of power in a central government that is remote from the people and relatively immune from popular restraints; it also recognizes the principle that essentially local problems are best dealt with by the people most directly concerned. Who knows better than New Yorkers how much and what kind of publicly-financed slum clearance in New York City is needed and can be afforded? Who knows better than Nebraskans whether that State has an adequate nursing program? Who knows better than Arizonans the kind of school program that is needed to educate their children? The people of my own State—and I am confident that I speak for the majority of them—have long since seen through the spurious suggestion that federal aid comes "free." They know that the money comes out of their own pockets, and that it is returned to them minus a broker's fee taken by the federal bureaucracy. They know, too, that the power to decide how that money shall be spent is withdrawn from them and exercised by some planning board deep in the caverns of one of the federal agencies. They understand this represents a great and perhaps irreparable loss—not only in their wealth, but in their priceless liberty.

Nothing could so far advance the cause of freedom as for state officials throughout the land to assert their rightful claims to lost state power; and for the federal government to withdraw promptly and totally from every jurisdiction which the Constitution reserved to the states.

✤ *D O C U M E N T   3*

Heart of Atlanta Motel v. United States, 1964

Mr. Justice Clark delivered the opinion of the Court.
... The case comes here on admissions and stipulated facts. Appellant owns and operates the Heart of Atlanta Motel which has 216 rooms available to transient guests. The motel is located on Courtland Street, two blocks from downtown Peachtree Street. It is readily accessible to interstate highways 75 and 85 and state highways 23 and 41. Appellant solicits patronage from outside the State of Georgia through various national advertising media, including magazines of national circulation; it maintains over 50 billboards and highway signs within the State, soliciting patronage for the motel; it accepts convention trade from outside Georgia and approximately 75% of its registered guests are from out of State. Prior to passage of the Act the motel had followed a practice of refusing to rent rooms to Negroes, and it alleged that it intended to continue to do so. In an effort to perpetuate that policy this suit was filed.

The appellant contends that Congress in passing this Act exceeded its power to regulate commerce under Art. I, 8, cl. 3, of the Constitution of the United States; that the Act violates the Fifth Amendment because appellant is deprived of the right to choose its customers and operate its business as it wishes, resulting in a taking of its liberty and property without due process of law and a taking of its property without just compensation; and, finally, that by requiring appellant to rent available rooms to Negroes against its will, Congress is subjecting it to involuntary servitude in contravention of the Thirteenth Amendment.

The appellees counter that the unavailability to Negroes of adequate accommodations interferes significantly with interstate travel, and that Congress, under the Commerce Clause, has power to remove such obstructions and restraints; that the Fifth Amendment does not forbid reasonable regulation and that consequential damage does not constitute a "taking" within the meaning of that amendment; that the Thirteenth Amendment claim fails because it is entirely frivolous to say that an amendment directed to the abolition of human bondage and the removal of widespread disabilities associated with slavery places discrimination in public accommodations beyond the reach of both federal and state law. ...

The Act as finally adopted was most comprehensive, undertaking to prevent through peaceful and voluntary settlement discrimination in voting, as well as in places of accommodation and public facilities, federally secured programs and in employment. Since Title II is the only portion under attack here, we confine our consideration to those public accommodation provisions. ...

This Title is divided into seven sections beginning with 201 (a) which provides that:

"All persons shall be e ntitled to the full and equal enjoyment of the goods, services, facilities, privileges, advantages, and accommodations of any place of public accommodation, as defined in this section, without discrimination or segregation on the ground of race, color, religion, or national origin."

There are listed in 201 (b) four classes of business establishments, each of which "serves the public" and "is a place of public accommodation" within the meaning of 201 (a) "if its operations affect commerce, or if discrimination or segregation by it is supported by State action." The covered establishments are:

"(1) any inn, hotel, motel, or other establishment which provides lodging to transient guests, other than an establishment located within a building which contains not more than five rooms for rent or hire and which is actually occupied by the proprietor of such establishment as his residence;

"(2) any restaurant, cafeteria ... [not here involved];

"(3) any motion picture house ... [not here involved];

"(4) any establishment ... which is physically located within the premises of any establishment otherwise covered by this subsection, or ... within the premises of which is physically located any such covered establishment ... [not here involved]." ...

The sole question posed is, therefore, the constitutionality of the Civil Rights Act of 1964 as applied to these facts. The legislative history of the Act indicates that Congress based the Act on Section 5 and the Equal Protection Clause of the Fourteenth

Amendment as well as its power to regulate interstate commerce under Art. I, 8, cl. 3, of the Constitution. ...

The Senate Commerce Committee made it quite clear that the fundamental object of Title II was to vindicate "the deprivation of personal dignity that surely accompanies denials of equal access to public establishments." At the same time, however, it noted that such an objective has been and could be readily achieved "by congressional action based on the commerce power of the Constitution." ... Our study of the legislative record, made in the light of prior cases, has brought us to the conclusion that Congress possessed ample power in this regard, and we have therefore not considered the other grounds relied upon. This is not to say that the remaining authority upon which it acted was not adequate, a question upon which we do not pass, but merely that since the commerce power is sufficient for our decision here we have considered it alone. Nor is 201 (d) or 202, having to do with state action, involved here and we do not pass upon either of those sections. ...

In light of our ground for decision, it might be well at the outset to discuss the Civil Rights Cases, ..., which declared provisions of the Civil Rights Act of 1875 unconstitutional. ... We think that decision inapposite, and without precedential value in determining the constitutionality of the present Act. Unlike Title II of the present legislation, the 1875 Act broadly proscribed discrimination in "inns, public conveyances on land or water, theaters, and other places of public amusement," without limiting the categories of affected businesses to those impinging upon interstate commerce. In contrast, the applicability of Title II is carefully limited to enterprises having a direct and substantial relation to the interstate flow of goods and people, except where state action is involved. Further, the fact that certain kinds of businesses may not in 1875 have been sufficiently involved in interstate commerce to warrant bringing them within the ambit of the commerce power is not necessarily dispositive of the same question today. Our populace had not reached its present mobility, nor were facilities, goods and services circulating as readily in interstate commerce as they are today. Although the principles which we apply today are those first formulated by Chief Justice Marshall in *Gibbons v. Ogden,* 9 Wheat. 1 (1824), the conditions of transportation and commerce have changed dramatically, and we must apply those principles to the present state of commerce. The sheer increase in volume of interstate traffic alone would give discriminatory practices which inhibit travel a far larger impact upon the Nation's commerce than such practices had on the economy of another day. Finally, there is language in the Civil Rights Cases which indicates that the Court did not fully consider whether the 1875 Act could be sustained as an exercise of the commerce power. Though the Court observed that "no one will contend that the power to pass it was contained in the Constitution before the adoption of the last three amendments [Thirteenth, Fourteenth, and Fifteenth]," the Court went on specifically to note that the Act was not "conceived" in terms of the commerce power ...

Since the commerce power was not relied on by the Government and was without support in the record it is understandable that the Court narrowed its inquiry and excluded the Commerce Clause as a possible source of power. In any event, it is clear that such a limitation renders the opinion devoid of authority for the proposition that the Commerce Clause gives no power to Congress to regulate discriminatory practices now found substantially to affect interstate commerce. We, therefore, conclude that the Civil Rights Cases have no relevance to the basis of decision here where the Act explicitly relies upon the commerce power, and where the record is filled with testimony of obstructions and restraints resulting from the discriminations found to be existing. We now pass to that phase of the case. . . .

While the Act as adopted carried no congressional findings the record of its passage through each house is replete with evidence of the burdens that discrimination by race or color places upon interstate commerce. . . . This testimony included the fact that our people have become increasingly mobile with millions of people of all races traveling from State to State; that Negroes in particular have been the subject of discrimination in transient accommodations, having to travel great distances . . . to secure the same; that often they have been unable to obtain accommodations and have had to call upon friends to put them up overnight, . . . ; and that these conditions had become so acute as to require the listing of available lodging for Negroes in a special guidebook which was itself "dramatic testimony to the difficulties" Negroes encounter in travel. . . . These exclusionary practices were found to be nationwide, the Under Secretary of Commerce testifying that there is "no question that this discrimination in the North still exists to a large degree" and in the West and Midwest as well. . . . This testimony indicated a qualitative as well as quantitative effect on interstate travel by Negroes. The former was the obvious impairment of the Negro traveler's pleasure and convenience that resulted when he continually was uncertain of finding lodging. As for the latter, there was evidence that this uncertainty stemming from racial discrimination had the effect of discouraging travel on the part of a substantial portion of the Negro community. . . .

That Congress was legislating against moral wrongs in many of these areas rendered its enactments no less valid. In framing Title II of this Act Congress was also dealing with what it considered a moral problem. But that fact does not detract from the overwhelming evidence of the disruptive effect that racial discrimination has had on commercial intercourse. It was this burden which empowered Congress to enact appropriate legislation, and, given this basis for the exercise of its power, Congress was not restricted by the fact that the particular obstruction to interstate commerce with which it was dealing was also deemed a moral and social wrong. . . .

It is said that the operation of the motel here is of a purely local character. But, assuming this to be true, "[i]f it is interstate commerce that feels the pinch, it does not matter how local the operation which applies the squeeze." . . .

Thus the power of Congress to promote interstate commerce also includes the power to regulate the local incidents thereof, including local activities in both the States of origin and destination, which might have a substantial and harmful effect upon that commerce. One need only examine the evidence which we have discussed above to see that Congress may—as it has—prohibit racial discrimination by motels serving travelers, however "local" their operations may appear. . . .

We, therefore, conclude that the action of the Congress in the adoption of the Act as applied here to a motel which concededly serves interstate travelers is within the power granted it by the Commerce Clause of the Constitution, as interpreted by this Court for 140 years. It may be argued that Congress could have pursued other methods to eliminate the obstruction it found in interstate commerce caused by racial discrimination. But this is a matter of policy that rests entirely with the Congress not with the courts. How obstructions in commerce may be removed—what means are to be employed—is within the sound and exclusive discretion of the Congress. It is subject only to one caveat—that the means chosen by it must be reasonably adapted to the end permitted by the Constitution. We cannot say that its choice here was not so adapted. The Constitution requires no more.

   Affirmed.

Mr. Justice Douglas, concurring.

Though I join the Court's opinions, I am somewhat reluctant here, as I was in *Edwards v. California*, … , to rest solely on the Commerce Clause. My reluctance is not due to any conviction that Congress lacks power to regulate commerce in the interests of human rights. It is rather my belief that the right of people to be free of state action that discriminates against them because of race, like the "right of persons to move freely from State to State" (*Edwards v. California* …), "occupies a more protected position in our constitutional system than does the movement of cattle, fruit, steel and coal across state lines." Moreover, … the result reached by the Court is for me much more obvious as a protective measure under the Fourteenth Amendment than under the Commerce Clause. For the former deals with the constitutional status of the individual not with the impact on commerce of local activities or vice versa.

   Hence I would prefer to rest on the assertion of legislative power contained in 5 of the Fourteenth Amendment which states: "The Congress shall have power to enforce, by appropriate legislation, the provisions of this article"—a power which the Court concedes was exercised at least in part in this Act.

   A decision based on the Fourteenth Amendment would have a more settling effect, making unnecessary litigation over whether a particular restaurant or inn is within the commerce definitions of the Act or whether a particular customer is an interstate traveler. Under my construction, the Act would apply to all customers in all the enumerated places of public accommodation. And that construction would put an end to all obstructionist strategies and finally close one door on a bitter chapter in American history.

✣ *D O C U M E N T   4*

Congress Protects the Victims of Gender-Motivated Violence, 1994

Title 42 > Chapter 136 > Subchapter III > Part C > § 13981 § 13981. Civil rights

(a) Purpose

Pursuant to the affirmative power of Congress to enact this part under section 5 of the Fourteenth Amendment to the Constitution, as well as under section 8 of Article I of the Constitution, it is the purpose of this part to protect the civil rights of victims of gender motivated violence and to promote public safety, health, and activities affecting interstate commerce by establishing a Federal civil rights cause of action for victims of crimes of violence motivated by gender.

(b) Right to be free from crimes of violence

All persons within the United States shall have the right to be free from crimes of violence motivated by gender (as defined in subsection (d) of this section).

(c) Cause of action

A person (including a person who acts under color of any statute, ordinance, regulation, custom, or usage of any State) who commits a crime of violence motivated by gender and thus deprives another of the right declared in subsection (b) of this section shall be liable to the party injured, in an action for the recovery of compensatory and punitive damages, injunctive and declaratory relief, and such other relief as a court may deem appropriate.

(d) Definitions

For purposes of this section—

(1) the term "crime of violence motivated by gender" means a crime of violence committed because of gender or on the basis of gender, and due, at least in part, to an animus based on the victim's gender; and .

(2) the term "crime of violence" means—

(A) an act or series of acts that would constitute a felony against the person or that would constitute a felony against property if the conduct presents a serious risk of physical injury to another, and that would come within the meaning of State or Federal offenses described in section 16 of title 18, whether or not those acts have actually resulted in criminal charges, prosecution, or conviction and whether or not those acts were committed in the special maritime, territorial, or prison jurisdiction of the United States; and

(B) includes an act or series of acts that would constitute a felony described in subparagraph (A) but for the relationship between the person who takes such action and the individual against whom such action is taken.

(e) Limitation and procedures

(1) Limitation

Nothing in this section entitles a person to a cause of action under subsection (c) of this section for random acts of violence unrelated to gender or for acts that cannot be demonstrated, by a preponderance of the evidence, to be motivated by gender (within the meaning of subsection (d) of this section).

(2) No prior criminal action

Nothing in this section requires a prior criminal complaint, prosecution, or conviction to establish the elements of a cause of action under subsection (c) of this section.

(3) Concurrent jurisdiction

The Federal and State courts shall have concurrent jurisdiction over actions brought pursuant to this part.

(4) Supplemental jurisdiction

Neither section 1367 of title 28 nor subsection (c) of this section shall be construed, by reason of a claim arising under such subsection, to confer on the courts of the United States jurisdiction over any State law claim seeking the establishment of a divorce, alimony, equitable distribution of marital property, or child custody decree.

✥ *D O C U M E N T   5*
_____

United States v. Lopez, **1995**

...Chief Justice Rehnquist delivered the opinion of the Court.

In the Gun-Free School Zones Act of 1990, Congress made it a federal offense "for any individual knowingly to possess a firearm at a place that the individual knows, or has reasonable cause to believe, is a school zone." 18 U.S.C. § 922(q)(1)(A) (1988 ed., Supp. V). The Act neither regulates a commercial activity nor contains a requirement that the possession be connected in any way to interstate commerce. We hold that the Act exceeds the authority of Congress "[t]o regulate Commerce ... among the several States. ... "

We start with first principles. The Constitution creates a Federal Government of enumerated powers. See Art. I, § 8. As James Madison wrote: "The powers delegated by the proposed Constitution to the federal government are few and defined. Those which are to remain in the State governments are numerous and indefinite." The Federalist No. 45, pp. 292–293 (C. Rossiter ed. 1961). This constitutionally mandated division of authority "was adopted by the Framers to ensure protection of our fundamental liberties." *Gregory v. Ashcroft, ...* "Just as the separation and independence of the coordinate branches of the Federal Government serve to prevent the accumulation of excessive power in any one branch, a healthy balance of power between the States and the Federal Government will reduce the risk of tyranny and abuse from either front." ...

The Constitution delegates to Congress the power "[t]o regulate Commerce with foreign Nations, and among the several States, and with the Indian Tribes." Art. I, § 8, cl. 3. The Court, through Chief Justice Marshall, first defined the nature of Congress' commerce power in *Gibbons v. Ogden, ...* :

> "Commerce, undoubtedly, is traffic, but it is something more: it is intercourse. It describes the commercial intercourse between nations, and parts of nations, in all its branches, and is regulated by prescribing rules for carrying on that intercourse."

The commerce power "is the power to regulate; that is, to prescribe the rule by which commerce is to be governed. This power, like all others vested in congress, is complete in itself, may be exercised to its utmost extent, and acknowledges no limitations, other than are prescribed in the constitution." ... The *Gibbons* Court, however, acknowledged that limitations on the commerce power are inherent in the very language of the Commerce Clause. ...

In *Wickard v. Filburn*, the Court upheld the application of amendments to the Agricultural Adjustment Act of 1938 to the production and consumption of home-grown wheat. ... The *Wickard* Court explicitly rejected earlier distinctions between direct and indirect effects on interstate commerce, stating:

> "[E]ven if appellee's activity be local and though it may not be regarded as commerce, it may still, whatever its nature, be reached by Congress if it exerts a substantial economic effect on interstate commerce, and this irrespective of whether such effect is what might at some earlier time have been defined as 'direct' or 'indirect.'" ...

The *Wickard* Court emphasized that although Filburn's own contribution to the demand for wheat may have been trivial by itself, that was not "enough to remove him from the scope of federal regulation where, as here, his contribution, taken together with that of many others similarly situated, is far from trivial." ...

Jones & Laughlin Steel, Darby, and *Wickard* ushered in an era of Commerce Clause jurisprudence that greatly expanded the previously defined authority of Congress under that Clause. In part, this was a recognition of the great changes that had occurred in the way business was carried on in this country. Enterprises that had once been local or at most regional in nature had become national in scope. But the doctrinal change also reflected a view that earlier Commerce Clause cases artificially had constrained the authority of Congress to regulate interstate commerce.

But even these modern-era precedents which have expanded congressional power under the Commerce Clause confirm that this power is subject to outer limits. In *Jones & Laughlin Steel*, the Court warned that the scope of the interstate commerce power "must be considered in the light of our dual system of government and may not be extended so as to embrace effects upon interstate commerce so indirect and remote that to embrace them, in view of our complex society, would effectually obliterate the distinction between what is national and what is local and create a completely centralized government." ... Since that time, the Court has heeded that warning and undertaken to decide whether a rational basis existed for concluding that a regulated activity sufficiently affected interstate commerce. ...

JUSTICE BREYER rejects our reading of precedent and argues that "Congress ... could rationally conclude that schools fall on the commercial side of the line." ... Again, JUSTICE BREYER's rationale lacks any real limits because, depending on the level of generality, any activity can be looked upon as commercial. Under the dissent's rationale, Congress could just as easily look at child rearing as "fall[ing] on the commercial side of the line" because it provides a "valuable service—namely, to equip [children] with the skills they need to survive in life and, more specifically, in the workplace." ... We do not doubt that Congress ... has authority under the Commerce Clause to regulate numerous commercial activities that substantially affect interstate commerce and also affect the educational process. That authority, though broad, does not include the authority to regulate each and every aspect of local schools.

Admittedly, a determination whether an intrastate activity is commercial or noncommercial may in some cases result in legal uncertainty. But, so long as Congress' authority is limited to those powers enumerated in the Constitution, and so long as those enumerated powers are interpreted as having judicially enforceable outer limits, congressional legislation under the Commerce Clause always will engender "legal uncertainty." ...

These are not precise formulations, and in the nature of things they cannot be. But we think they point the way to a correct decision of this case. The possession of a gun in a local school zone is in no sense an economic activity that might, through repetition elsewhere, substantially affect any sort of interstate commerce. Respondent was a local student at a local school; there is no indication that he had recently moved in interstate commerce, and there is no requirement that his possession of the firearm have any concrete tie to interstate commerce.

To uphold the Government's contentions here, we would have to pile inference upon inference in a manner that would bid fair to convert congressional authority under the Commerce Clause to a general police power of the sort retained by the States. Admittedly, some of our prior cases have taken long steps down that road, giving great deference to congressional action. ... The broad language in these opinions has suggested the possibility of additional expansion, but we decline here to proceed any further. To do so would require us to conclude that the Constitution's enumeration of powers does not presuppose something not enumerated, ... and that there never will be a distinction between what is truly national and what is truly local,. ... This we are unwilling to do.

For the foregoing reasons the judgment of the Court of Appeals is *Affirmed.*

Justice Breyer, with whom Justice Stevens, Justice Souter, and Justice Ginsburg join, dissenting.

The issue in this case is whether the Commerce Clause authorizes Congress to enact a statute that makes it a crime to possess a gun in, or near, a school. ... In my view, the statute falls well within the scope of the commerce power as this Court has understood that power over the last half century. ...

To hold this statute constitutional is not to "obliterate" the "distinction between what is national and what is local," ... nor is it to hold that the Commerce Clause permits the Federal Government to "regulate any activity that it found was related to the economic productivity of individual citizens," to regulate "marriage, divorce, and child custody," or to regulate any and all aspects of education. ... First, this statute is aimed at curbing a particularly acute threat to the educational process—the possession (and use) of life-threatening firearms in, or near, the classroom. The empirical evidence that I have discussed above unmistakably documents the special way in which guns and education are incompatible. ... This Court has previously recognized the singularly disruptive potential on interstate commerce that acts of violence may have. ... Second, the immediacy of the connection between education and the national economic well-being is documented by scholars and accepted by society at large in a way and to a degree that may not hold true for other social institutions. It must surely be the rare case, then, that a statute strikes at conduct that (when considered in the abstract) seems so removed from commerce, but which (practically speaking) has so significant an impact upon commerce.

In sum, a holding that the particular statute before us falls within the commerce power would not expand the scope of that Clause. Rather, it simply would apply pre-existing law to changing economic circumstances. See *Heart of Atlanta Motel, Inc. v. United States,* . ... It would recognize that, in today's economic world, gun-related violence near the classroom makes a significant difference to our economic, as well as our social, well-being. In accordance with well-accepted precedent, such a holding would permit Congress "to act in terms of economic ... realities," would interpret the commerce power as "an affirmative power commensurate with the national needs," and would acknowledge that the "commerce clause does not operate so as to render the nation powerless to defend itself against economic forces that Congress decrees inimical or destructive of the national economy." ...

✣ D O C U M E N T   6

Printz v. United States, 1997

Justice Scalia delivered the opinion of the Court.

The question presented in these cases is whether certain interim provisions of the Brady Handgun Violence Prevention Act, ... commanding state and local law enforcement officers to conduct background checks on prospective handgun purchasers and to perform certain related tasks, violate the Constitution.

I

The [Brady] Act requires the Attorney General to establish a national instant background-check system by November 30, 1998, ... and immediately puts in place certain interim provisions until that system becomes operative. Under the interim provisions, a firearms dealer who proposes to transfer a handgun must first: (1) receive from the transferee a statement (the Brady Form), ... containing the name, address, and date of birth of the proposed transferee along with a sworn statement that the transferee is not among any of the classes of prohibited purchasers, ... verify the identity of the transferee by examining an identification document, ..., and (3) provide the "chief law enforcement officer (CLEO) of the transferee's residence with notice of the contents (and a copy) of the Brady Form, ... With some exceptions, the dealer must then wait five business days before consummating the sale, unless the CLEO earlier notifies the dealer that he has no reason to believe the transfer would be illegal. ...

The Brady Act creates two significant alternatives to the foregoing scheme. A dealer may sell a handgun immediately if the purchaser possesses a state handgun permit issued after a background check, ..., or if state law provides for an instant background check, ... In States that have not rendered one of these alternatives applicable to all gun purchasers, CLEOs are required to perform certain duties. When a CLEO receives the required notice of a proposed transfer from the firearms dealer, the CLEO must "make a reasonable effort to ascertain within 5 business days whether receipt or possession would be in violation of the law, including research in whatever State and local recordkeeping systems are available and in a national system designated by the Attorney General." ... The Act does not require the CLEO to take any particular action if he determines that a pending transaction would be unlawful; he may notify the firearms dealer to that effect, but is not required to do so. If, however, the CLEO notifies a gun dealer that a prospective purchaser is ineligible to receive a handgun, he must, upon request, provide the would-be purchaser with a written statement of the reasons for that determination. ... Moreover, if the CLEO does not discover any basis for objecting to the sale, he must destroy any records in his possession relating to the transfer, including his copy of the Brady Form. ... Under a separate provision of the GCA, any person who "knowingly violates [the section of the GCA amended by the Brady Act] shall be fined under this title, imprisoned for not more than 1 year, or both." ...

Petitioners Jay Printz and Richard Mack, the CLEOs for Ravalli County, Montana, and Graham County, Arizona, respectively, filed separate actions challenging the constitutionality of the Brady Act's interim provisions. ...

It is incontestible that the Constitution established a system of "dual sovereignty." ... Although the States surrendered many of their powers to the new Federal Government, they retained "a residuary and inviolable sovereignty," The Federalist No. 39, at 245 (J. Madison). This is reflected throughout the Constitution's text, ..., including (to mention only a few examples) the prohibition on any involuntary reduction or combination of a State's territory, Art. IV, § 3; the Judicial Power Clause, Art. III, § 2, and the Privileges and Immunities Clause, Art. IV, § 2, which speak of the "Citizens" of the States; the amendment provision, Article V, which requires the votes of three-fourths of the States to amend the Constitution; and the Guarantee Clause, Art. IV, §4, which "presupposes the continued existence of the states and ... those means and instrumentalities which are the creation of their sovereign and reserved rights," *Helvering v. Gerhardt,* .... Residual state sovereignty was also implicit, of course, in the Constitution's conferral upon Congress of not all governmental powers, but only discrete, enumerated ones, Art. I, §8, which implication was rendered express by the Tenth Amendment's assertion that "[t]he powers not delegated to the United States by the Constitution, nor prohibited by it to the States, are reserved to the States respectively, or to the people."

The Framers' experience under the Articles of Confederation had persuaded them that using the States as the instruments of federal governance was both ineffectual and provocative of federal-state conflict. See The Federalist No. 15. Preservation of the States as independent political entities being the price of union, and "[t]he practicality of making laws, with coercive sanctions, for the States as political bodies" having been, in Madison's words, "exploded on all hands," ... the Framers rejected the concept of a central government that would act upon and through the States, and instead designed a system in which the State and Federal Governments would exercise concurrent authority over the people—who were, in Hamilton's words, "the only proper objects of government," The Federalist No. 15, at 109. We have set forth the historical record in more detail elsewhere, see *New York v. United States,* ..., and need not repeat it here. It suffices to repeat the conclusion: "the Framers explicitly chose a Constitution that confers upon Congress the power to regulate individuals, not States.". ... The great innovation of this design was that "our citizens would have two political capacities, one state and one federal, each protected from incursion by the other"—"a legal system unprecedented in form and design, establishing two orders of government, each with its own direct relationship, its own privity, its own set of mutual rights and obligations to the people who sustain it and are governed by it.". ... The Constitution thus contemplates that a State's government will represent and remain accountable to its own citizens. ... As Madison expressed it: "[T]he local or municipal authorities form distinct and independent portions of the supremacy, no more subject, within their respective spheres, to the general authority than the general authority is subject to them, within its own sphere." The Federalist No. 39, at 245.

This separation of the two spheres is one of the Constitution's structural protections of liberty. "Just as the separation and independence of the coordinate branches of the Federal Government serve to prevent the accumulation of excessive power in any one branch, a healthy balance of power between the States and the Federal Government will reduce the risk of tyranny and abuse from either front." *Gregory,* ... To quote Madison once again: ...

> "In the compound republic of America, the power surrendered by the people is first divided between two distinct governments, and then the portion allotted to each subdivided among distinct and separate departments. Hence a double security arises to the rights of the people. The different governments will control each other, at the same time that each will be controlled by itself." The Federalist No. 51, at 323.

... The power of the Federal Government would be augmented immeasurably if it were able to impress into its service—and at no cost to itself—the police officers of the 50 States.

We have thus far discussed the effect that federal control of state officers would have upon the first element of the "double security" alluded to by Madison: the division of power between State and Federal Governments. It would also have an effect upon the second element: the separation and equilibration of powers between the three branches of the Federal Government itself. The Constitution does not leave to speculation who is to administer the laws enacted by Congress; the President, it says, "shall take Care that the Laws be faithfully executed," Art. II, § 3, personally and through officers whom he appoints (save for such inferior officers as Congress may authorize to be appointed by the "Courts of Law" or by "the Heads of Departments" who are themselves Presidential appointees), Art. II, § 2. The Brady Act effectively transfers this responsibility to thousands of CLEOs in the 50 States, who are left to implement the program without meaningful Presidential control (if indeed meaningful Presidential control is possible without the power to appoint and remove). The insistence of the Framers upon unity in the Federal Executive—to ensure both vigor and accountability—is well known. ... That unity would be shattered, and the power of the President would be subject to reduction, if Congress could act as effectively without the President as with him, by simply requiring state officers to execute its laws.

The dissent of course resorts to the last, best hope of those who defend ultra vires congressional action, the Necessary and Proper Clause. It reasons, ... that the power to regulate the sale of handguns under the Commerce Clause, coupled with the power to "make all Laws which shall be necessary and proper for carrying into Execution the foregoing Powers," Art. I, § 8, conclusively establishes the Brady Act's constitutional validity, because the Tenth Amendment imposes no limitations on the exercise of *delegated* powers but merely prohibits the exercise of powers "*not* delegated to the United States." What destroys the dissent's Necessary and Proper Clause argument, however, is not the Tenth Amendment but the Necessary and Proper Clause itself. When a "La[w] ... for carrying into Execution" the Commerce Clause violates the principle of state sovereignty reflected in the various constitutional provisions we mentioned earlier, ... it is not a "La[w] ... *proper* for carrying into Execution the Commerce Clause," and is thus, in the words of The Federalist, "merely [an] ac[t] of usurpation" which "deserve[s] to be treated as such." The Federalist No. 33, at 204 (A. Hamilton). ... We in fact answered the dissent's Necessary and Proper

Clause argument in *New York*: "[E]ven where Congress has the authority under the Constitution to pass laws requiring or prohibiting certain acts, it lacks the power directly to compel the States to require or prohibit those acts. ... [T]he Commerce Clause, for example, authorizes Congress to regulate interstate commerce directly; it does not authorize Congress to regulate state governments' regulation of interstate commerce." ...

The dissent perceives a simple answer in that portion of Article VI which requires that "all executive and judicial Officers, both of the United States and of the several States, shall be bound by Oath or Affirmation, to support this Constitution," arguing that by virtue of the Supremacy Clause this makes "not only the Constitution, but every law enacted by Congress as well," binding on state officers, including laws requiring state-officer enforcement. ... The Supremacy Clause, however, makes "Law of the Land" only "Laws of the United States which shall be made in Pursuance [of the Constitution]," Art. VI, cl. 2, so the Supremacy Clause merely brings us back to the question discussed earlier, whether laws conscripting state officers violate state sovereignty and are thus not in accord with the Constitution. ... Today we hold that Congress cannot circumvent that prohibition by conscripting the States' officers directly. The Federal Government may neither issue directives requiring the States to address particular problems, nor command the States' officers, or those of their political subdivisions, to administer or enforce a federal regulatory program. It matters not whether policymaking is involved, and no case-by-case weighing of the burdens or benefits is necessary; such commands are fundamentally incompatible with our constitutional system of dual sovereignty. Accordingly, the judgment of the Court of Appeals for the Ninth Circuit is reversed.

✠ D O C U M E N T   7

United States v. Morrison, **2000**

Chief Justice Rehnquist delivered the opinion of the Court.

In these cases we consider the constitutionality of 42 U. S. C. § 13981, which provides a federal civil remedy for the victims of gender-motivated violence. The United States Court of Appeals for the Fourth Circuit, sitting en banc, struck down § 13981 because it concluded that Congress lacked constitutional authority to enact the section's civil remedy. Believing that these cases are controlled by our decisions in *United States v. Lopez,* ... *United States v. Harris,* ..., and the *Civil Rights Cases,* ..., we affirm. .

Every law enacted by Congress must be based on one or more of its powers enumerated in the Constitution. "The powers of the legislature are defined and limited; and that those limits may not be mistaken, or forgotten, the constitution is written." *Marbury v. Madison,* ... Congress explicitly identified the sources of federal authority on which it relied in enacting § 13981. It said that a "Federal civil rights cause of action" is established "[p]ursuant to the affirmative power of Congress ... under section 5 of the Fourteenth Amendment to the Constitution, as well as under section 8 of Article I of the Constitution." .... We address Congress' authority to enact this remedy under each of these constitutional provisions in turn.

II

Due respect for the decisions of a coordinate branch of Government demands that we invalidate a congressional enactment only upon a plain showing that Congress has exceeded its constitutional bounds.... With this presumption of constitutionality in mind, we turn to the question whether § 13981 falls within Congress' power under Article I, § 8, of the Constitution. Brzonkala and the United States rely upon the third clause of the section, which gives Congress power "[t]o regulate Commerce with foreign Nations, and among the several States, and with the Indian Tribes."

As we discussed at length in *Lopez*, our interpretation of the Commerce Clause has changed as our Nation has developed.... We need not repeat that detailed review of the Commerce Clause's history here; it suffices to say that, in the years since *NLRB v. Jones & Laughlin Steel Corp.*,..., Congress has had considerably greater latitude in regulating conduct and transaction under the Commerce Clause than our previous case law permitted....

Lopez emphasized, however, that even under our modern, expansive interpretation of the Commerce Clause, Congress' regulatory authority is not without effective bounds....

As we observed in *Lopez*, modern Commerce Clause jurisprudence has "identified three broad categories of activity that Congress may regulate under its commerce power."... "First, Congress may regulate the use of the channels of interstate commerce."... "Second, Congress is empowered to regulate and protect the instrumentalities of interstate commerce, or persons or things in interstate commerce, even though the threat may come only from intrastate activities."... "Finally, Congress' commerce authority includes the power to regulate those activities having a substantial relation to interstate commerce,... *i.e.*, those activities that substantially affect interstate commerce."...

Petitioners do not contend that these cases fall within either of the first two of these categories of Commerce Clause regulation. They seek to sustain § 13981 as a regulation of activity that substantially affects interstate commerce. Given § 13981's focus on gender-motivated violence wherever it occurs (rather than violence directed at the instrumentalities of interstate commerce, interstate markets, or things or persons in interstate commerce), we agree that this is the proper inquiry....

With these principles underlying our Commerce Clause jurisprudence as reference points, the proper resolution of the present cases is clear. Gender-motivated crimes of violence are not, in any sense of the phrase, economic activity. While we need not adopt a categorical rule against aggregating the effects of any noneconomic activity in order to decide these cases, thus far in our Nation's history our cases have upheld Commerce Clause regulation of intrastate activity only where that activity is economic in nature....

Like the Gun-Free School Zones Act at issue in *Lopez*, § 13981 contains no jurisdictional element establishing that the federal cause of action is in pursuance of Congress' power to regulate interstate commerce. Although *Lopez* makes clear that such a jurisdictional element would lend support to the argument that § 13981 is sufficiently tied to interstate commerce, Congress elected to cast § 13981's remedy over a wider, and more purely intrastate, body of violent crime.

In contrast with the lack of congressional findings that we faced in *Lopez*, § 13981 *is* supported by numerous findings regarding the serious impact that gender-motivated violence has on victims and their families. ... But the existence of congressional findings is not sufficient, by itself, to sustain the constitutionality of Commerce Clause legislation. ...

In these cases, Congress' findings are substantially weakened by the fact that they rely so heavily on a method of reasoning that we have already rejected as unworkable if we are to maintain the Constitution's enumeration of powers. Congress found that gender-motivated violence affects interstate commerce

> "by deterring potential victims from traveling interstate, from engaging in employment in interstate business, and from transacting with business, and in places involved in interstate commerce; ... by diminishing national productivity, increasing medical and other costs, and decreasing the supply of and the demand for interstate products." ...

Given these findings and petitioners' arguments, the concern that we expressed in *Lopez* that Congress might use the Commerce Clause to completely obliterate the Constitution's distinction between national and local authority seems well founded.

We accordingly reject the argument that Congress may regulate noneconomic, violent criminal conduct based solely on that conduct's aggregate effect on interstate commerce. The Constitution requires a distinction between what is truly national and what is truly local. ...

III

Because we conclude that the Commerce Clause does not provide Congress with authority to enact § 13981, we address petitioners' alternative argument that the section's civil remedy should be upheld as an exercise of Congress' remedial power under § 5 of the Fourteenth Amendment. ...

As our cases have established, state-sponsored gender discrimination violates equal protection unless it " 'serves "important governmental objectives and ... the discriminatory means employed" are "substantially related to the achievement of those objectives." ' " ... However, the language and purpose of the Fourteenth Amendment place certain limitations on the manner in which Congress may attack discriminatory conduct. These limitations are necessary to prevent the Fourteenth Amendment from obliterating the Framers' carefully crafted balance of power between the States and the National Government. ... Foremost among these limitations is the time-honored principle that the Fourteenth Amendment, by its very terms, prohibits only state action. ...

Shortly after the Fourteenth Amendment was adopted, we decided two cases interpreting the Amendment's provisions, *United States v. Harris*, . . ., and the *Civil Rights Cases*, ... In *Harris*, the Court considered a challenge to § 2 of the Civil Rights Act of 1871. That section sought to punish "private persons" for "conspiring to deprive any one of the equal protection of the laws enacted by the State." ... We concluded that this law exceeded Congress' § 5 power because the law was "directed exclusively against the action of private persons, without reference to the laws of the State, or their administration by her officers." ...

We reached a similar conclusion in the *Civil Rights Cases*. In those consolidated cases, we held that the public accommodation provisions of the Civil Rights Act of 1875, which applied to purely private conduct, were beyond the scope of the § 5 enforcement power.... Section 13981 is not aimed at proscribing discrimination by officials which the Fourteenth Amendment might not itself proscribe; it is directed not at any State or state actor, but at individuals who have committed criminal acts motivated by gender bias....

Petitioner Brzonkala's complaint alleges, that she was the victim of a brutal assault. But Congress' effort in § 13981 to provide a federal civil remedy can be sustained neither under the Commerce Clause nor under § 5 of the Fourteenth Amendment. If the allegations here are true, no civilized system of justice could fail to provide her a remedy for the conduct of respondent Morrison. But under our federal system that remedy must be provided by the Commonwealth of Virginia, and not by the United States. The judgment of the Court of Appeals is *Affirmed*.

✤ E S S A Y S

Steven G. Calabresi, a professor at Northwestern University School of Law, offers a defense of state sovereignty and traditional federalism. Examining the principles and practicalities of preserving state power, Calabresi argues that the Court's recent federalism decisions are good for the republic. Catherine A. MacKinnon, a professor at the University of Michigan Law School, takes a completely different position. Focusing her analysis on the *Morrison* decision, MacKinnon claims that the Court's return to federalism not only set aside decades of precedent but also affirmed male sovereignty.

In Defense of Federalism

STEVEN G. CALABRESI

Supreme Court enforcement of the boundaries of the commerce power and of Congress's Section 5 power to enforce the Fourteenth Amendment presupposes that federalism is important. One possible justification for the Supreme Court's refusal to enforce these boundary lines between 1937 and 1995 could be that it was not worth the Court's time to fill its docket with commerce power cases.... I submit that constitutional federalism is very important by several measures and that it thus is deserving of the Court's time and attention. In fact, I think federalism is more important to our constitutional order than are many other doctrines that the Court does not hesitate to police and enforce.

Constitutional federalism should seem important to the Supreme Court for at least four different reasons. First, and most obviously, it should seem important because it is a major theme of the constitutional text. The text of the amended Constitution is only several thousand words long, and it is overwhelmingly concerned with federalism boundary line problems. ... Article I, Section 8, for example, contains 18 clauses enumerating and listing the powers of Congress. Other provisions of the Constitution list and enumerate the powers of the President and the jurisdiction of the federal courts. The original Constitution of 1787 was thus overwhelmingly concerned with federalism problems. The Bill of Rights, as is well known, was added as an afterthought to help secure the enthusiastic ratification of all 13 of the original states. The Framers of the Constitution bequeathed to us a document that is far more concerned with federalism than it is with judicially protected individual rights. To the extent that the text of that document still matters—and constitutional theorists usually concede that the text matters at least to some extent—there is simply no escaping the fact that our constitutional text devotes a lot of attention to federalism boundary line problems. Federalism, thus, mattered to the Framers of our Constitution and for that reason should matter to the present Supreme Court.

Second, federalism should seem important to the justices because it is an important feature of the landscape throughout the contemporary world in which we live. Our world is filled with stories about newly emerging federalisms, both because of the growth of new confederal international trading arrangements like the European Union and the North American Free Trade Agreement and because of the dissolution of once-unitary nation-states into new federalist entities, as is happening in Spain and Great Britain. These two developments suggest that we are living in what could be called an Age of Federalism, in which once-unitary nation-states are increasingly losing importance as some functions like trade and national defense get pushed up into the hands of new confederal decision makers, while other functions, like culture and education, get devolved down to new regional authorities. . . .

This does not, of course, prove that federalism is still important in the United States, but it should predispose a fair-minded observer to the possibility that something that is terribly important in many other contexts might also be important in the context of American politics. We are living in a global Age of Federalism as nation-states increasingly dissolve, and the same economic forces that are producing federalist solutions in other countries remain at work in the United States.

Third, the economics of federalism suggest at least four well-known reasons why constitutionally mandated decentralization is a good thing in the United States, just as it is in Canada, Spain, or Great Britain. . . .

1. The decentralization of decision making allows for decision makers to be responsive to local tastes and conditions. If one area of a country is filled with smokers, for example, and another area has few smokers, then statewide laws discouraging smoking may make more sense than one national law. . . . State laws can be designed to vary with local tastes and conditions, while national laws must be uniform nationwide. The more heterogeneous a nation is, the more desirable decentralization will be. Since the United States is a large, continental-sized nation with a population of 284 million people, some degree of constitutionally mandated decentralization is likely to be even more important for us than for less populous nations like Spain and Great Britain.

2. Constitutionally mandated decentralization encourages competition between jurisdictions. . . . If local tastes and conditions vary between jurisdictions, and if some degree of decentralization of decision making is required, then jurisdictions will compete with each other to offer optimal laws so that they can attract taxpaying citizens and industries.

3. Constitutionally mandated decentralization encourages experimentation. In a competitive situation, the states must constantly improve the quality of their laws and government programs so that they attract new taxpayers and businesses or they will lose out to their neighbors. ... The end result is a race to the top between jurisdictions, with market forces encouraging a constant improvement in the quality of state governmental programs.

4. Constitutionally mandated decentralization keeps government nearer the people, where it can be watched more closely and where it is more likely to have good information about popular preferences as to good policy. ... In economic terms, monitoring, agency, and information costs all should be lower at the state level because there is a closer identity of interests between state governments and the governed than is possible at the national level, where government is inevitably more remote from the citizenry.

These four economic arguments for decentralization are not always dispositive, because there are economic reasons why some measures need to be handled at the national rather than at the state level: for example, because, like national defense or space exploration, they are characterized by increasing economies of scale ...; because, like telecommunications regulation, the states would face a collective action problem if they attempted to do the job; because state regulation—of the environment, for example—would generate negative external effects or spillovers ...; or because, as in the case of protection of minorities' civil rights, history suggests that the national government is more sympathetic. ... Cumulatively, however, what emerges from this economic analysis of federalism is that there is a strong prima facie economic case for constitutionally mandated decentralization, which can be overcome when economies of scale, collective action problems, externalities, or civil rights issues are raised.

A fourth and final reason the justices of the Supreme Court ought to think federalism is important is that the specific issues that the Court's federalism case law touches upon implicate serious concerns about the dangers of overweening national power. *Lopez, City of Boerne,* and *Morrison* dealt with the constitutionality, respectively, of the Gun-Free School Zones Act, the Religious Freedom Restoration Act, and the Violence Against Women Act—all federal statutes that sought to expand the reaches of the federal police power. *Lopez,* in particular, involved an attempt by Congress to expand the federal criminal law by outlawing the bringing of a gun within 1000 feet of a school, an action that had already been outlawed by more than 40 states. One issue, thus, which is inescapably raised by *Lopez* is the continuing federalization of the criminal law. This federalization refers to the process by which more and more ordinary state law crimes are relabeled as federal crimes by Congress in its eagerness to show voters that it is tough on crime. ...

Federalizing ordinary state law crimes transfers power and work from state prosecutors to federal prosecutors, from state police forces to the Federal Bureau of Investigation, and from state courts to federal courts. This process raises valid concerns about the sweeping power of the federal government and implicates genuine issues of that civil liberty which is protected by federalism. It is not too difficult in light of this to see why the Court thought the *Lopez* case was an appropriate one in which to draw a line. Had the Court upheld Congress's statute in *Lopez,* it would have been difficult to imagine any federalization of the criminal law that would not be deemed to pass constitutional muster.

City of Boerne and *Morrison* raise slightly more complicated issues because in those cases, the federal laws struck down involved novel expansions of civil rights. In *City of Boerne,* the Court declined to allow Congress to create a new civil right for protecting religion, which would have trumped ordinary state laws, and in *Morrison* the Court declined to allow Congress to create a new civil right for private acts of violence against women. In both cases, the Court's reason for declining to allow the congressional extension of the federal police power was that the states were already adequately protecting the civil rights of religious people and of women that were in question. In essence, the Court found that there was no ongoing deprivation by the states of civil rights protected by Section 1 of the Fourteenth Amendment that permitted congressional remedial legislation under Section 5 of that amendment.

City of Boerne and *Morrison* thus raise the same problem that *Lopez* raises because they involve congressional efforts to expand the federal police power by regulating traditional state law matters in a situation where the states are already doing a good job. Obviously, Congress cannot be allowed to federalize the law under the guise of expanding civil rights into wholly novel areas. That in essence is what the Court concluded Congress was doing in these two cases and why these portions of the Religious Freedom Restoration Act and the Violence Against Women Act were struck down.

My arguments above about the importance of federalism presuppose that it is important that decentralization be constitutionally mandated. One possible response to the argument thus far might be to concede that decentralization is a good thing but to contend that it ought to be done by Congress as a matter of national grace. Simply proving that decentralization is good, without more, does not establish that constitutionally mandated and judicially enforced federalism is also desirable. ...

One advantage of constitutionally mandated decentralization is that it is more entrenched and is harder to dispense with than is decentralization done as a matter of national legislative grace. Requiring decentralization in a written constitution makes it more likely that it will actually occur, and that increases the chance that the benefits of decentralization will be experienced. We protect First Amendment freedoms in our written Constitution because we rightly fear that without constitutional and judicial protection, we will not get enough protection of freedom of speech and of the press. The same argument works to justify the need for constitutional and judicial protection of federalism. ... Without constitutional and judicial protection of the values of decentralization, we will get too much national lawmaking and especially too much federalization of the criminal law. We need decisions like *United States v. Lopez* to counterbalance the enormous pressure that Congress feels to expand the federal criminal law into new areas that had traditionally been regulated by the states.

... We are thus faced with the urgent question of whether the courts can protect federalism, at least to some degree, without any serious adverse effects. If so, we would appear to have some prima facie arguments in favor of the judicial policing of federalism boundary lines. If federalism values, like First Amendment values, are important and are underprotected in Congress, then perhaps some modicum of judicial policing of federalism boundary lines would be a good thing. What then of the institutional argument for judicial policing of federalism boundary lines?

To begin with, it is perhaps somewhat surprising that so many modern commentators take the position that the Supreme Court lacks the institutional competence to police federalism boundary lines.... For 150 years, from the time of the Founding up through 1937, we had judicial enforcement of federalism boundary lines in well-known and much discussed decisions like *McCulloch v. Maryland, Gibbons v. Ogden, United States v. E. C. Knight, Champion v. Ames*, and *Hammer v. Dagenhart*. It seems a little far-fetched for modern commentators to argue that the Supreme Court is institutionally ill equipped to decide a category of cases that it very visibly handled for the first century and a half of our national existence....

[T]he Court ought to approach enforcement of the commerce clause and Section 5 power with restraint and that only in cases of egregious overreaching should acts of Congress be struck down. Congressional efforts to enforce the commerce clause or Section 5 deserve to be given the benefit of the doubt both because of Congress's greater information about the real world and because Congress is a coequal interpreter of the Constitution to the Supreme Court. But giving Congress the benefit of the doubt does not mean rubber-stamping everything that Congress has tried to do, as happened from 1937 to 1995. Sometimes in extreme cases, it is valuable for the Court to remind Congress of the constitutional values of federalism, and this is what I think has happened in *Lopez, City of Boerne*, and *Morrison*. In each of these cases, Congress was attempting novel federal solutions to problems that a majority of the states seemed to be handling very well. It was accordingly appropriate for the Court to slow Congress down by forcing it to take a second look at what it had in haste done in each of these areas....

The modern Supreme Court is highly unlikely to overenforce the commerce power or to trigger a modern version of the constitutional crisis of 1937. The justices of the Supreme Court are officers of the national government, whose work is covered and critiqued in the national press and in the elite law reviews of national law schools. The incentive and reward structure of Supreme Court justices is heavily tilted in a nationalist direction, and, for this reason, they are a somewhat biased umpire for state-national disputes... Far from posing a serious threat of disruption akin to that raised by the old Supreme Court prior to 1937, the new Rehnquist Court federalism is a mild corrective to a half century of steady and sometimes ill-considered expansions of national power.

Federalism and the Protection of Male Sovereignty

CATHARINE A. MACKINNON

In 2000, in *United States v. Morrison*, The Violence Against Women Act (VAWA) civil remedy provision making gender-motivated violence federally actionable became one of only two federal laws against discrimination to that date to be invalidated by the United States Supreme Court since Reconstruction. In passing the VAWA, Congress sought to remedy well-documented inadequacies in existing laws against domestic violence and sexual assault—acts of which women are the principal victims and men the principal perpetrators—by providing a federal civil cause of action for sex discrimination that victims could use directly against perpetrators in state or federal court. Congress passed the statute under the authority of both the Commerce Clause and the Enforcement Clause of the Fourteenth Amendment. In a one-two punch, the 5-to-4 *Morrison* majority held that neither clause constitutionally authorized the VAWA. Congress's commerce power, the Court said, reaches only those private acts that are "economic in nature," which violence against women, despite its impact on interstate commerce, was deemed not to be. Congress's equality power, the Court ruled, is limited to addressing state acts, a limit the VAWA, in reaching what were termed private actors and private acts, was found to transgress.

On its most obvious level, *Morrison* represented a high-water mark of this Court's specific notion of federalism. Shield and sword, this sweeping doctrine and sensibility protects states as sovereign both in dominating their traditional legal domains and in avoiding accountability for their acts. In *Morrison*, this doctrine exceeded its previous limits to invalidate a federal law passed to fill a void the states had left in an area of their traditional prerogatives. When it has commanded a majority, this sensibility has damaged equality rights in particular, including by defining state responsibility for equality violations extremely narrowly. *Morrison* went further still by preventing the federal government from legislating equality rights in an area that states have inadequately protected.

But there may be a yet more direct relation between the denial of equality and the Court's new view of the formal doctrine of federalism. On a deeper level of law and politics, and seen against a historical backdrop of the use of federalism to deny racial equality and enforce white supremacy, *Morrison* can be seen to employ ostensibly gender-neutral tools to achieve a substantive victory for the socially unequal institution of male dominance. Read substantively, *Morrison* is not an abstract application of neutral institutional priorities but a concrete refusal to allow Congress to redress violence against women—a problem of substantive sex inequality that the Court declined to see as one of economic salience or national dimension. In *Morrison*, the Court revived and deployed against women as such the odious "states' rights" doctrine, the principal legal argument couched in institutional abstraction for the substantive maintenance of slavery that was used to deny equality rights on racial grounds well into the twentieth century. Combined with the Court's evolving equal protection jurisprudence—the "intent" requirement, which has made it increasingly difficult to hold states responsible for equal protection violations committed by state actors—*Morrison* leaves women who are denied the effective equal protection of state criminal laws against battering and rape without adequate legal recourse.

In this wider perspective, the Supreme Court, having already kept women from holding states to effective standards of sex equality protection in its equality jurisprudence, moved in *Morrison* to preclude Congress from helping to fill the gap the Court had left. Doubly shut out, violated women were, in essence, told by the *Morrison* majority—a majority that did not mention them once—that this legal system not only need not, but by virtue of its structural design may not, where gender-based violence is concerned, deliver meaningful equal protection of the laws to them. . . .

The *Morrison* majority found gender-motivated crimes of violence beyond Congress's power to regulate under the Commerce Clause because such acts, in its view, were not "economic in nature" and lacked "commercial character." The Court also held that to legislate federally against gender-based assault would violate the "distinction between what is truly national and what is truly local," exceeding the constitutional bounds on the federal legislative power and disturbing federal-state comity.

With respect to the Court, there is no economy in nature. The Court's economic essentialism devalued women's material activity and contributions and erased the documented financial losses caused by women's violation. Its narrow notion of the economic served specifically to evade the massive congressional record evidencing the impact of gender-based violence on women's economic opportunities, including lost work, lost productivity, lost mobility, and medical and other costs and expenses. Justice Souter strongly protested the "devaluation" of Congress's conclusions that gender-based violence affected commerce in the majority's embrace of a narrowly categorical approach toward what was commerce and what was not.

Stripping violence against women of its amply evidenced economic impact also provided a pretext for not applying the empirical test for regulation of commerce established in 1964 in the *Heart of Atlanta Motel* case: whether the activity involves commerce in "more States than one" and "has a real and substantial relation to the national interest." That satisfied, Congress was also allowed to legislate to right "a moral and social wrong"—in *Heart of Atlanta Motel*, it was racial discrimination in public accommodation—that did not need to be confined to the commercial. The combined evils the VAWA sought to address are strikingly similar. As Justice Souter observed, gender-based violence operates much like racial discrimination in its substantial effect on interstate commerce. Although public accommodations may initially seem more inherently commercial, violence against women has a price as well as a toll, visible once women are seen as active participants in the marketplace. The economic effect of dropping out of school, as Christy Brzonkala [the rape victim whose case became *United States v. Morrison*] did because of her rape, is a case in point.

But violence against women remained, to the *Morrison* Court, noneconomic in essence no matter its economic costs or consequences. The ideologically gendered lenses through which the majority viewed the factual record becomes apparent when comparing the facts of sex-based violence with the facts of *Wickard v. Filburn*, a 1942 case that both Justices Souter and Breyer discussed in their dissents. In *Wickard*, growing wheat at home for home consumption, an activity purposefully outside the stream of commerce and determinedly domestic, was found subject to regulation under the Commerce Clause because, when aggregated, it produced a substantial economic effect. The *Morrison* Court expressly declined to aggregate the documented effects of violence against women into a national impact because it did not see them as economic effects. It rejected what the Court called "the but-for causal chain" in which "every attenuated effect" of violent crime on interstate commerce would have, in the Court's view, permitted Congress "to regulate any crime as long as the nationwide aggregated impact of that crime has substantial effects on employment, production, transit, or consumption."

As a logically prior matter, it was unclear why, if substantiality of effect on commerce was what mattered, the Court confined aggregation to activity considered commercial, yet, if the commercial nature of the activity were what mattered, why its effects need to be aggregated when they are direct. The same logical slip was visible in *Lopez*: "[t]he possession of a gun in a local school zone is in no sense an economic activity that might, through repetition elsewhere, substantially affect any sort of interstate commerce." If an activity is in no sense economic, no amount of repetition makes it so. If, however, its location in the stream of commerce is recognized, the act itself is economic, without regard to aggregate impact.…

Converging with the Court's rejection of the national impact of violence against women in its discussion of the Commerce Clause was the repeated description of sex-based violence as "local" in the Court's discussion of federalism. The fact that violence against women, to the extent it has been legally addressed, has historically been a crime addressed by each locality was used as a reason to refuse to face its society-wide uniformity and national scale. When Justice Souter contested the Court's "step toward recapturing the prior mistakes of the pre-1937 Courts to Commerce Clause review," specifically referring to its invalidations of federal laws that tempered the abuses of industrialization, he attributed the Court's revival of this long discredited jurisprudence to its interest in the new federalism. Since its 1995 decision in *Lopez* cast doubt on half a century of Commerce Clause jurisprudence, the Court has expressed recurring concern that federal enactments may endanger traditional state legislative preserves and disrupt federal-state relations. The VAWA heightened those fears. Even before it became law, the VAWA's supposed "potential to create needless friction and duplication among the state and federal systems" was publicly attacked by Chief Justice Rehnquist. The *Morrison* majority expressed concern about the Court's future ability to limit congressional power in areas "where States historically have been sovereign" if the VAWA was upheld.

How a federal law that duplicated no state law in theory, design, or remedy, a law with federalism-friendly concurrent jurisdiction that provided merely a supplementary civil option while leaving state criminal remedies in place, threatened to compete with state law was not clarified. How it threatened the states, thirty-six of which supported the provision in the Supreme Court, was also not addressed.…

Is it any wonder that women seeking sex equality, having been abandoned by states and the federal judiciary alike, would turn to Congress? Divorcing women have no more interest in a federal remedy or forum as such than violated women do; it is the discrimination encountered in some legal forums that impels women to seek justice in others. The Court's federalism discussion, denying them this access, was afflicted by a nominalism similar to that on display in its discussion of commerce. By example, how a rape becomes "purely intrastate" challenges the imagination. A new and compelling case for reconsidering the federal balance was presented by enfranchised mobilized women challenging violence against women as inequality.

Women's change in status from silent chattel to full citizen called for questioning systemic norms and substantive law alike. When long ignored, urgent, and pervasive injury, predicated on historic exclusion of a subordinated group from the legal system, reaches the Court for the first time, as it did for violated women in *Morrison*, surely it is inadequate to respond that the laws on the subject have been this way for some time.

Short of such reconsideration, the *Morrison* Court might have found the limit it desired on the commerce rationale in the VAWA's equality purpose by drawing on the Commerce Clause's history in upholding legislation for social equality. The VAWA did not have to be justified under *either* the Commerce Clause *or* the Fourteenth Amendment. A rationale crafted by combining the two could have provided both the basis and the desired limiting construction consistent with the precedents and purposes of both clauses—the Commerce Clause enabling Congress to reach private acts substantially affecting the economy across the nation and the equality clause confining this particular rationale for exercise of legislative authority to equality questions recognized within Section 1. On just such a theory, Justice Douglas, concurring in *Heart of Atlanta Motel*, traced the "dual bases" in commerce and equality of the public accommodations legislation upheld there, observing that, "[i]n determining the reach of an exertion of legislative power, it is customary to read various granted powers together." ...

Instead, the *Morrison* majority revived a long-discredited tradition of striking down socially progressive legislation, a tradition that, in Justice Souter's words, "comes with the pedigree of near-tragedy." This tradition's application to violence against women—something no legal system has ever effectively addressed—comes closer to post-tragedy. Under the majority's approach, Justice Souter predicted a standardless interregnum in commerce cases like the one in obscenity law between *Redrup* and *Miller*, when every sexually explicit book or film was potentially susceptible to Supreme Court review case by case. Strikingly supporting this parallel is the utter indifference to violence against women exhibited in both areas of law. In both, it took violence against women in the facts, and ignoring it in law, to push an already questionable doctrinal structure into breakdown mode. Sex-based violence in reality may raise issues that legal doctrines did not have in mind but elide at their peril.

Under every doctrine it deployed, the Court minimized and domesticated violence against women. Under the Commerce Clause, it had no national impact. Under the rubric of federalism, it was local. Under Section 5 of the Fourteenth Amendment as well, the Court distinguished the VAWA from civil rights laws it found properly limited to localities. But unlike in those cases, violence against women and ineffectual law enforcement against it were found across the country. Moreover, Reconstruction legislation against the Ku Klux Klan and kindred terrorist organizations, legislation that the VAWA more closely parallels, applied nationwide even though most racist terrorism at the time was confined to the South. Gender-based terrorism today is unconfined to any locality. No legal precedent requires a remedy to a nationwide problem be legislated state-by-state—precisely where *Morrison* leaves violated women. ...

To the ear of violated women, the same obligato in two different keys plays beneath the *Morrison* majority opinion: keep her at home. In the *Morrison* Court's view, to address violence against women federally was to make a category mistake: to treat the local as if it were national, the noneconomic as if it were economic, the private as if it were public. The VAWA just felt wrong to them. These conventional reflexes were by no means universally shared, just as the outcome was by no means doctrinally preordained, the dissenters made clear. Justice Souter could not see why wheat and corn are national but women are not, or why wheat grown for consumption "right on the farm" was reachable under the commerce power but domestic violence was not. Justice Breyer queried why drugs for home consumption and home fireplaces were federally regulable but violence against women in the home was not.

Given that the VAWA civil remedy could readily have been upheld on precedent, why did the Supreme Court majority prevent violated women from pursuing accountability for bigoted violence against them? The answer may lie less with the imperatives of institutional forces the majority invoked than with the gender relations that impel those forces. The institutional doctrines on which the majority relied to invalidate Section 13981 are observably built on underlying social arrangements of male power. That is, the "traditional" allocation to state authorities of the governmental response to men's violence against women, an allocation respectfully invoked by majority and dissenters alike, is built on nothing more than that: a historical tradition of men (men who had power among men) dividing up power among themselves under conditions in which women had no authoritative say and over which no substantive sex equality principles reigned or, since *Morrison*, yet reign. What "has always been," whether addressed from a gray stone building in Washington, D.C., or a red brick building upstate, is nothing more than that: two "spheres" from which women "ha[ve] always been" excluded, and in which they are not yet at home.

Categorical formalism may have become newly attractive in service of this particular federalism, but what explains the attraction of this particular federalism? Do its categories cover substance with form? If so, what substance? Analyzing substantively the abstract institutional commitments in the name of which the VAWA civil remedy was invalidated requires asking what this federalism is concretely about, specifically whose interests its dynamics are constructed to favor. Could it be that men keep their power over women by keeping it local and private? Is male dominance served by ensuring that men keep control of certain things, including the terms of their relations with women, at close range? If so, federalism is an abstract institutional arrangement embodying judgments of those concerns that men want to control closely, and those over which they are willing to share control with other men farther removed. The VAWA squarely confronted this gentlemen's agreement by creating an entitlement to an equality for women that has not "always been." On this analysis, gender may be driving this federalism, explaining as sexual politics a result that otherwise eludes satisfactory explanation. On this reading, *Morrison* is not just another case in the march of the new federalism. It may be its bottom line.

Put another way, doctrine required the Court to confront, under the Commerce Clause, whether the economy is hurt by violence against women, and, under the Fourteenth Amendment, whether the states are hurt by the VAWA. (The answers were, respectively: yes, but that does not make it economic; and yes, whether they think so or not.) But no doctrine required the Court even to ask whether women as such are hurt by invalidating this law against violence against women. Leaving the answer to the political branches, as Justice Breyer advocated, would at long last have saved a provision like this one, but is no answer when a doctrine like federalism, built in women's silence and on women's exclusion, and the constitutional standards for what is and is not economic, which do not value women's material contributions, can set the terms under which Congress's decision is authoritatively judged. This is not to say that the Court correctly assessed the VAWA's constitutionality under existing federalism, commerce, or equality doctrines. It did not. It is to observe that no doctrine—not federalism, not commerce, not commerce, not yet equality—requires that women's interest in living as equals free from gender-based violence be judicially accorded the same level of constitutional priority as the states' interests in their traditional sphere of action or localities' interests in their economic autonomy. Nothing in the design of the system exposes the gender bias built into the history and tradition of the Constitution's structure and doctrines. Nothing requires that women's interests as such be given any consideration at all.

One way to describe the process of change in women's legal status from chattel to citizen is as a process of leaving home. The closer to home women's injuries are addressed, the less power and fewer rights women seem to have; the farther away from home the forum, the more power and rights women have gained—and with them freedom of action, resources, and access to a larger world. In experiential terms, women are least equal at home, in private; they have had the most equality in public, far from home. It is in the private, man's sovereign castle, where most women remain for a lifetime, where women are most likely to be battered and sexually assaulted, and where they have no recourse because the private, by definition, is inviolable and recourse means intervention. For physically and sexually violated women, going public with their injuries has meant seeking accountability and relief from higher sovereigns, men who have power over the men who abused them because they are above, removed from, hence less likely to be controlled by those abusers. This process has meant encountering systemic barriers to access at each higher level—pressures, it is said, that have nothing to do with gender but simply reflect the way the system works. Systemically, the preferred jurisdiction of resolution is always the closest to the abuser. In effect, at each level, women are told to go back where he rules. One way to describe this dynamic is to observe that men often respect other men's terrain as sovereign in exchange for those other men's respect for their own sovereignty on their own terrain. As a result of such balances that men with power strike among themselves, represented in the shape of public institutions, men have the most freedom at home, and women gain correspondingly greater equality, hence freedom, the farther away from home they go.

"Why is it that women do not dispute male sovereignty?" Simone de Beauvoir once asked. Battered and raped women *have* disputed their various male sovereigns.

Their advances in human status can be tracked in space and time up an ascending jurisdictional ladder. After failing for centuries to stop domestic violence and marital rape in their own families, women sought relief outside the family in the legal system. First, they moved out from the home, where they had had no rights except by grace, to acquire recognition of harms done to them as women under local and state law. Achieving enforcement of state laws against domestic battering was a major step. Applying state rape laws to rape in marriages was another step up. When the law of sexual assault continued to fail women, a partial remedy for some rapes was found under civil rights laws in the form of claims for sexual harassment, achieving some national recognition for these injuries. Increasingly, international remedies are sought by women claiming a human right not to be violated because they are women. Thus, Bosnian women sought relief from genocidal rape not in their own postgenocidal legal system, but in another country, far from home, under international law. With the VAWA, women disputed male sovereignty itself.

As each jurisdiction fails them, and when they can, women seek accountability and relief in superior forums, disputing male sovereigns by appealing to higher male sovereigns. And at each level, women confront jurisdictional and systemic barriers as they are told in various terms that they do not belong there and should go back home where they belong.

Men have long fought over who has power over whom and what, battles of which institutions and doctrines like federalism and separation of powers are results. The women they victimize have no stake in whether their injuries are addressed by state or federal governments, by the Court or by Congress. What women do have a stake in, so long as men perpetrate violence against them on the basis of sex, is in having those injuries addressed: in effective and equal enforcement of laws against the acts that injure them. This concrete and urgent need, not any position on men's turf battles and not a desire for positive symbolism, produced the VAWA. It is in light of this concrete and urgent need that the *Morrison* outcome is most vicious. *Morrison* sent women back home, to their violators. Its constitutional message to violated women is: only the states can take your equality rights away, and only the states can give them back to you. If the states could have given women equality, they would have, and there would have been no VAWA because there would have been no need for one.

As post-Reconstruction courts obstructed racial equality, so the *Morrison* Court obstructed sex equality, and by the same means. The Court did not even do what it could. It reduced women claiming the most basic rights of citizenship to standing on ever narrower and shakier ground, ground now all but disappeared. Not one member of the Supreme Court argued that the rights the VAWA civil remedy gave women were constitutional under the Constitution's equality guarantee. Justice Breyer came closest in the part of his dissent that Justices Ginsburg and Souter declined to join. Perhaps the Constitution cannot be retrofitted adequately to address sex-based violations. An Equal Rights Amendment designed to promote equality of the sexes horizontally in society as well as vertically under law could. International law could also provide new ground for violated women to stand on. ...

United States v. Morrison closed a crucial avenue of access to equality under law and dealt a devastating blow to the development of women's human rights against sex-based violence. *Morrison* was a major battle in women's civil war: a battle at once over the structure of the union and the status of the sexes in civil society. It addressed ground zero for citizenship—physical security—and ground zero for women's human status—sexual inviolability. At stake was nothing less than whether women are full citizens and full human beings: equals. The VAWA civil remedy stood for the principle that a woman could not, with impunity, be assaulted anywhere in this nation simply because she is a woman. It put the power to dispute male sovereignty in women's hands. The *Morrison* majority decided that the union could not permit that and be the same union it was. The ruling thus raised, as no case before it has, the question whether the structure of a nation organized to preclude relief for the violation of one half of its people by the other should survive.

✠ F U R T H E R   R E A D I N G

Baker, Lynn A. and Ernest A. Young. "Federalism and the Double Standard of Judicial Review," *Duke Law Journal*, 51 (2001): 75–164.

Bansal, Preeta D. "The Supreme Court's Federalism Revival and Reinvigorating the 'Federalism Deal'," *St. John's Journal of Legal Commentary*, 21 (2007): 447–460.

Barrett, John Q. "The 'Federalism Five' As Supreme Court Nominees, 1971–1991," *St. John's Journal of Legal Commentary*, 21 (2007): 485–496.

Belsky, Martin, ed. *The Rehnquist Court: A Retrospective* (2002).

Bradley, Craig, ed. *The Rehnquist Legacy* (2006).

Claeys, Eric R. "Raich and Judicial Conservatism at the Close of the Rehnquist Court," *Lewis and Clark Law Review*, 9 (2005): 791–822.

Clayton, Cornell W. and J. Mitchell Pickerill. "Guess What Happened on the Way to Revolution? Precursors to the Supreme Court's Federalism Revolution," *Publius: The Journal of Federalism*, 34 (2004): 85–114.

Conlan, Timothy, *New Federalism: Intergovernmental Reform from Nixon to Reagan* (1988).

Diamond, Martin. "The Federalist on Federalism: 'Neither a Nation Nor a Federal Constitution, But a Composition of Both,'" *Yale Law Journal*, 86 (1997): 1273–1285.

Donahue, John D. *Disunited States* (1997).

Elazar, Daniel J. *Exploring Federalism* (1987).

Ferejohn, John and Barry R. Weingast, eds. *The New Federalism: Can the States Be Trusted?* (1997).

Frickey, Philip P. and Steven S. Smith. "Judicial Review, the Congressional Process, and the Federalism Cases: An Interdisciplinary Critique," *Yale Law Journal*, 111 (2002): 1707–1756.

Goldwin, Robert A., ed. *A Nation of States: Essays on the American Federal System* (1974).

Hensley, Thomas R. *The Rehnquist Court: Justices, Rulings, and Legacy* (2006).

Scheiber, Harry N. "Redesigning the Architecture of Federalism—An American Tradition," *Yale Law and Policy Review/Yale Journal on Regulation*, 14 (1996): 227–296.

Scheiber, Harry N. and Malcolm M. Feeley, eds. *Power Divided: Essays on the Theory and Practice of Federalism* (1989).

Schroeder, Christopher H. "Causes of the Recent Turn in Constitutional Interpretation," *Duke Law Journal*, 51 (2001): 307–361.

Schwartz, Herman, ed. *The Rehnquist Court: Judicial Activism on the Right* (2003).

Shapiro, David L. *Federalism: A Dialogue* (1995).

Walker, David B. *The Rebirth of Federalism: Slouching toward Washington* (1999).

Weissman, Deborah. "Gender-Based Violence as Judicial Anomaly: Between the Truly National and the Truly Local," *Boston College Law Review*, 42 (2001): 1081–1159.

Whittington, Keith E. "Taking What They Give Us: Explaining the Court's Federalism Offensive," *Duke Law Journal*, 51 (2001): 477–520.

Yarbrough, Jean. "Federalism in the Foundation and Preservation of the American Republic," *Publius: The Journal of Federalism*, 6 (1976): 43–60.

Yarbrough, Tinsley E. *The Rehnquist Court and the Constitution* (2001).

CHAPTER
15

Presidential Power from the Cold War to the War on Terror

One of the most astonishing constitutional developments of the past 75 years has been the dramatic increase in the power and influence of the American presidency. The founders had, at best, mixed feelings about executive power. Many were suspicious of concentrating too much power in any one individual because of their experiences with a British monarch. But after the Articles of Confederation proved unworkable as a plan of government, in part because it included no provision for an executive, the framers came to believe that a chief executive was a necessary ingredient for a successful republic. Although strong presidents were rare during the nineteenth century, the twin crises of the Great Depression and World War II allowed President Franklin D. Roosevelt, more than any of his predecessors, to establish the presidency as the center of national leadership. The Supreme Court, moreover, affirmed the president's key role, at least in foreign affairs, in United States v. Curtiss-Wright Export Corporation (1936), when it described the office as "the sole organ of the federal government in the field of international relations."

The Cold War accentuated the powers of the position. Beginning in 1946, the United States and the Soviet Union—the world's two remaining military superpowers after World War II—opposed and confronted each other around the globe. For at least the first two decades of this struggle, the United States pursued a bipartisan foreign policy based on aggressively containing the spread of communism. As various foreign crises arose, a succession of presidents from both parties claimed that national security required a strong executive who could respond swiftly to external threats. Given the president's role as commander-in-chief and his constitutional authority to negotiate treaties, Congress generally acquiesced in the expansion of these powers.

However, in the early 1970s, the Vietnam War and the Watergate scandal dissolved the bipartisan consensus in American foreign policy and with it Congress's role as a willing accomplice in the growth of executive power. As victory in Vietnam became elusive and American involvement more unpopular, a Democratic Congress opposed to Republican President Richard M. Nixon asserted its war powers and circumscribed the president's ability to dispatch military forces. At the same time that Vietnam prompted a reassertion of congressional power over foreign affairs, a domestic political scandal further eroded presidential authority. Beginning in the summer

518

of 1972, over a period of several months, a pair of intrepid journalists gradually exposed Nixon's role in covering up White House involvement with a break-in at the Democratic National Committee headquarters at the Watergate complex in Washington, D.C. Evidence of Nixon's direct involvement in the cover-up became apparent when the Supreme Court, in United States v. Nixon, *ordered that he surrender tapes of White House conversations. After the House of Representatives initiated impeachment proceedings in the summer of 1974, Nixon became the only American president to resign from office. The effects of Vietnam and Watergate on the presidency were immediate. In the next few years, Congress enacted a host of reforms, including legislation to increase disclosure of federal campaign contributions, affirm ethics in government, and provide public access to presidential records. The "Imperial Presidency," as historian Arthur Schlesinger termed it, was dead.*

Several years later, after the Cold War ended, a combination of presidential misbehavior, intense partisanship, and increased terrorist activity directed at the United States reignited conflict over presidential power. In 1998, after Democratic President Bill Clinton had a sexual dalliance with a White House intern and lied about it in a legal deposition, the Republican-led House of Representatives impeached him, although the Republican Senate voted not to remove him from office. More significantly, after the Islamic extremist group al-Qaeda carried out a major terrorist attack against the United States on September 11, 2001, President George W. Bush claimed extraordinary powers as commander-in-chief. Congress passed a resolution authorizing the president to respond, and Bush used the resolution to claim arguably unprecedented authority both to retaliate against al-Qaeda and to prevent future acts of terrorism. Because the "war on terror" appears destined to continue for some time, the debate over presidential power will surely continue as well.

What are the constitutional roles of the president and Congress in the realm of war-making and foreign policy? Does it matter that only Congress under the Constitution has the power to "declare war"? What are the limits to the president's authority as commander-in-chief of the armed forces? How independent is the executive branch from the legislative branch? Does the aggregation of presidential power pose a threat to civil liberties? How will President Barack Obama shape executive power in the coming years?

✚ D O C U M E N T S

The Cold War spawned numerous situations in which the president deployed military troops. When North Korea invaded South Korea in 1950, President Harry S. Truman committed U.S. forces to repel the attack under the authority of a United Nations resolution. A few years later, in the midst of the conflict, American steelworkers went on strike, and Truman cited wartime emergency as the basis for ordering a takeover of steel plants pending a labor settlement. Truman invoked the concept of "inherent" executive powers and his role as commander-in-chief to support the seizure. By a 6-3 vote, the Supreme Court rejected this view in *Youngstown Sheet & Tube Company v. Sawyer*, Document 1. Justice Hugo Black authored the majority opinion and Chief Justice Fred Vinson wrote the dissent. Justice Robert Jackson's concurrence was especially significant in elaborating various levels of presidential authority. Later, President Lyndon B. Johnson pursued military action in Vietnam. Following an alleged attack by North Vietnamese gunboats on U.S. destroyers in the Gulf of Tonkin in 1964, Congress passed the Tonkin Resolution, Document 2. The resolution amounted to a *de facto* declaration of war, especially because Congress continued to appropriate ever larger amounts of money to pay for the build-up of U.S. forces in Southeast Asia.

Victory eluded Johnson, and in 1969 President Nixon inherited the Vietnam War upon entering office. By that time, criticism of the war—coming from both home and abroad—had reached a fever pitch. At the same time that he began a phased withdrawal of American troops, Nixon expanded the conflict by ordering the bombing of North Vietnamese base areas in neutral, neighboring Cambodia, a fact which he initially kept secret from the public. Congress responded to Nixon's unilateralism by repealing the Tonkin Resolution in 1971 and a few years later by passing the War Powers Resolution over Nixon's veto. The Resolution, Document 3, established clear guidelines for the use of presidential war-making power (although subsequent presidents did not always abide by its terms). Nixon overplayed his hand at home as well as abroad, and his cover-up of the Watergate break-in brought the principle of executive privilege before the Supreme Court. In *United States v. Nixon*, Document 4, the Court unanimously (with Justice William Rehnquist, a former Nixon aide, recusing himself) ordered Nixon to turn over the audiotapes of his conversations with his close advisors. Chief Justice Warren Burger authored the Court's opinion.

Terrorist attacks against the United States revived the debate over the extent of the president's war powers. Within days of 9/11, President Bush addressed a joint session of Congress, which quickly passed a joint resolution, Document 5, authorizing the use of force against terrorists. After Bush dispatched American troops to hunt down al-Qaeda terrorists in Afghanistan and around the world, Alberto R. Gonzalez, then serving as Counsel to the President, asked the Department of Justice for its opinion on standards for interrogating suspected terrorists outside of the United States. John Yoo, then deputy assistant attorney general in the Office of Legal Counsel at the Department of Justice, responded with a memo, excerpted as Document 6, which offered both a narrow definition of what constituted torture and an expansive interpretation of the president's power as commander-in-chief. Sometimes known as the "Bybee Memo," it bore the signature of Assistant Attorney General Jay S. Bybee, although Yoo later revealed his authorship. (Bybee's successor later withdrew the opinion.)

Within a few years, the Supreme Court heard a significant challenge to Bush's pursuit of the war on terror. In *Hamdi v. Rumsfeld*, in a 6-3 decision, the Court held that due process demands that a defendant be given an opportunity to contest his detention as an "enemy combatant." Justice Sandra Day O'Connor wrote the opinion, excerpts of which are Document 7. In *Hamdi*, the Court began to reign in a president who had stretched to the limits the powers of his office.

✣ *D O C U M E N T   1*

Youngstown Sheet & Tube Co. v. Sawyer, 1952

Mr. Justice Black delivered the opinion of the Court.

We are asked to decide whether the President was acting within his constitutional power when he issued an order directing the Secretary of Commerce to take possession of and operate most of the Nation's steel mills. The mill owners argue that the President's order amounts to lawmaking, a legislative function which the Constitution has expressly confided to the Congress, and not to the President. The Government's position is that the order was made on findings of the President that his action was necessary to avert a national catastrophe which would inevitably result from a stoppage of steel production, and that, in meeting this grave emergency, the President was acting within the aggregate of his constitutional powers as the Nation's Chief Executive and the Commander in Chief of the Armed Forces of the United States. ...

The President's power, if any, to issue the order must stem either from an act of Congress or from the Constitution itself. There is no statute that expressly authorizes the President to take possession of property as he did here. Nor is there any act of Congress to which our attention has been directed from which such a power can fairly be implied. Indeed, we do not understand the Government to rely on statutory authorization for this seizure. ...

It is clear that, if the President had authority to issue the order he did, it must be found in some provision of the Constitution. And it is not claimed that express constitutional language grants this power to the President. The contention is that presidential power should be implied from the aggregate of his powers under the Constitution. Particular reliance is placed on provisions in Article II which say that "The executive Power shall be vested in a President ... "; that "he shall take Care that the Laws be faithfully executed," and that he "shall be Commander in Chief of the Army and Navy of the United States."

The order cannot properly be sustained as an exercise of the President's military power as Commander in Chief of the Armed Forces. The Government attempts to do so by citing a number of cases upholding broad powers in military commanders engaged in day-to-day fighting in a theater of war. Such cases need not concern us here. Even though "theater of war" be an expanding concept, we cannot with faithfulness to our constitutional system hold that the Commander in Chief of the Armed Forces has the ultimate power as such to take possession of private property in order to keep labor disputes from stopping production. This is a job for the Nation's lawmakers, not for its military authorities.

Nor can the seizure order be sustained because of the several constitutional provisions that grant executive power to the President. In the framework of our Constitution, the President's power to see that the laws are faithfully executed refutes the idea that he is to be a lawmaker. The Constitution limits his functions in the lawmaking process to the recommending of laws he thinks wise and the vetoing of laws he thinks bad. And the Constitution is neither silent nor equivocal about who shall make laws which the President is to execute. The first section of the first article says that "All legislative Powers herein granted shall be vested in a Congress of the United States. ... " After granting many powers to the Congress, Article I goes on to provide that Congress may

> make all Laws which shall be necessary and proper for carrying into Execution the foregoing Powers, and all other Powers vested by this Constitution in the Government of the United States, or in any Department or Officer thereof.

The President's order does not direct that a congressional policy be executed in a manner prescribed by Congress—it directs that a presidential policy be executed in a manner prescribed by the President. The preamble of the order itself, like that of many statutes, sets out reasons why the President believes certain policies should be adopted, proclaims these policies as rules of conduct to be followed, and again, like a statute, authorizes a government official to promulgate additional rules and regulations consistent with the policy proclaimed and needed to carry that policy into execution. The power of Congress to adopt such public policies as those proclaimed by the order is beyond question. It can authorize the taking of private property for public use. It can make laws regulating the relationships between employers and employees, prescribing rules designed to settle labor disputes, and fixing wages and working conditions in certain fields of our economy. The Constitution does not subject this lawmaking power of Congress to presidential or military supervision or control.

It is said that other Presidents, without congressional authority, have taken possession of private business enterprises in order to settle labor disputes. But even if this be true, Congress has not thereby lost its exclusive constitutional authority to make laws necessary and proper to carry out the powers vested by the Constitution "in the Government of the United States, or any Department or Officer thereof."

The Founders of this Nation entrusted the lawmaking power to the Congress alone in both good and bad times. It would do no good to recall the historical events, the fears of power, and the hopes for freedom that lay behind their choice. Such a review would but confirm our holding that this seizure order cannot stand.

The judgment of the District Court is

Affirmed.

Mr. Justice Jackson, concurring in the judgment and opinion of the Court....

The actual art of governing under our Constitution does not, and cannot, conform to judicial definitions of the power of any of its branches based on isolated clauses, or even single Articles torn from context. While the Constitution diffuses power the better to secure liberty, it also contemplates that practice will integrate the dispersed powers into a workable government. It enjoins upon its branches separateness but interdependence, autonomy but reciprocity. Presidential powers are not fixed but fluctuate depending upon their disjunction or conjunction with those of Congress. We may well begin by a somewhat over-simplified grouping of practical situations in which a President may doubt, or others may challenge, his powers, and by distinguishing roughly the legal consequences of this factor of relativity.

1. When the President acts pursuant to an express or implied authorization of Congress, his authority is at its maximum, for it includes all that he possesses in his own right plus all that Congress can delegate. In these circumstances, and in these only, may he be said (for what it may be worth) to personify the federal sovereignty. If his act is held unconstitutional under these circumstances, it usually means that the Federal Government, as an undivided whole, lacks power. A seizure executed by the President pursuant to an Act of Congress would be supported by the strongest of presumptions and the widest latitude of judicial interpretation, and the burden of persuasion would rest heavily upon any who might attack it.

2. When the President acts in absence of either a congressional grant or denial of authority, he can only rely upon his own independent powers, but there is a zone of twilight in which he and Congress may have concurrent authority, or in which its distribution is uncertain. Therefore, congressional inertia, indifference or quiescence may sometimes, at least, as a practical matter, enable, if not invite, measures on independent presidential responsibility. In this area, any actual test of power is likely

to depend on the imperatives of events and contemporary imponderables, rather than on abstract theories of law.

3. When the President takes measures incompatible with the expressed or implied will of Congress, his power is at its lowest ebb, for then he can rely only upon his own constitutional powers minus any constitutional powers of Congress over the matter. Courts can sustain exclusive presidential control in such a case only by disabling the Congress from acting upon the subject. Presidential claim to a power at once so conclusive and preclusive must be scrutinized with caution, for what is at stake is the equilibrium established by our constitutional system.

Into which of these classifications does this executive seizure of the steel industry fit? It is eliminated from the first by admission, for it is conceded that no congressional authorization exists for this seizure. . . .

Can it then be defended under flexible tests available to the second category? It seems clearly eliminated from that class, because Congress has not left seizure of private property an open field, but has covered it by three statutory policies inconsistent with this seizure. In cases where the purpose is to supply needs of the Government itself, two courses are provided: one, seizure of a plant which fails to comply with obligatory orders placed by the Government; another, condemnation of facilities, including temporary use under the power of eminent domain. The third is applicable where it is the general economy of the country that is to be protected, rather than exclusive governmental interests. None of these were invoked. In choosing a different and inconsistent way of his own, the President cannot claim that it is necessitated or invited by failure of Congress to legislate upon the occasions, grounds and methods for seizure of industrial properties.

This leaves the current seizure to be justified only by the severe tests under the third grouping, where it can be supported only by any remainder of executive power after subtraction of such powers as Congress may have over the subject. In short, we can sustain the President only by holding that seizure of such strike-bound industries is within his domain and beyond control by Congress. Thus, this Court's first review of such seizures occurs under circumstances which leave presidential power most vulnerable to attack and in the least favorable of possible constitutional postures. . . .

Nothing in our Constitution is plainer than that declaration of a war is entrusted only to Congress. Of course, a state of war may, in fact, exist without a formal declaration. But no doctrine that the Court could promulgate would seem to me more sinister and alarming than that a President whose conduct of foreign affairs is so largely uncontrolled, and often even in unknown, can vastly enlarge his mastery over the internal affairs of the country by his own commitment of the Nation's armed forces to some foreign venture. I do not, however, find it necessary or appropriate to consider the legal status of the Korean enterprise to discountenance argument based on it.

Assuming that we are in a war *de facto*, whether it is or is not a war *de jure*, does that empower the Commander in Chief to seize industries he thinks necessary to supply our army? The Constitution expressly places in Congress power "to raise and *support* Armies" and "to *provide* and *maintain* a Navy." (Emphasis supplied.) This certainly lays upon Congress primary responsibility for supplying the armed forces. Congress alone controls the raising of revenues and their appropriation, and may determine in what manner and by what means they shall be spent for military and naval procurement. I suppose no one would doubt that Congress can take over war supply as a Government enterprise. On the other hand, if Congress sees fit to rely on free private enterprise collectively bargaining with free labor for support and maintenance of our armed forces, can the Executive, because of lawful disagreements incidental to that process, seize the facility for operation upon Government-imposed terms?...

That military powers of the Commander in Chief were not to supersede representative government of internal affairs seems obvious from the Constitution and from elementary American history. Time out of mind, and even now, in many parts of the world, a military commander can seize private housing to shelter his troops. Not so, however, in the United States, for the *Third Amendment* says,

> No Soldier shall, in time of peace be quartered in any house, without the consent of the Owner, nor in time of war, but in a manner to be prescribed by law.

Thus, even in war time, his seizure of needed military housing must be authorized by Congress. It also was expressly left to Congress to "provide for calling forth the Militia to execute the Laws of the Union, suppress Insurrections and repel Invasions...." Such a limitation on the command power, written at a time when the militia, rather than a standing army, was contemplated as the military weapon of the Republic, underscores the Constitution's policy that Congress, not the Executive, should control utilization of the war power as an instrument of domestic policy....

We should not use this occasion to circumscribe, much less to contract, the lawful role of the President as Commander in Chief. I should indulge the widest latitude of interpretation to sustain his exclusive function to command the instruments of national force, at least when turned against the outside world for the security of our society. But, when it is turned inward not because of rebellion, but because of a lawful economic struggle between industry and labor, it should have no such indulgence. His command power is not such an absolute as might be implied from that office in a militaristic system, but is subject to limitations consistent with a constitutional Republic whose law and policymaking branch is a representative Congress. The purpose of lodging dual titles in one man was to insure that the civilian would control the military, not to enable the military to subordinate the presidential office. No penance would ever expiate the sin against free government of holding that a President can escape control of executive powers by law through assuming his military role. What the power of command may include I do not try to envision, but I think it is not a military prerogative, without support of law, to seize persons or property because they are important or even essential for the military and naval establishment....

Mr. Chief Justice Vinson, with whom Mr. Justice Reed and Mr. Justice Minton join, dissenting.

In passing upon the question of Presidential powers in this case, we must first consider the context in which those powers were exercised.

Those who suggest that this is a case involving extraordinary powers should be mindful that these are extraordinary times. A world not yet recovered from the devastation of World War II has been forced to face the threat of another and more terrifying global conflict.

Accepting in full measure its responsibility in the world community, the United States was instrumental in securing adoption of the United Nations Charter, approved by the Senate by a vote of 89 to 2. The first purpose of the United Nations is to

> maintain international peace and security, and, to that end, to take effective collective measures for the prevention and removal of threats to the peace, and for the suppression of acts of aggression or other breaches of the peace....

In 1950, when the United Nations called upon member nations "to render every assistance" to repel aggression in Korea, the United States furnished its vigorous support. For almost two full years, our armed forces have been fighting in Korea, suffering casualties of over 108,000 men. Hostilities have not abated. The "determination of the United Nations to continue its action in Korea to meet the aggression" has been reaffirmed. Congressional support of the action in Korea has been manifested by provisions for increased military manpower and equipment and for economic stabilization, as hereinafter described.

Further efforts to protect the free world from aggression are found in the congressional enactments of the Truman Plan for assistance to Greece and Turkey and the Marshall Plan for economic aid needed to build up the strength of our friends in Western Europe. In 1949, the Senate approved the North Atlantic Treaty under which each member nation agrees that an armed attack against one is an armed attack against all. Congress immediately implemented the North Atlantic Treaty by authorizing military assistance to nations dedicated to the principles of mutual security under the United Nations Charter. The concept of mutual security recently has been extended by treaty to friends in the Pacific.

Our treaties represent not merely legal obligations, but show congressional recognition that mutual security for the free world is the best security against the threat of aggression on a global scale. The need for mutual security is shown by the very size of the armed forces outside the free world. Defendant's brief informs us that the Soviet Union maintains the largest air force in the world, and maintains ground forces much larger than those presently available to the United States and the countries joined with us in mutual security arrangements. Constant international tensions are cited to demonstrate how precarious is the peace.

Even this brief review of our responsibilities in the world community discloses the enormity of our undertaking. Success of these measures may, as has often been observed, dramatically influence the lives of many generations of the world's peoples yet unborn. Alert to our responsibilities, which coincide with our own self-preservation through mutual security, Congress has enacted a large body of implementing legislation....

Congress also directed the President to build up our own defenses. Congress, recognizing the "grim fact ... that the United States is now engaged in a struggle for survival" and that "it is imperative that we now take those necessary steps to make our strength equal to the peril of the hour," granted authority to draft men into the armed forces. As a result, we now have over 3,500,000 men in our armed forces.

Appropriations for the Department of Defense; which had averaged less than $13 billion per year for the three years before attack in Korea, were increased by Congress to $48 billion for fiscal year 1951 and to $60 billion for fiscal year 1952. A request for $51 billion for the Department of Defense for fiscal year 1953 is currently pending in Congress. The bulk of the increase is for military equipment and supplies—guns, tanks, ships, planes and ammunition—all of which require steel. Other defense programs requiring great quantities of steel include the large scale expansion of facilities for the Atomic Energy Commission and the expansion of the Nation's productive capacity affirmatively encouraged by Congress.

Congress recognized the impact of these defense programs upon the economy. Following the attack in Korea, the President asked for authority to requisition property and to allocate and fix priorities for scarce goods. In the Defense Production Act of 1950, Congress granted the powers requested and, *in addition*, granted power to stabilize prices and wages and to provide for settlement of labor disputes arising in the defense program. The Defense Production Act was extended in 1951, a Senate Committee noting that, in the dislocation caused by the programs for purchase of military equipment "lies the seed of an economic disaster that might well destroy the military might we are straining to build." Significantly, the Committee examined the problem "in terms of just one commodity, steel," and found "a graphic picture of the over-all inflationary danger growing out of reduced civilian supplies and rising incomes." Even before Korea, steel production at levels above theoretical 100% capacity was not capable of supplying civilian needs alone. Since Korea, the tremendous military demand for steel has far exceeded the increases in productive capacity. This Committee emphasized that the shortage of steel, even with the mills operating at full capacity, coupled with increased civilian purchasing power, presented grave danger of disastrous inflation.

The President has the duty to execute the foregoing legislative programs. Their successful execution depends upon continued production of steel and stabilized prices for steel. Accordingly, when the collective bargaining agreements between the Nation's steel producers and their employees, represented by the United Steel Workers, were due to expire on December 31, 1951, and a strike shutting down the entire basic steel industry was threatened, the President acted to avert a complete shutdown of steel production. ...

A review of executive action demonstrates that our Presidents have on many occasions exhibited the leadership contemplated by the Framers when they made the President Commander in Chief, and imposed upon him the trust to "take Care that the Laws be faithfully executed." With or without explicit statutory authorization, Presidents have at such times dealt with national emergencies by acting promptly and resolutely to enforce legislative programs, at least to save those programs until Congress could act. Congress and the courts have responded to such executive initiative with consistent approval. ...

And many of the cited examples of Presidential practice go far beyond the extent of power necessary to sustain the President's order to seize the steel mills. The fact that temporary executive seizures of industrial plants to meet an emergency have not been directly tested in this Court furnishes not the slightest suggestion that such actions have been illegal. Rather, the fact that Congress and the courts have consistently recognized and given their support to such executive action indicates that such a power of seizure has been accepted throughout our history.

History bears out the genius of the Founding Fathers, who created a Government subject to law but not left subject to inertia when vigor and initiative are required.

Focusing now on the situation confronting the President on the night of April 8, 1952, we cannot but conclude that the President was performing his duty under the Constitution to "take Care that the Laws be faithfully executed"—a duty described by President Benjamin Harrison as "the central idea of the office."

The President reported to Congress the morning after the seizure that he acted because a work stoppage in steel production would immediately imperil the safety of the Nation by preventing execution of the legislative programs for procurement of military equipment. And, while a shutdown could be averted by granting the price concessions requested by plaintiffs, granting such concessions would disrupt the price stabilization program also enacted by Congress. Rather than fail to execute either legislative program, the President acted to execute both.

The absence of a specific statute authorizing seizure of the steel mills as a mode of executing the laws—both the military procurement program and the anti-inflation program—has not until today been thought to prevent the President from executing the laws. Unlike an administrative commission confined to the enforcement of the statute under which it was created, or the head of a department when administering a particular statute, the President is a constitutional officer charged with taking care that a "mass of legislation" be executed. Flexibility as to mode of execution to meet critical situations is a matter of practical necessity. . . .

Whatever the extent of Presidential power on more tranquil occasions, and whatever the right of the President to execute legislative programs as he sees fit without reporting the mode of execution to Congress, the single Presidential purpose disclosed on this record is to faithfully execute the laws by acting in an emergency to maintain the *status quo*, thereby preventing collapse of the legislative programs until Congress could act. The President's action served the same purposes as a judicial stay entered to maintain the *status quo* in order to preserve the jurisdiction of a court. In his Message to Congress immediately following the seizure, the President explained the necessity of his action in executing the military procurement and anti-inflation legislative programs and expressed his desire to cooperate with any legislative proposals approving, regulating or rejecting the seizure of the steel mills. Consequently, there is no evidence whatever of any Presidential purposes to defy Congress or act in any way inconsistent with the legislative will. . . .

The Framers knew, as we should know in these times of peril, that there is real danger in Executive weakness. There is no cause to fear Executive tyranny so long as the laws of Congress are being faithfully executed. Certainly there is no basis for fear of dictatorship when the Executive acts, as he did in this case, only to save the situation until Congress could act.

✠ *D O C U M E N T   2*

Congress Gives Authority to President Lyndon B. Johnson to Wage War in Vietnam, 1964

Joint Resolution

To promote the maintenance of international peace and security in southeast Asia.

Whereas naval units of the Communist regime in Vietnam, in violation of the principles of the Charter of the United Nations and of international law, have deliberately and repeatedly attacked United Stated naval vessels lawfully present in international waters, and have thereby created a serious threat to international peace; and

Whereas these attackers are part of deliberate and systematic campaign of aggression that the Communist regime in North Vietnam has been waging against its neighbors and the nations joined with them in the collective defense of their freedom; and

Whereas the United States is assisting the peoples of southeast Asia to protest their freedom and has no territorial, military or political ambitions in that area, but desires only that these people should be left in peace to work out their destinies in their own way: Now, therefore be it

Resolved by the Senate and House of Representatives of the United States of America in Congress assembled, That the Congress approves and supports the determination of the President, as Commander in Chief, to take all necessary measures to repel any armed attack against the forces of the United States and to prevent further aggression.

Section 2. The United States regards as vital to its national interest and to world peace the maintenance of international peace and security in southeast Asia. Consonant with the Constitution of the United States and the Charter of the United Nations and in accordance with its obligations under the Southeast Asia Collective Defense Treaty, the United States is, therefore, prepared, as the President determines, to take all necessary steps, including the use of armed force, to assist any member or protocol state of the Southeast Asia Collective Defense Treaty requesting assistance in defense of its freedom.

Section 3. This resolution shall expire when the President shall determine that the peace and security of the area is reasonably assured by international conditions created by action of the United Nations or otherwise, except that it may be terminated earlier by concurrent resolution of the Congress.

✣ *D O C U M E N T   3*

Congress Reasserts Itself in the War Powers Resolution, 1973

Joint Resolution

Concerning the war powers of Congress and the President.

Resolved by the Senate and the House of Representatives of the United States of America in Congress assembled, ...

Purpose and Policy

SEC. 2. (a) It is the purpose of this joint resolution to fulfill the intent of the framers of the Constitution of the United States and insure that the collective judgement of both the Congress and the President will apply to the introduction of United States Armed Forces into hostilities, or into situations where imminent involvement in hostilities is clearly indicate by the circumstances, and to the continued use of such forces in hostilities or in such situations.

(b) Under article I, section 8, of the Constitution, it is specifically provided that the Congress shall have the power to make all laws necessary and proper for carrying into execution, not only its own powers but also all other powers vested by the Constitution in the Government of the United States, or in any department or officer thereof.

(c) The constitutional powers of the President as Commander-in-Chief to introduce United States Armed Forces into hostilities, or into situations where imminent involvement in hostilities is clearly indicated by the circumstances, are exercised only pursuant to (1) a declaration of war, (2) specific statutory authorization, or (3) a national emergency created by attack upon the United States, its territories or possessions, or its armed forces.

Consultation

SEC. 3. The President in every possible instance shall consult with Congress before introducing United States Armed Forces into hostilities or into situation where imminent involvement in hostilities is clearly indicated by the circumstances, and after every such introduction shall consult regularly with the Congress until United States Armed Forces are no longer engaged in hostilities or have been removed from such situations.

Reporting

SEC. 4. (a) In the absence of a declaration of war, in any case in which United States Armed Forces are introduced—

> (1) into hostilities or into situations where imminent involvement in hostilities is clearly indicated by the circumstances;
> (2) into the territory, airspace or waters of a foreign nation, while equipped for combat, except for deployments which relate solely to supply, replacement, repair, or training of such forces; or
> (3) in numbers which substantially enlarge United States Armed Forces equipped for combat already located in a foreign nation; the president shall submit within 48 hours to the Speaker of the House of Representatives and to the President pro tempore of the Senate a report, in writing, setting forth—
>
> > (A) the circumstances necessitating the introduction of United States Armed Forces;
> > (B) the constitutional and legislative authority under which such introduction took place; and
> > (C) the estimated scope and duration of the hostilities or involvement.

(b) The President shall provide such other information as the Congress may request in the fulfillment of its constitutional responsibilities with respect to committing the Nation to war and to the use of United States Armed Forces abroad

(c) Whenever United States Armed Forces are introduced into hostilities or into any situation described in subsection (a) of this section, the President shall, so long as such armed forces continue to be engaged in such hostilities or situation, report to the Congress periodically on the status of such hostilities or situation as well as on the scope and duration of such hostilities or situation, but in no event shall he report to the Congress less often than once every six months.

Congressional Action

SEC. 5. (a) Each report submitted pursuant to section 4 (a) (1) shall be transmitted to the Speaker of the House of Representatives and to the President pro tempore of the Senate on the same calendar day. Each report so transmitted shall be referred to the Committee on Foreign Affairs of the House of Representatives and to the Committee on Foreign Relations of the Senate for appropriate action. If, when the report is transmitted, the Congress has adjourned sine die or has adjourned for any period in excess of three calendar days, the Speaker of the House of Representatives and the President protempore of the Senate, if they deem it advisable (or if petitioned by at least 30 percent of the membership of their respective Houses) shall jointly request the President to convene Congress in order that it may consider the report and take appropriate action pursuant to this section.

(b) Within sixty calendar days after a report is submitted or is required to be submitted pursuant to section 4 (a) (1), whichever is earlier, the President shall terminate any use of United States Armed Forces with respect to which such report was submitted (or required to be submitted), unless the Congress (1) has declared war or has enacted a specific authorization for such use of United States Armed Forces, (2) has extended by law such sixty-day period, or (3) is physically unable to meet as a result of an armed attack upon the United States. Such sixty-day period shall be extended for not more than an additional thirty days if the President determines and certifies to the Congress in writing that unavoidable military necessity respecting the safety of United States Armed Forces requires the continued use of such armed forces in the course of bringing about a prompt removal of such forces.

(c) Notwithstanding subsection (b), at any time that United States Armed Forces are engaged in hostilities outside the territory of the United States, its possessions and territories without a declaration of war or specific statutory authorization, such forces shall be removed by the President if the Congress so directs by concurrent resolution. ...

Interpretation of Joint Resolution

SEC. 8. (a) Authority to introduce United States Armed Forces into hostilities or into situations wherein involvement in hostilities is clearly indicated by the circumstances shall not be inferred—

(1) from any provision of law (whether or not in effect before the date of the enactment of this joint resolution), including any provision contained in any appropriation Act, unless such provision specifically authorizes the introduction of United States Armed Forces into hostilities or into such situations and stating that it is intended to constitute specific statutory authorization within the meaning of this joint resolution; or

(2) from any treaty heretofore or hereafter ratified unless such treaty is implemented by legislation specifically authorizing the introduction of United States Armed Forces into hostilities or into such situations and stating that it is intended to constitute specific statutory authorization within the meaning of this joint resolution.

(b) Nothing in this joint resolution shall be construed to require any further specific statutory authorization to permit members of United States Armed Forces to participate jointly with members of the armed forces of one or more foreign countries in the headquarters operations of high-level military commands which were established prior to the date of enactment of this joint resolution and pursuant to the United Nations Charter or any treaty ratified by the United States prior to such date.

(c) For purposes of this joint resolution, the term "introduction of United States Armed Forces" includes the assignment of member of such armed forces to command, coordinate, participate in the movement of, or accompany the regular or irregular military forces of any foreign country or government when such military forces are engaged, or there exists an imminent threat that such forces will become engaged, in hostilities.

(d) Nothing in this joint resolution—

(1) is intended to alter the constitutional authority of the Congress or of the President, or the provision of existing treaties; or

(2) shall be construed as granting any authority to the President with respect to the introduction of United States Armed Forces into hostilities or into situations wherein involvement in hostilities is clearly indicated by the circumstances which authority he would not have had in the absence of this joint resolution.

Separability Clause

SEC. 9. If any provision of this joint resolution or the application thereof to any person or circumstance is held invalid, the remainder of the joint resolution and the application of such provision to any other person or circumstance shall not be affected thereby.

Effective Date

SEC. 10. This joint resolution shall take effect on the date of its enactment.

✤ *D O C U M E N T   4*

United States v. Nixon, 1974

Mr. Chief Justice Burger delivered the opinion of the Court.

This litigation presents for review the denial of a motion, filed in the District Court on behalf of the President of the United States, in the case of *United States v. Mitchell* ... to quash a third-party subpoena duces tecum issued by the United States District Court for the District of Columbia, ... The subpoena directed the President to produce certain tape recordings and documents relating to his conversations with aides and advisers. The court rejected the President's claims of absolute executive privilege, of lack of jurisdiction, and of failure to satisfy the requirements of Rule 17 (c). The President appealed to the Court of Appeals. We granted both the United States' petition for certiorari before judgment ... and also the President's cross-petition for certiorari ... before judgment ... because of the public importance of the issues presented and the need for their prompt resolution. ...

On March 1, 1974, a grand jury of the United States District Court for the District of Columbia returned an indictment charging seven named individuals 3 with various offenses, including conspiracy to defraud the United States and to obstruct justice. Although he was not designated as such in the indictment, the grand jury named the President, among others, as an unindicted coconspirator. 4 On April 18, 1974, upon motion of the Special Prosecutor, ... a subpoena duces tecum was issued pursuant to Rule 17 (c) to the President by the United States District Court and made returnable on May 2, 1974. This subpoena required the production, in advance of the September 9 trial date, of certain tapes, memoranda, papers, transcripts, or other writings relating to certain precisely identified meetings between the President and others. 5 The Special Prosecutor was able to fix the time, place, and persons present at these discussions because the White House daily logs and appointment records had been delivered to him. On April 30, the President publicly released edited transcripts of 43 conversations; portions of 20 conversations subject to subpoena in the present case were included. On May 1, 1974, the President's counsel filed a "special appearance" and a motion to quash the subpoena under Rule 17 (c). This motion was accompanied by a formal claim of privilege. At a subsequent hearing, 6 further motions to expunge the grand jury's action naming the President as an unindicted coconspirator and for protective orders against the disclosure of that information were filed or raised orally by counsel for the President.

On May 20, 1974, the District Court denied the motion to quash and the motions to expunge and for protective orders. ... It further ordered "the President or any subordinate officer, official, or employee with custody or control of the documents or objects subpoenaed," ... , to deliver to the District Court, on or before May 31, 1974, the originals of all subpoenaed items, as well as an index and analysis of those items, together with tape copies of those portions of the subpoenaed recordings for which transcripts had been released to the public by the President on April 30. The District Court rejected jurisdictional challenges based on a contention that the dispute was nonjusticiable because it was between the Special Prosecutor and the Chief Executive and hence "intra-executive" in character; it also rejected the contention that the Judiciary was without authority to review an assertion of executive privilege by the President. ...

The District Court held that the judiciary, not the President, was the final arbiter of a claim of executive privilege. The court concluded that, under the circumstances of this case, the presumptive privilege was overcome by the Special Prosecutor's prima facie "demonstration of need sufficiently compelling to warrant judicial examination in chambers. ... " ... ... The court held, finally, that the Special Prosecutor had satisfied the requirements of Rule 17 (c).

Justiciability

In the District Court, the President's counsel argued that the court lacked jurisdiction to issue the subpoena because the matter was an intra-branch dispute between a subordinate and superior officer of the Executive Branch and hence not subject to judicial resolution. ...

Our starting point is the nature of the proceeding for which the evidence is sought - here a pending criminal prosecution. It is a judicial proceeding in a federal court alleging violation of federal laws and is brought in the name of the United States as sovereign. ... Under the authority of Art. II, 2, Congress has vested in the Attorney General the power to conduct the criminal litigation of the United States Government. ... It has also vested in him the power to appoint subordinate officers to assist him in the discharge of his duties. ... Acting pursuant to those statutes, the Attorney General has delegated the authority to represent the United States in these particular matters to a Special Prosecutor with unique authority and tenure. 8 The regulation gives the Special Prosecutor explicit power to contest the invocation of executive privilege in the process of seeking evidence deemed relevant to the performance of these specially delegated duties. ...

The demands of and the resistance to the subpoena present an obvious controversy in the ordinary sense, but that alone is not sufficient to meet constitutional standards. In the constitutional sense, controversy means more than disagreement and conflict; rather it means the kind of controversy courts traditionally resolve. Here at issue is the production or nonproduction of specified evidence deemed by the Special Prosecutor to be relevant and admissible in a pending criminal case. It is sought by one official of the Executive Branch within the scope of his express authority; it is resisted by the Chief Executive on the ground of his duty to preserve the confidentiality of the communications of the President. Whatever the correct answer on the merits, these issues are "of a type which are traditionally justiciable." ... The independent Special Prosecutor with his asserted need for the subpoenaed material in the underlying criminal prosecution is opposed by the President with his steadfast assertion of privilege against disclosure of the material. This setting assures there is "that concrete adverseness which sharpens the presentation of issues upon which the court so largely depends for illumination of difficult constitutional questions." ... Moreover, since the matter is one arising in the regular course of a federal criminal prosecution, it is within the traditional scope of Art. III power. ...

In light of the uniqueness of the setting in which the conflict arises, the fact that both parties are officers of the Executive Branch cannot be viewed as a barrier to justiciability. It would be inconsistent with the applicable law and regulation, and the unique facts of this case to conclude other than that the Special Prosecutor has standing to bring this action and that a justiciable controversy is presented for decision. ...

The Claim of Privilege

A

Having determined that the requirements of Rule 17(c) were satisfied, we turn to the claim that the subpoena should be quashed because it demands "confidential conversations between a President and his close advisors that it would be inconsistent with the public interest to produce." ... The first contention is a broad claim that the separation of powers doctrine precludes judicial review of a President's claim of privilege. The second contention is that if he does not prevail on the claim of absolute privilege, the court should hold as a matter of constitutional law that the privilege prevails over the subpoena duces tecum.

In the performance of assigned constitutional duties each branch of the Government must initially interpret the Constitution, and the interpretation of its powers by any branch is due great respect from the others. The President's counsel, as we have noted, reads the Constitution as providing an absolute privilege of confidentiality for all Presidential communications. Many decisions of this Court, however, have unequivocally reaffirmed the holding of *Marbury v. Madison,* ... that "[i]t is emphatically the province and duty of the judicial department to say what the law is." ...

No holding of the Court has defined the scope of judicial power specifically relating to the enforcement of a subpoena for confidential Presidential communications for use in a criminal prosecution, but other exercises of power by the Executive Branch and the Legislative Branch have been found invalid as in conflict with the Constitution. *Youngstown Sheet & Tube Co. v. Sawyer,* ...

Our system of government "requires that federal courts on occasion interpret the Constitution in a manner at variance with the construction given the document by another branch." ...

Notwithstanding the deference each branch must accord the others, the "judicial Power of the United States" vested in the federal courts by Art. III, 1, of the Constitution can no more be shared with the Executive Branch than the Chief Executive, for example, can share with the Judiciary the veto power, or the Congress share with the Judiciary the power to override a Presidential veto. Any other conclusion would be contrary to the basic concept of separation of powers and the checks and balances that flow from the scheme of a tripartite government. ... We therefore reaffirm that it is the province and duty of this Court "to say what the law is" with respect to the claim of privilege presented in this case. ...

B

In support of his claim of absolute privilege, the President's counsel urges two grounds, one of which is common to all governments and one of which is peculiar to our system of separation of powers. The first ground is the valid need for protection of communications between high Government officials and those who advise and assist them in the performance of their manifold duties; the importance of this confidentiality is too plain to require further discussion. ...

The second ground asserted by the President's counsel in support of the claim of absolute privilege rests on the doctrine of separation of powers. ...

However, neither the doctrine of separation of powers, nor the need for confidentiality of high-level communications, without more, can sustain an absolute, unqualified Presidential privilege of immunity from judicial process under all circumstances. The President's need for complete candor and objectivity from advisers calls for great deference from the courts. However, when the privilege depends solely on the broad, undifferentiated claim of public interest in the confidentiality of such conversations, a confrontation with other values arises. Absent a claim of need to protect military, diplomatic, or sensitive national security secrets, we find it difficult to accept the argument that even the very important interest in confidentiality of Presidential communications is significantly diminished by production of such material for in camera inspection with all the protection that a district court will be obliged to provide.

The impediment that an absolute, unqualified privilege would place in the way of the primary constitutional duty of the Judicial Branch to do justice in criminal prosecutions would plainly conflict with the function of the courts under Art. III. In designing the structure of our Government and dividing and allocating the sovereign power among three co-equal branches, the Framers of the Constitution sought to provide a comprehensive system, but the separate powers were not intended to operate with absolute independence. . . .

To read the Art. II powers of the President as providing an absolute privilege as against a subpoena essential to enforcement of criminal statutes on no more than a generalized claim of the public interest in confidentiality of nonmilitary and nondiplomatic discussions would upset the constitutional balance of "a workable government" and gravely impair the role of the courts under Art. III.

C

. . . The expectation of a President to the confidentiality of his conversations and correspondence, like the claim of confidentiality of judicial deliberations, for example, has all the values to which we accord deference for the privacy of all citizens and, added to those values, is the necessity for protection of the public interest in candid, objective, and even blunt or harsh opinions in Presidential decision-making. A President and those who assist him must be free to explore alternatives in the process of shaping policies and making decisions and to do so in a way many would be unwilling to express except privately. These are the considerations justifying a presumptive privilege for Presidential communications. The privilege is fundamental to the operation of Government and inextricably rooted in the separation of powers under the Constitution. . . .

But this presumptive privilege must be considered in light of our historic commitment to the rule of law. This is nowhere more profoundly manifest than in our view that "the twofold aim [of criminal justice] is that guilt shall not escape or innocence suffer." . . . We have elected to employ an adversary system of criminal justice in which the parties contest all issues before a court of law. The need to develop all relevant facts in the adversary system is both fundamental and comprehensive. The ends of criminal justice would be defeated if judgments were to be founded on a partial or speculative presentation of the facts. The very integrity of the judicial system and public confidence in the system depend on full disclosure of all the facts, within the framework of the rules of evidence. To ensure that justice is done, it is imperative to the function of courts that compulsory process be available for the production of evidence needed either by the prosecution or by the defense. . . .

In this case the President challenges a subpoena served on him as a third party requiring the production of materials for use in a criminal prosecution; he does so on the claim that he has a privilege against disclosure of confidential communications. He does not place his claim of privilege on the ground they are military or diplomatic secrets. As to these areas of Art. II duties the courts have traditionally shown the utmost deference to Presidential responsibilities. ...

No case of the Court, however, has extended this high degree of deference to a President's generalized interest in confidentiality. Nowhere in the Constitution, as we have noted earlier, is there any explicit reference to a privilege of confidentiality, yet to the extent this interest relates to the effective discharge of a President's powers, it is constitutionally based.

The right to the production of all evidence at a criminal trial similarly has constitutional dimensions. The Sixth Amendment explicitly confers upon every defendant in a criminal trial the right "to be confronted with the witnesses against him" and "to have compulsory process for obtaining witnesses in his favor." Moreover, the Fifth Amendment also guarantees that no person shall be deprived of liberty without due process of law. It is the manifest duty of the courts to vindicate those guarantees, and to accomplish that it is essential that all relevant and admissible evidence be produced.

In this case we must weigh the importance of the general privilege of confidentiality of Presidential communications in performance of the President's responsibilities against the inroads of such a privilege on the fair administration of criminal justice. ... The interest in preserving confidentiality is weighty indeed and entitled to great respect. However, we cannot conclude that advisers will be moved to temper the candor of their remarks by the infrequent occasions of disclosure because of the possibility that such conversations will be called for in the context of a criminal prosecution. ...

On the other hand, the allowance of the privilege to withhold evidence that is demonstrably relevant in a criminal trial would cut deeply into the guarantee of due process of law and gravely impair the basic function of the courts. A President's acknowledged need for confidentiality ... in the communications of his office is general in nature, whereas the constitutional need for production of relevant evidence in a criminal proceeding is specific and central to the fair adjudication of a particular criminal case in the administration of justice. Without access to specific facts a criminal prosecution may be totally frustrated. The President's broad interest in confidentiality of communications will not be vitiated by disclosure of a limited number of conversations preliminarily shown to have some bearing on the pending criminal cases.

We conclude that when the ground for asserting privilege as to subpoenaed materials sought for use in a criminal trial is based only on the generalized interest in confidentiality, it cannot prevail over the fundamental demands of due process of law in the fair administration of criminal justice. The generalized assertion of privilege must yield to the demonstrated, specific need for evidence in a pending criminal trial. ...

Since this matter came before the Court during the pendency of a criminal prosecution, and on representations that time is of the essence, the mandate shall issue forthwith.

Affirmed.

✤ *D O C U M E N T   5*

Congress Authorizes President George W. Bush to Fight International Terrorism, 2001

S.J. Resolution 23—Authorization for Use of Military Force (Enrolled Bill); September 18, 2001

…Joint Resolution

To authorize the use of United States Armed Forces against those responsible for the recent attacks launched against the United States.

Whereas, on September 11, 2001, acts of treacherous violence were committed against the United States and its citizens; and

Whereas, such acts render it both necessary and appropriate that the United States exercise its rights to self-defense and to protect United States citizens both at home and abroad; and

Whereas, in light of the threat to the national security and foreign policy of the United States posed by these grave acts of violence; and

Whereas, such acts continue to pose an unusual and extraordinary threat to the national security and foreign policy of the United States; and

Whereas, the President has authority under the Constitution to take action to deter and prevent acts of international terrorism against the United States: Now, therefore, be it

Resolved by the Senate and House of Representatives of the United States of America in Congress assembled,

Section 1. Short Title.

This joint resolution may be cited as the 'Authorization for Use of Military Force'.

Sec. 2. Authorization for Use of United States Armed Forces.

(a) IN GENERAL—That the President is authorized to use all necessary and appropriate force against those nations, organizations, or persons he determines planned, authorized, committed, or aided the terrorist attacks that occurred on September 11, 2001, or harbored such organizations or persons, in order to prevent any future acts of international terrorism against the United States by such nations, organizations or persons.

(b) War Powers Resolution Requirements—

    (1) SPECIFIC STATUTORY AUTHORIZATION—Consistent with section 8(a)(1) of the War Powers Resolution, the Congress declares that this section is intended to constitute specific statutory authorization within the meaning of section 5(b) of the War Powers Resolution.

    (2) APPLICABILITY OF OTHER REQUIREMENTS—Nothing in this resolution supercedes any requirement of the War Powers Resolution.

Speaker of the House of Representatives.
Vice President of the United States and
President of the Senate.

＃ D O C U M E N T   6

The Justice Department Asserts that Enforcement of Federal Anti-Torture Laws Would Violate the President's Powers as Commander-in-Chief, 2002

Memorandum for Alberto R. Gonzales Counsel to the President

Re: Standards of Conduct for Interrogation under 18 U.S.C. §§ 2340–2340A

You have asked for our Office's views regarding the standards of conduct under the Convention Against Torture and Other Cruel, Inhuman and Degrading Treatment or Punishment as implemented by Sections 2340–2340A of title 18 of the United States Code. As we understand it, this question has arisen in the context of the conduct of interrogations outside of the United States. We conclude below that Section 2340A proscribes acts inflicting, and that are specifically intended to inflict, severe pain or suffering, whether mental or physical. Those acts must be of an extreme nature to rise to the level of torture within the meaning of Section 2340A and the Convention. We further conclude that certain acts may be cruel, inhuman, or degrading, but still not produce pain and suffering of the requisite intensity to fall within Section 2340A's proscription against torture. We conclude by examining possible defenses that would negate any claim that certain interrogation methods violate the statute.

In Part I, we examine the criminal statute's text and history. We conclude that for an act to constitute torture as defined in Section 2340, it must inflict pain that is difficult to endure. Physical pain amounting to torture must be equivalent in intensity to the pain accompanying serious physical injury, such as organ failure, impairment of bodily function, or even death. For purely mental pain or suffering to amount to torture under Section 2340, it must result in significant psychological harm of significant duration, e.g., lasting for months or even years. We conclude that the mental harm also must result from one of the predicate acts listed in the statute, namely: threats of imminent death; threats of infliction of the kind of pain that would amount to physical torture; infliction of such physical pain as a means of psychological torture; use of drugs or other procedures designed to deeply disrupt the senses, or fundamentally alter an individual's personality; or threatening to do any of these things to a third party. The legislative history simply reveals that Congress intended for the statute's definition to track the Convention's definition of torture and the reservations, understandings, and declarations that the United States submitted with its ratification. We conclude that the statute, taken as a whole, makes plain that it prohibits only extreme acts. . . .

The Commander-in-Chief Power

It could be argued that Congress enacted 18 U.S.C. § 2340A with full knowledge and consideration of the President's Commander-in-Chief power, and that Congress intended to restrict his discretion in the interrogation of enemy combatants. Even were we to accept this argument, however, we conclude that the Department of Justice could not enforce Section 2340A against federal officials acting pursuant to the President's constitutional authority to wage a military campaign.

Indeed, in a different context, we have concluded that both courts and prosecutors should reject prosecutions that apply federal criminal laws to activity that is authorized pursuant to one of the President's constitutional powers. This Office, for example, has previously concluded that Congress could not constitutionally extend the congressional contempt statute to executive branch officials who refuse to comply with congressional subpoenas because of an assertion of executive privilege. We opined that "courts...would surely conclude that a criminal prosecution for the exercise of a presumptively valid, constitutionally based privilege is not consistent with the Constitution."... Further, we concluded that the Department of Justice could not bring a criminal prosecution against a defendant who had acted pursuant to an exercise of the President's constitutional power. "The President, through a United States Attorney, need not, indeed may not, prosecute criminally a subordinate for asserting on his behalf a claim of executive privilege. Nor could the Legislative Branch or the courts require or implement the prosecution of such an individual."... Although Congress may define federal crimes that the President, through the Take Care Clause, should prosecute, Congress cannot compel the President to prosecute outcomes taken pursuant to the President's own constitutional authority. If Congress could do so, it could control the President's authority through the manipulation of federal criminal law.

We have even greater concerns with respect to prosecutions arising out of the exercise of the President's express authority as Commander in Chief than we do with prosecutions arising out of the assertion of executive privilege. In a series of opinions examining various legal questions arising after September 11, we have explained the scope of the President's Commander-in-Chief power. We briefly summarize the findings of those opinions here. The President's constitutional power to protect the security of the United States and the lives and safety of its people must be understood in light of the Founders' intention to create a federal government "cloathed with all the powers requisite to the complete execution of its trust." *The Federalist* No. 23, at 147 (Alexander Hamilton). ... Foremost among the objectives committed to that trust by the Constitution is the security of the nation. As Hamilton explained in arguing for the Constitution's adoption, because "the circumstances which may affect the public safety" are not "reducible within certain determinate limits,"

> it must be admitted, as a necessary consequence, that there can be no limitation of that authority, which is to provide for the defence and protection of the community, in any matter essential to its efficacy. ...

The text, structure and history of the Constitution establish that the Founders entrusted the President with the primary responsibility, and therefore the power, to ensure the security of the United States in situations of grave and unforeseen emergencies. The decision to deploy military force in the defense of United States interests is expressly placed under Presidential authority by the Vesting Clause, U.S. Const. Art. I, § 1, cl. 1, and by the Commander-in-Chief Clause, *id.*, § 2, cl. 1. This Office has long understood the Commander-in-Chief Clause in particular as an affirmative grant of authority to the President.... The Framers understood the Clause as investing the President with the fullest range of power understood at the time of the ratification of the Constitution as belonging to the military commander. In addition, the structure of the Constitution demonstrates that any power traditionally understood as pertaining to the executive—which includes the conduct of warfare and the defense of the nation—unless expressly assigned in the Constitution to Congress, is vested in the President. Article II, Section 1 makes this clear by stating that the "executive Power shall be vested in a President of the United States of America." That sweeping grant vests in the President an unenumerated "executive power" and contrasts with the specific enumeration of the powers—those "herein"—granted to Congress in Article I. The implications of constitutional text and structure are confirmed by the practical consideration that national security decisions require the unity in purpose and energy in action that characterize the Presidency rather than Congress.

As the Supreme Court has recognized, the Commander-in-Chief power and the President's obligation to protect the nation imply the ancillary powers necessary to their successful exercise. "The first of the enumerated powers of the President is that he shall be Commander-in-Chief of the Army and Navy of the United States. And, of course, the grant of war power includes all that is necessary and proper for carrying those powers into execution." *Johnson v. Eisentrager,* ... In wartime, it is for the President alone to decide what methods to use to best prevail against the enemy.... The President's complete discretion in exercising the Commander-in-Chief power has been recognized by the courts. In the *Prize Cases,* ..., for example, the Court explained that whether the President "in fulfilling his duties as Commander in Chief" had appropriately responded to the rebellion of the southern states was a question "to be *decided by him*" and which the Court could not question, but must leave to "the political department of the Government to which this power was entrusted."

One of the core functions of the Commander in Chief is that of capturing, detaining, and interrogating members of the enemy.... It is well settled that the President may seize and detain enemy combatants, at least for the duration of the conflict, and the laws of war make clear that prisoners may be interrogated for information concerning the enemy, its strength, and its plans. Numerous Presidents have ordered the capture, detention, and questioning of enemy combatants during virtually every major conflict in the Nation's history, including recent conflicts such as the Gulf, Vietnam, and Korean wars. Recognizing this authority, Congress has never attempted to restrict or interfere with the President's authority on this score....

Any effort by Congress to regulate the interrogation of battlefield combatants would violate the Constitution's sole vesting of the Commander-in-Chief authority in the President. There can be little doubt that intelligence operations, such as the detention and interrogation of enemy combatants and leaders, are both necessary and proper for the effective conduct of a military campaign. Indeed, such operations may be of more importance in a war with an international terrorist organization than one with the conventional armed forces of a nation-state, due to the former's emphasis on secret operations and surprise attacks against civilians. It may be the case that only successful interrogations can provide the information necessary to prevent the success of covert terrorist attacks upon the United States and its citizens. Congress can no more interfere with the President's conduct of the interrogation of enemy combatants than it can dictate strategic or tactical decisions on the battlefield....

✣ D O C U M E N T   7

Hamdi v. Rumsfeld, 2004

Justice O'Connor delivered of the opinion of the Court

On September 11, 2001, the al Qaeda terrorist network used hijacked commercial airliners to attack prominent targets in the United States. Approximately 3,000 people were killed in those attacks. One week later, in response to these "acts of treacherous violence," Congress passed a resolution authorizing the President to "use all necessary and appropriate force against those nations, organizations, or persons he determines planned, authorized, committed, or aided the terrorist attacks" or "harbored such organizations or persons, in order to prevent any future acts of international terrorism against the United States by such nations, organizations or persons." Authorization for Use of Military Force ("the AUMF"), ... Soon thereafter, the President ordered United States Armed Forces to Afghanistan, with a mission to subdue al Qaeda and quell the Taliban regime that was known to support it.

This case arises out of the detention of a man whom the Government alleges took up arms with the Taliban during this conflict. His name is Yaser Esam Hamdi. Born an American citizen in Louisiana in 1980, Hamdi moved with his family to Saudi Arabia as a child. By 2001, the parties agree, he resided in Afghanistan. At some point that year, he was seized by members of the Northern Alliance, a coalition of military groups opposed to the Taliban government, and eventually was turned over to the United States military. The Government asserts that it initially detained and interrogated Hamdi in Afghanistan before transferring him to the United States Naval Base in Guantanamo Bay in January 2002. In April 2002, upon learning that Hamdi is an American citizen, authorities transferred him to a naval brig in Norfolk, Virginia, where he remained until a recent transfer to a brig in Charleston, South Carolina. The Government contends that Hamdi is an "enemy combatant," and that this status justifies holding him in the United States indefinitely—without formal charges or proceedings—unless and until it makes the determination that access to counsel or further process is warranted....

The threshold question before us is whether the Executive has the authority to detain citizens who qualify as "enemy combatants." There is some debate as to the proper scope of this term, and the Government has never provided any court with the full criteria that it uses in classifying individuals as such. It has made clear, however, that, for purposes of this case, the "enemy combatant" that it is seeking to detain is an individual who, it alleges, was "'part of or supporting forces hostile to the United States or coalition partners'" in Afghanistan and who "'engaged in an armed conflict against the United States'" there.... We therefore answer only the narrow question before us: whether the detention of citizens falling within that definition is authorized.

The Government maintains that no explicit congressional authorization is required, because the Executive possesses plenary authority to detain pursuant to Article II of the Constitution. We do not reach the question whether Article II provides such authority, however, because we agree with the Government's alternative position, that Congress has in fact authorized Hamdi's detention, through the AUMF....

The AUMF authorizes the President to use "all necessary and appropriate force" against "nations, organizations, or persons" associated with the September 11, 2001, terrorist attacks. ... There can be no doubt that individuals who fought against the United States in Afghanistan as part of the Taliban, an organization known to have supported the al Qaeda terrorist network responsible for those attacks, are individuals Congress sought to target in passing the AUMF. We conclude that detention of individuals falling into the limited category we are considering, for the duration of the particular conflict in which they were captured, is so fundamental and accepted an incident to war as to be an exercise of the "necessary and appropriate force" Congress has authorized the President to use....

In light of these principles, it is of no moment that the AUMF does not use specific language of detention. Because detention to prevent a combatant's return to the battlefield is a fundamental incident of waging war, in permitting the use of "necessary and appropriate force," Congress has clearly and unmistakably authorized detention in the narrow circumstances considered here....

Even in cases in which the detention of enemy combatants is legally authorized, there remains the question of what process is constitutionally due to a citizen who disputes his enemy-combatant status. Hamdi argues that he is owed a meaningful and timely hearing and that "extra-judicial detention [that] begins and ends with the submission of an affidavit based on third-hand hearsay" does not comport with the Fifth and Fourteenth Amendments. ... The Government counters that any more process than was provided below would be both unworkable and "constitutionally intolerable." ... Our resolution of this dispute requires a careful examination both of the writ of habeas corpus, which Hamdi now seeks to employ as a mechanism of judicial review, and of the Due Process Clause, which informs the procedural contours of that mechanism in this instance.

It is beyond question that substantial interests lie on both sides of the scale in this case. Hamdi's "private interest ... affected by the official action," ... is the most elemental of liberty interests—the interest in being free from physical detention by one's own government....

Moreover, as critical as the Government's interest may be in detaining those who actually pose an immediate threat to the national security of the United States during ongoing international conflict, history and common sense teach us that an unchecked system of detention carries the potential to become a means for oppression and abuse of others who do not present that sort of threat. ...

We reaffirm today the fundamental nature of a citizen's right to be free from involuntary confinement by his own government without due process of law, and we weigh the opposing governmental interests against the curtailment of liberty that such confinement entails. ...

Striking the proper constitutional balance here is of great importance to the Nation during this period of ongoing combat. But it is equally vital that our calculus not give short shrift to the values that this country holds dear or to the privilege that is American citizenship. It is during our most challenging and uncertain moments that our Nation's commitment to due process is most severely tested; and it is in those times that we must preserve our commitment at home to the principles for which we fight abroad. ...

With due recognition of these competing concerns, we believe that neither the process proposed by the Government nor the process apparently envisioned by the District Court below strikes the proper constitutional balance when a United States citizen is detained in the United States as an enemy combatant. That is, "the risk of erroneous deprivation" of a detainee's liberty interest is unacceptably high under the Government's proposed rule, while some of the "additional or substitute procedural safeguards" suggested by the District Court are unwarranted in light of their limited "probable value" and the burdens they may impose on the military in such cases. ...

We therefore hold that a citizen-detainee seeking to challenge his classification as an enemy combatant must receive notice of the factual basis for his classification, and a fair opportunity to rebut the Government's factual assertions before a neutral decisionmaker. ... These essential constitutional promises may not be eroded.

In sum, while the full protections that accompany challenges to detentions in other settings may prove unworkable and inappropriate in the enemy-combatant setting, the threats to military operations posed by a basic system of independent review are not so weighty as to trump a citizen's core rights to challenge meaningfully the Government's case and to be heard by an impartial adjudicator.

In so holding, we necessarily reject the Government's assertion that separation of powers principles mandate a heavily circumscribed role for the courts in such circumstances. Indeed, the position that the courts must forgo any examination of the individual case and focus exclusively on the legality of the broader detention scheme cannot be mandated by any reasonable view of separation of powers, as this approach serves only to *condense* power into a single branch of government. We have long since made clear that a state of war is not a blank check for the President when it comes to the rights of the Nation's citizens. *Youngstown Sheet & Tube,* ... Whatever power the United States Constitution envisions for the Executive in its exchanges with other nations or with enemy organizations in times of conflict, it most assuredly envisions a role for all three branches when individual liberties are at stake. ... Likewise, we have made clear that, unless Congress acts to suspend it, the Great Writ of habeas corpus allows the Judicial Branch to play a necessary role in maintaining this delicate balance of governance, serving as an important judicial check on the Executive's discretion in the realm of detentions. ... Thus, while we do not question that our due process assessment must pay keen attention to the particular burdens faced by the Executive in the context of military action, it would turn our system of checks and balances on its head to suggest that a citizen could not make his way to court with a challenge to the factual basis for his detention by his government, simply because the Executive opposes making available such a challenge. Absent suspension of the writ by Congress, a citizen detained as an enemy combatant is entitled to this process. ...

✦ E S S A Y S

John Yoo, an official of the Justice Department in the Bush Administration from 2001 to 2003 and a professor of law at the University of California, Berkley, makes the case for an energetic executive with wide authority in the realm of foreign affairs. As a conservative who believes that the original intent of the framers ought to guide constitutional interpretation, Yoo attempts to reconcile the founders' Constitution with the recent growth of executive power.

Peter Irons, a professor emeritus of political science at the University of California, San Diego, and a well-known civil libertarian, takes the opposite position. Believing that the Constitution gives the war powers to Congress, Irons sharply criticizes the Bush Administration for its forceful expansion of executive power and its zealous pursuit of the war on terror.

The President Possesses the Constitutional Power to Wage War on Terrorism

JOHN YOO

...Whether by constitutional intention or by its functional superiority in acting swiftly, secretly, and with unity, the executive branch controls the day-to-day operation of American foreign policy. The president and his subordinate officers develop the nation's foreign policy, communicate with foreign nations, negotiate international agreements of all kinds, and command U.S. officers abroad to take action. In the course of managing relations with the world, the executive branch must interpret treaties, and international law for that matter, on a daily basis. Congress cannot monitor or participate in the many ways that the executive branch interprets treaties in forming and executing foreign policy, and it does not have any formal constitutional authority to issue binding interpretations on its own. It can, however, make its cooperation in foreign policy contingent on the executive's agreement with its views on treaties, such as by withholding funding from executive foreign policy.

From Yoo, John, *The Powers of War and Peace: The Constitution and Foreign Affairs After 9/11.* The University of Chicago Press, 2005. Reprinted with permission.

Even on the difficult question of the domestic legal effect of treaties, the branches have developed a settled practice that emphasizes flexibility. Sometimes treaties are thought to take direct effect in American domestic law, even though they are created by the president and two-thirds of the Senate without the participation of the House. At other times, however, courts consider treaties to be obligations between nations under international law, and refuse to give them effect in suits brought by individuals. The political branches also pursue a course of non-self-execution, particularly when it comes to human rights treaties such as the International Covenant on Civil and Political Rights, the Genocide Convention, or the Torture Convention, by rendering them nullities as a matter of domestic law. In ratifying a treaty, for example, the president and Senate often attach reservations, understandings, or declarations that preclude treaty provisions from taking effect as domestic law and prevent the courts from enforcing them. The political branches attach such reservations to prevent treaty provisions from intruding into areas that are subject to congressional regulation or the reserved powers of the states. Non-self-execution, however, is not so much a denial of the Supremacy Clause as a vital means whereby the Congress can check the executive branch. By preventing the nation from carrying out the legislative elements of its international obligations, Congress can check efforts by the executive branch to achieve a certain treaty-based foreign policy.

The exclusivity of the treaty power itself is a last area where practice has given the political branches more discretion than that initially suggested by the constitutional text. In the early period of the nation's history, the treaty process held a virtual monopoly on the making of agreements. In recent years, however, the federal government has used simple statutes—known as congressional-executive agreements—to enter into some of our most significant international obligations. Several recent agreements of significance, such as the U.S.-Canada Free Trade Agreement, NAFTA, and the WTO agreement, have undergone this statutory process, as have America's earlier entry into important elements of the global financial system, such as the International Monetary Fund and the World Bank. While in its first fifty years the nation concluded twice as many treaties as nontreaty agreements, since World War II the United States has concluded more than 90 percent of its international agreements through a nontreaty mechanism. Under international law, either mechanism is sufficient to enter into an international agreement, but under domestic constitutional law this practice seems to run counter to the Treaty Clause. While some prominent scholars, such as Laurence Tribe, suggest this represents an end-around the Treaty Clause, congressional-executive agreements also preserve Congress's control over the subjects that fall within its domestic competence. Hence, congressional-executive agreements, as we will see, usually are used in areas where implementing legislation would normally be necessary to execute the international obligation.

Constitutional Text, Structure, and History

These results might initially appear inconsistent with the plain meaning of the constitutional text. Congress, for example, has the power to declare war. Shouldn't that provision require Congress's pre-approval for military hostilities? The Senate gives its advice and consent to the making of treaties. Should that not give the Senate an equal say with the president as to making, interpreting, and terminating treaties?

The Supremacy Clause makes treaties the laws of the land. Why shouldn't all treaties take immediate effect as domestic law? The Treaty Clause provides the only explicit means for making international agreements. Should it not be the exclusive method for entering into binding obligations with foreign nations? Doesn't practice, in other words, run directly counter to the Constitution? ...

My argument is that the Constitution, in particular the dynamic manner in which it balances the executive against the legislative branches, can be read to permit existing practice. ... Rather than foreclose the reading of the constitutional text and structure proposed here, historical evidence tends to support a more dynamic and open struggle between the executive and legislative powers over foreign affairs.

... Many of the leading theories about foreign affairs assume that the Constitution's text is incomplete. Many significant foreign affairs powers, such as the authority to develop foreign policy, to communicate with foreign nations, to make nontreaty international agreements, and to break international agreements, are not specifically enumerated in the constitutional text. The Constitution "seems a strange, laconic document," says Professor Lou Henkin, characterized by "troubling lacunae" that leaves "many powers of government ... not mentioned." The Constitution's silence has led many commentators to fall back on extraconstitutional sources, practice, or inferences from the Constitution's structure to support their preferred system for managing foreign affairs. Because of the "astonishing brevity regarding the allocation of foreign affairs authority," Professor [Harold] Koh concludes that a "normative vision of the foreign policy making process," implicit in the constitutional structure, must govern. Analogizing to the constitutional structure governing domestic affairs, he argues that Congress must authorize policy and that the president simply implements it. Professor Henkin believes that due to the Constitution's gaps, the management of foreign affairs should be determined in accordance with "the facts of national life [and] the realities and exigencies of international relations."

Rather than reading the Constitution to suffer from such significant oversights, it is more fruitful to take a closer look at the text and structure to discern its deeper patterns. As many have observed since the time of Hamilton's *Pacificus* essays, the Constitution provides a general grant of executive power to the president. Article II, Section 1 provides that "[t]he executive power shall be vested in a President of the United States." As Justice Scalia has written, this "does not mean *some of* the executive power, but *all of* the executive power." By contrast, Article I, Section 1 gives to Congress only those legislative powers "herein granted." In order to give every word in the Constitution meaning, we must construe "herein granted" as limiting Congress only to those powers enumerated in Article I, Section 8. Article II's Vesting Clause, by contrast, grants to the president an unenumerated executive authority. By analogy, Article III vests an unspecified "judicial power" of the United States in the Supreme Court and inferior federal courts, which some have read to give the judiciary certain core judicial powers.

If we assume that the foreign affairs power is an executive one, Article II effectively grants to the president any unenumerated foreign affairs powers not given elsewhere to the other branches. This understanding is further reinforced by the structure of Article II, which in Section 2 grants the president the power of commander in chief as well as the power to make treaties with the Senate's advice and consent. These powers were specifically included in Article II, rather than subsumed into the general Vesting Clause, because parts of these once plenary executive powers have been transferred to other branches or have been altered by participation of the Senate. While the Constitution does not embody a pure separation of powers in which each branch solely exercises all functions peculiar to it, the Senate's participation in treaty-making and appointments reflect an effort to dilute the unitary nature of the executive branch, rather than to transform these functions into legislative powers. When the Constitution, for example, grants the executive a power that is legislative in nature, such as the veto power, it does so in Article I, not in Article II. Participation of the Senate in treatymaking does not transform treaties into legislative acts, just as its role in appointments does not make the appointment of officers legislative in nature.

There are two sources of support for reading Article II as vesting the bulk of the foreign affairs power in the President. First, ... the executive power was understood at the time of the Constitution's framing to include the war, treaty, and other general foreign affairs powers. Both political theory, as primarily developed by thinkers such as Locke, Montesquieu, and Blackstone, and shared Anglo-American constitutional history from the seventeenth century to the time of the framing, established that foreign affairs was the province of the executive branch of government. Thus, when the Framers ratified the Constitution, they would have understood that Article II, Section 1 continued the Anglo-American constitutional tradition of locating the foreign affairs power generally in the executive branch.

Second, we might classify the conduct and control of foreign policy as inherently "executive" in nature due to practice and function. In terms of early practice, presidents from the very beginning of the Republic have exercised a general foreign affairs power, and the executive power has been understood to grant the president control over the conduct of foreign relations. As Thomas Jefferson, then the secretary of state, observed during the first Washington administration, "[t]he constitution has divided the powers of government into three branches [and] has declared that 'the executive powers shall be vested in the president,' submitting only special articles of it to a negative by the senate." Due to this structure, Jefferson continued, "[t]he transaction of business with foreign nations is executive altogether; it belongs, then, to the head of that department, except as to such portions of it as are specially submitted to the senate. Exceptions are to be construed strictly." In defending President Washington's authority to issue the Neutrality Proclamation of 1793, Alexander Hamilton came to the same conclusion regarding the president's foreign affairs powers. As Pacificus, Hamilton argued that Article II "ought ... to be considered as intended ... to specify and regulate the principal articles implied in the definition of Executive Power; leaving the rest to flow from the general grant of that power...." Hamilton further contended that the president was "[t]he constitutional organ of intercourse between the UStates [*sic*] & foreign Nations...." As future Chief Justice John Marshall famously declared a few years later: "The President is the sole organ of the nation in its external relations, and its sole representative with foreign nations.... The [executive] department ... is entrusted with the whole foreign intercourse of the nation...." Rather than a congressional ministry of foreign affairs, the president and his subordinates have exercised primary responsibility for the direction of foreign policy. A general glance through any standard diplomatic history text will show that presidents have historically played the leading role in setting foreign policy, while congressional influence has waxed and waned.

A functional analysis of the conduct of foreign affairs should also lead to the classification of foreign affairs as an executive power. If we assume, as many scholars do, that the international system is governed by anarchy in which nations seek to maximize their security and power (realism), or even that nations can cooperate in various ways to escape a prisoner's dilemma (institutionalism), then the demands of the international system promote vesting the management of foreign affairs in a unitary, rational actor. The rational actor can identify threats, develop responses, evaluate costs and benefits, and seek to achieve national strategic goals through value-maximizing policies and actions. Only a limited set of institutional designs will lead to the most effective exercise of national power necessary to achieve these foreign policy objectives. As Thomas Schelling has written, a nation-state would want "to have a communications system in good order, to have complete information, or to be in full command of one's own actions or of one's own assets." While bureaucratic or political imperatives may distort policy, or domestic interest groups may at times overcome the national interest, a unitary rational actor remains an ideal to guide foreign policy. It seems obvious that the presidency best meets the requirements for taking rational action on behalf of the nation in the modern world. As Edward Corwin observed, the executive's advantage in foreign affairs include "the unity of office, its capacity for secrecy and dispatch, and its superior sources of information, to which should be added the fact that it is always on hand and ready for action, whereas the houses of Congress are in adjournment much of the time."

One can see the influence of this ideal in the American legal system even before its formal expression in modern political science. Federalists defended the centralization of the executive power in the president precisely in order to enable the federal government to respond to the unknowable threats of a dangerous world. As Hamilton noted in *The Federalist* No. 70, "Energy in the executive is a leading character in the definition of good government. It is essential to the protection of the community against foreign attacks." This point applies perhaps most directly in war than in any other context. "Of all the cares or concerns of government, the direction of war most peculiarly demands those qualities which distinguish the exercise of power by a single hand," Hamilton wrote in *The Federalist* No. 74. "The direction of war implies the direction of the common strength," wrote Hamilton, "and the power of directing and employing the common strength forms a usual and essential part in the definition of the executive authority." It was for this reason, Hamilton argued, that the Constitution vested executive authority in one person, rather than the multimember executives of the Continental Congress and the states. Again, in *The Federalist* No. 70, he wrote: "Decision, activity, secrecy, and dispatch will generally characterize the proceedings of one man in a much more eminent degree than the proceedings of any greater number."

Supreme Court opinions have followed this line of thought beyond the context of war. In *Curtiss-Wright*, for example, the Supreme Court famously observed: "In this vast external realm, with its important, complicated, delicate and manifold problems, the President alone has the power to speak or listen as a representative of the nation." Quoting from a Senate report, Justice Sutherland further explained that "[t]he nature of transactions with foreign nations ... requires caution and unity of design, and their success frequently depends on secrecy and dispatch." Because of the unitary executive's perceived superiority to other approaches for addressing the dangers of the international world, the Framers maintained the executive's commander-in-chief power, its power to make (with the advice and consent of the Senate) treaties, and its power to conduct diplomatic relations. As Professor Koh describes it, "[h]is decision-making processes can take on degrees of speed, secrecy, flexibility, and efficiency that no other governmental institution can match." As a result, both the structural advantages of the executive branch and the functional exigencies of international politics have led to the centralization of foreign affairs power in the president. The history of American foreign relations has been the story of the expansion of the executive's power thanks to its structural abilities to wield power quickly, effectively, and in a unitary manner. ...

President Bush's War on Terrorism Has Hijacked the Constitution

PETER IRONS

No one disputes that protecting the nation against terrorist attacks has become an urgent need. Considering, however, that only a handful of those detained in the recent terrorist sweeps were later charged with anything more than immigration offenses, the question remains whether the Bush administration fired this "loaded weapon" without a plausible reason. One indication of the government's trigger-happy approach came in a speech by [Attorney General John] Ashcroft in October 2001, in which he vowed to use "aggressive arrest and detention tactics in the war on terror." The attorney general sounded like a Wild West marshal. "Let the terrorists among us be warned," he said. "If you overstay your visa—even by one day—we will arrest you. If you violate a local law, you will be put in jail and kept in custody as long as possible. We will use every available statute. We will seek every prosecutorial advantage. We will use all our weapons within the law and under the Constitution to protect life and enhance security for America." Apparently Ashcroft viewed the Constitution not as a guarantee of individual rights but as a license to lock up suspected terrorists for "as long as possible," with no regard for the due process clause of the Fifth Amendment. ...

But the treatment of prisoners in federal jails, most of whom were later released without being charged, paled in comparison to the mental and physical abuse inflicted on those who had been seized by U.S. troops during the war in Afghanistan and later in Iraq. Hundreds of actual and suspected al Qaeda and Taliban fighters, along with many civilians, found themselves bundled onto military planes, hooded and shackled, and transported to a military detention center at the U.S. naval base in Guantánamo Bay, at the eastern end of Cuba. As we saw earlier, the United States had forced the Cubans to grant a perpetual lease for this base as a condition of American recognition of Cuba's independence. More than six hundred prisoners, of some forty-four nationalities, including citizens of Australia and Britain, were held as "enemy combatants" at the infamous Camp X-Ray on the Guantánamo base. Many Americans were shocked by photographs of prisoners confined outdoors in steel-mesh cages, exposed to searing heat, forced by shackles to crawl on their knees, their heads covered by hoods or helmets that blocked out all light. U.S. officials defended these conditions as necessary to prevent the prisoners from attacking guards or communicating with one another. Defense Secretary Rumsfeld called them "hardened criminals willing to kill themselves and others for their cause," while Vice President Cheney described them as "the worst of a very bad lot. They are very dangerous."

The Camp X-Ray inmates no doubt included some hardened al Qaeda and Taliban fighters, but others quite obviously posed no threat to anyone, and many had been simply bystanders or innocent villagers when they were grabbed by American troops in Afghanistan. The release of three Afghani men, after eleven months of detention at Camp X-Ray, revealed that mistakes had been made. David Rhodes, a *New York Times* reporter, described one prisoner, who said he was 105 years old: "Babbling at times like a child, the partially deaf, shriveled old man was unable to answer simple questions." Rhodes described another, who said he was ninety, as a "wizened old man with a cane" who had been arrested when U.S. troops raided his village. Despite these belatedly admitted mistakes, U.S. officials claimed that harsh conditions and forceful interrogation techniques were necessary to extract information from al Qaeda members who might have knowledge of future terrorist attacks or the whereabouts of Osama bin Laden and key lieutenants who remained at large.

There is little question that the president's war powers as commander in chief allow him to authorize military officials to detain "enemy combatants" and subject them to interrogation. But there is also little question that presidents and their subordinates are bound by the provisions of international laws and treaties that provide for humane treatment of people captured on the battlefield or in theaters of war. The key issue here is whether the alleged al Qaeda and Taliban fighters were, in fact, entitled to be treated as prisoners of war and accorded the protections of the Geneva Conventions, a treaty the United States ratified in 1949. Under these stipulations, captured members of a "regular" army or supporting militia must be allowed to communicate with family members and representatives of their governments, and brought before a "competent tribunal" to determine their legal status if "any doubt" is raised about that status. The Bush administration flatly refused to abide by the Geneva Conventions in detaining the Camp X-Ray prisoners, simply asserting that al Qaeda and Taliban prisoners were not "regular" military troops. Thus the prisoners could be held indefinitely, without access to family or legal counsel, and with no recourse to challenge their detention in federal courts. In effect, much like President Lincoln during the Civil War, Bush suspended the writ of habeas corpus for as long as he—or his successors—determined that the war on terror was being fought.

In making this decision, Bush relied for legal advice on White House counsel Alberto Gonzales, a close friend and confidant from the president's years as governor of Texas; Bush later named Gonzales to replace John Ashcroft as attorney general in his second term. In January 2002, shortly after the first batch of prisoners arrived at the Guantánamo base, Gonzales drafted a memorandum to Bush, backing the president's decision not to treat the Camp X-Ray inmates as prisoners of war under the Geneva Conventions. In his memo, Gonzales made three main points. First, he said, giving the detainees POW status would increase the danger of "vague" charges being leveled against American military personnel for such violations of the Conventions as "outrages upon personal dignity" and "inhuman treatment" of prisoners. Second,

Gonzales wrote, "it is difficult to predict the needs and circumstances that could arise in the course of the war on terrorism" ("needs" that presumably included forceful methods of interrogation). And third, Gonzales worried about possible charges against military personnel under the War Crimes statute, Section 2441 of the federal criminal code. This law includes violations of the Geneva Conventions as criminal offenses. "It is difficult to predict the motives of prosecutors and independent counsels who may in the future decide to pursue unwarranted charges based on Section 2441," Gonzales wrote to Bush. "Your determination would create a reasonable basis in law that Section 2441 does not apply, which would provide a solid defense to any future prosecutions." ...

The connection between the "inhuman" treatment of Camp X-Ray inmates at Guantánamo Bay and the torture and murder of Abu Ghraib prisoners in Iraq reveals the perils of an imperial presidency that treats the Constitution with disdain, even contempt. That connection ran from the Justice Department to the White House, through another memorandum, written in August 2002 by Jay Bybee, who then headed the Office of Legal Counsel under Attorney General Ashcroft. Bybee had been delegated to prepare a legal analysis of the Geneva Convention Against Torture and Other Cruel, Inhuman, and Degrading Treatment or Punishment, a treaty ratified by the Senate in 1949, with the binding force of U.S. law. His task was to provide a legal definition of "torture" that would set parameters for military and CIA interrogators at Camp X-Ray who were charged with extracting information from suspected al Qaeda and Taliban prisoners. Sitting in his air-conditioned office in Washington, just blocks from the White House but more than a thousand miles from the sweltering human cages at Camp X-Ray, Bybee drafted a memo for Bush that was Orwellian in both style and substance. Although the dictionary definition of "torture" is "the inflicting of severe mental or physical pain to force information or confession," Bybee wrote his own definition, under which the infliction of severe mental pain "not intended to have lasting effects" would not be classified as torture. In other words, the infliction of "temporary" mental pain—produced by threats of death, for example—would be an acceptable interrogation technique. So would the infliction of severe physical pain, unless the interrogators intended to cause "serious physical injury such as death or organ failure." According to Bybee's definition, beating a prisoner into unconsciousness, or breaking bones, would also be acceptable. Only acts "intended" to cause the prisoner's death, or beatings "intended" to cause a kidney or spleen to burst, according to Bybee's definition, would subject the interrogator to possible charges under military or federal law. In his memo Bybee explained to Bush that his purpose was to "negate any claims that certain interrogation methods violate the statute" making torture a crime. He was, in effect, preparing a brief for lawyers defending U.S. soldiers or CIA agents charged with torturing prisoners.

It is, of course, impossible to link Bybee's memo—and its virtual invitation to employ interrogation techniques not "intended" to maim or kill prisoners—with the subsequent revelations that such brutal methods were actually used in Afghanistan and at Camp X-Ray. But the document certainly reflected the Bush administration's attitude that suspected terrorists could be abused with impunity....

Nevertheless, the Bybee memo may have had the unintended effect of stiffening the backbone of the Supreme Court. The memo, along with revelations about the

Abu Ghraib torture scandal, hit the front pages while the justices were considering three cases that challenged the government's power to detain, indefinitely and without recourse to family members, lawyers, or the federal courts, those whom the White House identified as "enemy combatants." Ruling in June 2004, the Court firmly rejected the Bush administration's claims of "inherent" presidential power to hold anyone—U.S. citizens and foreign nationals alike—without some kind of meaningful, neutral judicial review of their detention. The Court's decisions in these cases delivered the sharpest blow to the imperial presidency since its *Youngstown Sheet & Tube* ruling, in 1952, stating that Harry Truman had no "inherent" power as commander in chief to seize the nation's steel mills.

Two of the "enemy combatant" cases involved American citizens, Yaser Esam Hamdi and Jose Padilla, with similar claims to habeas corpus protection but with very different circumstances. Hamdi was born in 1980 in Louisiana to parents from Saudi Arabia; his father worked in the oil fields. The Fourteenth Amendment confers citizenship on "all persons born or naturalized in the United States," regardless of their parents' nationality. Hamdi returned to Saudi Arabia as a child and most likely never thought about his citizenship until he was seized in Afghanistan as a suspected Taliban fighter and shipped to Guantánamo Bay. Once his American birth and citizenship came to light, Hamdi was transferred to a Navy brig in Virginia. Padilla, in contrast, was born and grew up in Chicago, before he converted to Islam and supposedly joined al Qaeda; he received training in Pakistan and Afghanistan before returning to Chicago in 2002. Federal agents grabbed Padilla when he got off the plane, and Attorney General Ashcroft promptly called a news conference to announce that Padilla had plans to set off a "dirty bomb" that would scatter radioactive debris across an American city. Dubbed by the press as the "dirty bomber," Padilla was hustled to the Navy brig in Norfolk, Virginia, and later transferred to one in Charleston, South Carolina. The third "enemy combatant" case involved more than six hundred prisoners at Camp X-Ray, none of whom—after Hamdi was shipped to the Virginia naval brig—held U.S. citizenship.

After months of detention, Yaser Hamdi became the first "enemy combatant" to drag the Bush administration into federal court, through a habeas corpus petition filed on behalf of his father against Defense Secretary Rumsfeld. District Judge Robert Doumar, named to the bench by President Reagan, appointed a federal defender, Frank Dunham, Jr., to represent Hamdi, although government lawyers refused to allow Dunham to meet with his client. At the first hearing before Judge Doumar, he asked the Justice Department's lawyer, Gregory Garre, to explain the government's decision to detain Hamdi without charges or access to counsel. Garre handed Doumar a two-page affidavit by Michael Mobbs, identified as a "special advisor to the undersecretary of defense for policy." Mobbs had never met Hamdi, but his affidavit claimed that a "review" of government records convinced him that Hamdi had been "seized while fighting with the Taliban in Afghanistan." Hamdi had supposedly turned over a Kalashnikov rifle when he was captured by troops of the American-backed Northern Alliance. Judge Doumar noted that every statement in the Mobbs affidavit was hearsay, based on unidentified sources and with no supporting documentation. "I'm challenging everything in the Mobbs declaration," Doumar told Garre. "Indeed, a close inspection of the declaration reveals that [it] never claims that Hamdi was fighting for the Taliban, nor that he was a member of the Taliban." Garre replied that revealing the records Mobbs had relied on might endanger government agents or compromise intelligence sources. Nonetheless, Doumar ordered the government to turn over the records for his inspection. With the courtroom temperature rising, Garre declined to comply. "The present detention is lawful," he doggedly insisted. Doumar had one final question: "So the Constitution doesn't apply to Mr. Hamdi?" Garre had no answer.

After that judicial standoff, Frank Dunham—still refused access to his client—filed an appeal with the Fourth Circuit, reputedly the most conservative federal court of appeals in the country. A three-judge panel answered Doumar's question with a firm "no." ...

When Hamdi's appeal from the Fourth Circuit reached the Supreme Court, along with similar appeals from Jose Padilla and the Camp X-Ray inmates, government lawyers repeated their claim that Bush had the "inherent" power as commander in chief to detain any person, anywhere in the world and for any period, whom he designated as an enemy combatant. The attorneys made ... further arguments. The first was that Congress had, in fact, given Bush the right to detain suspected terrorists when it passed the Authorization for Use of Military Force Resolution in September 2001, allowing the president "to use all necessary and appropriate force against those nations, organizations, or persons he determines" had any role in planning, carrying out, or aiding the 9/11 attacks on the World Trade Center and the Pentagon. ... [The other argument] relied on the hairsplitting claim that federal judges could not rule on the habeas petitions of the Camp X-Ray inmates, because the Guantánamo naval base, they claimed, was actually on Cuban territory, outside the reach of federal courts.

Lawyers for the prisoners in all three cases disputed the claim that Congress had authorized the president to go beyond the use of military force in Afghanistan, certainly not to detain anyone for an indefinite period. They pointed the justices to the federal habeas corpus law, which gives courts jurisdiction over "any person who claims to be held in custody in violation of the Constitution or laws or treaties of the United States." The term "any person" would cover foreign nationals as well as American citizens, lawyers for the Camp X-Ray inmates argued; if the Guantánamo naval base was not within U.S. jurisdiction, they added, it would be a "lawless" territory. Presumably, inmates could be tortured or even murdered with impunity. Padilla's lawyer told the justices that Rumsfeld was a proper defendant because he had decided where Padilla would be held, and the naval brig warden acted under his command.

It took the justices three months to weigh these conflicting arguments and write opinions in the three cases. When the Court issued its rulings in June 2004, reporters quickly skimmed through more than one hundred pages of opinions, crammed with footnotes and citations to dozens of prior cases. They found their lead in Justice Sandra Day O'Connor's opinion in *Hamdi v. Rumsfeld*, in which she declared that "a state of war is not a blank check for the president when it comes to the rights of the Nation's citizens." The bottom line of the Court's ruling was that the Constitution afforded Hamdi a right to challenge his detention "before a neutral decision-maker." But these words left undecided the crucial questions of who that decision-maker might be, and what kind of proceedings Hamdi would be entitled to in pursuing that challenge.

In fact, the justices were sharply divided over the first issue addressed in O'Connor's opinion, the validity of Hamdi's detention in the first place. On this question, only Chief Justice William Rehnquist and Justices Anthony Kennedy and Steven Breyer joined this part of her opinion, holding that the congressional Authorization for Use of Military Force had granted President Bush sufficient leeway to detain suspected "enemy combatants" seized in Afghanistan, even American citizens, such as Hamdi. "Because detention to prevent a combatant's return to the battlefield is a fundamental incident of waging war, in permitting the use of 'necessary and appropriate force,' Congress has clearly and unmistakably authorized detention in the narrow circumstances considered here," O'Connor wrote. But her conclusion was not at all clear to the four justices who dissented on this issue. Not surprisingly, two of the Court's most liberal members, David Souter and Ruth Bader Ginsburg, disagreed with O'Connor. The Use of Force resolution "never so much as uses the word detention, and there is no reason to think Congress might have perceived any need to augment Executive power to deal with dangerous citizens within the United States," Souter wrote for himself and Ginsburg. Souter also cited the "cautionary example" of the *Korematsu* case, noting that President Roosevelt in that case and Bush in *Hamdi* had invoked "the same presidential power" as commander in chief. The Court had upheld FDR's authority, ratified by Congress, to detain Japanese American citizens for an indefinite period, but Souter and Ginsburg found no such ratification in the Use of Force resolution on which the Bush administration relied. ...

Despite their lack of agreement on the president's authority to detain Hamdi, eight justices rejected the Bush administration's claim that "enemy combatants" had no access to judicial review of their detention; Clarence Thomas stood alone in dissenting from this holding. His agreement that Congress had authorized President Bush to detain "enemy combatants" had provided O'Connor with the necessary majority on this issue, but Thomas disagreed with his fellow conservative, Justice Scalia, that government lawyers should either bring criminal charges against Hamdi or release him from custody. President Bush's determination that Hamdi was an enemy combatant, Thomas wrote, "should not be subjected to judicial second-guessing." Thomas, in effect, would allow the president to detain American citizens suspected of committing or aiding terrorist acts for the rest of their lives.

None of his colleagues shared Thomas's complete deference to executive power during wartime. Writing for a plurality of four, O'Connor held that "a citizen-detainee seeking to challenge his classification as an enemy combatant must receive notice of the factual basis for his classification, and a fair opportunity to rebut the Government's factual assertions before a neutral decision-maker." In other words, Judge Doumar had correctly ruled that the Mobbs affidavit, by itself, lacked enough supporting evidence to decide whether Hamdi's detention was lawful. Significantly, O'Connor quoted from Justice Frank Murphy's 1944 dissent in the *Korematsu* case, in which he argued that "the military claim must subject itself to the judicial process of having its reasonableness determined and its conflicts with other interests reconciled." O'Connor was saying, in effect, that the majority decision in *Korematsu*, upholding the wartime internment of Japanese Americans, was no longer a precedent the Court would follow.

The Court's decision that Hamdi was entitled to judicial review of the legality of his detention, however, did not free him from military custody. At the first hearing in Hamdi's case, Judge Doumar had asked the Justice Department lawyer how long the government could detain him: "A year? Two years? Ten years? A lifetime? How long?" The answer, it turned out, was three years. In September 2004, bowing to the Supreme Court's ruling, the Bush administration grudgingly released Hamdi from the navy brig. To gain his freedom, Hamdi agreed to return to Saudi Arabia and to renounce his American citizenship. "He has always thought of himself as a Saudi citizen," said his lawyer, Frank Dunham, "and he wasn't willing to spend another day in jail over it." After his return to Saudi Arabia, Hamdi expressed no bitterness at his treatment and simply said, "I am an innocent person." Whether he was innocent of any terrorist acts, of course, was a question the Bush administration had refused to permit a court to decide. ...

Whether the Court will someday depose the imperial presidency, and return the Constitution's war powers to their rightful place, in Congress, remains to be seen.

✤ *F U R T H E R   R E A D I N G*

Adler, David Gray and Michael A. Genovese, eds. *The Presidency and the Law: The Clinton Legacy* (2002).

Ball, Howard. *Bush, the Detainees, and the Constitution: The Battle Over Presidential Power in the War on Terror* (2007).

Berger, Raoul. *Executive Privilege: A Constitutional Myth* (1974).

―――. *Impeachment: The Constitutional Problem* (1973).

Bernstein, Barton J. "The Road to Watergate and Beyond: The Growth and Abuse of Executive Power Since 1940," *Law & Contemporary Problems*, 40 (1976): 58–86.

Bickel, Alexander. "Congress, the President and the Power to Wage War," *Chicago-Kent Law Review*, 48 (1971): 131.

Bradley, Curtis A. and Jack L. Goldsmith. "Congressional Authorization and the War on Terrorism," *Harvard Law Review*, 118 (2005): 2048–2133.

Cole, David. *Enemy Aliens: Double Standards and Constitutional Freedoms in the War on Terrorism* (2005).

Cooper, Phillip. *By Order of the President: The Use and Abuse of Executive Direct Action* (2002).

Cronin, Thomas. *The State of the Presidency* (1975).

Crotty, William, ed. *The Politics of Terror: The U.S. Response to 9/11* (2004).

Dudziak, Mary L., ed. *September 11 in History: A Watershed Moment?* (2003).

Ely, John Hart. *War and Responsibility: Constitutional Lessons of Vietnam and Its Aftermath* (1995).

Fisher, Louis. *Constitutional Conflicts Between Congress and the President*, 5th ed. (2007).

Goldsmith, Jack L. *The Terror Presidency: Law and Judgment Inside the Bush Administration* (2007).

Hassler, Warren W., Jr. *The President as Commander in Chief* (1971).

Henkin, Louis. *Foreign Affairs and the United States Constitution* (1996).

Irons, Peter. *Justice at War* (1993).

Koh, Harold H. *The National Security Constitution* (1990).

Kurland, Philip B. *Watergate and the Constitution* (1978).

Kutler, Stanley I. *The Wars of Watergate* (1990).

Marcus, Maeva. *Truman and the Steel Seizure Case: The Limits of Presidential Power* (1977).

Milkis, Sidney M. and Michael Nelson. *The American Presidency: Origins and Development, 1776–2002*, 4th ed. (2003).

Neustadt, Richard E. *Presidential Power and the Modern Presidents: The Politics of Leadership from Roosevelt to Reagan*, rev. ed. (1991).

Perkins, Gerald M. and Richard F. Grimmett. *The War Powers Resolution After Thirty Years* (2006).

Posner, Richard A. *An Affair of State: The Investigation, Impeachment, and Trial of President Clinton* (1999).

Pyle, Christopher H. and Richard M. Pious. *The President, the Congress, and the Constitution: Power and Legitimacy in American Politics* (1984).

Reveley, W. Taylor. *War Powers of the President and Congress: Who Holds the Arrows and the Olive Branch* (1981).

Rossiter, Clinton. *The Supreme Court and the Commander in Chief* (1976).

Rozell, Mark J. and Clyde Wilcox, eds. *The Clinton Scandal and the Future of American Government* (2000).

Schlesinger, Arthur. *The Imperial Presidency* (2004).

Smith, J. Malcolm and Stephen Jurika. *The President and the National Security State: His Role as Commander-in-Chief* (1972).

Streichler, Stuart M. "Mad About Yoo, or, Why Worry about the Next Unconstitutional War?" *Journal of Law and Politics*, 24 (2008): 93–128.

Woodward, Robert and Carl Bernstein. *All the President's Men*, 2nd ed. (1994).

APPENDIX I

Constitution of the United States

We the People of the United States, in Order to form a more perfect Union, establish Justice, insure domestic Tranquility, provide for the common defence, promote the general Welfare, and secure the Blessings of Liberty to ourselves and our Posterity, do ordain and establish this Constitution for the United States of America.

Article I.

Section 1. All legislative Powers herein granted shall be vested in a Congress of the United States, which shall consist of a Senate and House of Representatives.

Section 2. The House of Representatives shall be composed of Members chosen every second Year by the People of the several States, and the Electors in each State shall have the Qualifications requisite for Electors of the most numerous Branch of the State Legislature.

No Person shall be a Representative who shall not have attained to the Age of twenty five Years, and been seven Years a Citizen of the United States, and who shall not, when elected, be an Inhabitant of that State in which he shall be chosen.

[Representatives and direct Taxes shall be apportioned among the several States which may be included within this Union, according to their respective Numbers, which shall be determined by adding to the whole Number of free Persons, including those bound to Service for a Term of Years, and excluding Indians not taxed, three fifths of all of all other Persons.][1] The actual Enumeration shall be made within three Years after the first Meeting of the Congress of the United States, and within every subsequent Term of ten Years, in such Manner as they shall by Law direct. The number of Representatives shall not exceed one for every thirty Thousand, but each State shall have at Least one Representative; and until such enumeration shall be made, the State of New Hampshire shall be entitled to chuse three, Massachusetts eight, Rhode-Island and Providence Plantations one, Connecticut five, New-York six, New Jersey four, Pennsylvania eight, Delaware one, Maryland six, Virginia ten, North Carolina five, South Carolina five, and Georgia three.

When vacancies happen in the Representation from any State, the Executive Authority thereof shall issue Writs of Election to fill such Vacancies.

The House of Representatives shall chuse their Speaker and other Officers; and shall have the sole Power of Impeachment.

Section 3. The Senate of the United States shall be composed of two Senators from each State, [chosen by the Legislature thereof,][2] for six Years; and each Senator shall have one Vote.

---

[1] Changed by Section 2 of the Fourteenth Amendment.

[2] Changed by the Seventeenth Amendment.

Immediately after they shall be assembled in Consequence of the first Election, they shall be divided as equally as may be into three Classes. The Seats of the Senators of the first Class shall be vacated at the Expiration of the second Year, of the second Class at the Expiration of the fourth Year, and of the third Class at the Expiration of the sixth Year, so that one third may be chosen every second Year; [and if Vacancies happen by Resignation, or otherwise, during the Recess of the Legislature of any State, the Executive thereof may make temporary Appointments until the next Meeting of the Legislature, which shall then fill such Vacancies.][3]

No Person shall be a Senator who shall not have attained to the Age of thirty Years, and been nine Years a Citizen of the United States, and who shall not, when elected, be an Inhabitant of that State for which he shall be chosen.

The Vice President of the United States shall be President of the Senate, but shall have no Vote, unless they be equally divided. The Senate shall chuse their other Officers, and also a President pro tempore, in the Absence of the Vice President, or when he shall exercise the Office of President of the United States.

The Senate shall have the sole Power to try all Impeachments. When sitting for that Purpose, they shall be on Oath or Affirmation. When the President of the United States is tried, the Chief Justice shall preside: And no Person shall be convicted without the Concurrence of two thirds of the Members present.

Judgment in Cases of Impeachment shall not extend further than to removal from Office, and disqualification to hold and enjoy any Office of honor, Trust or Profit under the United States: but the Party convicted shall nevertheless be liable and subject to Indictment, Trial, Judgment and Punishment, according to Law.

Section 4.   The Times, Places and Manner of holding Elections for Senators and Representatives, shall be prescribed in each State by the Legislature thereof; but the Congress may at any time by Law make or alter such Regulations, except as to the Places of chusing Senators.

The Congress shall assemble at least once in every Year, and such Meeting shall be [on the first Monday in December,][4] unless they shall by Law appoint a different Day.

Section 5.   Each House shall be the Judge of the Elections, Returns and Qualifications of its own Members, and a Majority of each shall constitute a Quorum to do Business; but a smaller Number may adjourn from day to day, and may be authorized to compel the Attendance of absent Members, in such Manner, and under such Penalties as each House may provide.

Each House may determine the Rules of its Proceedings, punish its Members for disorderly Behaviour, and, with the Concurrence of two thirds, expel a Member.

Each House shall keep a Journal of its Proceedings, and from time to time publish the same, excepting such Parts as may in their Judgment require Secrecy; and the Yeas and Nays of the Members of either House on any question shall, at the Desire of one fifth of those Present, be entered on the Journal.

---

[3] Changed by the Seventeenth Amendment.

[4] Changed by Section 2 of the Twentieth Amendment.

Neither House, during the Session of Congress, shall, without the Consent of the other, adjourn for more than three days, nor to any other Place than that in which the two Houses shall be sitting.

Section 6.   The Senators and Representatives shall receive a Compensation for their Services, to be ascertained by Law, and paid out of the Treasury of the United States. They shall in all Cases, except Treason, Felony and Breach of the Peace, be privileged from Arrest during their Attendance at the Session of their respective Houses, and in going to and returning from the same; and for any Speech or Debate in either House, they shall not be questioned in any other Place.

No Senator or Representative shall, during the Time for which he was elected, be appointed to any civil Office under the Authority of the United States, which shall have been created, or the Emoluments whereof shall have been increased during such time; and no Person holding any Office under the United States, shall be a Member of either House during his Continuance in Office.

Section 7.   All Bills for raising Revenue shall originate in the House of Representatives; but the Senate may propose or concur with Amendments as on other Bills.

Every Bill which shall have passed the House of Representatives and the Senate, shall, before it becomes a Law, be presented to the President of the United States; If he approve he shall sign it, but if not he shall return it, with his Objections to that House in which it shall have originated, who shall enter the Objections at large on their Journal, and proceed to reconsider it. If after such Reconsideration two thirds of that House shall agree to pass the Bill, it shall be sent, together with the Objections, to the other House, by which it shall likewise be reconsidered, and if approved by two thirds of that House, it shall become a Law. But in all such Cases the Votes of both Houses shall be determined by yeas and Nays, and the Names of the Persons voting for and against the Bill shall be entered on the Journal of each House respectively. If any Bill shall not be returned by the President within ten Days (Sundays excepted) after it shall have been presented to him, the Same shall be a Law, in like Manner as if he had signed it, unless the Congress by their Adjournment prevent its Return, in which Case it shall not be a Law.

Every Order, Resolution, or Vote to which the Concurrence of the Senate and House of Representatives may be necessary (except on a question of Adjournment) shall be presented to the President of the United States; and before the Same shall take Effect, shall be approved by him, or being disapproved by him, shall be repassed by two thirds of the Senate and House of Representatives, according to the Rules and Limitations prescribed in the Case of a Bill.

Section 8.   The Congress shall have Power To lay and collect Taxes, Duties, Imposts and Excises, to pay the Debts and provide for the common Defence and general Welfare of the United States; but all Duties, Imposts and Excises shall be uniform throughout the United States;

To borrow Money on the credit of the United States;

To regulate Commerce with foreign Nations, and among the several States, and with the Indian Tribes;

To establish an uniform Rule of Naturalization, and uniform Laws on the subject of Bankruptcies throughout the United States;

To coin Money, regulate the Value thereof, and of foreign Coin, and fix the Standard of Weights and Measures;

To provide for the Punishment of counterfeiting the Securities and current Coin of the United States;

To establish Post Offices and post Roads;

To promote the Progress of Science and useful Arts, by securing for limited Times to Authors and Inventors the exclusive Right to their respective Writings and Discoveries;

To constitute Tribunals inferior to the supreme Court;

To define and punish Piracies and Felonies committed on the high Seas, and Offenses against the Law of Nations;

To declare War, grant Letters of Marque and Reprisal, and make Rules concerning Captures on Land and Water;

To raise and support Armies, but no Appropriation of Money to that Use shall be for a longer Term than two Years;

To provide and maintain a Navy;

To make Rules for the Government and Regulation of the land and naval Forces;

To provide for calling forth the Militia to execute the Laws of the Union, suppress Insurrections and repel Invasions;

To provide for organizing, arming, and disciplining, the Militia, and for governing such Part of them as may be employed in the Service of the United States, reserving to the States respectively, the Appointment of the Officers, and the Authority of training the Militia according to the discipline prescribed by Congress;

To exercise exclusive Legislation in all Cases whatsoever, over such District (not exceeding ten Miles square) as may, by Cession of particular States, and the Acceptance of Congress, become the Seat of the Government of the United States, and to exercise like Authority over all Places purchased by the Consent of the Legislature of the State in which the Same shall be, for the Erection of Forts, Magazines, Arsenals, dock-Yards and other needful Buildings;—And

To make all Laws which shall be necessary and proper for carrying into Execution the foregoing Powers, and all other Powers vested by this Constitution in the Government of the United States or in any Department or Officer thereof.

Section 9.   The Migration or Importation of such Persons as any of the States now existing shall think proper to admit, shall not be prohibited by the Congress prior to the Year one thousand eight hundred and eight, but a Tax or duty may be imposed on such Importation, not exceeding ten dollars for each Person.

The Privilege of the Writ of Habeas Corpus shall not be suspended, unless when in Cases of Rebellion or Invasion the public Safety may require it.

No Bill of Attainder or ex post facto Law shall be passed.

[No Capitation, or other direct, Tax shall be laid, unless in Proportion to the Census or Enumeration herein before directed to be taken.][5]

---

[5] See Sixteenth Amendment.

No Tax or Duty shall be laid on Articles exported from any State. No Preference shall be given by any Regulation of Commerce or Revenue to the Ports of one State over those of another: nor shall Vessels bound to, or from, one State, be obliged to enter, clear, or pay Duties in another.

No Money shall be drawn from the Treasury, but in Consequence of Appropriations made by Law; and a regular Statement and Account of the Receipts and Expenditures of all public Money shall be published from time to time.

No Title of Nobility shall be granted by the United States: And no Person holding any Office of Profit or Trust under them, shall, without the Consent of the Congress, accept of any present, Emolument, Office, or Title, of any kind whatever, from any King, Prince, or foreign State.

Section 10. No State shall enter into any Treaty, Alliance, or Confederation; grant Letters of Marque and Reprisal; coin Money; emit Bills of Credit; make any Thing but gold and silver Coin a Tender in Payment of Debts; pass any Bill of Attainder, ex post facto Law, or Law impairing the Obligation of Contracts, or grant any Title of Nobility.

No State shall, without the Consent of the Congress, lay any Imposts or Duties on Imports or Exports, except what may be absolutely necessary for executing it's inspection Laws: and the net Produce of all Duties and Imposts, laid by any State on Imports or Exports, shall be for the Use of the Treasury of the United States; and all such Laws shall be subject to the Revision and Control of the Congress.

No State shall, without the Consent of Congress, lay any Duty of Tonnage, keep Troops, or Ships of War in time of Peace, enter into any Agreement or Compact with another State, or with a foreign Power, or engage in War, unless actually invaded, or in such imminent Danger as will not admit of delay.

Article II.

Section 1. The executive Power shall be vested in a President of the United States of America. He shall hold his Office during the Term of four Years, and, together with the Vice President, chosen for the same Term, be elected, as follows

Each State shall appoint, in such Manner as the Legislature thereof may direct, a Number of Electors, equal to the whole Number of Senators and Representatives to which the State may be entitled in the Congress: but no Senator or Representative, or Person holding an Office of Trust or Profit under the United States, shall be appointed an Elector.

[The Electors shall meet in their respective States, and vote by Ballot for two Persons, of whom one at least shall not be an Inhabitant of the same State with themselves. And they shall make a List of all the Persons voted for, and of the Number of Votes for each; which List they shall sign and certify, and transmit sealed to the Seat of the Government of the United States, directed to the President of the Senate. The President of the Senate shall, in the Presence of the Senate and House of Representatives, open all the Certificates, and the Votes shall then be counted. The Person having the greatest Number of Votes shall be the President, if such Number be a Majority of the whole Number of Electors appointed; and if there be more than one who have such Majority, and have an equal Number of Votes, then the House of Representatives shall immediately chuse by Ballot one of them for President; and if no Person have a Majority, then from the five highest on the List the said House shall in like Manner chuse the President. But in chusing the President, the Votes shall be taken by States, the Representation from each State having one Vote; A quorum for this Purpose shall consist of a Member or Members from two thirds of the States, and a Majority of all the States shall be necessary to a Choice. In every Case, after the Choice of the President, the Person having the greatest Number of Votes of the Electors shall be the Vice President. But if there should remain two or more who have equal Votes, the Senate shall chuse from them by Ballot the Vice President.][6]

The Congress may determine the Time of chusing the Electors, and the Day on which they shall give their Votes; which Day shall be the same throughout the United States.

No Person except a natural born Citizen, or a Citizen of the United States, at the time of the Adoption of this Constitution, shall be eligible to the Office of President; neither shall any person be eligible to that Office who shall not have attained to the Age of thirty five Years, and been fourteen Years a Resident within the United States.

[In Case of the Removal of the President from Office, or of his Death, Resignation, or Inability to discharge the Powers and Duties of the said Office, the Same shall devolve on the Vice President, and the Congress may by Law provide for the Case of Removal, Death, Resignation or Inability, both of the President and Vice President, declaring what Officer shall then act as President, and such Officer shall act accordingly, until the Disability be removed, or a President shall be elected.][7]

The President shall, at stated Times, receive for his Services, a Compensation, which shall neither be increased nor diminished during the Period for which he shall have been elected, and he shall not receive within that Period any other Emolument from the United States, or any of them.

Before he enter on the Execution of his Office, he shall take the following Oath or Affirmation:—"I do solemnly swear (or affirm) that I will faithfully execute the Office of President of the United States, and will to the best of my Ability, preserve, protect and defend the Constitution of the United States."

Section 2.   The President shall be Commander in Chief of the Army and Navy of the United States, and of the Militia of the several States, when called into the actual Service of the United States; he may require the Opinion, in writing, of the principal Officer in each of the executive Departments, upon any Subject relating to the Duties of their respective Offices, and he shall have Power to grant Reprieves and Pardons for Offenses against the United States, except in Cases of Impeachment.

He shall have Power, by and with the Advice and Consent of the Senate, to make Treaties, provided two thirds of the Senators present concur; and he shall nominate, and by and with the Advice and Consent of the Senate, shall appoint Ambassadors, other public Ministers and Consuls, Judges of the supreme Court, and all other Officers of the United States, whose Appointments are not herein otherwise provided for, and which shall be established by Law: but the Congress may by Law vest the

---

[6] Changed by the Twelfth Amendment.

[7] Changed by the Twenty-Fifth Amendment.

Appointment of such inferior Officers, as they think proper, in the President alone, in the Courts of Law, or in the Heads of Departments.

The President shall have Power to fill up all Vacancies that may happen during the Recess of the Senate, by granting Commissions which shall expire at the End of their next Session.

Section 3. He shall from time to time give to the Congress Information of the State of the Union, and recommend to their Consideration such Measures as he shall judge necessary and expedient; he may, on extraordinary Occasions, convene both Houses, or either of them, and in Case of Disagreement between them, with Respect to the Time of Adjournment, he may adjourn them to such Time as he shall think proper; he shall receive Ambassadors and other public Ministers; he shall take Care that the Laws be faithfully executed, and shall Commission all the Officers of the United States.

Section 4. The President, Vice President and all civil Officers of the United States, shall be removed from Office on Impeachment for, and Conviction of, Treason, Bribery, or other high Crimes and Misdemeanors.

Article III.

Section 1. The judicial Power of the United States, shall be vested in one supreme Court, and in such inferior Courts as the Congress may from time to time ordain and establish. The Judges, both of the supreme and inferior Courts, shall hold their Offices during good Behaviour, and shall, at stated Times, receive for their Services, a Compensation, which shall not be diminished during their Continuance in Office.

Section 2. The judicial Power shall extend to all Cases, in Law and Equity, arising under this Constitution, the Laws of the United States, and Treaties made, or which shall be made, under their Authority;—to all Cases affecting Ambassadors, other public Ministers and Consuls;—to all Cases of admiralty and maritime Jurisdiction;—to Controversies to which the United States shall be a Party;—to Controversies between two or more States;—[between a State and Citizens of another State;—][8] between Citizens of different States,— between Citizens of the same State claiming Lands under Grants of different States, [and between a State, or the Citizens thereof, and foreign States, Citizens or Subjects.][9]

In all Cases affecting Ambassadors, other public Ministers and Consuls, and those in which a State shall be Party, the supreme Court shall have original Jurisdiction. In all the other Cases before mentioned, the supreme Court shall have appellate Jurisdiction, both as to Law and Fact, with such Exceptions, and under such Regulations as the Congress shall make.

The Trial of all Crimes, except in Cases of Impeachment; shall be by Jury; and such Trial shall be held in the State where the said Crimes shall have been committed; but when not committed within any State, the Trial shall be at such Place or Places as the Congress may by Law have directed.

---

[8] Changed by the Eleventh Amendment.

[9] Changed by the Eleventh Amendment.

Section 3.   Treason against the United States, shall consist only in levying War against them, or in adhering to their Enemies, giving them Aid and Comfort. No Person shall be convicted of Treason unless on the Testimony of two Witnesses to the same overt Act, or on Confession in open Court.

The Congress shall have Power to declare the Punishment of Treason, but no Attainder of Treason shall work Corruption of Blood, or Forfeiture except during the Life of the Person attainted.

Article IV.

Section 1.   Full Faith and Credit shall be given in each State to the public Acts, Records, and judicial Proceedings of every other State. And the Congress may by general Laws prescribe the Manner in which such Acts, Records and Proceedings shall be proved, and the Effect thereof.

Section 2.   The Citizens of each State shall be entitled to all Privileges and Immunities of Citizens in the several States.

A Person charged in any State with Treason, Felony, or other Crime, who shall flee from Justice, and be found in another State, shall on Demand of the executive Authority of the State from which he fled, be delivered up, to be removed to the State having Jurisdiction of the Crime.

[No Person held to Service or Labour in one State, under the Laws thereof, escaping into another, shall, in Consequence of any Law or Regulation therein, be discharged from such Service or Labour, but shall be delivered up on Claim of the Party to whom such Service or Labour may be due.][10]

Section 3.   New States may be admitted by the Congress into this Union; but no new State shall be formed or erected within the Jurisdiction of any other State; nor any State be formed by the Junction of two or more States, or Parts of States, without the Consent of the Legislatures of the States concerned as well as of the Congress.

The Congress shall have Power to dispose of and make all needful Rules and Regulations respecting the Territory or other Property belonging to the United States; and nothing in this Constitution shall be so construed as to Prejudice any Claims of the United States, or of any particular State.

Section 4.   The United States shall guarantee to every State in this Union a Republican Form of Government, and shall protect each of them against Invasion; and on Application of the Legislature, or of the Executive (when the Legislature cannot be convened) against domestic Violence.

Article V.

The Congress, whenever two thirds of both Houses shall deem it necessary, shall propose Amendments to this Constitution, or, on the Application of the Legislatures of two thirds of the several States, shall call a Convention for proposing Amendments, which, in either Case, shall be valid to all Intents and Purposes, as Part of this

---

[10] Changed by the Thirteenth Amendment.

Constitution, when ratified by the Legislatures of three fourths of the several States, or by Conventions in three fourths thereof, as the one or the other Mode of Ratification may be proposed by the Congress; Provided that no Amendment which may be made prior to the Year One thousand eight hundred and eight shall in any Manner affect the first and fourth Clauses in the Ninth Section of the first Article; and that no State, without its Consent, shall be deprived of it's equal Suffrage in the Senate.

Article VI.

All Debts contracted and Engagements entered into, before the Adoption of this Constitution, shall be as valid against the United States under this Constitution, as under the Confederation.

This Constitution, and the Laws of the United States which shall be made in Pursuance thereof; and all Treaties made, or which shall be made, under the Authority of the United States, shall be the supreme Law of the Land; and the Judges in every State shall be bound thereby, any Thing in the Constitution or Laws of any State to the Contrary notwithstanding.

The Senators and Representatives before mentioned, and the Members of the several State Legislatures, and all executive and judicial Officers, both of the United States and of the several States, shall be bound by Oath or Affirmation, to support this Constitution; but no religious Test shall ever be required as a Qualification to any Office or public Trust under the United States.

Article VII.

The Ratification of the Conventions of nine States, shall be sufficient for the Establishment of this Constitution between the States so ratifying the Same.

> *Done in Convention by the Unanimous Consent of the States present the Seventeenth Day of September in the Year of our Lord one thousand seven hundred and Eighty seven and of the Independence of the United States of America the Twelfth In Witness whereof We have hereunto subscribed our Names,*

[signed by]
Go. WASHINGTON
Presidt and Deputy from Virginia
[*and thirty-eight others*]

Amendments to the Constitution of the United States

Amendment I.[11]

Congress shall make no law respecting an establishment of religion, or prohibiting the free exercise thereof; or abridging the freedom of speech, or of the press, or the right of the people peaceably to assemble, and to petition the Government for a redress of grievances.

---

[11] The first ten Amendments (Bill of Rights) were ratified effective December 15, 1791.

Amendment II.

A well regulated Militia, being necessary to the security of a free State, the right of the people to keep and bear Arms, shall not be infringed.

Amendment III.

No Soldier shall, in time of peace be quartered in any house, without the consent of the Owner, nor in time of war, but in a manner to be prescribed by law.

Amendment IV.

The right of the people to be secure in their persons, houses, papers, and effects, against unreasonable searches and seizures, shall not be violated, and no Warrants shall issue, but upon probable cause, supported by Oath or affirmation, and particularly describing the place to be searched, and the persons or things to be seized.

Amendment V.

No person shall be held to answer for a capital, or otherwise infamous crime, unless on a presentment or indictment of a Grand Jury, except in cases arising in the land or naval forces, or in the Militia, when in actual service in time of War or public danger; nor shall any person be subject for the same offence to be twice put in jeopardy of life or limb, nor shall be compelled in any criminal case to be a witness against himself, nor be deprived of life, liberty, or property, without due process of law; nor shall private property be taken for public use without just compensation.

Amendment VI.

In all criminal prosecutions, the accused shall enjoy the right to a speedy and public trial, by an impartial jury of the State and district wherein the crime shall have been committed; which district shall have been previously ascertained by law, and to be informed of the nature and cause of the accusation; to be confronted with the witnesses against him; to have compulsory process for obtaining witnesses in his favor, and to have the assistance of counsel for his defence.

Amendment VII.

In Suits at common law, where the value in controversy shall exceed twenty dollars, the right of trial by jury shall be preserved, and no fact tried by a jury shall be otherwise re-examined in any Court of the United States, than according to the rules of the common law.

Amendment VIII.

Excessive bail shall not be required, nor excessive fines imposed, nor cruel and unusual punishments inflicted.

Amendment IX.

The enumeration in the Constitution of certain rights shall not be construed to deny or disparage others retained by the people.

Amendment X.

The powers not delegated to the United States by the Constitution, nor prohibited by it to the States, are reserved to the States respectively, or to the people.

Amendment XI.[12]

The Judicial power of the United States shall not be construed to extend to any suit in law or equity, commenced or prosecuted against one of the United States by Citizens of another State, or by Citizens or Subjects of any Foreign State.

Amendment XII.[13]

The Electors shall meet in their respective states, and vote by ballot for President and Vice President, one of whom, at least, shall not be an inhabitant of the same state with themselves; they shall name in their ballots the person voted for as President, and in distinct ballots the person voted for as Vice-President, and they shall make distinct lists of all persons voted for as President, and of all persons voted for as Vice-President, and of the number of votes for each, which lists they shall sign and certify, and transmit sealed to the seat of the government of the United States, directed to the President of the Senate;—The President of the Senate shall, in the presence of the Senate and House of Representatives, open all the certificates and the votes shall then be counted;—The person having the greatest number of votes for President, shall be the President, if such number be a majority of the whole number of Electors appointed; and if no person have such majority, then from the persons having the highest numbers not exceeding three on the list of those voted for as President, the House of Representatives shall choose immediately, by ballot, the President. But in choosing the President, the votes shall be taken by states, the representation from each state having one vote; a quorum for this purpose shall consist of a member or members from two-thirds of the states, and a majority of all the states shall be necessary to a choice. [And if the House of Representatives shall not choose a President whenever the right of choice shall devolve upon them, before the fourth day of March next following, then the Vice President shall act as President, as in the case of the death or other constitutional disability of the President—][14] The person having the greatest number of votes as Vice-President, shall be the Vice-President, if such number be a majority of the whole number of Electors appointed, and if no person have a majority, then from the two highest numbers on the list, the Senate shall choose the Vice-President; a quorum for the purpose shall consist of two-thirds of the

---

[12] The Eleventh Amendment was ratified February 7, 1795.

[13] The Twelfth Amendment was ratified June 15, 1804.

[14] Superseded by Section 3 of the Twentieth Amendment.

whole number of Senators, and a majority of the whole number shall be necessary to a choice. But no person constitutionally ineligible to the office of President shall be eligible to that of Vice-President of the United States.

Amendment XIII.[15]

Section 1.   Neither slavery nor involuntary servitude, except as a punishment for crime whereof the party shall have been duly convicted, shall exist within the United States, or any place subject to their jurisdiction.

Section 2.   Congress shall have power to enforce this article by appropriate legislation.

Amendment XIV.[16]

Section 1.   All persons born or naturalized in the United States and subject to the jurisdiction thereof, are citizens of the United States and of the State wherein they reside. No State shall make or enforce any law which shall abridge the privileges or immunities of citizens of the United States; nor shall any State deprive any person of life, liberty, or property, without due process of law; nor deny to any person within its jurisdiction the equal protection of the laws.

Section 2.   Representatives shall be apportioned among the several States according to their respective numbers, counting the whole number of persons in each State, excluding Indians not taxed. But when the right to vote at any election for the choice of electors for President and Vice President of the United States, Representatives in Congress, the Executive and Judicial officers of a State, or the members of the Legislature thereof, is denied to any of the male inhabitants of such State, being twenty-one years of age, and citizens of the United States, or in any way abridged, except for participation in rebellion, or other crime, the basis of representation therein shall be reduced in the proportion which the number of such male citizens shall bear to the whole number of male citizens twenty-one years of age in such State.

Section 3.   No person shall be a Senator or Representative in Congress, or elector of President and Vice President, or hold any office, civil or military, under the United States, or under any State, who, having previously taken an oath, as a member of Congress, or as an officer of the United States, or as a member of any State legislature, or as an executive or judicial officer of any State, to support the Constitution of the United States, shall have engaged in insurrection or rebellion against the same, or given aid or comfort to the enemies thereof. But Congress may by a vote of two-thirds of each House, remove such disability.

Section 4.   The validity of the public debt of the United States, authorized by law, including debts incurred for payment of pensions and bounties for services in suppressing insurrection or rebellion, shall not be questioned. But neither the United

---

[15] The Thirteenth Amendment was ratified December 6, 1865.

[16] The Fourteenth Amendment was ratified July 9, 1868.

States nor any State shall assume or pay any debt or obligation incurred in aid of insurrection or rebellion against the United States, or any claim for the loss or emancipation of any slave; but all such debts, obligations and claims shall be held illegal and void.

Section 5.   The Congress shall have power to enforce, by appropriate legislation, the provisions of this article.

Amendment XV.[17]

Section 1.   The right of citizens of the United States to vote shall not be denied or abridged by the United States or by any State on account of race, color, or previous condition of servitude.

Section 2.   The Congress shall have power to enforce this article by appropriate legislation.

Amendment XVI.[18]

The Congress shall have power to lay and collect taxes on incomes, from whatever source derived, without apportionment among the several States, and without regard to any census or enumeration.

Amendment XVII.[19]

The Senate of the United States shall be composed of two Senators from each State, elected by the people thereof, for six years; and each Senator shall have one vote. The electors in each State shall have the qualifications requisite for electors of the most numerous branch of the State legislatures. When vacancies happen in the representation of any State in the Senate, the executive authority of such State shall issue writs of election to fill such vacancies: *Provided,* That the legislature of any State may empower the executive thereof to make temporary appointments until the people fill the vacancies by election as the legislature may direct.

   This amendment shall not be so construed as to affect the election or term of any Senator chosen before it becomes valid as part of the Constitution.

Amendment XVIII.[20]

[**Section 1.**   After one year from the ratification of this article the manufacture, sale, or transportation of intoxicating liquors within, the importation thereof into, or the exportation thereof from the United States and all territory subject to the jurisdiction thereof for beverage purposes is hereby prohibited.

---

[17] The Fifteenth Amendment was ratified February 3, 1870.

[18] The Sixteenth Amendment was ratified February 3, 1913.

[19] The Seventeenth Amendment was ratified April 8, 1913.

[20] The Eighteenth Amendment was ratified January 16, 1919. It was repealed by the Twenty-First Amendment, December 5, 1933.

Section 2.   The Congress and the several States shall have concurrent power to enforce this article by appropriate legislation.

Section 3.   This article shall be inoperative unless it shall have been ratified as an amendment to the Constitution by the legislatures of the several States, as provided in the Constitution, within seven years from the date of the submission hereof to the States by the Congress.]

Amendment XIX.[21]

The right of citizens of the United States to vote shall not be denied or abridged by the United States or by any State on account of sex. Congress shall have power to enforce this article by appropriate legislation.

Amendment XX.[22]

Section 1.   The terms of the President and Vice President shall end at noon on the 20th day of January, and the terms of Senators and Representatives at noon on the 3d day of January, of the years in which such terms would have ended if this article had not been ratified; and the terms of their successors shall then begin.

Section 2.   The Congress shall assemble at least once in every year, and such meeting shall begin at noon on the 3d day of January, unless they shall by law appoint a different day.

Section 3.   If, at the time fixed for the beginning of the term of the President, the President elect shall have died, the Vice President elect shall become President. If a President shall not have been chosen before the time fixed for the beginning of his term, or if the President elect shall have failed to qualify, then the Vice President elect shall act as President until a President shall have qualified; and the Congress may by law provide for the case wherein neither a President elect nor a Vice President elect shall have qualified, declaring who shall then act as President, or the manner in which one who is to act shall be selected, and person shall act accordingly until a President or Vice President shall have qualified.

Section 4.   The Congress may by law provide for the case of the death of any of the persons from whom the House of Representatives may choose a President whenever the right of choice shall have devolved upon them, and for the case of the death of any of the persons from whom the Senate may choose a Vice President whenever the right of choice shall have devolved upon them.

Section 5.   Sections 1 and 2 shall take effect on the 15th day of October following the ratification of this article.

---

[21] The Nineteenth Amendment was ratified August 18, 1920.

[22] The Twentieth Amendment was ratified January 23, 1933.

Section 6. This article shall be inoperative unless it shall have been ratified as an amendment to the Constitution by the legislatures of three-fourths of the several States within seven years from the date of its submission.

Amendment XXI.[23]

Section 1. The eighteenth article of amendment to the Constitution of the United States is hereby repealed.

Section 2. The transportation or importation into any State, Territory, or possession of the United States for delivery or use therein of intoxicating liquors, in violation of the laws thereof, is hereby prohibited.

Section 3. This article shall be inoperative unless it shall have been ratified as an amendment to the Constitution by conventions in the several States, as provided in the Constitution, within seven years from the date of the submission hereof to the States by the Congress.

Amendment XXII.[24]

Section 1. No person shall be elected to the office of the President more than twice, and no person who has held the office of President, or acted as President, for more than two years of a term to which some other person was elected President shall be elected to the office of the President more than once. But this Article shall not apply to any person holding the office of President when this Article was proposed by the Congress, and shall not prevent any person who may be holding the office of President, or acting as President, during the term within which this Article becomes operative from holding the office of President or acting as President during the remainder of such term.

Section 2. This article shall be inoperative unless it shall have been ratified as an amendment to the Constitution by the legislatures of three-fourths of the several States within seven years from the date of its submission to the States by the Congress.

Amendment XXIII.[25]

Section 1. The District constituting the seat of Government of the United States shall appoint in such manner as the Congress may direct: A number of electors of President and Vice President equal to the whole number of Senators and Representatives in Congress to which the District would be entitled if it were a State, but in no event more than the least populous State; they shall be in addition to those appointed by the

---

[23] The Twenty-First Amendment was ratified December 5, 1933.

[24] The Twenty-Second Amendment was ratified February 27, 1951.

[25] The Twenty-Third Amendment was ratified March 29, 1961.

States, but they shall be considered, for the purposes of the election of President and Vice President, to be electors appointed by a State; and they shall meet in the District and perform such duties as provided by the twelfth article of amendment.

Section 2. The Congress shall have power to enforce this article by appropriate legislation.

Amendment XXIV.[26]

Section 1. The right of citizens of the United States to vote in any primary or other election for President or Vice President, for electors for President or Vice President, or for Senator or Representative in Congress, shall not be denied or abridged by the United States or any State by reason of failure to pay any poll tax or other tax. Section 2. The Congress shall have power to enforce this article by appropriate legislation.

Amendment XXV.[27]

Section 1. In case of the removal of the President from office or of his death or resignation, the Vice President shall become President.

Section 2. Whenever there is a vacancy in the office of the Vice President, the President shall nominate a Vice President who shall take office upon confirmation by a majority vote of both Houses of Congress.

Section 3. Whenever the President transmits to the President pro tempore of the Senate and the Speaker of the House of Representatives his written declaration that he is unable to discharge the powers and duties of his office, and until he transmits to them a written declaration to the contrary, such powers and duties shall be discharged by the Vice President as Acting President.

Section 4. Whenever the Vice President and a majority of either the principal officers of the executive departments or of such other body as Congress may by law provide, transmit to the President pro tempore of the Senate and the Speaker of the House of Representatives their written declaration that the President is unable to discharge the powers and duties of his office, the Vice President shall immediately assume the powers and duties of the office as Acting President. Thereafter, when the President transmits to the President pro tempore of the Senate and the Speaker of the House of Representatives his written declaration that no inability exists, he shall resume the powers and duties of his office unless the Vice President and a majority of either the principal officers of the executive department or of such other body as Congress may by law provide, transmit within four days to the President pro tempore of the Senate and the Speaker of the House of Representatives their written declaration that the President is unable to discharge the powers and duties of his office.

---

[26] The Twenty-Fourth Amendment was ratified January 23, 1964.

[27] The Twenty-Fifth Amendment was ratified February 10, 1967.

Thereupon Congress shall decide the issue, assembling within forty-eight hours for that purpose if not in session. If the Congress, within twenty-one days after receipt of the latter written declaration, or, if Congress is not in session, within twenty-one days after Congress is required to assemble, determines by two-thirds vote of both Houses that the President is unable to discharge the powers and duties of his office, the Vice President shall continue to discharge the same as Acting President; otherwise, the President shall resume the powers and duties of his office.

Amendment XXVI.[28]

Section 1.   The right of citizens of the United States, who are eighteen years of age or older, to vote shall not be denied or abridged by the United States or by any State on account of age.

Section 2.   The Congress shall have power to enforce this article by appropriate legislation.

Amendment XXVII.[29]

No law, varying the compensation for the services of the Senators and Representatives, shall take effect, until an election of Representatives shall have intervened.

---

[28] The Twenty-Sixth Amendment was ratified July 1, 1971.

[29] Congress submitted the text of the Twenty-Seventh Amendment to the States as part of the proposed Bill of Rights on September 25, 1789. The Amendment was not ratified together with the first ten Amendments, which became effective on December 15, 1791. The Twenty-Seventh Amendment was ratified on May 7, 1992, by the vote of Michigan.

APPENDIX II

Justices of the U.S. Supreme Court

Name	Party	State	Replaced	Service	Years
APPOINTED BY GEORGE WASHINGTON, FEDERALIST OF VIRGINIA (1789–1797)					
• *John Jay*	Federalist	NY		1789–1795	6
• John Rutledge	Federalist	SC		1789–1791	1
• William Cushing	Federalist	MA		1789–1810	21
• James Wilson	Federalist	PA		1789–1798	9
• John Blair	Federalist	VA		1789–1795	6
• James Iredell	Federalist	NC		1790–1799	9
• Thomas Johnson	Federalist	MD	Rutledge	1791–1793	2
• William Paterson	Federalist	NJ	Johnson	1793–1806	13
• *John Rutledge*	Federalist	SC	Jay	1795	1
• Samuel Chase	Federalist	MD	Blair	1796–1811	15
• *Oliver Ellsworth*	Federalist	CT	Rutledge	1796–1800	4
APPOINTED BY JOHN ADAMS, FEDERALIST OF MASSACHUSETTS (1797–1801)					
• Bushrod Washington	Federalist	VA	Wilson	1799–1829	31
• Alfred Moore	Federalist	NC	Iredell	1800–1804	4
• *John Marshall*	Federalist	VA	Ellsworth	1801–1835	34
APPOINTED BY THOMAS JEFFERSON, DEMOCRATIC-REPUBLICAN OF VIRGINIA (1801–1809)					
• William Johnson	Demo-Rep.	SC	Moore	1804–1834	30
• Henry Brockholst Livington	Demo-Rep.	NY	Paterson	1807–1823	16
• Thomas Todd	Demo-Rep.	KY	new seat	1807–1826	19
APPOINTED BY JAMES MADISON, DEMOCRATIC-REPUBLICAN OF VIRGINIA (1809–1817)					
• Gabrial Duval	Demo-Rep.	MD	Chase	1811–1835	23
• Joseph Story	Demo-Rep.	MA	Cushing	1812–1845	34
APPOINTED BY JAMES MONROE, DEMOCRATIC-REPUBLICAN OF VIRGINIA (1817–1825)					
• Smith Thompson	Demo-Rep.	NY	Livingston	1824–1843	20
APPOINTED BY JOHN QUINCY ADAMS, DEMOCRATIC-REPUBLICAN OF MASSACHUSETTS (1825–1829)					
• Robert Trimble	Demo-Rep.	KY	Todd	1826–1828	2

Name	Party	State	Replaced	Service	Years

APPOINTED BY ANDREW JACKSON, DEMOCRATIC-REPUBLICAN OF TENNESSEE (1829–1837)

Name	Party	State	Replaced	Service	Years
• John McLean	Democrat (later Repub.)	OH	Trimble	1830–1861	32
• Henry Baldwin	Democrat	PA	Washington	1830–1844	14
• James M. Wayne	Democrat	GA	Johnson	1835–1867	32
• *Roger B. Taney*	Democrat	MD	Marshall	1836–1864	28
• Philip P. Barbour	Democrat	VA	Duvall	1836–1841	5
• John Catron	Democrat	TN	new seat	1837–1865	28

APPOINTED BY MARTIN VAN BUREN, DEMOCRAT FROM NEW YORK (1837–1841)

Name	Party	State	Replaced	Service	Years
• John McKinley	Democrat	KY	new seat	1838–1852	15
• Peter V. Daniel	Democrat	VA	Barbour	1842–1860	19

APPOINTED BY PRESIDENT JOHN TYLER, WHIG FROM VIRGINIA (1841–1845)

Name	Party	State	Replaced	Service	Years
• Samuel Nelson	Democrat	NY	Thompson	1845–1872	27

APPOINTED BY JAMES K. POLK, DEMOCRAT FROM TENNESSEE (1845–1949) *[typo]*

Name	Party	State	Replaced	Service	Years
• Levi Woodbury	Democrat	NH	Story	1845–1851	6
• Robert C. Grier	Democrat	PA	Baldwin	1846–1870	23

APPOINTED BY MILLARD FILLMORE, WHIG FROM NEW YORK (1850–1853)

Name	Party	State	Replaced	Service	Years
• Benjamin R. Curtis	Whig	MA	Woodbury	1851–1857	6

APPOINTED BY FRANKLIN PIERCE, DEMOCRAT FROM NEW HAMPSHIRE (1853–1857)

Name	Party	State	Replaced	Service	Years
• John A. Campbell	Democrat	AL	McKinley	1853–1861	8

APPOINTED BY JAMES BUCHANAN, DEMOCRAT FROM PENNSYLVANIA (1857–1861)

Name	Party	State	Replaced	Service	Years
• Nathan Clifford	Democrat	ME	Curtis	1858–1881	23

APPOINTED BY ABRAHAM LINCOLN, REPUBLICAN FROM ILLINOIS (1861–1865)

Name	Party	State	Replaced	Service	Years
• Noah H. Swayne	Republican	OH	McLean	1862–1881	19
• Samuel F. Miller	Republican	IA	Daniel	1862–1890	28
• David Davis	Republican (later Independent)	IL	Campbell	1862–1877	14
• Stephen J. Field	Democrat	CA	new seat	1863–1897	34
• *Salmon P. Chase*	Republican	OH	Taney	1864–1874	8

Name	Party	State	Replaced	Service	Years

APPOINTED BY ULYSSES S. GRANT, REPUBLICAN FROM ILLINOIS
(1869–1877)

Name	Party	State	Replaced	Service	Years
• William Strong	Republican	PA	Grier	1870–1880	11
• Joseph P. Bradley	Republican	NJ	new seat	1870–1892	21
• Ward Hunt	Republican	NY	Nelson	1873–1882	9
• *Morrison R. Waite*	Republican	OH	Chase	1874–1888	14

APPOINTED BY RUTHERFORD B. HAYES, REPUBLICAN FROM OHIO
(1877–1881)

Name	Party	State	Replaced	Service	Years
• John Marshall Harlan	Republican	KY	Davis	1877–1911	34
• William B. Woods	Republican	GA	Strong	1881–1887	6

APPOINTED BY JAMES GARFIELD, REPUBLICAN FROM OHIO
(MARCH–SEPTEMBER 1881)

Name	Party	State	Replaced	Service	Years
• Stanley Matthews	Republican	OH	Swayne	1881–1889	8

APPOINTED BY CHESTER A. ARTHUR, REPUBLICAN FROM NEW YORK
(1881–1885)

Name	Party	State	Replaced	Service	Years
• Horace Gray	Republican	MA	Clifford	1882–1902	21
• Samuel Blatchford	Republican	NY	Hunt	1882–1893	11

APPOINTED BY GROVER CLEVELAND, DEMOCRAT FROM NEW YORK
(1885–1889)

Name	Party	State	Replaced	Service	Years
• Lucius Q.C. Lamar	Democrat	MS	Woods	1888–1893	5
• *Melville W. Fuller*	Democrat	IL	Waite	1888–1910	22

APPOINTED BY BENJAMIN HARRISON, REPUBLICAN FROM INDIANA
(1889–1893)

Name	Party	State	Replaced	Service	Years
• David J. Brewer	Republican	KS	Matthews	1890–1910	20
• Henry B. Brown	Republican	MI	Miller	1891–1906	15
• George Shiras	Republican	PA	Bradley	1892–1903	10
• Howell E. Jackson	Democrat	TN	Lamar	1893–1895	2

APPOINTED BY GROVER CLEVELAND, DEMOCRAT FROM NEW YORK
(1885–1889)

Name	Party	State	Replaced	Service	Years
• Edward D. White	Democrat	LA	Blatchford	1894–1910	17
• Rufus W. Peckham	Democrat	NY	Jackson	1896–1909	14

APPOINTED BY WILLIAM MCKINLEY, REPUBLICAN FROM OHIO
(1897–1901)

Name	Party	State	Replaced	Service	Years
• Joseph McKenna	Republican	CA	Field	1898–1925	27

Name	Party	State	Replaced	Service	Years

APPOINTED BY THEODORE ROOSEVELT, REPUBLICAN FROM NEW YORK (1901–1909)

Name	Party	State	Replaced	Service	Years
• Oliver W. Holmes	Republican	MA	Gray	1902–1932	29
• William R. Day	Republican	OH	Shiras	1903–1922	20
• William H. Moody	Republican	MA	Brown	1906–1910	4

APPOINTED BY WILLIAM H. TAFT, REPUBLICAN FROM OHIO (1909–1913)

Name	Party	State	Replaced	Service	Years
• Horace H. Lurton	Democrat	TN	Peckham	1910–1914	5
• Charles E. Hughes	Republican	NY	Brewer	1910–1916	6
• *Edward D. White*			Fuller	1910–1921	10
• Willis Van Devanter	Republican	WY	White	1911–1937	26
• Joseph R. Lamar	Democrat	GA	Moody	1911–1916	5
• Mahlon Pitney	Republican	NJ	Harlan	1912–1922	11

APPOINTED BY WOODROW WILSON, DEMOCRAT FROM NEW JERSEY (1913–1921)

Name	Party	State	Replaced	Service	Years
• James C. McReynolds	Democrat	TN	Lurton	1914–1941	26
• Louis D. Brandeis	Democrat	MA	Lamar	1916–1939	22
• John H. Clarke	Democrat	OH	Hughes	1916–1922	6

APPOINTED BY WARREN G. HARDING, REPUBLICAN FROM OHIO (1821–1923)

Name	Party	State	Replaced	Service	Years
• *William H. Taft*	Republican	CT	White	1921–1930	8
• George Sutherland	Republican	UT	Clarke	1922–1938	15
• Pierce Butler	Democrat	MN	Day	1923–1939	17
• Edward T. Sanford	Republican	TN	Pitney	1923–1930	7

APPOINTED BY CALVIN COOLIDGE, REPUBLICAN FROM MASSACHUSETTS (1923–1929)

Name	Party	State	Replaced	Service	Years
• Harlan F. Stone	Republican	NY	McKenna	1925–1941	16

APPOINTED BY HERBERT HOOVER, REPUBLICAN FROM CALIFORNIA (1929–1933)

Name	Party	State	Replaced	Service	Years
• *Charles E. Hughes*			Taft	1930–1941	11
• Owen J. Roberts	Republican	PA	Sanford	1930–1945	15
• Benjamin N. Cardozo	Democrat	NY	Holmes	1932–1938	6

APPOINTED BY FRANKLIN D. ROOSEVELT, DEMOCRAT FROM NEW YORK (1933–1945)

Name	Party	State	Replaced	Service	Years
• Hugo L. Black	Democrat	AL	Van Devanter	1937–1971	34
• Stanley F. Reed	Democrat	KY	Sutherland	1938–1957	19
• Felix Frankfurter	Independent	MA	Cardozo	1939–1962	24

Name	Party	State	Replaced	Service	Years
• William O. Douglas	Democrat	Conn.	Brandeis	1939–1975	37
• Frank Murphy	Democrat	MI	Butler	1940–1949	9
• James F. Byrnes	Democrat	SC	McReynolds	1941–1942	1
• *Harlan F. Stone*			Hughes	1941–1946	5
• Robert H. Jackson	Democrat	NY	Stone	1941–1954	13
• Wiley B. Rutledge	Democrat	IA	Byrnes	1943–1949	7

APPOINTED BY HARRY S. TRUMAN, DEMOCRAT FROM MISSOURI (1945–1953)

• Harold H. Burton	Republican	OH	Roberts	1945–1958	13
• *Fred M. Vinson*	Democrat	KY	Stone	1946–1953	7
• Tom C. Clark	Democrat	TX	Murphy	1949–1967	18
• Sherman Minton	Democrat	IN	Rutledge	1949–1956	7

APPOINTED BY DWIGHT D. EISENHOWER, REPUBLICAN FROM NEW YORK (1953–1951)

• *Earl Warren*	Republican	CA	Vinson	1953–1969	15
• John M. Harlan	Republican	NY	Jackson	1955–1971	16
• William J. Brennan	Democrat	NJ	Minton	1956–1990	34
• Charles E. Whittaker	Republican	MO	Reed	1957–1962	5
• Potter Stewart	Republican	OH	Burton	1958–1981	22

APPOINTED BY JOHN F. KENNEDY, DEMOCRAT FROM MASSACHUSETTS (1961–1963)

• Byron R. White	Democrat	CO	Whittaker	1962–1993	31
• Arthur J. Goldberg	Democrat	IL	Frankfurter	1962–1965	3

APPOINTED BY LYNDON B. JOHNSON, DEMOCRAT FROM TEXAS (1963–1969)

• Abe Fortas	Democrat	TN	Goldberg	1965–1969	4
• Thurgood Marshall	Democrat	MD	Clark	1967–1991	24

APPOINTED BY RICHARD M. NIXON, REPUBLICAN FROM CALIFORNIA (1969–1974)

• *Warren E. Burger*	Republican	MN	Warren	1969–1986	17
• Harry Blackmun	Republican	MN	Fortas	1970–1994	24
• Lewis F. Powell, Jr.	Republican	VA	Black	1972–1987	16
• William H. Rehnquist	Republican	AZ	Harlan	1972–1986	15

APPOINTED BY GERALD R. FORD, REPUBLICAN FROM MICHIGAN (1974–1977)

• John Paul Stevens	Republican	IL	Douglas	1975–	

Name	Party	State	Replaced	Service	Years

APPOINTED BY RONALD REAGAN, REPUBLICAN FROM CALIFORNIA (1981–1989)

Name	Party	State	Replaced	Service	Years
• Sandra Day O'Connor	Republican	AZ	Stewart	1981–2006	25
• *William H. Rehnquist*			Burger	1986–2005	19
• Antonin Scalia	Republican	VA	Rehnquist	1986–	
• Anthony M. Kennedy	Republican	CA	Powell	1988–	

APPOINTED BY GEORGE H. W. BUSH, REPUBLICAN FROM TEXAS (1989–1993)

Name	Party	State	Replaced	Service	Years
• David H. Souter	Republican	NH	Brennan	1990–	
• Clarence Thomas	Republican	VA	Marshall	1991–	

APPOINTED BY WILLIAM J. CLINTON, DEMOCRAT FROM ARKANSAS (1993–2001)

Name	Party	State	Replaced	Service	Years
• Ruth Bader Ginsberg	Democrat	DC	White	1993–	
• Stephen G. Breyer	Democrat	MA	Blackmun	1994–	

APPOINTED BY GEORGE W. BUSH, REPUBLICAN FROM TEXAS (2001–2009)

Name	Party	State	Replaced	Service	Years
• *John G. Roberts*	Republican	NY	Rehnquist	2005–	
• Samuel A. Alito	Republican	NJ	O'Connor	2006–	

Italicized names are those of the chief justices.